TRADITIONAL LIFEWAYS OF THE SOUTHERN MĀORI

TRADITIONAL LIFEWAYS OF THE SOUTHERN MĀORI

THE OTAGO UNIVERSITY MUSEUM
ETHNOLOGICAL PROJECT, 1920

James Herries Beattie

Edited by Atholl Anderson

OTAGO UNIVERSITY PRESS
Te Whare Tā o Te Wānanga o Ōtākou
IN ASSOCIATION WITH TŪHURA OTAGO MUSEUM

Published by Otago University Press
Te Whare Tā o Te Wānanga o Ōtākou
533 Castle Street, Ōtepoti Dunedin 9016
P.O. Box 56, Ōtepoti Dunedin, New Zealand
www.oup.nz

Published in association with
Tūhura Otago Museum

First published 1994, reprinted 1995, 2009
This edition 2024

Copyright © Atholl Anderson 2024

ISBN 978 1 99 004863 0

Front cover: The 'Taiaroa Map' filled in by Ngāi Tahu in 1879–80 at the instigation of H.K. Taiaroa, the member for Southern Maori (see p. 233). Hori Kerei Taiaroa Collection, Canterbury Museum 19XX.6.1.

Printed in China through Asia Pacific Offset

CONTENTS

- 7 Foreword: *Sir Tipene O'Regan*
- 9 Introduction
- 32 Acknowledgements
- 33 Murihiku
- 221 Canterbury
- 469 Nelson
- 519 Westland
- 535 Appendix 1
  Edited remains from first draft of Murihiku volume
- 579 Appendix 2
  Glossary of names for flora and fauna
- 604 References
- 608 Index of Names
- 613 Index of Place Names
- 620 General Index

Detailed contents lists for each geographical section appear at the beginning of that section

Modern poha-titi (container for muttonbirds – see p. 177), made by Mrs Flora Reiri.

FOREWORD

Modern Ngāi Tahu owe Herries Beattie an enormous debt. The mountain of papers he placed in the Hocken Library is recognised by those familiar with it as one of the most important bequests that our people will ever receive. At a critical phase in our history, when much of our custom and tikanga was being discarded as of no future relevance, Beattie was assiduously collecting the remnants of information on our past which have become part of the foundation of the redevelopment of Ngāi Tahu culture in our generation.

Atholl Anderson, in his scholarly introduction, attests to Beattie's honesty and integrity as a recorder. Whilst there might be debate about some of Beattie's interpretative judgements, we must remember that he was, after all, a person of his time and that he had feelings of extreme deference to the senior scholars of his period. Those early giants of the Polynesian Society were rampant theorists about Māori origins and ethnology, and one feels that Beattie was, sometimes, over impressed with them. However, it would be a brave person who could confidently assert that Beattie was wrong in terms of a fact or statement he recorded. It is my view that if he wrote something down which turned out, later, to be unsupported by other facts he would have written it down only because someone told him. It is that willingness to laboriously note what people said and to laboriously transcribe what they had written that is his most important gift to us.

This volume is full of fascinating details, many of which will challenge, in some respect, what are now received truths about ancestors, nomenclature and custom. Some of these will promote vigorous discussion and debate – that is healthy and will do our cultural redevelopment process no harm.

Beattie, of course, left us far more than this 1920 volume. His laborious transcriptions of whakapapa and tradition and his voluminous cross references on traditional historical notes in the manuscript whakapapa also survive. They are a major source of knowledge for those of us who are privileged to be initiated in Ngāi Tahu and South Island Māori studies. The volumes of placenames and general Southern Māori nomenclature are a bountiful complement to the extensive recording done by our tūpuna in support of different aspects of Te Kerēme, the Ngāi Tahu claim.

Beyond Beattie, however, we are presented here with the equally diligent scholarship of Atholl Anderson, another of the great benefactors of Southern Māori studies. Anderson's introduction is, arguably, one of the best scholarly treatments of Southern Māori historical and ethnographical sources we are liable to encounter. His enormous outpouring of scholarly writing is the modern equivalent of the voluminous recording and note-taking of Beattie. We are blessed in them both.

Ngāi Tahu will be the richer for the emergence of this remarkable text. Māori studies, in general, will be the richer. The texture of Southern knowledge will be better etched in our landscape.

Kia ora tātou

SIR TIPENE O'REGAN
FORMER CHAIR
NGĀ TAHU MĀORI TRUST BOARD

INTRODUCTION

JAMES HERRIES BEATTIE AND THE 1920 PROJECT

Between 1955 and 1965, James Herries Beattie sent some fifty parcels of his papers to the Hocken Library and others were added after his death in 1972. These contained many notebooks recording his interests in local and natural history, collections of waiata, whakapapa and Māori vocabulary, records of interviews with early settlers, correspondence and drafts of published and unpublished works (McDonald 1974). Amongst the latter are extensive handwritten results of an ethnological field project undertaken between Foveaux Strait and north Canterbury for the Otago University Museum, as it was then commonly called, in 1920 (the original name, Otago Museum, was reinstated by H.D. Skinner in 1936). Together with a draft publication of the results for the Murihiku region, sent to the Hocken Library in the 1920s, these writings comprise manuscript 181: the most important single work resulting from Beattie's long involvement with southern Māori. He mined it repeatedly in writing his popular books and pamphlets, but it was never published.

The growing interest in Māori traditional ways during recent years has brought manuscript 181 a level of deserved scholarly attention and respect from academic and other researchers, not least Māori, beyond any that it had in the past. This is reason enough to make it more widely and easily accessible, but as the manuscript is also becoming fragile from handling it seems an appropriate time to carry out Beattie's original intention and get it into print. How much more or less valuable the work is now, more than seventy years later, is for readers to judge, but H.D. Skinner, who was Beattie's supervisor and mentor in the conduct of the project, wrote in his report to the University of Otago (Otago University archives [OUA], 1920), 'the information collected exceeds by many times all that had been previously placed on record by other observers, and ranks as one of the most important contributions made to the ethnology of the Maoris.'

A BIOGRAPHICAL NOTE

James Herries Beattie MBE, usually known as Herries Beattie, was born in Gore on 6 June 1881, the eldest son of a pioneer family. His father James Beattie JP (1839–1935) was born in Kirkcudbrightshire, Scotland, and came to Port Chalmers in 1862, bringing merinos for Watson Shennan's Galway station on the Dunstan. This was at the height of the Otago goldrushes and James succumbed briefly to the dream before returning to sheepfarming, at first on

D'Urville Island as a manager and then on his own farm at Jacob's River, Southland. He later opened a general store in Winton, progressing to a larger business in Gore, where he became a well-known figure in the community and Mayor for four terms. Herries Beattie's mother, Mary Roden Thomson (1848–1934), was a Galloway lass who came to Dunedin with her parents in 1862. They purchased land at Maungatua, from John Shennan, made their own bricks and built a house at The Banks, West Taieri, where Mary and James were married in April 1874 (Hocken ms 582/L/31).

The Beatties had nine children, four of whom died young – three in an epidemic in April 1882 – leaving three sons and two daughters (Hocken ms 582/A/12). They were a religious family, Presbyterian at first, then Congregational when the church opened in Gore in 1892. Herries Beattie professed his belief in 1902, at the age of twenty-one, and later, at the urging of his wife, joined the Brethren church in Oamaru. A strong personal faith and the willingness to share it – he was a Sunday school teacher in Gore, New Plymouth and Waimate for more than forty years – remained central to his life.

With the unshakeable convictions of Scottish Protestantism went a high regard for learning, though rather less for schooling. Herries was sent to Gore School in December 1886 and quickly developed a strong interest in natural and local history. He was not an outstanding student in the usual academic subjects, although he had a broad general knowledge and was good at games, especially rugby and cricket. He failed the scholarship examination for free entry to secondary school in 1894 and did not enjoy his subsequent two years at Southland Boys' High School, Invercargill, where he dropped Latin, taking Bookkeeping and Shorthand in its place. Although offered a free year of schooling in 1897, he left gladly to begin work in his father's shop as an assistant and message boy. There he met Mary McKenzie, a seventeen-year-old tailoress from Riverton who came to work as a vest-hand, and whom he married in May 1910 after six years of courtship. They built a house, 'Dalzien', in a field below the Beattie home, 'Dalbeattie', and four children (Mary, Christina, Herries and Margaret) were born between 1911 and 1918.

The family business slumped at the turn of the century and was taken over in 1903 by cousins from Invercargill, trading as Thomson and Beattie. Herries Beattie remained in it until 1916, though with increasing dissatisfaction. His annual salary, £156 in 1910, was modest and his intellectual ambitions unfulfilled. He studied to become a schoolteacher but failed the examination. At the end of 1916, however, he accepted a substantial drop in salary to become a proofreader and reporter on the *Mataura Ensign*. He remained with the newspaper until 1919, but his wife and children had left Gore that year to live with Mary's parents at Oamaru, and Herries was anxious to join them, especially since Mary was in poor health. He left the *Ensign* in January 1920 and, after a frustrating search for work in Dunedin, was employed by the Otago University Museum. His base that year was a small farm at Weston, near Oamaru.

At the conclusion of the Museum project, Henry Skinner recommended him to his father, William Skinner, for the position of librarian and ethnologist in the Carnegie Institute at New Plymouth (subsequently divided into the Public Library and Museum). Beattie held the position for a year but became ill and, worried also that New Plymouth would not suit Mary's delicate state of health, turned down a further term and salary increase to return to Oamaru and search again for work. Unsuccessful in this, he finally scraped together his resources in 1922 to purchase Manchester's bookshop and stationery business in Waimate, which he ran until selling it in 1939, the earliest opportunity he could find to get an acceptable price after the Depression (Hocken ms 582/L/30).

Herries Beattie continued to live in Waimate and devote himself full time to writing and publication. This career prospered and he became increasingly well-known and respected. He had been elected to the Polynesian Society as early as 1914 and elevated to corresponding membership in 1920. W.W. Smith, the secretary, wrote (5 July 1920, JPS collection ATL): 'The Society consider that your contributions to the South Island history are most valuable and hence wish to mark their sense of value by the appointment.' In 1950 Beattie was awarded the Stephenson Percy Smith medal for achievements in anthropology. In the Queen's Birthday Honours, June 1967, he received the MBE in recognition of his long years of historical research and writing. He died on 11 May 1972 in Timaru Hospital and was buried at Waimate (*Otago Daily Times* 12 May 1972).

HIS ETHNOLOGICAL WRITINGS AND THE 1920 PROJECT

Alongside an undistinguished business career, Herries Beattie maintained a highly productive avocation in historical research and publication. From early childhood he had been keen on writing. He tried his hand at poetry and nursed a teenage ambition to write a New Zealand novel (amongst his papers are the drafts of twenty-three short stories and three novels); but after an early foray into writing about birds, his lifelong attention was captured by pioneer history and the historical traditions and ethnology of the South Island Māori.

At the age of ten he started the first of many notebooks kept during his teenage years recording historical recollections of pioneer families about Gore and those of the surviving whalers and other old identities at Bluff and Riverton. He had an excellent memory and was able to write up these conversations in remarkable detail, the first being a biography of his uncle William Adam of the Taieri. Adam was the most important influence on Beattie's nascent historical and Māori interests. As a child, Beattie spent a number of holidays at his uncle's house at Otokia and through him first came to meet some of the Māori residents of south Otago. Adam had been taught Māori methods of fishing and fowling by a Māori shepherd, Paul (Tuheke) in 1858–1859, and went on to form a strong acquaintance with Henley Māori, notably Tiori or Turia, from whom he gained a detailed knowledge of traditions and lifeways.

In 1898, at the instigation of J.A. Forbes, Beattie compiled a short history of Gore for the *Gore Standard*, his first published work. His history of early settlers was largely published in *Pioneer Recollections* (1909, 1911). However, it was in the years 1917 to 1921, when he took the plunge to leave drapery for journalism, that his historical interests in Māori history and ethnology really began to flourish.

A major series of southern Māori traditions, history and placenames was published in the *Journal of the Polynesian Society* between 1915 and 1922. Thereafter came a flood of small books and pamphlets, most concentrating on Māori placenames, history and lifeways. The most important were: *Tikao Talks* (1939, republished 1990), *Moriori* (1941), *Maori Placenames of Otago* (1944), *Maori Lore of Lake, Alp and Fiord* (1945), *Maori Placenames of Canterbury* (1946), *The Maoris and Fiordland* (1949), *Our Southernmost Maoris* (1954), and his edited volume, *Folklore and Fairy Tales of the Canterbury Maoris* (1957). Some of the material for these, and many of the contacts with Māori informants to whom he returned on many visits, had been made during the 1920 project.

After leaving the *Ensign* in January 1920, Beattie tried to find work in Dunedin at journalism, the libraries, the Public Trust and elsewhere, but without success. At the Early Settlers Museum, he proposed that they employ him to interview surviving gold miners but was apparently told that there was nothing left to collect, Dr Hocken having got it all. At the Otago Museum, however, Assistant Curator Henry Skinner had a job for him. In fact, he was probably not at all surprised that Beattie turned up to enquire. In correspondence during 1919, Beattie had asked about finding Museum employment and proposed taking a year off from journalism to 'rescue facts about the southern Maoris before it is too late ... if anyone would find the necessary wherewithal, say £250' (Beattie to Skinner 23 June 1919, Otago Museum Archives, OMA). Later he dropped a broader hint by telling Skinner that he was soon to leave Gore, with no definite plans, and noting that the Government had allocated £200 to the Otago branch of the New Zealand Institute for research (Beattie to Skinner 21 August 1919, OMA).

Beattie already knew that Skinner was most anxious to have someone go around the South Island Māori settlements and collect information about traditional lifeways, material culture and settlement patterns, because Skinner had furnished him with a list of pertinent questions at Easter 1919 (Beattie to Skinner 3 February 1920, OMA), and raised the possibility of a collaborative project. He probably knew as well that Skinner's interest was quite specifically concerned with a debate about the status and origins of 'Moriori'. Unlike Elsdon Best, Percy Smith, Peter Buck and other established authorities, Skinner was convinced that the earliest people in New Zealand came from East Polynesia – a 'quaint theory' in Best's opinion (Skinner 1974: 15). Since a

Beattie's uncle William Adam and his friend Tiori, 1869. Burton Brothers photograph, Box-002-035, Hocken Collections Uare Taoka o Hākena, University of Otago.

'Moriori' element (here meaning descendants of a supposedly Melanesian population) was supposed to survive more strongly in South Island Māori, and since native Chatham Islanders were regarded as 'Moriori' descendants in the same way, Skinner's attention was drawn particularly to these areas. If he could show that in neither of them was there a case for other than East Polynesian culture, anciently or traditionally, then the 'Moriori' argument in general would be difficult to sustain. He went to the Chathams in 1919, subsequently arguing that Moriori (in the present sense of original settlers of the Chathams), were of East Polynesian ancestry and culture (Skinner 1923). He kept an eye on the archaeological work of David Teviotdale on old coastal middens in the South Island, especially at Shag Mouth, and engaged his interest in questions about the material culture of the moa-hunters, concluding that it too was of East Polynesian type. To complete the case, he wanted a thorough survey of traditional southern Māori culture.

In March 1920, Skinner approached the Chancellor of the University of Otago – at that time Otago Museum was administered by the University and Skinner held appointments as Assistant Curator, Hocken Librarian and Lecturer in Ethnology – and argued successfully for a grant of £50 to employ Beattie, offering him £5 a week as a temporary member of the staff of the University Museum. Skinner (to Chancellor 24 March 1920, OUA), argued that Beattie:

has already collected more information about the South Island natives than all previous investigators put together, and in quality his work leaves nothing to be desired. Within a very few years all such information will have vanished, and no sum of money and no amount of research will retrieve it.

The Chancellor was willing to fund the project more substantially, but Skinner assured him that Government money was in the offing through the New Zealand Institute. In June, Mr W. H. Skinner donated £25 to the University to continue the research. This attracted a matching government subsidy and a grant of £200 was also awarded by the Minister of Internal Affairs, through the New Zealand Institute, thus providing a total of £300 (Skinner to Beattie 24 March, 20 May, 21 June 1920, OUA).

As the project became formalised, Beattie supplemented the 1919 list of questions with a notebook containing several hundred more about ethnological matters. Skinner instructed Beattie to concentrate upon them and not to collect information about migrations, battles, whakapapa and history (Beattie continued, nevertheless, to collect information on traditional history). The notebook can no longer be found and, in any event, the lists were continually revised as interviews developed further leads and Skinner perused the results. Beattie asked sixty-five questions at Temuka in April 1920, took 187 to begin his Canterbury work in July and added another 100 during it (Beattie to Skinner 29 April, 29 August 1920, OMA). By the time he was interviewing his Nelson informant his 'query book' began with 500 questions and ended with over 1000. Skinner also instructed Beattie to buy items of interest to the Otago Museum, and Beattie obliged with purchases of various small artefacts including fish traps, baskets, sandals, adzes, handles, beaters and clubs.

It was intended that Beattie's material would be published at the conclusion of his field work. Skinner (to Chancellor 21 June 1920, OUA), had suggested initially to the Chancellor that Beattie's work should be published as a bulletin of the University Museum, but the response was unencouraging, perhaps because there was no manuscript to consider. There was also some uncertainty about who was responsible for the material. Skinner hoped that Beattie would prepare it for publication, while Beattie (to Skinner 5 October 1920, OMA) hoped that Skinner would take on an editorial role – 'I believe some 'good fairy' will provide the funds necessary, and also that you will produce a 'classic' in New Zealand anthropology' (Beattie to Skinner 10 November 1920, OMA). As it happened, the task of collating notes was then delayed by the New Plymouth appointment and Beattie became resigned about the prospects of publication, writing to Skinner (Beattie 28 November 1921, OMA), 'I believe that when the time is ripe for the South Island material in the Hocken Library [it] will be published.'

It was July 1922 before Beattie had a manuscript of the first regional survey prepared (the Murihiku results), and by that stage Skinner was already putting some of the material to use in publications, notably his paper on culture areas in New Zealand (Skinner 1921). He remained optimistic that the B.P. Bishop Museum, Honolulu, whom he had approached for fieldwork and publication funding in 1920, albeit fruitlessly, but which had published his own B.A. research thesis on Moriori culture (Skinner 1923), was a likely possibility. Others were the Polynesian Society and the newly established Ethnological Research Board, when either had cleared their current commitments to publish works by S. Percy Smith and Elsdon Best respectively.

Skinner, however, was not prepared to edit Beattie's work. He read it and made considerable alterations to the first few pages, but then cautioned Beattie that the manuscript needed substantial abbreviation because 'publication is so expensive a matter now-a-days that if you do not study brevity your editor will do it for you ruthlessly, and often without much discretion' (Skinner to Beattie 22 September 1923, OMA). Other critical comment to the effect that the writing was 'too slangy' and the material repetitious, prompted Beattie to rewrite the Murihiku manuscript and place it in the Hocken Library in the hope that they might eventually find an opportunity to publish it. This never happened, although Beattie continued to hope and even listed the projected works (*The Maoris of Otago – Their Manner of Life and Their History; The Maoris of Canterbury – Their Life and History; Maoris of Nelson and Westland – Life, History and Place-names*), in his later publications (e.g. Beattie 1941: 72). In 1957, when he no longer saw any likelihood of publication, he sent the material discarded in rewriting his Murihiku manuscript, together with his 1920 Canterbury, Nelson and Westland notes collated into the same form as the Murihiku manuscript, to the Hocken Library for safekeeping. He remained philosophical about the lack of publication, noting that if the Murihiku manuscript had been published, 'it would have been the first book of its kind in New Zealand, for there is nothing resembling it in print' (Beattie, February 1957, foreword to 1920 project material, ms 181).

THE FIELDWORK AND INFORMANTS

Beattie's 1920 diary (Hocken ms 582), records that he was at Māori settlements for 127 days between 23 February and 31 December and spent eighty-three days writing up his notes, which he kept in a vault of the Bank of New South Wales in Gore during periods of fieldwork. He travelled by train and bicycle, often cycling twenty or thirty miles to visit outlying settlements. Skinner and he had hoped to cover all of the South Island but in the event their attention was restricted to the east coast between Foveaux Strait and Rangiora, although at Tuahiwi he met several Westland Māori who were able to provide information on that district, and at Kaiapoi a valuable informant about Nelson.

He might also have visited some settlements not recorded in his diary but mentioned in the Murihiku manuscript and shown on its accompanying map: Otakou (he certainly visited Karetai's house in January 1921 [Hocken ms 582/L/16] but it is not clear that he met his intended informant), Ruapuke Island and Stewart Island. However, no 1920 informants are recorded for these places and it is likely both that some informants elsewhere were familiar with those places and that information collected on pre-1920 visits to them was added in for the sake of completeness, as in the case of Waikawa (which Beattie noted in his introduction to the Murihiku draft manuscript). Skinner had encouraged him to add in earlier material and Beattie (to Skinner 29 August 1920, OMA) told him that in one batch of his Murihiku results he had 'incorporated many notes from my old notebooks of years gone by. Some of the men and women who gave the information have since passed away.' Beattie also added some notes collected as late as 1936 to his otherwise meagre Westland material.

Beattie's fieldwork had the qualities of 'social tact, ability and untiring industry' as Skinner (7 July 1920, OMA) observed, and he seems to have had little difficulty in making productive contacts in the Māori community, many of which lasted for more than thirty years. Considering his limited means, Beattie was generous to his hosts, if in ways which are easily misconstrued nowadays: 'when I go among the Natives (who live in poor circumstances as a rule) I take a supply of gifts – fruit, biscuits, tobacco etc., and give the children money.' However, he did not pay for information and he did pay for items collected on behalf of the Museum. Of the latter, he was alarmed to learn that old relics were seldom cared for and sometimes burnt – "no good in these days" they say' (Beattie to Skinner 29 April 1920, OMA).

The extent of Beattie's fieldwork in 1920.

Traditional knowledge was also fast disappearing, it seemed. Everywhere he went 'people deplore the fact that no one came to collect information forty, thirty or even twenty years ago' (Beattie to Skinner 29 April 1920, OMA). This was not entirely true. From the 1840s onward, substantial information about traditions, genealogy and lifeways was given to European explorers and surveyors, notably Shortland (1851). In addition, Ngāi Tahu elders had made a concerted effort to set down placenames and associated data about settlements and former activities, in 1879–80 (much of it published by Beattie 1944, 1946), and had repeatedly given extensive evidence about the past in commissions of enquiry. Around the turn of the century, as well, there had been Pākehā collectors of southern Māori traditional lore – notably W.H.S. Roberts, James Cowan and Frederick Chapman, and prominent informants such as Tame Parata M.H.R. Nevertheless, the impression of loss or impending loss was evidently general in the Māori communities and many were anxious to see what remained being written down. Of his major informant, Beattie (to Skinner 11 October 1920, OMA) wrote, 'my friend Tikao feels that he should perpetuate his knowledge as he is the alloted span, so as none of his descendants care a straw about it he is giving it to me – I tell him he will make me a tohunga yet if he does not stop.'

Beattie's research was generally conducted in English, for although he seems to have had a working knowledge of written Māori he was not a confident speaker. Beattie asked his questions, often repeatedly until he was sure of the answer, and attempted to write down information as nearly as possible in the language used by his informants. His training in shorthand must have been of considerable assistance.

It is difficult to say how much, if anything, was lost in translation. Often the children or other younger relatives of an informant assisted in the interviews, and this must have helped to ensure the accuracy of communication. In a foreword to his 1957 gift to the Hocken Library of the remaining 1920 notes he insisted:

I went among them with no preconceived notions, no theories to uphold, and no previous knowledge to colour what was told me. I relegate myself to the background, and keep to the simplicity of my informants, and neither overstate nor understate the information given me. It is a faithful record.

Of course, this was an overstatement on all counts and by the time he had reworked his notes and collated them under the numerous headings of his draft manuscripts, both the flavour of the spoken word and the identity of the informants concerning particular items had been largely lost. Yet there can be no doubt that Beattie was a scrupulously honest reporter whose appreciation of the privilege he was accorded by Māori elders was repaid by assiduous attention to getting their information down accurately, even when he thought his informants were wrong or confused.

In addition to fieldwork, Beattie visited libraries to compare his information

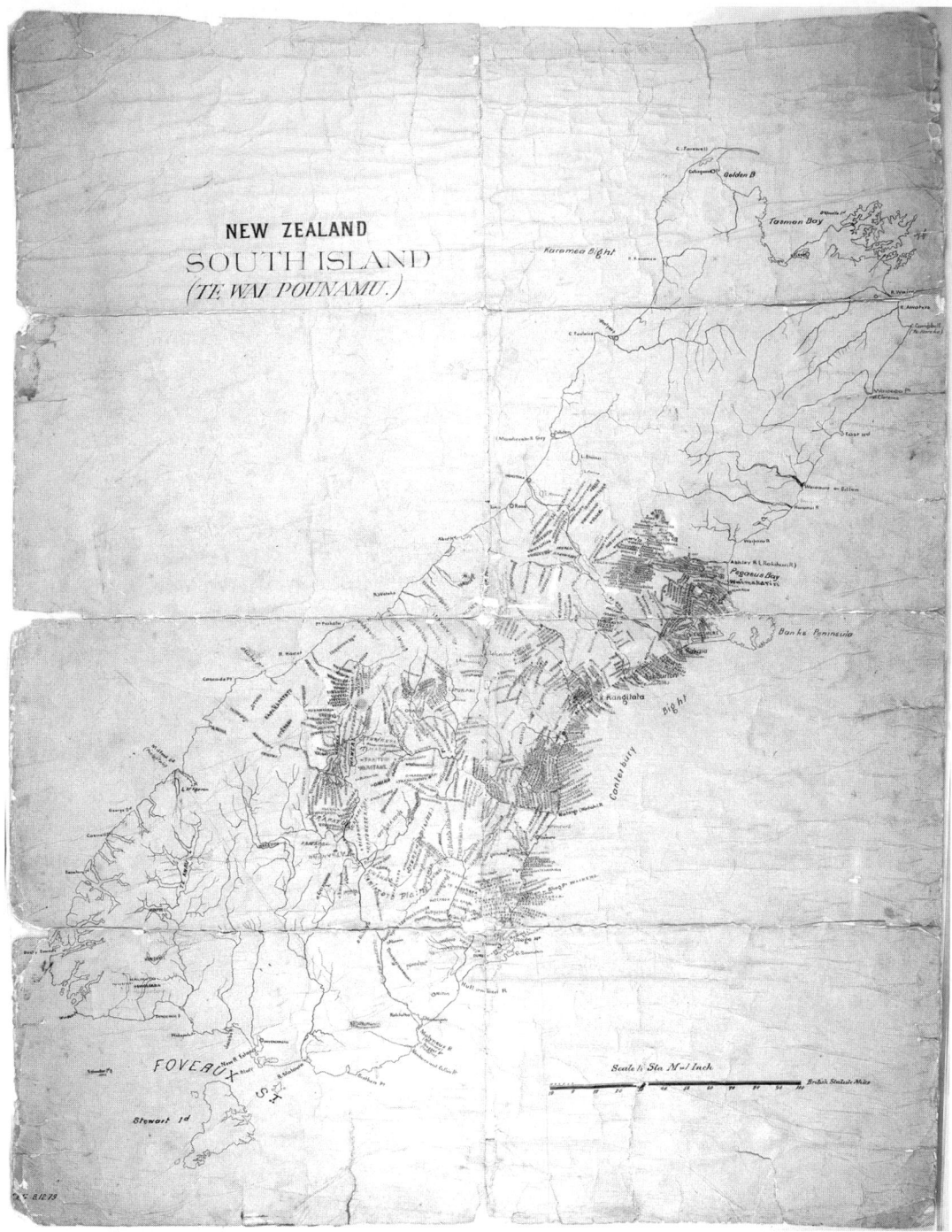

The 'Taiaroa Map' filled in by Ngāi Tahu in 1879–80 at the instigation of H.K. Taiaroa, the member for Southern Maori (see p. 233). Details appear on the following pages.
Hori Kerei Taiaroa Collection, Canterbury Museum 19XX.6.1.

INTRODUCTION 19

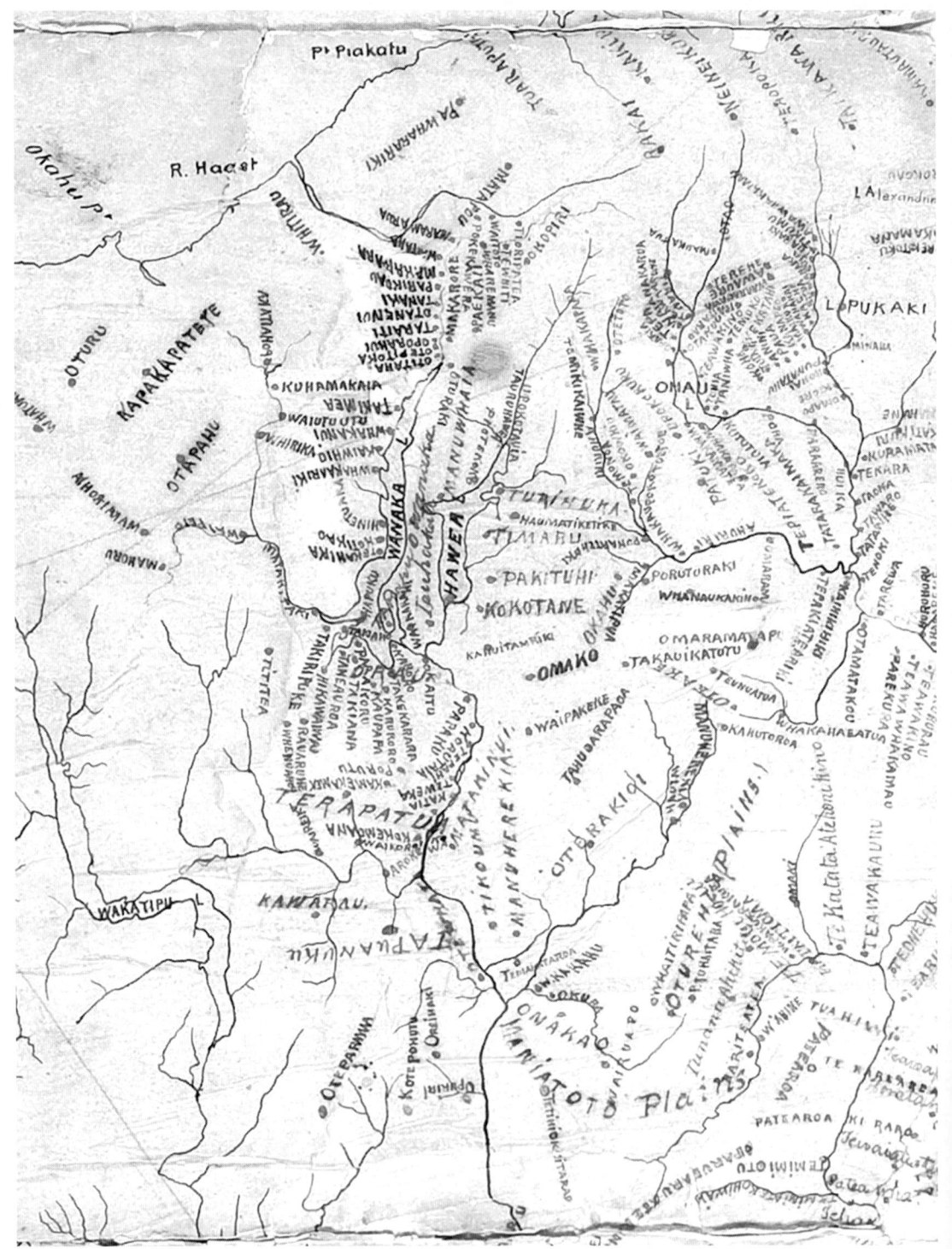

Central Otago and the South Westland coast.

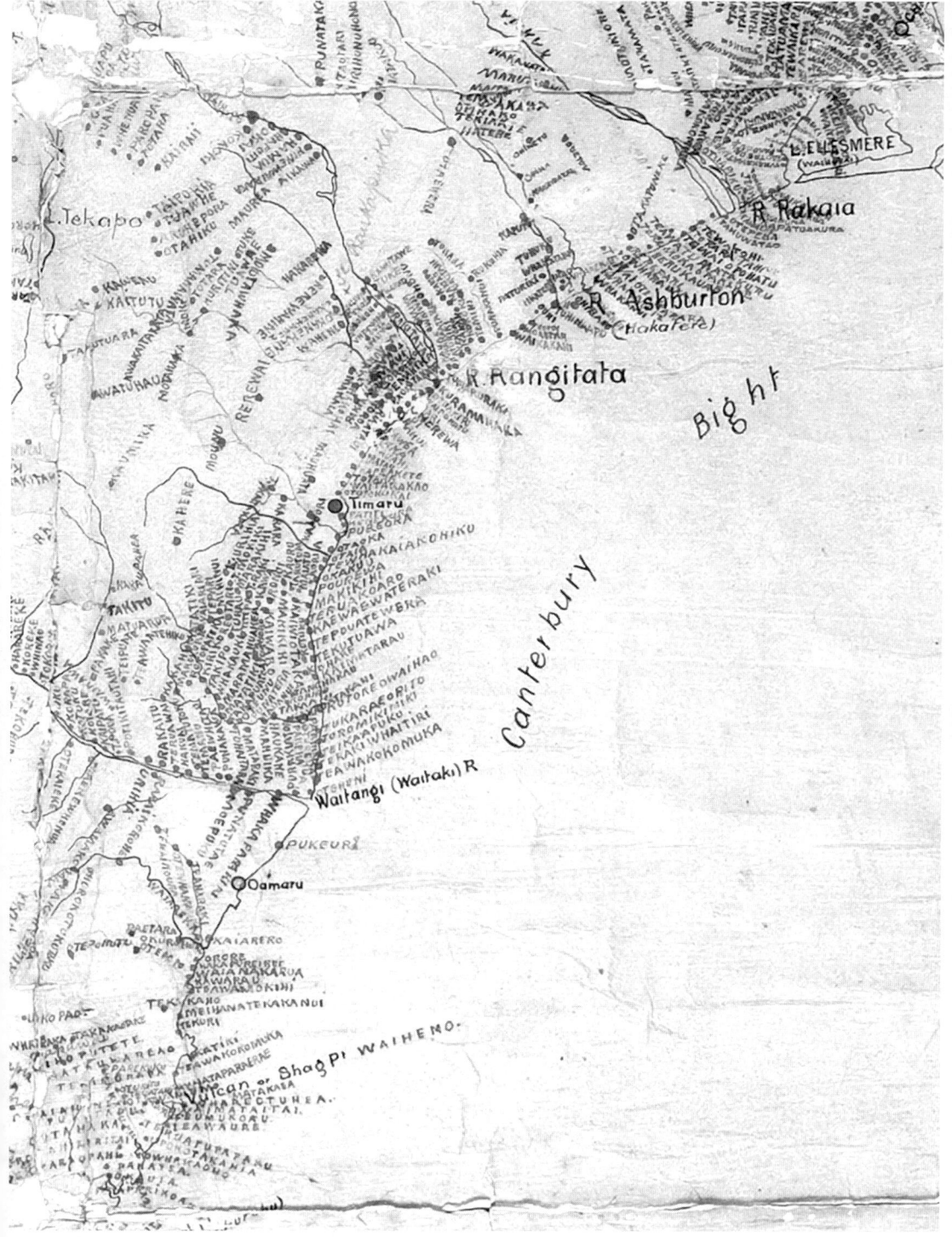

The South Canterbury and North Otago coast inland to Lake Tekapo.

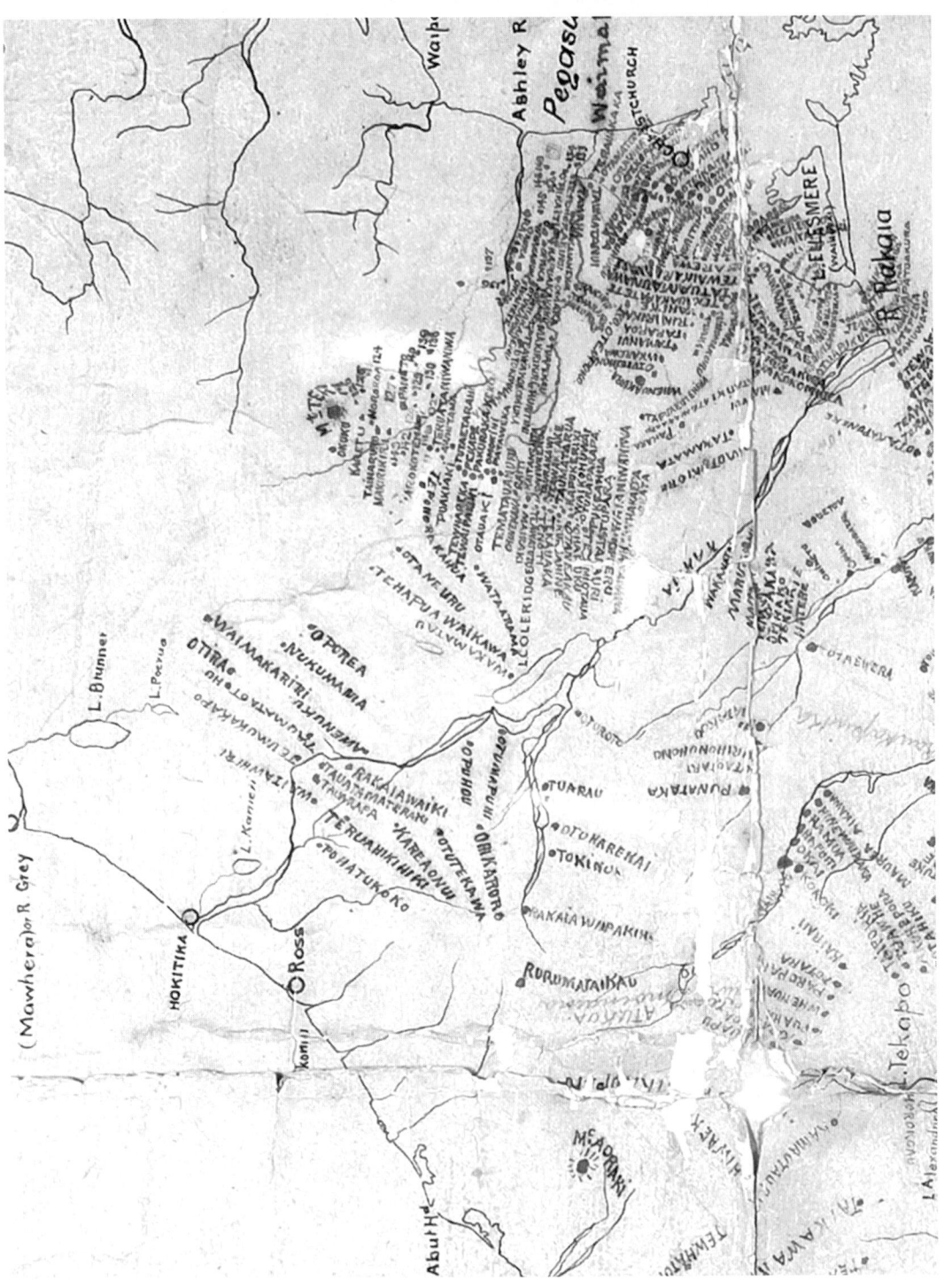

Central South Island, from Hokitika on the west coast to the Waimakariri River on the east.

with that compiled by Percy Smith, John White and other authorities and spent a week with informants (Rehu and King) in the Otago Museum recording southern Māori names for fauna and artefacts; there are various references in the text to the information obtained in this way. He also visited some traditional pā sites, learnt the elements of Museum accessioning and referencing from Skinner – with a view to improving his prospects of employment at the conclusion of the project (Beattie to Skinner 30 June 1920, OMA) – and copied out notebooks lent to him by informants, notably Hoani Korehe Kahu's 1880 notebook of mahinga kai (food-gathering places), lent by the Kahu and Paipeta family at Temuka, and T.E. Green's manuscript lent by the Pitama family at Tuahiwi. (These are not included in the manuscript, although Beattie acknowledges the use of material from them in various places.)

The fieldwork was divided broadly into two sections: from February to mid-July, he worked at the settlements between Foveaux Strait and Temuka; thereafter, he worked between Temuka and Rangiora. Most time was spent at Tuahiwi and elsewhere in the Rangiora district (twenty-five days), followed by Rāpaki (twenty-four days) and Temuka (about twenty days). He was at Bluff and Kaka Point for about a week in each case and spent one to three days at each of another sixteen localities. All his main informants and some of the minor contributors are recorded for each visit, but Beattie attended tangi and other large gatherings where he spoke to many people and did not record the source of every piece of information. Further, since his original notebooks were evidently disposed of when he had transferred his information into systematic notes, it is no longer possible to match particular pieces of information with specific informants. Nevertheless, an approximate attribution can be attained by consulting his diary and noting other comments in his writings and letters to H.D. Skinner, which record his main sources. Described below are the principal informants he consulted in the 1920 project. It is worth noting that both before and after it he also had other important informants such as Erute Poko Cameron, Taare Reweti Te Maihāroa and Tuhituhi Te Marama, to name only a few.

Beattie lists the Murihiku informants in his draft manuscript and provides additional lists from which the Canterbury and other informants can be deduced in his later placenames volumes (Beattie 1944, 1946). The names were checked in the Ngāi Tahu kaumātua lists (Ngāi Tahu Tribal Trust Board 1963, 1967) and genealogical information sought in Garven (1974), and in the records compiled by Mrs June McDougall (see Anderson 1991). In many cases, there is additional information elsewhere in Beattie's writings, especially in his unpublished notes and newspaper clippings (Hocken ms 582) and his newspaper series (Beattie 1931).

Bluff

The main informant seems to have been Tiemi Haereroa Kupa, born about 1849.

He was the son of Atiru Te Mahana and Stewart Coupar, a whaler. They were living at The Neck, Stewart Island in 1844, and subsequently at Arowhenua, during Kupa's early years, before settling at Colac Bay (Beattie 1931, 1946, Hocken ms 582/E/7). Another informant from whom Beattie obtained considerable information was Tiori Mahure (George Mahure Newton), born at Mason Bay, Stewart Island in 1843. He was the son of George Newton, a Codfish Island sealer, and Wharetutu (Anderson 1990). They lived at Murray's River (Stewart Island) and The Neck. Mahure was married to Arihia Whaitiri, daughter of another prominent southern Māori family (Dawson n.d.). A third major informant was Wiremu Te Paro (William Spencer, William Power), born in 1844 at the Bluff. He was the son of James Spencer, a whaler, and Tinirauwaho Qane Rawaho). He married Louisa Coupar, daughter of Te Mahana and Stewart Coupar (above). Te Paro was a regular visitor to Fiordland and Stewart Island and an authority on the military history and maritime knowledge of southern Māori (Beattie 1931, Hocken ms 582/A/13, 23.) It was probably at Bluff as well that Beattie interviewed Hoani Kaiporohu, born Stewart Island in 1848, who was knowledgeable about Māori seafaring, muttonbirding and southern traditions and placenames (Beattie 1931).

Kapuka

At this inland Southland settlement Beattie interviewed Hoani Tamahika Matiu, born 1854 at the Karitane mission station and a recognised authority on southern traditions (Beattie 1931, 1944. See p. 97).

Tuturau

This was another small inland settlement, where Beattie met Mrs Takai Whaitiri (Elizabeth Wesley; John Takai Wetere was her husband), a daughter of Mere Wehikore who was a first cousin to Kohikohi, the wife of Captain Howell of Riverton (Hocken ms 582/A/13; G/l).

Kaka Point

One of Beattie's most important informants was 'King', or Ruru (Eruete Kiingi Kurupōhatu, King Ruru, Kīngi Ruru Kurupōhatu). Beattie rated him second only to Tikao in the abundance and value of his knowledge. He was born about 1839, the son of Ruru and Hinewahia, the former a grandson of Taikawa. His cousin, Te Uira, was married to Tuhawaiki. 'King' gained his nickname from a jocular remark by W.B.D. Mantell, who saw him as a youth at Henley in 1854 and asked him if he was 'king of the Maoris' in those parts. Beattie had known King since about 1913 and refers to him at various points as 'the mine of information'. From him Beattie obtained information in 1920 about children's games, plant foods and scents, clothing, eeling, fishing, lizards and mythology (Beattie 1931, Hocken ms 582/E/7,8; G/l. See p. 50). Another valued informant at Kaka Point was Rakiraki (Hoani/Teone Puao/Puahu Rakiraki, John Lakitap, Jack Raki), born in 1855 at Maranuku (Molyneux), the son of Wild and Haimona Rakiraki (Rakitapu), who was known for his knowledge of the inland South Island. John Rakiraki spent his life in South Otago, mainly in the Māori village at Wilsher Bay, and was a noted fisherman and hunter (Beattie 1931, 1944, Hocken ms 582/A/6; E/8. See p. 115).

Henley

Beattie interviewed here Mrs Martin (also seen again at Tuahiwi, below), Mrs Elizabeth Crane, born 1838 to Tīti (Kuini) and William Palmer at the Tautuku whaling station (Beattie 1931), and Mrs Kui Tanner, her sister born in 1843 (Beattie 1931, Hocken ms 582/E/7). Mrs Martin (see also Tuahiwi below) was the widow of Korako Matene or Matene Korako Tumeke ('Old Colac' or 'Old Martin'), said to be a chief of Ngāti Māmoe, who died in 1896. Beattie also obtained

From left: Tiemi Haereroa Kupa, Tiori Mahure, Wiremu (Wiriama) Te Paro, and Turia Morokiekie Te Kene, photographed at Bluff in about 1935. All were valued informants of Herries Beattie. Photographer unknown, Box-003-021, Hocken Collections Uare Taoka o Hākena, University of Otago.

information from Jack Connor (Tieke Kona/Kana), born 1841 on Stewart Island. His father drowned when he was an infant and when his mother, Tarewati, remarried he went to live with Nicholas Robelia and a northern Māori woman, Romatiki. He travelled widely and in 1892 became a Māori J.P. He was especially knowledgeable about southern genealogies and place names (Beattie 1931, Hocken ms 582/E/7).

Puketeraki

At this east Otago settlement near Karitane, Beattie met Mrs Mary (Meri) Harper (see p. 65), who was born about 1842 at Waikouaiti, the daughter of Caroline Punahere and Elisha William Apes, a whaler. He also spoke to a Mrs Woods, probably Hanna Te Wahia, an elderly woman who died soon after in 1922.

Moeraki

Henare Te Kooti Rehu, born approximately 1850 at Moeraki, gave Beattie much information about north Otago during meetings at Moeraki and Tuahiwi (Beattie 1931. See p. 51.)

Waimate

Beattie spent several days here, or at nearby Waihao, with Mr and Mrs H. Te Maire (Harry Davis). Te Maire was born about 1844, the son of Rawiri Te Maire, a noted informant of Chapman and Parata in the late nineteenth century (see portrait, opposite). He was particularly knowledgeable about the interior and had

Rawiri Te Maire, n.d.
Photographer unknown, P1951-004/2-001, Hocken Collections Uare Taoka o Hākena, University of Otago.

been living there at the time of Te Puoho's raid in 1836. From H. Te Maire, Beattie learnt about planting by the phases of the moon, plant foods, fungi, scents, lizards and burial customs (Beattie 1931, 1946, Hocken ms 582/A/6; e/7). Probably at Glenavy, near Waimate, Beattie interviewed 'Te Ururaki' (judging from Beattie [1946], probably either Nani, born 1874 or Teone, born 1879, both of whom lived at Glenavy, but possibly Mihiata Te Ururaki, born 1868, who lived at Rāpaki).

Temuka

The main informant here was evidently Mrs Tiriata Kahu, born about 1845. She was a daughter of Te Maiharoa and married Hoani Korehe Kahu of Arowhenua (Hocken ms 582/E/7). She was assisted in the interviews by her daughter Wikitoria, who was the wife of Pita Paipeta (Hocken ms 582/A/13; E/7). Beattie also met a Mrs Karihana and 'Ryan' (possibly Piripi Ryan [Beattie 1944], born 1840 at Otago Heads).

Little River

Beattie obtained information about fishing in particular from 'Tom Billy' (Hoani Haupere) of this settlement (Beattie 1946).

Leeston

Here Beattie met Mrs Tini Kerei Taiaroa of Taumutu, born 1840, and her son Richard (Riki). He talked with them and visited traditional fisheries and pā sites (Beattie 1946. See portraits, pp. 233 and 309).

Rāpaki

Teone Taare Tikao (Hoani/John/J.C. Tikao), was Beattie's most important informant in all his ethnographical research (see portrait, p. 227). In the space of thirteen days of interviews (in his Murihiku manuscript Beattie says it was nineteen days), he provided most of Beattie's information about Canterbury. Tikao was born in 1850 at Tikao Bay, Wainui, near Akaroa, the only child of Rahera and Tamati Tikao. His father, a chief of the Irakehu hapu of Ngāi Tahu, had been captured as a youth by Te Rauparaha and upon release was educated in James Stack's mission school at Wairau. Tamati later established the first school at Wairewa, Banks Peninsula; and in about 1858 followed up his interest in education by sending Teone to study traditional lore and history with the two remaining tohunga in the district, Koroko and Tuauau. Ten years' studentship with them, the knowledge he gained from his father and uncle who had become Land Court assessors, and from other tribal elders such as Pāora Taki, together with his own

Carte de Visite of Paora Taki (Paul) from Port Levy, c.1870. Heslop Brothers photograph, Canterbury Museum, 19XX.2.868.

interest in genealogy and tribal politics, including a leading role in the Māori parliament of the 1890s at Papawai, Wairarapa, gave him an unparalleled understanding of traditional ways (Beattie 1939, 1990, Hocken ms 582/A/5; E/7, 8). Also at Rāpaki, Beattie interviewed Reihana Tau, born 1854 and Teone Watson, born 1853 (Beattie 1946). In Rāpaki Beattie usually stayed with Mrs Couch, and in Christchurch with her son Wira Couch.

Tuahiwi

Beattie interviewed 'the Henley lady', Mrs Martin (Hinehou Matene), on several occasions. She was visiting Tuahiwi from her usual home at Henley. She had been born about 1845 at Moeraki and was married to Matene Korako Tumeke, a descendant of Te Rakīhia. Mrs Martin was assisted in her recollections by Henare Matene and his wife Ripeka Karetai. From these sessions Beattie obtained information on childbirth, games, perfumes, burial customs and seasonal hunting trips in the Strath Taieri (Beattie 1944, 1946, Hocken ms 582/E/7). Another relative, Mrs Teripa Te Hauraraka Pitama (nee Puru Matene), born in 1881 (Beattie 1946), lent T.E. Green's manuscript to Beattie. Several other informants at Tuahiwi were 'Reuben' (possibly Hamuera Te

Aomutu Pupene, in Beattie 1946) and 'Maka' (possibly Epipha Maaka [Beattie 1946], born 1849). At Tuahiwi, Beattie also met Peter Roberts (Te Kahupuku), who had been born at Whakapuaka, Nelson, and lived for twenty-five years in the district before moving to Kaiapoi. He was recommended to Beattie by Tikao and from him came all the Nelson information. He is probably Pita Te Kahupuku Hohapata, born 1872 (Beattie 1946).

Nearly all of Beattie's informants, and certainly all the major figures, were seventy to eighty years of age. Their information, it may be assumed, had been acquired largely at a time when southern Māori fortunes were at their lowest ebb. By the late nineteenth century, nearly all the land had been alienated, the population was falling and traditional resource gathering was severely curtailed by difficulties of access to former fishing and hunting grounds. Intermarriage with Pākehā was already well advanced (Anderson 1991), and southern Māori language, custom and traditional belief were in decline. Not surprisingly, then, Beattie's detailed and persistent probing located various gaps and numerous minor contradictions in the evidence he received; but it is also apparent from the sheer quantity and variety of information and its consistency between regions, that many people of his informants' generation, perhaps the last to do so in such numbers, had made a particular effort to retain traditional knowledge.

EDITING OF MS 181

The manuscript was written on loose pages of a lined exercise book (200 mm x 260 mm) with each section held together by a brass split pin. Some pieces have been pasted on. The writing is neat and legible but has faded to grey from its original blue. So far as can be determined, the full manuscript still exists, although in the Murihiku part there is neither title page nor content for Section XII 'Greenstone'. This gap is puzzling, the more so because there is a section on greenstone amongst the material remaining from Beattie's revision of the original manuscript (Appendix 1). Beattie's own analysis of these revisions (Hocken ms 181) shows that the revised Murihiku text on greenstone contained one page of new material and nothing from the first draft. It seems probable that the new page has somehow been mislaid. However, since Beattie (1920) published his findings about greenstone up until 1919, and the original Section XII for Murihiku still exists (see Appendix 1) to show his results obtained in 1920, it may be that little, if anything, has actually been lost.

The full manuscript is 1049 pages long and divided into six parts: Murihiku (which is in a more polished form and slightly different format to the rest), Canterbury, Nelson, Westland, Traditions of Murihiku and Murihiku remainders. Traditions of Murihiku (sixty-four pages) are not included here. They were published exactly as in the manuscript by Beattie (1922). The Murihiku remainders (233 pages, 65,600 words), now stored with Hocken Library manuscript

582, consist of material left over when Beattie revised his first draft of the Murihiku volume. Much of it, which simply repeats material in the text, has not been included here. The balance of new material has been reordered as an appendix to Murihiku (Appendix 1). Where a phrase or sentence also found in the main body of the text is left in Appendix 1 to assist intelligibility, it is marked there by { }.

Within the text, Beattie occasionally added a comment of clarification or judgement within [ ] brackets, and translation or descriptive comment in ( ) brackets. These have been left intact. His marks to indicate where additional words or notes were to go have been removed and the material added as intended. Similarly, odd words and sometimes sentences crossed out have been removed where it is apparent that this was intended and no loss of content or meaning ensues. Beattie also used vertical lines through his text to indicate passages that he had already published. But he evidently intended that these would remain in the text and they have been kept in but marked by * at the beginning and ** at the end. Abbreviations such as etc. and c.f. have been left but &, vol. and directions (s.w., n.e. etc.) rendered in full. Spelling, cases capitalisation and grammar remain as in the original, except for minor corrections of obvious errors, or additions of a word or two where the sense of the text is otherwise obscured. Beattie's writing exhibits various idiosyncrasies, one of the more obvious being his preference for '…or' over '…our' in such words as behaviour, colour and armour. Where Beattie has used a macron in a Maori word this has been replaced by a double vowel. He underlined all Māori in the original, but seventy years on this seems pedantic and underlining or italics has not been added. Editorial comments, which have been kept to a minimum, are shown enclosed by [[ ]].

The references listed on p. 604 include those to works noted in the text by Beattie. It will be seen that Beattie had decided preferences in comparative material, relying especially on Tregear's 1891 *Dictionary* and 1904 volume, *The Maori Race*, together with Stack's (1893) *Kaiapohia*. Of course he did not have available, in 1920, the later Elsdon Best volumes, such as: *The Maori* (1924), *The Maori Canoe* (1925), *Games and Pastimes of the Maori* (1925), *Fishing Methods and Devices of the Maori* (1929), and *Forest Lore of the Maori* (1942), nor such useful compendia as: Buck's (1949) *The Coming of the Maori*, Oppenheim's (1973) *Maori Death Customs*, Makereti's (1938) *The Old-Time Maori*, and Phillipps's (1952) *Maori Houses and Storehouses*. These works and some others, notably Harlow's (1987) *A Word-list of South Island Maori* and Starke's (1986) edition of Boultbee's *Journal of a Rambler*, provide a useful introduction to comparative material for the modern reader.

The map that accompanied the Murihiku text has been redrawn to show the places Beattie visited in Canterbury as well (see p. 17), and occasional diagrams in the text have been re-drawn and placed in their original positions. Faunal and floral names and binomials, with suggested modern equivalents, are in Appendix 2, which also has a separate reference list (p. 606).

Houses & Villages

In a kaika (village) some of the buildings were of the familiar ∧ shape whilst others were circular or almost so. The former were the more important; the latter were the abode of the common people. Descriptions of the houses (whares) written by Europeans in 1823 and 1830, are to be found in "Murihiku" (1st edition) pp 215 and 264, and these can be compared with Maori traditional lore. The largest building in a village would be the meeting-house (called variously whare-huika; whare-huihui or whare-runaka). One named "Matiti", constructed at Korotuaheka (Waitaki Mouth), had walls (tara) of 4 or 5 feet high built of sods (pae) through which raw posts (poupou o te tara). It had several poutokomanawa (centre posts) but being made as late as the "sixties" it had no carvings. It was opened with considerable ceremony but later was destroyed by fire.

In such a building the wall-plate was called paetara; the window, matao; the door, tatau; doorstep, paepae; roof, tahu; rafters, heke; battens, kaho; while the end of the house opposite the door was tuaroko. After the rafters & battens, were on the roof this was covered with pukakaho reeds & thatched with patiti (tussock). The pukakaho the collector was told is the reed of the toetoe plant, the name toetoe belonging to the clump from which the reed springs, while the fluff at the top is its huruhuru (hair). In former days meeting-houses often had on top a carving known as the "tiki o te whare". The house at Temuka was carved in places, & inside it the poutokomanawa posts were carved in the likeness of tupuna (ancestors) both male & female. Gable ends were called matapihi, the verandah te maihi & the small wall before it, paepae.

A well-equipped kaika had also to have a wharepuni for visitors to sleep in. To make the wharepuni snug & warm the foundation was dug in the ground, while two of the old men also asserted that the roof was covered with earth (in some cases at least). Against this one of my aged informants considered that wharepunis were confined to the North Island.

The chiefs and upper class usually had houses of the ∧ shape and if these were of fair size they were sometimes designated whare-nui to distinguish them from the round houses, which were also called whare, although their particular name was porotaka. A chief's house usually had four poupoutokomanawa or mainposts — one supporting the verandah, one the rear wall & the other two standing in the interior, these usually being carved.

A page from manuscript 181. 'Houses & Villages', from 'Record of interviews with South Island Māori, entitled, "The Maori in Murihiku", sections 1 to 15 (1920)', James Herries Beattie papers, MS-0181/001, Hocken Collections Uare Taoka o Hākena, University of Otago.

ACKNOWLEDGEMENTS

Permission to transcribe and publish the Beattie manuscript was given by Mr Stuart Strachan, Hocken Librarian, and Ms Margaret Beattie (Waimate). I am indebted to them and also to Mr Douglas Girvan, Registrar, and Mr Richard Cassels, Director, who permitted respectively the use of University of Otago and Otago Museum archives. Mr Peter Miller and Mr David MacDonald were particularly helpful at the Hocken Library, and Mr Graeme McKinstry (Computing Services Centre) and the late Mrs Jacqui Pilditch (Anthropology Department) assisted with transcribing difficulties. For useful advice on technical or historical matters I thank Associate Professor Hel-en Leach and Mr Graeme Mason (Anthropology Department), Mr Richard Cassels and Dr Tipene O'Regan (Wellington). For assistance with illustrations, I thank Mr Leslie O'Neill and Mr Martin Fisher (Anthropology Department). The project was supported by Te Rūnanga ō Ōtākou. Ms Carolyn Campbell (Dunedin) transcribed the manuscript and carried out many research tasks. I am indebted to her for care, diligence and willingness of a high order. Her work was funded by the University of Otago, the 1990 Commission, the New Zealand Employment Service and the New Zealand Lottery Grants Board. Ms Wendy Harrex and Dr Helen Watson White of University of Otago Press provided valuable editorial advice. A handsome contribution towards the cost of publication was made from the de Beer Family Publications and Research Fund by the Otago Museum Trust Board. This assistance is gratefully acknowledged.

ATHOLL ANDERSON

MURIHIKU

CONTENTS

Section		Introductory Remarks 35
		Foreword written in February 1957 40
	I	Habitations, Sleeping Places, Storehouses, Fortifications 41
	II	Clothing 46
	III	Flaxwork 52
	IV	Personal Adornment 54
	V	Paints, Dyes, Colours, Perfumes 59
	VI	Tattooing, Wood-Carving 64
	VII	Play, Games, Pastimes, Recreation, Amusements, Entertainments, Water-Sports, Musical Instruments, Singing and Dancing 67
	VIII	Medical Lore 82
	IX	Disposal of the Dead 88
	X	Customs 93
	XI	Weapons 100
	XIII	Canoes and Paddles, Torches and Torching, Spades and Digging 108
	XIV	Domestic Science 111
	XV	Vegetable Foods, etc. 117
	XVI	Fish, Eels, Sharks, Whales, Shellfish 129
	XVII	Birds 163
	XVIII	Insects, Worms, Lizards 185
	XIX	Dogs, Rats, Bats 187
	XX	Trees, Shrubs, Plants, Tussocks, Ferns 191
	XXI	Winds, Weather, Rainbows, Stars, Seasons 196
	XXII	Wharekura, Tapu, Karakia, Tuahu, Tohukas, Witchcraft, Omens 204
	XXIII	Folk Tales 215
	XXIV	Table giving names of Relationships (South Island dialect) at Oraka (Colac Bay), Waikouaiti, Moeraki and at Temuka kaikas 218

MAORI IN MURIHIKU

Oral Traditionary Lore gathered From the Maoris and Halfcastes of Murihiku, New Zealand, (viz., From Stewart Island to Temuka, Canterbury), By H. Beattie, Collector, Acting under the authority and direction of H.D. Skinner Lecturer on Ethnology at the University of Otago.

INTRODUCTORY REMARKS

The following information was gathered from the Southern Maoris in the year 1920. Owing to the collector's imperfect knowledge of spoken Maori all my informants gave their answers in English. Some of the descriptions and passages may be criticised from the literary standpoint but the collector pleads that he has kept as nearly as he could to the language used by the old Maori men and women he consulted and this fact should be remembered all through. Whenever he was doubtful of the meaning he kept questioning until he was convinced he had satisfactorily grasped what his informants intended to convey.

The information contained in this memoir is supplementary to the writer's previous collection which has been published in the *Journal of the Polynesian Society* (1917–23) and in the *Transactions of New Zealand Institute* (Volume LII).

If there is a certain amount of duplication in the present memoir it should be remembered that the information was gathered in twenty-three localities ranging over a distance of three hundred miles, and at intervals during a period of twelve months. Hence the information varied a good deal, principally in details, but it was thought advisable to err on the side of reiteration rather than miss any shade of opinion.

The collector met with a kindly reception from the Maoris, most of whom were glad to assist the quest. He doubts whether he would have been equally well received by a similar number of Europeans or as patiently endured during long and tiresome cross-examinations. Here the lack of time-sense on the part of the Polynesian (a defect shared by most other primitive peoples) was an asset, but the good breeding of the Maori was also constantly in evidence. Courtesy and hospitality are two features in the traditional etiquette of the Maori and the Collector here records his grateful appreciation of them. Although the older Maoris are becoming sophisticated by contact with civilisation they still retain many of the characteristics of those whom Kipling designates the childlike races. In many things the Maori is like a grown-up child, but contrary to the precept 'Familiarity breeds contempt', the collector ended his work among them with the most genuine regret and will always remember the folk he worked among with affection and respect.

Prior to setting out on this quest (which was arranged and organised by Mr

H.D. Skinner) the collector filled a notebook with many hundreds of questions arranged under headings and this formed the basis of his work. As an indication of the length of the discussions involved, it may be mentioned that it took an intelligent old Maori and the collector nineteen days (of an average of eight or nine hours each) to work through the list.

The collector would further like to say that he considers it a wonderful thing that so much information can even at this late date be gathered from Southern sources. A sealing gang operated at Preservation Inlet in the year 1792 and from that time onward the Murihiku Maoris have been in contact with white men. Thus we find that they seemed to lose their traditional lore so completely that a European writing in the *Otago Witness* in 1856 says that the few Maoris then resident in Otago and Southland appeared to have even forgotten their own language, and could speak nothing but a broken English. Similarly Colenso writing in 1881 said that no South Island Maori could then be relied on for accurate information regarding his race. Yet the experience of the collector in 1920 showed what an amount of material could be accumulated even at so late a date. The memories of some of the old people were getting rather shaky and this doubtless accounts for some of the apparent discrepancies but this detracts little from the remarkable feat of memory of this scanty remnant of a race which has associated with the white race for over a century.

Another thing which calls for comment is the limitation of the Maori alphabet by those responsible for committing it to paper. Twenty years ago the collector was on a visit to Stewart Island and asked a very intelligent Native what the Maori name of Rabbit Island was. 'Falafala,' he replied. The collector incredulously stated that there was no 'f' or 'l' in the Maori language and that 'Falafala' sounded like a Samoan name. His informant laughed and replied, 'You white people would spell it w-h-a-r-a-w-h-a-r-a. When I was a boy the old people called Stewart Island "Lakiula". Then when I was middle-aged they were calling it "Rakiula", and now we all say "Rakiura" the same as the white man.'

Not only was 'l' used in the South Island but also, the collector believes, in the North Island. Reverend Joseph King, the veteran missionary of Samoa, told me that he once informed the principal of Te Aute College that the Maoris used 'l' as well as the Samoans. The principal called a senior boy and asked him. To his surprise the lad replied that the Maoris did use 'l', and the principal chaffed him that it was a modern Maori addition. 'Not so,' stoutly maintained the youth, 'it is only the very old people who use it.'

In addition to the usual fifteen letters of the written Maori alphabet [A, E, H, I, K, M, N, Ng, 0, P, R, T, U, W, Wh] the collector believes that to make it really representative of the phonetic sounds of the Maori tongue (as spoken in the South at least) it should include B, D, F, G, L, and V. This belief may incur the scorn of some excellent Maori scholars but on the face of it it seems ridiculous to hold that the Maori was incapable of using vowel and consonantal sounds common to Samoans, Tahitians, Hawaiians and other branches of his wide-flung race.

Herries Beattie, Waimate. James Herries Beattie papers, MS-582/R/1, Hocken Collections Uare Taoka o Hākena, University of Otago.

Reverend J.F.H. Wohlers for forty years a missionary among the Foveaux Strait Maoris says the Murihiku dialect was an uncouth one. So it was compared to Northern speech; the Southern Maori readily admits this; but it seems to the collector this was occasioned by its admixture of the old Moriori tongue with the language of their Maori conquerors. The Moriori strain was always strong in Murihiku according to the traditions and its presence is indicated by letter-changes such as 'hotu' for 'whatu'; 'horau' for 'wharau', etc., and by the clipping of words, such as kaik for kaika, halakek for harakeke, and so on.

It must be noted by readers of these Maori narrations and descriptions that the vowels A, E; and A, O; and E, I; and I, U; and O, U; are interchangeable. A is frequently used in South Island where E fulfils a similar function in the North Island and the collector noticed that some villages pronounced E where others used I. This accounts for what may seem vagaries of spelling in the various accounts. Another point the collector noticed was that where two H's occur in a word the first is often dropped as in koikohi for kohikohi, tapiapiha for tapihapiha (a fish's gills), and so on.

A point that the collector has never seen stressed in any publication and which is absolutely essential for a thorough grasp of Maori names of birds, fish, trees, etc., is that the same names are used for totally different objects in the North and South Islands respectively.

Thus the kuaka of the North Island is the godwit, and the kuaka of the South is a kind of muttonbird, the godwit being called powaka or poaka. The piopio is a thrush in the North Island, but it is a morepoke owl in the South Island. The pipi of the North Island is a completely different shellfish to the pipi of the South, and so on through scores of instances. The kahikatea (white pine) of the North Island is the kahika (white pine) of the South Island. The people of Murihiku did not use the word koromiko at all, the shrub of that name being called kokomuka, but the Railway Department in its wisdom has imposed the name Koromiko on a siding near Orepuki. This difference in the Maori identification of many objects common to both islands must never be forgotten by anyone desirous of accuracy.

Another thing which should be remembered is that the Murihiku Maori had to scratch hard for vegetable additions to his menu as the kumera did not grow south of Lake Ellesmere, while the Karaka with its edible fruit was not found south of Banks Peninsula. This was the southern limit also of the titoki tree whose berries yielded oil, and the beautiful nikau palm's natural southern limit was Akaroa.

The Southern Maori became, perforce, a mighty hunter of birds and a bold fisherman. In his frail canoes he braved the tempestuous seas round his home and this hardihood in seafaring was a source of admiration to early white men. F.T. Bullen in his 'Cruise of the Cachalot' pays a just tribute to the skill and daring of the Maori and half-caste crew of the celebrated Captain Paddy Gilroy.

The Murihiku Maori was also a fighter and when Te Rauparaha devastated Canterbury the natives from Foveaux Straits went all the way to Marlborough to meet him and they had the better of the fighting when they met. This warlike trait led to many a sanguinary encounter with the early sealers in Southern waters.

It was to the present-day representatives of this historic people that the collector went with his array of notebooks and the result is embodied in the following pages.

Note: The information which immediately follows was collected from the Maoris of Southern New Zealand in January, February, March 1920. The Maoris who gave information are mostly between sixty and ninety years of age, their names being:

Mesdames	Tiriata Kahu	Temuka
	P. Piper	Temuka
	H. te Maire	Waimate
	Inehou Matene	Taiari
	Mere Tanner	Taiari
	T. Whaitiri	Tuturau
Messrs	Henare te Maire	Waimate
	Henare te Kooti Rehu	Moeraki
	Tieke Kona	Taiari
	John Puahu Rakiraki	Maranuku
	Eruete Kinihi Kurupohatu	Maranuku
	Tiemi Kupa Haereroa	Oraka
	Wiremu te Paro	Bluff
	George Newton	Ruapuke
	_____ te Ururaki	Ruapuke
	Hoani Matiu	Kapuka
	Hoani Kaiporohu	Rakiura
	etc.	

See end of Canterbury information. H.B. Note: A full list will be supplied at conclusion of the research. H.B.

FOREWORD WRITTEN IN FEBRUARY 1957

In sending the first (or what we can call the rough) copy of my Murihiku fieldwork to the Hocken Library a few words of explanation may be advisable. I wrote at the time:

'Of its honesty I am fully convinced. It is so easy to give a little extra polish to the philosophy of a savage race. I went among them with no preconceived notions, no theories to uphold, and no previous knowledge to colour what was told me. I relegate myself to the background, and keep to the simplicity of my informants, and neither overstate nor understate the information given me. It is a faithful record. Herries Beattie.'

This was against it being published as a scientific work, as one critic described it as 'too slangy', and another said that in giving the various answers of my aged friends there was too much re-iteration, and I was told to re-write it.

This I did and placed the manuscript in the Hocken Library where it still is. Needless to say it was not published – if it had been it would have been the first book of its kind in New Zealand for there is nothing resembling it in print.

When I re-wrote the work I used as much as I could of the first copy and what was left is now forwarded to you. Some of this unused information is not in any of my other writings and may be worth preserving, notably the tales told in Section 23 and Section 28 which is intact and items in Section 1 and 12, etc.

All the pages stroked off in red ink were used and could be burned; where there is a sentence or two not stroked out these could perhaps be typed before burning.

The proposed introductory preface is included for its explanatory value.

JAMES HERRIES BEATTIE

SECTION 1

HABITATIONS, SLEEPING PLACES, STOREHOUSES, FORTIFICATIONS

HOUSES AND VILLAGES

In a kaika (village) some of the buildings were of the familiar ⋀ shape whilst others were circular or almost so. The former were the more important; the latter were the abode of the common people. Descriptions of the houses (whares) written by Europeans in 1823 and 1830, are to be found in *Murihiku* (1st edition) pp. 215 and 264 [[McNab 1907]], and these can be compared with Maori traditional lore. The largest building in a village would be the meeting house (called variously whare-huika, whare-huihui or whare-runaka). One named 'Matiti', constructed at Korotuaheka (Waitaki Mouth), had walls (tara) of four or five feet high built up of sods (pae) through which ran posts (poupou o te tara). It had several poutokomanawa (centre posts) but being made as late as the 'sixties' it had no carvings. It was opened with considerable ceremony but later was destroyed by fire.

In such a building the wall-plate was called paetara; the window, matao; the door, tatau; doorstep, paepae; roof, tahu; rafters, heke; battens, kaho; while the end of the house opposite the door was tuaroko. After the rafters and battens were on the roof this was covered with pukakaho reeds and thatched with patiti (tussock). [The pukakaho the collector was told is the reed of the toetoe plant, the name toetoe belonging to the clump from which the reed springs, while the fluff at the top is its huruhuru (hair).] In former days meeting-houses often had on top a carving known as the 'tiki o te whare'. The house at Temuka was carved in places, and inside it the poutokomanawa posts were carved in the likeness of tupuna (ancestors) both male and female. Gable ends were called matapihi, the verandah te maihi, and the small wall before it, paepae.

A well-equipped kaika had also to have a wharepuni for visitors to sleep in. To make the wharepuni snug and warm the foundation was dug in the ground, while two of the old men also asserted that the roof was covered with earth (in some cases at least). Against this one of my aged informants considered that wharepunis were confined to the North Island.

The chiefs and upper class usually had houses of the ⋀ shape and if these were of fair size they were sometimes designated whare-nui to distinguish them from the round houses, which were also called whare, although their particular name was porotaka. A chief's house usually had four poupoutokomanawa or mainposts – one supporting the verandah, one the rear wall and the other two standing in the interior, these usually being carved.

To construct a round whare (in which no centre pole is used) timber with a curve or bend in it is sought. This timber is known as whiti and the cross pieces as kaho. It is thatched with wiwi (rushes), patiti (tussock), or similar vegetation this thatch being called rau. A hole called putaka-au or sometimes koroputa is left in the top to let in light and let out smoke. A fireplace guarded by stones (called pae by one of my informants) was in the centre of the floor and this fireplace was called taukahi according to two of the old men and takuahi according to others. An old lady said to me: 'I have seen a whare with a hole in the roof for smoke and light, but that was only a hut – a whare-rau – one with grass on'. She went on to say that (though the North Islanders said that the buildings in the South were different to theirs) the whares of old were well made of wood with totara bark round and roofed with cane and wiwi. The people were industrious and employed skill and energy in house-building as in other pursuits. Several of my informants said that round whares made on the old traditional lines are yet to be seen on the Titi Islands (off Stewart Island), the timber used being tupari, titiaweka and inaka, thatched with tataki grass and having grass doors, the huts so made being warm.

A door was tatau and when there was no door, the doorway was still called tatau, the post on each side being called te roro o te whare (the brains of the house). When there was no rakau (wood) door the opening was hung with a tiaka mat, this mat being often called a pahuri although this name pahuri rightfully denotes a shelter of branches, rushes, flax, grass, etc., run up in the bush or on river banks when travelling about birding or fishing. The pahuri had no front in it but it was made to suit the prevailing weather conditions. It is described as having been both sheltering and warm. The Maoris nowadays usually call such shelters 'maimai' but my aged friends consider that this is a 'foreign word'. [The collector thinks it an Australian aborigine word introduced by the early runholders who came from Australia to Southland.] One of my informants said the first house he had after being married was a round whare.

A European who visited the Taieri [My informants say spelling Taieri is correct according to the Southern dialect.] kaika in 1858 tells me the whares were ∧ shape, constructed of bark tied with flax, and were snug and waterproof.

In Tregear's [[1891]] *Dictionary* 'tako' is given as the common house of a community, especially of the young men and Reverend Wohlers is quoted as using the term whare-tako in this connection. The collector inquired regarding this word but could find no one who knew it. An old man who was born on Ruapuke Island did not know it and added that he had heard a building set apart for the young people to amuse themselves in, called a whare-takaro (play house) or a wharehaka or wharehanga (dancing house). He had heard the term niu used to describe a house where people could meet, but he had heard it very seldom and thought it was perhaps a Northern name for a meeting house.

Another aged man said he had not heard of the whare-tako, nor had he heard the expression whare-hanga (this is the Murihiku rendering of wharehaka) used in Southern New Zealand. It might be used in other parts of the country but he had certainly not heard this name used in Canterbury, Otago nor Southland. On the other hand he had heard a meeting-house called a whare-korero, but more recently Halls on the European plan had been built in most Maori centres and each hall had a name of its own, mostly given in honour of renowned ancestors.

In regard to the pronunciation of the word whare, the collector found it was invariably pronounced as spelt in old colonist documents, i.e. 'warrie'. The Southern Maori usually pronounces 'wh' as 'f' but the collector never heard 'fare' but always 'ware'. The word whakapapa follows the same rule being pronounced wakapapa. Whata on the other hand is always pronounced fata, gutturally, sounding like 'futtah'. A description of the whata will be given later on in this section.

Travelling parties sometimes carried flax or aka-tororaro (a kind of creeper) to tie the sticks and bind the thatching for pahuri or maimai. These shelters could be made of poles, branches, poka (treeferns), leaves, rushes, tussock, manuka or other materials available and would keep the rain and wind out for several days if well-made by competent persons.

SLEEPING PLACES

In a round whare the fire was in the centre and the sleeping-places (moeka) were ranged round, with sticks (pae) in the ground to keep them in place. Scrub or sometimes flax was laid on the ground and thickly spread with patiti (white tussock) and covered with a tiaka mat on which the sleeper lay, covering himself with kakahu or taniko mats as his station in life permitted. One of my informants said that the moeka was sometimes filled in with fern but two of the others (whom the collector saw together) considered that scrub and tussock were more commonly used. Sticks called pae were driven into the ground to keep this bedding from scattering over the floor.

The whare-nui for the aristocracy had beds, continued my informants, and they maintained these were used before the pakeha came to New Zealand. These beds were called rara and (so far as the collector could understand) poupou (posts) were driven into the ground and battens (rauraho – pronounced laulaho) were tied on to them with flax. These battens were covered with rushes (wiwi) over which was spread tussock, (mania or patiti) and on this were laid two tiaka (mats). The under one was a tiaka-wahi (of unscraped green flax) while the one above it on which the sleeper lay was a tiaka-haro, or mat of fine scraped flax. This flax was as a rule steamed in an umu (earth-oven) and was very white and soft. The bed coverings were several mats of the softest whitau (prepared flax fibre). These bed mats were called kakahu, the same as the mats worn by persons, but were larger (and sometimes differently made) than the ones for personal wear.

Great pains were taken to have the beds comfortable. 'The people of old were never idle and did their work without fuss or urging.'

One of my informants had when a boy slept in such a bed as described and he says the flax kakahu were 'fine, soft and warm'. He stoutly maintained they were as good as pakeha blankets.

Each rara was apportioned to a definite person as his or her property. In accordance with traditional etiquette a kauati (fire-stick) was placed at the side of each bed and no one else was permitted to touch another person's rara or kauati. Pillows were for the aged alone and only some used them. The pillow (uruka) was a suitable piece of wood or stone with a mat over it, it is said, but sometimes a doubled mat or a clump of clean tussock covered with a folded mat would be used.

An old woman said she had never seen fern beds but the down of the bulrush (raupo) was cleaned and used for moeka. She had seen titi feathers put in flax mattresses. Even to this day some of the old people prefer the ancient method to European beds, and sleep on earthern floors using modern blankets instead of flax mats.

STOREHOUSES

No kaika (village) would be complete without its storehouses, the general name for which is whata. The name can be applied to anything which holds food or to which food is suspended. Thus if two posts are erected with a cross beam between and eels are hung to it, this is called a whata. The ordinary storehouse (wharepu) is built sometimes on two and sometimes on four posts and is within ordinary reach. The boards that form its floor are called papaka and are lashed with aka vine. The little sliding door is called tatau, the same as the doors of houses. My informants had not heard the name pataka applied to any form of whata.

Another form of storehouse (or rather the previously described form in a more elevated position) is called whata-teitei (high whata) and was used to store food for winter. It was reached by an arawhata (literally 'road to whata' – a name now applied to any ladder). This was a log flattened on the back and with steps (pae) cut up the front side. When not in use this arawhata was taken down so that rats would not climb up and it was sometimes hidden so that thieves would not be tempted to steal.

The wharepu built on the whata of ordinary height was well within the reach of marauding rats so a temporary expedient or procedure called 'whena te pou' was sometimes adopted. This was to tie green harakeke (flax) up the posts of the whata lengthwise and the rodents' feet could get no purchase on the slippery surface. The ends of the flax were bent outwards.

A whata found by Europeans on the Waimea Plains in the 'fifties' had deep notches round its legs or posts to keep the rats from climbing up. One old Maori said he had seen whata 'legs' with niches to keep the kiore (rats) out, but he forgot what the old people called those notches. Another supplied the name as whati-whati and added that the cut was slanted up from the bottom and made abrupt at the top. In addition the papaka (floor) was projected over the pou (posts) to further frustrate the attempted inroads of the rodents.

Over at the Titi Islands some of the Natives call the stage erected to hang the birds on, the whata, although its correct name is tirewa or tiroa.

FORTIFICATIONS

The Southern Maoris never constructed fortifications as frequently or as elaborately as their Northern brethren did. There was not the same need. The people were fewer in number and lived much further apart. The pa outlines so familiar on suitable ground in the North Island are few and far between in the South Island and the fingers of Time have mostly effaced the evidences to such an extent that the olden earthworks are now so faintly visible as to be deciphered with difficulty. Such evidences still exist at Kartigi, Waikouaiti, Purakanui, Henley and Orepuki.

According to my informants the line of main defence in a pa was the tuwatawata or palisading, usually of totara posts strongly bound with the tough creeper known as akatotara. Earth was thrown up against this palisade on both sides and a ditch called aparua was formed. A lighter palisade known usually as a takitaki (but sometimes as aria) was outside the main defence. In the tuwatawata at intervals there were huge posts which were simply called poupourahi (big posts). Some had a carving or whakapakoko at the top. You could not scale the palisading without an arawhata (ladder) and here and there on the inside were puhara (platforms) for the purposes of defence. A taumata or watch-tower was built up within the pa while ngutu or gateways, usually two or three in number, were placed at convenient sites.

Wohlers [[1874]] in *Transactions of the New Zealand Institute* Volume 7 page 32 gives patatara as 'an old house' but one of my informants said the word meant the 'parapet of a pa'. Another man said the banks of the trench were called tauapa and that alternate names for the ditch itself were paruarua and oruarua.

When there was not time to build a proper pa a temporary defence was to erect a pikiraki or pekeraki. There was no trenching work done – it was simply a protective fence. One old man called the big posts in a fortification, taki.

SECTION II

CLOTHING

[CLOTHING]

It was necessary that the Murihiku Maori should have warm clothing to protect him from the elements. The principal item of clothing was the mat (kakahu) usually made of flax although other supplementary things were used.

Sharp stones or flakes called mata were used to cut the flax, which was then scraped (tika-whitau) with the shell of the pipi (*Mytilus lutus*). [[Note that here and elsewhere Beattie's 'pipi' shell is the mussel shell.]]

The undressed flax was called harakeke and the dressed fibre whitau [or muka in North Island talk]. Scraping flax was also called haro and the refuse left was known as toreka.

It was the whitau that formed the basis of most Maori clothing and if skilfully woven (whatu) it made warm, comfortable and supple garments. It was woven on two sticks called poupou-whatu (or sometimes turuturu) and the first line of weaving was called aho. A string connected the two sticks and on this string the weaving commenced. Ordinary whitau was white in colour but if it was dyed, the introduction of the dyed whitau into the work in progress was called taniko.

Kakahu were the same for man (tane) and woman (wahine).

Those who have noticed early European descriptions of Murihiku call flax mats 'kakahow', will be interested to know that some of the old Maoris occasionally pronounce the word something like that.

Kakahu is the general name for all kinds of woven mats whether used for bedding or for personal wear and the name is now applied to all clothes but the collector was told that weruweru was the correct name for clothing. The following are mats mentioned by my informants: Kakahu taniko is a plain mat with a border marked ⌒⌒⌒⌒ in black. Kakahu torotoro is a mat that is relieved with wavy markings called weuweu. Kakahu korowai (no description was given of this mat). Kakahu miromiro is a whitau mat adorned with black thrums (miromiro). These thrums are put on the knee and rolled (miromiro) and they are then knotted at the ends. This is said to have been a very quick method of pleating and effective because it never comes undone unless the string breaks.

Kakahu ihupuni (also uhupuni) is a dogskin mat. It has a whitau foundation to which are attached narrow strips of dogskin – about twelve inches long by half an inch wide, said one old man. He further added that these strips were sewn on in layers like thatching a house and that feathers were sometimes inserted here and there for decorative effect.

Kakahu topuni is a feather mat, according to several of my informants. It is usually made of kiwi and toroa (albatross) but other feathers can also be utilised, one aged man mentioning one of weka skins. Against this opinion however, must be recorded the description given by an intelligent woman that the topuni is a rough flax mat. Flax that dries in the bush is called koka and this would be cut and beaten (patu) between two stones (pohatu) and then steeped in water for two or three days – ka potia roto wai. It was then washed (horoi) and then spread out (horahia) in the sun until dried sufficiently, when it was taken and woven (whatu) into a garment. It was rougher and darker than whitau, was not dyed, and made a rainproof mat suitable for winter wear. That was the real topuni. [The conflict between these two descriptions is interesting and may be susceptible of explanation, although the collector has no further information on the subject at present. It may be added that the former opinion was gathered round Foveaux Strait and the latter one about two hundred miles north of it. Tregear's [[1891]] *Dictionary* gives the meaning of topuni as a black dogskin mat. It seems to me that the weight of opinion in the South is on the side of topuni being a feather cloak and that the garment described by the lady would be a kakahu-koka.]

Kakahu-tikumu is a mat of flax fibre into which is worked the soft white down scraped off the leaves of the mountain daisy (tikumu).

Kakahu-houi is a mat made of ribbonwood bark (kiri houi). This bark can be scraped, dried and beaten into a kind of material suitable for making mats (kakahu), baskets (kete), poi balls, fillets (kopare), belts (tatua), piupiu for haka dancing, and, in recent years, smoking caps. One of my informants deplored the fact that the houi (ribbonwood) was now so scarce that the New Zealand Government would not permit 'Tihore te rakau' (barking the trees). The bark, it is said, was not dyed in olden days but is coloured now to make fancy articles for modern use on a small scale. None of my informants had seen a whole kakahu made of houi – the knowledge of such is traditional. Kakahu-koroiti (or Kakahu-iti) is a short shoulder cloak but no particulars were given as to its manufacture.

Pins made of bone were sometimes used to hold the two ends of kakahu fastened over the chest, and these fastenings were called tui or titia. Many kakahu had strings attached to them.

RAINCOATS

Pokeka-tikumu is a rainproof cloak of flax fibre and mountain daisy leaves. The whitau is woven (whatu) as in ordinary mats but rows of big tikumu leaves are attached with aho (threads) of fine whitau. This coarse cloak is designed to protect the wearer from rain (awha or ua) and snow (huka). Pokeka-toi is made of whitau to which is attached the big leaves of the titoi tree. This tree is a kind of dwarf ti (cabbagetree) and its very wide flaxlike leaves (called toi) are excellent for warding off showers. Pokeka-patiti is a waterproof cloak of whitau laid over with layers of tussock (patiti).

Pokeka-pikao was described to me as follows: 'The pikao is a cutty-grass that grows by the seaside; it is not the ordinary cutty-grass which is called matoreha. The women put it in a waka (wooden basin) in which kiripokaka (pokaka bark) was steeping. This was to soften the pikao for pleating (whatu). It was then put to dry (pehi) and was afterwards woven into a pokeka to keep off the rain.'

Pokeka-koka is made of koka or flax that has died in the bush. The rotten part at the end of the dead leaves is cut off with a pipi shell or a stone knife (parihi pohatu) and the remainder is used to make a rough cloak.

On a cold wet day the kakahu mats could be brought closer to the body with tatua (belts) and this enabled the pokeka to be slipped on over them easier. All my informants united in praising the waterproof qualities of a good pokeka. An aged native of Stewart Island said he had seen pokeka-toi and could speak of their excellent qualities. He had also experienced the benefit of using a pokeka made of pieces of flax which had been scraped (tika) into a rough whitau. This had then been 'sewed overlapping like the shingles on a roof' and added the old man in picturesque vein, 'No rain from heaven could penetrate it.'

WAIST MATS

Kinikini is correctly a waist garment or kilt. Statements made to the collector at Moeraki and Puketiraki that it could also be hung on the shoulder (so that if a person had two, one could be suspended from the shoulder and the other from the waist) did not meet with approval generally and finally it was unanimously agreed that the correct usage was as a kilt. Ocular demonstrations were given to show that although the kinikini could be hung from the shoulder it would not hang properly except when worn as originally intended. It is made of dried flax, not koka but harakeke maroke (flax dried after cutting) and this curls up like long quills. Each of these hard quills is 'pinched' at regular intervals into short sections of soft threads. The word kini means 'to pinch' and the process is done with pipi shells. All the quills are then put in parapara (black mud dye) but the hard portions will not take the dye, only the soft 'pinched' sections doing so. The consequence is that the hard portions remaining white, and the soft portions turning black, form an attractive striped pattern of alternate white and black. The waistband to which these long, dangling quills are attached is called te hope. When the wearer of one of these garments moves about, the quills rattle against one another and this is considered to be a help to effectiveness when the owner is dancing the haka.

Pakipaki is a waist mat said to have been mainly worn by the women. It is made of ti (cabbage tree leaves) or flax and is not intended to make a noise when the wearer moves about although the present meaning of the work pakipaki is 'to clap hands'.

Piupiu is a waist mat which seems to serve two purposes. It can be made of whitau in the roll or twist known as the miro fashion, or of the prepared bark of the ribbonwood. Made thus it is practically a silent garment but it can also be made of dried flax to make a swishing, rustling sound when the owner is engaged in hakas or in twirling the poi balls.

Maro is the name of a loin cloth made of soft, flexible whitau. It used to be worn by men in warfare when it was fastened to a tatua (belt) but very little is known about it. The maro for women is different from that for the men and the pakipaki is intended to be worn over it.

Tatua (belts) were sometimes made of houi (ribbonwood) or kauheke, but far more commonly of whitau. Those belonging to famous chiefs are referred to in the history of the South Island Maoris a number of times.

Kauheke is a small tree, 'something like an apple tree', whose bark is very similar to that of the ribbonwood and which can be used for similar purposes to that of the latter in making kopare (hair fillets) tatua (belts) and piupiu mats. It may even have been used for garments but its use in any case is very much less than that of the ribbonwood for it grows on the hills and is consequently harder to procure.

MAORI CLOTHING IN OTAGO MUSEUM

The following were the names supplied by two old Maoris [[King and Rehu]]: D10.236 Kinikini, D10.237 Kinikini, D10.232 Kakahu miromiro, D10.233 Kakahu miromiro, D10.230 Ihupuni, D10.231 Weruweru taniko, D10.227 (name forgotten), D10.238 Pokeka, D10.239 Pokeka (made of snowgrass). [[Also, no accession numbers:]] Pokeka-toi (rough raincoat), Kakahu-houi (ribbonwood garment), Piupiu (waist garment), Topuni (feather mat).

Tregear makes a statement that kahu-kekeno (cloaks of sealskin) were made by the Maori 'but were rare except in the extreme South'. Inquiries revealed the fact that the olden Maoris had been in the habit of singeing off the skins of the various seals they killed and eating the carcases, but the oldest man interviewed said that he had heard that in exceptional cases the skin of the fur seal (kekeno) had been made into mats. He had further heard that in the earliest sealing days the kekeno skins had been made into potae (hats) for both races alike.

HEADWEAR

An old man who had been reared at Otago Heads said that when he was a small boy he had seen the old Maori people wearing a flax hat called the whareama. It was round in shape, high in the centre of the crown and afforded no shade to the eyes. It was made of whitau (dressed flax fibre) which was twisted and pleated roughly to the shape of the head. He considered it was derived from an idea given to the Maoris by the earliest whalers.

All my informants concurred in the opinion that the whareama copied a Pakeha (European) custom, and that, correctly speaking, there was no ancient

Beattie's 'mine of information', Kingi Ruru (above) and Henare Te Kooti Rehu (right), who supplied much information about north Otago. The two men also visited the Otago Museum with Beattie, identifying artifacts and supplying names and information. Ruru photo: photographer unknown, P1951-003/1-155, Hocken Collections Uare Taoka o Hākena; Rehu photo by W. A. Taylor, Canterbury Museum, 1968.213.3214.

Maori hat. Widows wore a mourning cap called a potae and sat mourning in a building called a wharepotae. It appears that when the Maoris first saw the caps and headgear of the sailors on the first ships to come round our coasts they called the strange head-coverings potae after the ancient name for the widow's mourning cap and that from this simple beginning the practice spread until now any hat is called potae.

None of my informants except the one aged man already mentioned had ever seen a whareama but all had heard of it. The men and women of old before the Pakeha came had no need of hats, they said, as they had long hair and were hardy,

but when they saw the Europeans wearing hats they began to think their heads were cold without such protection and so they made flax hats.

In the dictionary the word kopare is translated 'a shade or veil for the eyes', but all my informants agreed in describing it as a fillet or hair-binding or headband. It could be made of undressed flax or of whitau or of ribbonwood. One old man contradicted a statement that kopare could be made of toatoa. The bark of this tree could be pulled but it was unlike houi and was not suitable. The bark of the kauheke, however, could be pleated into bands for hair-binding. The kiri, or bark, of the houi and kauheke, as far as the collector could ascertain, were the only ones used for kopare.

FOOTWEAR

To protect the feet in walking over rough, stony or thorny ground the Maoris in the south wore what they call paraerae (sandals). These were usually made of flax although plenty were made of ti (cabbage-tree) leaves, the latter kind being more durable. When completed the sole is called papanui the same name as the sole of the foot. The sides are called ka-taha-o-te-paraerae and when the sandal has an upright piece for the heel to rest against this is called whaka-reke (reker-eke being the heel of the foot). The flax fastenings across the paraerae to keep the foot in place are known as kaakau while the string to fasten round the ankle is simply called tau.

Taupa (leggings) were worn by the men in warfare when in rough country and also when passing through tumatakauru (Wild Irishman). These taupa were made of tikumu, whitau or patiti and were designated in consonance with the material employed, taupa-tikumu, etc. The ones of tikumu leaves are said to be the best and an old Maori offered (if he was provided with the tikumu) to make the collector a pair.

The women (as a rule) not wearing leggings, but occasionally needing protection for the legs when in thorny localities, devised stockings for themselves of the silver tussock (patiti). This tussock was placed in the paraerae (sandal) and the foot inserted. Then the tussock was brought up the leg and tied above the ankle. This protection was called puru and the sandals were then known as tupuru.

It is interesting to note that the Southern Maoris called pakeha stockings 'puru' but the younger generation is now saying 'takini' for their hosiery.

The two old Maoris called the binding behind the heel of the paraerae in the Museum whakareke, the strings tau, and the toe part, moremore. This last word, they explained, meant the ihu (nose) of anything, or the snout of an animal.

SECTION III

FLAXWORK

FLAX

All my informants were agreed that there was only one kind of flax and that it was called harakeke or harareke. What is called pao or harakeke-pao is not a separate kind but is merely a leaf or two on an ordinary flaxbush which has turned brown – a freak of nature. This pao was prized by the basket-makers as it allowed them to introduce some variety into their patterns and they used it effectively.

The collector tried a number of the names given by Tregear as varieties of flax but the Murihiku Maoris repudiated them all and stoutly maintained there was but the one variety, the harakeke. What is called falariki (wharariki) or mountain flax was not regarded as a flax apparently.

When the people were going out cutting flax the elders would say, 'Don't cut the matua'. The matua is the oldest blade of flax in a bunch, hence the warning.

When the flax was cut it could be used either as it was, or be scraped and prepared. Its use in the former case for making kopare (head bands) or kete (baskets) is only a temporary expedient for the flax soon dries and becomes useless. Large loosely-made kits (kete-harakeke) for gathering shellfish, potatoes, etc. are made of the unprepared flax and do good service, but the finer kits and baskets require whitau.

An ordinary kit for shellfish is called kete but when double-plaited it is called ketepu. Plaiting the flax is called rereka (or sometimes raka), but plaiting the fibre is called whatu.

To get the fibre out of the flax the shell of the pipi (*Mytilus lutus*) was used as a scraper. Big pipi shells (called in the North Island kuku) were used as the smaller pipi shells were not strong enough to stand the strain. A woman who was left-handed (maui) would use the opposite side of the pipi bivalve to one who was right-handed (katau). In scraping flax (haro) the blade of flax was pulled with one hand through between the first and second fingers of the other hand where it was pressed against the scraper held firm by the thumb. In the old days the flax was pulled through the toes when being scraped. Comparatively little refuse came off but it seemed to render the flax supple and a basket made of scraped flax is said to have lasted twice as long as one made of green flax.

Tika-whitau is when the fibre is scraped out of the flax. The fibre was always got from the 'inside' of the flax-blade, the part of the blade left (the back) being called toreka. This process was done with a pipi shell.

The soft and silky whitau (fibre) was now ready to be woven (whatu) into kakahu (mats) fine baskets and similar articles. A statement that the tohungas used to teach the girls weaving was unknown to my informants, it being understood that the older women expert at such work did the teaching.

Flax also provided the Maori with his table dishes. Small baskets were made of whitau, were filled with kai (food) and were handed round to the guests. These neat baskets were called rourou and the handle was called katau. Rourou were also made of pukakaho (the stem of the toetoe plant) but whitau ones were much commoner.

Bone needles (au) were used in olden times for sewing, etc, and varied in size from tiny ones to big ones. One of my informants had seen an old man putting holes through needles and described the process as follows: 'He laid the bone flat in a niche in wood cut just to fit it exactly and he used a stick whose name I did not hear. At the point of the stick was fastened a sharp pointed mata (flint) and up near its top was a wooden wheel to make it spin. The stick was worked by a string and revolved and soon bored the hole. Holes were bored through greenstone the same way.'

It has been mentioned that formerly flax was scraped with pipi shells but now European knives are used. Formerly the flax was heated (ina) before a fire when it would steam (tokoahi) but now if the whitau is wanted very soft and white it is boiled. Some of the work done under modern conditions is very artistic and dainty.

Floorcloths (whariki) and sails (ra) were both made of tiaka (matting) and were interchangeable. They were made square. To make one the plaiter used to raka (plait) the flax the width required for the floor and as it reached the ends of the lengths a joining (morua) was required. Each section or strip of mat between the rows of morua was called a papa and it depended on the number of these sections what size the mat was. The band along the top is called whiri and is four or five inches wide. The timata (start) of the mat is called whakawa and flax was split (toitoi) and worked through it. In a tiaka the ends of the flax project underneath and that side is rough but the papa side is smooth. A similar mat, the papaki, is made of coarse flax woven like a tiaka.

The collector left some whitau and toreka at the Otago Museum, also a kete made of boiled flax into which some pao is nicely worked. In that kete there is a whiri (twist) round the top, while that kind of handle is called whaitau. In the Museum the small food basket there named 'kete-kai' is a rourou, the rough basket is a ketewahi, while four well-made baskets (one numbered D10.50) are of the kind known in Murihiku as tewhatewha. The flax belt is a tatua. The shoulder straps are called kawe and their ends tau. The floorcloth is a whariki.

SECTION IV

PERSONAL ADORNMENT

PERSONAL ADORNMENT

Ear ornaments were common in Murihiku. Holes were bored in the ears and were known as tarika-poka, and the ancient Maori would be proud to have a bunch of prized feathers dangling from his ears. Such a bunch was called pohe, and toroa (albatross) feathers were in demand for this purpose. A string of bones (usually of the seal) was also sometimes attached to the ear and was known as

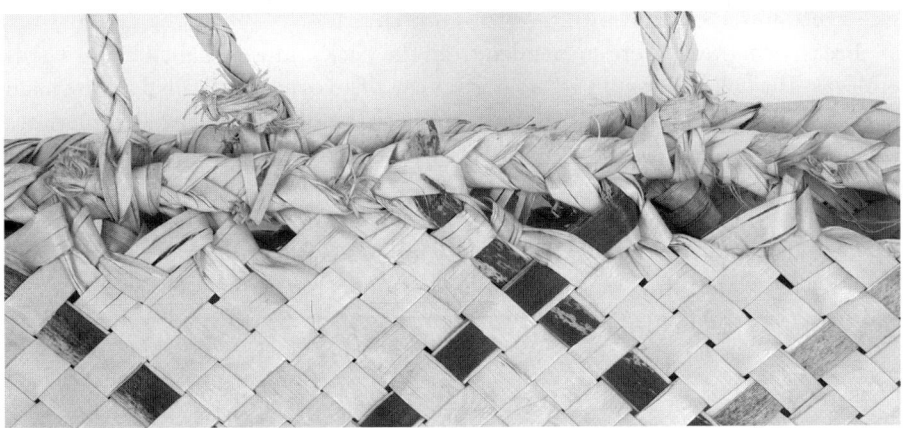

A kete made of boiled flax into which pao has been worked – collected by Beattie and mentioned on page 54. Tūhura Otago Museum Collection, D21.234. With kind permission of Te Rūnanga o Arowhenua.

a tautarika. Ear ornaments were also made of greenstone and of bone. In the former case they were known as whakakai (and this name is now applied to European earrings) while ornaments of shark's teeth were called makotaniwha. The use of seahorses as pohe for the ears did not seem to be known among my informants.

Nose ornaments were not so common but still some people had their nostrils pierced (ihu-poka). When a string of bones or teeth was attached to the nose the name has been forgotten but may possibly have been tau-ihu. A much more common ornamentation of the nose was to insert through the ihu-poka a long thin piece of greenstone, a polished bone ornament or feathers. 'My father had a hole through his nose,' said an aged taua (grandmother) to the collector, 'And he wore a raukura of kotuku (white heron) feathers through it on special occasions. He sometimes put pieces of greenstone in it as an ornament.'

Necklaces were not unknown. A favorite device was to procure the knotted bones of the vertebrae of certain seals and string them on a whitau thread and hang this as chain round the neck. This necklet was called taukaki (literally 'neck string').

Wristlets were sometimes made with a string of bones which was too short to go round the neck but would compass the tauri (wrist). This bracelet was called taurika.

Haircombs were also used and were called heru. When the hair was put up in the form known as koukou it was held by a piece of iwi (bone) variously called a titi, titia or tiatia which was inserted in the knot. It is also said these names could be applied to the act of fastening a heru (combs in the hair). The hair was called huruhuru in the South Island (and makawe in the North Island) and adorning it with the feathers of the koekoea (longtailed cuckoo) or the kotuku (white heron) was a recognised custom with the well-born class.

Breast ornaments were suspended from the neck and were called hei in a general way. The collector could get no particulars of an ornament called a hei-matau but a hei-mata was known. It is made in the shape of a curve and is sometimes called heipiko (bent hei) but hei-mata is the correct name. The collector was shown a long straight hei made of greenstone, and a hei made of the niho (tooth) of a sperm whale. In olden days some long pins made of bone had holes (poka) in them and could be used for the double purpose of hei or as clothes fasteners. If used as the latter they were then called titia; if as the former they were known as aurei, a general name for bone ornaments.

HEITIKI

Heitiki is the name of the best-known of all ornaments of the Maori yet there is much ignorance on the part of the Maori generally as to how it originated and its significance. The collector visited fifteen kaika (villages) of the Maori in

Murihiku and in every one he pursued his inquiries about this subject but with little success in the main. All the old people were agreed in one point and that was that the wearing of the heitiki was confined to the upper classes and was a mark of good breeding. They were almost all agreed further that although men, women and children wore heitiki their use strictly speaking should properly be confined to women. Heitiki were worn suspended from the kaki (neck) by a taura (string) of whitau (dressed flax fibre).

Heitiki were usually made of greenstone and were objects of great veneration, prized ones being handed down as valuable heirlooms from generation to generation. They were also made of whalebone and one of my informants, a very old woman, added that some had been made from moa bones. The oldest man interviewed said, on the other hand, that heitiki were made solely from greenstone and as greenstone was found in the South Island it was an open question where the heitiki had originated. Against this, again, a man usually reliable in his information said that not only were heitiki made of greenstone and bone but also pawa shell and even of wood. Another aged man said that in rare cases pieces of pawa shell had been let into the greenstone to form kanohi (eyes). He had never seen such a heitiki but he had heard that such had been manufactured.

All my informants seemed more or less aware of the fact that there was some signification underlying the making and wearing of heitiki and that it was more than a mere ornament yet most of them seemed to have only vague ideas about what that signification could be. One aged woman said she had heard no traditions as to its origin or purpose but she thought her heitiki was an ugly thing of uncanny import and she was glad to get rid of it by giving it away. Another of my informants said the heitiki was a sign of rank but he had never learned its origin or purpose although some of the old people called it an atua (evil spirit). At another village the collector was told that women and children usually wore the heitiki because there was an idea prevalent that it was not supposed to be worn by males after they had grown to manhood. At another place it was stated that although both men and women wore heitiki it was noticeable that if an old person left one to a mokopuna (grandchild) this was almost invariably a girl.

At last the collector met a woman who seemed to know more about the heitiki than any of his previous informants, although it is probable she acquired the information while on a visit to the North Island. She said that hei denoted a neck ornament and that Tiki was the first man. Continuing she said the heitiki were very sacred objects and were handed down as heirlooms in rakatira families. The heitiki were only to be worn by high-class women and more especially when they were expecting children. The wearers would karakia (repeat charms) to the revered emblems they were wearing in the expectation that they would have an easy childbirth. If a high-born young married woman was not the owner of a heitiki, and particularly if she was expecting her firstborn, it was considered a kindly office for someone to lend her one to wear, and to repeat karakia over, until the child was born.

Most of my informants considered that a heitiki could be classed as a sacred thing, but some added that it could not be and never was regarded as a god. When it was being made the maker would say karakia (invocations) to Raki, to Tane and to other powerful gods. The Maori had never been in the habit of bowing (koropiko) to idols and would not do so to a heitiki although they might say karakia to the gods who had most mana (power).

The inference recorded above that heitiki were made as symbols of Tiki the first man received attention from several of my informants. They said that some of the old Maoris had upheld this theory but that others had denied it, so they did not know what the truth was in regard to this matter. Tiki was generally regarded as a god but he was as much a god of men as of women. One old man reverently said that Tiki was the supreme God, being superior to Raki and other gods, but how the heitiki first came to be made, or when, or what it meant, he had never heard.

Add to Heitiki

Asking a well-informed kaumatua about the heitiki he said: 'Tiki was a god and had something to do with women. Tiki-au-waha or Tiki-auha was Tane's offspring but was a god. I have heard that Tiki was the name of Tane's ure. Tane was one of Raki and Papa's sons, the second I think, and he knew more than the others. When big he felt the inclinations of nature and wanted to ai or moe [not puremu which is adultery] his mother, and she would not let him so he made a woman out of wet mud, blew his breath into her mouth till he felt her moving, and then hid to watch her. By-and-by she sat up and began moving about. Her name was Hine-hau-one, or Hine-ahu-one, and her first child was Hinetitama by whom Tane had a son whom he called Tiki. Once when Tane was away visiting his elder brother Rehua in the tenth heaven Hinetitama asked a tipuna, perhaps Papa, who her father was and after some pressing she learnt that her father and husband were one. She was very ashamed and went away and some of her family went with her. She became Hine-nui-o-te-po but that is a long story. The Maoris used to karakia to Rehua, Tane and others but I never heard of karakia to Tiki nor of a ceremony called tua. Tua means the back of anything and if you asked where a man was I might reply "kai tua ra" (behind there). The word tua was used in karakia if for a person behind you. Tiki is the god of the ure and Io is the god of the thigh. If you see a woman you like your person (Tikiauwaha) will yearn for her but this learning was not much known among the Maoris. Perhaps the heitiki is meant as a representation of Tiki but I never heard any legends as to its origin. I think the legs are curved beneath to get the whole figure in a handy position to carry about.'

A venerable Maori said the heitiki was also a hei-whakapakoko but he did not know why the legs were bent or the head to one side. They were made in the image of an atua. Tuterakihuanoa, a devil, first made them and he was the first to make carvings. He was cast out from the heavens and came to earth and made whakapakoko (images or carved figures).

From the foregoing information it will be seen how little the present Maoris know of the origin of the heitiki. The collector had given up hope of getting any real information about what it represented when he paid a flying visit to Colac Bay to see an aged man about various items of Maori lore. This was the man who first pointed out to the collector some things in the Maori account of creation that would puzzle the average white man. He apologised for knowing so little about the heitiki saying that the Southern Maoris had never dwelt on the signification of tiki, but what little he had heard from the lips of the wise men in his youth he recounted as already recorded. Although he was correct about tiki he was ignorant as to the purport of the peculiar shape of the heitiki.

Mr Elsdon Best has an able paper on 'Maori Personifications' in the *Journal of the Polynesian Society*, June 1923, and two sections dealing with 'The Inner Meaning of the Tiki Myth' and 'The Tiki Neck Pendant: Its origin and purport' are well worth studying by anyone interested in the heitiki. According to this paper the true sacerdotal term for the male organ of generation is tiki; superior teachings recognise that Tiki was no real person; Tiki and Tane really represent the same thing, the male procreative element; the heitiki is nothing less than a phallic symbol, though named after the phallus it is not fashioned in the form thereof, but in the cramped, doubled-up form of the human embryo.

From these extracts it will be recognised how intense is the ignorance of the average Maori as to the significance of one of his most treasured and prized works of art, the heitiki.

SECTION V

PAINTS, DYES, COLOURS, PERFUMES

PAINTS

Maukoroa, a red paint, was formerly used to paint houses, canoes and carvings; to mark the 'men' in the game of draughts; to smear on the face and clothes and for other decorative and preservative purposes. The maukoroa is a haematite found at Moeraki, at Waikouaiti, at Kaitangata and elsewhere. It was pounded on a flat stone and at various old kaika (villages) reddish stones, used for this purpose for many generations, are pointed out. After being ground down it was mixed with oil; with shark oil if near the coast and such was procurable, and with bird oil if inland. One of my informants said it was burnt before being pounded and he added that oil from the ate (liver) of the shark was easily the best of all oils to mix with it. He spoke from practical experience and could affirm that shark oil mixed better than any other oil and produced the strongest and most lasting paint. It was painted on carvings to keep them from cracking and it had a good preservative effect on all woodwork. The act of painting was called pani. It is traditional knowledge that the olden Maoris used red paint freely to keep the maeroero (wild men of the woods) away. These uncanny visitors were said to have a special abhorrence of anything red and one of my best informants considered that was why red paint was so freely used in former times. The only name for this paint in Murihiku is maukoroa but further north according to my informants it is called horu and kokowai.

It has been stated in print many times that Otakou received its name because the Maoris got takou a red ochre from a hill on the Otago Peninsula. Mr Hansard, a school teacher at Otakou for many years, told the collector he had seen the place where the takou had been procured. My informants, on the other hand, declared that they had no such word in their vocabulary and further that if there is any red ochre at Otago Heads it did not originate the name. The word 'Otakou' probably came from Hawaiki and was applied to a rip in the channel near the mouth of the Otago Harbour and it was the whalers who applied the name to a piece of land.

Mr S. Percy Smith says that horu is a red ochre procured from the bed of streams. My informants all said that maukoroa was got from cliffs so it is a question if the two names should be regarded as synonymous.

In *Murihiku* by R. McNab (1st edition 1907) on page 264 is given the opinion of Captain Morrell who visited Port Molyneux in January 1830. He says: 'The same material which they [the Maoris] used for daubing their faces they also used for painting their whares red and black.'

Here black paint is mentioned but none of my informants described it, although one man casually referred to black effects being produced by charcoal. A blue clay (paruparu) was found at Moeraki and my informants said it was used to paint chimneys in the whaling days but they could not ascribe any ancient use to it. Uku is the name of a yellow clay but my informants had not heard of its use either as a paint or dye.

The word pani besides meaning 'painting' can be applied as a general name to any kind of paint, and you can say pani ma, pani whero and pani maku for white, red, and black paint respectively.

One of my informants had seen whata (storehouse) legs at Purakaunui which had been painted red with maukoroa – probably to preserve them. Another aged man said he had never used maukoroa paint nor had he seen it made, but he had seen canoes which had been painted with it many years before.

DYES

Toatoa is the dye made of the tree of the same name. The bark was placed in an ipu (wooden basin) in which water was heated by dropping in hot stones. These stones had been made red hot (te aroaro) in an umu (oven). The first lot of stones would not extract the colour from the bark but as they cooled a fresh lot would be put in. The stones might be in the water five or ten minutes but the process was continued until the colour was right. This was proved by putting in whitau and if it absorbed the colour the dye was correct. The stones were then taken out and the flax fibre was left in with the bark until dyed, when it was taken out. The stones were heated again and put in the ipu with more whitau and this process was repeated until the bark would give off no more dye when a fresh lot of bark would have to be used. [The foregoing is an authoritative account of the making of toatoa dye, but it may be added that two of my informants said that the bark of the small tree called toatoa was gathered and pounded and soaked in cold water for two days, the result being 'an everlasting dye of brownish colour'.]

Kamahi or Kamai is the dye from the tree of the same name. The bark was soaked in an ipu in which the water had been made to boil (pupu) by dropping in hot stones, and it was left in the ipu for two or three days after the water became cold. The dye was of a reddish colour (whero) and of a lasting nature. It was regarded as having a preservative effect and fishing lines were sometimes soaked in it to preserve them, and mats were stained with it.

Pokaka is another dye extracted from the bark of a tree by the procedure of steeping in boiling water, but whitau (flax fibre) soaked in it has to have a further process of being soaked in black mud (paruparu) before the dye becomes permanent.

As one of my informants said: 'The pokaka will not dye without paruparu nor will the paruparu dye without pokaka.' The whitau was put to soak in the pokaka juice for a day and was then soaked in the paruparu mud bath for two days. It was then taken out, rinsed in water to remove the particles of dirt, hung up in the sun to dry and the result was the flax fibre had been dyed a black colour that would not wash out. Pokaka dye itself is said to be a cream or pale yellowish colour, but the fibre turns black in it, although this black is not 'fast' until the mud, got from certain swamps, has been used. [An informant said the bark was beaten when in the ipu to help extract its juice; the mud used was an uku; that the flax fibre after being two days in the mud was washed and put back in the dye for another day; that it was hung out to dry in the shade and not in the sun. Another said that the juice of a tree, whose name was not available, when mixed with the juice from the pokaka bark made a brown dye.]

Kokihi is the name of a plant found on the seacoast – inland the frost kills it. It has a red berry from which a red dye could be made, but the dye was not permanent, only lasting a certain time. The berries were merely soaked in water and squeezed to make the dye. In recent times the berries have been used to make a red ink for the Maori children to rule their school lessons.

Pukepito is a blue dye made out of the tawai (beech or birch). A piece of that wood that had gone rotten would be well shaken to get the dust out of it. This dust was moistened with water and then mixed with either fish oil or muttonbird oil. The resultant liquid could be used for blue dye or could be thickened to paint with. [So said a reliable informant of mine, but the knowledge did not seem common property. Tregear says, 'Pukepoto – a kind of dark-coloured earth formerly used as a pigment'.]

COLOURS

It must be admitted that the Maoris of Murihiku seem to be uncertain about colours – either that or their definitions in English are at fault. For instance the collector was told by different informants that toatoa dye was red, yellow, brown or reddish-brown. They themselves candidly admitted that their parents and elders had given them very little traditional knowledge about colours.

Reverend J.A. Stack [[1879]] wrote in *Transactions of the New Zealand Institute* Number 12 pages 153–158 that the Maoris knew little about colours but he drew on himself a very full rejoinder from Reverend W. Colenso [[1881]] in *Transactions of the New Zealand Institute* Number 14 pages 49–76 in which his critic infers that that observation applies only to the South Island Maoris. Whether that be so or not the collector cannot say but the Murihiku Maoris concede their ignorance on the matter. After much questioning the collector elicited the following list of colour names: Hinamoki – gray, Kiri – yellowish, kiriwhero – light red, kura – red, kakariki – green like a parrokeet, ma – white, maku – black, pakaka – yellow, pako – black or dark-blue, pounemu – green like greenstone, waikurakura – light red, waimarima – a translucent shade in greenstone, waituko – yellow, waitukokiri – shade of yellow, whero – reddish.

My informants agreed in affirming that they had never heard the older generation give any name to the blue caused by tattooing, the green of trees, or the blue of ocean or sky. They never said 'the blue of the sky' but referred to the sky unobscured by clouds as tihore te raki an expression denoting a fine day, while kiko-o-te-raki was indicative of the usual appearance of the sky. The present generation sometimes call a cloud he ao, but paiao was the old correct name and to distinguish between them dark clouds were called paiao-maku, light fleecy clouds paiao-ma while clouds with a reddish glow or red fringes were known as paiao-whero. It was also permissible to use the term pukeao for masses of thick, heavy clouds.

None of my informants seemed to regard tea as a name for white or light colours using ma instead. Maku was freely used to indicate black or dark colours as kirimaku for a dark skin and waimaku for the sea when it was a sombre colour.

A red sky was called raki-tahutahu or raki-tututu. [Tahutahu means 'to kindle fires' or 'to burn' but tututu is a more uncommon word and the nearest approximations to its meaning found in Tregear's [[1891]] *Dictionary* are the Tongan and

Marquesan and more particularly the Mangarevan comparatives made under the word tutu.]

PERFUMES AND SCENTS

Taramea was the commonest perfume prepared in Murihiku. It was the work of the women to prepare it and they went about this in the old time-honoured way. They would find suitable taramea plants (speargrass) and would light a bunch of dry grass under them because the heat of the fire draws the juice of the plants. This they did in the evening and in the morning they would go and gather (uru) the juice (waiwhenua). This juice or gum was mixed with woodhen oil (hinu-weka) and was used to dress the hair and to rub on the body. When cold this perfume would harden and was sometimes worn suspended round the neck in a scent bag (hei-taramea). When so worn the heat of the body caused the scent to melt a little and a pleasant perfume from the bag rose into the wearer's nostrils. When gathering the taramea gum the gatherers had to sleep in the orthodox way prescribed by custom. They had to adopt the traditional posture of sleeping with the knees drawn up (moe-tuturi or moe-pepeke) for if they slept lying straight out (moe wharoro) it was a sign that the gum would fall down from the plants and be lost.

Toatoa, the tree from which the dye of that name was procured, has a very pleasant smell and the Maoris used to carry bits of its bark about as a scent. It is a tree somewhat like manuka, and the wind would waft its aroma abroad, serving as a guide to its whereabouts. [One informant said the toatoa tree could be used for making a perfume like the taramea but if so the collector has no particulars of it.] Any scent or perfume was called kakara.

Kopuru is the name of a fine textured, sweet-scented moss which grows on rocks at the seaside. It was sometimes placed with taramea gum in the sachets suspended from the neck, but more often it was gathered in rourou (flax plates) and saturated with hinuweka (woodhen oil), the resultant perfume being put in a taha (gourd) and kept. The shell of the kina (sea-egg) was also used as a convenient storage receptacle for kopuru and taramea perfumes. [One informant thought kopuru was probably 'mountain musk'. He described it as bearing a very tiny flower, and as keeping close to the ground. In summertime it has a very nice smell and the old Maoris put it in hinu-weka to preserve its odour.]

Naupiro (anise) has an aromatic smell but none of my informants included it among the scents used by the olden Maoris.

Karetu is said to be a scented grass used by North Island Maoris, but none of my informants knew of its use in such a connection. The karetu grass which was formerly plentiful in Murihiku has no scent. [Probably what is called karetu in the North Island is a different grass to what is called karetu in the South Island.]

Mokimoki does not seem to be known in Murihiku although one of my informants had handled and smelled some brought from the North Island.

Certain mountains in Murihiku are said to have given to the breezes in summertime a pleasant and distinctive aroma. The Takitimu range is especially famous for its fragrance, and several mountains in Central Otago are also named as sending forth a delightful odour. The shepherds on the sheep-runs call sweet-smelling leaves 'Maori scent', but my informants could not name the plants which gave to those mountains their particular fragrance, except that the sweetest-smelling shrub of all was traditionally called karo. The word karo means 'lost' and none of my informants had seen it, those who searched for it having failed to find it.

SECTION VI

TATTOOING; WOOD-CARVING

Karehu was the name of tattooing ink. It was made from the gum (mapara) out of the red pine (rimu) which when burnt created a thick black smoke. The soot from this could be caught in branches or flax matting and was placed in an akapawa (pawa shell). It could be mixed with hinu-weka (woodhen oil) or hinu-tuna (eel fat) or hinu kereru (pigeon fat) or hinu putakitaki (paradise duck fat) or with any other suitable oil, grease or fat to make tattooing ink. The ink so made tattoos a dark blue colour (maku). [One informant, usually well-informed, said that the karehu (ink) was got from the soot of the mako wood.]

Ta ki te moko was how the Murihiku Maoris designated the process of tattooing. A certain number of fine bone points were grouped together, dipped into the pawa shell or little ipu (wooden basin) which held the tattooing ink and were then placed in the position required and tapped with a tapping hammer (patu). The bone points were usually from bones of the albatross and were known as iwi-toroa. They were sometimes tied in a little cluster for certain marks but generally were put in a row and attached to a wooden handle to form a sort of heru (comb). The number of points was usually four but three would be used on occasions, and sometimes five or six. It was naturally a very painful process and made the face bleed. Karakia (invocations) were repeated all the time to allay the pain of the operation. When it was completed a man might sometimes lie for weeks before his face properly healed.

Some of the olden Maoris had their faces tattooed in spirals, one of my informants saying her poupou (father-in-law) who died at Waikouaiti had been fully tattooed with scroll designs (whakairo), but a more common style in Murihiku was the ancient Waitaha method of dots and straight lines (tuhi). A woman whose

Mere Harpur (Harper) of Karitane, born in Waikouaiti and interviewed at Puketiraki. This photo was published in the *Otago Witness*, 24 June 1924, after her death. S17-031a, Hocken Collections Uare Taoka o Hākena, University of Otago.

father had been tattooed in this style described it to the collector as follows: 'Two straight lines ran across each cheek with dots between them at intervals. There were perhaps six dots on each cheek. These dots were called tiatia and the lines tuhi. The tattoo was of a greenish shade and this colour was said to be got from fernroot but I never heard how it was made. An old man named Kainawe did it with toroa (albatross) bone and said karakia to take away the pain. This karakia must have been like Pakeha chloroform because father said he knew nothing during the act of tattooing. The ink was held in a little ipu (basin) into which the bone points were dipped and then they were tapped into the skin with a piece of wood. The tattooing showed plainer when he lay dead than it did during life. The dots were like star points and seemed to me to have been made by tying three or four points together in a bunch. Father never said why he had been tattooed in the tuhi style, but he was born on Ruapuke Island, and I have heard that style was the custom there.'

Tattooing was also done on the body to a considerable extent in olden times, and one of my informants considered some of it was done as a mark of mourning for the dead. Be that as it may all my informants had heard that body tattooing was quite common at one time. The only name for this work that was given to the collector was papatea and that was the name that was applied to tattooing from the waist to the knees. It is said that flints were used to make the cuts into which the tattooing pigment was dropped or rubbed, the flint being quicker where you could cut in straight or long lines as on the thighs.

All the foregoing information about tattooing is traditional. Not one of all the collector's informants had seen the act of tattooing performed so it was impossible to get the account of an eye-witness, and very few of them seemed to have had the operation described to them. The custom of tattooing died out in Murihiku soon after the sealers came round the coasts and with the recent deaths of very old people it is extremely doubtful if any man or woman with tattoo is now living in South Canterbury, Otago, Southland or Stewart Island. The collector knows of none and has heard of none.

The last two men with tattooed faces died at Moeraki a dozen years ago and the last woman (aged about 97) at Puketiraki a year ago (in 1919). All these were tattooed in the tuhi fashion.

A good many years ago some women tried the experiment of being tattooed with the red juice from the kokihi berries. One of my oldest informants had seen some of them. The red effect was striking and looked well but did not last, fading away after a number of years.

One of my informants picturesquely designated tattooing as face-carving. He was asked about carving and queried, 'Do you mean wood-carving or face-carving?' The former is called whakairo and the spirals tattooed on the face also bear the name whakairo.

CARVING

Carving was never so much done in the South as in the North but some was done and was called whakairo. One man said: 'Chisels (whao) were used to carve wood and were hit with a club (patu). My uncle used to carve finials for (modern) houses and he used a gouge or pakeha chisel and hit it with a wood hammer made in pakeha fashion. The old wood hammer of the Maori was often just a tree root of hard wood and was called pokuru.' The collector was told at Puketiraki: 'Most of the whakairo (carving) here was done with the mataa (flint) but it was so long ago we cannot describe it.' Some of the figureheads of canoes were carved but often they were just painted with red maukoroa. Some of the chiefs' houses and the meeting-houses had carvings on them. The poupou-toko-manawa (or pouto-komanawa, centre posts) were sometimes carved and in a meeting-house at Kaiapoi the first post was carved as a man and was called Tutekawa after the historic personage of that name while the second post carved as a woman was called after his wife Tukorero. Carvings over doorways are said to have been called huataki. An old man said 'The whao was the chisel for the whakairo (carving) and was tapped with a hammer. This was usually a piece of rakau (wood) with a lump on it at the end. The whao was usually made of pounemu (greenstone).'

A well-informed kaumatua (elderly man) at Colac Bay said he had never seen anyone doing Maori carving, nor had he heard descriptions of how it was done in the olden days. Another Foveaux Straits veteran remarked that there used to be two carved tauihu (canoe-bows) lying at Ruapuke Island when he was a boy. He could not say what became of them.

SECTION VII

PLAY, GAMES, PASTIMES, RECREATION, AMUSEMENTS, ENTERTAINMENTS, WATER-SPORTS, MUSICAL INSTRUMENTS, SINGING AND DANCING

TOPS

Tops were called potaka and were made out of the hard wood of the matoi tree, said one old man, but another said they were usually made of kapuka (broadleaf). The latter informant added that he had never seen tops spun any otherway than as the pakeha does. One man said: 'The potaka of old was made with a dent in the middle for the string. The flax was wound round this with one end tied to a stick and this was pulled one way and the top spun. The top could be whipped along.

I never heard a name for the stick employed but whipping the top was called ta-potaka.' This whipping is said to have been the occasion of much fun and merriment, and it is also said that competitions were held between villages as well as between individuals. In the far South the collector was told that the stick and whip for the top was known as raukaka and that to whip the top along was called haua. It was further said that the best wood of which to make tops was the ramarama (peppertree). A little further North an old man said the ancient top was lashed with a hau (whip) and spinning it was called haupotaka. The rohutu was a good wood to make tops from and he would make one for the Museum. At Temuka the collector was told that a Maori top made in the old style had been in existence up to a year or two before. It had a big head, was about ten inches long and it was plain, having no dents. Its point was called mata – 'taka koikoia te mata' = sharpen the point. The whip was of a number of flax-strings – or often a piece of flax split into divisions, the butt being tied to a stick (te kakau) – but its name is forgotten. To whip the top was called 'te whiu o te potaka' but it was also called ta, and it would be kept going many minutes. It was done on hard, beaten tracks which had been swept with kakaukore (literally 'without handle' and here applied to a handful of scrub used as a broom). This sweeping was called tahia or ope. Within the recollection of my informants one old man used to show the children a way of setting the top going. He held it in the air and gave it a hit with the whip, after which it would land on the ground spinning and he would continue to whip it up.

An aged couple at the Bluff said that spinning tops were also called pirori although this name really belonged to little flax windmills. An old lady of Otago Heads said the whip was called whiu and whipping haua. Many a fight or quarrel took place over top contests. The teetotum was called potaka the same as the top.

WINDMILLS

Toy windmills were made and were called pepepe. These windmills were made of harakeke (flax) twisted into a star shape. A small stick could be inserted through each windmill and a string could be tied to this stick, but more often the stick was withdrawn and a string (subsequently knotted) was thrust through the aperture. In a wind the flax 'star' or pepepe revolved freely and could be tied to a tree or carried by the child as he ran along.

SKIPPING STONES

Skimming stones over water was called tipi by one aged person and kaitipitipi by another. Pohatu-papa (flat stones) were searched for as pohatu-puku (round stones) were useless. The sport was carried out on rivers and lagoons, and as far as can be ascertained the number of skips was not counted, the winner being the one who made the stone travel furthest over the surface of the water.

CAT'S CRADLE

Cat's Cradle was called whai and was played with thin flax string, but very little information was forthcoming. An old woman said she had seen the game of whai when she was a child but she had not learnt any of it. An aged couple of Ruapuke Island said that various moves in this pastime were called Whai-o-Tane, Whai-o-Tura and others whose names they had forgotten. It was not a popular game in Murihiku as it was considered to bring on rain, wind, and bad weather. A well-informed old man of South Otago said he only knew two figures at whai, one being tawhiti-kuri (the dog trap) and the other representing a house. It was very little performed in the South, but he had not heard that it brought rough weather. Others said that sometimes in olden days a number of people would endeavour to copy the evolutions of a leader (whose title is forgotten). In the South the following moves formed a favorite opening: 1. Ka Moana. 2. Tawhititara. 3. Ka Kawe Tupapaku (carrying the corpses). The names of the succeeding movements are forgotten. An ancient woman said she could not do whai, but when she was a girl she had heard the names of some of the manipulations. One was Tawhititara, another Kawe-tupapaku, another Ka-mahaka-koko (the tui snares) and another Ka Moana. The last was for two players. This is all the Murihiku information about cat's cradle that the collector could gather. He could get no ocular demonstrations of it and considers it died out early in the South.

WRESTLING

Wrestling was called mamau according to most of my informants but very few of them knew anything about it but the name. One old man, indeed, was not sure if it was an ancient pastime or introduced by the white man. He said the expression used for tripping up another person was 'koheke tetahi ki raro'. The only man who seemed to know a little about Maori wrestling said it was called takaro, the catch-as-catch-can style being known as tikawe while the Cumberland style was called te raka. To place a foot behind your opponent's was called whiri and to cross-buttock him was raka.

TOBOGGANING

Tobogganing was called panukunuku and was popular in suitable localities. Young ti (cabbage trees) were used, the tobogganist sitting on the leaves and holding up the stem between his legs before him. The leaves being slippery great speed was attained down steep hillsides. At Henley some serious accidents were narrowly averted when the sport was revived and booming in the 'sixties and 'seventies. Maori boys who wore the seats of their pants out and would not desist from panukunuku had their nether garments patched with highly-coloured cretonnes and prints and gradually this cured the boys of their tobogganing propensities. So the indignant Maori mothers of Henley coped with this revival of an old-time sport. At the Otago Heads the children would beg or borrow tiaka mats and would kai-panukunuku on them down the big sandhills of that locality.

STONE-SWINGING

A great diversion with the boys, said one old man, was to tie two stones in flax strings and swing both with one hand, each stone going the opposite direction to the other. He gave an adroit exhibition of this para (play) but had forgotten its name. It was a form of poi swinging. Another old man confirmed this by saying the stone swing was one of the moves in the so-called poi dance. Two potatoes could be used equally as well as two stones for the purpose of swinging. The older women were appealed to but although all knew the pastime its specific name could not be ascertained.

SWINGS

Swings were used in olden times, said an aged couple. A whitau rope would be tied to a lofty tree and a loop (karu-mahaka?) would be made to sit in and swing. On Ruapuke Island this was called kaitarere. An old man said he had heard that the kaitarere was a swing made of whitau hung from a branch, the swinger probably sitting in a loop, but he had never seen one in operation, his sole acquaintance with swinging being on the familiar pakeha swing. An old woman said that swings of all descriptions were called kaitaurere. She had heard of the name moari for swings but it was a North Island word. Another old lady brought up as a child at Moeraki said that seventy years previously the Maori swings were called kaitaurere.

SEESAWS

Seesaws are stated to have been used in ancient Maori villages, but my only two informants differed on this point, one considering that the seesaw was not a Maori idea or game at all, the other holding that it had been performed in ancient times, a stick over a log being sufficient, and the name of the seesaw being morere.

KITES

Kites were called manu but there was another name which has been forgotten. They were made of raupo but had a hardening or stiffening (moroto) of sticks. These were two (rua) in number and were shaped something like this ⊤.

They were called rakau-he-whaka-maroo (maloo – long 'o'). The raupo was woven (whatu) from top stick in two separate divisions until halfway down centre stick when they were united and gradually tapered down to a point. The raupo was decorated with the huruhuru (feathers) of the kaka and kotuku (and other birds in some cases), and had a waero (tail) of whitau. The taura (string) was also of whitau and was attached to the centre stick about its middle (probably just above where the two sides join). It was a long string and kite was flown when the wind was suitable. The kite fliers were mostly young men but some elders and also women participated. Competitions were held in Temuka and elsewhere in the olden days.

An old man remembered the sport of manu (kite-flying). When he was a lad he was at Port Molyneux and an old man named Ohua made a kite and flew it. It was made of the leaf of the koareare (raupo) and was held by a long taura (string). Its tail was called waero. There was a stick round the top whose name he had forgotten but the centre stick was called a kaukau, or kaokao. (The old man did not say kakau.) The kite flew very well.

REVOLVING TOYS

Another children's game was pirori (the proper pirori is a revolving drill to bore the pounemu (greenstone)). The old people used to make circular rolls of flax and put strings through so that they could be revolved. They gave these to the tamariki (children) and on rainy days playful combats were arranged. The children were arranged in pairs and their spinning piroris were allowed to fight (kakari) until one or other was pakaru (broken). The one whose pirori lasted the longest was winner. When this game was played in a whakatika (correct) manner it caused fun and laughter but of recent years it fell into disuse because quarrelsome children would become impudent (whakatoi) and when their piroris were worsted would whakateke (slap) one another. The action of working the hands out and in and so causing the toy pirori to rotate was called kukume.

ARCHERY

Paketekete was something like the pakeha bow and arrow. Pirita (supplejack) or stout vines were bows and whitau or thin wiry vines were used as strings. The arrows were sharpened kaikatoa (manuka) sticks and were shot at kaka parrots, koko (tui) kereru (pigeons) and other birds. This was used at Temuka seventy years ago in the recollection of one venerable dame who has a mokopuna-tuatoru (great, great, grandchild) and she considered it an olden Maori pastime. An old man in the extreme South remembered the boyish game of bows and arrows. The bow was called pakete and the arrows mata. The bows were made of manuka, the string being whitau, but they were not strong enough for man's use, so were delegated almost entirely to the boys. Yet they could do damage on occasions and a Maori boy at Riverton many years ago lost an eye through an arrow striking it.

HOOPS

Hoops were unknown to one informant except as a Pakeha plaything, but an aged couple said: 'Take the karetu grass and bend it into hoops or potaka five or six inches across. Let the wind blow it and after a time it will land on its side and run along the sand or hard ground until it falls over. The one which goes furthest wins the race (kai tata whaika). The famous Maui [pronounced by them Ma-oo-ee] and a brother were once out at play and the father said that the one who could throw a karetu potaka on to the matao (window) of his grandfather's house would be a great king. The brother's hoop fell far short but Maui's one touched the mark and he became great as the history tells us'.

The same aged pair also mentioned that in olden times the people would gather thistledown and light fluffy stuff which they would softly press into light-as-air balls and liberate when the wind was blowing right for adjacent villages. This pastime was called karere (messengers).

VARIOUS PASTIMES

Skipping ropes were called kaiwhiuwhiu said the old Taieri lady, while an old Moeraki lady gave it as the name of the skipping itself.

Stilts were called pourewa according to the first of these two informants but at Moeraki the name given to the collector was waewae-rakau (wooden legs). The collector unfortunately got no description of the Maori form of stilts.

Hide-and-seek was called whakamomoka by the first of these two informants (at Henley) but the second one (at Moeraki) called this game whaimomoka.

Romping on sandy beaches was a favorite occupation of the Maori children, even as it is with children of all maritime races, but no particular name was given to this para (sport) or takaro (play). When the children wished to clamber over the rocks along the beaches they often made themselves temporary paraerae (sandals) by slitting suitable kelp and inserting the foot.

DRAUGHTS

Draughts is a game for adults and opinions differ as to its antiquity in New Zealand. At Temuka the collector was told that Kaimu was the Maori game of draughts and stones were used for men. It could be played on tiaka mats or on boards. Suitable boards (paparakau) were chipped out of totara wood with a toki-pounemu. Some squares were marked black with karehu (charcoal) the others being left white or the natural color. Black is called maku and white ma but the name of the squares was not remembered. The men were pohatu (stones) of flat shape and one player would have plain stones while those of the other would be coloured red with maukoroa paint. The men were called kai and this name is still used in playing pakeha draughts when you will hear one player say to another, 'nekehia tou kai' = shift your man.

The oldest resident at the Taieri reserve could only say about the game – 'draughts were called mu', while an old lady brought up at Otago Heads remembered that she had seen North Island visitors playing mu but she did not know the names of the board, the men, nor the moves. The oldest Maori in North Otago said: 'I never heard of a Maori form of draughts – if such was played it was before my time,' and this opinion was backed up by the oldest Maori in South Otago who said: 'I never knew a Maori game of draughts – our people must have learned it from the Pakeha.'

The collector has always understood the Maori form of draughts was very ancient, but Te Rangihiroa (Dr P. Buck) informed him that he considered the game a European innovation in New Zealand and that the Maori name mu was simply an adaptation of the English word 'move'. This sounds feasible enough but further research is necessary before the question can be regarded as settled. A little further information about draughts from a Maori standpoint will be found in the Kaiapoi section (to be published later).

'CHUCKY-STONES'

Ruke, or to give it its long name, he-ruke-mo-te-raraki, was a favorite game of old and was of a similar nature to the game of 'chucky-stones' played by white children. The first informant said he had played it when a child. It was played with five or six pebbles. Four of these as a usual rule were placed on the ground at fixed intervals apart and one in the hand was tossed up in the air while one of those down was picked up before catching the one in the air. This was repeated twice and then two stones were picked up and then three and so on until the player picked up the whole four or five on the ground before catching the stone tossed up. In ruke there were different figures such as koruru, koriwha, tiwi (pronounced tivi) and others and each figure was played twice.

At Temuka the game was described as follows: The first move is to place two stones in one place and two in another, the odd one of the set of five being used to throw up and catch. The next move is takirua, the next takitoru, and the next takiwha, each move being done twice. Each stone is picked up in turn. After the takiwha comes the koriwha when all the stones are held in the hand and one is thrown up and caught. Then comes the ruke for the raraki (pronounced 'ralak') in two twos again. Then the four stones are placed separately and each one is brought into the centre in four successive throws, and the whole four are picked up together the next throw. This is called koruru and each move is done twice, the missing of a stone at any stage of the game ruling a player out. Other movements are now forgotten.

It appears that this game was not known in every village in Murihiku. An intelligent old man informed the collector that he was born on Ruapuke Island in or about 1839 and he had never played ruke nor had he ever seen any games played with stones when he was a boy. Recently, however, he had visited Temuka and there he saw the children playing these old stone games.

Another old man referred to the fact that a boyish pastime of his was to throw up pebbles and catch them on the back of his hand. An aged couple at the Bluff called this game pirihapara, but at Temuka the collector was told, 'Huripoki is a variation of ruke and consists of throwing up the five stones and catching them on the back of the hand. After the whalers came the Maoris used to gamble on these games'. An old man said there were other variations of these pebble-tossing games but he could not remember them.

TOY CANOES

Amongst a bold, seafaring people like the Maoris it was only to be expected that the children would emulate their parents' example, hence we find that big tio (oyster) shells were used by children for floating in water as a game. Toy canoes were also used for the same purpose. The old men would make quite elaborate little waka for their favorite children. These canoes had no sails but on windy days would be set in line in a hapua (lagoon) and let go. This was a great amusement for the children but the races often attracted the old people and a graphic description of this was given to the collector. The old people would get very excited as the canoe of this or that mokopuna (grandchild) was leading and would rush along as fast as they could shouting encouragements to the particular craft they were favouring. A old man who had been brought up in the Port Molyneux district recalled the fact that when he was a boy he and his mates sailed waka-harakeke (flax canoes) on Karoro Creek in races. This sport they simply called poti which is a Maoricised form of the English word 'boat'.

ATHLETICS

Athletic pastimes were not overlooked. One aged man said: 'We call a race pure but sports are kahau. Wi is a kind of game of the prisoners' base style with plenty of running in it and when I was a boy I have even seen the men playing at it.' Another old man said: 'A race was he oma and to the winner you would probably say, ko koe te mea tere and of the loser ko maui ki muri.' My Taieri informant was the only one to mention somersaults and said that the name for them was the same as for standing-on-the-head, viz. kai-tu-poupou, but the fact needs corroboration before it can be implicitly accepted. Another informant said that tupou was to stand on the head. Leaping, one informant considered, was a Pakeha idea, but the long jump was called rere, while another gave rere as the name of any kind of jump.

WATER SPORT

The young Maoris liked to sport in the water. Diving was called he ruku (the word ruku being frequently pronounced luku) and many excelled at it. Ducking was also indulged in with boisterous mirth, the usual name for this vigorous water sport being puharu although the word rumaki was sometimes used to define it, notwithstanding that one of my informants considered rumaki a North Island word. Ducking could not have been very common because one at least of the aged people had never heard of it, let alone seen it.

DART THROWING

Projecting darts along sandy beaches or over flat ground was a favourite amusement of old and was mentioned by several of the old people but it is difficult to dovetail the information given into concise form. The first man who mentioned it said that a suitable piece of koauau kelp would have pukakaho (stems of the toetoe grass) inserted through it, thus forming a kind of dart which could be projected with the aid of a stick. He thought a good dart might travel two hundred yards. He was not sure of the name of this pastime but fancied it might be retired, while the stick could be called a whana he thought. It may be added that this informant was rather partial to North Island phraseology at any time, so that these two words may not have been used in Murihiku in this connection. Another old man had heard of boys sending darts from a stick by a flax string but could not name nor describe the method, but the oldest woman at Temuka said projecting darts was anciently called toropenepene and could be done several ways. One way was to take koauau kelp and put a stick through it and kokiri it. (Kokiri is an underarm throw – paka is an overarm throw.) This was done on the beach to see who could throw it furthest. Another way was to put pukakaho reeds through the koauau and tie it loosely on a stick and project (pakaina or whiua) it, the stick remaining in the hand. None of the other aged people interviewed had heard the name toropenepene but as it is mentioned in an episode that occurred before the Maoris came to New Zealand it is clearly a very old name of this very old pastime. Projecting pukakaho reeds on the beach was just a para (sport) with no particular name said the other old people. Another form of this pastime was introduced to the collector's notice as follows: 'Take koauau kelp and push two pukakaho stalks through it at an angle to meet at a point in front and then propel it along with a stick. I do not know its name – it was just a para (play).' A very old man said: 'Paku was a game of driving sticks along a beach or piece of flat ground. Two sticks are joined like ∠ , and another stick is inserted at the point and they are tossed along, sometimes in a race. It was once a favourite boyish amusement.' Another opinion stated: 'The dart called koauau was simply flicked forward with a short stick – this was called paka-te-koauau.' The aged couple whom the collector saw at the Bluff said 'Pakupaku is played on the sand in races. You join two sticks together into a point where you insert a stick held in the hand and flip it along the sand as far as it will go. You then rush up, insert the stick again and repeat the performance until the mark is reached.'

The projection of a stick called a timata was also referred to by several informants. One old man said: 'For timata you take a stick about a foot long with a cavity in one end, and you place the end of a manuka wand about three or four feet long in this cavity and hurl it away from you to see who can send the timata furthest.' From a roomful of Maoris at Temuka the collector heard that you could hurl a timata a long way by putting flax round one end of it and projecting it. This was to werohia (cast) the timata but the collector could not ascertain the exact method of projection nor any specific name for it. None of the people present had heard of such projection having been used in warfare but only as a pastime.

A well-informed kaumatua (elder) recalled the use of what must have been a form of sling. He said: 'When we were boys we used to roll stones in flax – no sticks were employed – and throw them by this means. This we called kotaha.'

NOTES

In the Christchurch Museum there is a bull-roarer (called purerehua or mamae in the North Island) but not one of my informants had heard of such a thing. There is also a wooden spinning toy. [string/wood sketch] It is probable that the spinning-toy of flax which was made in the South Island was an adaptation of the wooden one. It could be hung to revolve in the wind and was called pirori the same as the 'fighting windmills' (see ante), and one form of it was called pepepe. Jumping jacks also seemed to be unknown in Murihiku and the collector could get no account of 'hunt the pebble' or similar games. Ancient riddles also seemed to be unknown and one or two of the old people seemed to consider riddles a Pakeha introduction. One ancient woman had seen the childish games of lacing fingers, etc., but she forgot what they were called. Another remembered the game of making your hands do the opposite to your opponent's while singing at the same time, but she had forgotten its name. The concluding note the collector has is to the effect that an intelligent old man who was brought up in that stronghold of Southern Maoridom, Ruapuke Island, says that he could remember only a few games being played when he was a boy. This explains the meagreness of the information along certain lines.

SURFING AND WATER SPORT

To go surfing, said a poua, or grandfather take two pohas (kelp-bags) and blow them up tight. Tie (tauhere) the two together and put the string over the kaki (neck) and a poha under each arm. Go out into the moana (ocean) and come in over the breakers like a bird. The sport was called kaukau. The word pala (para) meant skylarking or playing but he did not think a surf-board was used by the Maori until after the Europeans came.

A venerable woman said the sport of surfing was generally called kaukau. Two poha-hau (bladders blown up) were used with a piece of flax between and the surf-bathers usually came in on the surf lying with their breasts on the connecting piece of flax between their buoyant supports. She had not seen surfing where wood was used but had heard of the sport being carried out with logs some of which were in their rough state while others had been chipped. These logs would sometimes come in straight and sometimes they would turn round in the karu (waves) and roll over. This was fine sport and was known as pala (para) a word applied to any game or pastime, or as kaukau. Small waka, usually known as tawai, were given the children to sport (para) with in the water. The young people bathing in hapua (lagoons) used pohahau and papa (planks) to quite recently, if not to this day, and they called this water-sport, the old name, kaukau. Kaupo is a method of swimming upright. A stick (tokotoko) usually of kahikatoa or toatoa, but any kind of stick would do, would be put on the water and the swimmer would place his hands on it and keeping the body upright would swim with his waewae (feet). Another form of kaupo was done without a stick. The swimmer would fold (whakapiki) his arms and keeping the body erect with the water up to his elbows would swim with his feet. The narrator concluded her remarks by saying that a stick lying on the ground was called rakau, but if it was picked up and used by anybody it became a tokotoko.

If the Maori had any business on the sea he went quietly, said one old man. He made those bathing go quietly or the sea would rise (tu-te-tai or tu-moana). The old people used to make the titi hunters land quietly on the islands so that the sea would not be rough. A woman said she had seen both kaupo and kautapapa swimming and thought former the faster. (Kautapapa is swimming in flat position.)

MUSICAL INSTRUMENTS

One poua said: 'I never heard of a wooden drum being used by the Southern Maoris but there was a koauau or flute which was made of bone. I think it was made of the wing bone of a toroa (albatross) and I heard it played at Waikouaiti. It had three holes at the bottom and one at the top and was a little bigger than your thumb. It was probably called koauau because it could be made of koauau kelp. It was also made of wood. The sound was much the same from each kind and it could be blown with the nose if one wished. The porutu is a bigger flute and has six holes and it could accompany singing. There is a short song that was often sung into the porutu and I have heard my mother sing it but I never learned it. I never heard of shells being used as horns but there was a pukaea, or trumpet, made of flax which was used for calling. I have heard the name of putorino given to an instrument of old but I never saw one. The word means "to make the ears ring" so it must have made a loud noise or a sharp one.'

A taua (grandmother) said: 'I never heard of a wooden drum or gong or of a putatara trumpet but I have seen pukaea of flax and of bone. The pukaea-iwi (bone trumpet) I saw was very old and only the old people knew how to blow it. I think it was made of whalebone. In the old days a man stationed on a taumata (platform) in a pa would blow one if he saw the foe coming. I have also seen a putorino but I was so small that I do not recollect it to describe it. The porutu had four, five, or six holes and was made of rakau (wood) – a koari (flax-stick) would do. Another flute was the koauau and it was four or five inches long, had three keys and was made of wood or kelp. I heard an old man play it with his nose. He had a hole through his nostrils and stuck the koauau through it and played away. It was only the koauau which was played with the nose, the porutu being for the mouth. The people used to use toitoi shells to blow on. These are something like koruru shells and some were blue and some white. The ones they blew are not like the ones I see picked up now but were longer. I do not know the name of that instrument but tunes could be played on it.' There was an old porutu kept at Temuka until recently but it disappeared a year or two ago.

Add to Musical Instruments

Not one of the old people interviewed in the South had heard of a wooden drum or gong as being used down here, but a well-informed kaumatua said that he had heard kanakas who came on whaling vessels (in the sixties) speak of such things as being used in the islands from which they came.

A venerable Murihiku Maori said that he had never heard of a wooden drum among the people of old but they had flutes and suchlike. The koauau was often made of bone and had three holes. The porutu was made of tutu-rakau wood and had four holes but he considered the former flute (three holes) a better instrument and more tuneful. (The tutu-rakau, he explained, was another species of the tutu plant and grew into a tree.) Another instrument for producing music in the old days was the putorino. It was often made of albatross (toroa) bone and was a sort of whistle.

A woman over seventy who has been in Southland all her life said she never at any time had heard anyone playing on the old Maori flute, or indeed on any Maori instrument. The whalers founded the town of Riverton in 1837 and since then European things have always been procurable.

Tradition records that Te Taoho, who was killed at Orautahi on Stewart Island, was a renowned player on the flute (koauau). My informant thought that Taoho's celebrated instrument was of bone, but personally he had heard ones made of kelp. They sounded like a tin whistle. There was a bigger instrument of six holes called a porutu and it was more like a European flute than the koauau was. The people of old also made a flax trumpet called a pukaea for the purpose of sounding out a big noise.

Add to Musical

In his remarks on the music of the Ancient Maori Tregear [[1904]] in *The Maori Race* says that pakuru consisting of hitting two resonant sticks, one held in teeth, together to time; that the Maoris had a harp (roria) made of supplejack; and that the South Island Maoris had a trumpet worked like a trombone – it was made of tutu or mako wood and 'packed with delicate flax tubing!' The collector asked his two aged lady friends about these facts:

The taua (she is a great-grandmother) from Henley said she had never heard of the pakuru in the South, but the roria was a long thing held across the waha (mouth) and hummed on. The pukaea was a flax trumpet easily made and blown. The porutu was a flute made of tuturakau or mako wood, and the koauau was a small flute made of kelp but she had never heard of a flax tubing in either. The tune of anything played or sung was called raki or te-raki-o-te-waiata.

The other great grandmother who was brought up at Moeraki and Otago Heads said that the tune or air of any music was raki or te-raki-o-te-waiata. Roria was the Jew's harp but further than this she did not know. The porutu was made of wood and had three or four holes to regulate the sound. She had heard it and it was a nice sound. She had never known or heard of a flute packed with flax lining. Koauau, she thought, was a North Island name for a flute. The pukaea was made of flax and could produce a big noise. These pukaea were quickly made and she could make one if she had the material.

In the Maori Room of the Christchurch Museum is exhibited a long wooden 'flageolet'. The collector described it to an old Maori deeply versed in ancient lore and asked its name. He said it might be a koauau, some of which were long. Some old people were wont to say the koauau sounded better than the Pakeha flute. The koauau for the mouth and the ones for the nose had just the same name as far as he knew. He had not heard of shell trumpets similar to the one the collector saw in the Christchurch Museum marked 'A Shell War Trumpet'.

Add to Musical

The collector tried to find out if there had ever been a musical instrument called the putara in southern New Zealand but none of his informants had ever heard this name. The best of his informants had heard of the pukaea and putorino but not of the putara. An aged Waihao Maori had not heard of the putara either, nor had he heard of the pakuru (hitting two sticks together). He had never heard of a 'trumpet worked like a trombone and packed with a delicate flax tubing' [like what Tregear says South Island Maoris had] but he had often heard of the pukaea, an ordinary trumpet made of flax. He could not say if the roria (Maori form of Jew's harp) was a genuine old Native instrument or if it was modelled on ones brought by the whalers.

Even the principal informant (in Canterbury) in all his varied travels had never heard of the putara, but an old man spoke as if he had heard vaguely of it but he said it was not a South Island instrument.

One man referred to whaka-oriori (which he pronounced whakao-ri-ori) or lullabies to stop children from crying when being nursed; and also to relate old history. Some of these lullabies were composed ten generations or so ago. At the request of the collector he supplied a very long and very ancient song of this description to Mr S. Percy Smith.

The use of musical instruments of primitive construction seems to have persisted among the Maoris to a later date than did the use of many other of their arts and crafts, inasmuch as every aged person interviewed seemed to know something about the subject, and most of them had actually heard the instruments played. One of the old men told the collector that when he was a boy it was a common pastime to make horns or trumpets of flax. If rightly made these uncouth instruments could produce a surprising volume of sound and they were called pukaea the same name as the war trumpets of old. This and the romantic associations traditionally connected with their modes of music have helped to preserve an interest in the subject.

POI

The subject of the poi cropped up in conversation and the collector was told that the poi in the olden days was much simpler than now, and that the old style of doing it was different in the South from the North. A well-informed old man said that the poi balls in the south were usually made of bulrushes – not the koareare or bottom part but were made of the raupo or top part. The balls had a string attached and were thrown out and brought back, and caught in the other hand sometimes, in a way unlike the North Island poi. Sometimes two balls without string were tossed up and caught with alternate hands but he never heard the old Maori name of this. Altogether as far as he was aware poi was not done much down here – it was more a North Island pastime. Another old man said that all he knew about the poi was that it was played with the players kneeling and using their hands to hit the balls about. Boys and girls played it together. A woman told the collector that the southern poi was different from the northern. Down here they stood in two rows facing each other and threw across balls and sang. There were no strings attached to the poi balls when this was done.

She had never learnt the old songs that accompanied the game. She had heard this game was not known in Hawaiki but started at Opunake in Taranaki. A girl named Pari lived at the Tahi-marae pa near Parihaka and as she was getting raupo in a swamp she worked some of it into balls for amusement and when she heard the other girls singing she would juggle these balls about in time to the music. The word poi once meant singing and this new game was called poi because it went with singing. Pari's father heard of her new accomplishment and got her to do it before him. Then at a big gathering of people he commanded her to show this entertainment and she, all shy and nervous, did so and it 'caught on' and gradually made its way all over New Zealand. This was the story told her by Taranaki people but whether it was correct the narrator had no idea.

An old man wrote out an ancient South Island poi waiata (song) as follows: 'E poi ana au i taku poi nei nokaira amiti no katara mea kea mehea te upoko nui o te ruru tere ko'. The old people at Temuka thought the last words of the above fragment belonged to a proverbial saying about the morepork and they gradually remembered the ancient poi waiata which they sung with fine effect and which was written down for me as follows:

E poi ra taku poi na kaia Rawhitu na kaia Rameho kia a me hoa. E wai tu pa whakapatito mai te huruhuru tuke te rikarika whakarautoka te poroa o te makariri e koakoha kite wai e Tahuri atu tahuri mai e korero na te hikaka na te reua kahara mai tenei ka kukuru ... (last word forgotten).

The old time Southern poi, the collector was assured, differed from the Northern one in several aspects but principally in that a long string was used as against the short string of the Northern poi ball. The participants would stand in two rows and throw the balls across to each other, the long strings allowing this. It is said that an ancient form of poi was without strings at all, the balls being thrown, and caught and returned, the players singing meantime, but later long strings came into favor and these in turn were superseded fairly recently by the short strings. The long string (taura) form of poi was also played sitting, the player throwing the ball upward and forward. The short taura (string) was also used long ago but it was only recently it ousted the other altogether. One or two of the old people remember the long string poi and also the standing poi and they say the poi waiata (songs) were the same for all varieties – a good waiata was suitable for only the standing or sitting poi. (The one given above was sung to the collector 'both standing and sitting' – the singers adopting both positions.)

DANCING

In regard to dancing, remarked an ancient dame, the hanga [This is a Southern form of word haka. H.B.] was danced down here. One portion of it was called horu – that was the finishing piece. A Southern Maori said that in the older kaiks there was a wharehaka, or concert house, where singing and dancing could be enjoyed in the long winter evenings. Koekohe (or kohekohe) is said to have been a kind of haka where the arms moved a lot.

SECTION VIII

MEDICAL LORE

MEDICAL LORE

Medical lore does not seem to have been very extensive in Murihiku. Living near to Nature the people were relatively healthy but occasionally illness crept in and had to be relieved with the few simple remedies known, or on the other hand left to Nature to kill or cure. Physical defects were also comparatively rare but were not unknown. Wounds, cuts and injuries were common to an active, warlike people but were usually borne with stoicism and healed with a rapidity astonishing to civilised man.

The following are some of the diseases mentioned by the old people of Murihiku, supplemented, where possible, with the few details of treatment that have been traditionally preserved.

Asthma was called hu. Colds and coughs were treated with drinks made from the juice of the pouaka grass or from the steeped bark of the kowhai tree. Before the Pakeha runholder came with his cattle and his annual spring fires the pouaka was plentiful. It was gathered, soaked in water and then squeezed, the resultant juice being called te wai pouaka. The kowhai or kohai bark was steeped in water which extracted the juice and te wai kohai was a favorite remedy for colds and for various ailments.

Consumption was called mate-kohi or mate-tarai (or sometimes merely kohi or tarai) and is said to have been very rare. The bark of the karamu shrub was gathered, beaten, and soaked in water. The fluid thus produced (wai-karamu) was poured in the ears and nostrils and in the worst cases the sufferer was turned face downward and the remedy was poured into the kotore (anus). A course of this drastic treatment together with appropriate karakia (invocations) pronounced by a tohuka is said to have brought about some wonderful cures, but now the people have mostly lost faith in the remedies of their forefathers and seek the chemist's shop instead of the forest herbs.

Costiveness [[constipation]] was relieved by swallowing flax root or koareare (the edible lower part of the raupo bulrush). In the former case the flax root was roasted in the ashes of a fire, left to cool and then cleaned and opened, the white part inside being extracted. This tasted sweet, said my informants, but was so strong in its action that a very small piece would relieve the most obstinate case of constipation. The koareare also had a very sweet taste but was not so powerful in its effects as flax root which one of the aged men termed the Epsom salts of the Maori. He went on to say that when he was a boy at the Otakou Kaik the old people if they felt out-of-sorts would ask the young people to procure and bring to them the koareare to chew. Opening medicine of a gentle nature for mate-tiko (constipation) could also be made by steeping the leaves of the manuka shrub or the burrs of the piripiri (bidibid) in water and drinking the infusion.

Cuts (motu), scratches and wounds were treated with various healing agencies according to which was most convenient at the time and place. Flax gum (pia-harakeke) was extensively used. A European who came to Otago in 1857 told me that following the Maori example he used flax gum for cuts, binding it round with whitau (dressed flax) and that he found it very efficacious. Weka (woodhen) oil was used by the Maori and was considered to be good for taking the inflammation out of wounds and for rapid healing. It is said to have acted quicker when heated than when cold. The collector was assured that an excellent remedy for cuts was wai-rakau or water in which the bark of trees had been soaked. One could soak the aka vine in water for this purpose but the tree most commonly favoured was the kowhai. One aged man narrated the case of a Maori who had been with him on a sealing hunt. This man suffered very nasty injuries when his face unfortunately came between the teeth of a kekeno (fur seal). As soon as possible waikohai (kowhai juice) was poured into the wounds and in two or three days the man was right again. My informant considered that without this bush remedy the man's eyes would have remained closed for several days and that his recovery would have taken a fortnight at the very least. Maukoroa or red paint was used for slight cuts, scratches or for cracks in the skin. One man who championed its usefulness maintained that if you had a crack in the skin and put on maukoroa at bedtime you would wake up next morning to find the skin healed. It was also painted on exposed parts of the skin to keep the cold out. The presence of shark or bird oil in the paint no doubt contributed to its curative properties.

Deafness was called turi. This was not a common complaint but ear-ache (tarika-mamae) is said to have been one of the commonest ailments in the olden days. The oil out of eels (hinu-tuna) was regarded as the best cure, a drop or two in the ear being generally sufficient to alleviate the pain.

Diarrhoea was called terehi and to cure it the leaves of the kokomuka shrub were chewed – a procedure still followed by the Maori and Pakeha bushmen. This shrub is called koromiko in the North Island. The berries of the kirimoko, a kind of small manuka, were also chewed to stop diarrhoea.

Dropsy [[fluid accumulation in tissues]] was called matewaewae by an ancient woman at Otago Heads and kohao by an equally venerable dame at Henley, but neither described any ancient method of treatment.

Eye troubles came to the ancient Maori through sitting in smoky dwellings, and ophthalmia or inflammation of the eyes resulted in certain cases. This inflammation was called kukura and when old age came on sometimes led to blindness (pohe).

Fever is nowadays called pewa by the Maori but they claim that typhoid fever was brought into Murihiku by the white man. At the same time it is acknowledged that certain complaints of the olden time brought on a feverish condition in the sufferer. On Stewart Island and the Titi Islands the tree called titiaweka has scented leaves and these were used to allay high temperatures and reduce fever. These leaves are also said to have a beneficial effect on sick persons who put them in a bath or who steam them.

Gout may be a modern complaint. A Maori who had it told the collector he had puhipuhi i tana waewae (gout in his feet). Puhipuhi is a name for any swelling.

Itch, often called The Maori Itch [[scabies]] by Europeans nowadays, was a troublesome complaint of the olden Maori. It was called hakihaki in Murihiku and the people used to boil the leaves of the kaio tree and apply them to relieve the intolerable itchy feeling. My informants seemed to regard titi as an allied skin trouble, describing it as a rash which would break out into small sores, forming numerous small scabs. Harehare or areare was a name applied to breaking sores. Leprosy was a rare disease in Murihiku. It was called tuhawaiki. Ringaringa Beach at Stewart Island is called after a man whose hands had rotted away to stumps through the ravages of this fell disease.

Paralysis was called maro according to one of my informants, and rikapeke according to another.

Rheumatism was simply called mate, the collector was told, or more commonly now rumatiki. The ancient name seems to have been forgotten, one veteran terming it an iwi-mamae (pain in the bones). Hinu-weka or woodhen oil was the best remedy the Maori knew for this painful ailment.

Ringworm was called pakewakewa. It is said that the ancient Maori clapped the runa (a water plant) on the afflicted spot as a remedy.

Sore throat was an old-time trouble and was called katirehe. Waikohai or kowhai juice was sometimes used to give relief, but an old man who had recently had katirehe used another old palliative. This was 'to take the breath from the ihu (nose) and place it on the throat'. He blew through his nostrils on to his fingers which were then rubbed on his neck outside the sore place. He was careful to use the maui (right hand) and not the tahae (left hand). The latter would be no match for the spirits (wairua) but they are afraid of man's strong right hand. He was pleased to say his observance of the old rite had cured him.

Stoppage of the bowels was called papapuni and several of the old people had heard of it traditionally but they could recall no other case than the historic one of Tukete who lived on Stewart Island about nine generations ago. He could not evacuate his bowels but got a little relief from vomiting (ruaki). He became prodigiously stout and when his enemies killed him they got four or five baskets of fat from his body.

Swellings of any sort or inflammatory gatherings were termed pupuhi and the invaluable waikohai (kowhai juice) if applied promptly was considered a sure and swift cure. It may be recorded here that in all cases of extracting juice for medicinal purposes from trees and shrubs the Maori was careful to take the bark from the sunny side of the tree.

Thrush is the name of a rash in the mouths and on the tongues of infants, and the old-time Maori babe was not immune from it. The Pakeha uses borax and honey for a remedy but the Maori took pouaka grass, pounded it and then wrung the juice out, using the juice as a mouth-wash with excellent results as a rule. The name of the trouble was called haha.

Toothache is said to have been a very rare affliction in olden days. It was called nihotuka. Juice from the flax root, so the collector was told, if poured into the ear would make the recipient give a cold shiver, but in about twenty minutes time it would cause the toothache to depart.

Worms in children were called noke, the same name as denoted earth-worms, but the collector got no details as to treatment.

In his book, *The Maori Race*, Tregear [[1904]] gives a list of the diseases and physical defects said to have existed among the Maoris when the missionaries first went among them. Out of this list it was noted that the Murihiku Maori people considered that they did not know scrofula and epilepsy.

Of deficiencies of the senses the cases of deafness and blindness have been mentioned, but obstructions of the organ of speech sometimes existed. To be dumb was known as kaiaia or muhako, but is generally called tami in these modern days of English contact. One informant said that wahaku meant silence and wahakaka was when a person stammered, but another added that stammering was often called nanu and lisping wahananu.

Certain physical defects or peculiarities cropped up occasionally in olden days, some by birth and others by accidents and by wounds in warfare. A hunchback was called kunu, and a clubfoot, hape. To be bowlegged was waewaepiko, one leg shorter than the other was waewaepoto, while limping or lameness was variously called waewaekoki, haerekoki or koki. A person with six fingers or six toes was called he rapa or erapa, although one of my informants considered it should be taotao-ono (six toes or six fingers).

Mental deficiencies were not common but a few odd cases occurred. The collector was informed that a person who was silly was called karearea, but idiocy was known as karakiraki or pororirori.

Fainting was called poki but could not be regarded as at all common. Iwikore was the name applied to a languid, listless state that sometimes preceded illness. A party of Maoris told the collector that not only was illness rare in the old days but that the principal remedy was karakia (invocations). Kokomuka (veronica), kowhai, and flax root were only efficacious in some cases. The true remedy was to appeal to the tohuka to exercise his powers to drive away the illness (mate-atua or mate-kikokiko).

[The dictionary gives one of the meanings of kikokiko as 'flesh', which would be appropriate here, but it may be further suggested that in Murihiku kikokiko also means the evil spirits that proceed from unborn children or from the menses (mate-wahine) of women and that these may have been anciently regarded as causing sickness. According to the older Maoris the designation mate-atua implied that illness was the work of evil spirits.]

One old man said that in pre-pakeha days the people might take four or five months travelling from Murihiku to Kaikoura, or vice versa, but the walking and the change of scene was health-giving. He considered that this travelling was one of the things that kept the ancient Maori healthy. The advent of the white man largely stopped this roaming activity and the new-comer introduced quite a number of diseases previously unknown, and defects such as baldness (hore) which was never known in the old hatless days.

Some of the people in Murihiku had never heard of rewharewha, but at last one aged woman said it was a kind of influenza which swept the North Island in the whaling days. Others told the collector about a deadly disease called whiu brought into Murihiku by the whalers. It was responsible for many deaths, and so also was the measles (mitara) which ravaged the southern coasts and played havoc with the uncomprehending Maori.

At one of the more important villages in Murihiku all that the collector could garner about medicinal lore was that the principal remedy in the old days was karakia or invocations and that the principal means of cure was resort to the tohuka (priest). 'It was the tohukas and certain old people who did the curing and they were separated from the rest of the people as it was a sort of secret process. They had some way of trying those ill and if they thought they could not cure the sick person they did not try to. Almost all of those treated were cured, but now our people take pakeha (European) medicines and everyone knows with what result.'

During the monthly courses of women, fine whitau (dressed flax) the softest thing the olden Maoris knew, was placed inside the maro (loin cloth) and was burnt after use. Now the maro is only worn during menses, or the cloth so worn is designated by this ancient name. In the old days men and women wore maro, the ones for the men being larger than those for the women. These maro were wound round the hips and then up between the legs, one of my informants alluding to them as 'napkins' and another as 'trunks'. The correct olden name for the fine maro worn by women during their periods was marototo and tradition avers that the great Maui came from a marototo cast away by his mother. Another form of marototo was made by the women placing fine moss in their ordinary maro during the mate-wahine or woman's sickness and this moss was later thrown away. The phrase, 'Kai te mate te wahine I te pakaruhaka toto' meant that the woman referred to was undergoing the menstrual discharge, but the collector ascertained no specific name for menstruation itself.

A Pakeha remark that the Maoris had flat foreheads, flat noses and flat feet was scornfully repudiated by three Maori matrons. They instanced cases where some of the old Maoris had Roman noses and features of a decidedly Hebraic cast, and also of cases of high insteps, although these latter are rare.

Historians have asserted that the Maori decreased, after European contact, by reason of very small families. This is absolutely incorrect of Murihiku. The number of offspring per union is large but there is an awful leakage through early deaths. A Native schoolmaster says the local graveyard is full of his former pupils.

POISONS

Poisonous things were not common in Southern New Zealand. The best-known case was the purapura (seeds) in the hua (berries) of the tutu plant. These seeds were called kakata and to be poisoned with them was called kai te hori, or sometimes kai te hori te tutu. Adults usually avoided these poisonous seeds but occasionally a tamaiti (child) would swallow them and be taken with convulsions. The treatment was to purua te waha (insert a stick in the mouth) so that the sufferer would not bite the arero (tongue) during paroxysms, and this rakau (stick) was held there until the huka (froth) came and the patient vomited the tutu pips.

An old man said that the berries of the mikimiki (or stinkwood) were a favourite food with the weka (woodhen) but were poisonous to human beings. The older people would say to the children, 'Do not eat those berries or they will kill you.'

Katipo spiders do not seem to frequent Otago and Southland but are found on the sea-coast of South Canterbury. Their bite seemed not to affect certain people very badly but was very serious, if not fatal, to others. The collector was told of one woman who narrowly escaped death through a bite on the shoulder. The ancient Maori antidote was waipuha (juice of the sowthistle). The puha, or thistle, was put on the fire until half-cooked and then it was twisted and the juice so extracted was rubbed into the bite. After the whalers came gunpowder steeped in water was used and proved a good remedy.

One aged man casually mentioned that in the olden days some of the spear points were said to have been poisoned. One poison was said to have come from the stingray. The name of the fish was whai and its tail or spine was called tete. It was from this spine the poison was supposed to come, the poison also being called whai. He had grave doubts if it was poisonous at all. [Note: Some of the South Sea Islanders used the spine of the stingray to point their spears, and wounds from these caused great inflammation but there is no evidence the point was smeared with poison. Tregear gives tete as 'the head of a spear'. The Katimamoe used spears with tete-whai points in very early battles with the Kaitahu tribe and the latter said the spears were poisoned. This seems to be the origin of this particular legend.]

SECTION IX

DISPOSAL OF THE DEAD

DISPOSAL OF THE DEAD

The ancient Maori in Murihiku could, within the bounds of possibility, have disposed of his dead in the following seven methods: 1. Tree burial. 2. canoe burial. 3. water burial. 4. earth burial. 5. cave burial. 6. cremation. 7. mummification. The collector asked after all methods but could find no Murihiku Maori who had heard of placing dead bodies on stages in or among trees, except one man who had a dim recollection of hearing that bodies were laid on platforms in the bush to await a bone-scraping ceremony, but he had absolutely no details of this, and may have heard it during a visit to the Gisborne district.

The Maoris of Murihiku acknowledge their relationship to the Morioris of the Chatham Islands, but the custom of the latter in sometimes placing a corpse in a canoe which was let drift to sea, seemed to be altogether unknown in Southern New Zealand, although water burial was quite common in former days. Along the seacoast the body was deposited in the sea, but inland it would be placed in a lagoon, a burial spring or a deep waterhole. The tupapaku (corpse) was weighted with pohatu (stones) and sunk in the particular spot chosen. This style of burial was called heke or whakaheke and a number of place-names perpetuate its memory. [A quantity of detail about it will be given in the Kaiapoi information still to be published.]

Cave burial was a favourite method of disposing of the dead where there were caves, but some districts were notably devoid of such convenient chambers to lay the dead in, and in these localities the people seemed unaware of the practice of old in more-favoured vicinities. In one caveless district the people had not heard of cave burial but had been told of a huge waro (hole) in a hillside near Lyttelton Harbour from which numerous skeletons had been uncovered in recent years. In mountainous areas the dead were sometimes carried up mountain sides and deposited in holes in the rocks, and this was usually done secretly in the night-time.

Cremation was a recognised form of disposing of the dead but different localities differed somewhat in their traditionary descriptions of the event. At Puketiraki the collector was told that there was a spot at Purakanui where bodies were burnt. These bodies were rolled in mats and everything was consumed, the ashes being subsequently buried. Further north the collector was told that it had been quite common to burn the dead, any kind of wood being used and the act being usually done in the evening, just before sunset. The fire was generally made and lighted by a tohuka or by a tuakana (senior relative) of the deceased. The ashes were buried near the spot and my informants had never heard of the ashes being sent to relatives at a distance, or being kept as a memento of the dead. At Henley this conclusion was confirmed, my informants further remarking that the ashes were sacred and were buried. The fact the ashes were not stored away was further confirmed by a well-informed man. The dead who were cremated, he said, were burnt by the tohuka who carefully covered the ashes so that they would not be blown away. This was done in a secret place, not openly in the marae. The takihaka (tangi) would be held when the body was lying in the marae, but the corpse was carried away secretly at night and burnt. The ashes were not kept in wooden boxes but were reverently committed to the ground. The ceremony of burning the dead was usually done in the very early morning when nearly everyone was asleep. Mummification was a process about which little seems to be known nowadays to the descendants of those who practised it. The first of my informants considered that the corpse was disembowelled but in this he was contradicted by every other informant. Not one of all my informants could detail the exact process of embalming but all were familiar with the fact that it was a priestly operation of ancient times and that it was called whakatamiro (also wakatamiro and whakataumiro). The process was done by a tohuka and it was only the bodies of important personages that were treated. The piro (intestines) were not removed and the tinana (body) was rubbed with taramea oil said one informant, and another gave the further information that after the body had been anointed it was painted with maukoroa or haematite. The corpse was taken to a cave or to the coolest place possible and would be left sitting upright for the people to view it. The people would go there in the early mornings and would weep over the dead and would cut themselves with mata (flints). In other cases the bodies were left standing upright against papa (boards) which were leaning against the cliffs or they were lashed to posts to keep them upright and so give the people a better view. How long the bodies preserved in this manner would keep was unknown to my informants but they were all agreed it was quite a number of weeks. Then, when the tohuka decided the body had been kept sufficiently long, the head was severed and (probably) smoke-dried while the body was either buried or burned.

The preservation of heads was mentioned by several of the old people of Murihiku but with the exception of the one statement that the heads were smoke-dried none of my informants gave details of how the heads were preserved. The head of the dead person would be cut off by a tuakana (senior relative), the body buried, and the head taken round from village to village.

This was only done in the case of high-born people. The head was preserved by karakia (invocations) said one informant, and was then placed in a net and called rara. It was taken from place to place where takihaka (tangis) would be held over it, after which it was ultimately buried or burned. Another informant said that the heads were preserved by a process called rara but unfortunately he did not describe the operation. [Note: 'rara' usually means a stage, but here seems to coincide with the Samoan 'atualala – to embalm a dead body'; and the Rarotongan 'rara – to desiccate'. Of course, the stage on which the head was set may have originated the name of the process].

Most of the population of Murihiku lived round the seacoast and here the form of earth burial was to place the corpses in sandhills. An early settler told the collector that in the fifties the Maoris round Foveaux Strait buried their dead in a sitting posture, wrapped in mats and with a greenstone toki in one hand and a club or spear in the other, and that food was buried with them. My Maori informants ridiculed most of this statement, but they acknowledged the correctness of the contention that the bodies were wrapped in mats and that formerly weapons were buried with dead warriors. In war days burials were necessarily in secret so that enemies would not know the spot and dis-inter the remains for purposes of insult. As a rule the dead were buried lying flat and with due regard to decorum, but this was not so in the case of slaves or of persons of the lowest rank. One aged woman told me that when she was a girl she was left in a village with several women, all the rest of the people being away. An old woman of no consequence died and was straightway buried without any ceremony. A hole was dug, the body was rolled in a tiaka mat all doubled-up, no effort being made to straighten it out, and was dumped into the hole in a very casual manner.

Not one of my informants had heard of burial chests, nor of receptacles to hold the bones of the dead. The nearest approach to a coffin or burial chest that the collector could hear about was the papa (boards) against which mummified corpses were placed upright in caves. An aged man said that in the West Coast Sounds there was a cave where the dead were placed upright against the cliff. The corpse was lashed to two poles – one on each side – and these were propped against the side of the cave.

A dead man's weapons were buried with him – 'tapuketia atu tona rakau'. If a chief died his widow wore a kopare-potae (mourning hat) made of houi (ribbonwood) bedecked with kotuku (white heron) plumes, and she cut (haehae) her face with kohairiki or mata (kinds of flints) or akapipi (mussel shells). Other names for the widow's mourning cap were given to me as parepare and kopare-taki (headband for the tangi). This was sometimes just a strand of vine wound round the head but more usually was made of houi with green leaves – frequently those of the kaio or ngaio tree – intertwined. After the burial a widow's cap called a wahine-potae was made of tikumu, ti or toi and was worn for a long time. The house in which the widow sat mourning was called a wharepotae. Sometimes the widows cut their hair in memory of their dead husbands and sometimes the hair was pleated to hang hei (ornaments) on as a whakamahara (remembrance). The men as a rule did nothing to show mourning in any special way, but occasionally if a favourite wife died a chief would wear her kopare (headband) not over his head but tied with a string under his chin as a mark of grief. One informant said: 'The people would wear a kopare (circlet) of kakaha – not kauheke – leaves round their heads as a sign of mourning for those who died in war.'

Most New Zealanders are familiar with the 'tangi' of the Maori. In Murihiku the lamentation for the dead was called taki or takihaka. One of my informants, an exceptionally well-informed man in most things, said that at the takihaka speeches were made about the dead. He had never heard poetic phrases advising the soul to take its departure to Hawaiki, but only sorrowful laments for dead ancestors. Against this opinion the collector was told by several other aged people that the dead were told to take their flight to the various Hawaikis, the ancient homes of the race. A very ancient dame said that when she was a small girl she had heard the mourners, when wailing, tell the soul of the dead person to haere, or travel away, away to the very far distant Hawaikis, and the oldest man interviewed, corroborated this statement. At a taki the principal men made speeches called whaikorero and farewell addresses to the dead were called poroporoangi or poroporoaki. As each lot of manuhiri (visitors) arrived at the place of mourning they were welcomed by the head man and their leader replied and when departing the headman bade them farewell and their leader responded. This farewelling was called korero-whaka-haere and 'te tewe muri nei' was a figurative reference to the people left behind in a place when the visitors departed. A lady who was brought up at Otago Heads told the collector that girls in their teens were put to assist the old women in taki and by this means they were taught ancient songs and apakura (laments). A poroporoangi addressed to the corpse of an unmarried girl was one she thus learned at an early age. It ran: 'Haere atu ra, E Hine, haere atu ra. Haere atu ra ki ou tipuna; haere atu ki te kopu o te whenua. Haere atu ra.' (Depart thou, O Maid, depart. Go to thy ancestors; go to the womb (or belly) of the earth. Depart.) She did not remember any of the words of the apakura but they were extremely pathetic. In the olden days people never cried nor wailed in the house – it was done out on the marae. As visitors arrived the men of the place would taki (make gesticulatory speeches), each speaker flourishing a taiaha staff to lend emphasis to his efforts to 'haeremai' (welcome) the visitors, and later a visitor would 'return thanks' or karaka mai as it was called. This ceremonial welcome would probably extend over a whole afternoon. She remembered as a child running away afraid when the old men donned a kakahu (mat) or a blanket and began to taki vehemently. One fierce old man in particular used to bound about in a frantic manner shouting 'ka'aka mai' very excitedly. The people used he raurau (green leaves) as a kopare of mourning. The widows and female relatives would haehae (gash) their bodies with sharp stones and would go about with the blood streaming down as a mark of grief and abandonment. The narrator's grandmother was much marked on her body through this old custom.

Another aged lady brought up near Dunedin said that kopaki was to present clothes to a mourning family as a sign of sympathy with them in their bereavement. In the old days a family might go to a tangi with a bundle of Maori clothing and present them in a proper and ceremonial style to the bereaved. It was a sign of grief and respect from one great family to another equally great family. The gift was spread in front of the dead person (or the coffin since European ways came in). It would sometimes be re-given to a visiting family but these would return it to the family in mourning. In the event of another person dying the mats, etc., could be given to his or her family by the first recipients of the gift, or if the death was in the ranks of the family who first made the gift, it was a graceful act for their gift to be re-bestowed on them or an equivalent gift supplied. There was nothing in convention or tradition to prevent the clothes being worn by the various recipients.

Clippings of hair were not kept in remembrance of the departed, the idea being repugnant to the Maori mentality. Where such locks were known to exist they were not burned but were buried with due solemnity. The collector was told of the case of a Maori from Otago who died in Mexico and whose relatives here received some of his hair forwarded in a letter. The relatives cried over this memento of the deceased and then ceremoniously took the hair to a cemetery and buried it.

The Murihiku Maoris still observe a little of the traditional idea of family precedence in regard to burials. To lay a corpse out in observance of etiquette it requires an elder brother or sister, or a member, even though younger in years, of an older branch of the family. The custom of burying their possessions with the dead or of burning the deceased's property seems to have died out in the South, as well as other customs connected with the wailing for the dead. Some of the old men, however, will not take pipes, tobacco nor matches into cemeteries, one remarking to the collector that such things would contaminate the graveyard and pollute the dead. Whether the men wore greenery on their heads as a sign of mourning in pre-European days the collector cannot say but some of them place green leaves in their hat-bands at funerals in modern days. A funeral is called uhuka and a burial ground is usually called urupa, but also unu or unu-tupapaku.

SECTION X

CUSTOMS

Childbirth – Maori women, even to this day, have a decided objection to going to a Nursing Home to give birth to children, fearing that the doctors and nurses may burn the whenua (afterbirth) and not bury it as per immemorial custom. To burn it is terrible in Maori eyes. The correct procedure is to carry the whenua forth before dawn the next morning after the birth and bury it in the whenua (ground) at sunrise. Sunrise is the most propitious time as it is believed the child grows in vigour even as the sun increases in strength from sunrise to its zenith.

Rocking Baby – In the olden times, said a man of over seventy summers, babies were sometimes put in a kete (flax basket) and this was suspended to a branch of a tree, or ridgepole or a lofty whata (storehouse) by ropes, two in number he thought, to one of which a taura (rope or string) was tied and given an occasional pull to swing the baby about. The only name he knew for this was kaitaurere or kaitarere, a name applicable to all kinds of swings.

Nakedness – Of old, said an ancient dame, the children ran naked together and thought no harm of it but for years past the people had conformed to Pakeha ideas in this respect. When she was a small girl she ran naked with the rest. An old man also referred to the fact that the maids and youths bathed together in the nude.

Whistling – One aged man said he had not heard that whistling was abhorrent to the people of old. He had whistled when he was a boy and it had not been forbidden. Two aged women, however, remembered that the old people disliked people whistling. One recalled the fact that as children they were not allowed to whistle at night. The other remarked that whistling was called kowhiowhio but she had not heard the reason the old people looked on it with disfavour. An old man said he had heard in a casual way that whistling brought spirits about. Spitting, if not actually forbidden, was very much disliked. One lady said she had heard no definite reason for this and another informant considered it was because of some Northern superstition that had drifted down South, but the rest of my informants had heard it was because the older generation were afraid an enemy might makutu (bewitch) the spittle and cause serious harm to the spitter. Spitting was called tuha or tuhatuha or sometimes huare.

Salutations – The greeting to one person is tena-koe and the reply is tena-koe (literally 'that is you' but equivalent to our 'good-day' or 'hullo'). The greeting to two persons is tena-korua and to three or more tena-koutou. After a visit and when the visitor is departing the host says 'e haere ra' and the guest replies 'e noho ra' or often just 'e noho'. This means 'Depart thou' and 'Stay thou' and is a polite form of etiquette.

Rubbing Noses – An old man at Stewart Island called this custom hoki but offered no comments about it. A mainlander called it tukuihu and said that the hand-grasp accompanying it was called ru. The collector was under the impression that this venerable custom had died out in Murihiku but on the return of the mutton-birders he saw plenty of it at the Bluff. True, one or two halfcaste women did salute one another with a halfhearted kiss on a supercilious cheek, but nearly all indulged in the hoki. To see two bearded veterans pressing noses on the main thoroughfare of Southland's principal port might seem ludicrous to those not privileged to see it in actuality, but the entire lack of self-consciousness gave the ceremony a certain touch of dignity. While you are pressing noses you state your relationship to the other person such as taku hakoro (my father) or taku mokopuna (my grandchild) as the case may be, or if you are not related you may say tena koe or kia ora or other suitable greeting. The collector could find no history or tradition bearing on this ancient custom as none of his informants had heard how it originated.

Suicide – This was not a common Maori custom but a certain number committed suicide, mostly through thwarted love affairs. The collector asked what the Murihiku Maoris called suicide and could get no direct name for it. He was told that the phrase 'Nana noa i a kai kino' was said if persons committed suicide or did bodily harm to themselves. In addition to the few who took their own lives a few came to their ends by sitting down and moping – 'willing themselves to die' – a strange Polynesian ability which has no English counterpart.

Ohu – This is the name of a custom whereby a number of Maoris agree to do a certain work by assembling and working together. Cases of ohu occur several times in the narration of Murihiku history.

Tapui, said a well-informed kaumatua, was the name applied to a girl reserved as a bride or a young man reserved as a bridegroom. The parents made the selection and the young people had to obey. If they objected very much their only escape was in flight. If a girl did so and later married another man leaving a chief to lament her defection, the deserted one might kill some servants or slaves of her people as a solace for his insulted feelings. In the old days wars even started through the actions of tapui persons absenting themselves to prevent such arrangements being fulfilled. These arrangements were sometimes made long before and according to one of my informants if any objection was made when the time for fulfilment came it was usually the man who was fractious and who emphasised his objection by hurriedly leaving the locality.

Marriage – In Murihiku genealogies marriage is generally designated 'i moe i' or 'ka noho'. It was by no means an elaborate ceremony and was briefly disposed of by one of my informants as follows: 'For a marriage to take place get the friends together and when both families agree they say to the young couple "i moe korua" and by thus sleeping together they are regarded as married.'

Hereditary succession – In regard to the question of father-right versus mother-right as interpreted in varying parts of Oceania it is interesting to note that in the South as well as the North of New Zealand the upoko-ariki (head chief) of a tribe could be either a male or female according to birth. In one village visited by the collector he was interested to observe that a young woman, wise and discreet beyond her years as it happens, was appealed to for advice by those much older than she was. Inquiry revealed that she was, by line of descent, tuakana (or 'elder') to nearly everybody in the village. The name tapairu given in the North Island to the eldest-born daughter of the highest chief of a tribe appeared to be absolutely unknown in Murihiku. In regard to the esteem in which women were held, one aged man pointed out that proverbs detailing the prowess of various celebrated warriors always alluded to them as the sons of their mothers quoting the mother's name. He quoted three such sayings about Rakaitauheke, Maru and Te Kaue to prove his statement. He knew of no reason for this custom except as a tribute to the mother. The collector has noticed in genealogies, however that where two men of the same name are mentioned, the names of the respective fathers are added for purposes of identification.

Rights in Children – In some parts of the Pacific the mother's brothers had certain rights as to the children but as far as the collector could ascertain these were nil in Murihiku. My informants considered that the Maori custom was for the parents and grandparents to have all the say as to the children. If a chief's daughter married a lower-class man against the wishes of her father, the latter could exercise a considerable sway in regard to the children's upbringing. In any case grandparents very often brought up the children and their rights in this respect were generally conceded.

Plurality of Wives – Polygamy was not as common as it might have been but still was a well-recognised custom. On the authority of Wohlers it is said that when a man had several wives, the relationship of one wife to another was called taokete, but the collector has no information on this point.

Rights re widows – One aged man recalled the fact that in the olden times if a married man died leaving a brother, the latter was supposed to take the widow to wife or to add her to his stock of wives. My informant did not know the name of the custom, but a well-informed man said it was called putao. Your brother's widow is your putao and you have the disposal of her. Fighting used to sometimes occur over this custom in the old days.

Genealogies – A custom deeply ingrained in the Maori was the readiness and ability to recite his whakapapa or wakapapa (family tree) when need arose. Wonderful fluency was attained and the strictest accuracy was demanded (and in the old days was enacted at the weapon's point). Even to this day the recital of any genealogy is subjected to keen scrutiny and searching criticism. If found correct it is 'kai te tika'; if in the slightest degree wrong it is 'kai te he'. Although a woman could be an ariki yet the Maori likes to pride himself on unbroken lines of male descent. A line in which every name is a male one is a whakatutane and for a man to be a whaka-tu-tane from some illustrious chief is a source of great pride.

Taunting – The old, old habit of casting up the deeds and misdeeds, the misfortunes or the mode of death of ancestors still breaks out on provocation and then the taunt of taurekareka (slaves) is freely bandied about. An old and respected Native of Murihiku told the collector that his mother used to teach him when he was a little boy to answer taunts about slain ancestors with the words 'ki taurekareka'. The name really meant a prisoner, he thought. This custom of teaching children retaliatory abuse is also called mokai. If there is anything detrimental in either party's ancestry this is sure to be brought forward in these quarrelsome vilifications. This custom of taunting will have to die out ere the apostolic advice to live peaceably with all is fully obeyed by the Maoris. It must be candidly admitted that the women are the worst offenders [See Stack's [[1893]] *Kaiapohia*, pp. 50–51]. Old intertribal and inter-family jealousies are at the bottom of most of the quarrels.

Rahui – the meaning of this word is to preserve anything and it can be applied to a game reservation or a fishing reserve and also to a custom whereby a chief sometimes preserved the life of a man whom a taua (war-party) might wish to slay. This man became a rahui of his preserver and his descendants were liable to be taunted as taurekareka (slaves) when wordy feuds broke out and bygone events were raked up.

Taunaha – This was the custom of proclaiming what was one's own or what one intended to be his own. If a tribe conquered another, the conquering chiefs would taunaha, or bespeak, the parts of the conquered territory they wished to hold or intended to be kept for themselves and their posterity.

Plucking beards – In the old days the male Maori was beardless because tattooing prevented the growth of beards. With the advent of the whaler and the decline in tattooing, beards grew freely and were dealt with by the painful custom of hutia-te-pahau (pulling the beard), a practice also called takina, which my informant said meant 'snatching'. He had seen the process when a boy at Otago Heads and pulling the hairs out one by one was tedious as well as painful. It was done with a bivalve before the two sides of it got dis-united and this natural tweezers was closed on each hair and given a sharp tug. The face would bleed a little and if the performance became too sore it was carried out in instalments.

Fishermen's Return – When the fishermen came home from the sea, said a Maori lady to the collector, the custom was for the unused bait (fish) to be given to the children to eat, but she as tuakana (oldest) of her family did not get any – only the taina (those younger than her) were permitted to eat it. Her father was very strict about this old prejudice being observed and as she thought she was being deprived of some treat she would go away and shed tears. This relic of the old caste observances bore hardly on her, she considered.

Hoani Matiu of Karitane, photographed in 1937, a recognised authority on southern traditions and one of Beattie's informants. E.A. Phillips photograph, P1951-003/2-001, Hocken Collections Uare Taoka o Hākena, University of Otago.

Passing each other – One of my informants said it was customary in the olden times for one man to pass another on his right side. The right side was considered the more powerful – it was the tahatane the man's side whereas the weaker left side was the tahawahine, the woman's side. In the same way there were certain things a man did with his right hand (maui) and not with his left (tahae). The origin of these observances was the belief that wairua (spirits) were more afraid of your strong right hand than of your weaker left one, and so superstition dictated some customs.

Customs not Known – It is a custom with some savage peoples to file the teeth but none of my informants had heard of teeth-filing. That circumcision was practised to a limited extent among the Maoris we know and there is a place-name in Otago bearing a reminder of the custom but none of the old men the collector interviewed in Murihiku could give any information about it. It was a custom in the North Island to keep elaborately carved boxes to hold feathers and one such box is in the Christchurch Museum, but none of the oldest people in the South of the South Island had heard of such boxes, let alone seen them.

Porterage – In the old days big pohas (kelp bags) and potted foods were carried on men's backs long distances to feasts. Three sticks or 'legs' dangled from the load and were used when the porter required a rest. Many of the loads were so heavy that the carrier could not have hoisted them up unaided. My informant saw pohas borne thus to the tangi for Hoani Korako at Otakou, but he never heard the name of the three sticks (which presumably form what Stack calls 'a porter's stool'). It is said that it took the porters three weeks to bring their loads from Riverton to Otago Heads.

Genealogical Records were sometimes kept on rakau-whakapapa (notched ancestral sticks). One belonging to the Taiaroa family is said to be deposited in the Bank of New Zealand at Dunedin. It is described as three-sided with a row of notches down each ridge, each notch representing an ancestor. It is further said to be the only one now in existence in the South Island.

CUSTOMS

Tangis – If the average Pakeha was asked to name any Maori customs he would probably say 'Tangis and haka' – and then stop. The former observance has largely died out in Murihiku, particularly the wailing that was so marked a feature when a corpse was carried out for burial. A generation ago at a Maori burial in Otago the wailing was of such a poignant and piercing a character that it was heard well over two miles away, but nowadays silence is mostly observed the same as at a European funeral. Often, however, something like a traditional Irish wake is held in the house of mourning the night before the burial and sorrowful dirges are sung. The Murihiku name for a tangi is takihaka.

Hakas – The average white man considers the haka to be a war-dance, but from the little the collector could glean in Murihiku and the South Island generally, it is really a part of the ceremony of welcome or for entertaining visitors. My main informant had never heard of hakas being given in Otago in the olden days, but another well-informed man said it used to be performed. Some of the performers would be on their knees and some standing. He had never heard of it immediately preceding a fight but occasionally it would be done prior to a war party setting out and if a hitch or a mistake occurred in its presentation, the warriors would say that was a bad omen and refuse to go to war. It was sometimes danced at peace-making ceremonies too. The collector failed to get any of the words sung or shouted to it. In modern days if the Murihiku Maoris wish to give a haka they import one from the North as a rule. It may be mentioned that the older people in Murihiku call it a hanga.

A Warrior's Death – In the olden days it was the ambition of every warrior to die a proper death, that is fighting. The olden Maoris believed it was unnatural for a man to die a natural death. To die naturally was called mate te fala (mate te whara) and was to be avoided wherever possible. 'They believed in death in battle', said one of my informants.

The fingers – In Maori carvings showing the hand there are usually only three fingers but the collector heard no explanation of this peculiar fact. Persons with six fingers or six toes were supposed to be particularly favoured by Nature. In counting the fingers the collector observed two procedures. An ancient dame at Taieri started at the little finger and counted thus: taotao-iti; taotao-rua; taotao-toru; taotao-wha; konui (thumb). An aged man from Otago Heads began at his thumb and enumerated: konui, koroa, mapere, manawa, koiti (little finger). He thought mapere meant boy's marbles and that it was so called because it was used in that game, but he could not say why the first finger was called 'long' nor where the other names came from. [This derivation of mapere from marbles was merely ascribing a modern explanation to what is probably an ancient term. It seems to the collector that the former count is modern and the latter count is ancient.]

Steeping in water is a Maori custom that interests and puzzles white people. The Maori used to steep various things in water as recorded elsewhere in this series and when maize was introduced he steeped it too. Maize did not grow in Murihiku but potatoes did and the Maori steeped them in water, calling the softened and bleached result by the name of kopi.

Salt was not used by the olden Maoris. They would soak crayfish, etc. in fresh water to get rid of any taste of the sea. Most of the older Maoris will not use salt to this day but the younger generation is adopting Pakeha customs.

Buried Treasure – It was customary to bury weapons with a chief, but many a living man would bury some treasured object. If he died without revealing the secret hiding-place the object was not recovered and this explains why the Pakeha every now and then unearths some relic of the former owners of the soil, other than at ancient burial grounds.

SECTION XI

WEAPONS

WEAPONS

The weapons of the Southern Maori are described as follows: Taiaha – same as the Northern weapon of this name, Maipi – practically the same only a Katimamoe name, Pou-whenua – somewhat like two foregoing but with one end pointed, Patu-pounemu – synonymous with the northern mere, Patu-paraoa – a mere made of whalebone, Patu-uri (or patu-pohatu) a mere made of stone, Kauri – a mere (or patu) made of black stone, Patu-Rakau – a mere made of wood, Toki-pounemu – an axe or adze of greenstone (seldom used in warfare), Toki-uri – an axe or adze of dark stone (seldom used in warfare), Paiaka – synonymous with northern tewha-tewha, Tokotoko – a stout stick used as an emergency weapon, Timata – a short spear for throwing, Toro – a short spear for throwing, Huata – a long spear for thrusting (syn. tao), Panehe – an axe or adze of any kind (an emergency weapon), Patu – a rough club of wood (an emergency weapon), Toki-pohatu – an axe of light grey stone (an emergency weapon), Hoe-waka – canoe paddles sometimes used as an emergency weapon, Kauri pohatu – stone fernroot beater sometimes used as an emergency weapon, Pukahu – a sharpened stick sometimes used as an emergency weapon. Rakau was a general name for all weapons.

THE TAIAHA

The taiaha or taieha was also called maipi throughout Murihiku. The weapon was generally made of rata wood in the South or of maire wood further north. This well-known weapon consisted of a head te reke and a blade te rapa and was carried with the blade up and the head down. The head had a koroputa (hole) bored through it and in this was inserted a string of whitau (dressed flax) to hold a bunch of kaka, kakapo, kakariki, koekoea or ruru feathers. This feather bunch was called puhi, te puhi or taupuhi and was only for ornament, being removed in warfare. The head was carved in such a manner that it more or less resembled a human face. The eyes were equipped with the irridescent shell of the koeo, a small and pretty variety of the well-known pawa, or sometimes tio (oyster) shell or pipi shell; and in olden times were gummed in with tarata (white maple gum) or flax gum (piaharakeke or piaharareke). Hold the blade uppermost and the Maori sees the facial representation. The puhi of feathers hanging down represented human hair. The 'forehead' was called te rae the eyes kanohi while the 'eyebrows' were called tukemata and the 'lip edge' under the kanohi was called ka kutu, the remainder of the countenance being the arero or tongue. The portion under the kanohi (eyes) was called puheke-o-te-arero. The puheke is really part of the human throat (pukorokoro) and the name pukorokoro was sometimes applied to the part of the weapon rightly called puheke. The end of the arero was called maripi (a cutting edge) while the flat end of the rapa was called puhaki-o-te-maipi. The part where the hand held the weapon was called maukarika [maungaringa = carrying in the hand].

In using a taiaha a warrior did not cut down at a foe, but slashed sidewise to get the whole length of his opponent's body to hit at. He did not parry with the weapon but moved his body, arms or head to correspond with his opponent's attack. His opponent might feint with the rapa and suddenly jerk up the arero aimed at his stomach, or he might feint with the arero and swiftly slash with the rapa, but in either case the experienced fighter changed his position with speed to meet, or inaugurate, each attack. This was what was assiduously practised, and only competent men were supposed to carry such a weapon.

THE MERE OR PATU

The term patu covers a wide range in Murihiku and may mean anything from a rough, knotted wooden club to a beautiful mere made of greenstone. To define the various classes of patu with exactitude a qualifying descriptive word was added as

patu-pounemu, a mere made of greenstone
patu-paraoa, a mere made of whalebone
patu-uri, a mere made of a black stone (also called kauri)
patu-pohatu, a mere made of any other kind of stone
patu-rakau, a mere made of wood.

The Northern name for this well-known weapon, mere, was gradually invading southern precincts in recent generations, the collector was informed, and was being applied to the highest form of the weapon, viz. greenstone. Thus it had become correct to say mere pounemu or patu pounemu to identify one made of greenstone, but it was still quite impermissible to say mere paraoa, mere uri or mere rakau when speaking of a patu paraoa, patu uri or patu rakau.

The knob at one end was called te upoko, the handle, kakau, and the blade te arero. A hole (koroputa) was bored through the handle and through this ran a string (taupatu) to attach it (kia mau ai) to the wrist or tatua (belt) so that it could be grasped quickly when most needed.

Some fighters would throw it forward three or four feet and recover it by the string but others would use shorter strings only permitting a throw of one foot perhaps. It was really a weapon for hand-fighting and when held in the hand the patu was thrust (whaka-oho) at the enemy (hoariri). It was a dangerous weapon if effectively used and even the ones made of heavy wood were formidable.

My informants had not seen carved specimens of patu, but added that a decorative touch was added by tying bunches of whitau (dressed flax), coloured black and white, or red, to the handle.

Some of the patu in the Otago Museum are very rough and my informants called these uncouth specimens patupaiarehe and added that tradition said they were the weapons of the maeroero.

SPEARS

The collector has heard a certain amount of comment dealing with the absence of throwing weapons among the Maoris but anyone who subscribed to that view might have modified or revised his conclusions somewhat if he had interviewed the Murihiku Maori.

Nearly all my informants seemed to have heard of the throwing of spears in the old days of warfare. It would be strange indeed if they had not for spear throwing is mentioned at least seven times, if not more, in the South Island record of fighting; four times recording the deaths of the chiefs at whom the spears were thrown, twice describing spear throwing contests and once relating the timely evasion and escape of the chief at whom the missile was hurled. The spear that was thrown is usually called timata nowadays but the collector was told that this word really applies to the act of throwing, the correct name for the spear being toro. It was usually made of manuka, the bark being singed off with fire and the rod scraped with kohairaki (a kind of quartz). The mata (point) of the rod was hardened in the fire (me tahuru ki te ahi), and if done properly the point could be made like steel and of very penetrative qualities. When hardening spear points the manuka would sometimes make a whistling noise called toi and this was regarded as a very good omen for the user of that spear.

In addition to the toro or timata there was a longer spear called huata (which is probably synonymous with the North Island tao) and although primarily intended for thrusting it could also be thrown if occasion warranted.

My informants agreed in giving the length of the throwing spear as six or seven feet, with some up to eight feet for tall men. There was more diversity of opinion over the length of the huata estimates ranging from nine feet to fifteen feet with a preponderance of belief that twelve feet was a fair average.

AXES AND ADZES

These were both termed toki and although they were not so much used in fighting as in peaceful pursuits they can be classed under the heading of weapons for history records the use of toki in warfare. In pre-pakeha days the use of a toki in the form of a European axe was rare, the general use being in adze form. So much was this the case that one well-informed old man told the collector that he had never seen the toki attached to wood in other than the adze form. A few of the oldest people, however, had seen the toki utilised in an axe form and it was then a toki-titaha for splitting (wawahi), the adze being a toki-tarai for chipping. The toki-titahi was usually big and heavy and was lashed to the handle with vines and flax. A woman who had seen her father split wood with a stone axe said he lashed the toki firmly between two sticks, a long and a short one, using the longer one as the axe handle – a simple but effective plan. Some of the old-fashioned kakau-paneke (axe handles) were in existence until recent years but they have now all disappeared. The collector was told that toki was the head of the axe or adze, its handle was kakau while the whole axe or whole adze was called panehe.

The toki varied in their composition, the toki-pounemu being of greenstone, the toki-pohatu of ordinary stone, while the toki-uri was frequently made of the kind of dark stone called kara, and was said to be better than the greenstone one for chopping trees (topea te rakau). One of my aged informants went into the bush behind his hut, made a rough kakau (handle), lashed a toki-uri to it and gave the collector a practical demonstration of tree cutting. That rough-and-ready adze is now in the Otago Museum.

Some toki had an upoko (head) and kaki (neck) to enable them to be more firmly lashed to the arero part of the kakau but most were plain. The lashing was called kaui or kau-wi and was usually of whitau (dressed flax). The handle for the adze was generally procured by cutting off a suitable branch and with it and attached to it at an angle a piece of the tree, this piece forming a convenient face to which to lash the toki. For an axe a stout stick, smoothed a little where the toki was attached, was sufficient.

It was pointed out to the collector that both sides of a toki were not evenly balanced, one being flatter than the other. In lashing a toki to an adze handle the flat side was put next the wood so that in using the implement it came in the under position. The bulge in the other side of the toki was called the uma and in using the adze the uma faced the user leaving the flat side of the toki down on the surface being adzed, with a corresponding advantage that the chip made by the cut was forced upward by the shape of the uma.

Quite considerable trees were chopped down with these stone adzes and the stumps left in several instances were in existence after the white settlers came to Otago. Before the tree fell the olden Maori would shape the end of the canoe on it and also chip it out as high as they could reach and one of my informants surmised that the toki-titaha would be a very suitable implement for this work. When the tree was felled little fires of chips were used to reduce the trunk. This burning (tahuna te ahi) charred the wood and the adzes were used to chop out the chars (taraitia ka karehu) and so hollow the trunk.

Another use for adzes is said to have been in digging difficult ground for house foundations or pa earthworks. As a weapon a famous chief was killed with a toki on Otago Peninsula, and the favourite weapon of another historic chief was a toki, but history does not record if these weapons were in the shape of axes or adzes.

In the Otago Museum there are a number of small toki which are hard to place. My informants considered these had been made for boys. The elders would show the youngsters how to use the toki and if they showed carelessness, indifference or inaptitude after the lesson the learners were likely to receive a hearty cuff. One of my informants who gave much information about weapons generally said, 'I have heard of rough clubs of wood and stone having occasionally been used in fighting, but I never heard of either panehe or toki being used as weapons.' This opinion is contradicted by the information already given but it shows how otherwise well-informed men can lack information on certain points and also how difficult it is to collect authentic details.

THE PAIAKA

was described by one man as a 'long stick with a slab at one end'. After hearing several of the aged Maoris describe the weapon they called paiaka, the collector came to the conclusion it was the same as the North Island tewhatewha, and this surmise was confirmed when he took an old Maori into the Otago Museum and showed him the exhibit there named tewhatewha, for the veteran straightway called it a paiaka.

The flat portion that forms the chief characteristic of this weapon was generally called te rapa, although one of my informants said it was an arero. In comparing two of these weapons the olden people would say, 'the rapa of this paiaka is larger than the rapa of that one', and so on. It is said that when carried the paiaka was held about the centre with the rapa up and the point down. This point (mata) was useful in fighting for stabbing, while the rapa end was for dealing blows. There was often a carved piece on the handle (maukarika) and this is traditionally said to have originated to give a firmer grasp and to prevent the hand slipping as it would be wont to do on a polished surface. In common with most of the other weapons the paiaka was frequently adorned with a puhi of bird feathers. The paiaka was made of rata (ironwood), manuka or kahikatoa (a big kind of manuka) and was made all in one piece. It was not such a common weapon as the taiaha, mere or spear, nor is its ancient use so well-known as that of the toki. One man, indeed, who drew a rough drawing of a paiaka for the collector, considered it was used by the women and that the taiaha was used by the men. Another old man was under the impression that the paiaka and maipi were the same weapon, but most of the others interviewed knew a little better than that and gave the information recorded above.

THE POU-WHENUA

was a weapon that seemed unknown to the majority of the old Maoris and half-castes whom the collector interviewed. Some had never even heard the name while others professed to have casually heard the word but added that they were unable to describe such a weapon. At length the collector met two men who knew something about the pou-whenua, but there seems to be no doubt that its occurrence in Murihiku must have been very rare.

One old man said the pou-whenua was a big taiaha with the difference that where the latter had a 'tongue', the former had only a sharp point. It was ornamented with a puhi (bunch of feathers) and was usually six or seven feet long – about the same length as a large taiaha.

The other informant said that the pou-whenua was similar to a taiaha but it had no carved head. The blade (rapa) was like that of a taiaha but from there it ran to a point for stabbing. In warfare the pou-whenua was used like the maipi (taiaha). Although it looks blunt the arero of a maipi would cut a man like a knife. In place of the arero the pou-whenua had a sharp point which could do equally effective work if suddenly stabbed into an opponent's puku (stomach). The rapa (blade) was used exactly the same as that of the taiaha. The pou-whenua could also be used for a staff when its owner was walking, and when so used the rapa was kept downward while the sharp end was pointing upward.

EMERGENCY WEAPONS

were occasionally brought into use by the olden Maori when necessity arose. Such was the tokotoko a stout manuka stick used as a walking staff. One end was sharpened and hardened in the fire and if the need occurred this end could be used as a stabbing point while the remainder of the stick could be used to lay on or ward off blows. It is said to have been usually six or seven feet long and when used for walking the sharp end was kept uppermost. Exhibit D10.68 Otago Museum is a tokotoko.

Hoe-waka (canoe paddles) were sometimes used as weapons. A blow from te rapa o te hoe (the blade of the paddle) dealt by a strong man was a serious, if not a deadly, matter for the recipient. One of my informants remarked 'The oar was a very nasty weapon to meet in a tight pinch'.

The Murihiku Maoris used long stones for beating fernroot and these rude stone clubs were called kauri pohatu or patu aruhe. Wooden clubs were also in use for this purpose but they were not so effective as the stone ones. It is said that these clubs were occasionally pressed into service as temporary weapons. The pukahu, a stick sharpened at both ends and used to spear eels, etc. was also an emergency weapon for history records the death of a great chief at the battle of Tarahaukapiti through one.

VARIOUS INQUIRIES

were made about the following items but with little result: Toki-poutangata – was a name unknown to any of the old people interviewed. Dagger – this weapon was unknown and was considered to be not a Maori idea. Oka – was not a weapon, but to stab with a sharp point was called 'oka'. Maripi – was not a weapon, but was applied to any cutting edge and it now signifies a pakeha knife. Kotaha – this was unknown to most of those interviewed but one old man said: 'I have heard of the kotaha, and "paka ia te kotaha" was to use it. It was a sort of a sling but I cannot describe it. The darts were called timata. I have seen men take a short stick with a notch in it and project spears straight for a long way – further than by hand – but I do not know its name and I never heard of its being used in fighting.' Kauri – this weapon is mentioned in the history of the fighting in the South Island, about two hundred and fifty years ago, but only one of those interviewed had heard of it. He says it was made of black stone in the shape of a patu or mere, so probably the name patu-uri is synonymous with it. Whao is the name of the old stone chisel of the Maori but whether such were ever used as emergency weapons in a crisis cannot be said.

REMARKS CONCERNING WARFARE

While the collector was interrogating the aged people about the ancient weapons of their race, they let fall sundry remarks about the use of the weapons and about the old-style fighting generally and these stray remarks have been gathered together here.

'Before a young man,' remarked one informant, 'was allowed to fight for his tribe or take his place as a warrior the tohuka (priest) took him to a pool and sprinkled him with water by means of a branch or a bunch of grass. As far as I can recollect this ceremony was called patukatapu. The tohuka called on the tribal atua to strengthen the young man and make him a worthy warrior.'

'When they were fighting,' said another, 'the men used to koukou their hair up into a bunch so that it would not get in the way or blind them. They wore feathers stuck in it. As far as I know men not only wore the maro (loin cloth) when fighting but all the time. When thoroughly aroused the warriors often stripped and fought kiri-tahaka (naked). I never heard of the Maori having a dagger of bone, wood or stone. The word oka means to stab and is now applied to sticking a pig. The action of a man thrusting with a taiaha or pou-whenua was called werohia or tapahia. The men used to dance the haka down here but I cannot say in what it differed to a North Island haka.'

Most of the old men seemed to have a fondness for the taiaha as a typical Maori weapon yet the collector was unable to ascertain the names of the various feints and movements connected with its use, except that the Southland place-name Tamaipi means 'to strike with a maipi'. Very few of the narrators had ever seen the taiaha in actual use, but one veteran described with great glee the manner in which the chief Pukurakau, using a stick as a taiaha, warded off and scared away a bulldog which attacked him at Kohurau (now called Kurow). My oldest informant had seen an exhibition of spearcraft by a chief of Waitaha-Katimamoe descent and it so impressed him that he considered in the event of a duel it would be superior to the taiaha unless an extremely able exponent was handling the latter weapon. At the same time he reckoned that a man armed with a short spear could beat a man with a long spear, other things being equal.

Quite a number of those interviewed could say nothing about the maipi or patu, but nearly every one had heard of the throwing spear. It was responsible for the deaths of too many prominent men of old to be overlooked or ignored and yet no one seemed to know how far it could be thrown in a trial nor its effective range in combat. It appears to the collector to have been largely a Katimamoe weapon and that it fell into disuse when the Kaitahu and Katimamoe tribes amalgamated.

One intelligent old man said: 'The huata was a lance twelve or fourteen feet long but it was not much used as it was too dangerous for the wielder to use at close quarters. The patu or mere was the best weapon for close fighting. The timata was a spear seven or eight feet long to hurl at the enemy. It was not very much used as the Maori did not believe in his weapon being out of his hand or thrown out of his reach. He liked to feel he had a grasp of what he was fighting with.'

Another old man championed the hand-to-hand fight too. He put in a good word for the fighting qualities of the maipi in its twofold use, and then proceeded to refer to the paiaka as a good fighting weapon also, concluding with the remark: 'It was used with both hands – that's how the Maori had such command of his weapon.' The last of my notes on weapons concerns an exhibit in the Otago Museum, where it is thought to be an oar weapon. The two aged men [[King and Rehu]] who visited the Museum with me thought it might be a takoko for making holes in soft ground or for digging pa-kanakana (lamprey weirs). At the same time it might have been used as a weapon for many an unusual implement was pressed into service in the old-time fighting days.

SECTION XII

GREENSTONE [[SEE APPENDIX 1]].

SECTION XIII

CANOES AND PADDLES; TORCHES AND TORCHING; SPADES AND DIGGING

PADDLES AND PADDLING

The name for the paddle was hoe and one old man said it was usually five or six feet in length and made of kahikatoa (or kaikatoa) which is a kind of big manuka tree.

Asking a kaumatua how the Maori propelled a canoe in which only one man was sitting, he, and a younger man with him, agreed in stating that the paddling (hoetia) was done on only one side of the canoe. The occupant sat in the stern of the waka (canoe) and by giving a 'side-flick' to his paddle at the end of a stroke he also steered (whakatere) his bark. Going against a current this was sometimes very difficult to do but a skilful man could hold a very straight course. This informant said he had seen a canoe sent along by a takoko, which he described as a scoop with a handle on it and used for digging ditches. This was an emergency method of rowing, however.

Another poua differed from the last man in describing the paddling of a one-man canoe, the rower, he said, using the paddle so many times on one side and so many on the other and so on alternately. The blade of the hoe was called rapa, he continued, and usually had a bend forward near the point to get a 'better grasp' of the water when rowing. Some of the hoe had a ridge down them to strengthen them, and some were carved all over and looked beautiful. He remembered when he was a boy seeing at the Bluff forty or fifty Maoris paddling a canoe sixty or seventy feet long and made of totara. The sides of the canoe were heightened with boards but he forgot the name these were called. Such a sight, with so many rowers all keeping time, was unforgettable and the pity was it was a thing of the past. An old lady said the hoe (paddles) she had seen in the South were straight but she fancied the North Island ones had a slight bend in them. The collector has a further note that waka (canoes) were usually made out of totara trees. Among the Kati-Mamoe tribe the old men who mended canoes were called pateketeke, according to Stack, but the present collector has no information on this point.

Add to Canoes

One old man said: 'When I was a boy I saw a waka-unua (double canoe) which had arrived from Codfish Island (Foveaux Strait). The two canoes were much about the same size and were perhaps four or six feet apart and joined. The tiaka (sail) was square like the topsail on a pakeha schooner and had a boom along the top and along the bottom of it, and a mast (hua) in the centre.

Poles called rauraho ran across from canoe to canoe and were lashed on with whitau. The two rauraho nearest the bow and the two nearest the stern ran right across both canoes and were fastened with whitau, while the rest of the rauraho ran from edge to edge of the canoes. Raupo was built on the platform so that no waves would come up between the spaces between the rauraho. The mast was placed between two strong rauraho and ropes ran from it to the ihu (bow) and to te ta (the stern). Two men were steering, one at the rear of each canoe and each held big hoe (paddles) to steer with. In the old days the bow and stern pieces were carved with spirals and such designs. I never saw an outrigger used, nor have I heard of such having been used'. It is said to have been common in the South for the canoes to be daubed with red paint, but the collector has no further record of this custom.

There were two kinds of mokihi. In the proper kind you would not get wet but in the other, a makeshift, you sat astride a bundle of korari and paddled with your legs. A good mokihi (or moki) could be constructed of raupo, as well as the commoner one of the buoyant korari sticks.

An old man said: 'Some canoes had one portion of their bottoms made deeper than the rest to allow water to gather there to be easier bailed but other canoes had no hollow like this and were plain throughout. The ordinary tataa (bailer) is made like a canoe paddle and can throw water out of the canoe. The takoko has a deeper scoop and also a handle. It can be used to scoop sand or to bail canoes.'

An old woman said: 'The ipu for bailing canoes was smaller than the usual household ipu.' It thus appears that a variety of articles could be used for bailing – anything that would lift water would do in an emergency but the tata is the correct baler.

Add to Canoes

One well-informed kaumatua said: 'The sails of canoes were made of flax mats but I never heard the shape. Perhaps they were square but I never heard how they were fastened to the mast. When I was a boy I was at Temuka and have seen outriggers (keakea) used. We went for wood to a lagoon near the sea and it was a ticklish job in the river current so a log of totara about four or five feet out from our canoe was used as an outrigger. The log was a few inches through and was roughly shaped like a canoe but you could not carry anything in it. I have also seen one used at Parika (Paringa in Westland a place which is named after a chief who went over from Waitaki and had a fight there). At Temuka, old Te Maiharoa had made a log canoe to hold five or six people and the keakea was about half its length and was held to the canoe by two sticks, one at each end. A hole was put through the gunwale so as to put string through to tie poles down and the same was done in the keakea. The poles went right across the top of the canoe. In seagoing trips two canoes were used, one being larger than the other. They were perhaps three feet apart and a platform was made of sticks and whariki (a kind of flax matting). Holes were made in the gunwales to put ropes through to tie poles down. I do not know where the mast was put or if there were more than one mast. I do not know if the platform extended over both canoes or not, nor its name but the space under it was called aroa. In single canoes the sides could be made higher by boards and these were called rauawa. I only saw one such; it was at Temuka and was said to be from the North Island. It had carvings on both ends.'

An old man (seventy seven years old) said he had never seen the waka-unua (double canoe) nor had he heard a great deal about them but to construct the platform they must have put the poles on which it was built across both canoes as to lay them from one side of one canoe to the near side of the other would put too great a strain on those sides. He reckoned the ra (sails) were square and they must have been run up and down, as to attach them fast to the mast would render them unworkable. Probably the hua (mast) had a forked top through which to run a rope. He understood that to make the platform, poles were laid across the canoes and holes (rua or koroputa?) were made through the canoe gunwales (te papa) and the poles were lashed down with whitau. This lashing was called aukaha. In his seafaring days if two men were engaged in lashing one would say 'kia kaha' as he pushed the aho (line) through and then as both pulled together the other would say 'au kaha'. If four or more were hauling on a rope the word aukaha was a signal for all to haul together. He had used the old Maori hoe (paddle) and it was shaped like this ●━━━◯ . The handle was called kakau but he forgot the name of the knob. The paddle part was hollowed to give a better 'hold' on the water. It was usually made of hard wood. The takoko (scoop) was made somewhat similar but rough while the hoe was made finer. The hoe was also used to bale canoes. It was perhaps six feet long and he had seen them used to propel log wakas (canoes) in his time. This was on the Taieri River and these canoes held two men. He has himself rowed with the hoe in a whaleboat after the black whale (kewa). They faced the way they were going and the pakehas in the boat used the hoe the same way as the Maori. They rowed almost as fast as with the best pakeha oars used in good rowlocks.

Two old Maoris, eyeing the canoe in the Otago Museum, said the bow was ihu (nose) (and if there had been a bow-piece it would have been called tauihu), the gunwale was kiato, the keel was tuara-o-te-waka, the hollow was riu, the sides taha while if bunches of raupo or tussock had been put in as seats these would be called whariki. It is about twenty eight feet long and three or four men would fish in one that size. One informant had a canoe forty feet long on the Clutha River but some white men let it go out to sea – much to the owner's disgust when he found out. The bailers in the Museum = tata and their handles = puritakarika (hand-grasp). The blades of the paddles = te papa and the handles = kakau. The big paddles – tiroa – were used for steering while the small ones – hoe – were used for rowing. They considered sails were square (and were called ra-kurupae or ra-whakapae). No tacking was done. If the wind was too strong let the string go and the sail flap. Run before it. The 'leg-of-mutton' sail was a pakeha sail in their estimation.

SECTION XIV

DOMESTIC SCIENCE

The principal method of preparing food for human consumption in ancient Murihiku was the familiar earth-oven called umu or oumu. When food was placed in the umu it was wrapped in a roll of flax called a whena or was put in a basket called a tapora. This kind of basket was made of ti (cabbage tree) leaves, of rerewaka or tutuna grass, or of koareare (raupo shoots) and was always made for use in the umu and for no other purpose. Sometimes if the food was very moist so that the juice permeated the tapora, the latter was eaten as well as the food it contained. To cook in the umu was called tao and food so cooked, or rather steamed, is very palatable. On special occasions in modern days as many as forty or fifty cakes have been done in an umu at one time and cake so made has a great reputation. Paapaa is the name for Pakeha bread and to bake it or cakes in an umu is called papatao.

To get boiling water the ancient Maori had to resort to a certain amount of ingenuity. As he had no pottery nor metal utensils he had to use a wooden vessel sometimes called a waka but more commonly known as an ipu. This was sometimes a tree trunk hollowed out and sometimes it was a receptacle made of totara bark in such a way that it would hold water. The usual way to make these vessels was to bark a totara tree and lay the bark in strips overlapping each other. The ends were tied with flax and a string ran from end to end as a handle (tau o te ipu). The ones for the women to use were usually small or medium sized, but some big ones were kept which could only be handled and carried by strong men. To make the water in an ipu boil (pupu) heated stones (werawera) were dropped in. These stones were heated in an umu and when hot enough were rolled out of it with a rakau (stick) and then rolled into a takoko (a wooden scoop) and were then carried to the ipu and deposited therein. A succession of these hot stones caused the water to boil. [In regard to the ipu an old Murihikian said that the North Islanders had gourds (hue) and used them to carry water, but the hue never grew in the South hence the term hue was not used for water vessels, but ipu or sometimes opu or upu.]

A common method of cooking food was to impale the bird, fish or eel on a stick slanting over an open fire (ahi). This roasting or toasting process was called kohiku.

An allied method was to place the food on a rara or stage just over the flame and so murumuru (grill) it. The rara was made of manuka and was handy and efficient. The collector was told that the kind of eel called kotokoto tasted very good when done on this rude gridiron. The old people interviewed seemed to consider this was a different way of cooking food to the kohiku although the collector thought it was merely a variation. Nowadays these rara are made of wire and one such is said to be still used at Temuka in the eel season. At Moeraki the collector was told that the best way to cook kakihi (sea limpets) was to put them in a poha (kelp bag) and roll it over and over in the fire, this method being called murumuru te poha. Occasionally the bag bursts and then its contents have to be raked out of the fire as quickly as possible. There is a doubt if this method is really ancient as one of my informants saw some pakehas following this mode at Lyttelton and was assured by them it was a European way. More information is needed on this point.

While speaking about cooking one aged woman mentioned as an interesting fact that the whaiuku (a species of stingray) had e rua ate (two livers). She had seen one opened and it seemed to have two livers joined into one. These were placed in a tapora or cooking bag and steamed and had a very nice kakara (smell). The other species of ray, the whaiporapora, has a long tail with spikes on it and its body was eaten but the liver was all that was eaten of the whaiuku.

A European settler told the collector that in the fifties the Maoris used sometimes to cook eels in the ashes, but my informants denied all knowledge of such a proceeding. At the same time they had seen birds occasionally done in the ashes and this, they said, scorched the feathers off, made the skin easy to remove and rendered the bird edible. To cook damper in the ashes as per the old colonial style was called komuka. Scorching a bird's plumage off in the flames prior to cooking was called hunua.

The collector was curious to get the truth (or otherwise) of a Pakeha statement that the Maoris rolled rats in mud and so baked them, the mud bringing the rodent's skin off neatly. Some of my informants had never heard of such a procedure, but one old man had seen birds baked in clay. This, he said, was called komuka and he considered it was a thing introduced into New Zealand. He had seen old Rakiraki at Port Molyneux do it very well, and that venerable man had told him it was a whaler's fashion. A well-informed old Maori briefly dismissed

Jack Rakiraki of Kaka Point, known for his knowledge of the inland South Island and a noted fisherman and hunter. Photographer unknown, P1951-003/2-024, Hocken Collections Uare Taoka o Hākena, University of Otago.

the subject by saying: 'Baking manu (birds) in clay was not a Maori work'.

In the old days the Maori used to taona te weka (cook the woodhen) as follows according to an aged man: 'Take the birds and bone them (ohori or kohori – Tregear gives 'kohure'). Then kari i te rua mo ka weka (dig the trench for the woodhens) with ko and kaheru (digging implements) and put pouaka (a kind of grass) in it. Keep the birds in the rua or trench for some days wrapped in the grass and then put them in an ipu in which hot stones have heated the water and keep them there until the fat is all out of them and lying on the bottom of the ipu. The birds are now ready to be put in the poha (kelp bag) to be kept until wanted. I have eaten them done this way and to my taste they were like titi (muttonbirds). The titi were done in the same way and are now a delicacy to the Pakeha.'

Before the neolithic Maori could cook his food he had to produce fire and this was done by rubbing the point of one stick up and down the groove made in another stick. My informants said that if the firemaker could not get a male or female companion to takahi kauati or tread on the grooved stick to keep it steady, he laid it on the ground before him, held it as well as he was able and proceeded to hika or rub as best he could. When a flame came, or rather a smouldering spark, it was fed with wisps of dry inflammable wood such as mikimiki in the bush or korokio scrub and tumatakuru on the open flats. The kotukutuku or fuchsia was not to be burned [see Superstitions] but all other kinds of timber or wood could be freely used. The grooved stick used in the procuring of fire was called kaueti or kauati, while the process itself was called hinga or hika.

My informants were all of one mind that the word 'kohua' was not used in Murihiku to define the hole made in the ground for an earth-oven, nor was it used in any way in regard to cooking or preparing food. [The whaler's term 'goashore' for a cooking pot is said to be a corruption of the Maori word 'kohua' but this seems very far-fetched.] Some of the earth-ovens were very big and were really well made – so much so that a few of them are still extant in a fair state of preservation.

In addition to cooking in the umu, to roasting or toasting at the open fire and to boiling, food could be sun-dried, or, as in the case of some shellfish, soaked in fresh water for some days and eaten raw. Of course any food could be eaten raw if dire necessity dictated such a course, but naturally a certain amount of culinary treatment was usually sought after.

The two old Maoris who visited the Otago Museum with the collector said that exhibit D10.54 was a proper old Murihiku ipu. D10.98 is an ipu also and could be used to carry oil, fat, etc. D10.44 they called a taha and said it was one of a kind used to carry oil or water. The wooden club in this section they called a patu.

The Maori did not cook in his dwelling, but outside, or in a special cooking shed. Someone suggested that this shed was called wharau but a well-informed old man differed from this suggestion. The wharau-tuna, he said, was an outhouse where eels were stored, but the shed where they were cooked was called orau [Note: Wharau has become Horau or Orau in the extreme South of New Zealand. (Compare the Moriori change of whaka to hoko).] In Canterbury he-wharau-tuna means a cooking shed for eels but in Southland the term did not seem to be used and one man said that he-wha-rau-tuna meant 'four hundred eels!'

An old settler who knew many of the Otago Maoris and sometimes travelled with a Maori companion, told the collector that when he was bullock-driving in 1858 and camping out for weeks, he received many tips from the Maoris as to how best to live on the country. One of these tips was to catch eels with a flax and worm bob and to place the eels over-night in the ashes of his campfire. He acted on this advice and invariably found the eels done to a turn and tasting delicious. From information subsequently given to the collector by aged Maoris it appears that this cooking in ashes was learned by the Maori people from seeing the whalers baking damper.

A white man whose Maori wife had recently died at the allotted span of seventy years told the collector that he had never known her to skin an eel. She split them down and took out the backbone. Like all the other old-time Maoris she did not use salt but as a concession to her husband's tastes she sprinkled some salt on eels intended for his use. Little sticks were inserted across the eels to keep the flesh spread out. When they were about half-dried they were spitted over the fire and although the skin was charred the flesh came out clean, sweet, fresh, and lovely to eat.

Jack Rakiraki (left) and his dog, with Denham Faitt and Colin Harper of Gore, outside his cottage at Kaka Point, c.1910–1930. Photographer unknown, Box-002-025, Hocken Collections Uare Taoka o Hākena, University of Otago.

COOKING EGGS

'Numerous eggs were broken into poha (kelp-bags),' said a venerable Maori to the collector, 'and as these bags would burst in the fire, the pohas were put to tao (steam) in the umu (earth-oven). They were left in the umu for five hours or so, when all the eggs formed into a hard lump called kaika. This lump could be kotikotia (cut) into slices or any way you wished. It was eaten cold and tasted very well – at least I liked it. This was the way the Maoris treated eggs when they found plenty of them in the old days as far as I know.'

Long ago a full-blooded Maori told the collector that Maoris did not cook duck or any other eggs in umus or otherwise – they waited until the eggs were hatched and took the young birds before they could fly. This was also the collector's belief, but it must be said that the last-named Maori (now dead) was not near so well-informed as the aged man quoted above.

DRYING FISH

At Otago Heads, said a Maori, the people used to put makaa (barracouta) on a stage, remove the bones, split the fish into layers two inches thick, plait these together, steam and hang up for the sun to dry. It was then packed away and would keep a long time. It was called paku; maraki being the name of fish sun-dried in a raw state. Maraki was not subject to fly-blow – neither was shark, probably because of its strong smell. Pawhera is barracouta which has been split and then dried in the sun. The people also used to string flounders up on a line to dry in the sun. The only name he knew for this was patiki-maroke (dried flounders). [Although this informant does not state so, maraki is the dried flesh of the groper. H.B.]

DOMESTIC UTILITIES

'The pipi shell was very useful to the olden Maori,' said one taua (grandmother), 'and you would often hear the old people say to the children "Haere tikina te pipi", go and fetch a pipi shell. It was used to tika (scrape) flax. It was used to cut the navel string (pito) of new-born babes. It was used to scrape new potatoes, waruwaru taiawa or waruwaru mahitau as the kind might be. It was the spoon of the old people and its edge was their knife.' Useful as the pipi was the Maoris are said to have had a maripi or stone knife and the collector sought information about it with very discouraging results (such as 'I do not know what the maripi was', etc.) until he met two old people at Temuka who said 'Maripi is an old name used for anything to cut flax, open fish and birds, etc. It could be a pipi or a pohatu (stone) or pounemu. If the last-named the edge was not at the end but along the side. In some cases it was not polished but it could be sharpened on a hoaka (Maori 'grindstone'). It was often just haea or wahia (split) off a lump, but the best maripi of all was the parihi pohatu (split stone) which is also called a mataa. Another name for the mataa was kohairaki. The mataa is a flint and was often fastened in a cleft in a stick, usually of manuka, and lashed in with whitau fibre. It was then used as a knife and would not hurt the hand. The proper name when used in such a fashion is kohairaki. Any sharp, cutting edge was called maripi and this name is now given to pakeha knives.' The patu-aruhe was a stone beater for feraroot, the collector was told, and it was often just a common stone picked up on the beach. The fernroot, another said, was first roasted at a fire and then put on a big stone and pounded. Stone beaters were called kauri but you could use any lump of wood to patu aruhe (beat fernroot). Long stones, said another, are to-day known as kauri but the proper kauri was very dark. 'The one my father had was dark and he latterly used it to drive in the stakes (poup-ou-pa) for the hinaki (eelpot) in the pa-tuna (weir). It is lost now.' Kara is a black stone and kurupakara a white stone and these were the only stones used in umus (ovens) as they kept their heat well and the fire did not crack them. A well-informed kaumatua said the mataa was used to drill holes in wood, cut flax, etc. He had never heard of it being put on a handle to use.

SECTION XV

VEGETABLE FOODS, ETC.

EDIBLE BERRIES

The Murihiku Maori ate many kinds of berries to eke out his fare, but there is so much ambiguity about which berries he considered edible and which he regarded as non-edible that the collector is forced to the opinion that in some parts of the country the same berries went under different names. We know that this is the case with white bushmen so perhaps the Maori is to be excused. The tutu berry is said to have been the only really poisonous berry, and then only when the seeds were consumed, but some of the other berries had injurious effects or were so nasty and unpalatable that they were not eaten.

Matai (black pine) berries were eaten. Tataraheka (lawyer) berries were eaten and a woman added that they make good jam. Tataramoa (bramble) berries were eaten. An old woman said the tataramoa did not bear fruit, but an old man said it bore bigger berries than the tataraheka.

Pikiraki – a very old woman who gave some good information supplied this name as that of a berry that was eaten. The pikiraki is a mistletoe or parasitic growth high up on trees and my principal informant had never heard of the berries being eaten; he thought they were poisonous.

Kotukutuku is the well-known fuchsia-tree and its berries were called hua-kotukutuku and not konini as in the North Island. It is very abundant and a prolific bearer – the berries being ripe about January.

Kareao is the name of the edible berry of the pirita (supplejack); also called hua-pirita. Mako berries were eaten. Miki shrubs bear 'hinamoki ka hua' (grey berries) said an old man and he added that those berries tasted good. The woodhens were very fond of these berries.

Mikimiki is said to be the stinkwood of the bushman and to bear a red poisonous berry, yet at Puketiraki the collector was told that the 'white mikimiki berries were eaten'. There is evidently here some confusion. White people sometimes call the miki the mikimiki and apparently my informants in this case had done the same. One of my informants said that mikimiki wood sinks in water.

Rehua is a spreading plant on the sea-beach. It bears greyish berries which are good to eat. Patotara is a small plant said to come out of the ground in summer and to die away in winter. It bears a small red berry which has a small black spot known as its konohi (eye). The berry is edible.

Tapuka is the Murihiku name of the familiar snowberry, so sought after by back-country musterers, by kea parrots and by weka (woodhens). It has a pleasant taste.

Takapo is the name of a shrub about two feet high. It has a white-and-red berry about the size of the tapuku and it can be eaten also.

Kakaha is a flaxy-like plant with red berries and these were included in a list of edible berries with a question mark attached. At Puketiraki the people were not sure if the berries were eaten or not, and at other places the replies were indefinite, but at Moeraki the old people said the name was rightfully takakaha and that the berries were poisonous. At the Bluff the Maoris said the kakaha is the nearest approach in the South to the kiekie; its red berry is not poisonous although it does not look inviting.

Kokihi is a seaside plant with red berries and these could be eaten as they were harmless.

Poroporo grew on the Otago Peninsula, according to an old Maori who was brought up there, and the fruit was eaten when ripe. This was about March and April in an average year. The fruit was yellow and sweet and were about the size of a gooseberry and hence the settlers often referred to them as Maori gooseberries. Some Southern Maoris pronounce the word as bolobolo.

Kahika (white pine) berries were eaten by the old-time Maoris. Totara berries were eaten by the Maoris and some Europeans in recent years have acquired a liking for them. No doubt many other berries were also eaten, but no further names were mentioned in conversation.

FLAX HONEY

In an old Maori Manuscript book giving a list of places where food could be procured, one class of place was defined as 'He taaka korari'. The collector made inquiry about this definition and at Moeraki was told that taka meant 'shaking' and that he taka korari was a place where suitable flax grew, and that the flax stems were broken to get the honey out. Down in Southland, however, none of the Natives questioned had heard the term taka korari, but one well-informed kaumatua (elder) added that ru koari was to shake the honey of the flax into kauru to add to the latter's taste. Flax honey will be mentioned again later on in this section.

THE SOWTHISTLE

played a not unimportant part in providing vegetable food for the ancient Maori. It grew plentifully in the bush (and hence is often called bush thistle by settlers) and the aged people at Temuka enumerated at least three kinds, viz. the rauriki, a very fine soft variety; the ordinary puha; and the puha-taratara, a coarse kind of recent appearance in that district. Further South the people appeared to have just the one name, puha (often pronounced buha in the extreme south). They mentioned its down (puawai) as containing the purapura (seeds) and as blowing about with every breeze that blew. On a windy day the elders would exclaim 'Na rere atu ra ka puawai' (the thistle down is flying).

The collector was told of two ways of preparing this thistle for food. The first ran: 'The old way of treating the puha was to put the stems in an ipu (wooden basin) and pound them to get the bitter white juice or waiu out of them. The stalks were then eaten raw like what the Pakeha eats cress.' This information was collected from an old man who was born on Ruapuke Island in Foveaux Strait but further North the following description of the thistle's preparation was given: 'The puha was gathered and put with tuna (eel) or poaka (wild pig) in a whena or tapora [See Cooking Section] in an umu. The thistle and the flesh blended well and gave one another additional relish. The juice of the thistle (te au o te puha) was sour or bitter, and was squeezed out and thrown away but sometimes when the people were lazy they left it in and ate the puha as usual although not with the same enjoyment as when the juice was absent. Nowadays the puha is boiled in European fashion just like cabbage.' It may be added here that the introduced Scots thistle is called Kotimana (Scotchman) by the Maoris but like all the thistles brought into the country it is useless for human food.

ANISE

The fragrant anise plant was called naupiro in Murihiku and was sometimes eaten. One ancient man said he had chewed it himself when shepherding on the hills over sixty years ago.

INTRODUCED PLANTS

The general name for potatoes in the North Island is said to be taewa and in the South Island mahetau. The latter word means 'a string of sinkers' and was applied because the Southern Maori on seeing the first potatoes they had grown pulled up out of the ground, likened the hanging cluster of tubers to a string of fishing-line sinkers.

The Maori in Murihiku had for long generations been out of touch with kumera cultivation, but it is noticeable that when potatoes were introduced he began to grow them in puke or heaps according to the traditional method of growing the ancient kumera. The Maori soon became expert at cultivating the potato and it quickly became a staple article of food, but his ideas of preparing it for food along certain lines were distinctly different to European ideas. For instance the method called kopi was thus explained to the collector: 'The potatoes were left in a spring or in running water for from four to six weeks according to the quality of the water. The skins were left on but became very loose and the potatoes became very white. Formerly we used to tao (cook) these steeped potatoes in the umu but now we just whena [See Cooking Section] them close to the fire and the result tastes lovely. We use fat and sugar with the kopi now, but in the old days it was eaten just naturally. If the kopi is done correctly there is no offensive smell about it.'

In passing it may be said that the same idea of steeping was also used with maize, but as maize did not flourish in Murihiku it is outside present consideration.

To keep potatoes until required as food, one old man said the Maoris used to sometimes pack them away in kits stored in earth tunnels. A heap of potatoes in a pit was called taiki.

When the first white settlers came to Otago a plant called 'Maori Cabbage' was very prevalent along the edges of water-courses. Cabbage is called paparaki nowadays but the wild 'Maori Cabbage' was called pora while a sort of wild swede turnip was called kawakawa and my oldest informant considered that both these plants were brought in by Captain Cook. In this connection it is worthy of note that when the Murihiku Maoris first saw a European ship they called it a pora.

Two further varieties or variations of the pora were called pohata and paritea. White settlers say that the so-called 'Maori cabbage' was really a turnip that had run wild and become degenerate, merely consisting of long leaves and a thin wiry root. It was the leaves that the Maori ate and my informants said that the pora, pohata, paritea and kawakawa were all eaten in the same manner as the puha or sowthistle.

PUNUI

is the name of a big leaf of a vivid green colour that is eaten on the Titi Islands and some of the muttonbirders bring bundles of it back to the mainland to serve as a sort of cabbage. It is said that in the olden days food was wrapped in these big leaves and placed in the umu (ovens), the leaves being eaten as a kinaki (relish) to the food. The leaves are used extensively by the muttonbirders, being as handy as paper for wrapping and for spreading things on. On one island the people call it, or a variety of it, punawe (pronounced boon-a-way), but the general name is punui (pronounced bunui).

PAPAII

is the species of speargrass that constituted part of the vegetable foods of the Maori. The ordinary speargrass (taramea) was too bitter to eat but the papaii was good. An old lady said the Maoris cooked and ate the roots of the papaii, but a well-informed old man described the process more fully: 'It has a hollow stem and could be eaten from where the root begins up to about a foot above ground. Waruwaru (shave or scrape) the spears off the stem, skin it and eat the rest. To me it tasted good – better than English turnips. Some people used to put it with tuna (eel) in the umu with a tapora over it and it ate well.' Another man said, 'The papaii comes up in Spring and you break the stalk and eat it. This does not kill the plant, and it still keeps on growing.'

PURAUM

This vegetable food did not seem to be as well-known as most of the others mentioned. One old lady said the purau plant was put in the umu to prevent the kauru [see later] being burnt by the heated stones. At length the collector secured a few particulars from a very old man. The purau is a plant about two feet high, with yellow leaves and no flowers. It grows in bunches and was formerly plentiful at Pomahaka and elsewhere. The root is like wee onions and was the part eaten. Personally he did not like the flavour but old Takatahuruhuru and other real old-time Maoris relished it.

PITAU

was another vegetable food of the Maori that seemed little-known in the South, or it is probably known by another name there. One exceptionally well-informed old man told the collector he had heard the name pitau but he had never tasted it and could not describe it. He was of the opinion that it grew on the West Coast like the kiakia [kiekie H.B.] did. The mystery was solved by a South Canterbury native who said the pitau was the top portion of the koareare (part of the raupo stem) and was pulled out of the water and eaten when young and tender in the Spring. Later it gets thick and has to be skinned.

KATOTE

Many people are aware that the ferntree was included in the list of Maori vegetable foods, but few know the particular kind that furnished part of the native dietary. The familiar poka (known as ponga further north and called the bungee by white bushmen) was no good from a food standpoint. An old lady said to the collector: 'It was the katote kind of ferntree that was a kai (food) – you cut it and ate it like an apple. It was also sometimes put in the umu with a papaki [see Cooking Section] over it.'

KAUHEKE

This form of vegetable food seems to have been better known in Southland than elsewhere and two of the old men referred to it. The kauheke, said one, was a sort of ribbonwood and you could tihori (strip) its kiri (bark) off and chew the inside skin as a food. The kauheke, said the other informant, is a small tree like an apple tree and its bark could be used the same as houi (ribbonwood) to make kopare (head bindings) and piupiu [See Clothing Section]. The Maori also got a kind of flour out of the kauheke and it was eaten raw. The flour was called kauheke too, and the Maori was fond of chewing it.

KIEKIE

The kiekie (which some of my informants called kiakia and others giegie) does not grow on the east or south coasts of the South Island but as it grows as far south as Dusky Sound on the West Coast it comes within the territorial bounds of Murihiku. The few of my informants who had been round in the Fiords appeared to be the only ones who had tasted this fruit, and one narrated: 'The sprout (wharawhara) of the kiekie is sweet and I have sucked the juice. The tongue which projects at the top is called the tawhara-kiekie and lower down there came a growth like a pineapple which was called taureure and was eaten as a fruit. I liked it and thought it tasted well.'

NATURAL HONEY

was found in the puawairata (rata blossom) and besides the kaka birds being fond of this juice or wairata, the people would sip it also. A sweet juice was also found in the korari or flaxstick and waikorari was a dainty morsel to the Maori. An old man remarked to the collector: 'The flaxstick is bitter to the taste; the bark of the rata is the same, yet the juice in both is sweet'. Taka-korari is the operation of shaking the honey out of the flax-stick over the kauru (or edible part of the cabbage tree) to give it a sweet flavour. Since the advent of the white man there has been such an astonishing influx of insect pests that it is said you cannot now use this honey.

FOODS (VEGETABLE FOODS)

Pukapuka – Bread from the Raupo

In the Christchurch Museum in the Maori Section there is an exhibit marked 'Bread from the pollen of the raupo'. The collector asked an old Otago woman about this and she said they used to eat the koareare or raupo root but they made no bread. That, she considered, was a Pakeha idea. My best informant, however, knew the bread in question. On the top of the raupo plant grow brownish or yellowish seeds – 'about the color of mustard', he added as an afterthought – and many years ago he used to see the women at Lake Waihola shake 'te upoko o te koareare' (raupo heads) into a tipaki (flax matting). This shaking brought out a flour and water made this flour into a paste like dough. This was put in flax baskets into the umu where it was left three or four hours until cooked. Then it was taken out, laid by, and eaten when cold, as all Maori food usually was. This informant laid stress on the ancient Maoris eating their food cold and to this he attributed their good teeth, but the statement requires modification for some Maori food was eaten hot from the umu. It was a kind of bread and tasted all right – very sweet and not as dry as one might expect. It was known as pukapuka [Tregear gives 'pua' and 'pungapunga' as bread made from the pollen of the raupo or bulrush. H.B.]. Koareare was just pulled up and chewed – the raupo was not destroyed by this pulling as it grew again from the root.

Aruhe – Fernroot

In an old Maori Manuscript book the collector copied there was a list of 'mahi-ka-kai' or places where the Maoris of old could get certain foods. Some places were described as 'koutu aruhe', others as 'para kauru' and still others as 'ka rauiri', and so on. Those were the three designations that concern this phase of this investigation so the collector was curious to have them defined by the surviving old people. The collector has just two Maori opinions to offer about the first of these terms. 'Koutu aruhe simply means to kari (dig) fernroot'. 'Koutu aruhe. The word "koutu" means "scooping". It means to dig fernroot up.' An old man who spent many years at Otago Heads said that when he was a boy there the people of the Kaik ate plenty of fernroot – it was both good and abundant.

A woman said that when she was a girl at Korotuaheka (Waitaki Mouth) aruhe was eaten but was never cooked on the range or fire inside the house but on a special fire outside. If this was not done (i.e. cooking fernroot out in the open air) it was said that the fishermen would catch no fish. Te Aruhe-a-Pora was the Maori name of Pigroot, Central Otago. History records that the early inhabitants of Ruapuke Island once ran short of aruhe and sent a canoe to the mainland to procure some – about two hundred and fifty years ago.

None of the Southland Maoris had heard the word 'koutu'.

Edible fernroot is called aruhe, said one man, and the fern itself is called rauaruhe down here but it is known as rarauhe further North. The best kind of fernroot to eat is the papaka, a kind that was once common at Waihao (Morven) in South Canterbury. Another kind, the aruhe-rakau has a black streak in it, but he had forgotten the other fernroot names.

Another old Maori said he had eaten fernroot at Waipouri (Hillgrove) North Otago, when he was younger. It was dug out of the ground with a typical old kaheru (shaped stick).

A well informed man said: 'I have eaten fernroot. It was dug, then dried in the sun and then stored in the whata (storehouse). To get it ready for eating it was tied in a bundle, soaked in water, and then roasted by rolling it over on the cinders – not in an umu. It was beaten after this. If a husband wanted some for a meal he would say to his wife 'Haere patua mai e aruhe ma tatau' (go and beat some fernroot for us). It used to be beaten into a lump, and waikorari (flax honey) was dripped on it to make it sweet. Much of it was constipating, but in that case flax root was used as a purgative. Long-shaped stones were used in the old days to beat it but any suitable stone from a river-bed would do for a patu-aruhe (fernroot beater). Wooden clubs were not often used for this work.'

Another old man corrected the statement that flax honey was dripped into the aruhe, which he said did not need it as it was sweet. It was the kauru (or cabbagetree) which needed the honey.

Kauru – Cabbage tree

In regard to the term 'para kauru' the collector was told that it meant that each party had a different pala (para) or section.

The old man mentioned before as having been brought up at Otago Heads said that perhaps why they ate so much fernroot in that locality was that they did not get so much kauru, as ti (cabbage-trees) were scarce on the Peninsula.

In regard to the word Rauiri the collector was told the word denoted a reserve. There were two kinds of reserves – Rauiri-tuna and Rauiri-whenua. The former was a reserve for eeling or fishing; the latter was a reserve for birds or for the products of the land (such presumably as aruhe and kauru). One old man said 'A rauiri was a reserve for fishing, for birds and for pora (the so-called Maori cabbage)'.

An old woman mentioned the ti (cabbage palm) and how the kauru part of it was eaten. This kauru was a young shoot at the side of the tree and she had never seen anyone eat the root as kauru. If the tree was cut down but the root left in the ground, the tree would grow again. The collector may have misunderstood this informant, but her information requires some modification about the kauru being a young shoot from the tree.

From subsequent inquiries it appears that there were at least three ways of getting kauru. (1) When travelling cut down young trees, strip the bark off and eat the remainder. (2) When travelling cut down old trees and eat the roots and a part away up at the top of the tree. (3) Select a suitable place and make an 'orchard' of the ti, by cutting down all the young trees to a suitable height, leave them two years and then harvest the result. The growth from these 'pruned' trees was so suitable for food you merely scraped it and ate the lot.

It seems probable that the third method was more in operation on the East than on the South Coast for up the former the operation of cutting the ti was called parahia and a place where the trees had been cut was a para-kauru, while among genuine South Coasters the word para-kauru is held to denote the part you ate. One man explained it thus: 'Para means dust and the shreds were thrown away. You chew aruhe (fernroot) and eat it, but you chew kauru and reject the fibre, the maka-kauru. The maka is the chewed lump which is not swallowed, but the para-kauru is the softer portion which is swallowed.'

EDIBLE SEAWEEDS

The kelp (rimu) was put to various uses in the South. Boiled with tutu wine it formed the edible rehia. In its green state it was used to steam shellfish in – a process called murumuru te poha (singeing the kelp), and in its dried state it furnished fine receptacles for the preservation of food. The membranous interior of kelp is called puka and the kind of kelp with this is known as rimupuka while that without it is rimurapa. To push the hand into kelp opening it is called koko-poha.

A kelp bag in its green state was poha-mata but after being dried it was a poha-maroke. One of the old men said he had heard that of old the people ate part of the root of the kelp when it was properly dry. Another confirmed this saying that it was the piece between the root end (which was cut off) and the rimu itself which was eaten. It was simply roasted on the open fire and was called rimu. Kareko was the kind of kelp used for carragen but the kelp for making rehia was thicker than kareko. Still another said 'Kareko is a fine seaweed which is pulled off the rocks, soaked in fresh water and cooked. It is mixed with tutu to make rehia. The weed the pakeha calls carragen was called rimurimu by the Maori.'

'What the white people calls carragen we call kaleko (kareko) which is perhaps a modern word I cannot say as to this. The young Maoris boil it in milk nowadays. I have heard that the old people ate it but I do not know the history of it,' said another. My principal informant said: 'The Maori took what you call carrageen, put it in fresh water for two or three days to take the salt out and then chewed it. It was called rimurimu while the ordinary kelp was rimu. The tangle of weeds cast up by the sea is koauau and was used for nothing that I know of. Another name for weeds cast up by the sea is parariki and the Maori would pick out the white pieces to chew or to steam in the umu. The pink-colored seaweed was called rimurimu the same as carrageen. A thin kind of kelp as wide as your hand was known as kareko and it was cooked in the umu and eaten. After the pakeha came it was sometimes laughingly called kapiti (cabbage) but its old name was kareko.' From this it appears that to say carrageen is kareko is simply a misapplication of a genuine old name. The collector may add that he had some carrageen in his pocket and he gave some to the old man who chewed it without more ado. He added that kelp was sometimes used as 'he mau wai' (a water-carrier). Holes were left in the kelp at the top to carry it by and it carried water all right. He considered the spongy interior of kelp was called rapa.

Add to Seaweeds

Asking after edible seaweeds the Maoris at Temuka said that the heaps of weeds (apparently flotsam and jetsam of the tides) which wash ashore and which include greenish and reddish colored stuffs are called kareko. They are gathered and dried until so dry that the kareko will crack in the fingers. It is not boiled but is put in a frying-pan with hinu (grease), pepper and salt and is fried. This is a modern dish. My oldest informant said she had never heard of the people of old eating it in South Canterbury but had heard it said that it was eaten in the North Island. At Puketiraki the collector was told that kareko was much more eaten in the North than in the South. If any North Island people come down to Otago on a visit and go to the seashore they get quite excited over the amount of kareko going to waste, and busy themselves collecting it. They then fry it and eat it with great gusto – rather to the wonderment of the prosaic southerner. Koauau is the kelp with 'crackers' hanging in strings but it is not eaten.

Rimupuka is the kind of kelp that is eaten with the tutu wine in the rehia (described elsewhere). Takakau rimu is the butt end of the rimu after the portion for the rehia jelly has been taken off. It is cooked in the ashes for some hours and is then put in water for some days. Next the exterior blackened by the ashes is scraped off and the interior lies revealed; it is nice and soft, and according to my informants 'tastes lovely'.

When near the beach fresh water used to be carried in rimu (kelp) say my Temuka friends. A piece of kelp was slit, the water poured in, the top tied, the kelp placed in a flax bag or basket and carried on the back. Although this was 'green' rimu it could be repaired the same as the dried rimu in the poha bags – by putting 'tiwha' patches over the hole. The kelp used was just the ordinary rimupuka of which the poha-titi ('muttonbird bladders') are manufactured.

Fanny and Mohi Te Wahia at Puketeraki, 1907. W.A. Taylor photograph, Box-196-005, Hocken Collections Uare Taoka o Hākena, University of Otago.

CHEWING-GUM

The old Maori who was my principal informant, in reply to a question said he had never heard of a weapon called kauri but he had heard of a deep-sea fish of that name and he proceeded to relate the following extraordinary fact. This fish, the kauri, had 'no fins nor legs but a round body and a round mouth, and it was sometimes washed ashore at high tides. The people of old would pick it up alive and would carry it into the bush where they would feed it on the leaves of the makamaka shrub until it died. The fish was then cut up into pieces which were used as kao (chewing gum).' He had never seen the fish, but once he had tasted the gum and it was 'all right'. You could chew away at it until you were tired and then put it by until another time.

At Puketiraki the collector was told that there were two 'chewing-gums'. The first was the puha or sowthistle. The top was pulled off and the juice formed into a white wax, also called puha. The second kind was the kauri. This was a shellfish with a small shell on it. [Note difference from the account above. H.B.] It was fed on the makamaka and when it died it formed a black chewing-gum. My informant had chewed it 'often enough', but it had not much flavour.

A European tells me that he saw the Maoris at Riverton in 1865 chew 'sowthistle gum', but he did not try it himself to see what attraction it possessed.

[The kauri is evidently synonymous with the Northern mimiha, also called, I think, the kauritawhiti. H.B.]

Add to Chewing-Gum

At the Bluff the collector was told there were several varieties of sowthistle but all were known by the one name – puha (pronounced 'buha'). If the puha stem is broken the gum or milk of the plant collects at the break and hardens into a white ball which is chewed.

The kauri, the old man continued, was a puzzle as no one seemed to know what it was (or is). It is as black as tar, and is picked up on the sea beach and could be chewed right away. He had sometimes picked up pieces when proceeding along the sands and had straightway put it in his mouth and chewed away. It had no taste at all as far as he recollected. The story about carrying it into the bush and feeding it on makomako leaves was a very old yarn, and might have been due to a strange fancy on the part of the olden Maoris but there was no doubt it was put on the branches of the makomako tree although what effect this had on it he did not know from personal experience but he had heard it was done as a habitual custom by the old people.

MUSHROOMS

An old woman said she considered the mushroom (whareatua) was in New Zealand before the pakeha came but it was not regarded with much favor. Its name meant 'devil's house' and the old people would say to anyone who gathered it 'Throw it away – a devil lives in it'. The poketara is the puffball and came in thunderstorms. It would grow as big as your head and was roasted and eaten. The peelings were taken off and the inside eaten – she had eaten them and they were sweet. The weho is a kind of mushroom that grows in a heap. It often grows in sandy places and has a stem but no top. It used to be cooked at the fire and eaten.

An old man said the only place he had seen the weho was at Temuka. It grows on a knob and when the skin is pulled off it is slimy inside yet it was cooked and eaten. As for the 'devil's house' – the whareatua – some Maoris would not eat it, himself included.

Another old man considered the whareatua, weho and poketara were all native to the country.

A settler who came to Otago in January 1858 says he considers the darker coarser mushroom was a native as he found it in the backblocks in remote situations and he ate them as a welcome addition to his larder; but he had been in the country some years before he saw the whiter, smoother kind. Before puffballs became powdery they were good to eat and he had cooked and eaten them. They were white and in favorable conditions grew as big as a small football.

An intelligent old Maori said he had never eaten the fungi which grows on the trees in the bush and he did not think the olden Maori ate them either. He was not familiar with the names hakekakeka and harore [said to be used further North]. The only name he knew for mushrooms was whareatua.

A South Canterbury Maori said he had a faint recollection of having heard the names harore and hakekakeka and he thought that one or other, if not both, was eaten at one time. The only kind he ate personally was the whareatua which grows on the plains. As far as he knew mushrooms grew in New Zealand before the Pakeha came.

The Maoris interviewed added a warning note against eating whareatua which were white inside, as they were injurious.

SECTION XVI

FISH, EELS, SHARKS, WHALES, SHELLFISH

FISHING

The name for fishing was hiika or hi-ika.

The collector asked diligently at every coastal settlement of the Maori round Murihiku if the people had ever been in the habit of using paawaa shell on their fish-hooks. The reply was unanimously in the negative, the explanation being that the fish, the kahawai, which was caught on the line with pawa-inlaid hooks in the North Island was only caught in nets in the South Island, and then not in great numbers.

None of the old men had heard of using bone gorges to catch fish.

An intelligent old man residing near Foveaux Straits said: 'I never heard of fish-gorges but you could take a piece of wood, called pekapeka, with five or six hooks attached to it and a mahe (sinker) tied on a line below the hooks. You could catch any kind of fish with it – any of the smaller kinds, not groper. The olden Maoris used it often but I forget its name.'

In South Canterbury the collector was told that the old people were wont to take a stick and tie three or four hooks to it. A sinker was then fastened to the aho (fishing line) and this pulled the stick and its baited hooks down. Blue and red cod, trumpeter, butterfish and other similar fish could be caught with this simple and effective device. This kind of multiplex fishing was called panapana in contradistinction to ordinary fishing which was called hi-ika.

The rock called John Bull's Head, on the Taieri river near its mouth, was called by the Maori Whaka-renga-mahe or Whaka-renga-pohatu, a name which signifies 'Casting away the sinkers'. Mahe, also called maahi, is a sinker. When the canoes came in from the sea-fishing the fishers dropped their sinkers at this rock. There was seldom a groove round these sinkers – they were in nets whose name the old man forgot. There was deep water there but a line led up from the sinkers to the surface and it was tied to a floating stick. Probably spare sinkers were kept at this convenient spot also.

The sinkers in the Otago Museum (exhibit D10.132) are called mahi (or mahe).

To express the idea of a shoal of fish the Murihiku Maori said 'Kai te poke te ika'.

If there are plenty of koladi (korari) it is said to denote a good year for any fish or for fishing, in sea, lake, river or surf (beach). The pukakaho (toetoe stalk) is said to foretell similarly.

MURIHIKU NAMES OF FISH

The Collector accompanied an old Maori through the Otago Museum and secured as many of the names as he could remember and other information.

Red Cod (*Physiculus bacchus*) = hoka
— [[no common name given]] *(Trachichthys elongatus)* = puramorehu
— (*Mendosoma lineatum*) = koihi
— (*Paratrachichthys trailii*) = patohe
Kelp fish *(Odax vittatus)* = marari
Trevally (*Caranx platessa*) = kopapa (Auckland Island)
— (*Galaxias brevipinnis*) = hiwihiwi (can be caught in Murihiku)
Frost fish (*Lepidopus caudatus*) = paara
Bullhead (*Gobiomorphus gobioides*) = kokopu
Pigfish (*Congiopodius leucopuecilus*) = puramorua
— (*Leptoscopus macropygius*) = toro
— (*Cheimatrichthys forsterii*) = piripiripohatu (It clings to rocks)
Elephant fish (*Callorynchus antarcticus*) = makorepe
Spiny Dogfish (*Squalus fernandicus*) or its mate
— (*Galeus australis*) = makohuarau
Lamprey (*Geotria stenostama*) = tuere (Blind eel found in rivers as well as sea)
Conger eel (*Leptocephalus*) = koiro
New Zealand Ling (*Genypterus blacodes*) = rari (also the macruroros novae zealandiae)
Kingfish (*Auxis* Species) = maka-taharaki
Skipper (*Scombresox forsterii*) = moeanu ('sand fish' = fishermen's name)
— (*Geniagnus maculates*) = moamoa

Maori Chief (—) = patutuki
Warehou (*Seriolella brama*) = tarakihi.

In regard to the other fish my informant said the Maoris classed the turbot as a patiki (flounder). The *Galaxias alepiclotus* called 'kokopu' in Museum records he said was a 'kokopara' but the specimens labelled *Galaxias fasciatus* are kokopu. The minnow (*Galaxias attenuates*) is the Maori inaka while the whitebait (young of the *Galaxias attenuates*) is the famous mata. The *Galaxias lynx* from Lake Wakatipu he considered to be a young kokopara (cockabully) while the mudfish (*Neochannea apoda*) he thought was a young upokororo and the next fish (the grayling) he reckoned was a big upokororo.

Among fish which did not come under our notice at the Museum the following names were added: Trumpeter = koikohi, Schnapper = tamuri, Blue Cod = Rawaru, Soldier Fish = Puaihakarua (also called the Red Jacket Fish), — Moki or Mogi (no English name), Mullet = Aua. At Moeraki the Maoris differed slightly from the foregoing lists and for the sake of comparison the few differences will be noted here. The moeanu was called Sandfish and not Skipper; the patutuki was the rock cod; the tarakihi was the bream; the maka-tahalaki (maka taharaki) was the Jew fish, although sometimes this was known as the Kingfish; and they added that the butterfish was called matohe and the conger eel was koiro. The tuere is a blind eel, similar to the tuna eel in a way but soft and slimy. Like the kanakana lampreys they have no bones. They are not usually found in rivers but in the sea and the tide washes them ashore. Some Maoris eat them freely but my informant did not like them.

An old man, a native of Otago Heads, said: 'The moenu is a fish which lives in the sand, while the patutuki is what the Pakeha calls Maori Chief. It lives among the rocks and has tattoo marks round its face.'

THE BARRACOUTA

The barracouta (makaa) has a certain notoriety in the South as it was the only fish to be caught with a rod in pre-pakeha days. The rod was called matere and was often made of the wood of the kaii (this tree is something like a totara but has a finer leaf). The jigger (pa) was made out of towai a tree which grows in Otago and its timber was even carried up into Canterbury for this purpose. If it was not available light totara was used. The hook (matau) was of bone and was tied (taka) on with whitau. The string from the rod to the pa was called aho. The reason a rod was used was that it threw the line further out than by hand and also served to give the desired rotatory motion to the pa. The makaa thinking it a smaller fish snaps at it and is hooked. Sometimes it is caught by the gills (tapiapiha).

Io, who is mentioned in mythology as one of the first of created human beings, is the god of the barracouta, but why the collector does not yet definitely understand. In those days the mako (shark), hapuku (groper) and other big fish sent out the makaa (barracouta) to scout, but it took its own way and finding a shoal of marakuha (sardines) fell to eating them. Others were sent out and brought the makaa back in disgrace and it was punished by its bones being made like the tao or huata (spear) which was thrust through it. Those iwi (bones) are now just the shape of a huata and the flesh is called io when hung up to dry (paku). 'Io is said to be the parent of the barracouta and is the head leader of that fish to this day.' The makaa is a strong swimmer and may run out on the current perhaps forty miles in June when spawning. 'They are then thin and full of worms (kahio). The best time to catch them is March when they are in good condition and close in shore. When caught, cut off the heads and tails and leave the bodies in the umus for five or six hours and then let the flesh get cold and eat (if required at once). When soaked in fresh water and dried the flesh is called moi. When cooked and taken out in sections and laced in flax and dried it is called paku,' said one old man.

Here are three recipes as given to me in the simple phraseology of my informants: Moi or Moe – Take the barracouta of poor quality, behead them and hang till almost rotten. Then put them in running water, kept down with stones or heavy wood for four days. Then clean and hang them in the whata (storehouse). When wanted put on the fire and cook them, or, as is done nowadays, roast them.

Pawhera or pawhera-makaa – When you catch barracouta hang them up by the tails two by two on a drying stage. They are too slippery to cut at first. They are not ripped up but when dry you cut out the kumu (navel) and then when the head is cut off you can tuaki or pull the innards out at the same time. Now clean the fish in water and again hang on the whata or stage. Next day you take the fish and pawhera (split) them on a papaki (mat) made of patiti (tussock) and then you hang them with the split side to the sun. Three or four days later you string them and hang them out during the day with the flesh to the sun and at night you turn them with the skin out and you repeat this for about a fortnight. You cover them with papaki mats if it rains during the day or if there is dew at night, but you can use sacks for covering nowadays. Then you put the dried fish away in the storehouses and they can be kept a year or they may be eaten at once if you wish.

Paku – Dry the barracouta on a gallows and cut the belly pieces. In cutting this piece two cuts are made and the piece pulled off is called parooaroo and the rest of the fish is called io. Cut round the navel and pull the skin off leaving the ribs showing. Place the io on its back and upon it place another io belly to belly. Put three or four pairs in a bundle and tie up in kakaha grass. Put these bundles in the umu or earth oven in this manner – a layer of hot stones, then fish, then, stones, then more fish and cover with tussock and kelp and heap over with earth. It must be made so that no steam will escape and it is left all night. Next morning the umu is opened and the fish are put on a tipaki mat and placed in the storehouse. Next day all the skin portions or shiny parts are carefully scraped off and put to one side. This scraping is called makiri. The parooaroo has also been cooked and this together with all the scrapings is now placed in a poha or kelp bag to be preserved until winter when it forms a tasty dish. The flesh that has been taken out of the umu is called paku and it is now put in the storehouse until required.

THE GROPER

The groper, known to the Maori as hapuku or hapuka, is a well-known table fish and in pre-Pakeha days was eagerly sought by the Maori for the twin reasons of size and flavour. To catch the weighty groper a big wooden hook known as a maka-hapuka was employed. This had a bone point called a matau, and nowadays English hooks are known to the Murihiku Maori by this name. To make groper hooks, ironwood or kowhai roots were usually selected, cut out, taken home and shaped. These roots often grow above ground and sometimes are near the required shape naturally. A great deal of crude ingenuity was exercised in some cases in getting the roots into the shape of hooks and some fine examples of this workmanship can be seen in our Museums. A visit to the Otago Museum in this connection will well repay the visitor.

The barb on the matau point was called kaniwha and sometimes there were two or three barbs on the one hook. When a hapuka was caught it was hauled up and hit on the head with a patu or club to kill it (patua kia mate) before it was dragged into the waka (canoe). One of these clubs is now on exhibition in the Otago Museum.

Hapuku-upoko or Upoko-hapuku (groper's head) was a great delicacy among the olden Maoris, and the aged people would wait for the boats to come in to secure the heads. Even to this day they will say to returned fishermen, 'Give us a fat kanohi' (or eye piece) as they dearly love the fat around the eye.

To preserve the flesh of the groper for keeping a while, its head was cut off, its puku or stomach was taken out and it was hung up by the tail to dry. When taken down it was split in one slice of the knife as two cuts might haggle the flesh about. The skin part was called pakeka and the flesh when dried was known as maraki. At Stewart Island an old man had some maraki suspended in an old-fashioned wide chimney and as he was chewing it himself his native politeness led him to grope up the chimney and to present the collector with a piece. Two of the old Maoris said that they had advised European fishermen that winter is the best time to catch groper and also when the tide is running and that since then the pakehas have fished with good results.

NETS AND NETTING

The North Island Maori in catching the strong-running kahawai used pawa shell on the fishhook to attract the fish. The kahawai was not so big at the southern end

He patu (club) for killing hāpuku mentioned in the text on page 133. Balclutha, South Otago. Tūhura Otago Museum Collection, D20.131. With kind permission of Te Pae Ārahi o Tūhura.

of the South Island nor so numerous as in the North Island. What kahawai were caught down here were caught with the kaka – a net made of green flax and split (toetoe) fine and then plaited (whatu te kaka = plait the net) close like a basket. It was about five feet high and one or two chains long and had a pole at each end. The kahawai will run up the Opihi (when it is running full) and Rakitata rivers in Canterbury but from there to the Mata-au (Molyneux) the only river with enough current to attract it is the Waitaki. The Mataau is too deep to net but this disability does not apply to the Waitaki where one man could hold the poupou-uta (land pole) on shore and the other, holding the poupou-waho (sea pole) wade out and encompassing many fish return to land with bigger or lesser bags according to the run of the fish. A good bag would include many kinds of fish besides the kahawai. The kaka, as a rule, was for freshwater fish, and was of smaller size and with a finer mesh than the net for saltwater fish. One of my informants had caught paraki (a small kind offish) in Lake Forsyth (Wairewa) with a kaka weighted with pohatu (stones) at the bottom. One held the shore end and the other went out and round and swept in good catches. Another had seen kaka used on the mud flats in the estuary at Riverton years ago when they secured baskets and baskets of inaka, paraki, patiki and kokopu. The latter is small but the kokopara is a big fish living among the eels – he never saw either kokopu or kokopara at sea. This informant went on to say he had seen the nets (kupeka) for sea fish several chains long and had helped to use one of them on Riverton beach, the catch being mostly flounders.

In R. McNab's [[1907]] *Murihiku* (First edition p. 216) we read of the Foveaux Strait Maoris in 1823 having fishing nets from one to two miles long and between ten to twelve feet wide and made of green flax. The biggest net seen by any of my informants was seven or eight chains long and was made at Korotuaheka (Waitaki Mouth) the year Te Maiharoa died (about 1886). It is said to have been the last (Maori) net pulled there. Henare te Maire records that Arama Karaka and he took this net out on mokis (koradi rafts sat astride) on the current and worked round to the shore again. There was a number of men there to pull the net in and it needed them for the haul was large including a number of groper and three or four sharks. The kupeka had a rope at the top and bottom, the former being called tatu and the latter karihi. There were weights on the bottom line which were called puka, perhaps, but my informant remembered no floats on the nets. It was plaited in the same manner as the puraki net on the head of an eelpot but it had a bigger mesh.

An old seafaring man said that what he called 'seines' (kupeka) had floats made of mako wood. These floats had a groove (pakaru) in the side to lash a rope to. To make a seine two men would start from the centre 'manufacturing' each way. He had never heard of it being made in sections. Every ten feet or so the seine would have upright sticks (pou-kupeka) but it was so long since he saw one he forgot the names of the parts.

This last fact was also what troubled another old seadog whose memory was not equal to recalling the various names. The biggest kupeka he had seen was one for flounders at Taumutu over fifty years ago.

Another of the old men brought up a mythological connection between two names of parts of the kupeka and the heroes of old by saying that Karihi, the brother of Tawhaki, was named after the bottom line of a net and Puka, another brother, after the weights (stones) tied on in front of the bottom line. He was not sure if they were named after the net or the net parts after them but he thought the former was the way of it. The top line was called tatu and floats (poito) of koradi were tied here and there lengthwise on it. The mesh was called mata (mutta). About 1887 he saw a big kupeka at Waitaki Mouth. It was ten or twelve feet wide but how long he could not say for he never saw it fully extended. The bottom line of the kupeka, said an old lady, was karihi but the stones along it were called paririhi – each weight was called parihi (plural paririhi). The action of netting was called kohao and this was also the name of a kind of net. 'The kohao,' said an old man, 'was a scoop net for any fish. It had a ring round its mouth and a pole attached but I never saw it used.' Another said the kohao was built like a crawfish net (taruki). It had a supplejack round its mouth and was mainly used for eels. It was on a long stick and was dragged along creeks. Another man would poke the banks and as the eels came out the kohao was guided over them and they were deposited on terra firma.

Add to Nets

The collector read to seven Maoris at Temuka Shortland's names of parts of nets (as collected from Gisborne Maoris in 1842) to spur their memories. They are as follows: Kupenga – a seine (Shortland Manuscript page 130) 1 Ngaki the centre piece. 2 Matakeke pieces next centre. 3 Tuara-matakeke pieces next in order. 4 Heketanga pieces at extremities. 5 Pourakau, the wood spreaders. 6 Karihi, line and sinkers at bottom of net. 7 Kaharunga the top line. 8 Pouto the floats. (These are the Maori names, Poverty Bay, in 1842.)

The Temuka Maoris said that making a kupeka was called honohono, or rather this is the operation of knotting, the mesh being called mata (mutta). If a net is not big enough and a fresh row is started to make it larger this row is called tihoi. A kupeka could be made by several men working simultaneously. The top line was called tahatu and the bottom one karihi while the weights along the bottom were karirihi if whole stones and paririhi if split stones. The wood 'spreader' at the shore end was pou-uta and at the sea-end pou-waho. The floats which were usually of korari wood were called puarewa. The only other name they said they had was that 'the belly of the net' was waekanui.

An old man in the South said he had seen a kupeka to catch kahawai at Waitaki about 1879. It was made by Wi Pokuku and others, some splitting (toea) flax and others knotting. It had a pole at each end and was four or five feet wide. It was perhaps fortyfive feet (? yards) long and was taken out on a 'mogi' (raft of korari). They had horses ready to attach to it but the sea brought it in as well as the people pulling. He thought the floats were called poitu and the weights, puka.

Another man had seen a kupeka about fifty yards long at Purakaunui (near Dunedin). It was for flounders, the short nets (kaka) being mostly for whitebait in the streams. A woman said, 'The kohao was to catch fish and the stick which formed its handle was te kakau o te kohao. The mesh was of flax and was much the same as the puraki one in an eelpot. The mouth of the net was kept circular by a rim (called kaututu) of supplejack, aka or the tororaro vine. The people used to make a hole (parua) in creek-beds and dip the kohao in and koko (scoop) the fish out with it.' The traditional description for a beach which was suitable for netting was He-paeka-kupeka (a landing place for the big sea nets.)

KOKOPU AND KOKOPARA

Kokopu – My informants had nothing to say of this fish which was one of the few found in inland waters before the Pakeha introduced trout.

Kokopara or Kokopura – These names in the rude speech of the old Maoris sounded like kokobala and kokobula and hence we get the familiar name 'Cockabully' known to all New Zealand boys. A lot of these fish, some of fair size, can still be found in the Oraka Creek at Colac Bay, while the Maori name of the creek in the Waimate Gorge is Waikokopura because of their prevalence in it. The flesh of the kokopara is sweet but it is unusually full of bones. The old Maoris say these bones can be successfully dealt with by cooking the fish, splitting it open and lifting out the ribs and frame in one mass. This fish was formerly common in the Taieri River in the lagoons near it, but mining silt and drainage operations seem to have made it vanish. The trout are no doubt aiding its disappearance from other streams.

Panako is the name of a sort of kokopu said my informant and another added that it is like a kokopu but is of a different colour. This fish can be seen mostly after Christmas time – about Autumn. At other times you only see occasional odd ones.

Pipiki is a fish about which there is some uncertainty. One informant said it was like a smelt or inaka, while the other said it was like a panako, only larger. The former is probably correct. These two fish (the pipiki and panako) at one time enjoyed a great reputation because they were the only ones to swim over the hiku (tail) of the pounemu (greenstone) lying in the bed of a river. As far as the collector can gather they were once regarded as sacred, apparently being the only fish to secure such an honour. A song was composed about this famous exploit of which only the last line seems to be remembered, viz. 'Nana ika ke hiku o te taniwha'. The greenstone is here alluded to as a taniwha, or water demon.

SMALL FISH

In gathering information about the fish of ocean and stream the collector had to rely on his aged informants for both the English and Maori names of the fish which were mentioned, so that while every care was taken to secure information as accurate as possible, the identity of several of the fish may not be firmly established.

Notwithstanding this fact and considering the divergencies that exist when Pakeha fishermen discuss the various kinds of fish it must be conceded that the Maori was keenly interested in every denizen of the deep and very observant of all details thereabout, and that his general accuracy as to what he has observed is unimpeachable.

Let us deal first with their observations about the smaller fish. Kouraraki is a tiny inhabitant of the sea and is known to the Pakeha as whalefeed. It is not eaten by man but is chased by the barracouta. It is of a red colour and is the shape of a koura (crayfish) but is extremely tiny. Marakuha is the name of what white fishermen call sprats or sardines.

Koroamo is the name of a similar small fish. These small fish were got by the ancient Maori when the muttonbirds pursued them and drove them ashore, and white people go out on the beaches and collect them nowadays. As far as my informants knew the olden Maoris did not dry or preserve these fish to keep anytime but used them at once. Neinei is a small fish whose English name was unknown to my informants. Waharoa is like a sardine – only longer. Inaka is the minnow, celebrated as the parent of the mata (whitebait) and of this famous pair my informants had much to say.

Add to Fish

The inaka, said the old man from Otago Heads, spawned in the sea. Its spawn must have something to hold to or rest on, or it would be carried by the tides and washed ashore and perish. Therefore it spawned on the rimu (kelp) something like the bot-fly laid its eggs in horse's manes. After it spawns the inaka (minnow) dies and its eggs (like those of the groper in the deep-sea kelp) hang on to the kelp until they become fish when they come up the rivers as whitebait. No matter how rough the sea is those eggs cannot be swept off the kelp to which they cling and on which they feed as they grow bigger into mata (whitebait). Te mata, te tamaiti o te inaka (the whitebait is the child of the minnow). He had never heard of the inaka spawning in the mouths of rivers and could not conceive of them doing so through not reaching the sea in time. The inaka knew its seasons just like, or better than, a woman, and made for the salt water in ample time. The various kinds of patiki (flounders or flat-fish) such as the raututu, the mohoao, and the horihori would spawn anywhere in either salt or fresh water. There was kelp on the bottom of the sea well out from the coast and the fish spawned there. It was not the right rimu (kelp) but was more a weed growing on the flat or rocky bottom of the ocean. The best fishing-grounds were directly over such spawning-grounds. The inaka (minnow) spawned in the proper kelp along the sea-coast, the bigger fish out in the weeds further out. He never saw spawn (hua) so he could not describe it.

Contrary to the opinion expressed above that the inaka did not sometimes spawn before reaching the sea, a well-informed old man told the collector that the Matainaka lagoon at Waikouaiti was named from the young of the minnow and that he had seen part of the edge of the lagoon white with the spawn of minnows. Also near the mouth of the Puerua stream which runs into the Molyneux River near the sea the rushes would be surrounded by water white like milk with the spawn of minnows which had spawned before reaching the sea. These minnows then went on out to sea and the spawn was carried down by tides. The spawn came back as mata (whitebait) and from this grew into minnows.

'To catch inaka,' said one old man, 'use a close net, the kaka, with a pou (pole) at each end. A man holds each pole and drags the net along enclosing the fish. We call this dragging rau. Then when plenty of inaka are enclosed, pull the kaka on shore and secure the catch.'

In addition to the awa or channels made to catch eels it is said that drains were dug to catch the whitebait. These ditches were made along a river bank but the mouth was facing downstream and not upstream as in a awa-tuna (eel channel). The tiny fish, said one informant, were caught in a net with a round mouth which was put in the drain, filling it from side to side, and through which the water flowed.

A woman said: 'We used to catch inaka with a basket called a koko-harakeke. It is closely woven – there is no mesh. The aho (string) of which it is made is wound round the flax whenu (string running lengthwise) strand after strand. The first string is called the aho-tahei until it is tied on two posts when it is called timata (beginning) and then aho after aho is added. If the mat is made long enough it is doubled and the sides sewn, leaving the top open as a waha (mouth). If it is knit in two parts separately, one of these is placed on the other, the sides are sewn and one end also and there you have your koko-harakeke. If the mouth requires stiffening use pirita (supplejack). The basket is tied to a pole and if taken to a potirimata (shoal of whitebait) and put in the water you can koko (scoop) the whitebait out easily.'

An intelligent elderly man said to the collector: 'About February you will see the minnows (inaka) rushing to the sea, and the Maori caught them with kaka (nets). At Washdyke (Waitarakao, in South Canterbury) I have seen the net laid flat at the lake end nearest the sea and tapered to a spout. There is a fair drop to sea-level and rocks were put under this spout to keep it fairly level. Closely-knit baskets (kete-putaputa) were placed under this spout and as each filled with inaka, another was substituted until thirty, forty or fifty baskets were filled as required and then you stopped. These kits were often sent as a kaihaukai (gift of food) to other kaika (villages). The people prepared gravel beds (wahi taurakitaka inaka) to dry the inaka in the sun (tauraki=drying) and the little fish were spread on these drying grounds, which were commonly known as ka-wa-inaka. Two or three good days will dry them, but you must hurihuri or keep turning them. The inaka are going to the sea to spawn. When they return their name is paraki; there is now no spawn in them and they look brighter. The paraki come up in shoals and can be netted with the kaka. This net may be from half-a-chain to a chain long and you may get as many paraki in it that it will be very heavy to handle. The paraki are dealt with the same way as the inaka. When properly dried they will keep for years and although not cooked they eat well. Some people soften them in water before a meal but I prefer them hard and dry. The waharoa is like a sardine and it is caught in the kaka with the paraki and the inaka. The mata is the whitebait and I consider it is the same all the time and never grows bigger. A koko-mata or net fastened to a pole was used to catch them and they were scooped out in large quantities. I hear that up North nowadays they cut small trenches from the rivers to catch whitebait as they think the old fashion is too slow, but I have only seen the koko-mata method myself. There is a lagoon near Waikouaiti called Mata-inaka but I do not know how it got its name. Mata means "raw" or "the face" and has other meanings as well as being the name of the whitebait. Nor do I know about the spawning habits of these little fish.'

This informant stands alone in considering the whitebait as a different fish to the minnow – all the others who gave information were positive the whitebait is simply the young of the minnow.

MISCELLANEOUS INFORMATION

Upokororo – one of my informants mentioned this as a fish found in rivers. In appearance, he said, it was like a herring or mullet. Ikamaru – this name was once given to me as the name of a small fish like the minnow, but the collector could get no corroboration of the assertion, although it was mentioned that a Waitaha chief called Te Ikamaru once lived in Otago. Kiore-tawhiti was the Murihiku name of the seahorse. The ancient Maori had no horse to compare this strange marine creature to, so he compared it to the kiore or rat. Kina – was the name of the sea-egg, but the collector gathered no further information about it than its old-time name. Patakaroa – 'This was our name for the starfish', said a reliable informant, but another man said it was kotore-moana. There is no doubt the former is the genuine old name.

EELS AND LAMPREYS

The eel, and to a lesser extent the lamprey, was an item of great importance on the bill-of-fare of the ancient Maori. In a country where freshwater fish were so few, the presence of great numbers of eels in up-country rivers, lagoons and lakes was a boon to the Maori travelling inland. The rich sweet flavour of eel flesh appealed with irresistible charm to the Maori palate and the collector, himself a lover of the epicurean delights of the tasty eel, found many evidences of the esteem in which this food, so despised by the prejudiced white man, was held by the modern as well as the ancient Maori.

Mythologically eels are said to have originated in the time of Maui, who killed Tuna and cut him in half, the tail flying off into the open sea and forming the koiro or conger eel, and the head flying off inland and forming the tuna or ordinary eel. Hence the latter can spawn in fresh water if necessary, said my informant, although the eels that do so, afterwards proceed to the sea for 'a taste of saltwater'.

The question of how the eels reproduced their kind proved a prolific source of controversy among the older Maoris, the question being amicably discussed by a number of them at various times before the collector, but without coming to any finality.

The old man from Otago Heads who gave the collector much information about fish and sea lore said he could not definitely say about the spawning of the eel as he never saw one with young. Englishmen said that eels came from horsehair but he had heard the old Maoris claim that eels came from mud. The tuna had no mother but was just formed in the mud, so the old people said, and he was inclined to believe them as no matter where one went every lagoon had eels in it. Another Maori at a place two hundred miles distant from the last informant also considered that eels did not spawn as little eels were found in lagoons and waterholes where the most diligent search failed to find big ones. The roe of fish is called hua or ka-hua but he had never found it in eels, so he did not know what to make of it.

A well informed old man said to the collector: 'When we caught eels about November and opened them to gut them I used to particularly notice the windbags (whose Maori name escapes me) because in them you would see small black things crawling about. We reckoned these were young eels so they must breed there in the windbag but I do not know much about the subject. We could not tell the male and female in eels although we could of some sea fish.'

My principal informant said he was a believer in the old belief that the little eels come out alive from the mother eel. Some sharks produce their young alive so why not eels? The makohuarau, a small kind of shark, produces its young in this way and he considered that eels do the same. The tiny eels when in the mother eel are in the layer of fat, the pua, and come out of this into the water looking like a lot of little pins, the fat being still inside the parent eel. These tiny eels are not to be found in small-sized eels but in the great big ones which apparently are the breeding eels. All eels, he added, will go to the sea at or about the breeding time as a taste of salt water seems vital to them.

Other Maoris took it for granted that the heke or migration of the eels to sea when they trapped such vast quantities of them in the old days was for the purpose of breeding but they could not settle the question of spawn versus birth so the matter must be left open as far as they are concerned. One or two thoughtful Maoris considered that a few eels spawned up country but they could give no details. Others considered that some huge eels lived in holes for years without going to the sea, but the general opinion seemed to be that annual trips were the rule, and that sooner or later every eel had to respond to the call of the sea.

In regard to the kanakana (lamprey) the collector has two opinions as to where it spawns. The first runs: 'The kanakana goes up the rivers and spawns in springs, the old ones die and the young, called wairaki-kanakana, are carried by freshes or floods to the sea where they grow and then they come up the rivers next year to spawn. The old Maoris seemed to be firmly of this opinion but they were not at all sure about eels.'

The second proceeds: 'The kanakana has a bag near its throat and this bag is called purehe. When it goes up the rivers it has no visible purehe but then this swells up and the kanakana goes back to the sea and "lays its eggs" in the sand. It spawns in salt water like the minnow and other fish and to say anything else is to tell lies.'

It will be noticed that the two statements are in direct opposition. Both were made by aged men who gave good information, but it must be added that the former would undoubtedly excel in all-round reliability. In addition the former contention was corroborated by two or three other Maoris who stated that the kanakana went up the rivers to spawn, one of them stating that the tiny little fry was known to the olden Maori as kanakana-wairaki. The collector regrets that he did not stress the question more when he was with his informants and secure further information as to what they knew of the range inland of the kanakana migration, the localities and extent of spawning operations and kindred topics.

The kanakana could only be counted as a food-producing asset during one season of the year but the eel in one or other if not all its varieties could be counted on all the year practically. The Maoris say the eels had a special fondness for frequenting certain spots in lakes, lagoons and streams and could always be found there. One of these spots is a hole at Omata up the river Purupurukene (now called Pourikino by the residents); another is a spring near Wyndham and another is in Lake Waihola. In this lake the eels loved to lie under a fine weed known, like kelp, as rimu, but perch and trout ousted them and now occupy this site. Many other spots throughout Murihiku were known of old as noted eel resorts.

The Maori had various ways of securing eels. One of these was by 'bobbing'. A bob was made of worms threaded with flax strings and this was dropped into the water. The eel sank its teeth into the bob and was hauled out before it could let go. A white settler who learned bobbing from the Maoris in 1858 told the collector, 'it was all right for small eels but it was not too good a method for catching big eels'. An aged Maori woman told the collector that sometimes a piece of mikimiki wood, which sinks in water, would be tied to a string hanging a few inches below the bob. This bob was usually called mounu in Murihiku, but she had heard it was called putinoke in the North Island. When the tuna was pulled out, the piece of mikimiki used as a sinker could be utilised to stun or kill the eel, or, of course, a separate stick for this purpose could be kept handy on the bank. Eels could also be secured by a procedure similar to what the English call 'tickling' or the Scots 'guddling'. It was known as rapu by the Maoris. About April the eelers would feel under the grassy banks ki tahaka (at the sides of rivers) and would lift out their victims. The collector was told of a Maori woman jumping into a pond where the water was up to her hips, groping round with her hands and throwing out quite a number of eels.

The Maoris would sometimes dive for eels which were resting on the bed of a river and would come to the surface with one. A Temuka lad had recently performed this feat. Old Kokoro of Temuka has left a wonderful reputation for getting eels in any weather, at any place, under any conditions and with any or every kind of method.

The spearing of eels with the eel-spear known as a matarau is probably centuries old and it is still carried on 'with modern improvements'. The collector was shown a hayfork with some additional, and barbed, points attached, which had done duty quite recently. In the old days the matarau was often made of manuka and some of my informants had seen them used. The eels were speared crosswise, the spearman then putting his foot on them and threading them on a string which he trailed after him. Although the general name for the eel-spear is matarau, said an old man, this name really applied to the fork-like prongs, the handle being called kauho. They were used for spearing patiki (flounders) as well as tuna (eels). Spearing is still pursued but the old wooden prongs have been replaced by barbed iron ones. Spearing was done both by day and night, rama (torches) being used in the latter case. The old man added that his father when a boy was taught in common with other boys to throw spears and he could spear an eel with accuracy at about thirty feet, sometimes giving an exhibition of his prowess in this respect. Another informant recalled the fact that a chief of old, Urihia by name, had quite a historic reputation for spearing eels. He was taught by his father, Te Kapo, and could throw a spear accurately. Tradition said he generally used a tokotoko (stick) with a bone point (piauau). Spearing eels from a distance with single spear was called patia, but walking through shallow water and transfixing them with a matarau was called wero, or wero-tuna.

My informants were curious to know what is the biggest or heaviest eel caught in New Zealand. Tradition speaks of eels at Lake Wanaka being so big that the eelers could not hold them so they got away. A halfcaste who claimed to have seen an eel out of Lake Wakatipu weigh one hundred and twenty two pounds was regarded as a Maoriland edition of Baron Munchausen by my informants.

Eels when caught were frequently dried in the sun and wind, a mat of patiti (tussock) being suspended over them as a covering (uhi) to 'keep the rain and snow off and also to keep the night dews from settling on the tuna'. The drying process might take a week.

An old lady gave a graphic description of eel-spearing but words fail to portray her animation and vivid gestures. 'In wero-tuna,' she said, 'the matarau was used and if it was in the daytime the eels could be thrown out on the bank, but at night-time it was different. You could spear in a muddy creek in the daylight but at night you sought running water. I remember so well spearing in the Waihemo River at night. I had a matarau in one hand and a rama (torch) in the other. I had a taura (string) of whitau (dressed fibre – it was used because the harareke or flax was too bitter and would taste the eels), and this whitau was wound round my torch hand and trailed away behind in the water. As I speared each eel I stuck an au (bone needle) through its tail and threaded it on to my taura. Soon I had plenty of eels following me. It was too dark to throw them out on the bank and besides it was easier to trail. To-haere-muri means "dragging behind" and that's what we call this. When caught I gave the eels' heads a patu or bang on the matarau to kill them but it only seemed to stun them in many cases. Anyway they seemed to have enough sense left to come along without any trouble and most of them must have been swimming after me judging from their lightness in the water. I speared a few patiki (flounders) and threaded them on too. I have heard of a man trailing four hundred eels. How many I got that night I do not know. They were light in the water but were a very heavy weight to pull out on the bank.'

The Maori divides the eel tribe into many divisions. At Moeraki the hao was placed first for its flavour, while the tuna-rakau (wooden eel) was so-called because it remains hard and tough even after it is cooked. Other eels were known as papaaka; tunatai, a yellow eel; matamoii, a grayish eel; horihori-wai, a white-bellied eel found in gravel creeks; horepara, a big black eel, round-shaped and fat; and the kirirua, a big black eel, noted for its thick skin. At Temuka the kinds named were the hao, classed as the most delicious to eat and which grows big in time; the winiwini-hao, a small hao which never grows any larger; the kouka, said to be 'te tipuna o ka tuna', the biggest of the eels, as it runs up to twenty pounds and more; the kotokoto, a small kind, very fat and suitable for the rara, or Maori gridiron; the arokehe, no description; the manawa, something like the kotokoto, fat and with a fine skin. It was added by my informants that the hao 'has nothing in its piro or its puku', that is, it needs no cleaning. A man at Colac Bay who had been round the West Coast Fiords in his youth said that two kinds of eels found round there are called kokekehe and riko (or reko). He further said: 'Personally I do not care for saltwater fish unless they are fat, but I could eat eels all the year round. Some Maoris won't eat one kind of fish and some won't eat another, but I do not know any kind that all would refuse to eat. Eels taste better than fish.'

The collector will now stand aside and let his informants tell in their own way how the Maori of old made eelpots, eeling canals and eel weirs, and of the various methods adopted to enhance the Maori's food supply by trapping eels during the great eel migrations. Slight differences in the descriptions of patuna and pakanakana are in all probability due to a difference of methods adopted in Southland, Otago and Canterbury in building eel and lamprey traps and weirs according to the depth, width and strength of the various rivers.

EELS AND EEL-CATCHING

To make eelpots (hinaki), pirita (supplejack) could be split and used; korari (flax sticks), aka vine, tororaro (a vine which grows on flats) could be used also. The mouth of the pot was of flax and was called puraki and the flax part which led from the puraki into the pot was called te rohe. The hinaki is long and round and

The hīnaki made in Temuka mentioned on page 146. Tūhura Otago Museum Collection, D31.1334. With kind permission of Te Rūnanga o Arowhenua.

good ones were made of aka vine, so good that North Islanders have expressed admiration of them as better made than their own and the South Islanders in return admit that they are not as expert in catching eels in other ways as their visitors. To keep the framework of aka in place, hoops (potaka) of pirita or big branches of aka are inserted at necessary intervals. The big opening at the front of the hinaki is called te-rae-o-te-hinaki or te-kutu-o-te-hinaki while the small opening at the rear end is known as te-kumu-o-te-hinaki. The puraki is the mouth through which the eel enters the te rohe and from latter it passes into the pot and cannot return. The loose flax strings which are its doom are called ka-mata-o-te-puraki, and without the hinaki the rest of the trap is called kaitara.

In regard to the different sizes of hinaki a divergency of opinion exists. One man said: 'Small hinaki were made for travelling and not specially for catching the kanakana. Being small they were easier to carry and they were set at nights. Big hinaki were for fixed settlements. They were made of tororaro, also called moeraro, the most durable vine in the bush. It creeps along the ground, hence its name tororaro (creeping). Other vines will not last anything like it. Very few vines are left now; probably the sheep have eaten them out.'

As against this opinion the small hinaki made in Temuka and now in the Otago Museum is definitely stated to have been intended for catching kanakana. Further the collector asked a roomful of Maoris regarding sizes of hinaki and was told that the hinaki for eels was the same for both travelling and stationary use, but that the hinaki for the kanakana were smaller in size and were made somewhat differently.

The modern Maoris use eelpots made of wire netting but with the old-time flax mouthpiece. The collector saw one with a sugar bag tied to it, and he heard of one where a stocking with the foot cut out comprised the rohe! The old name of the method of making a puraki for an eelpot was waikoruru. Besides eels the following fish were sometimes caught in the eelpots – panako, pipiki, upokororo, kanakana and others.

Add to Eels and Eeling

Kaitara. The collector's education was extended at Temuka. 'The kaitara is used for catching eels at any time, the hinaki is only used in the heke. The hinaki is made of vine but the kaitara of papaki (close woven flax) with rings of vine to keep it taut. The mouth (te waha) is of flax and is much the same as the rohe of the hinaki. The puraki (mouth) of the hinaki can be made any size by extending or shortening the ring of pirita (supplejack) but the kaitara has a fixed mouth. Both hinaki and kaitara have a net over the kumu or rear-end but I forget its name. The kaitara is put in the water with its mouth downstream and bait inside. Nowadays we use kaitara made of wire netting with sacking tied round to keep the light out and also to help keep the smell of the bait in it.'

It is said that the common eels can be caught at any time, the others in their seasons.

The collector especially inquired for eeling-canals. At Moeraki he was told, 'Drains to catch eels were made at Little River, and at Washdyke (Waitarakao). They were made from the far end, twenty eight to thirty feet perhaps, towards the lake and then opened up one night when ready. The water in the race runs into a big hole and drains away leaving the eels stranded. It can't be worked in the daytime as there is too much light. Near the eel-races pahuris (shelters) were built and fires were made where the glow would not show to the eels and the people would sit there waiting for the eels. No torches were used and no people stood by the race to alarm the eels but at the hole the eels were collected as fast as possible in the dark. This was done at Waimataitai (a lagoon at Goodwood – not the Timaru lagoon which has the same name) but we do not know of any further South. The sea comes into all these places in the wintertime but at other times is blocked by sandbars. The ditch made is called an awa. In the old days hinaki and puraki were used in the races but now this is too much trouble so holes are dug. The channel used to be made with tataa (bailers) and takoko (a scoop with a handle) as these shovelled the sand all right. March, April and May are the months for this work. In March you can get hao and tunarakau and in April papaka, tunatai, matamoi, horihoriwai and horepara. In May you catch a few tunarakau and papaka but more kirirua ('double skin'). If these last named eels are split open, dried, cooked and preserved in a poha kelp bag for about six months they eat all right.'

At Puketiraki the collector was told: 'Eel canals or trenches were dug in the sand. The hao a small eel about the size of the kanakana, goes to the salt water to spawn. It won't go into the hinaki (eelpots) set upstream but comes down to the sea in shoals and is caught in these trenches: The Maoris made a trench (korere-wai) with a puna (hole) in it. It was always opened up at night. White stones were put on the bottom of the trench at one part and if you could not see these you knew the eels were passing over. When plenty of eels were in, the water was cut off by blocking the mouth of the ditch and when it was dry the eels were secured. The ditch was made instead of constructing a pa-tuna or fence as it suited the conditions better. The channel was made so that the current took the hao in. This method of getting eels was called whakaheke.'

The old people of Temuka narrated: 'At the Washdyke, three miles north of Timaru, is the Waitarakao lagoon and channels called awa were made from it to catch eels. The sand was dug with a takoko (a scoop of manuka made like a short canoe paddle), or if it was soil it was dug with a pukahu (a sharpened stick). Some awa were made just wide enough for a hinaki to go in and some were made wide enough to place three or four hinaki side by side. In the latter case ka poupou (posts) were placed between the hinakis to fasten the purakis of each hinaki to the front of the posts. You could catch kokopu, eels and inaka in well-made hinaki at Washdyke. The awa were made long enough to "ia te wai" (create a current) to sweep the fish in. No bait (moenu) was used as it was not needed as the eels thought they were going to the sea. A parua (hole) was made at the end of the awa and eels were scooped (koko) out of it with a kohao [see Nets]. We never heard of taking them by hand out of the trench or hole, but by the hinaki and the kohao. White stones or white bones were put on the bottom of the awa to let the people know if the eels were travelling (heke). When the hinaki was going to be lifted out a papaki mat was placed over the mouth of the channel to keep mud, eels, kohuwai (moss) or refuse out of the channel. When the hinaki was replaced the papaki was lifted out. Beside the poupou (posts) put in at front of hinaki, another is put in at the back to tie the string to stretch the net out. If this is not done the net crumples up and you will hear the old people say "Ka puru i te waha i te hinaki" (the mouth of the pot is blocked). Some of the hinaki are small and are for one man to handle, but the big sizes take several men. The mouth of the hinaki is turned upstream. They can be seen used at Otipua (St. Andrews), Pareora, Opihi, Ohapi and other rivers whose mouths are suitable. The hao, the best eel of all, is only caught in the autumn. It cannot be caught in the moonlight as it won't travel then, or if it does happen to travel in the atamarama (moonlight) the least shadow makes them frightened (wheata – this is an old term, pronounced "feeat"). If the day has been rough with a south west wind and the night is dark (hinapouri) the hao can be caught in abundance, but if on such a night the sea comes over the spit it is a "caution". The coming down of the eels is called "heke" and the catching of them then in the awa is called whakaheketuna.' In regard to pa-tuna (eel-weirs) not much information was forthcoming. It is said that only in the case of the kanakana was a 'fence' made across the river, and as the lampreys are coming up the rivers the mouths of the hinaki (pots) are turned towards the sea, that is downstreams. The pa-kanakana is built to suit the current but the one at Opihi was made straight across the river with hinaki at intervals. In recent years wire netting has been used but in the old days stakes were driven into the riverbed and rauaruhe (fern-leaves) and patiti (tussock) were placed against them.

Whakapipipohatu means to 'heap up stones' and this was done next, the whole forming a paewai. One of my informants had seen a fence with six hinaki close to one bank. For the tuna no fence was built but a 'pa' was made in centre of river with hinaki in the strength of the current. The eels come up the centre of a stream and when the collector was at Temuka (May 26, 27, 28, 29) the arokehe was said to be doing so. It was added that the kanakana comes up the Opihi in June, whereas in Southland it goes up the rivers in September.

Add to Eeling

A well-informed kaumatua said: 'I never saw a patuna (eel weir) in the South but I saw it at Temuka long ago. To catch hao you can stretch a long net across creeks and small rivers leaving a place for the hinaki or eelpot. In big rivers don't put fences across at all but simply set pots to each side and catch what you can. The hinaki was used in hekes (migrations) but you set the kaitara with bait inside and without nets or fences leading to it. Up at Lake Ellesmere and Little River channels were made leading so far and then stopping. The eels would swarm into these and finding no outlet would turn back for the lake and would be caught in a kohao held in the water by a man. They used to put whalebone down on the beds of these channels so as to tell if the eels were passing in the dark. Perhaps ten of these awa (channels) would be made in a suitable vicinity for this was the easiest way of all to catch eels. I do not know what "whakapuni tuna" is but it might be making a channel from a creek like and then block up both ends and you have the eels in the blocked part. I saw this done long ago at Temuka but I do not know if it was called "whakapuni tuna". I have never seen patunas or eel channels in Southland but I believe that such may have existed once from what old Sandfly (Rawiri te Awha) told me. He said that at the Upper Mavora Lake which our people called Manawapore or Manawapopore – I have heard both names – there was a stone eel trap. It may be there yet but I have never been up to see. He called it a whakapapa (c.f. papa – flat slabs of stone) and told me the name of the Katimamoe man who built it but I have forgotten his name. You could block the mouth and get hundreds of eels. It was builded against the bank and there was a hole at each end and probably one in the middle. It was covered with slabs of rock and the eels were bound to go into such a tunnel – anything like that always attracts them. After blocking the mouths you could lift up the stones – the puru (plugs) – and see the eels in it and get more than you could carry. I think they will be there yet – those stone wharetuna. We call spots where eels congregate wharetuna, and I know several such resorts. In October and November, before the shearing season, we used to catch eels in Ourawera (Lake George at Colac Bay) with a kaitara. These were made of miro bark, of totara bark or of korari or toe stalks with potaka (rings) of he aka (vine). The net at the rear end is called te kumu and has to be well-made as the eels try to escape there. These kaitara are also called hinaki but the former name is more correct. We used a bait in the kaitara but not in the proper hinaki.'

A well-informed old man said to the collector: To make a pakanakana, place two puti (kits filled with stones) in such position as to direct the current and with a cross piece (whatitau) and attach the hinaki to pou (posts) right where the puti concentrate the current. The pakanakana only occupies a part of the river but a patuna is built in quiet water and goes right across. Put poupou (posts) across the stream and place scrub before them (whakapurupuru). Do this in October when the eels are migrating (heke) to the sea. Perhaps you might have two or three hinaki instead of one. No moenu (bait) is needed for hinaki but only for the kaitara. The only patuna he had seen was in the Auahituroa channel at Roto-nui-a-Whatu (Kaitangata). Rakiraki, Takatahuruhuru, Ohua, Te Haere, Rotopikoro,

Kaikoura and other old men made it. It was a great place for tunarakau, horepara, and other eels, as well as for kokopala, patiki and other fish. It took two or three men to handle the big hinaki. It was carried ashore and emptied into a parua (hole) made for the purpose and was then carried back and replaced. The eels were then secured and knocked on the head. He had seen kaitara used at various places but the one at Kaitangata was his sole experience of an old-fashioned patuna. One old man said that in the Mataura river at Tuturau stood some posts in the river with stones built against them. This was permanent and was called a taumanu. Then in the kanakana season a wing-dam (taupatupatu) was built of manuka to obstruct the rest of the river and hinaki were set in beside the East bank. So very uncommon were pa-tuna or pa-kanakana in Murihiku since the white man came that an old Maori seventy seven years old told the collector that he had never seen one. He heard that one existed in the Mataura River near Tuturau so when he visited that locality he made a special trip to see it but found that very little of it was remaining then.

After ceasing to build the pa-kanakana the Maori mainly relied on getting the lampreys from the various falls which obstructed some of the rivers up which the migrations went. An old woman mentioned to the collector that when a girl she had accompanied parties going to the Opurere Falls on the Pomahaka River, but she gave no fresh details about the expeditions.

Add to Eels

A Maori whom the collector met in Canterbury graphically narrated his experiences in the South after lamprey eels (kanakana). Some eighteen years ago he and another Maori caught nine sacks full in one night at the Mataura Falls. They 'fished' both sides of the river and probed it in daytime to see the extent of their operations and at night waded in river and pulled the kana off the rocks and put them in sacks. A light was held on top of bank – not much, just enough to see by. They had gloves on and pulled the fish off with a sharp jerk. As each was displaced another would occupy its place. You might sometimes catch five of six of them in one grasp and could fill a sack in an hour going steadily. When a sack was full enough it was taken to a big purua (hole) near the bank which they had made to hold their catch and there it was emptied into it. Narrator was lowered over the edge down a rocky face, about twenty feet high on the Freezing-Works side, sitting meantime in a loop of the rope. He would stand on a ledge and fill his sack. They did not go down when the Works were going (which was up until midnight at that particular time) as the force of water would wash them away, but went down when the Works ceased operations for the night. If the rope broke 'you were a goner'. Only two volunteered to go down – the lightest two as it happened – and that is how he and the other man got nine sacks as he had told me. Near the Works they only got wet to the knees there was no spray there but further down-river from the Falls they would be up to the neck in water before they would strike a ledge to stand on. He did not remember it as being cold in the water, but he worked hard tugging kana off the rocks to which their sucker mouths hung. The kanakana has no stomach and no bones, and is better than eels to eat but he had never heard of anyone dying from a surfeit of them [See *Maori Race* by Tregear. [[1904]] H.B.]. The kanakana comes up from the sea to spawn up the rivers but he did not know its food – probably the froth of the water. He had heard the old people say it lived on foam or froth, but beyond this he knew nothing of what it ate.

The old man who had been born and bred at Otago Heads also recalled trips he had made to Mataura in the brief 'kanakana seasons' years ago. He said he had secured numerous kanakana off the wheel of the Mataura Paper Mill in the early morning before the mill started work. The opening into the wheel was too small for a man to pass through to pull the lampreys off the wheel so they were poked off with a long stick and fell into the channel in which he and companions had set three hinaki made of tororaro and flax. The kanakana lives on water, not on the hukahuka (foam or spume), as it did not come to top of water but kept below. The Maoris used to get free passes on the railway for mahi kai (seeking food) or for tangis, but such privileges were withdrawn years ago. This mahika-kai was worked on co-operative lines as each kaik would get five or six railway passes and the whole kaik would contribute the out-of-pocket expenses of those who went for them and the whole result (in food) of the trip was divided pro rata. This is not done now.

In regard to the foregoing information the collector would add that the Mataura Paper Mill was started about 1876 and the Southland Freezing Works on the opposite side of the falls about 1882 so the two industries very seriously cramped eeling operations at the actual falls, but the rocky walls of the small gorge below the falls was still available. Then about the year 1900 dredging operations so contaminated the water with silt and mining refuse that the Mataura River practically ceased to be regarded by the Maoris as a kanakana fishery.

[Note by collector: The question of eel-weirs and eel-catching is, if anything, more fully gone into in the Kaiapoi section than in these Murihiku notes.]

Add to Eeling

In an old Manuscript account of places where the Maoris got food in Otago and Canterbury the names 'tunga hinaki' or 'turaka hinaki', and 'whakapuni tuna' occurred frequently as defining places where the Maoris got eels. 'Turaka or tunga hinaki' is easily understood as a place where hinaki (eelpots) were 'stood' or set, but what was 'whakapuni tuna'. The old woman who lent the collector the book to copy made the following remarks: '"Whakapuni tuna" was to block a creek by making a pa or fence and putting hinaki down. It means the same as pa-tuna. In a stream of fair size the pa is in the centre and the rest of the river is open, so at certain times the old people put a papuni (blockage) across the river to block the free passage of the eels. A paewai was made of rauaruhe, patiti, etc., loaded down with stones. Sometimes, if the current was strong, poupoupa (weir-posts) were put in behind the paewai to hold it in position.

"Turaka hinaki" was to reserve a place, or spot, to put eelpots down. In autumn you faced the hinaki upstream to catch the eels and in spring (September) you faced it downstream. Turaka was the place where the eelpots were set.'

An old man said: 'The words tunga-hinaki mean an eel-weir or patuna, while whakapuni-tuna is the place where it was set. A creek would be blocked and a hinaki set at its only outlet. The eels went into the waha (mouth) or properly speaking here, the kaututu of the puraki and so into the hinaki from which they could not escape. I never heard the name whakapepepa applied to the catching of eels by a pa-tuna but the word whakapipi was a term meaning the damming or blocking of a creek by placing a pa across it.'

It is worthy of note that the two opinions given above were spoken by the two oldest Maoris interviewed and that they seemed to be the only ones who had heard and knew the terms. One other old man said that whakapuni tuna meant blocking up eel's holes but he could give no further information about it, and all the others admitted their ignorance.

Rauiri is defined as 'a small patuna' in Williams' [[1917]] *Dictionary* but my informants said that to them ka rauiri meant hunting grounds for birds or places for catching fish.

FLOUNDERS AND SOLES

My informants said there was only one kind of sole but three kinds of flounders. The correct name of the sole was horihori but it was often known as the kutuhori, a word meaning 'bent jaw' because of the shape of its mouth. One man classed the sole among the flounders calling it the patiki-horihori but the rest seemed to regard it as separate. The soles, so the collector was told, seldom go up the rivers but one of his informants had seen them several miles up the Taieri River – this was regarded as unusual.

The general name for flounders was patiki and the old men made comments about the following varieties: Poroporo is small and white, according to one man. None of the other men included this as a variety, and at Moeraki the people said that porapora-patiki meant 'small flounder'. Raututu is a kind of flounder with a yellow belly. It lives in the sea but comes up the rivers. Mohoao is a big spotted flounder which has left the sea and has been in fresh water for a long time, said one man. Another said the mohoao is a freshwater flounder marked with brown spots; and another said that the mohoao with its spotted back is practically a freshwater fish. Patiki-wai-maori is said to be a freshwater flounder. Patiki-wai-whai (or the Waiwhai) has a white belly and is a saltwater flounder. Patotara is a yellow-bellied flounder. It is said to spend half its time in fresh water and the other half in salt water.

An interesting point about the information given about the flounders is herewith appended to show local variations in nomenclature. Nearly every old man interviewed maintained that there were three kinds of flounders and they named them as follows: 1. Poroporo mohoao name forgotten. 2. Patiki-wai-maori mohoao patiki-horihori. 3. Patiki-wai-whai (white) mohoao (spotted) patotara (yellow). 4. Patiki mohoao raututu.

The collector would add that to his knowledge the poua (grandfather) who gave the third list was a man well-versed in Nature and that probably his division is the most authoritative. At the same time there was nothing to prevent the people at one village calling a flounder by one name and the people at another place one hundred miles distant calling it a different name altogether.

OCTOPI

'The muheke,' said an old seafarer to the collector, 'is the squid that the whales eat, but I never saw it used as human food. The squid has just one kawai (arm) but the wheke (octopus) has several. Some people are frightened of the wheke and will not touch it but it eats very well. Cut the arms off and boil it or murumuru (roast) it on the embers – it tastes like koura (crayfish) but is somewhat salty. The wheke has the impudence to catch hold of people gathering kelp for pohas and some women are frightened of it but it is easily managed. You simply put your fingers in its mouth and pull out its teeth and it is done for. It has teeth the same as those of the kina (sea-egg) and many a one I have killed. Avoid its kaka-shaped beak and its teeth are soon wrenched out. We hear stories of big wheke in other lands but I never saw the big kind round Murihiku.'

SHARKS

received but little mention from my informants and it seems that these tigers of the deep did not figure on Murihiku menus as much as they did on those of the North Island Maoris, although they were not despised as food. Even white men who have tasted shark flesh admit it is good eating as one or two of the aged Maoris pointed out with a gratified air. What little was said here follows: Mako, a small shark, could be caught with line and hook if necessary. At Moeraki the collector was told the mako is the blue shark. Tatare, a small kind of shark, is probably the dog-fish. Tupa is said to be a yellow shark, the biggest of those found round southern coasts, running up to eighteen feet and weighing up to two tons, said my informant. Mako-huarau, a small kind, the spiny dog-fish. Mako-ururoa, a bigger kind, said to be very fierce. Mako-repe a small kind known as the elephant fish. Sometimes, said one man, when walking along the beach you came across a black, brittle framework like a piece of dried kelp, or like a black hairbrush's back but with scalloped edges. The old people used to call it Te Whare-o-Makorepe because they said it was hatched out of the body of the species of shark known as repe or mako-repe. At one time it would be filled with eggs and as these hatched out they form tiny sharks and grow into mako-repe. The whare or case, emptied of its living contents becomes the sport of wind and wave and being cast on shore constitutes part of the familiar flotsam and jetsam of the tides.

WHALES

A well-informed old man referred to the traditional lore that in storms at sea an efficient tohuka (or tohunga) could call up great fish to protect the canoe. Even the fierce shark, the mako-ururoa could be made to obey the will of the tohuka. Any whale, or shark, or big fish, or taniwha, or monster of the deep thus called up was called a takaroa, or tangaroa, and all were 'paid with a hair from the human head' [See Section XXII for details of this].

Tuterakihaunoa was the name given in ancient days, said my principal informant, to what the whalers called the 'sparm' whale (the spermwhale). Paikea, said the same informant, was the olden name of the 'humpback' whale. Kewa is a big whale. 'I think it is your Right Whale' said my informant.

Raratawhiriwhiri – there was some difference of opinion about this name. One man said 'In the Otago Museum is a seal, brown, very wide, and fully nine feet long. It is a raratawhiriwhiri.' Another man who gave good information said: 'The raratawhiriwhiri is the black fish and you would sometimes get a tun of oil out of one. You sometimes find them stranded where they have run ashore.'

Raratahurihuri – 'I do not know the name raratawhiriwhiri you mention,' said one veteran, 'but the raratahurihuri is the finback, or possibly the black fish. The finback is the longest whale but the biggest is the bowhead, which was unnamed by the olden Maoris as it is too far South for them to know.'

Te Aitaka-a-Puka is 'a sort of whale, perhaps the cowfish', said one informant, but a well-informed old man said the correct name of the cowfish was upokohue. An old woman said that sometimes the Maori would find paikea, kewa or other kind of whale cast up on shore. The flesh would be cooked in the umu oven. She had eaten it and it was 'kapai' (very good). Terehu is the porpoise. One man called it the popokarua.

CRAYFISH AND CRABS

Koura is the name for crayfish, or crawfish, whether found in fresh water or salt water. It is said the sea ones grow much larger and are redder in hue than the ones inland. The sea koura when caught was put in fresh water prior to being eaten. They were tied by string looped round their bodies and fastened across a stream to stones, branches or grass on either bank. Perhaps a dozen or so would be on one string and they soon died. Eels would not touch them while they had their shells on. When taken out of the fresh water they could be eaten raw or be hung up on lines to dry, or again the shells could be removed and the flesh steamed in an umu (oven) and either eaten at once or be stored away in poha (kelp bags) to be kept until required. The koura-waitai (sea crayfish) can be caught in traps called taruke (or sometimes taruki), a round-shaped affair made of pirita (supplejack) bound with tutaekereru vine and with a koroputa (hole) in the top for the koura to enter. One of these old-fashioned taruke was made over at Ruapuke Island a few months ago. A place near Temuka is called Punakoura because the koura-wai-maori or freshwater crayfish can be taken there. It is caught by hand. There are no koura-wai-tai or saltwater crayfish to be found along the coast in this locality so the taruke or lobster pot was not made in this district.

The collector accompanied a venerable Maori through the Otago Museum and the old man was much interested in the koura. He said it grew to a great size and sometimes was speared with a sharp stick. He had once killed one in this manner near Colac Bay. It was a veritable monster and he considered it was quite double the size of the largest one in the Museum. The collector asked him the name of a lobster pot and he replied taruke yet when he was shown one in the case [Exhibit D10.243] he called it a tatakoura. He also said that Exhibit D10.195 was a net to catch the koura. A bait was placed in it and when the koura entered it was hauled up.

The collector asked an intelligent old man at the Bluff the Maori name of a lobster pot or crayfish trap and he replied taruki; yet three months later he professed not to have heard of such a name, but said that a tata for koura was made of pirita (supplejack) in the shape of a 'rat cage' and was called tatakoura.

The collector must frankly admit he was puzzled at these seemingly inexplicable and contradictory comments by two such reliable and trustworthy men and he has not solved the mystery yet, but he recognises firstly that very old people suffer from sudden lapses of memory and secondly that there is a distinct possibility that the taruke and the tatakoura are two different forms of trap.

An old Maori mentioned to the collector that crabs were not found inland. This statement was volunteered because of the loose phraseology of the colonial youth some of whom claimed to have caught crabs sixty or seventy miles up-country. The koura was found very far inland, however, and was treated, cooked and eaten in the same manner as the sea crayfish. The crab, he explained, had legs and the koura a tail.

Another aged Maori corroborated this statement – the koura could be found in streams in the far interior of the country, but the crab was a sea dweller.

The crab (*Prionorhynchus edwardsii*) exhibited in the Otago Museum was called a papaka by two Maoris who accompanied the collector through the museum, but later the collector was told that papaka was a general name for all kinds of crabs.

STINGRAYS

At Moeraki the collector was told that there are two kinds of 'stingaree', viz., the whai-uku and the whai-porapora. At Colac Bay the principal informant said, 'I never heard of the whai-uku and whai-porapora but simply the whai. The word uku means "clay". I have seen the whai eaten, but I never tried it myself.'

SEALS AND SEALING

Kekeno is the name of the fur seal. The white sealers called the males 'wigs' and the females 'clapmatches' but the Maori did not distinguish between the sexes by giving separate names. My informants said that the seals were clubbed in pre-pakeha days the same as they are now. A hard, heavy stick was used, varying in length according to necessity. 'We used a short club (patu) for the kekeno as we crawled into their caves after them,' said one veteran, while another added: 'The kekeno is found in caves and on the rocks only. At Otago Heads there was a rookery of fur seals where they bred in the rocks there. I have never heard of the olden Maoris using the skins of either the fur or hairseal but in the whaling days we sewed the skins up into moccasins to protect our feet.'

Popoikore is the hair seal according to my principal informant and it was preferred for food. It is a very mild and sleepy creature and boys were wont to climb on its back in sport.

Pakake, in common estimation, is the hair seal but my principal informant said it was a general name for all seals. Giving the name in its popular usage one old man said: 'The hair seal or pakake lies on the sands sunning itself and does not frequent the rocks. It breeds up in the bush by ponds (hapua) and makes a track called he ara pakake from there to the sea.' The saying 'He-takotoraka-pakake' means a lying-place for hair seals; it describes sandy beaches of easy access.

Rapoka is the sea-leopard, also known as the sea-devil. It is not so fearsome as its name and one veteran remarked, 'An old woman could kill the rapoka it is so easily dealt with.'

Whakahao or whakahau is the sea-lion and it is noted for the great disparity in size between the sexes. So marked is this disproportion that the Maoris gave the female the separate name of Kaki. A huge lion is an awe-inspiring sight and Te Wera may be pardoned for thinking discretion the better part of valour. From this historic incident two proverbial sayings arose and translated they run, 'Te Wera never flinched from the point of a weapon but he fled from a sealion', and 'The foe of Te Wera was a sea-lion'. Yet up to this formidable creature the Murihiku Maori walked with a club (patu) made of manuka or other hard wood and killed it by hitting its nose. There are still a few Native veterans surviving of those who took part in such encounters. One veteran said the Maoris who tackled the sea-lion were active on their feet and expert at dealing blows. The club was usually rough and knotted but not too heavy for instant use. It was frequently referred to as a rakau (stick) and the action of hitting was called poi. 'We used a short club for the fur seal,' said another grizzled veteran, 'but big, long clubs were needed to fight the sea-lion. There was a knack in killing them and it took practice to acquire it. If you ran, the whakahao chased you and he would make you travel too as he moves with surprising speed for such a big, awkward-looking fellow. The best way to escape was to run towards the sea and then to one side and he could go on to the water.' Another retired seafarer said, 'I went sealing for some seasons when I was a young man. We used a heavy rata club small at one end for the hand to grasp and with a knob at the other end. If the whakahau saw you were afraid he went for you at once and he could move very fast. If you hit him on the nose you stunned him, but it might take a dozen good blows to kill him. It also took several hits to kill the much smaller pakake and kekeno as a rule.'

Ihupuku is a big kind of seal, said one man, but another added that the ihupuku (swelled nose) is the sea-elephant. 'It has a trunk,' he continued, 'but I have never seen one, as these huge creatures live down at Macquarie Island.' The collector has read that there is a proverbial saying, 'Te konohi kai nukere' (the eye of the sealer). My friends explained that nukere meant rookery and that the purport of the saying was looking into a rookery to see the seals assembled there.

There is a 'whaling club' in the Otago Museum. My informants considered it had no special name but was merely a patu. They mostly defined the killing weapon by the name of the species of seal killed with it as patu-pakake, patu-kekeno or patu-whakahau, and so on.

OYSTERS AND SHELLFISH

The claim by some whalers that they introduced oysters into Foveaux Strait did not find favor with the old Maoris. The latter say they have had tio (oysters) for centuries past but mostly rock oysters found on the beaches. They all considered the oyster a natural product but admit that the older people did not know of the existence of the Foveaux Strait bed. 'The Maori knew rock and mud oysters – both called tio,' said one old sea-farer. 'The mud oysters are found in the bays at Rakiura (Stewart Island). If you tap their edges on the stones they can soon be opened and eaten.'

'The oysters were not brought by the whalers,' said another venerable mariner. 'Our people knew the tio long ago and found tio-pohatu on the rocks and tio-paruparu in the bays at Rakiura and also on the shores near the Bluff. The tio-paruparu is the same kind as the oysters out in the straits but the latter being in deeper water do not taste so good as the ones in the shallow water. I never heard of them being put in umu (ovens) but that they were broken and eaten raw or else roasted in the ashes.' 'Oysters (tio) were found on the rocks and were opened with stones. There used to be a lot at the end of Colac Bay. I do not know how the people cooked them before the pakeha came.' Another old man who is a mine of information about ancient things said: 'The tio could be eaten raw after being bashed open between two stones, like mussels (pipi) and like the latter could also be put in the umu and steamed for an hour or so with grass, not earth, on top when they would be ko maoka (cooked) and ko hamama (gaping open). Tio were gathered on the rocks into a kete (basket of flax) and were soaked in a freshwater creek (te wai maori) as a rule before being eaten raw or steamed. The tio were much scarcer than the pipi.' A veteran sea-dog said: 'A man named Charlie Britt found the Foveaux oysters when trawling and got a cutter to go oystering and I was with him. We took oysters to Dunedin and Invercargill in 1863 or '64 and that was the start of the present industry. At first hand dredges were used and in Port Adventure we used to fasten a rope to a tree to help us work the dredge. Then we shifted out to the straits and others came oystering also.'

The pawa was a welcome addition to the native larder and could be eaten either raw or cooked. Like most sea products eaten by the Maori the pawa was first soaked in fresh water, usually in a stream near the sea-coast. Hence we find the name Waipawa applied to a creek some miles from the mouth of the Taieri River, to a creek on the Bluff hill near the reservoir and to brooks elsewhere. 'If you wished to preserve them,' said an old man, 'you cooked them and then strung them on a line with "he au" (a needle) made of bone or wood. You would hear the old people say "Homai te au iwi" (give me the bone needle) or "homai te au rakau" (give me the wood needle) and they would soon thread the pawa up on a line to dry. The pawa were then put away in baskets in a whata to be eaten when wanted.'

Dealing with shellfish 'the mine of information' continued: 'Pawa were eaten raw after being soaked in wai maori (fresh water). The kakahi is a shellfish found inland; the toretore is the shape of the kakahi but is found in salt water; the pukanikani is slightly different from the toretore and is fastened (mau) very hard on the rocks. It is stuck so tight that it is hard to gather (uru). The koeo is like a pawa but smaller and its shell is prettier. It is very good to eat raw as it is soft, while the pawa is tough. The rori is black like a pawa but it has a small white shell. There used to be plenty at Colac Bay and it is good to eat raw or cooked. The pupu or periwinkle was sometimes broken and eaten raw and again it was put in fresh kelp and stuck in the umu and steamed. Tahoehoe is white and has a double shell (I never heard of any name for the spring which opens double shells) and it can be eaten. The tuaki or cockle is smaller than the tahoehoe. It is soaked in fresh water and eaten raw. The kina, or sea urchin, is eaten raw, not cooked. I saw some eaten recently when I was visiting Colac. The tupehokura has a double shell, very long and of a bluey color. It is found in the sand at low tide and can be eaten raw or steamed. Some of the Maori younger people don't soak them nowadays but boil them at once.' Another old man said: 'Mussels were not eaten raw but were put on the fire. Cockles (tuaki) and clams (roroa) were eaten raw. Big clams (taiwhatiwhati) were roasted or put in fresh water till they opened. The best way to cook any shellfish was to put them in green kelp-bags (poha-mata), put them on the fire and steam till the contents were done. This was called "murumuru te poha" and did them nicely.'

The whakaira-tama, a white mussel, is good to eat. An intelligent travelled Maori said: 'The shellfish which is called toheroa at the Bay of Plenty is called tohemango at Otaki and tupehokura in Otago.' [See discussion on this point later in this section.]

Add to Shellfish

Inquiring if the roukakahi (cockle-rake) was used in the South the collector at Moeraki was assured it was not – the kakahi was gathered by hand. One man added: 'Kakahi were in the rivers and were felt in the mud with the feet and were then picked up. As soon as you touched it, it closed up. It does not open up sidewise (kohera) but at the point and its arero (tongue) comes out to feed and drink. The pipi on the beach does the same, as well as the whakai-a-tama and the taiwhatiwhati but when the weather is hot and they are out of the water they kohera (gape) for moisture. The kakihi is the saltwater limpet and the shells are used to make a quick tiwha (patch) on the pohas (kelp bags) at the Titi Islands. Always turn the open side of the shell to the inner side of the poha and it makes a better and neater job. Flat stones picked up on the beach are also used as tiwhas on pohas.'

He continued: 'The shells with whorls from bottom to top are karuru. Koeo is a small kind of paua but has a different fish in it. Most Maoris will not eat the rori shellfish because the children get "slawery mouths" and water runs out. This is ware-waha (running mouth). (Ware is a running gum, pia is a dry gum). When you eat tio (rock oysters) throw the shells away carefully as if you throw them in the fire they may fly out and blind you. The tuaki cockle has a rough shell; the whakai-a-tama is bigger and has a smooth shell, and one like it but flatter is taiwhatiwhati. The name Whakai-a-tama means "feed the son". The pipi and kuku are the same shell but the latter is bigger. The small black shell like this is called toritori. The tuke is a cockle with one side ridged. The hinge of a double shell is called kotiri and to place two against each other and twist them open is called kohiti. I forget the name of periwinkles. The bubu (pupu) is a black, round shellfish good to eat. The door of its house forms the "kanohi pupu", or "cat's eye" as the pakeha calls it. A shell was said to come off the kaio (ngaio) or "bullkits" as you pakehas call them, but I forget its name. Quite a number of seashells I never heard the Maoris give a name for and some I did know I cannot recollect.

One kind of bubu (pupu) carries its shell on its back till it is old and then it drops it and the old people used to say it went away either flying through the air or swimming as a fish. I forget its name then but it is finally said to go into a sort of crab. I do not know the proper story about it. The toheroa is a big form of the taiwhatiwhati and the shellfish called tohemaunga in the North Island is by us called roroa.' At Temuka, however, the collector was handed a shell which was said to be a 'tohemango' from the North Island (but which the people at Temuka said they would call a big roroa) so the Northern name of this shellfish may vary in different localities in the North as well as be different from the Southern name. The collector was also given (for the Museum) the biggest shell he has seen from any South Island coast. It was picked up on the beach near Wainono (Lake Studholme). The Temuka people say it is a very big pipi and call it a hoemoana (oar of the ocean). The ordinary pipi rolls in to the shore on the tide but the hoe-moana comes in standing upright and the Maoris say it is walking. The present Maoris say the older people informed them this shellfish travelled in the sea this way.

At Puketiraki the collector saw some very black and hard-looking round things hanging on a line and was informed they were dried paawaa shellfish. They had first been boiled and then had been strung on the line.

An old man said he reckoned the pipi was the same kind of shell as the kuku only bigger. The small, blue, plain shell of the same kind was called toretore and the small blue ones with the ridges in the shell are pukanikani. He wrote the name of another shell in it, viz. tuupehukura. Continuing he said that whetiko is the name of a kind of pupu. The mythological name of the cat's eyes on the pupu is 'konohi Tawhaki' because that hero of old used them when in a tight fix. He told his brother Karihi to gather some of those 'eyes' on the rocks as he had a premonition the old witch Matakarepo intended to kill them. The brothers could not keep awake but took the wise precaution of fastening these 'eyes' over their eyelids and every time the old dame stirred the fire and glanced at them she saw the 'eyes' shining and thought the men were awake and watching her.

One man said the only bird he knew which carried up mussels in the air and dropped them on the rocks to break them and open them was the karoro, or seagull.

An old woman said the term pupu nowadays embraced a lot of shellfish – some are called 'big pupu', and others, 'little pupu'. The whetiko is a kind of pupu. A long, thin shell is called toitoi; there is also another kind with the same name. These shell-fish were picked out with a thin bone pin whose Maori name she forgot.

Add to Shellfish

One of the middle-aged Maoris said that he had visited Napier and had heard what was called roroa here called pipi there. They had not mussels there but three sorts were found in Foveaux Strait viz. toritori, black and smooth; pukanikani, blue and corrugated and the kuku is big with a shell of yellowish edge. The kuku is the same shell as the pipi only larger. A small kuku would be a big pipi or vice versa in southern phraseology. Aka means a shell or any shell. He considered that shellfish such as the pawa, etc., were soaked in fresh water to make them soft, not to get any salt taste out of them.

Asking a well-informed kaumatua regarding the roukakahi (rake for mussels) he said it was not used down here although the word rou could be used for scraping or raking a thing out as in 'e rou mai'. They gathered the kakahi by hand down here as sufficient could be collected that way to suffice for all the needs of the people – the kakahi was not much eaten in Murihiku; it was not considered very tasty.

In regard to a question he did not know the Maori name of the common shell, the 'fan', but he considered that each of those shells once had meat in it but as this was always missing when it reached the shore the Maori could not eat same and so gave the shell no name. The Foveaux dredges bring up big ones with meat in them but as the old Maori did not know these large fans they had no name for them. The paua and koeo, he continued, were eaten. The mariri is a small pawa and was gathered and eaten by the children, the adults not bothering about it. It is very seldom seen compared with the two other kinds. Pawa shell was used to put kanohi (eyes) in whakairo (carvings) and it was also used for water. He had seen a good shell taken and the holes laced tight with flax and this formed a convenient water receptacle.

An old man said that he never heard the term kuku for the mussel when he was young – they were all called pipi – but now big pipis were being called kuku – a word imported from the North Island. The following names were got in the Otago Museum:

Diplon (unio) lutulentus = kakahi (this is a freshwater kind)
Purpura striata = toitoi
Siphonalia mandarina = pupu koihi (koihi = pointed)
Apollo argus = pupu-ma-takata ('pupu for a man')
Astralium sulcatum = pupu kaiwhiri
Turbo granosus = pupu (common variety)
Monodonta covrosa = whetiko
Patella strigilis = kakihi (waitai = sea kind)
Plaxiphora suteri = haka hiwihiwi (= ridges)
Barnea similis = tetere moana
Chione stutchburyi = tuaki (this is the cockle)
Mactra discors = whakai-o-tama ('food of the son')
Standella elongata = tupehokura
Resania lanceolata = roroa
Mesodesma ventricosa = roroa (big).

'The official name of the Toheroa is *Mesodesma ventricosum*.'
Pinna Zelandica = hoe-moana
Mytilus lutus = pipi
Mytilus magellanicus = pukanikani
Mytilus edulis = toritori.

The last three are all varieties of pipi. In addition to the sea kakihi there is also (but not represented in Museum) a variety which moves along the rock (to which it attaches itself) and is called kakihi-tere.

In view of the diversity of information about the shellfish, the collector has thought it best to let his informants speak for themselves. The only way to thoroughly settle the question of the variations of shell nomenclature in the various parts of New Zealand would be to have a representative collection of shells bearing their correct Latin or scientific names taken round from district to district and have the local Maoris give their name for each individual shell. Failing this plan, one or two of the best-informed Maoris of each district could be accompanied to the nearest Museum which has properly classified shell exhibits and there name the various shells. By either of these means a lot of data would be acquired and it would serve to show the dialectal, tribal or local differences in the names bestowed on the shells which are such familiar objects round our coasts. The collector is sure that such a procedure and investigation would prove that the differences are far more surprising and extensive than many imagine.

In regard to the information recorded here the collector would like to add a few of his own conclusions. He found at each place that the people were alive to the fact that 'further North' the shellfish which they were trying to describe to the collector had different names and in some few cases they tried to record the difference, but with indifferent success. Thus one man said the Murihiku roroa was called the pipi in Hawke's Bay, but this is against the whole weight of southern evidence. If he had said toheroa in place of pipi he would have voiced the popular verdict. Another said the toheroa was called tohemango and tohemaunga in some parts of the North Island. As to this the collector cannot say. One man said the toheroa was called tupehokura in Otago and another described it as a big form of taiwhatiwhati, but the official name *Mesodesma ventricosum* identifies it as the Murihiku roroa and establishes the accuracy of those who stated such to be the case. The collector regrets that he cannot state what the Murihiku Maori called the shell known as pipi in the North Island, but it is now fairly well known that the shell known as kuku further North was round the Otago coasts invariably called the pipi and was used for scraping flax, etc.

SECTION XVII

BIRDS

BIRDS

Takahea – The takahea (*Notornis*) (strange to say the Southland Maoris call this rare bird takahea while the Canterbury Maoris know it as takahe) was just a big pakura (swamphen) said an old Maori. The people of old said it lived in the bush in the mountains and stayed in one place all its life. The late Rakitapu (who was a boy at Wanaka prior to Puoho's raid in 1836) had seen it caught. The bird could not fly and it had a cry like the pakura only louder and stronger. It slept during the day like the kakapo and at night-time came down to the little hapua (lagoons) near ka moana (the big lakes) where it fed on grass like the pakura does, being very fond of the koareare (bulrushes). It could be killed in the early morning, as it returned from the feeding-ground up to the hills, by kuri (dogs) bailing (hao) it up, when the men hit it on the head with a club. It could run very fast. It had an extremely strong beak but could be caught in a snare if the man would huna (hide) near and run out when it was entangled, otherwise it would cut the net like a knife with its beak and escape. You could not distinguish the sex by its appearance. Another well-informed kaumatua said he had never heard of snaring takahea but old Rawiri-te-awha had told him that it used to be caught at Lake Te Anau with the kuri which had been trained to catch weka (woodhens).

Kotuku – 'The white heron was as easily caught with snares as was the wild duck,' said one poua. 'The bird nested in trees but was caught on its beaten paths beside rivers or in swamps.'

'The kotuku was snared and its fine feathers plucked for piki (head-plume) and the bird was then let go,' said another. 'I never heard of them being eaten. I have heard the old people speak of a small crane but I forget its name. The matuku (bittern) was snared by the head like a duck and not by its feet. The only birds snared by the feet were the karoro and tarapuka – two kinds of seagulls.' 'The little blue kotuku was called kotuku-wai-tai,' said another informant. 'The white kotuku nested at Ourawera (Lake George at Colac Bay), Moeraki on the West Coast (in Westland), and elsewhere, and it could be caught by snares put on its nest. As it flew down the snare got round its neck. It used to be caught at the heronry at Oreti River' (near Wallacetown – eight miles from Invercargill).

Kamana – The crested grebe is a rare bird now although the Maoris say it was once common enough, particularly about Kaitangata and Waihola. It was caught with snares. The birds came alongside the banks for the night and the same snare, the kaha that caught ducks would catch the grebe. This bird, which used to figure on the Maori food list, was called kam-a-na, and the crest on its head was called koukou [probably after mode of dressing hair called by this name]. 'The male bird has the crest, the female very little if any,' said a well-informed Maori to the collector. 'It lives on little fish and is good at diving. There was another bird – the totokipio – which was also a great diver. It was small – about the size of a koreke (quail) – and lived on fish too. Both kinds were once plentiful.'

An early settler told the collector that he remembered the birds called 'divers' by the colonists. If fired at these birds could dive so fast that the shot did not hit them. The bird known to the Maori as the totokipio and to the settler as the diver is apparently the dabchick.

Kiwi – The oldest Maori interviewed said the kiwi was caught with kuri (dogs) as you could not find them otherwise. He had never heard of snaring them nor of waiting behind trees to club them. The birds were hunted in the daytime and the dogs would scent them out. The tokoeka is a kind of kiwi and could rip the dogs but these were trained to grab the birds from the back when they were powerless to do any damage with their kicking.

Kakapo – There was only one sort of this bird, said the previous informant, and it was often caught in the moonlight when it came out to eat. It lives on the bark of trees and on berries and when it begins to eat the harakeke (flax blade) it becomes poor and tastes of it – ugh! kaua (bitter). [Note: this word is usually rendered kawa – kava – but the old man pronounced it kau-a: cf. pawa and paua.] This poor condition is called maiki [the collector also has this name as maieki] and during it the bird is very quiet. The kakapo lives in rua (holes) made like umu (ovens) only deeper. The bird is only sought when it is fat as otherwise it is no good. It has a habit of jumping into its hole and shaking itself and the old people said it was trying to shake the fat out of itself and make itself maiki. This was what he had heard because he never saw them. The cock-bird has two or three hens and calls to them 'u' 'u' and they come into the rua and it is here they are caught. They cannot bite or kick and when the Maori located the hole he pulled the birds out and clubbed them. He had never heard the old people speak of the young birds so could not say about them.

Weka – The old man had never heard different names for the big yellow weka on the plains and the smaller dark weka of the bush. They were all just called weka. Koau – As far as the collector can gather koau seems to be the general name for shags in the South and one old man divided these birds into two divisions – koau-tai or sea shags and koau-mapua (freshwater shags living on the inland lakes). The young were eaten, he added. The principal informant said: 'The kahia is the white-bellied shag. It frequents rivers and Inch-Clutha used to be a great resort for them. The rori is a small sea shag of the black color. The male is smaller than the female and has a white breast. The koau-tai is the grey sea shag while the mapua is the big black shag which lives up-country. The kaha is also black but mostly lives on islands near the coast such as Okaihae (Green

Island near Dunedin) and has a crested head. The cock has a yellow stripe on its head but the other sex is plain. The female kaha also has a greyish breast. Of all the shags the only ones you can tell the cock from the hen at a glance are the rori and kaha.' Another old man said: 'Gull Rock on Stewart Island was called pohatu-koau (shag rock) by the Maori. We would go there at night and sneak up and knock the birds over with a patu (waddy). I remember we got one hundred shags one night. We cooked them in umu (ovens) or by kohiku method and ate the old as well as the young and they all tasted all right.'

Ducks – The black teal was called kukupako (one poua pronounced this gugupako); the little teal is patake; the grey duck is parera; the spoonbill duck is tataa; the blue mountain duck is whio; the paradise duck is putakitaki while the brown duck is hoho. An old woman took exception to a statement that the putakitaki was run down with canoes and hit on the head with sticks. It was true they were chased when moulting and she had assisted in driving them on shore at Manu-whaka-rau, at the North end of Lake Waihola. They were caught by good dogs as a rule. You could not hit them on the head with sticks as they buried their heads in the grass and rushes. When they were caught by hand their necks were wrung. She had never seen anyone killing these birds by biting the back of their necks. [This is the old manner of killing titi (muttonbirds).] The ducks were split open and were hung up in rows.

Penguins – The collector has hitherto never been able to gather any information about these birds but an ancient Maori came to the rescue. 'The tawaki is one kind of penguin – just the ordinary size – but I do not know its English name. Tokoraki is the King Penguin while the penu is a small kind with yellow eyebrows. The korora is the ordinary penguin and is much the same as the penu. These two kinds live in rua (holes) near the Muttonbird Islands and after the titi season was over the natives sometimes went and killed penguins. They were quite good to eat, in fact, when they were fat they tasted better than our present geese. The feathers would be burnt or scalded off and the birds roasted (kohiku) or put in the umu (tao).' One old man said that 'rock-hoppers' were called korora and the bigger penguins tawaki, but he did not think the Maoris knew the big penguin he had seen down at the Macquarie Islands.

Toroa – 'The toroa (albatross) was snared on some of the islands but I do not know how,' said one old man. 'I never heard of fish-gorges,' said the principal informant, 'but the toroa could be taken by swallowing a fish in which a stick had been placed and was then hauled in. You could not catch fish that way. When the people were out fishing the toroa would come round. A fish would have a stick or bone put in it and would then be tied to a line. The bird gulps the fish and is then pulled up to the canoe and clubbed. You could eat them, particularly the young ones. The feathers were used for pohe (ear ornaments) or were stitched on to mats where they looked very pretty.'

Seabirds – In the South the gannet was called tarawhakarara; the barracouta bird was tarapirohi while the ordinary gull was karoro. A dark kind of gull was called pohio while a bird of the sandpiper species was named kukuruwhitu. A bird like the torea or redbill was called powaka (or poaka), while a 'long-legged little bird, some grey and some black with a white belly and a long beak' which frequented the lakes was named rerewaka. Said the principal informant: 'We snared the karoro and the tarapuka (a small white gull) on the sand of the seashore. A hollow would be made and in it fishguts were placed as a bait. The snare was tied to a stone or a string could be laid to where a man was hidden. The birds were eaten. They were plucked cleaned and cooked at the fire on a kohiku stick or if a lot were caught they could be put in the umu.'

An intelligent Maori informed the collector that the black gull called pohio is merely a young karoro (seagull). Its plumage alters as it grows older. The bird known as the mollyhawk is called totoria according to one of my informants.

Small birds – The ground lark (pioioi) the collector was informed was snared and eaten but no particulars were available. One of the old men considered the native canary or whitehead was called riroriro but this is very doubtful. There is still a bird called mataa to be found in the swamps. It is about the size of a sparrow but with a longer tail and its call is 'koriti, koriti'. In another district the collector was told the mataa was a small bird like the sparrow but with feathers like the weka and that it had not been seen for years. It is probably the fernbird. The collector met no one who knew the southern Maori name for the ringeye. The northern name, Tauhou (meaning 'a stranger') was apparently not used. A small bird, the titiripounemu, is not now seen at Temuka and the Maoris there now call the ringeye (which they say is an imported bird) by this ancient name.

Kurupatu – What bird this is the collector cannot say. An old woman brought the name up as that of a bird she had not seen for many years. She said it did not fly off when disturbed but fluttered away through the re (swamp – synonymous with northern repo) in which it lived. It was about the size of a pigeon or guineafowl and dogs could catch it. An old man said he had heard the name when he was young. He understood the kurupatu was of the duck family. It was the color of a grey duck but as small as a little teal. My last informant had seen the kurupatu and described it as a small river bird, bigger than a pioioi, or lark, with a brown breast and for the rest coloured like the lark. It had not been seen by the Maoris in Murihiku for many years. [Note: It is probably one of the New Zealand rails that is meant. H.B.]

Koparapara – The bellbird is still to be found in the South and a Maori on Ruapuke Island killed three or four dozen the other day very simply. He built a pae on two posts and obscuring himself under branches called the birds by blowing on a leaf held between his lips. It is said any leaf will do to call the koparapara. When a certain number of birds were on the perch he swept it with a stick, killing or incapacitating the occupants. Another man told me of securing kakas this way (see next paragraph). Although the bellbird is called koparapara in Murihiku the collector was told it was also called makomako in Canterbury.

Kaka – This edible brown parrot is almost extinct in the South. The simplest and not least effective method of killing this bird was called patu kaka (strike kaka). Make a longish perch and have a stick (rakau patu kaka) ready to sweep it. Hide in the greenery underneath and call the birds. For this purpose a birdcall made of wood is said to have been used. When the birds congregated the perch was swept and the ones not killed were usually injured sufficiently to catch. My informant had seen good bags made in this way. Native Thrush – Some of the old men recalled the fact that they had heard the beautiful notes of this songster round in the Fiords but they could not recollect its Maori name. The name was certainly not piopio although this is the Maori name of Milford Sound. At last the collector met an aged man who was familiar with the bird and he said its old name in Murihiku was korowhio. [Tregear gives koropio and korohea as thrush names.]

Tomtit – This familiar little black-and-white bird was called miromiro, the general name throughout New Zealand, but none of my informants had heard the pleasant tradition mentioned by Tregear that formerly this bird was supposed to carry messages between lovers.

Moa – The moa has been extinct so long that my informants could say little about it. One had heard that a big range between Lakes Wanaka and Wakatipu was a favourite resort of these gigantic birds for it was very gravelly and, he gravely added, the moas liked this place for they lived on gravel. One solitary representative of the moas lived behind a waterfall in the Takitimu Range until about fifty years ago and some people saw it and ran away. Finally the big birds were lost from the land for they were killed out by karakia or incantations. The best of his informants said the moa was a bird of the very ancient times and very little was known about it except the proverbial statement that the kokomuka (the Murihiku name for the koromiko) was the timber to cook it. He had never heard any stories nor legends about the moa but he had heard mention of a big bird called the pouakai. It would carry away children or anyone it was capable of catching and holding. It was perhaps like an eagle. One was said to have been caught and killed on a hill near Clinton and it took four or five strong men to kill that big bird. That was all he knew of the great birds of old which once inhabited this land.

Karae – The Rainbird, a kind of petrel with a very harsh screech before rain, was called karae. Kaikorai at Dunedin should be written Kaikarae and must be added to the extensive list of Maori place-names in Otago which perpetuate the names of birds.

THE HAWKS

The common hawk or harrier was called kahu and my first informant said it was not caught or killed by the Maori as it was not eaten. This information has to be discounted, however, for my subsequent informants all agreed that the hawk had been sometimes eaten. One old man said the hawk was sometimes caught in snares and the people would eat it if very hungry. The prejudice against it was because it would eat men if it found dead bodies. He had never known nor heard of anyone eating the karearea or bush hawk, however. A well-informed old man said he had personally known some of the old generation to eat young hawks from the nest if they were plump and in good condition. Some of the hardier spirits would also eat hawks of any age but he would not do so himself. When he was a young man on eeling expeditions he would raid one or two hawk's nests built in the swamps handy to the streams and would use the nestling hawks as eel-bobs. The karearea, which he considered was called the sparrowhawk by the white man, he continued, was too swift to catch and he had never heard of them being snared. When he was with a Maori party which cruised round the Fiords in 1874 he saw a karearea at Piopiotahi (Milford Sound) soar up in the air and come down on a kereru (pigeon) and strike it into the water. His party picked up the pigeon still living and cheated the karearea of its prey. At a later date at Waikoula (Waicola, Southland) he saw a karearea chase a piopio (native lark) into a house that was being built. The piopio swerved to the floor and escaped while its pursuer tried to fly out a window but was so confused that the carpenters killed it.

An ancient place-name near Clinton is Awa-kaeaea (Sparrowhawk Stream) so that we know that kaeaea must have been an olden name for either the bush or sparrow-hawk, but my informants could not settle the identity of these two birds. (Note: The bird formerly called Bush Hawk is now more commonly called Quail Hawk.)

THE OWLS

The collector made diligent inquiry among the older Maoris as to whether there was any bird of fair size that they would not eat and thought he would find the owl family exempt but this was not so for one of his informants had eaten, and enjoyed the 'big morepork that lives among the rocks', while evidence was tendered that showed that daredevil Maoris would eat the ordinary morepork of the bush. This latter bird was called ruru and its hoot was known as koukou and there is a place near Colac Bay called Rurukoukou (the hoot of the owl). The 'big morepork' or open country owl was known as ruru-whenua in Murihiku, and also, but more rarely, as whekau. It lived mostly in the limestone cliffs of the inland country and had a terrible screechy laugh.

The morepork was also called piopio said one of my informants. He had never heard of the New Zealand thrush but he was positive he had heard the old Maoris call the owl piopio. Another man said the name was peopeo [Tregear says peho]. The bird was sometimes called this name from one of its cries. It would call 'peo peo, ko-u, ko-u' over and over again at certain times to the consternation of the superstitious.

Many stories are told of the uncanny nature of the ruru but one will suffice here. About seventy years ago a Maori ate part of the crop of a morepork which he had killed at Molyneux. The bird had been plucked and was opened and roasting by the fire when it suddenly flew off. After that sensational occurrence none of the Maoris in the district would kill a morepork purposely and if they accidentally killed one they would not touch it.

An old woman in the presence of the collector reproved some young muttonbirders for scoffing at the supernatural element in the stories current about the owl. 'Some moreporks are devils' she cried, 'they have he atua (an evil spirit) and you can hear some of them talk just like a man.' She gave some illustrations to clinch her contention and concluded by saying she had not heard of owls speaking to people in recent years but she was quite convinced and sure that they did so in some striking instances in years gone by.

THE KOREKE (QUAIL)

The quail has been extinct many years – a regrettable thing. A query from the North Island as to how the South Island Maori caught the bird drew the collector's attention to this phase of the subject. A European who lived among Maoris for years and who gave valuable information about what he had seen of Native methods of snaring, etc. said he had not seen them catch the koreke but he had been told that they laid bait on bare patch and sat to one side in flax or fern with a long rod. When the birds were feeding the man would bring the stick round with a circular sweep disabling or killing from twelve to twenty birds perhaps. He had heard that the koreke was a very tame bird and that when it was intent on feeding it took little notice of man. Not one of a dozen Maoris interrogated had heard of this method. They did not deny it was possible – they simply had not heard of it. Snaring was easier, surer and simpler. The bird made tracks through the grass, said the first man questioned, and snares were placed on these paths. Put up poupou (upright sticks) and tie grass round them as camouflage and then tie a flax line across and from this line suspend a number of slip nooses the height of the bird's head. The bird would walk under one or other of these, the noose would tighten on its neck as it stepped forward and there you were. A snare like this was called a kaha, the noose being known as mahaka.

An old woman added the further information that the birds came in the evening along the tracks they had made and walked into the kaha. The kaha was the name of the whole snare, sticks and all, but the noose itself was named koromahaka. The yarn about killing them with a stick was 'he korero palau' (a false story) as far as her district was concerned because the birds were far too wary, to be secured with such a simple device. An old man said that in some kaha a long stick acted as the cross-piece and from this perhaps a dozen mahaka (running loops) would be hung. Wild ducks could be caught in a similar way on riverbanks when they came ashore.

An aged woman said she knew little of the bird but remembered that when she was a girl she had found one of their nests and that in it were twelve spotted eggs. An old man said he never heard of koreke being killed with a stick – in fact the only bird he knew that was killed in this manner was the kaka, but another kaumatua related that the koparapara (bellbird) was also killed with a stick and possibly others might be too. One old man was inclined to think he had heard of killing koreke with sticks but his neighbor was emphatic that such a thing was beyond his experience or knowledge. The latter, however, added that dogs could catch the birds. An early settler with a large acquaintance with quails that had passed from a living state by means of guns, stones or dogs said that in the dozens he cleaned for the table he never found anything inside them but beetles and insects. This pioneer was a remarkably straight shot with stones and bowled over a number of quail this way.

Asked about what food the quail ate the Maoris all expressed ignorance except one ancient man who said he did not know the birds ate beetles but he knew they ate patotara berries, takapo berries, tapuku (snowberries) and vegetation. The knowledge about the quail is getting dim and remote for it is about fiftyfive years since the bird vanished.

A settler says the birds had a peculiar cry which they gave repeatedly about dusk and the colonists translated this sound as 'pretty quick', as far as memory goes.

An old Maori told the collector that he had heard that the koreke was still existent in the valleys north of Lake Wakatipu, but he added that this was on the testimony of a runholder as he personally had not seen the bird for many years.

MUSEUM SPECIMENS

Looking at the birds in the Otago Museum an old Maori named them as follows:
Black Backed Gull (*Larus dominicanus*) = karoro
Skua (*Megalestris antarctic*) = pohio
Dusky Plover (*Ochthodromus obscurus*) = totoripa
Pied Stilt (*Himantopus picatus*) = rerewaka
Godwit (*Limosa novae zealandiae*) = powaka
Shag (*Phalacrocorax chalconotus*) = kaha
Shag (*Phalacrocorax punctatus*) = koau tai
Shag (*Phalacrocorax brevirostris*) = rori
Shag (*Phalacrocorax carunculatus*) = kahia
Shag (*Phalacrocorax chaleconotus*) = mapua
Marsh Rail (*Porzana affinis*) = toitoi

(?) Caspian Tern (*Hydroprogne caspia*) = tara whaka rara
Whitefront Tern (*Sterna frontalis*) = tara pirohe
Black Bill Gull (*Larus bulleri*) = tara puka
Shoveller Duck = hoho
Big Kiwis = tokoweka
Small penguins = korora
Big penguins = tawaki
Sparrowhawk = karearea
Bush hawk = pouakai
Tomtit = miromiro
Robin = kakaruai
Rifleman = Titiripounamu
Yellowhead or Canary = tatariki
Kingfisher = kotare
Lark = pioioi
Bellbirds = koparapara
Grey warbler = riroriro
Fernbird = toitoi
Bush wren = hino (?).

He did not know the name of the New Zealand Creeper, nor of the Ringeye. The latter he did not know, but said it looked more like an English bird than a native one. Some people said the titiripounamu was the mother of the shining cuckoo (pipiwharauroa) (i.e. nested its eggs) but he did not believe it. The fantails were called pitakataka and he considered that the pied ones were females. He had seen two black ones together and two pied ones together also, but nevertheless he was sure the latter were female birds. When a boy he used to chase the toitoi (fernbird) until it tired, when it could be caught and eaten. It only flew a few yards at a time and when tired took refuge in the grass.

The bird called a merganser in the Museum he thought was the miuweka of the Titi Islands as it looked very similar. Unlike the more familiar weka it can fly a little.

The huruhuru-ma (white feathers) on the breast of the koko (tui) is its tohu (sign) but he had never heard any stories regarding this tohu. The white woodhens in the Museum are korako (albinos) and the olden Maori used to call them Ariki ko ka manu (the highest-born among the birds), but he had heard no stories nor superstitions about such abnormal birds. Similarly, the old man said, three reddish-and-whitish kakas in the Museum were 'te ariki o ka kaka'.

The laughing owl in the Museum was the ruru-whenua which he had known, and eaten, in days gone by. He fancied it was also called whekau. He did not know the Stitch Bird nor the Stephen Island wren (which he thought must be an English bird) but he recognised the takahea (*Notornis*) and koreke (quail) at once. Such was the information the collector garnered from the aged man of over eighty, and it is possible his identification of the specimens in the Museum is at fault in one or two instances after the lapse of so many years since he saw the corresponding living representatives of the various species. The Maori name of the New Zealand Creeper is usually given as toitoi but he could not place this bird at all and unhesitatingly applied the name toitoi as that of the fernbird and said it was also possibly one of the names of the marsh rail. He had not seen a bush wren for many years and thought it was called hino [Tregear gives heno]. The godwit which is called kuaka in the North Island is in Murihiku called powaka or pouaka, the name kuaka being reserved for a species of muttonbird. A most interesting point is that the old man straightway gave the name of the fierce-looking bush (or quail) hawk as pouakai (glutton) a name usually associated with the bird of prey of ancient tradition.

BIRD-CATCHING

The pakura (or swampturkey), said an ancient Maori, was caught with kuri (dogs) because its beak (kutu) was so strong and sharp that it would cut or bite through the strands of the snare. When moulting this bird could be patu'd (clubbed) like putakitaki (paradise ducks). The matuku (bittern) had a long beak but it was not strong like that of the pakura and hence it could be caught by the kaha-waewae (feet snare). The kotuku (white heron) could also be caught with a kaha-waewae. The snares of this description were placed on the ara (or paths) of the birds, some half-dozen snares or so at intervals. It was raised some inches off the ground and when the bird stepped in and kicked it in any way the cords closed on its legs. The kaha (snare) to catch parera (wild ducks) was often three or four chains long and was suspended over a river at about the height a bird's head would take the noose. The korora (little penguin) and tawake (big penguin) bred in Sandy Bay, Nuggets, and they could be caught in rua (holes) like titi (muttonbirds) were. The Maoris annually gathered so many of them. An island in Foveaux Straits was called Hoputoroa (to seize albatrosses) but my informant could not say how it came to be known by this title. An old white man married to a Maori woman and who had resided over fifty years with the Natives told the collector that forty years ago he had seen the Maoris catch as many as two hundred kakas in quick time. As the birds were left alive until snaring finished (for that time) there was a tremendous din. He forgot the Maori name of the Crested Grebe but he knew that these birds were caught down at Tokanui, but he could not describe the exact method. There was a clump of ti (cabbagetrees) near the Maori Reserve at Tuturau and at certain seasons of the year the pigeons just swarmed in throngs in the ti tops and as they were within easy reach of even short spears, great numbers were speared.

The collector has a note that about fifty years ago a novel contest took place near Riverton. A Pakeha boasted that he could account for more kakas with his gun in a stipulated time than any Maori would with his own methods. The challenge was taken up and the white man proceeded to the bush with a big supply of ammunition while the Maori got to work with his call-bird or decoy and his snare (called tuke or tuki). The time allowed was about two hours and the European shot about a hundred birds, but he was easily beaten by his brown rival who had secured over one hundred and fifty in the same time.

Mr H.W. Bishop, the S.M., states that he has known two hundred and fifty kakas to be caught in about an hour in the Nelson district, but probably several fowlers were at work to achieve this result.

BIRD SPEARS

Asking the old men after bird spears the collector was considerably astonished that not one of his informants had heard of bird spears being made in one straight piece but they all seemed to know the spear made in detachments like a chimney-sweep's outfit. They said the bush was too tangled to trail a long spear through so they went forth with a bundle of pukaikai under their arm. These pukaikai were usually made of mako wood cut into lengths. Take each length and extract the soft pith (kaikai) so far down at one end and sharpen the other, so that the various lengths can be fitted into each other.

Beside these pukaikai there is a length of manuka about ten or twelve feet long and at its end is a tara of bone with two or three barbs (kaniwha). This manuka wand has had its bark removed and has been hardened in the fire and like the bone point is called tara, and from this fact the whole spear is sometimes called tara as well as pukaikai.

When he went 'tara wero kereru' (spearing pigeon) the huntsman marked his bird and if the tara was not long enough he added a pukaikai and if that was not enough length he added another pukaikai and so on. The whole spear could be run up or taken to pieces in a few seconds. If any of the pukaikai ends were too loose they were bound with flax. The bone point had two or three notches so that it could be securely lashed to the manuka tara. The experienced man struck the bird between the legs where there is a 'sort of navel' called putaiti and if this was hit the bird expired with one flap. It was seldom that a bone point was broken. None of the old men had ever seen or heard of a string being attached in any way to any bird spear. One old man said the point of the tara was called mata.

Several of my informants had used a tara-kereru (pigeon spear) of the pukaikai kind, and one said that he had seen within recent years a pukaikai at Purakanui, near Dunedin, but he considered it was hardly likely to be in evidence yet as such things were usually destroyed when the owner died.

Add to Bird Catching

A white settler told the collector that in Southland in 1868 the kakas and pigeons were numerous and he saw the Native skill in securing them. The birds were just then keeping low in the goai bushes and an old Maori told him not to waste powder and shot on them. He affixed a piece of wire to a long stick and 'stuck' the kakas in great style. Then he made a running noose on a long stick which he put up behind the pigeons, carefully letting the noose drop over their heads and he soon had a big bag. The same Maori caught numerous woodhens by the familiar 'red rag' principle.

'To catch kakas,' said an old Temuka lady, 'in the old days at Arowhenua you could build a "kaka house" with four posts or you could select a forked tree, one with two or more branches (e rua tuke = two branches) and build a pourakaraka or "maimai" on a stage under them. The snares (koro-mahaka or karu-mahaka) are spread on the branches. The birds cannot see the men hiding on the stage and holding the strings of the karu-mahaka. The men, not using anything in the mouth, call "ke, ke", in imitation of the bird's cry and the first manu (bird) caught is used as a whakakeke or caller. If the birds are plentiful the men pull all the strings at once. When the birds are caught and tied together the bunch is called tahuikaka. Other men will go into the bush (kei te tahere manu i roto i te kaherehere) to catch birds and by calling them bring them low when they are caught in the pihere – a noose on a stick. Yes! Kai te tahere manu was good sport. Calling a bird with a piece of grass in the mouth was whakapipi. On the Titi Islands upoko-takata and tataaki grass were used to call weka. To call weka with a rolled (takai) piece of flax in the mouth is turutu. The only meaning of whakakeokeo I know is 'tickling'. In catching weka the stick with the red feather tied to it is paruru and the longer one with the noose is pihere, while the whakapipi is in your mouth.' The collector was told that a Waitaki Maori had made a birdcall (of korari) recently but the name of such calls seems to be forgotten. At Puketiraki it was said: 'Pihere is another name for the koro-mahaka. It can be made for koko (tuis), ducks, and other birds. At Pu-o-te-ra, near Omimi, there is a pool which was once a fine place for snaring tuis.' (It is said that pigeons have become so fat that when shot the fall to the ground bursts them, so the Maoris say). One kaumatua said: 'Tuke is the name of the snare for the legs of kakas. Tuki is the last stick on a pukaikai. It is longer, thicker and heavier than the others to give a better grasp for the hand. The word tuki (or tukia) means "to strike up".'

The collector was told that the word 'mu' meant the note of any bird – it was a general term for all sounds made by birds. The Maori was very skilful at imitating the various bird cries and often used leaves in his mouth to aid him in getting the required sound. Calling the weka or woodhen was known as whakakeokeo and the leaf used was a blade of kakaha grass doubled. The kakaha was described as a coarse grass which bore red berries which had leaves of a flaxy nature. A caller who knew his business could bring numerous woodhens around and it was a comparatively simple matter to snare them with the familiar noose looped on a stick five or six feet long. A shorter stick bore the wing of a bird or a bright object and this was enticingly waved before the inquisitive and pugnacious weka with a result that to get at it he put his head through the noose and was caught. From time immemorial the coastal Maoris made a habit of going inland after the weka in June and July when the birds were at their prime. The Maoris from Otago Peninsula and Henley went up the Strath-Taieri to the Maniatoto Plains and Central Otago. These annual expeditions were discontinued about fifty years ago but some of my informants had taken part in them in the days of their youth. The camp-shelters were made of patiti (tussock) and taru (grass) woven on sticks and were of a temporary nature merely designed to keep off the rain and wind. The weka was caught in great numbers as it simply teemed on the inland plains until grass fires, settlers and dogs almost exterminated them.

Another bird which furnished many a succulent meal to the ancient Maori was the tui, usually known as the koko in Murihiku. The traditional name for the spots where these birds were snared by nets set round pools of water used by the birds as drinking-places is wai-tahere-koko.

A place that was resorted to for snaring birds (or for catching fish) was called rauiri. The word seems to have the same significance as the description 'a game reserve'.

Add Birds Bird-Catching Extraordinary

Two old men told the collector of some unusual ways of getting birds to eat – quite outside the customary snaring and spearing. The easiest way to catch the tui was to cover its drinking place with piripiri (bidibidi). The bird rashly dives into this and gets its wings covered and cannot fly. The kaka and kereru are too strong to be caught this way and the kaka is too cunning as it will push the piripiri to one side before drinking but the koko (tui) simply dives right into the mass of clinging burrs. Then again in the winter-time go into the bush and see where the tuis sleep. They are very momona (fat) and sleepy. In the early morning go and light a fire where it will light up the vicinity sufficient to see by, and then shake the tree where the tuis are clustered. This sport is called ruiruia – ru = one shake but ruirui means several. The birds tumble out of the roost and fall to the ground. They won't fly and are easily secured being killed by a nip (with the teeth) on the head. My informants said they had known dozens of birds being got in this manner. In winters when the berries were very plentiful the kakas and kererus would gorge themselves until they could scarcely fly. When in this condition the Maori would go into the bush with a suitable patii or stick and kill the birds which were within reach. The kakas were easily hit as they tried to run up the trees using their claws and good bags were made. My informants had never heard any name for this method of slaughter but said it could only be done in special seasons. In cold winters when the birds were numb with cold they were often easily secured also. [Note by collector: Numerous notes about birds and descriptions of many methods of catching will be found in the Kaiapoi information.]

BIRD LIFE ON THE TITI ISLANDS

The Titi Islands lie round the coasts of Stewart Island and in the muttonbird season are visited by the Maori and halfcaste families whom the law recognises as owners. Some of these muttonbirders informed the collector that over on these islands are to be found birds not now to be seen on the mainland – birds such as the koka (native crow) and tieke (saddleback). They gave the following description of the birds they had met with on their muttonbirding excursions:

Miuweka is the name of a bird about half the size of a weka. It cannot really fly but hops about, and in colour is whakaporoporo (speckled). On some islands the Stewart Island weka has been introduced to keep down the spiders, leeches and rats but they have started killing the defenceless miuweka and there is a danger that the latter bird will become extinct on those islands. One of my informants said the miuweka was about the size of a tui and although it was the same general build as a weka it was not the same colour.

Bush snipe, a rare bird, is still to be found on Pukeokaoka Island but my informants did not know its Maori name. It flies only a few feet at a time, is much smaller than the miuweka and is more reddish in colour. Kakariki (parrokeets) are still fairly plentiful on the Titi Islands and the collector saw some pet ones that had been brought to the Bluff. The Maoris say the red-topped ones live longer than the other varieties. The koka (crow) is famous for its wattles and the Maori called these wiri-o-te-koka or were-o-te-koka. Kuruti is a little green bird – not the ringeye – which my informants had only seen on the Titi Islands.

Tutukiwi is a small flightless bird about the size of a well-developed chicken and with a long beak like a kiwi. On some of the islands is a bird called the 'tataki thrush' but whose olden Maori name the collector could not ascertain. It is a native bird, is of a brownish colour and about the size of an English thrush. It is something like a lark but has a few black feathers and it is also somewhat similar to the toitoi or fernbird of the mainland although it is not that bird. It lives on seeds and flies from tuft to tuft of the tataki grass, hence its modern name.

The kuaka is a small bird with a beak like the titi. Its nest is never found but it frequents the islands during the season, leaving when the titi does. The parara builds in holes in the rocks, not in the earth like the titi. They are caught by the aid of torchlight at night and parara stew is good. They are not caught in any quantity, however. The cry of the bird is parikoko and this name is also applied to it.

MUTTON-BIRDING

Last year (1919) the mutton-birders had not sufficient poha (kelp-bags) to hold all the titi (mutton-birds) they killed so this season (1920) they took time by the forelock and for months before the opening of the season (April 1 usually) scoured the coasts for suitable rimu (kelp). For weeks before the season you can pick out the Maori residences at the southern ports by the line of kelp bladders in the yard. These bladders blown up are called poha-hau and the place where each is tied up is te kutu (the lip). They are tied on to a round piece of wood called a tiwha which forms a plug like the cork of a bottle. If the bag bursts at one spot it may be repaired by another tiwha being inserted in the hole and the kelp being tied on to it. The poha was blown up by means of a pupuhi-rimu, a hollow tube which was inserted into the orifice alongside the tiwha. Some of the younger Maoris call this tube a koko, a word that may perhaps be compared to northern ngongo – to suck through a tube. A venerable Maori narrated: 'The pupuhi is often made of patete from which the pith (kaikai) has been taken by a small straight piece of manuka hardened in the fire. This was called a koko and pushing the pith out was koko kia puta. Since the pakeha came wire is used and the blowpipes are made longer. If one got tired blowing (puia te poha) and wanted a hokihoki (rest) he put his tongue against the hole. When the poha is filled put the tongue against the pipe and pull the poha off keeping tight hold and tie (here na kia mau) it tightly with harakeke, not whitau. This is the way people did of old.' Yes! but times advance. A modern mutton-birder said scornfully: 'Fancy a consumptive or asthmatical Native blowing through a koko into a poha! My party use a bike pump, and common bellows do quite well.'

The immemorial covering for the poha when it is full of preserved titi is kiri-totara (totara bark) but the Natives have had difficulty in getting it of recent years. It is said that Papatotara over the Waiau River was named because the Maori went there to get bark for the poha-titi. Of recent years the Maori has got his bark from the sawmills giving titi in exchange but even this supply is deficient so on some of the islands toi and raupo is being used as a substitute.

For weeks before the titi season the birds can be seen in countless multitudes round the coasts following the marakuha (sprats), sardines (koroama), makaa (barracouta) or any fish that goes about in shoals (poke). When the young birds (pi-titi) are in the rua (holes) the old birds feed them well to a certain day and then the latter disappear simultaneously. Where do they go? was the question asked the collector. They do not go to Tasmania, says the modern birder, for the muttonbirds there are of a different species. This is a question which has long puzzled the Southern Maori.

The hakuai is another mystery of the titi islands. At night this great bird shrieks 'hakuai' loudly three times in succession and then there follows a whirring noise like a hawser chain running out. A young Maori told the collector that the old people with whom he had been on the islands declared that the bird had two knots in its neck and a chain on its leg. An intelligent man said that no one had ever seen the hakuai and that the Government had offered one thousand pounds for one. Another man stated that on the nights when the bird came it repeated its performance seven times and then ceased for that night. The cry has never been heard in daytime so it must be a big night-bird.

The old custom of killing the mutton-birds was by biting the back of the neck and an old woman said this was to prevent the titi putting oil out of its mouth and soiling its feathers which could not then be cleaned. This information is doubtful because it is said the bird always ejects oil and the up-to-date Maori holds a basin to catch the oil which he makes the bird vomit before killing it with a stick. If this oil touches the feathers these cannot be plucked and the bird is spoilt. The feathers are used for pillows and the oil is splendid for harness, etc. Thus does the modern Maori utilise the by-products.

The cry of the young is 'kuaka, kuaka'. At the end of the season they are caught at night by torchlight but millions escape. 'How would wire-netting the islands do?' semi-jocularly asked a commercially-minded muttonbirder. In the old days it was a food undertaking – now it is a business enterprise. A well-informed kaumatua told the collector that in pre-European days the Maori did not go round to the southern and western islands for titi but just to the ones east of Stewart Island. It was only since the pakeha came, he said, that the industry had reached anything like its present dimensions.

A further note runs: 'The titi wahine (?titi-wainui) a species of mutton-bird makes a screeching cry at night, especially stormy nights.'

Mutton-birding is downright hard work and dirty greasy work at that. A Southland representative footballer says a night's torching is far more arduous than ninety minutes of strenuous football.

Add to Mutton-birds

At Moeraki the collector was given some tiwha made of wood that were left over when the muttonbirders departed and also a round stone suitable for the same purpose and these are now in the Otago Museum. Kakihi shells are also used for the same purpose. In repairing a hole in the poha (bag of dried kelp) the tiwha is put on from the inside and the kelp is tied behind it. In putting on a shell its open side is facing outwards as it makes a neater and surer job. At Moeraki there is a small titi (muttonbird) manu (preserve) on the little island of Maukiakia. From its steep sides ninety eight muttonbirds were taken this year (1920). Last year was a very bad season from the local standpoint as no birds were captured at all. The record number taken off this picturesque little isle is stated to have been one hundred and twenty one and while this is very small compared with the many thousands got at the titi-manu round Rakiura (Stewart Island) it is a very welcome addition to the Moerakian larders.

One old man in mentioning the kaheru (one form of Native spade – the ko has a step for the foot, the kaheru is a sharpened stick as far as the collector can ascertain) said he had seen one used to dig fernroot. It was a sharpened goai (kohai) stick, the one he saw. He added that these kaheru were still used over at the Titi Islands to dig out the muttonbirds when the burrows (ruas) fell in. He also added that wooden ipu (basins) were still in use at the Titi Islands. These had a spout (ko kutu) for the purpose of pouring the titi oil into the pohas for the preservation of the contents. The kaheru and the ipu were so used generations ago and are still in use on certain of the islands unless they have been recently superseded.

When counting muttonbirds, potatoes, etc., the addition of the word 'pu' doubles the number quoted at tahi-pu = two; rua-pu = four, and so on.

The present-day Maoris call a white muttonbird a 'jimmy-bird' but the collector could get no reason for this name, although his informants admitted it was given through a lingering superstitious dread of directly naming a thing of ill-omen.

Add to Muttonbirding

Some months before the titi (muttonbird) season the Southern Maori made and makes preparations for this annual harvest. About December or January they cut the rimu (kelp). The olden Maoris would take nothing but good-shaped kelp but now with the vast extension of the industry any kelp is taken so long as it can be utilised. It is said four or five pohas (bags) can be got from a good length of bull kelp. The kelp on the coast from Riverton Westward is harder than that round Bluff and some Natives esteem it better, but my Bluff informants prefer their own product as they say it is more elastic, softer and more pliable than the

The three wooden tiwha given to Beattie at Moeraki. Tūhura Otago Museum Collection, D20.215, D20.216, D20.217.

former kind. The kelp is koko'd (opened) by pushing the hand through carefully and care is taken not to push in too near the edges, but a fair margin is left to avoid any tendency for edges to split when drying. The sun and wind also koko the bag. Pupuhi (blow it up) when green and hang it up in the wind and sun (but not in the rain). It can be blown up with the mouth alone or with a pupuhi pipe (see Museum exhibits), a flax loop being round the poha mouth ready to tighten when blowing ceases. The tighter it is blown the better for the poha. It usually takes two to three days to dry but can be dried in one day in auspicious circumstances. It is then hung up inside for a day and then deflated to whakahau (soften) it. A wet muggy day might do this through the moisture in the air but it is usually laid on the grass (tarutaru) and covered with grass to take the hardness out. Water must not be let on it when hard and dry or it would be ruined. When the bag is pliable the edges are trimmed and the bag rolled up for future use. In olden days the bags were put in earth (tapuke = covered with earth) to soften them and the bag was worked till like 'elastic velvet' as one man termed it (and they do get velvety to the touch when well done). The mouths were stretched and the birds rammed in then, but now if the mouth is tight it is cut wider while the bags are often soaked in hot water to let the operators fill them quicker. The bag presented to the collector for the Museum is an excellent quality of kelp and was made from kelp got at or near Te Wai point, Bluff. It is a small poha for eighteen to twenty birds but bags are made to hold up to one hundred and ten birds although forty or fifty is the average size. The timu or stump of kelp where it grows from the rock is called more. In the poha the hard 'cord' of kelp where there is no fringe is called taha-rakau (wooden edge) and young searchers were enjoined to look for pieces with this edge.

So much for the bags – now for the contents. 'First catch your hare.' The titi lays its egg in a rua (burrow) in the earth and when the egg hatches the young bird is fed until it gets very fat and it is then game for the Maori birder. 'Ko tae mai te hakui ki te whakai a tana pi', is said of the mother bird feeding the young one but my informants thought both male and female sat on the nest and fed the young, but were not sure. These ruas may be in bush, in dense patches of vines, in among tussocks or on bare spots and it is hard work locating some of them, the best results being got by the headman of each party allotting the same ground to definite individuals year after year until they know every nook and cranny of it. A new person on that patch will not get so many birds or nearly so quickly as one familiar with it. The Maoris used to start away on April 1 but now go over about the twentieth of March, returning to civilisation about the first week in June.

The birder starts out early in the morning. Each hole he comes to (in his section) he kneels down and inserts his arm. If he can reach the bird well and good and his experienced hand angles round to get a hold where the sharp beak cannot peck him or the sharp toes scratch him. The best hold is to seize the beak and

The pōhā (bag) made from kelp got at or near Te Wai Point, Bluff. It now has the appearance of grey velvet. Tūhura Otago Museum Collection, D21.238.

haul. In the old days as the head emerged and while yet the body and legs were in the rua (hole) the bird hunter bent down and bit the crown of the head to kill the bird. (Now the sophisticated half-caste uses a waddy.) The bird is then pulled out and held head down and gently squeezed (name forgotten – not pehia which also means to press) to let the ruaruakakata (contents of stomach – mostly oil) run out. Great care is taken not to let this oil on any of the birds as they then could not be plucked and would have to be thrown away. As each bird is taken killed and squeezed it is laid down but not in a heap for fear of the oil contaminating one another. If the hole is too long for the birder's arm he puts in a stick (called koko – cf. kokomo a North Island word = to thrust in; to put in) and if there is down on its point he knows the bird is at home. Estimating the distance in from the mouth of the rua the birder begins to whakapoka (dig a hole) to reach the bird. He used (in old times and a few are still extant) a kaheru (a digging implement of wood) said to be short for this work: two feet long or so, half of this being handle and half blade. The handle is round and the blade flat and of an oval-shape. He goes down through the earth and reaches the bird. In rare cases a man has had to whakapoka twice to strike the end of a long tunnel (rua). After taking the bird out he plugs up the whakapoka hole (whakapurutia te rua) and next year all he need do is to go and lift the plug (puru) and there is his bird beneath him. Sometimes when the koko (stick) reaches a bird it is twirled (kowhiri) round and round and entangles in the bird's down and the bird (pi-titi) is then pulled out but the collector is not satisfied but that this is a modern innovation. The bird is covered with a white down called hukahuka in the early part of season but later soft feathers appear.

In the old days the birds underwent titi-tahu. Wooden basins (known variously as opu, upu or ipu) were used and heated stones put in with the birds already in them. The birds so cooked were then put in pohas (kelp bags) and fat was poured in, the top of the bag tied to exclude air and there was your titi-poha. It was left till cold and then totara bark was tied round to protect the kelp. A flax basket (konae) is placed on the ground and the poha with the upright strips of totara round it is placed in it and then the bands are tied round (ta te poha). The basket so attached to the foot of the bag is called a papa-poha. It is said that in the old days the birds were tahu'd in their down (hukahuka) without cleaning but now they are plucked and cleaned. A certain number are still cooked in fat for Maori consumption but of those for pakeha delectation most are now simply salted and put in pohas. This is modern for the old Maoris never used salt.

The couple to whom the collector is indebted for the foregoing particulars had only once seen a white titi. It is an omen of disaster but they forgot the old Maori name for it.

An old man said the old Maori name of Long Island was Te Kanawera and then he named eighteen manu or birding-grounds on it. An old name for these preserves was rahui but they are generally called manu (bird) now. Almost all these manu are named after tipunas (ancestors). Evening Island is called Poutama and like Long Island is divided into various reserves.

A Kaiapoi native who has gone muttonbirding since 1909 says this year (1920) is the best he has experienced. All accounts agree this is an excellent season. A Southland native says her party of five got about ten thousand birds and her cheque (for about three months' work) was eighty four pound equalling one pound a day. It is rough, arduous, and dirty work. None of her party got a pure white bird but a black and white one was caught. The white titi (an atua or 'jimmy-bird') was an evil omen. Catching birds by day was nao nao (cf. northern 'nanao' – to pull out from a hole) and at night it is rama. [This name was also given me as nanahu or nanao. Nanao is correct. H.B.] A person could take eighty to one hundred and fifty birds per day and two torching at night might get two hundred or more. The birds caught in the early part of the season are more oily than later. Very little Maori, she said, was now spoken on the Titi Islands. On the island she went to no old-fashioned things were preserved but they used European things.

The collector could find no one who knew any traditions how the use of kelp bags was discovered or by whom. From a roomful of aged and middle-aged people he heard this: The titi is handled sixteen times from its catching to its placing in the poha. At one stage it is hung on a gallows formed by crossing two sticks with a cross stick and other sticks can be lashed down the four legs if desired to have more 'hanging' lines. This is called a tirewa (or sometimes indifferently tirea or tiroa). If the birds are boned this is called ohori. While the titi are suspended on the gallows the kakariki (parrokeets) come and if they get a chance eat into the breast of the titi. Some of the islands still have rough huts of round shape on them and some still use wooden ipu with spouts (kokutu) on them. One of these ipu was described as standing on four legs (peke-karara). Kaheru are still in use on Papatea (Green Island) and one of these is promised to the Museum but the old dames who owned the ipus would not part with them as they are valued for associations with departed relatives. It is said a takoko or scoop is used on one island to poke up the fire and shovel away ashes but the collector could get no further particulars *re* it. This year one party got a bird out of a rua which was regarded as a freak. Nature had plucked it – it had no down and it was let go, ostensibly because it was too small.

Regarding the Hakuai (the famed bird of the Titi Islands), one intelligent man said he fancied the hakuai was a kind of titi. He had read somewhere it was a small bird of great speed. It was only at the end of the season it was heard rushing about in the air and always at night.

Asking the roomful of returned birders about the hakuai it was said it was heard this year as usual. The old people said it had eight joints (pona) but some said six. The grandmother of one ancient dame was asserted to have once seen one which she described as not the size of a goose, with very long wings and six joints. This was on Green Island. To find one on the ground would be extremely bad – it would portend the death of not one but very many people. Some pakehas had tried to shoot one but could not. A man came all the way from England to try. He fired at the sound but all he shot was the rushing wind. All my informants agreed it was a manu-tapu but all declared they knew no folklore about it.

Titi. Not only were titi got on the islands but on the mainland. At Bobby's Head near Goodwood is a cliff inland from the sea. Titi bred there and men were lowered over with ropes to collect the pi (young birds). They don't go there now – weasels cleaned out the titi. Tieing the kiri-totara (totara bark) round the poha is called ta, so it is said.

Since the foregoing was written the collector has got the following additional particulars: It would be gulling the public to sell to them titi captured before April 1st as the birds would not be far enough advanced so the Commissioners fixed the date of starting birding as April 1, and no one can start before that date. The Natives go over about March 20th to get their houses fixed, to make tracks round the 'manu', and do other necessary work and it takes them all their time to be ready to treat birds by April 1st. For four weeks it is all day catching (nanao) but about the end of April the pi (young bird) comes out at night to shake the down out and let the feathers grow, and then it can be caught outside by torch-light (rama). It is easier to catch them outside so day catching is discontinued and torching goes on until about May 15 as a rule, after which date very few birds are taken. The young bird shaking itself = ta ka huruhuru. A good hand gets from eighty to one hundred and fifty birds per day but torching should get two hundred or more a night but catching is limited by the progress of preserving operations as it is useless to catch more than the party can possibly handle. It is not every bird which throws up oil. The bird is not squeezed but pressed gently, an operation called whakaruaruakakata. When the bird is laid down if oil is dribbling from its mouth a feather is pulled from the bird and put in its mouth and this stops the flow. This putting a feather in the bird's mouth (after its first vomit is over) is called purua-te-waha. The hakuai was apparently heard on some islands, and not on others, this year. Its identity is still as keenly discussed as ever. One party is said to have got a white titi this season and the outcome is awaited with interest. The Natives have gone to the Hokanui Hills for totara bark for years past. They do not take bark off right round the tree but only on one side so the tree wont die. At Kelvingrove this year a young man told me an old man pointed out a totara tree which had had one side barked by stone axes 'donkey years ago'. On the islands a thin pi (young bird) is called a kiaka while the mother bird is known as a kaiaki or kaieke. [Further Notes: In 1922 shoals of fish were absent and many young titi died of starvation and the Maoris had a very poor season, but in 1923 Nature regulated things as usual and an excellent season resulted.]

SECTION XVIII

INSECTS, WORMS, LIZARDS

INSECTS

Moths – The general name for moths was wairua-takata because of the old belief that they are the souls of persons who have passed away.

Butterflies – The name of the 'red and black' butterfly is mokarakara, a name which some of my informants pronounced mokalakala.

Flies – The only fly in New Zealand in pre-pakeha days as far as the old people knew was the rako, known to the pakeha as the blowfly or bluebottle. One old man said he did not know what the Maori of old did to combat its tutaerako or 'blow' because it must have often been troublesome where food was concerned. This 'blow' produced the maggot which was called iro. He had noticed that the 'blow' of the big rako never became alive but remained white and finally dried up. The 'blow' of the smaller flies came to life and from this he concluded that the big blue rako were the male flies and that the smaller, more dull-coloured ones were the female flies. Two of the old men remarked that the blowflies were not a nuisance in October, November and December but in the months of January, February and March they became a regular pest.

Fleas – The collector had a note about a controversy in Northern circles as to whether the flea was indigenous or introduced, some Maoris affirming it was brought in by the whaling ships. One old woman considered it was not found in southern New Zealand before the pakeha came, but two old men thought it a native, one basing his conclusion on the fact that it comes out of the hot sand and the other that if it was not a native it would have been given a European name, Maoricised, whereas it is called tuiau. Another old man recalled the fact that the place on Ruapuke Island known as Te Awa-tuiau (flea channel) was mentioned in the line of a song that ran 'The sea breaks at Te Awatuiau'. This song mentions the chief Pahi and also the girl Tokitoki who about the year 1815 married Jimmy the Boy (James Caddell) and how long before that the name of Te Awatuiau had been in existence he could not say.

Spiders – The general name for spiders was pukawerewere. The only other spider name the collector could get was katipo, which he was told, was not found in Murihiku but on the beaches up in Canterbury. Spider webs were known as whare-pukawerewere (literally 'house of the spider') and when the spider was spinning its web each strand was called he aho pukawerewere. The collector was told of one of the mutton-birders who caught a rarity in the spider line at the Titi Islands. It was a huge black and yellow specimen, 'spotted like a tiger shark', and was captured to bring to the mainland as a curio but was unfortunately mislaid in packing. It was an extraordinary pukawerewere.

Crickets were called kihikihi or kikihi according to my informants and the collector was told that the place-name Makihikihi meant a whitish or light-coloured specimen of this familiar green insect, but whether this is correct or not the collector cannot say. The name of the grasshopper was given as toetoe and one old man defined it as of a reddish colour or like the colour of a weka or woodhen. The collector found it much harder to get information in this section than it was to procure facts about birds, fishes and plants.

A big, black beetle with a hard back was called mata, while the ant was known as the upokorua. A caterpillar described as 'black and hairy' was called the toroku, and another kind was called whe but the collector could get no description of it. The so-called vegetable caterpillar is said to have been called tutae-kereru from its general resemblance to the excrement of the native pigeon. The collector was told that it was to be found on the tataramoa bramble and that plants sometimes grew from this strange creature. What the European calls the stick insect the Maori called the ro and there was a superstition that if it was seen as a Maori traversed the bush it was a sign of the death of some one near and dear to him. The collector was told that the word pukawerewere while specifically defining spiders was also used as a general term to roughly include all insects.

There was one grub which was an article of diet to the Maori and in Murihiku it was called tukarakau. This was the fat white grub with a blackish head that is to be found when pine trees are felled. The Maori ate it either raw or cooked in the ashes and the general opinion seems to be highly laudatory of its edibility and flavour.

On the Titi Islands there is said to be a small leech called the kata which occasionally burrows in under the toenails of children. The name kutu (lice) is to be found very far back in the narration of Maori history – even to a time before the people came to this land, but whether they brought it here or not my informant could not say. The familiar sandfly of Murihiku coast was called namu, the mosquito keroa while the swarms of midges which sometimes come out at eventide were called naonao.

In company with a Maori of eighty summers the collector visited the Otago Museum and the following names were secured during an inspection of the specimens in the insect section: Sand Wasp (*Pompilus monarchus*) = kohitihiti, White Wood Grub (*Hepiatus virescens*) = tukarakau, Dragon Fly (*Uropetalia*) = kikihiwaru, Weta (*Hemideina ricta*) = weta.

The old man remarked that the weta although ugly was harmless, would not bite when handled, but was not eaten by the Maori. The insect called Daddy Long Legs by the pakeha was known as Te-tatau-o-te-whare-o-Maui (the door of the house of Maui) in Murihiku because tradition said it was connected with the story of Maui, the demigod. He thought it had something to do with the hole in the floor of the house when the pole was moved to let Maui down into the world below, but he was not sure of its exact significance.

Worms – The collector found it as difficult to get information about worms as about insects. One old man said that the big white worm was called noki-waiu and the ordinary red worm noki-tuatara. Another informant added that there was also a kind of black worm called tuaraki. It was about the colour, he said, of a young kanakana (lamprey eel). It was bigger than the noki which was milky white in colour, but it was not used for eel-bait when bobbing as the eels seemed to prefer the noki to it. Noki is also rendered noke.

Lizards – This is also a difficult subject to collect information about as the average Maori shuns these harmless creatures through superstitious fears. The tree lizard was described as black, ugly and sluggish and its Maori name was given as mokopapa. An old man described a black lizard he had seen on one of the Titi Islands. It was about five inches long, was covered with short hair, and was remarkable in that it had a double tail. An old man identified this as a moko-huruhuru lizard and another old man who remarked that hairy lizards were repulsive called them moko-tua-huruhuru.

The collector saw an old Maori refuse to go near or touch a pet tuatara as he was still swayed by a remnant of the old superstitious beliefs. It is said that the tuatara has been seen in the Catlins district within recent years. Dr Fulton wrote, 'On the Rough Ridge you could see a larger lizard than the common brown one. It was eight or nine inches or more and had gaudy yellow markings'. One old Maori who had traversed all over Central Otago when he was a boy could not recall such a lizard, nor could any other of the old people interviewed. [Note: Probably if they saw the lizard in question they would recognise it at once – this is one of the difficulties of collecting information by oral description.] In the Otago Museum an old Maori saw the Spotted Lizard (*Lygosoma grande*) and said it was a karara-toro-pakihi. The Green Lizard (*Naultinus elegans*) he called a karara-moko-huruhuru, remarking that it could be found along the Taieri River.

SECTION XLX

DOGS, RATS, BATS

DOGS AND DOG-TRAPS

Only one of my informants had seen a kuri-maori (or native dog) and that was in Westland when he was a boy so very little information was forthcoming as to the animal's appearance and habits. So little is known about it that some of those interviewed were inclined to think Captain Cook had brought it to New

Zealand. So far as the collector can make out the Southern Maoris kept a few kuri in their kaika (villages) as pets and also to catch flightless birds at certain times, but besides these tame canines there were large numbers of kuri running wild and making a good living of the birds which swarmed everywhere. According to my friends many of these brutes were untamable and traps were set to catch them for eating.

This trap was made on the same principle as the one for kiore (rats) only much bigger and stronger. Both were called tawhiti – tawhitikiore in the one case and tawhitikuri in the other. The bait in the trap was called moinu and when the dog pulled this meat the snare was sprung and the noose attached to the whana (bent stick) soon strangled the animal. One old man said he had a boyish recollection of old Tangatahuruhuru setting a big tawhiti to catch wild dogs at Opurere on the Pomahaka River, and he further remembered that the old people called the tame dogs by crying 'moi, moi'. Another man recorded a much more recent use of the tawhiti-kuri than this, as about 1884 a Wakapatu Maori who was greatly bothered with dogs stealing his meat, etc., made a trap on the old principle but employing wire and other modern appliances. My informant did not see the trap and as he left the district just after he did not hear what results it achieved.

Another kind of trap was described by one informant. A whata was made and from this a toothsome barracouta was securely suspended. So that the dog would not sniff man's hand on the fish, the latter is suspended for some hours in water and is then attached to the whata without the man touching it. A small step was often made so that the dog had to put its fore feet on the step to reach the fish. When it got hold of the fish it held on like grim death and tugged and this liberated two heavy stones which were hung to each side of the whata in such a manner as to clash together below with a swing when let go simultaneously.

These stones weighed perhaps fifty or sixty pounds and if the dog was not killed it was badly maimed and so caught. My informant forgot the name of this trap but said he had heard of it being set to kill or injure thieves who were annoying villagers by their unwelcome attentions.

Not one of the other old folk had heard of such a trap although they did not deny it might have been used in olden days. One man said he had read of such a method being used in some parts of the world to kill or maim crocodiles. Another said that while he had not heard of the stone-crushing trap for either man or dog he had been told of traps for thieves. In one such case as the thief came feeling in the dark he would grip a fish which if pulled would bring a long, sharp stick into him. If he was not killed he was usually crippled or hurt and so would be known in the daytime if met. He had heard it said that sometimes the points of these sticks were poisoned.

Still another said he had heard of the tawhiti dog snare but never of man-traps. The tohukas could protect property by karakia and if thieves then stole, their mouths would go crooked or their hands and feet go wrong. The people believed this so much that they dare not steal such karakia'd goods.

Another method of catching wild dogs is said to have been to tie a tame bitch up at a likely place but none of my present informants had heard of this procedure either.

'Sometimes,' said one narrator, 'when my father would go inland after weka he would see thirty to forty wild dogs very fat from living on birds. Once he went up the Molyneux and found the weka very scarce so he knew wild kuri were there. He carried a pukahu (or pukau) a big, thick stick on his travels. His big dog grappled with a wild dog and he killed the latter with his stick.' The same informant said he had heard male dogs called both kuri-tane and kuri-toa, and female ones called kuri-wahine and kuri-uwha. This indicates a laxity of vocabulary which would have appalled old-time critical Maoris.

The collector could not ascertain what the olden Maoris called the howl of the kuri but now the bark of a dog is called pari and its growl kukuru. [At Temuka when dogs howl it is called whakapuolo (whakapuoro).] An old settler who saw some kuri sixty three years ago says they were white and also light brown. They were about the size of a collie but very unlike it otherwise.

An old Maori said one dog-trap was called karu-mahaka ('karu' he said meant the eyeball and 'mahaka' a noose). This trap was like the tawhiti, only it hoisted the kuri up in the air.

RATS AND RAT-TRAPS

The kiore-maori (native rat), said one of the old people, was bigger than the pouhawaiki (English rat). In color it was a lighter grey and it was better looking. It had a shorter ihu (nose) and a shorter waero (tail). [The word 'bigger' should probably be 'fatter'.]

The kiore, said an old lady who had seen them near Oxford in Canterbury, had a short ear and nose. It was almost the same color as the pouhawaiki being brownish on the back and grey elsewhere. It had a furry skin and was nice to look at. They were cleanly animals and ate the 'fruit' of the bush trees when it fell to the ground, being fond of the hua-matai (black pine berries) and the berries of the kahika (white pine), the tawai and other trees. They were potted at the proper season, the fat being gathered in a totara waka (receptacle of totara) and were put in poha (kelp bags) the same as the familiar mutton-bird. They tasted very nice.

The tawhiti (snare) to catch rats, said a veteran in these matters, was about eight or nine inches square as a rule, but bigger ones could be made to catch four rats. The square was formed by pegs stuck in the ground with a doorway in. The bait was fish, meat or roasted bird. There was a bent stick called whana with a line and noose to the bait. The tawhiti was generally made of mikimiki, and young ribbonwood and manuka would do for the whana. Two little hoops are made over the bait and if the rat touches a string the whana is released, the noose tightens over kiore's neck and pulls it up against the hoops where it is quickly suffocated, having just time, perhaps, to give the rat's cry 'ti, ti'. The sound (or 'ping') the trap makes as it goes off is called tuki. Other rats cannot go in to eat the bait for the dead rat blocks the way. An ingenious plan, the tawhiti!

'I never saw the kiore,' said an old man, 'as it was eaten out by the big pouhawaiki, but I have heard it was a white color. It got very fat and was preserved like the titi (muttonbird). Oxford was a great spot for them and it was nothing for a family to catch four hundred or five hundred in the season. Old Scotch John has told me that with four or five other whalers, he had to take refuge once at Taikunui (Tokanui). Food was short and they had to eat the kiore and they said afterwards they had never tasted anything better.' As a rule the Maoris would not eat the pouhawaiki but the collector was told of one case of it being eaten.

An old settler says the Native rat was like the English water-rat only not so fierce or big. It had a short head, a short tail, short ears, and was black. It was said that in every litter there is only one female. [Note: This black rat was likely an introduced species.] [For lengthy description of Native Rat see Kaiapoi Notes.]

BATS

As in the case of insects, worms and lizards it is also difficult to get information about bats. An old woman said she only knew one kind of bat, the pekapeka, and she knew no stories nor superstitions about it. It was not eaten by the Maori because, although it flew like a bird, it had no feathers on it. Another old woman said the pekapeka lived in trees that were rotting especially the kapuka or broadleaf and that they were very repulsive creatures, being dirty in their habits and creating an abominable smell. An old man said the name of bats was kopekapeka, a word which meant 'zigzagging about', but he had never had one in his hand nor had he been close enough to one to describe it. Another old man said that the pekapeka raised an awful smell. It had a skin like a kiore (native rat) or like a hinereta (English mouse). Some of them lived in the thatch of the whares (huts) on the Titi Islands and as far as he knew they are still to be found there, although they never were very welcome guests so near to human beings. He concluded by saying that some Maoris are frightened of bats even as they also are frightened of lizards.

SECTION XX

TREES, SHRUBS, PLANTS, TUSSOCKS, FERNS

PLANTS AND TREES

Walking through the bush with a very old Maori he gave the following names of trees and shrubs, etc. to the collector but unfortunately the latter is no botanist and cannot supply the Latin and often not even the English or the bush dweller's names for the various items: Ramarama = pepper tree. The leaves are hot to the taste. Kotukutuku = fuchsia, and hua-kotukutuku the edible berry thereof. A deciduous tree. Tatarahika = lawyer, and tataramoa is almost the same but with white bark. Mikimiki = stinkwood. The leaves and bark hauka (stink). Red poisonous berries. Rau tawhiri = black maple of the settlers. Tarata = white maple of the settlers. Matipo = a shrub or small tree and Mapou = a shrub or small tree (there is a difference between these two trees). Matoi = is a shrub with small leaves and hard wood. Kamahi or kamai is the tree commonly known by this name. Miki = different wood to mikimiki. It has a grey berry good to eat. Rehua = a spreading plant growing on the sea coast. Has grey berries. Kokihi = a shrub which grows by the seaside. It has red berries. Kokoeka = grass tree which grows in bush, (also called lance-wood I believe). Kaio = a small tree which grows near seaside (may be synonymous with northern Ngaio). Popohue (or popohua) is a climbing plant with round green leaves and white flowers (clematis). Tutaekereru is somewhat similar to popohue with longish green leaves and white flowers. Haki = Native Holly. Hakihaki is another tree. Pirita = supplejack. Kareao was name of its berry. Toatoa = a small tree somewhat similar to manuka. Has a pleasant scent. Haka = is said to be a white clematis. Kapuka = broadleaf. A very lasting timber, said my Maori friend. Mahinahina = a shrub (no particulars). From later information the collector believes it is also called hinahina and that it is what is called mahoe in the North Island.

VARIOUS TREES

Kahika – this is the familiar white pine of the settler. The Murihiku Maori never called this tree kahikatea as in the North Island – simply kahika. Kahikatoa or kaikatoa is the name of the big kind of manuka which grows to a great size. The kilimoko or kirimoko, a kind of small manuka, comes out in white flowers and later in berries. Towai wood was greatly favoured for making pa (jiggers used in catching the barracouta fish), but the place-name Papatowai is said to have been bestowed by Europeans. Houi is the common ribbonwood, but the place name

Houipapa is said to have been given by the white man. The Maori made various ornamental and useful things from the bark of the houi, also from the kauheke, a small kind of tree similar to ribbonwood. Totara bark was also extremely useful to the Maori. As an instance an old man told how he was travelling with several companions in the fifties when they were overtaken by night at the Otuwhata Bush near Waianakarua. They simply cut totara bark and made efficient shelters. Kaio or ngaio is a tree that grows along the coast but not inland. It was pointed out to the collector that it grew on the Otago Peninsula but not at Henley which is six miles inland with a range of hills intervening. On plains it may grow further inland than six miles (as at Papakaio up the Waitaki River and at Waimate in South Canterbury). One old man showed the collector a curiosity in a peculiar long piece of kaio tree which he picked up at Otago Heads. This piece has no leaves but has widened out to form a fibrous blade-like mass. Akerautaki is mentioned in an account of Southland's vegetation but my informants said it did not grow at all in the South Island except at Nelson.

Kokoeka is what the bushman calls the grasstree, and its long blade-like leaves were called rau like ordinary leaves. There is a long rib in this leaf its specific name forgotten, and it was sometimes used to make hinaki (eelpots), being very durable – as good as the tororaro vine so one of my informants averred. Another English name for the kokoeka is lance wood. Inaka is the name of a tree on the Titi Islands and some of my informants called it the grass tree, saying that the kokoeka was a tree in the bush. Calling it the grass tree must be a local usage as it is apparently quite different from the kokoeka.

Kiekie is the name of a famous fruit-bearing tree which is not found in Murihiku but is found in the West Coast Sounds and in Westland. The collector was once told of a small tree called kiakia from whose bark a dye could be extracted. Not one of his present informants had heard of such a name for a tree and one and all surmised that the word had been confused with kiekie. It may be mentioned that there is a beach and small island at Moeraki both known as Mau-kiakia but the origin and meaning of the name seems lost in antiquity. Some of the floors in Southern Maori homes were covered with handsome kiekie mats sent down as gifts by Northern friends.

Hinau – An old man who had been brought up at Otago Heads mentioned that hinau berries could be eaten, but he must have inadvertently inserted the name into his list of edible berries because of his later sojourn in the North Island, for every one of my other informants was emphatic in the opinion that the hinau tree was not to be found in Murihiku. [See Section 15 Vegetable Foods.]

Karaka – Similarly my informants said this tree was not in Murihiku – it does not seem to grow south of Banks Peninsula. Further north the berries were used for food. Titoki – This is another tree not found in Murihiku. One of my informants mentioned that the northerners got an oil from the titoki berries to rub on their bodies. Titiaweka and Tupari are two trees on the Muttonbird Islands.

They are nearly alike but the former is scented. Tawai is the name of the beech (or birch). Miro is a tree which a white bushman described as a cross between the red and white pine. The pigeons thrive and fatten on its bitter berries. Matai is the black pine. Rimu is the red pine. Korokio is the name of a common shrub. Turokio is said to be the name of another shrub, but the name may have been local as it did not seem to be generally known. Tumatakuru is the correct name of the Wild Irishman shrub and the Maoris have conjectural guesses as to where the Pakeha got 'matagowrie' from – some surmising Scotland. Rautawhiri, the black maple of the bushman, is often seen in hedge-form when it is called matipo by townspeople, the real matipo being a smaller shrub with finer leaves.

GENERAL REMARKS

'Ka hua a Tane' (the fruits of Tane) is a proverbial saying for all big trees as they are all the children of that god. He broadcast the forest, the potiki (last son) being the pikiraki (mistletoe) which was not planted in the cold ground but was flung up among the sheltering foliage of the older trees.

In the Christchurch Museum there is a good specimen of that strange plant, the 'vegetable sheep' but although the collector made most diligent inquiry he could find no one who knew its Maori name. Nor did any of the old people interviewed know the Maori name of the mountain musk.

Inquiries made as to any plant called pikiarero, or te rerewa were devoid of result. One aged woman had vaguely heard of the rekareka but she could not describe it or say where it grew. The other inquiries made have been answered to a greater or lesser degree in the information already detailed.

MALE AND FEMALE TREES AND SHRUBS

One old Maori told the collector that he considered that almost every tree has male and female specimens. As instances he quoted the ordinary manuka as the male and kirimoko as the female of that species of tree. [This kirimoko the collector has been informed is the small kind of manuka called 'kilmog' by the early settlers and it is said that Mount Kilmog between Dunedin and Oamaru was named because of its prevalence there.] The other instance he quoted was the matai (black pine) the male trees of which had narrow leaves and no berries while the female trees had broader leaves and berries.

Another man said he had heard the old people talking of the trees having sexes but only one instance had come under his notice. Mrs Cameron of Riverton [the halfcast daughter of the famous Captain Howell, a woman keen on preserving Maori lore] showed him two ramarama (pepper-trees) growing side by side on her lawn and asked him if he could see any difference between them. He replied that he could see quite a lot of difference, one being distinctly redder in the leaf than the other. She explained that it was the female shrub while the greener one was the male. If you put two red ones together there would be no fruition and two green ones would similarly fail, but place a red and a green one side by side and the red one would bear berries.

Another old man said he did not remember hearing the past generation speaking of male and female trees. The only rakau-toa (male tree) he knew about was that some trees made into spears better than others – they were trees for the toa or warrior.

A well-informed old man told the collector that he had heard the old people refer to toa-rakau and uha-rakau, or male and female trees. You could distinguish some by their berries. Such a tree was the kamai or kamahi, the berries being white for the female and red for the male trees, but in the case of many species of trees it was very hard to tell the difference between the two sexes.

VINES AND CREEPERS

Tororaro is a vine famous in southern circles for its suitability in the manufacture of eelpots. A stronger creeper is the aka-totara it is red inside and if used to bind anything becomes very tough and very hard to cut. Tutaekereru is a vine and received its name because its stalks are exactly the colour of the native pigeon's excrement. This vine will climb the highest tree in the bush and it can be used to tie post and rail fences. Popohue is another vine but its stalks are too short and brittle to be made use of by the Maori. This is called the white clematis by settlers. After the white man came the leaves of one clematis could be boiled for tea in emergency; it had no berries but pods with seeds inside. Tawhiwhi is a kind of fine vine with beautiful yellow flowers, said my informant. The children used to swing on it sometimes. Horokaka is a seaside plant with creeping characteristics. According to my informants it has 'pinkish-tinged stems and green pods'. Kokihi is a seaside plant which had red berries and these berries are sometimes used in these modern days by Maori schoolchildren to make a crude red ink.

FLOWERS

Puawai was formerly the correct name of the red blossom of the rata and 'Ko ahua te puawai' was the expression used to denote its breaking forth into flower – a gorgeous spectacle. The name was gradually extended to take in any bush blossom and is now applied to define all flowers.

The Maori love the aroma provided by Nature and some of the old people made most affectionate reference to the beautiful perfumes wafted by the evening breezes from some of the ranges whose sides were clothed with hakeke, taramea, karamu, anise, musk and other fragrant growths – now alas! vanished for ever for the sheep have eaten the old-time aromatic native vegetation.

GRASSES AND TUSSOCKS

Tarutaru was a name for grass. Tutaki is a kind of long coarse grass which grows on the Titi Islands. It is a suitable and convenient substitute to cover the kelp bags for muttonbirds if totara bark runs short. Te Haumaataa is a grass which grows very tall in swampy places. It is something like matoreha or cutty-grass but is not so sharp-edged. Pouaka is a grass which grew near or around water but it is rare now. Karetu grass grows long and the children used it as fishing lines to catch kokopu and inaka in the creeks. It has no smell (so apparently is not the scented karetu of the North Island). It is probably another grass altogether to the latter. Taru whenua is the ordinary grass of the plains. Ma uku uku or Mauukuuku is the common grass in swamps. Rerewaka is a kind of grass which grows near swamps. This name was given to one in South Canterbury but did not seem to be known further South, where the people said it was the name of a bird and not of a plant. Neither had they heard of ririwaka, said to be a sedge (Tregear's [[1891]] *Dictionary*). Tutuna is a kind of grass usually found near swamps.

Pikao is a coarse grass that grows by the sea. Its leaves are said to resemble those of the famous kiekie only they are of a brownish colour. The pikao was formerly made into rain-cloaks in Murihiku, but a modern use is to make it into ladies' hats. Matoreha is the familiar cutty-grass of the colonist. One informant gave it as the name of the 'niggerheads' in swamps, but all the rest united in saying it is solely the designation of cutty-grass. Turokio was a name given to me as defining a long kind of matoreha, but another said it was a scrub, and yet another said the word was turukio, a kind of fern.

Wi is the name of what the early settlers called snowgrass, athough one old man said it meant the rushes [see next word]. It is a very long grass and in the old days formed excellent material for thatching whares. If a thunderstorm came on when the people were after weka (woodhens) they could creep in under clumps of it for shelter, and it was also very handy for weaving into breakwinds and temporary shelters. Wiwi is the name of rushes. Patiti is the name of the common tussock. Maania is another name for patiti tussock, or it probably may be a somewhat different variety. Tarahikoau is a sort of tussock but does not grow so big as the patiti. Pupatiti is the name of the clumps or tufts of tussock which grow along the sand on the coast. Pukio (sometimes pukiu) is the Murihiku name for the niggerheads in the swamps. One old man considered that upokotakata was another name for them. Kopata is like a dock but has narrower leaves. My informant considered it a Native plant as it was formerly abundant inland at Pomahaka. When the whalers introduced tobacco, the Maoris would sometimes smoke kopata leaves when tobacco was scarce.

FERNS

The amount of information that could be gleaned is very small. Piupiu was given to me as the southern Maori name of the maidenhair fern. Turukio is a fern with a long leaf. Makamaka, said one of my informants, is a fern that is looped similar to supplejacks growing up a tree. It creeps over the bases of trees and over rocks, said another informant, and has two little round leaves on each side all the way along its stems. Rauaruhe is the fern, the root of which is eaten [See Vegetable Foods Section].

MOSSES

One of my informants considered that the correct name for the moss in swamps is pukahu, a word which he said meant spongy. Paku was given to me as the name of the moss that bedecks the tawai (beech or birch). This moss is famous for its celerity in kindling during the use of the kauati (fire-sticks).

Kohuwai or kohuai is the moss growing on the miki tree, said one man, but others give it as the name of a green scum that grows on stagnant water and on swamps. Not so, said my first informant, the moss that grows in water is really kokuta and this was sometimes said to be 'the eels' house' as they liked to frequent it and they could be readily speared among it. The red growth seen on swamps and sluggish water is known as rimurimu. Another of my informants said, 'Kohuai is a green stuff which grows on muddy water – it is a spongy growth in a layer'.

Re is a swamp on the low ground or flats, while nei is a swampy place in the hills, and one of my informants narrated the case of a shepherd who was drowned in one on a mountain-top.

SECTION XXI

WINDS, WEATHER, RAINBOWS, STARS, SEASONS

WEATHER, WINDS AND DIRECTIONS

An old man said the Maori had no fixed terms for east, west, north and south denoting fixed points of the compass but used words to express the general direction or idea of such wished to be conveyed. Then the North Island people, he had heard, had different ideas of what was 'up north' and 'down south' to what the South Island people had. Then he believed that the canoe Arai-te-uru famous in southern Maori history was in the Cook Islands known by the name

Arai-te-tonga. He had heard the old people in the South of New Zealand call the east, tairawhiti; the west, taihauauru; the north, taitokerau; and the south, taitoka. The winds according to Maori ideas did not come straight from these directions but came from 'between points'. Thus he did not know of any direct east wind as per the ideas of his ancestors but from the south-east came the winds Waihola (Waihora) and Autehi; from the north-east, whakarua; from a northerly direction, tawera; from a westerly direction, wawa; from the north-west, mauru or hauauru; from a southerly direction, toka; and from the south-west, ta. Two land-breezes were called tu-whenua and wawa. The former was bad in the Waitaki Valley and came off the snowy mountains and off the river very cold. When it blew South Canterbury was much colder than Southland. The people down the east coast of Otago said that the east winds, Waihola especially, were nice gentle winds and that the north-west and south-west were rough, boisterous winds. They therefore called the former potiki-wahine (a girl baby) and the latter potiki-tane (a boy baby).

It is noteworthy that in the stories of the destruction of giant ogres by fire the favorable wind sought for was the ma-uru (north-west).

An old Maori said that no one knew how to account for the winds as far as he could say. [An account is given in the Kaiapoi notes.] In explaining the word wawa to the collector an old man said that wawaa was the sound of anything but that waawaa was a northerly wind. At Moeraki the collector was told the north-east wind = whakarua; the south-east wind, waihola; the southerly wind, toka; the north-west wind mauru and south-west wind ta, the two last-named having the reputation of being the cold winds.

At Temuka the south-west wind is called toka when it blows ordinarily but when it increases to a gale it is called puaitaha and is reputed to be very cold. The nor-wester for which Canterbury is famous is here called wahanui apparently, but another north-west wind is the mauru while hauauru and ta are westerly winds and wawa is an easterly wind. At Arahuru, in Westland, it is said the south-west wind means fine weather but the north-west wind always brings rain, so the Temuka people had heard. When the wind flew fitful and sleety the old people would say, 'E takata nui ko mate ranei kai te mea rani ki a mate apopo ka roko tatau' (a great man will die – we will hear the tidings by and by).

If a chief died and shortly after the hau (wind) ua (rain) or whaitiri (thunder) came on the people would say 'E takata mana' meaning it was an expression of his mana (influence). Similarly if a high-born lady's demise was accompanied by similar natural manifestations the people would say 'E wahine mana' or if both a man and woman had died shortly before a thunderstorm the saying would be 'E takata mana, e wahine mana ranei'.

In Volume 52 of the *Transactions of the New Zealand Institute*, page 63, the collector [[Beattie 1920b]] gave a little of the weather lore of the Southern Maoris and some of their names for snow and ice, etc. The following is a little more of their weather observations.

Papahuka is the name of a thin crust of ice on water but the name is also applied to thick ice. Kopaka is frost and a hard, black frost is kopaka-whaka-rakau, while a misty rain is called punehunehu (a word signifying dust). The following are 'weather remarks': Kai te ua te awha = the rain is falling (or 'the raining of the rain' – ua here means 'to rain'). Kai te kotiti te awha = the rain is drizzling. Kai te taki te hau = the wind is blowing (The word 'kai' is South Island dialect for Northern word 'kei'.) Kai te oka te huka = the snow is falling (The word oka here is puzzling. One old man said it was only used for snow or for the stabbing of a pig. Perhaps the old people thought the snow stabbed the air.)

Add to Winds and Weather

In South Canterbury the south-west wind is (or was) called ta; the 'southerly' is toka; the south-east wind is waihora; the north-east one is whakarua; from a point further round, but still nor-east, is wawa; from a north-westerly direction is tawera; from a point further round, but still nor-west, is wahanui; and a westerly wind is mauru.

Of the characteristics of these winds an old woman gave a shrug (or shiver perhaps) and said waihora (south-east), whakarua (north-east), ta (south-west), and toka (south) were hau-makariri (cold winds or with a wintry feel) but mauru was mahana (warm) or werawera (heated). [Europeans speak of the 'warm nor-westers'. H.B.]

'Kai te taki te wahanui ki te toka; kai te tono atu ki te toka to taki' said the taua (grandmother). ('The cry of the nor-wester bidding the southerly to blow too' – is a rough but sufficient interpretation of the remark.) The saying is based on an old figurative allusion that when wahanui blows, 'te taki o te hau' (the sound of the wind) it is 'te tono o te toka' (the ordering of the south wind) to begin to blow; and true enough it is, that when the nor-wester does blow it is very often followed by a southerly wind. Tuwhenua is the name of a land breeze in the morning, concluded the taua, but she knew no stories nor whakatauki (proverbs) about the winds. Some years ago an aged Maori in speaking of a certain locality said there was a Maori cultivation there in 1840 and the whaling days. The garden was called Rakitamau (cloudy sky) but whether it was named after a man or the weather he did not know. The correct Maori name of the picturesque lake now usually called Hauroto is Hauloko (Hauroko, or in North Island dialect Haurongo) which means 'the sound of the wind', an appropriate name from its situation among towering peaks and deep valleys.

At Waikouaiti in 1840 the Reverend J. Watkin was told that rafiti and muahuboku were words denoting 'eastward', while toka meant westward. This information is interesting to compare with what the collector gathered eighty years later.

Add to Winds and Weather

H. te Maire said he had heard his late father (the well-known chief, Rawiri te Maire [[see photo, p. 26]]) speak about the weather in the region bordering on the lower reaches of the Waitaki River. If fog hung on the top of the range Tahu-a-Te-Kaumira near Waimatemate (Waimate) and then came down it was a certain sign of rain. [The day the collector saw him he foretold rain by this sign and the writer got drenched before he finished cycling to the railway at Waihao (Morven). H.B.] If fog hung on top of the hill Te Whiwhi (near Pukeuri, North Otago) this was regarded as a sure indication of rain. His father told him to watch these signs when he was harvesting. As to winds, toka was south-west wind; ta was the north-west one; mauru was a north-east one; and whakarua was the easterly wind. These were the four principal winds of the Lower Waitaki plains and it was more difficult to foretell weather by them than by the fogs on mountains, but their general characteristics were known. Mauru was a hot wind; whakarua was sometimes a wet wind and sometimes a dry one; Toka was the stormiest one of the lot and generally brought rain in its train but sometimes it was only wind, and passed gustily blowing itself out. His father was very good at weather lore and he regretted he had not learnt more of it from the old man while the latter was living at Waitaki Mouth. In regard to climate he thought it must have been drier before the Pakeha came or the olden Maori could not have travelled about as he constantly did, nor could he have lived in such frail shelters as the pahuri if the weather was as changeable as now.

As against this opinion my principal informant said he considered that the climate was wetter before the Pakeha came, but the people probably did not notice it so much as they would now. To see naonao (midges or gnats) flying about at dusk is generally a sign of fine weather, the collector was told. At Waikouaiti in 1840 Reverend J. Watkin was given the names of the directions from which winds came as follows: toka, south-east; ta, south-west; Waiora, east; fakarua, north-east; mauru, north-west. These are interesting to compare with what the collector was told in 1920.

Add to Winds

The following list was given by a venerable Maori: Whakarua = north-east wind – strong and boisterous, Rawaho = east-north-east wind – strong, Koio = south-east – coldish, Paretao = east-south-east wind – light, Waihola = south-east wind – mild, sometimes coldish, Toka = south wind – variable, Ta = south-west wind – hard, dry wind, Mauru = west wind – warm wind, Hauauru = north-west wind – strong wind, Tawera = north wind – strong wind.

This classification of winds is probably made from a knowledge of the South Otago district where this informant usually lives. It would not be correct in Southland. The informant added that any wind which came down a river was called Tuwhenua. One he knew came down the Waitaki and it had the reputation of being a disagreeable wind and like it the one which came down the Molyneux was a moist, cold wind.

RAINBOWS

'When they see rainbows,' remarked an old man, 'the Southern Maoris know that Te Ao-Matara, a tapu man of old mentioned in the Tuhaitara whakapapa (genealogy) is travelling about. It is his sign. His wife ran away but saw a rainbow and knew he was coming. After some trouble he got her back.' Another man said: 'Rakiora is a god of the rainbow. If the whaitiri (thunder) rolls in the daytime and you see two rainbows the smaller one is rakiora.' Another Maori said that Kahukura is the god of the rainbow. He had never heard of Rakiora and did not know what that name (or Rangiora) meant.

Add Rainbows

Asking regarding sky phenomena the collector was told by one ancient that rainbows were called atuaraki whether they appeared in the daytime or at night. He lives on Stewart Island but he could not remember ever having heard the Maoris give a name to the Southern Lights so often visible from there.

Another old man (who is from Ruapuke) said he had heard the rainbows just called atuaraki but he did not know the particular name of night bows. Shooting stars are called matakoke but he had never heard any name for the Aurora.

The kaumatua (from Colac Bay) said 'Kahukura (or Kaukura) is the god of the rainbow and as far as I know the correct name of rainbows is kahukura, as they are called after him. When you see a double rainbow the old Maoris would say the back one was Rokomai and the front one was his son Kahukura. (Rongomai or Rokomai was Kaukura's father). I never heard the word aniwaniwa for a rainbow and Wai-aniwa in Southland was not named because of rainbows but after an old chief called Tane-aniwa. Aniwa down here means a reflection, a light flashing by you or a sudden gleam past your eyes. Kahukura is the name for any rainbow but when only a small portion of a bow is visible it is known as a mutukou. You may understand this term better when I say that when half a finger is cut off, the stump is known to us as a rika-kou. Ka-tara-o-kai is the name of the Southern Lights but I never heard any legends regarding it.'

The principal informant also gave the name of the Aurora Australis as Ka-tara-o-kai. The only name he knew, however, for either day or night rainbows was Atua. When the Southern Lights were seen it was said to be a sign someone great was going to die. Rainbows were regarded as a sign that someone, connected in some way or other with the observer was travelling.

An old man said that if you saw a double rainbow the lesser arch was called rakiora, but another man, equally well-informed, said he had never heard of rakiora as a rainbow name, but only kahukura.

STARS AND SKY-LORE

One poua said, 'My father watched the stars, especially Autahi and Puaka, to see if the year was going to be a good or bad one. He would place a stick upright in the ground and would watch for several nights. If the star he was watching rose in the south it was a good sign but if it rose in the north it was a bad sign. This was because if the star rose in the south it meant the good weather was pressing the bad weather away south where it would not harm us, but if the star rose in the north it meant the bad weather was pressing the good weather away and coming on to us. I do not know the Wero stars as they only come out in a certain part of the year. I have heard the name Tokopa used for a star but I think it means a part of the sky.'

A well-informed old man said 'Autahi is a red star at the end of te ika o te Raki (the Milky Way) and Puaka used to be his wife but he went away and when he came back he found another star, Takurua, had her. So he left her with Takurua and he (Autahi) became te ariki o te-ika-o-Raki (King of the Milky Way). The star you call Jupiter we call Mirimiri.' The Murihiku Maoris now say for sunrise 'Puta mai te ra' (coming here the sun), but formerly they used the poetic or figurative expression 'Haea te pu ata' (tear open the dawn, or, split the dawn open). Ata is said to be really the reflection caused by the sun before it appears, but it is a word now often employed to express the idea of dawn. At Waikouaiti in 1840 Reverend J. Watkin was told that Puta mai te ra denoted sunrise while kua to te ra meant 'the sun has set'.

One old man considered that no one knew how far back the stars went. You might travel through the fourteen heavens of the Maori before you came to the one the Maori race came from and you might see the stars from there too. He had never learnt the name of the fourteen heavens but he thought they were in stars and that you must pass them till you came to the right one. (This may be a modern idea but he seemed sincere in thinking it an old belief.)

Add to Sky-Lore

My principal informant mentioned that when the old Maoris went fishing they usually went out from land with the morning star (kopuparapara). He had never heard the name Tawera used for the morning star in the south but it was mentioned in a North Island song. The Evening Star was called Haere-ahiahi, and perhaps it was identical with the one that rises in the morning. If the star Puaka rose in the north it was said to foretell good weather; if towards the south it indicated bad weather. Meteors were called matakokiri but he had heard no Maori names for comets nor eclipses of sun and moon. The old people used to say 'Ko puta mai te ra' for sunrise (Coming in sight the sun – literally) and 'ko to te ra' means the sunset.

A Waimate Maori said that with the exception that matakokiri meant meteors, he knew no names for comets, eclipses, etc. Navigation was accomplished by means of observing the stars and the moon. The people knew where the moon would rise and steered accordingly, and also the movements of the stars were familiar to them and served to guide them. The Maori came from Hawaiki-pamamao first but narrator could not say which stars he steered to or by. The only stars he knew they steered by in old days are Matariki, Puaka, Meremere and Autahi. He forgot the song which mentioned them, but the Takitimu canoe came by those stars. Narrator did not know the old Maori name of the Southern Cross – he had never learnt the star lore.

The Maoris of old did not know the earth is round like what the Pakeha says, remarked an old man. They thought it was flat and they considered the ra (sun) went down one side in the evening and up the other side the following morning.

An aged dame remarked that she used to ask her seniors where the sun went when it disappeared into te rua o te ra (the hole of the sun) every night but they could not tell her.

Add to Stars

The Wakahuruhurumanu, a spirit canoe, coming to New Zealand met fifty gigantic seas. These were very high and the Uruao (with people on board) would have been buried by them. The first-named canoe smoothed out these seas one after the other and so prepared the way for the Uruao and other canoes. Those early voyagers saw Kopuparapara (morning star = Venus, so the old Maoris said) in the morning and in the evening they saw other stars, notably Mirimiri, the Evening Star. There is one star that stands still – Autahi. All the others shift when Te Ika o te Raki (the Milky Way) does, but Autahi stands there and so is Te Ariki o te Tau (The Lord of the Year). The rainbow also pointed the way for those early navigators. You can see Kopuparapara at midday in January straight up above us and this was a good mark to go by. Puaka, another famous star, goes away for a while but comes again in July. Up at Kaikoura (it is said) the Omihi people when they see Puaka, who is a Upoko-ariki of theirs, make a sacrifice. They bake a bird, or a fish, or a potato in an umu and present the food to the appropriate god. It is said this is done even up to this day.

THE MOON

'Ko korohiti te marama' is said by Southern Maoris to indicate the new moon. 'Kai te haere te marama kia ohua' is said when the moon is just coming to the full, while 'Kai te haere te marama kia mate' is the expression to show the moon is going off or dying. 'Ko te hinapouri' is said of the dark nights when there is no moon. My informant, a venerable Maori, knew of no legends relative to the waxing or waning of the lunar sphere. Neither he nor another well-informed kaumatua knew the names of the days of the moon's age, nor had they heard the old people assign any reason for the tides of the sea. At Waikouaiti in 1840 Reverend J. Watkin was told that koroiti meant 'new moon'; korohiti te marama also had the same import, while the phrase katoa te marama designated 'full moon'.

THE SEASONS

The principal informant said the old Maori year had only ten months in it and he knew of two ways these were counted, viz. – Te Ka'uru = January/February, Ka'uru kai paeka = March/April, Te Torn = May, Ko Te Wha = June, Ko Te Rima = July, Ko Te Ono = August, Ko Te Whitu = September, Ko Te Waru = October, Ko Te Iwa = November, Ko Te Tekau = December. Te Rua = June, Te Torn = July, Te Wha = August, Te Rima = September, Te Ono = October, Te Whitu = November, Te Waru = December, Te Iwa = January, Te Kahuru = February/March, Te Kahuru kai paeka = April/May.

He had never heard any other names but these i.e. the kahuru for harvesting and kahuru kai paeka for storing food and then the other eight months counted. These months may have had proper names but he had never heard them. The seasons were roughly divided as: Makariri = Winter or practically May, June and July, Ko Mahana = Spring roughly August and September, Raumati = Summer roughly October and November, Kahuru = Autumn roughly December, January and February, while March and April were called Kai te haere as they were between potato digging and winter. The leaves of the kotukutuku (fuchsia) fall off and this is a warning winter is on. He did not know names of moon's age. A well-informed kaumatua said he had heard the names of the Maori months many years ago but he never learnt to repeat them.

Another aged man said the tau (year) was formerly divided into ten months but he did not know their names nor how they were denoted unless by counting tahi, rua, toru, wha, rima etc. In regard to the seasons ninihi meant the dead of winter; au-maria was about Christmas time or so; kokota denoted the springtime, while ahuru was about the height of summer. Te Waru was the time for tilling the ground when the pipiwharauroa (shining cuckoo) arriving in New Zealand told the people the advice of Maui about cultivating the soil, while kahuru was the season for gathering what had been planted.

INFORMATION GATHERED IN 1840

Reverend J. Watkin arrived at Waikouaiti in 1840 and to aid him in his study of the Maori language wrote out a vocabulary. Some time after the collector had finished his work among the Maoris, the Reverend Rugby Pratt forwarded him a typewritten copy of Watkin's Manuscript and it is interesting for purposes of comparison. The following is his list of the months of the year: Hiua = January, Kahuru = February and March, Matahi = April, Mania – May, Maruaroa = June, Toru = July, Fa = August, Rima = September, Ono = October, Fitu = November, Warn – December. It will be noticed that Mr Watkin has given eleven names as against the ten of my informants. Six of the names are identical with those of my informants' second list. Hiua is evidently intended for iwa, and mania is reconciliable with te rua; matahi stands for the same part of the year as kahuru-kai-paeka while maruaroa is the eleventh name not given to me. My list was procured eighty years later and one hundred miles further south than Mr Watkin's one.

EARTHQUAKES

Earthquakes were called ru, said the best of my informants, but he had never heard the old people tell of the origin or history of them. 'Te whenua kai te oioi' (the earth is shaking) is an expression used when ru is on. He thought these violent manifestations of Nature were caused by big fires underneath the earth's surface.

SECTION XXII

WHAREKURA, TAPU, KARAKIA, TUAHU, TOHUKAS, WITCHCRAFT, OMENS

WHAREKURA

The perpetuation of Maori religious ideas, scientific lore, art, mythology and history did not rely on any haphazard methods such as the father telling the son, nor on any adventitious circumstances such as tribal gatherings, feasts or similar meetings. It was based on well-thought-out lines and executed with rigid fidelity.

Briefly put, knowledge was perpetuated from generation to generation by what may be called the ancient Maori school system as represented by the wharekura and similar colleges. The brightest and most intelligent lads in each tribe were required to spend a certain time at these colleges under the most onerous conditions and rigorous supervision. The instruction given by the priests and learned men was oral and had to be memorised word for word under dire penalties for failure or departure from the strictest letter of the recognised recital. The amount memorised was simply prodigious to Pakeha ideas and it was faithfully transmitted generation after generation. When the sealers and whalers came round Otago and Southland, the wharekura ceased and the present Maoris retain very little knowledge of them, although spasmodic attempts were made to revive their influence and teachings.

Speaking at Taumutu to Mr R. Taiaroa he told the collector that he had been born at Otakou in 1868 and that about the years 1879–82 a wharekura was held at that place for the sons of chiefs. It was held in a cottage – a little one-roomed hall – which had two windows, one of which he accidentally broke, an occurrence which filled his boyish mind with dismay, for a time, as he thought he would fall a victim to the dread makutu. At that place he heard old stories, the Maori account of creation, and mythology but he was obliged to confess the things told there did not stick in his memory. There were four pupils: Tom Wesley (Morven), Maurice Topi (Bluff), Momo Taituha and himself and he was afraid none of them profited by the instruction as they all left Maori ideas completely and clung to Pakeha education thereafter. The tohuka was Hoani Korako, a fiery old gentleman of whom they stood in considerable awe, and who sometimes called himself Hoani Korako Wetere in full although he was no relation of Tare Wetere te Kahu. The wharekura taught at Otakou was probably the last one in the South Island, but he must add he thought its object – to teach Maori lore to the sons of chiefs – was not achieved to any extent.

TAPU

The collector [[Beattie 1917]] has previously written in the *Journal of the Polynesian Society* about the 'wharekura' at Moeraki about 1868–9. Speaking to Henare te Maire who is (as far as is known) the sole survivor of that historic institution, the collector asked how the tapu was taken off the pupils. His reply was that he was taken to the Kawa Creek where the tohuka dipped a peka (branch) of Rautawhiri or Tarata into the water and shook it over his head. He forgot just then the name of this ceremony but whiuwhiu-te-koe-ki-te-wai expresses the going to the water. For two days and one night he had nothing to eat (to keep his mind intent on retaining what he had heard) but now he was taken inside and then outside the 'wharetapu' to eat cooked food – some fish it was. 'Whakai koe kia noa ai koe' (you were fed and made 'un-tapu' or common – noa – again). As far as he knew water was used in every ceremony of the Maori. To sprinkle warriors going to war was called tohi. Fire was also used in many ceremonies [See Tuahu section. H.B.]. The building in which the teaching was done at Moeraki in 1868–9 was usually called Te Wharetapu, or Te Whare-korero, but any building constructed was a wharetapu until the tapu was taken off it, but he did not know how this rite was done. At Moeraki they wanted to make the wharetapu common (to be used as a meeting-house) so to make it free, water was heated and sprinkled over it. He saw the hot water being sprinkled but that was all he knew of what was done. Then the Uenuku Hall was built and later the old deserted wharetapu was burnt by some Maori larrikins.

A venerable Maori [[the mine of information]] said: To make a man tapu the tohuka would take him to a pool and sprinkle water on with his fingers. (He had never heard of karamu branches being used for sprinkling.) To take the tapu off, an umu would be made and four potatoes and some fish put in. The man would lie on this umu perhaps an hour or so. When the food was cooked all ate a little of it and the tapu was lifted, and the man was noa. This was called taowhakamoe and the karakia of that name was repeated during the ceremony. There were no tapu trees in the South Otago district that he could recall, but he had heard of such elsewhere although he could not say they were usually matai [As at Tuturau. H.B.]. As to why trees became tapu it was generally because the 'ghosts of the old people' had lain down behind such trees. Tapu trees were commonly big trees – that was all he knew about them.

The collector attended a religious service with a fine old Maori and noticed that he gravely placed his pipe, tobacco and matches in a hedge before entering the church grounds. He would not take them even into the grounds, let alone defile the sanctity of the Wharetapu (Church) with them.

Te Maire, questioned, said that taowhakamoe was to karakia and use the mind in secret but he forgot the details of the proper old ceremony connected with it.

Certain trees were regarded as tapu. A few of these trees, no doubt, were to be found near every ancient Maori settlement but the collector was only told of certain tapu trees at Riverton and Tuturau. Some, if not all, of these trees stood as long as the old generation lived but with the departure of the ancient Maori Mana, these monarchs of the bush have all fallen before the white man's axe. The coming of the Pakeha destroyed the original mana of the Maori, but one old man told the collector it would be revived. It appears there is a vaguely-worded tradition that the ancient tohukas foretold that the Maori Mana would depart for a time but would return and then 'the Maori people will be able to turn their minds to anything'.

KARAKIA

It has been stated in print that the Maoris believed that ghosts were afraid of cooked food and could be dispersed by such being taken to a haunted spot, but none of my informants seemed to know of it. One intelligent old woman said that to scare away ghosts or evil spirits the olden people said karakia. They relied on karakia to relieve them from all terrors of the seen or unseen – not on cooked food. If thunder or lightning or any other vivid natural manifestation frightened them, they said karakia, and they repeated karakia to drive away all ghostly visitants, to allay fear and to ward off all portents of evil.

Add to Karakia

Although the word karakia is sometimes translated 'prayer' it does not define what would be prayer to a Christian. A karakia is rather an invocation addressed to some particular god at some particular moment for some particular purpose. Thus a man going fishing or bird-hunting would ask the god appropriate to the occasion to give him a successful expedition; or one going on a journey would ask the god who had charge of travellers not to lengthen out the journey nor let harm befall him. A karakia being repeated in set terms gave it the effect of an incantation or charm in certain instances, an effect which was heightened by its mystic references and oft-times obsolete phraseology, but generally speaking a karakia was to invoke some god to let some wished-for thing come to pass, or some un-wished-for thing fail to eventuate or to hurt the one repeating the words. The words the apostle Paul wrote of Israel might be applied to the ancient Maoris – 'For I bear them record that they have a zeal of God, but not according to knowledge.'

The Maoris were a most religious people, said one veteran, 'for they never did anything without karakia (invocations). They prayed for everything and over everything they did. If we could go back to the old style we would thrive again. The Maoris never prayed to Maui, although he could do miracles, but to the proper gods. I do not know who Tiki was, for I never heard of karakia to a god of that name. The Maoris never worshipped images but prayed direct to the gods. On Ruapuke Island the people (after 1844) were frightened Reverend Wohlers would hear about their karakia so all who indulged in the ancient customs kept them secret. One belief was that if you burnt pikiraki (red mistletoe) and said the right karakia with it, the wind would be calmed. This was done before craft put to sea and the time I saw it done it was quite effective.'

The following is said to be a karakia and was recited by two old men: 'Haea a te ata, ka hapara te ata, ka koroki te manu, ka wairori te kutu, Ko te ata nui, ka hora ena, ka take te umere te awatea.' The collector knows the general meaning of these words but the old men could not or would not give the particulars of the translation and of the meaning attached thereto.

THE TUAHU

In a Maori manuscript list of places in Canterbury detailing where the Maoris procured various foods some places had written against them the words 'he tuahu tapu' (a sacred altar) implying that such altars had stood at those places. One old man said the tuahu tapu was where the 'tabooed devil' was; but a well-informed kaumatua said, 'The tuahu was tapu and it was said if you went there, not being authorised to do so, you would die. The tohukas used to go there to karakia. It depended for its situation on where the kaika or pa was located. If a big chief came on a visit to that place the people would take him there first to karakia before the entertaining took place. The tuahu might be a carving or a stone or a heap of stones perhaps. You would always see a stone at a tuahu in any case covering ashes or other things. Fires were used for some karakia and also to roast selected food to give the visitor to the tuahu a taste of tapu food during the performance of the karakia or ceremony connected with that place.'

Another well-informed man [[the mine of information]] said, 'The tuahu was a place of worship and was tapu. It was sometimes a tree or a rock. The tohukas sometimes made a sacred fire there and the stones there were sacred too. When visitors came to a strange kaika they were always told where the tuahu was situated, and although in wandering about they might go into the urupa tupapaku (burial ground) they would take good care not to approach the tuahu.'

Another Maori told the collector that the tuahu at Moeraki had been called Haere.

The tuahu, said an old woman whose father had been a tohuka (priest), was a very sacred spot. It was where they 'made karakia' (said the most solemn invocations) and made tapu (decided regarding restrictions). There was sometimes a building known as a whare-korero or whare-tuahu near it and to these places men would go to say karakia. They were places of korero-tapu (sacred talk). No one save the priests was allowed near the tuahu – it was extremely tapu.

Add to *Tuahu*

One of my informants [[the mine of information]] said: 'The tuahu is a flat stone with a fire below it and the karehu (embers) are karakia'd. Go back in ten years and the ashes are as potent as ever. If they are touched by anyone but the tohuka, that person will fall stone dead.'

A Waihao Maori [[Henare te Maire]] said: 'The words of a tohuka are ahi-tapu, as they are like a sacred fire when he is speaking for the gods. Learning a pupil to recite secret karakia or sacred words is ahi-tapu. "He ahitapu" is also a little fire near the tuahu – a very sacred spot. There are always stones at the tuahu – stones cannot be burnt like wood or worm-eaten. There are usually two or three big stones – not heaped up high – and some are flat. There was a tuahu at Punatarakao Creek near Morven and it was called Kai-a-te-Atua like the pa near it. When I was a young man we were warned not to go there as its mana still clung to it. I think I am the only one now living who knows where that tuahu is.'

POWERS OF THE TOHUKA

At sea the tohuka could call up whales and marine monsters to protect the canoes in storms, said an old Maori. The karakia would bring the whales who quietened the ocean. When near the shore the tohuka would take one hair from his head and put it in the sea before the whale, which would thus feel rewarded and disappear.

The tohuka did not use the hair to bring the whale, but only afterwards when the canoe was near the shore.

Another aged man referred to whales 'being paid with a hair' for stopping storms at sea; if a shark came up to a canoe to do harm to the crew the tohuka would give it a hair and it would go away. He had never heard of hairs from the body being used, but only those of the head.

The tohuka, he continued, could also do other wonderful things. He could put a person to sleep by karakia; he could fill the air with voices; he could perform divination; and he could karakia a stone and place it under your doorway so that when you stepped over it you came under the dread influence of makutu. There were women tohukas as well as male ones, but they acted in their own hapus (families) and not for the tribe generally. The tohuka was the proper person to cremate the dead and to cover up the ashes so that these would not be blown away by the winds of heaven. The tohuka was not allowed to wash his head in hot water or to cut his hair, as the head was so sacred that his power would be gone if he did. The tohuka would go to the tuahu alone and there at a sacred fire he would karakia. No offering was burnt at it but in his communings there the tohuka was the recipient of power and of secret knowledge. He told no one his secrets but he would give his warnings that certain things had to be done and the propitious time for performing them. He could take a hair of the head and touch your lips and give you the necessary power to do what was necessary – 'whakai koe kia mana ai koe' (feed you and give you power).

An old lady narrated: 'The well-taught tohukas had wonderful powers in the days of old. They did not reveal the source of their power to the common people – it was a secret work. The well-known chief, Tare Wetere of the Otago Heads, used to say that in the olden days the tohuka would keep alert and watch his chances to injure those opposed to him. If he saw the footsteps of those people in the soil or sand, he would karakia them and so kill his enemies. A great tohuka had a terrible power in bringing people to death. Some of the tohukas had also great powers in finding out hidden things and in revealing them. Others besides the tohukas have the power of finding lost possessions. At present Mrs Heuheu, of Taupo, is performing wonders in finding lost articles, but I know of no one in the South Island now with a similar gift.'

DIVINATION AND VENTRILOQUISM

The tohukas are credited with both these faculties but the collector could get but little information. One said: 'I never heard of Maori ventriloquism – voices coming from the roof or from the air above would be echoes. I never knew personally of whakaata (divination by water) but I have heard of it. Your shadow is called an ata and it is said it would appear in the pool where the tohuka gazed but I do not know the tohu (signs) of that work. Nor have I heard of divination by tossing sticks.' Another had heard of a tohuka filling the air with voices, but he did not know how it was done or what it was called. Divination by sticks was called rotarota but he did not know the procedure.

WITCHCRAFT

In discussing details of what is commonly called witchcraft my informants mentioned four kinds and following are their remarks under these four headings.

Rotu or Rotua – One old lady called this rotu, the rest of my informants terming it rotua, which is probably merely the passive form of the word, but in passing it may be recalled that the Canterbury Maoris called the bird, the *Notornis*, takahe while the Southland Maoris insist that the name should be takahea, so there may be more in the additional 'a' than meets the eye at first glance. The old lady said: 'Rotu is dozing. It is also to be put to sleep against your will. It can be done by karakia, by reciting a charm "rehua moe" against a person. The charm was handed down from generation to generation. The tohuka did not need to be gazing at you to put you to sleep. He could do it secretly at a distance. All the old Maoris did in such work was unseen – it was unknown to others.'

An old man said: 'Rotua was done by brainwork or heart knowledge. I have heard the tohuka could put a man to sleep but I believe it was more done in the North Island than down here. It was performed in the same way as the tohuka performed makutu.' Another said that for rotua-ki-moe he thought the tohuka procured something that had been worn on a person's head or that he put his hand on the head before the person went off into sleep but he was not sure of this. A well-informed man said: 'Rotua was to put to sleep but I never heard how it was accomplished. The person against whom the tohuka directed the rotua might never waken again or it might be only a short sleep.'

Another venerable man said that a prisoner might karakia and his captors falling asleep he would walk off. He escaped by rotua. This informant narrated a case where a tohuka pronounced a rotua against the dogs of a pa and their mouths were so closed that they could not bark while the enemy was stealing in on their masters.

Atahu – This was not well-known in Murihiku apparently for little information was forthcoming. [The collector got more information about it at Kaiapoi.] At length an elderly woman in South Otago referred to a charm to make one of the opposite sex respond to unreturned affection. If a young man desired a maid who was unresponsive to his wooing he could ascertain a pool or stream she visited and he could karakia the water so that when she looked at it she would fall under the charm and he could carry her away. There was a darker, more sinister, side to this form of witchcraft and she understood it was a form of makutu known as atahu in the North Island. [The Reverend R. Taylor in his book *Te-Ika-a-Maui* 2nd edition page 181 gives a charm or spell and says: 'Atu ahu is a charm to induce a stubborn woman to accept the person who is disliked by her as her husband. This charm is so powerful as to compel the lady to come from any distance. The offering made to the gods was called "manawa".]

Whaiwhaia is a form of witchcraft which bore a bad reputation in the old days. It is a curse which can be projected over any distance. A tohuka would have some cause of grievance against someone and would send a curse against the offending person so that the latter would suffer a disease or affliction of the body or some harm or hurt. Whakatau, a tohuka at Kaikoura, sent a whaiwhaia against Tunarere at Stewart Island and Tunarere's toes and fingers rotted off. The same amiable tohuka put a curse on Hakopa who lived at Makawhio in Westland and it twisted his victim's face into a very distorted shape. Some of my informants had seen Tunarere and Hakopa so they considered they had plain visible evidence of the dire results of this powerful form of witchcraft.

Makutu is considered to be the blackest form of the black art, the deadliest manifestation of wizardry. One of my informants, indeed, considered whaiwhaia and makutu to be much on a par, but the others gave the palm to makutu. They did not say much about it, one of my best informants dismissing the subject in these words: 'Whaiwhaia is to suffer bodily pain, but makutu is sudden death.'

OMENS

The collector asked the Maoris at Temuka concerning the belief in omens and elicited a little information. Omens were termed ka tohu ki te raki (signs from the sky) or ka tohu e pa ana ki te takata (the signs concerning the man). Such signs were many.

If the ruru (morepork) calls in a particularly hoarse manner it betokens a death. A strange thing about this cry is that some hear it while others as near do not. If the voice of the ruru is clear it is a good omen, kai te pai. If you are driving a horse and it stops and stands still it has a tohu and if you force it forward it will be bad for the animal. A Maori was driving a cart through his gateway when the animal stopped. He forced it to proceed and a little way along the road it dropped dead. It had received a tohu but its master disregarded it.

There is a bird called the karae, never seen in the daytime but heard at night. If it appeared to be going south and it was crying in a hoarse voice that portended a death in the South but if its voice was clear that was e pai = good (or in the vernacular kai te pai). If it was going North the same signs held good there as for the South. One taua (grandmother) had heard this bird's cry and said it was quite distinct from any other she had ever heard – it was very unlike the usual cry of any land or sea bird she knew of or had heard of. When the kiore (rat) goes kokoho (gives a gasping cry) it is a sign of death to some person and if the hinerata (mouse) gives a squeak like the tick of a clock it is likewise a bad sign indicating the probable death of some relation of the person who heard it. If you go fishing for hapuku (groper) and the maka (hook) catches on the pito (navel) of the fish it signifies death to a relative of the fisher.

The ruru (morepork) is credited with being an uncanny bird at the best of times and some members of the family have the reputation of being familiar spirits of certain tohukas and such atua birds are regarded as capable of giving warning of impending events or disasters. One of my esteemed informants related at some length how an atua bird had tried to warn her. She could not understand what it was trying to tell and was left in a state of nervous tension. Next day two of her relatives were drowned.

An old woman said: 'To find a white titi (muttonbird) is very uncommon. It is a sign of death.' The people of old would not eat before going fishing and would often set out with the morning star. They would on no account take a kauati (firestick) in their canoes on fishing trips as it would be very unlucky. My informants had not heard that cooked food would not be carried by bird-hunters going into the forest (*vide* Tregear) but they considered it might be correct as it seemed very like an olden idea.

Add to Omens

Sneezing – Matihe is sneezing. It is said if you sneeze from the right nostril it is a good omen but if from the left nostril it is a bad sign. Another old man said sneezing indicated if people were talking about you or it was perhaps a sign someone was going to die. If you sneezed on the right side someone was speaking evil about you, but if the sneeze was on the left side their talk about you was good. Another old man said he had always understood matihe was a good omen.

Dreams – An old taua (grandmother) said moemoea (dreams) could often be relied on. She believed in them since she (then at Ruapuke Island) dreamt a lad at Colac was dead and later word came verifying the dream. Hinehaka, a prophetess at Ruapuke, was noted for her dreams, notably one re Tahununu's fate (see H.B.'s articles Number X [[Beattie 1919 v28]] in *Journal of the Polynesian Society*). When word came that Puoho was coming South, Hinehaka was asked to prophesy. She laid down on a ra (sail) and going to sleep, dreamt. When she awoke she told the people Puoho would be killed at Tuturau. She also told them not to go on with the pa they had been building (it was the Rauparaha raid time) as it would stand and rot. Both predictions came true. A poua (grandfather) called dreams moe and said if you saw someone doing evil in a dream it might be an omen but he did not believe in dreams. All the same he would not do an act if he had a dream against doing it. Some Maoris attached importance to dreams. An old Maori told the collector that personally speaking he had found it unlucky to dream of coalpits or anything black; to dream of bees denoted his enemies were active and he had found it was bad to dream of any animal but the sheep. Dreams generally came true and if he dreamt he was swimming he would wake up to find it raining. The Maoris, he said, also believed in tohu (signs) to tell them whether to undertake journeys, etc., (but he gave no instances of these).

Another Maori said if you dreamt where a thing was that was lost, etc., you would have to get up at once and mark the place or else your dream-sign would be of no value to you. My informants related to me instances of how paint clay had been found at Kaitangata and greenstone in Westland by means of dreams.

WAIRUA AND ATUA

An inquiry as to what constituted the difference between these two terms brought forth a little information. One man considered that the two were interchangeable terms. He added that once when the whalers lived at Otaku (Murray River, Stewart Island) all the men, Europeans and Maoris alike, saw a spirit walking about. It was said to be the ghost of a man who had done away with himself. It was a wairua or atua.

Against this opinion the best-informed of the aged people took issue. One said: 'Wairua is the spirit of a man who is living or who has lived and is now dead, but an atua has not lived in a human form – it is simply a bad spirit.' Another narrated: 'Wairua is your spirit or the spirit of anyone. You may see a man's wairua when he is dying, or sometimes before this happens as when he is sleeping or in a trance, or after he is dead. Once at Wakapatu I was certain I saw a man moving in his garden and I mentioned the fact to a woman. She replied that he could not possibly be in his garden as he was far too ill to move out of bed. I would not believe her against the evidence of my senses and went over to his cottage to see, but sure enough when I got there I found he had just died and I had seen his wairua. On the other hand an atua was a demon, a ghost not of this world or a supernatural being. In the Maori Bible the word God is translated Atua but it is not a good nor correct name for Deity as we generally consider an atua an evil spirit'

THE TOHUKA'S WAIRUA AND AN ANGRY MAN

Once at Moeraki a tohuka brought up a shoal of small fish but the people said there were so many the fish would smell ere they could be eaten so the tohuka called up Ruatapu who sent a big sea and washed them off. The old man died and his face was painted with red maukoroa and he was stood upright against a papa (slab) and told to go and get satisfaction (tuhi-tokorau) for his death. [Kakemate or kakimate is to kill someone to avenge a death]. His spirit went forth and greatly annoyed a man carrying (kaweka) wood. The man tripped over the wood several times. He heard the deceased's spirit was out on a mission to obtain utu, so being a reckless fellow he took his taiaha and went and hit the corpse over the head with it. He threatened to repeat this performance so the relatives took the body away and burnt it.

SUPERSTITION

As with most uncivilised folk superstition was rife among the Maori. This is not to be wondered at considering the amount that still lingers among white people.

It was said by the Murihiku Maori that if you used kotukutuku (fuchsia) for firewood you would get puhipuhi (gout). An intelligent old Maori told the collector he had used it but had not got gout. How the superstition started he did not know. Recently a man who really had gout was told it was caused by wearing another man's shoes. He returned the shoes and the gout disappeared.

Moving trees – a story of trees moving about or travelling has been told about Banks Peninsula but none of my Murihiku informants had heard of any such occurrence.

Enchanted trees – None of these seemed to have been located in Murihiku. One man had heard of a magic tree 'up Rakitata way' which the people had tried in vain to hew down.

Taniwha or water demons were held to infest certain waters and also an aquatic monster called a pukutuora but none of my Southern informants had heard of the puku-atua a fierce marine demon mentioned in the Kaiapoi section.

It is recorded that Matamata the magic reptile guardian of the great Katimamoe chief, Te Rakitauneke, slept with lizards hanging to his nostrils, but my informants did not seem to have heard this statement. They had heard, however, that that noted karara would lick the blood oozing from wounds and heal them. By this means it is said to have stayed the flow of blood from its master, when his wounds were so severe that death seemed certain.

Warning Voices – In certain localities warning voices are supposed to come from the bush warning the Maoris when they have caught enough pigeons, enough eels, or cut enough flax, etc. The voice would command 'Kati ra' (Stop!) and the Maoris dared not disobey under fear of dire penalties. It was the maeroero who called out.

The Maeroero were wild men of the woods, a kind of uncouth fairies. It was they who forbade the Maori gather too much of the produce of the wild. They are not recorded in the Waitaki region, but down the east coast of Otago and most frequent in the Tautuku forests. They are described as wild hairy creatures but strange to say they play the flute beautifully. Old Rakiraki, when at Tautuku, heard the maeroero playing the putorino flute a long way off, and the soft cadences of the flute music is supposed to linger round many an Otago peak.

SECTION XXIII

FOLK TALES

A FOLK-TALE

The collector [[Beattie 1920b]] published (*Transactions of the New Zealand Institute* Vol. 52 p. 72) a folk-tale about the toroa (albatross) and the kakapo (ground parrot) as given him by an old man. Recently he heard two more bird stories but they are both variants of the former story but will be given here for illustrative comparison of how a story can degenerate when indifferently learned.

The first was given by an otherwise well-informed man who has given much valuable information to the collector at various times on many topics.

'The only tradition I know of birds is that the albatross wanted the kakapo to go to sea but the kakapo said, "No! We're better on shore." The albatross replied, "If we stop here someone will eat us," but the kakapo said "Not so! but if we go to sea we will be seen and eaten." So they parted company, the albatross going to sea while the kakapo now hides under the fronds of the piupiu fern.'

The collector asked a roomful of returned muttonbirders (June, 1920) if they knew any stories of birds and at length one middle-aged woman said: 'We call the mollyhawk, totoria, and once it lived on land where its white plumage made it easy to be seen and killed. The kakapo was then a seabird but its green colour was not thought so suitable for the sea as for the land. So the two changed places – the kakapo went to the forest which its green colour matched very well, while the totoria, white like the crest of the waves, sailed away over the big ocean. This was the story I heard the old people tell some years ago.'

TWO FOLK-TALES ABOUT BIRDS

Once the koka (Native Crow) and Tieke (Saddleback) had a discussion about the speed they could fly (rere) and to settle the matter agreed to have a race. This was at Rakiura (Stewart Island) and both started out level. Soon the koka missed the other and he felt well pleased with himself for he thought he was leading, but just then the tieke's whistle sounded away ahead in the bush. The tieke waited until he heard the lumbering flight of his rival and then he forged ahead and whistled again. Every time he heard the koka coming he flew forward and whistled again. Finally he stopped till the other came up. The tieke said, 'You cannot fly like me.' The koka replied 'I hurt my pakihau (wing).' The tieke laughed and said 'That is not so – I beat you.' After this race the tieke was recognised as the better flier of the two and crossed to the Titi Islands while the koka stuck to Stewart Island.

And that is why the tieke is found on some of the Muttonbird Islands while the koka is not.

Once upon a time the only bird in Aotearoa (New Zealand) which had red upon its plumage was the kaka. It was also the only bird with kutu (lice) upon it. The kakariki looked at the kura (red) of the kaka and longed to have it for its own, so it offered to pick the lice from the bigger bird. The kaka consented and the parrokeet set to work. After a time when the kaka was not looking the kakariki took a firm hold of all the red in the kaka's head and jerked it out. The parrokeet fled with its prize and the kaka pursued, calling out 'Whakahokia mai oku raukura' (return my red feathers) but the parrokeet was too fast and the kaka could not catch it. Hence it is now that the kakariki has the red on its head while the kaka has none on its head, but only some under its wings. (The Maoris said the parrokeets with yellow and orange heads are young females and that as these birds get older their heads will turn red. One Maori told a European this and the latter would not credit it but it is said the bird he had with yellow on it eventually turned red. Such is the Native belief.)

Add to Folk-Lore

'Now, you know,' said an intelligent old Maori, 'there are two kinds of shellfish with names almost similar but quite dissimilar in shape. One of these is the kakahi and the other is the kakihi. These two had a discussion as to where they would live. The kakihi said to the kakahi, "You go to the sea," but the latter replied "No! You go!" The kakihi urged, "You try the salt water," and the kakahi finally did so, but came back and said, "The sea is too kawa [bitter – but my informant in explaining the term said it meant the salt water tasted 'too strong' for its liking. H.B.] for me." The kakahi then said to the kakihi "You try it yourself," and the latter shellfish went off to the sea, remaining away for three or four days. When it came back the kakahi said, "I thought you were dead," and the kakihi answered, "No! I am not dead. I liked it very much and stayed on a while." Then the kakahi said, "You should now try the freshwater." The kakihi did so and after a trial said to the kakahi, "You can stick to your fresh water, the salt water for me." Both thereupon separated and went to the element they liked the better – the kakahi to the fresh water of the inland streams and the kakihi to the salt water of the ocean, and both have kept to their own sphere ever since.' The narrator added that the kakihi will rot in fresh water. He had eaten both kinds and found both good. He knew of no story where the karoro (seagull) took part, although this bird has a habit of taking shellfish up in the air and dropping them on the rocks to open them. It was because these birds used to do this often of a morning, or watch for fish each morning also, that Karoro Creek, near Port Molyneux, got its name.

THE SEAL AND THE QUAIL

The koreke (quail) and the pakake (seal) were friends, although one was a bird and the other a mammal. The pakake said to his friend, 'Let us go out to sea together.' 'No!' replied the koreke, 'We'll stop on land.' 'No!' said the pakake, 'We'll go out to sea.' With these words he began to move towards the ocean but the koreke caught hold of him to keep him back. Then the pakake began to tangi (cry) and sang a little lament as follows: 'Thou, O Quail, my friend, canst stop on land, but this is my lamentation. Alas! Alas! If I stay here I will be killed to be meat on the flaxen plate at Te Pariwhakatau.'

After this sorrowful farewell the pakake kept on his way and went out to sea while the koreke stayed on shore and turned inland.

This is a korero-tawhiti (fairy tale) of the Maori.

A TALE WITH A MORAL

A saying of old in the South was 'E kai ko maoka, ka kai Korekore' meaning 'the food that was cooked was the food of Korekore,' or that Korekore would eat. He was a tipuna but was a frightfully lazy one and it is told of him that he would set out to hunt (apparently) but when out of observation would sit down and scrape and fray his paraerae (footgear) to make them appear worn with much walking. Then he would quietly doze the day away and return (in time for the evening meal) to the kaika. The people would think he had been hunting wekas unsuccessfully and would give him some cooked ones. He was not only very lazy but very greedy and when the birds were handed out of the umu would gammon they were too hot to hold long enough to divide with anyone so slunk away with a lot unshared. The proverb quoted above by old people was to check and rebuke greediness on the part of children and to try and teach the young to be unselfish and to share with others.

SECTION XXIV

TABLE GIVING NAMES OF RELATIONSHIPS (SOUTH ISLAND DIALECT) AT ORAKA (COLAC BAY), WAIKOUAITI, MORAKI AND AT TEMUKA KAIKAS

Relationship	Speaker	Moeraki and Waikouaiti	Temuka	Colac Bay
Father		Hakoro	Hakoro or Matua hakoro	
Mother		Hakui		
elder Brother	ms	Tuakana		
elder Brother	ws	Tukane		
elder Sister	ms	Tuahine		
elder Sister	ws	Tuakana		
Father's brother		hakoro		
Father's b's child		Tuakana if brother is older, Taina if brother is younger		
Father's b's wife		Hakui keke (or matua whakai)		
Father's Sister		Hakui		(you could also say re her 'tuahine no taku hakoro')
Father's s's husband		Hakoro keke	Hakoro-keke or Matua whakai	(usually) Matua-whakai
Father's s's child		Tuakana if sister is older, Taina if sister is younger		
Mother's brother		Hakoro		
Mother's b's wife		Hakui (It is not good form to add 'keke' here)	Hakui or Matua-whakai	
Mother's b's child		Tuakana if brother is older, Taina if brother is younger		
Mother's Sister		Hakui		
Mother's S's husband		Matua-whakai or Hakoro-keke		
Mother's s's child		Tuakana if sister is older, Taina if sister is younger		
Father's father		poua		
Father's mother		taua		
Mother's father		poua		
Mother's mother		taua		
Husband	ws	Taku Tane		[I was told that taku hoa = North Island]
Wife's father		Poupou or Matua hukoi tane		(usually) Matua hukoi
Son		tama		

Relationship	Speaker	Moeraki and Waikouaiti	Temuka	Colac Bay
Daughter		tamahine		
Younger brother	ms	taina		(The last boy or girl is potiki)
Younger brother	ws	Tukane koroiti/ tukane iti or taina		
Younger sister	ms	Tuahine iti or taina		
Younger sister	ws	taina		
Brother's child	ms/ws	iramutu or Tamaiti		Tamaiti is a general term
Husband's b's child		iramutu or iramutu keke or tamaiti whakai		[Tamariki whakai is plural]
Wife's b's child		Tamaiti whakai		
Wife	ms	Taku wahine		
Sister's child	ms	iramutu		
Husband's S's child		Tamaiti whakai		
Wife's S's child		iramutu keke		
Son's child	ms	mokopuna		
Son's child	ws	mokopuna		
Daughter's child	ms/ws	mokopuna		
Daughter's husband	ms/ws	Hunoka		
Son's wife	ms/ws	Hunoka		
Wife's mother		Poupou or Matua hukoi	matua-hukoi-wahine	(usually) Matua hukoi
Husband's father		poupou	matua-hukoi-tane	...
Husband's Mother		poupou	matua-hukoi-wahine	...
Wife's brother		taokete		
Wife's sister		waiwahine		
Sister's husband	ms	taokete		
Sister's husband	ws	whaitane	whaitane	taokete tane or whaitane
Brother's wife	ms	Waiwahine	Waiwahine	Taokete wahine or waiwahine
Brother's Wife	ws	Taokete		
Husband's brother		Whaitane		
Husband's Sister		Taokete		
Wife's s's husband		Hoatane		
Husband's b's wife		Hoawahine		
Son's wife's Parents		not recognised		

[[ms = man speaking; ws = woman speaking; b = brother; s = sister. Unless shown otherwise, the term used at Moeraki and Waikouaiti is the same at Temuka and Colac Bay. Capitalisation as in original manuscript.]]

Notes: At Moeraki the collector was told that iramutu-tane = nephew and iramutu-wahine = niece. That keke meant 'armpit' and denoted a child next in kin to one's own. That taku ropa = my sweetheart. That putau was an old widow. That great grandfather = tipuna; that whai = step; and that an old maid = poueru.

At Temuka the informants said that kuia meant a very old wife, whaiereere a wife with a family, and pakoko or pukupa a wife with no family; that a stepfather or step-mother was called matua-whakai, matua meaning parent and whakai = feeding; that a woman speaking of both her father-in-law and mother-in-law would say 'aku matua hukoi'; that grandchildren were mokopuna tuatahi, great-grandchildren – mokopuna-tuarua and great-great-grandchildren = mokopuna-tuatoru. A woman at Temuka has a mokopuna-tuatoru.

At Colac Bay the collector was told that the real meaning of matua-whakai was to adopt children; that keke equalled 'step' such as step-mother or was a relationship term to show it came by marriage; that poupou for a father-in-law was slangy the correct term being matua-hukoi – you could use poupou in speaking of him to others, but hukoi when speaking personally to him; that tamaiti is used much more than tamaiti-whakai; that wahine-pa or sometimes pukupa, is a wife without children; that poueru is a widower; that wahine-poueru is a widow or old maid; that a married man or woman = maronui, a single one = poueru. End of 'The Maori in Murihiku' volume.

CANTERBURY

CONTENTS

Section
- I   Habitations 223
- II   Personal Wear and Clothing 232
- III   Flaxwork 238
- IV   Personal Adornment 241
- V   Paints, Dyes, and Scents 245
- VI   Tattooing and Wood-Carving 249
- VII   Games and Music 253
- VIII   Medical Lore 261
- IX   Disposal of the dead 269
- X   Customs 275
- XI   Weapons 281
- XII   Greenstone 284
- XIII   Canoes, etc. 286
- XIV   Domestic Science 290
- XV   Vegetable Foods 296
- XVI   Ichthyology 307
- XVII   Ornithology 334
- XVIII   Entomology 346
- XIX   Zoology 350
- XX   Botany 355
- XXI   Meteorology and Astronomy 359
- XXII   Religion 365
- XXIII   Mythology 383
- XXIV   Superstition 408
- XXV   Folk-Tales and Proverbs 423
- XXVI   History 425
- XXVII   Table giving names of Relationships at Rapaki, Taumutu and Tuahiwi [Canterbury], and also up in the Province of Nelson 448
- XXVIII   Information relating to Names of Things, etc., Contact with Pakehas, Some Interesting Words, Introduced Animals, Introduced Plants, Parts of the Human Body Named in Nelson, Canterbury, and Murihiku. See list. 451

SECTION I

INFORMATION RELATING TO HABITATIONS

Te Kaika or The Village — Whare-huihui or Meeting Houses — Wharepuni or Communal Houses — Niu or Guest Houses — Paepae or Latrines — Kaupapa or Food Platforms — Pa or Fortifications — etc.
Note: If the spelling of a word differs it is through the differing pronunciations of my Maori friends. Vowels are often interchangeable. Thus ipu, opu, and upu all denote the same object; and so on.

WHARES (AND KAIKAS)

Round-shaped whares were never or very seldom seen in North Canterbury, said my principal informant. (Rapaki, one of the chief settlements, was started after visit of Rauparaha to Akaroa and Kaiapoi in 1831). Prior to this date the head people at Kaiapoi had whare-whakairo (carved houses) ordinary houses not being carved. The wharepuni or communal sleeping house was dug into ground and was entered through a small door and steps (or arawhata) led down to floor. Very little of this building was out of ground. The whare-runaka (a recent name for a meeting-house, the older name being whare-huihui) was more modern than the wharepuni – both in point of time and manner of construction. Its poutokomanawa were carved. Some of these were square and carving on two sides would be men and two sides would represent women, or they might be round, alternate ones representing the sexes. There was plenty of carving in the old days – just as much as the North Island proportionately to population, but he had never seen it done although he drew plan for model pa for Christchurch Exhibition. He had seen whares at Onuku and Akaroa when a boy. The roof and ridgepole = tahu; walls of totara, kohai and other timbers = pakitara; the back wall = tuaroko; battens = kaho; window = matao; he forgot name of front wall and the verandah. He further added that over the verandah was carved a tiki, or figure to represent a man or woman. In speaking later he called part of the front of house (over verandah apparently) maihi.

An intelligent old man whose acquaintance with the Kaiapoi district dates back to 1857 as a small boy says he remembers the carvings on certain houses and also the wharepuni at Te Kai-a-te-Atua kaik. It was dug in the ground – the biggest part was in the earth, and roofed over. This was for warmth he thought. About two feet depth of wall showed from outside and below this inside wall were earth walls lined with pukakaho reeds cut off in about two feet lengths. The roof – tahu-o-te-whare – was lined with pukakaho (toetoe reeds) inside and pukio (niggerheads) and thatch outside. The back of the whare like the sides was earthed up too but there was a sort of verandah in front which he thought was called a marae. There was no window but only a door. It was dark inside but was only used as a sleeping house and the fire would give sufficient light. It was used in winter and not much in summer. The pukakaho for use in lining whares was gathered in autumn to keep dry for use. The old meeting-house (he forgot its name – it stood three miles from Tuahiwi) and the old church were made in Native style – or at least a Maori look was imparted by their being lined with reeds. In old days Kaiapoi Pa was principal settlement in district but there were minor villages at Tuahiwi and along the Cam River (Whakahume) at Ruataniwha (the north side of Kaiapoi Factory site) and further up that stream at Koau and Te Kai-a-te-Atua. No one now lives at these last three places but all the people are gathered on the Tuahiwi Reserve. This is said to be a very old place and after Kaiapoi was taken and burnt in 1831 the refugees returned to live at Tuahiwi and ever since it has been the principal settlement of North Canterbury. (Indeed it was the largest in South Island for years although it is believed Temuka is now more populous.) This informant had never heard of round houses except at the Titi Islands where the timber suits that style of dwelling as it is crooked and not tall. The trees usually used on the islands are tupari (most) and also inaka and titiaweka, and as they are usually bent by prevailing winds they are adapted to whare-potaka (round houses). He has assisted to build several on Titi Islands. There is a fine example of one standing at Puai on Taukiepa (or Kanawera he had heard it correctly called, Taukiepa being a corruption of English words South Cape) or Long Island on chart. It would not be so easy to build round whares on Banks Peninsula as it had a hard soil but on Titi islands the soil is soft and peaty and the tree branches can be pushed well in to form round house. He did not remember much about the ordinary whare of Canterbury except it was made of poles and reeds.

A woman who first saw Rapaki in 1878 says it looked a rough and ready place, the whares being clay, with thatched roofs. There was a long guest-house (niu) of poka (ferntrees) lined with clay. [Imitation pakeha wattle-and-daub. H.B.] It had an earth floor and roof of wiwi (rushes) and there was a door at each end. If visitors arrived the elders would cry 'Show them to the niu'. The wharerunaka (meeting-house) was, as far as she remembered, of poka and wiwi. It must have had a floor for she recollected a dance in it. All these buildings were gone long ago.

A Maori who saw Tuahiwi and Kaiapoi district in 1867 says he remembers the old wharehui (meeting-house) there. It was called Tutekawa but it has since been pulled down and a new one built (a la pakeha) called Tuahuriri. The old one was about thirty feet long and had low walls = ka tara o te whare. The posts (pou) supporting the walls were about five feet apart and along the top of them were laid round poles = paetara. The walls were a line of pukakaho reeds inside and patiti (tussock) outside – there was no timber among it. To support the roof there were two poutokomanawa; the first carved to represent Tutekawa, the second his wife (he forgot her name but other sources give it as Tukorero). The ridgepole = tahu; rafters = heke; battens = kaho. The roof was reeds inside and patiti outside. The tualoko (back wall) had a pole up its centre and rows of reeds inside and patiti outside. The rows of reeds inside had a nice effect – the joinings (called hono) were of flax. To get the picturesque black and white rings on the reeds, the toetoe (reeds) had flax wound round at regular intervals and was then scorched (tahutahu pukakaho) creating black rings where fire got at it and white where flax band had encircled it. The door was called a whatitoka [This may be genuine – he says it is but he has been twenty nine years at Wairarapa in North Island although he spent his boyhood at Kaiapoi. H.B.], the window, he thought was matapihi while he forgot what the people called the verandah of the house. After he left the district the old Native Hall was pulled down and a European one substituted for it.

The collector has a further note that the name of the Hall at Rapaki is Wheke.

Add to Buildings

A little whare (house), said the principal informant, built near the main whare of a chief and used for sleeping in was called a mahau. The veranda of a whare was called whakamahau. To raise the pou and poutokomanawa of a big house a platform (kaupapa) would be erected and the people on it would raise the big logs – this act was called tokorangi. The barge boards (maihi) crossed one another thus $\times$ and a carved figure, a tekoteko was put between at top. He never heard of a koruru board. This tekoteko or spire had another name which he forgot. It was fastened with aka vine. The tatau (door) slid open but he forgot the name of the sliding panel frame. There was no chimney on the oldtime whare – the smoke got out of the matapihi (window); the high window at front of house, not the low one at the back. The smoke blackened the walls in time. The fire in dwellings was just for warmth. One name for the fireplace was ahipaeinaina and ahitaina was another name but he forgot the principal name of the lot. Some whare had small openings near roof to let the smoke out – these 'smoke windows' were known as pihanga after the 'female mountain' of that name (Pihanga) in North Island which lets its smoke drift slowly and lazily out. [The collector read him the account of house-building given in Tregear's 'Maori Race' and he said he agreed with the list of names given there although some of them were new to him. H.B.] These house-building names seemed to him to be correct enough except he would say ruru-aho-tuhere (not ruruwaho-tuwhere) but that was a dialectical difference. He did not know some of the names but he could understand their meaning. The cord to fasten a door was not ruru-aho-tuhere in Canterbury but whakarawe. He had never heard of killing a man at a house-opening in the South Island. Such a custom must have been in the 'bush country' of the North

Island. In regard to other buildings the wharau was a sort of lean-to with an open front, used for camping sometimes. He had heard of it but never seen it. A whare-wharau would be run up when out hunting food but he forgot its North Island name. He had heard the name maimai used for a shelter but the origin of the word he knew not. [Australian Blackfellow term. H.B.] A potato, kumera or pora which had lain long in a koropu or storing pit, and become soft was called a maimai. The storing-pit was also called rua here and other names which he forgot. Besides whares the whatas were prominent in a village. The niches round the legs (pou) of the whata were to protect it against Pakeha rats – the Maori rat never went up the whatas; it was never in the pas but always kept to the bush. He did not know what these niches were called. The whata-tunga-kai or (sometimes) whata-punga-kai was a whare on papaka or plates resting on pou (posts) and used to place food in. Some whata stood on only one big post, others on two and some on four posts.

In every pa or village stood the paepae (latrine). He had heard name mianga used in his travels. The paepae was placed on side of lagoon or creek usually and was common to all. The board to sit on was carved and would accommodate several at once as no shame was felt over nature's actions. A poupou or handgrip (whose name he forgot) stood before each sitter to be grasped if required. The place was called whare-paepae, or paepae-tiko, or paepae-tutae but in these enlightened days the people thought these last two terms were 'slang – too rough altogether', so imported hamuti or paepae-hamuti, a North Island word, as more polite. In the old days if children dirtied the board they had to wash it clean. [His father said that at Kaiapoi he had seen the people use a manuka broom to sweep hamuti off surface before drawing water from the lagoon for domestic use. The people had no idea of sanitation in those days.]

A Maori said 'The whata was a stage to put food on, the pataka was a permanent storehouse on posts. There were also rua-kumera and rua-taewa to store kumera and potatoes in.' Every Maori building, said the principal informant, faced east or north, not west nor south, so that the souls of dead en route to Reinga would not enter them.

There is said to have been a niu (guest-house) in every kaik in the days of fifty or sixty years ago, and these were made of tree-trunks lined with clay. A wharepuni existed at Taumutu till fairly recent years.

The collector asked his various informants concerning the use of the buildings said to have been existent in ancient kaikas but got very little further forward. An old man who had spent much time in the South (and who is less tainted with North Island ideas and phraseology than most Canterbury Maoris) had never even heard the name Wharetako [Tako – See dictionary. H.B.]. The principal informant had just heard the word but considered it was 'children's talk', as was also the name wharehaka. He had heard of the niu. It was a round-shaped house and was used to sleep in. (The shape would be as convenient for sleeping in as is the bell-tent used by soldiers.) Another meaning of the word niu was to denote

Teone Taare Tikao (left) and Hoani Matui, 1908. Tikao was Beattie's principal informant on Canterbury traditions. H.J. Gill photograph, S23-030a, Hocken Collections Uare Taoka o Hākena, University of Otago.

a child's games like niti, or toropenepene, or teka. Perhaps the word whare-tako should read as whare-teka, the house where boys played games. You could make a sort of windmill and set it up on the peak of a niu or round-house, and it would revolve in the breezes. To take a man's wife away while he is looking is 'tako' and this might possibly be an origin of name Whare-tako. If the name was whare-taka it could mean rolling up one's possessions to go on a journey. Takapo Lake owes its name to such a circumstance. The people, Waitaha, he thought, heard of a defeat of their tribe at a distance and of the approach of a hostile force and 'bundled up their swags and cleared out at night'.

The pahuri, said an old man, was a temporary dwelling, or rather a shelter from the weather, built on journeys or on fishing, birding or ratting trips. It was made of boughs of trees, of toetoe, korari, tussock, reeds, saplings, or other material available according to the locality. 'You could not tie it without vines or flax,' he concluded.

BEDS AND BEDDING

It is getting increasingly hard to gather information on a subject like this in North Canterbury where the famous Kaiapoi mill has been turning out good Pakeha blankets since 1873. (Stack [[1893]] says it started in 1866 to deal with flax fibre – see *Kaiapohia* page 12). Following is the scanty information the collector gathered:

The principal informant said he had long ago slept on an old-fashioned rara bed. There were several in the whare. There were six pou (posts) and the framework (stretcher, hammock, call it what you will) was tied to these posts. This framework was made of supplejack, akatea and plaited flax and it was about two feet off the floor. The akatea made it springy. You spread the bed kakahu (which were made bigger than ordinary wearing kakahu) over the rara, or framework, and it was quite easy to sleep on. Some slept on the ground beside the fire and in the old days it was nothing unusual for a person to sleep kiri-tahanga (naked). In those days the skins of the people were hardened much more than now. They were inured to exposure in all kinds of weather and consequently did not feel the cold as now when used to Pakeha clothes. Hence for a person to sleep absolutely naked was no hardship. At the same time there was always plenty of kakahu mats about, but without prejudice to the excellence of flax mats it had to be admitted that blankets of sheep's wool are warmer.

A Rapaki Maori in referring to the abundance of feathers the old Maoris had said they were useful to make feather mats (kakahu) or to sleep on when they could be used as bedding.

A Kaiapoi woman referred to the fact that in old days the 'floors' of earth in whares were covered with whariki [Synonymous with tiaka. H.B.] as a rule. The joins in these whariki were called morua [At the tangi at Temuka the big hall (Te

Hapa o Niu Tireni) was used as a communal sleeping barracks. Straw was laid down each side and this was covered with a continuous line of tiaka mats, each one overlapping the last one. Blankets and pillows completed the bedding. H.B.]

STOREHOUSES

The principal informant had little to say regarding storehouses. Whata, he said were sometimes built on four legs and sometimes on two. Some were high and some were low but he had forgotten their different names. A storehouse in the earth to store kumera, pora, pohata and potatoes, etc. was koropu. [This may be a North Island word. H.B.]

An old Maori said there was only one way to make whata, and that was to put them on posts. A whata was usually put on two posts (pou), the floor being called kaupapa and the rafters kauwhata. A little house is built of wood or totara bark and roofed with raupo or bark. Food is stored in them. Some are quite big. They are put up high so that if anyone goes to them the person could be seen – this is a protection against robbery. A ladder or arawhata runs up to the high ones. It is a pole in which holes have been gouged out for footholds. It could be set upright to whata or on a slant as required. He had never heard of earth storehouses but a hole to pit 'spuds' was called rua.

In speaking of the drying and storing of kauru the principal informant mentioned 'open whatas' or 'drying whatas'. These apparently had a roof made on the principle of an open shed on a farm. Under this roof things could be hung to dry in the wind. These roofs were held up by four posts or two as the case might be. The roof was called a kaupapa although this word really means a floor. [Tregear gives Kaupapa – raised platform for storing food – and quotes a sentence from Wohlers' writings. H.B.] After food was through the 'drying whata' it was put in the 'store whata' and kept for future use.

FORTIFICATIONS

In regard to pas, said my principal informant, you first selected a site and then proceeded to surround it with two lines of palisading. He forgot the names of the inner and outer fences but a general name was tuwatawata. Some pas were round and others square while others were of irregular outline. The ditch was termed aparua and there were stages inside the fences for purposes of defence and he thought these were named taumata. This was all he could recollect hearing about the old-time pa.

The collector visited the Maori monument erected in 1898 in memory of the old Ngai-Tahu pa of Kaiapoi and was surprised to see a Maori fence along one side of the old pa site. This fence is of tall manuka and has thicker posts with knobs on top to represent old-time carvings. This fence is said to have been built some years ago or years after the stone monument was erected. The zigzag trench made by North Islanders from the only terra firma side ([[the]] rest [[is]] swamp) is no longer visible but rest of pa site is in a fair state of preservation. You can still see where the old palisading was burnt in 1831 and the collector got three small pieces (out of earthworks) for the Museum (Otago). He also secured some old ahi-pohatu (or umu stones) fragments, and also charred wood and bone, from old whare sites in the pa. He is sorry to add that mischievous boys have been defacing the stone monument with pocket-knives and lead pencils. Altogether the pa memorial is an interesting reminder of a troublous time in South Island history. The pa was situated (near Woodend) about five miles from the modern town of Kaiapoi and about a mile from the sea. The swamps are still there but old bush has vanished. [Note: It has occurred to collector that perhaps the fence is that which was round the Maori village at the Christchurch Exhibition in 1906-7 and that when Exhibition was over the fence (or part of it) was removed to pa site and erected there. This can be ascertained later. H.B.]

Add to Fortifications

The fences round a pa, said the principal informant, were called hokahoka and pekerangi. He had never heard of a kiritangata fence but it may have been where a pa had three fences as had some in North Island. He forgot the name of the figures carved on the palisading but it was not kahia (a North Island word). The banks were called maioro and the stages over main fence were puhara. As to the ditches he had never heard names awamate nor waikari but awakari, although, of course, the other names might be correct in the North Island. The awakari not only went round the fences but a branch channel was taken through the pa for 'rain' or watering purposes. At each of the several gates a deep hole was made the breadth of the gate and was crossed on a board which was taken away if need arose. He forgot the names; but he thought the hole was called awarua and the board papa-takiri (meaning it could be suddenly pulled away). The people of Rotorua and Wanganui built a pa for Christchurch Exhibition in 1906. He was on committee and said it was like a sheepyard and told them to stop. He knew nothing about pas except traditional lore but he drew a plan that was approved by Mr McGregor from Wanganui and accepted. He only knew of pas at Kaiapoi, Onawe, etc., from tradition. The old pa at Waikakahi [[Lake Ellesmere district]] was said to be the biggest pa in the South Island and probably eclipsed anything in the North Island also. The popular saying about it was that a child born at one end would be known at the other end by the time his beard grew. He had never heard of buildings of stone (but the tuahu was constructed of stone and wood) but the old people may have used a stone wall where handy at some part of a pa on rocky ground – this was only a suggestion. Stones could not have been much used, and certainly not all round a pa, or it would be traditionally known. He knew no instance in either island of stones being used.

The collector went over the sites of old pas at Taumutu with Mr R. Taiaroa. He called it the Gibraltar of the South Island as these pas stood between the sea, the southern end of the lake and the inland swamps – and raiding parties not wishing to make a very extensive detour inland had to pass here. The meeting house (called Moki after Moki the Second – Moki-a-Ruahikihiki not Moki-tawhiri-ruru) stands on the site of Te Pa-a-Moki and some of the old parekura or parepare (embankments) still surround the hall. The Church (Wesleyan) stands on the site of the Pa-a-Te-Ikamutu; you can still trace the mounds and banks and the old 'moat' where the water almost surrounded it. The parapets of these pas were burnt for firewood in the whaling days. Two other pas stood – one at the South end of lake and the other on sea-coast but both have vanished and left no trace. The old pa at the end of the lake has been washed away – he forgot its name but it was the principal pa centuries ago. Another old pa – Te-pa-o-Te-Korua – stood between his house and the lake and its site is now mostly in lake which, at the time of this pa's activity, was then nearer the sea and narrower – the 'break-outs' in the course of centuries have brought the sand in. This pa was the 'watch-tower' for the other old pa (the one at end of lake) – these were the two oldest pas in district. The seaward pa was built later – its site is now obliterated by the rolling sandhills until scarcely a vestige can be seen. Later still the two pas whose banks can still be traced were built – the one at Moki Hall being the landward 'watch-tower' of the other and bigger one. Waipupu (now the fishing camp and which commands a good view of lake) is said to have been occupied long ago by slaves and dependants as a look-out station.

The collector was told that the carved figure on top of the monument or column at the old Kaiapoi Pa was supposed to represent Turakautahi, the alleged founder of the pa [The collector considers it more likely that Turakautahi strengthened or rebuilt an existent fort as tradition says that Waitaha and Kati-mamoe lived there long before Turakautahi's time. The Kai-Tahu always say he founded Kaiapoi Pa, however. H.B.]

SECTION II

PERSONAL WEAR AND CLOTHING

Maro or Loin-cloths — Rapaki or Waistmats — Ihupuni or Dogskin Mats — Pokeka or Raincloaks — Whiri or Plaitings — Whatu or Weaving — Tahau-taupa or Shin-guards — etc.

CLOTHING

The principal informant said that the ihupuni and topuni were the same [see later on. H.B.] – both were dogskin mats. He showed me a photo of his wife in a kakahu-kiwi, so-called because it was made of the huruhuru (feathers) of the kiwi bird. The men of old wore the maro but of slightly different make to women's maro. A rapaki or waist mat was worn over the maro and the rest of the body was naked in warm weather or at the desire of wearer. Made of whitau. Feathers were interwoven here and there into maro and rapaki to beautify them. The latter is also called pakipaki (='crackling sound') but rapaki is its proper name and it was after a man who wore one of them that Rapaki got its name. [It is said he was fishing in creek and took his rapaki off as it got so wet. H.B.] Another waist garment is the kinikini which is hard and soft by turns [as explained in Otago Southern notes. H.B.] or this name is sometimes given to the rapaki. He knew no name for shoulder mats. At a later stage he said he thought hana was a shoulder mat and also the name of a bigger size. The Kai-Tahu brought all this kind of work from the East Coast of North Island with them ten generations ago. Ihupuni was a dogskin mat. The parawai is a big plain mat relieved by feathers. The hurukuri is a form of ihupuni – it is whitau with skin sewn on it. The taniko is mat with black border. The korowai has dark miromiro threads on it. All these mats have whitau as their foundation. The pokeka, or raincoat, is made of ti, koka or toi. The ti or toi leaves are soaked in water perhaps twelve months, and then beaten with patu (club) until only string is left and this string is whatu'd into the waterproof. Timaru was named because ti leaves were made into pokeka there as shelter; it was a good place for such work. Oamaru is nearly the same – it is a shelter from rain too. Topuni was a kind of dogskin (sic) mat between a pokeka and a kakahu. One kind is whitau, the other of ti leaves. The torotoro was a kind of kakahu but he could not describe it. Long ago he had seen his mother make some kakahu. She put up two pou (posts) and tied a string (kaha) between them to start. Some mats were entirely covered with feathers – principally kiwi. The strings to fasten these to mat were called aho or whenu. The bone needle used was an au. Some mats were fastened round the waist with a tatua or belt.

In speaking to two Maoris they mentioned the mountain daisy or tikumu, and how useful its big, white leaves were to the olden Maori. They could be used to make good pokeka (raincoats), poho-taupa (chest protectors, when fighting), taupa (leggings) or tahau-taupa (shin protectors, in thorny localities). The silvery part of the leaf is skinned off and used, the green residue being rejected. The white fluffy stuff is knitted into the flax whitau and is said to render the pokeka rainproof although my informants had not seen it tested. One man said the tikumu made the garment like a feather mat and that one he had seen so done

Tini Burns Taiaroa (right), was another Canterbury informant. In this photograph with grandchildren Riahiko and Tini, her husband Hori Kerei Taiaroa is wearing a cloak made with tikumu leaves, c.1890s. Photographer unknown, P1951-004/1-021, Hocken Collections Uare Taoka o Hākena, University of Otago.

was the prettiest mat he ever saw. Pokeka could also be made of dry flax (koka) and tussock and pikao and were regarded as thoroughly rainproof garments.

An old man said the people wore European clothes when he was a small boy but one or two of the very old people wore the old-fashioned mats for the twofold reason that they regarded them as comfortable and warm and because their forebears had done so.

One woman in mentioning rapaki said it was a loin cloth or trunks. She had an old piupiu made wholly of houi (ribbonwood) and was thinking of putting it under the copper when the collector spied it in the washhouse. Needless to add it did not suffer a fiery fate but is now in the Otago Museum. One old Maori when asked what was the name of a feather mat (he had referred to the use of feathers) said it had no special name but was simply called a kakahu.

Add to Clothing

Whiri is to plait, said the principal informant, and as far as he remembered whiri-rauru meant a plait of five strings, whiripapa four strings, whirituapoko or whirituamanga four strings or more. A round plait was denoted by last two names but former two were nearly flat. The plait with three strings was more nearly round than any of the others; some plaits were nearly four-cornered. There were at least four ways of making aho (strings) as recorded above. Whenu is the name of a single strand and miro is to roll two or more whenu on the knee into a twist. To miro whitau for kakahu take two very fine whenu and twist. He showed the collector a mat saying the whenu constituted the body of it and the aho were the transverse lines across it every half-inch or so. There were several kinds of whatu but he did not remember the names. They were largely the same but their working brought out differently-made mats. Taniko was very neat work and there were hana, porowai, torotoro and other mats whose names he forgot. He had never heard of a whare-pora [weaving-house – see Tregear's [[1904]] *Maori Race*. H.B.] and he did not think tohungas taught weaving but an old woman called a kai-whatu-kakahu taught the girls. The tohuka never came to karakia the work – it had nothing to do with him – what right would he have to interfere with the work of the women. Very few men learnt this craft of weaving.

In regard to some other things mentioned by Tregear he had never heard of a kahu-kekeno (cloak of sealskin) and indeed would flatly contradict the statement. He had never heard of a tahi-uru nor of a tapahu of dogskins, but he had heard of a tapahu made of koka or ti, soaked in water and beaten and then thickly and closely whatu'd for protection in war. Pauku or pukupuku were not flax armor but were two North Island names for the pake or pokeka, a sort of 'rain overcoat'. It was made like a blanket with a big-plaited string (whose name he forgot) for tieing (here) purposes. You could whatu dogskin in one way also.

A dogskin mat was ihupuni, topuni or kahu-kuri but the former name was correct. The topuni or kahu-topuni was made same way but not of dogskin. To fasten kakahu an aurei was often used. It was a pin usually of ivory or bone got from the tusk of a pig or from whalebone. The ordinary Maori pin of wood or bone was an au.

Add to Clothing

The attention of the two ladies quoted in 'Ornaments' section was directed towards clothes – a subject ever near to the feminine heart. They had not heard that the tohukas taught weaving, but that the old women transmitted their knowledge to the young ones. It requires patience as it takes a lot of time to weave a good mat. One's mother had once made three mats in a fortnight, but they were small – just one morua (joining) in each. 'Ko tahi te morua' was one joining; 'E rua ka morua' was two joinings and so on. Plaiting flax into kete and tiaka (floor-covering) was raraka; but weaving the whitau was called whatu. They thought that weaving was once called raraka and that whatu was really the hard binding at the top, but was applied to weaving later. (Whatu, they explained meant anything hard, hence is applied to hailstones and now to bullets, etc.) Be that as it may, weaving is now called whatu and is (if the collector understands aright) practically the same for all mats; the decorative effects making the difference in names of mats. Patterns are known as tanikoniko and constitute the different mats. [Note: the collector has a great difficulty in grasping their ideas of weaving. Probably they are in the dark themselves about it. H.B.]

Tregear's work states, 'Maori legends mention cloaks of sealskin (kaku-kekeno) but they were very rare except in far South.' My two friends had never heard of such mats and one said she recollected her father saying the old Maoris had no means nor knowledge of skinning seals until the Pakeha sealers came. Tregear also says: 'Bone needles, au or aurei, were mostly used as pins. Needles were the quills (tuaka), the thread being tied to the feather end; such needles were called toromuka.' My informants said that quills were called whatu-maro, a feather being called piki or pikihuruhurumanu. Piki are the big, hard feathers and huruhuru-manu the small, soft ones. They had never heard of quills being used as needles, which in the South are usually bone (au-iwi), a small manuka twig or stick (au-rakau) or of shell (au-paua). One informant had had one made of paua [or pawa. H.B.] shell and it should be somewhere yet. She would have a look for it at her next house-cleaning. Her taua (grandmother) had used it as a pin (au) for her rugs. Au were used to hold garments or mats together as well as strings and sometimes both were used in unison, prized au being tied to the strings to prevent their going astray or getting lost.

Another woman said the people of old used to beat their kakahu on the stones in creeks to wash them. This washing (horoi) was effected by beating, their only soap being uku, a bluish clay. This clay could be used not only as an aid for washing but also for dyeing – the same as black mud. To dye the whitau (flax fibre) they used pokaka bark and tawai-whero (red birch – now called black birch by settlers). Needles, she concluded, had a koroputa (eye) at one end and were usually called au, the act of sewing being known as tui. [The North Island name is tuitui. H.B.]

The collector went to see a collection of 'curios' left by a Native (deceased) at Temuka. The items comprised a taiaha (North Island); a greenstone mere; a bone mere; a stick carved by a son – but most of the remainder were mats. One of kiwi feathers was a nice mat; two were miromiro mats; another a taniko and others were ordinary kakahu adorned with Pakeha wool. There were also some kinikini and piupiu. Other things are now away with relatives but these will probably be returned in the whirligig of time, according to the custom prevalent. [See Former Notes, H.B.]

When speaking of ferns the name piupiu cropped up and the principal informant added: 'Piupiu is also a name for a war-belt or tatua – it is a sort of rapaki.'

FOOTWEAR AND LEGGINGS

In these days of dear boots and shoes the minds of the Maoris regretfully turn to the days when they got their footwear for nothing but the trouble of making them. At Colac Bay the collector saw an old man wearing roughly-made flax sandals over his woollen sox and at other places (including Canterbury) the old people shuffle about in slippers at home, only wearing boots or shoes when going to town. One or two of the oldest people (mainly women) go barefoot in the house (even in winter) and slip on slippers when going outside.

The principal informant said that paraerae (sandals) were made of harakeke (flax), ti (cabbage-tree leaves) and toi (leaf of the titoi plant – it is broader than flax). To make them of a single plait was called takitahi and double was torua. Koka (flax dried on bush) was stronger than harakeke and wore better. If soaked in water and made double they were nearly as good as ti (sandals). Leggings (whose name he forgot) were made of ti and flax. They were not much used as they were too heavy and warm for comfort. Patiti (tussock) was a fine thing to put in the paraerae to keep the feet warm and if one was wading it was warmer with patiti round the feet than without it.

Two Tuahiwi Maoris mentioned tikumu and the collector asked if they had heard of leggings made of it and they answered in the affirmative. These leggings (or leg-protectors when going over thorny ground) were called taupa but to distinguish them from the chest 'armour' – poho-taupa [See Weapons section, H.B.] they were called tahau-taupa (also rendered taupa-tahau). The word tahau means 'the skin' and the name is practically 'shin-guard'. [Owing to exigencies of time they did not enlighten the collector as to how the taupa were made but no doubt they were made of other materials (besides tikumu) such as ti, koka, patiti, pikao, etc. H.B.]

An old man at Kaiapoi mentioned paraerae, saying ti lasted much longer than flax.

Pāraerae (flax sandals) from Temuka, purchased through Beattie. Tūhura Otago Museum Collection, D20.129. With kind permission of Te Rūnanga o Arowhenua.

Add to Footwear and Leggings

The collector had a note, from Tregear's works, that in North Island rohe was a combined sandal and legging and that flax leggings were called parengarenga. The principal informant said he had never heard of rohe. The North Island, he thought, had no paraerae but in the South these were made of flax and ti (toi was not used for sandals although it was used for pokeka). The paraerae would last longer but the strings gave way first. He forgot the name of these strings but the heel was called whakareke. The North Island may have had leggings. Leggings (in South Island) were made from tikumu, whitau, koka, or ti. They were not like puttees but were made in one piece with strings at top, middle and bottom. They were not much used as they were too awkward for comfort and too cumbersome for light travelling. They were called taupa. There was no meaning in the word parengarenga and if the North Island or any other people used such a word they required education as to correct Maori terms.

A Maori said 'Skin the leaves of the mountain daisy and the tissue or white part is wharawhara and the green part is tikumu. The former is used in the hair and in the ear as ornamental while the latter is used for taupa. The tikumu lasts better when the down is taken away. The green leaves are dried and are then whatu (woven) into rough leggings to wear as a protection against thorns.'

SECTION III

FLAXWORK

Harareke or Flax — Wharariki or Mountain Flax — Kete or Baskets — Tika or Scraping, Au or Needles etc.

FLAXWORK

Up in North Canterbury as in Murihiku flax bags are called kete, the top rim is whiri and the handles tau. They are made in all manner of ways from the rough kete to hold potatoes to the dainty kete of finest white whitau two samples of which the collector secured for the Otago Museum (from Rapaki). The lady who made these also gave the collector a small kete-ti (bag made of cabbagetree leaves) made by another woman. She said she could not (although an expert at flaxwork) do the ti work and drew the collector's attention to the roll in the bottom of the kete from which it starts and says she never learnt how to make it for one thing.

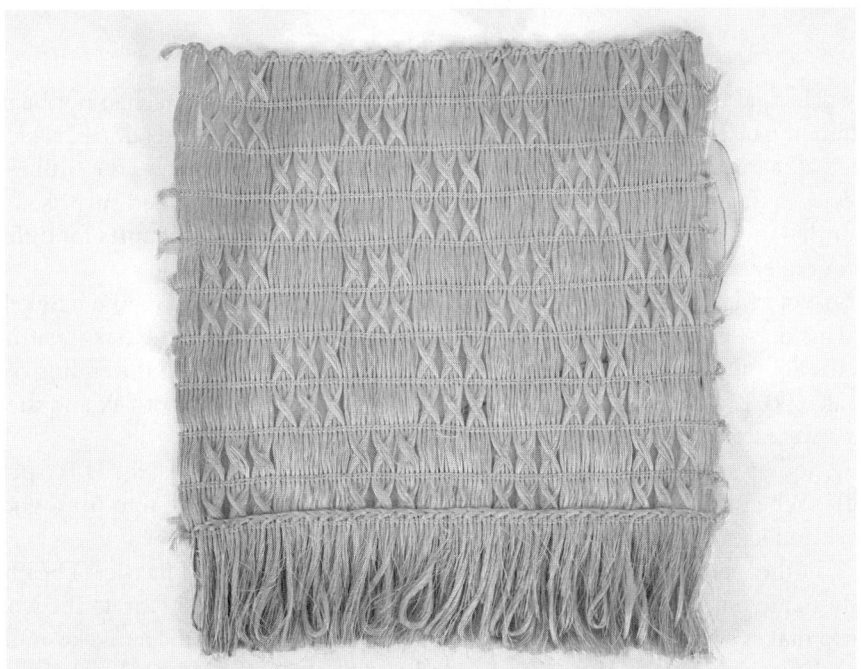

The two 'dainty kete of finest white whitau' from Rapaki, Banks Peninsula, mentioned on page 238. Tūhura Otago Museum Collection, D21.236, D21.237. With kind permission of Te Hapū o Ngāti Wheke Rāpaki.

My principal informant referred to the pao found among flax and said such leaves varied in color, being red, black or yellow and were very effective when I plaited into baskets. The two kinds of flax on Banks Peninsula were harakeke and wharariki. In old days flax was cut with pipi or mataa. Scrape it with pipi to get the sap and rough material out and put it in wai (water) and patu (beat) it to make it soft. (The patu is of wood the same as for aruhe or kauru beating.) It was beaten on wood not stone – on a tupararakau, a log which would wear hollow in the centre and which often had carved ends. He never saw one but heard of them. He forgot name of log. The beater was often carved at end and had a knob on handle but he never heard any name for this knob but the whole beater was usually named after a tipuna. Waru is scraping sap out and tika-whitau is scraping the second time. Then hang the fibre up to dry and it gets soft like wool. It may be beaten several times. Then it is made into kakahu. Raraka is plaiting flax and whatu is weaving whitau. Whenu is rolling the aho or long strings into 'worsted' ready for whatu-ing. Miromiro is to roll short lengths to attach to mats. To make fancy baskets for sale rito, the young, tender flax was cut and used. He thought the flax suffered in old days from pests even as now, being holed by caterpillars (toroku). To pull young flax-blades is called taki.

Add to Flaxwork

My principal informant, or indeed any of the various informants, had not heard different names for different kinds of flax (names such as oue and takirikau, etc.). They all agreed there were only two kinds of flax in Canterbury – the ordinary species, harakeke, and the 'mountain' flax, wharariki. They seemed surprised to hear that the olden Maoris in other parts had quite a number of names for different, or allegedly-different, varieties.

An old Maori said there was only two kinds on the Peninsula – the harakeke and a small flax which grew on rocky hillsides, the wharariki. The tiaka matting on his floor was made by his wife. The start was called timata and the ending of it whakapiki. It was made of strips each as wide as average length of flax and these papa were united by joins = morua.

Another said there was only one flax, the harareke [[consistent H.B. spelling]]. When the women were scraping it they would say kai te toto for a good piece and kaore te toto for a bad or poor piece.

Another said that a pokeka-toi (the toi is like a very broad flax-leaf) beautifully-made was taken Home by an Englishman who realised £50 for it. The wharariki makes a fine silky mat – there is no whitau (or muka) in it. Harakeke-muka makes very good mats. The pao, a vari-colored blade, is one kind of harakeke – it grows on a different root to the ordinary flax. [This is new to me. H.B.] He had seen one at Kaituna on the Peninsula twelve feet high and it was a very beautiful sight. It was a wonder to him the Botanical Gardens had not secured it.

The principal informant said he had never heard of tuaka or toromuka [See Tregear's works. H.B.] but he had heard of feathers being used as needles and also of needles of bone and wood, but he forgot the names. The aurei were mostly used for fastening mats, but may have been holed and used to sew sails, etc. They were generally made of the bone of the paikea (whale).

A Maori said he found a grand aui or au (bone needle) at Taumutu. It was in perfect condition and had the eyelet intact. It was 'pinched' (taken) by some old Maoris who visited him.

One man said whirituapuku was a round plait (not flat) of four, six, eight or twelve strands, while whirituamaka was a plait of three strands probably. [See Clothing H.B.]

SECTION IV

PERSONAL ADORNMENT

Hei or Pendants — Pare or Circlets — Piki or Plumes — Tautarika or Ear-rings — Heru or Combs — Whiriwhiri or Hair-pleats — etc.

ORNAMENTS

*The principal informant said that a circlet for the head was called pare and that you could stick a feather in it, the feather ornamentation being named after the bird, as parehuia (a feather of huia) parekotuku (white heron feather) and so on. The feathers of the cuckoos and also the tail of the kereru or pigeon, and plumage of other birds also, were sought after for this purpose. The soft feathers of the kotuku, etc., worn in the ear is a pohe. Feathers put through a hole in the cartilage of the nose was also a pohe. A hole in ear was called rua or koroputa and a hole in nose ditto. A dead chief's head would be cut off and whakatamiro'd (he forgot other name for preserving) and set up for exhibition adorned with pohe in ears and nose. Raukura was a red feather; the red in wing of kaka is called kura. The people brought kura from Hawaiki (which was perhaps America) and threw them away when they saw the pohutukawa here. One woman (Mahine-a-Rangi) a great granddaughter of Rakaihikuroa kept her kura. She married Turongo and Ngatikahungunu came from that line. That, the only kura brought to New Zealand, was lost long ago, he thought.

A Rapaki Maori said earrings were makotaniwha or tautarika. They were nearly all of bone (such as the teeth of sharks, etc.) and were tied on with whitau strings perhaps.

Two Tuahiwi Maoris said the heru was a comb of bone and some were plain and some were adorned with pawa shell. The hair was combed and then the comb was inserted in koukou (topknot – a bunch of hair is called puti). It was mostly worn by chiefs. Women wore their hair mahora (spread out) hanging down or in whiri or whiriwhiri (one or two plaits respectively). Koroputa-tarika is a hole through ear and a greenstone ornament for it is tauhei-tarika, or a shark's tooth one is mako-taniwha. Feathers in the ear = pohe-tarika. Holes in the ihu (nose) were, they thought, mostly Kanaka work but some Maoris did it although they (my informants) did not know the name of such perforation. It was said if an old-timer could sit on the marae with the feathers in his ihu (nose) kapakapa (waving) in the breeze it was considered very becoming. 'Taku raukura' was when a young man claimed a girl and stuck a feather in his hair and dared the world to take her.

HEITIKI

*'The heitiki,' said the principal informant, 'started from a woman many generations ago. She was a chief's daughter but her name eludes me. The heitiki takes its 'face-carving' or tattooing from that woman. It is a photo of her. A man carved it to represent her and it has kept the same shape ever since (in all its replicas). He carved it in commemoration of some feat of hers. She was tired so her head is to one side. Her legs are bowed beneath her but this was not explained to me. For men to wear this ornament is wrong – it is for women not men.** I never heard it was a likeness of Tiki nor that it had any special connection with women sexually. There was a god Tiki but I did not pick up that branch of knowledge. *I think that some said karakia to him.'** The collector asked him if he knew of a rite or ceremony called tua and he described a form of infant baptism. [See Maori College – Tohukas, H.B.] In answer to two queries he said he had heard the name hei-matau and that was all; and he knew nothing about a headless figure nor of its possible signification he had never heard of it.

A Rapaki Maori said he had seen greenstone tikis when a boy – not many as they seemed few in number – and he did not know how it got its name nor why it was so shaped.

Two Tuahiwi Maoris said a hei was any hanging ornament and heitikis were for ornamental purposes. They did not know why the head was to one side nor the legs bent but presumed it was ancient Maori art. It was not correct for men to wear it. It was for high-born families and chiefs tried to secure or retain them to give to their daughters. They had heard the name hei-matau but did not know what it was.

A Tuahiwi halfcaste reckoned he had a curiosity no one else (nor Museum) had in New Zealand. It was a tiki – a headless figure – picked up at Taumutu.

It must be very old. The old people gave him a name for it but it was a hard name to remember. He would try to ascertain it against the next visit of the collector. [Note: The collector told him (after above recital) of headless figure in Museum at Dunedin and promised to call and see him as soon as possible on his return to district. H.B.]

ORNAMENTS, TIKIS AND HAIR-DRESSING

*During the course of his remarks on numerous subjects the principal informant made passing references to the old Maori ideas of ornamenting and adorning the human frame.

The huruhuru (feathers) of birds were stuck in the hair. If of the white heron the plume would be called piki-kotuku or pare-kotuku. Piki, he understood, denoted one feather, pare a number. They used to skin bird and dry skin and cut a piece off and stick this to the head with a kopare (band). Raukura really means a red feather but latterly the name would be figuratively applied to white plumes. Red could be used in hair by highest people only – anyone else putting red on the head would be killed. As to modes of hair-dressing for girls to go round with a mass of curls was potikitiki as far as he remembered. The koukou (a sort of top knot) was common to both men and women as the former wore the hair long, and is mentioned in the history. There were other methods such as rahiri (in sheaf), tikitiki in a ring, and putiki, and others, but he had only heard names – he never saw them. He may have heard names in North Island. Combs of wood were made of manuka, maire and kohai and were called tiheru. He did not know how the states of wifehood or spinsterhood were shown by dressing the hair as such knowledge was not in his curriculum of learning, but the plaits so often seen now worn by Maori women were a modern innovation as far as he knew.** He had never heard of warplumes being called marereko – the only name he knew was piki. *He had heard of face being half-red and half-black to frighten the enemy but he did not remember the name of this fantastic performance.** He had not heard the names [See Tregear. H.B.] of tuhi-kohuru for diagonal streaks of red on face or tuhi-korae for horizontal red stripes but such-like things were done in the bad old days. *It was all devil-work. Now the people laugh but then it was a frightening thing but he was not sure of the definite object in all those weird decorations. He had seen one half the face black and other half red at a haka in the North Island but such had not been in the South Island 'since Christ came to New Zealand.' He told the young fellows at the haka to use burnt cork as charcoal was harder to remove off face. He had never heard of yellowing the face, but he had seen blue rings painted round the eyes in the North Island but he did not inquire the name of such freakish behavior. In the old days the Maoris, or such as were inclined, wore wristlets, and anklets, both being known as tauri.** Ones of flax, toi, or kakaha grass were for temporary wear but for longer use they were made of dogskin or whitau (dressed flax). He had never heard such a name as komori [See Tregear. H.B.] but children would wear shells as ornaments – there was no name for this and it was not worth mentioning. The Kanakas and darkies overseas would wear fish teeth as anklets and armlets but such was not a Maori mode. *In regard to tikis he thought the origin of the head of the heitiki being to one side was because the preserved heads stuck in the atamiro round a pa would often lose their erect position and recline to one side and the carvers had been stuck with this.**

The collector at Tuahiwi called in to see the headless tiki [See Previous Canterbury notes, H.B.]. It (the head) seemed to have been broken off long ago and then the tiki was polished in straight line across the pakihiwi (shoulders). An old Maori of seventy could give no name for it but said it was of aotea (pounemu variety) as was also a straight hei the owner of the tiki also had. He said he had been offered twenty five pound for it by a Christchurch gentleman but had not accepted it. The old Maori concurred with the collector's belief that the head was not purposely omitted but had been accidentally broken off.

A statement by Tregear that the kiore-moana (sea-horse) was dried and worn in the ear, was referred to the principal informant. He said the proper name of this creature was kiore-tawhiti as it came from a great distance. He had heard it was dried and used as an ear-ornament, but such usage, he understood, was mostly by children.

The collector was told a fine tiki was found at Taumutu some years ago. His informant thought that the tiki was made in likeness of some god – perhaps the god of war.

Add to Ornaments and Personal Adornment

The collector besought the good offices of two Maori ladies for the purpose of this section of the information and herewith gives the little additional material he was able to accumulate.

As far as they knew girls in the old days did not wear their hair different before and after marriage – you could not tell the married woman from her hairdressing. As for the styles of this; potikitiki was to make what are now known jocularly as 'bun loaves', because so shaped. Another style of winding the hair round was called taroi, but alas! the collector can supply no description of it. (Pictures or drawings would be only adequate way of illustrating such a topic.) Koukou was a style almost the same as the potikitiki. Plaits are called whiripapa or whiriwhiri and the women would wash in the river and then whiriwhiri their abundant, black locks. 'Ko tahi te whiri' is one plait; and 'e rua ka whiri' is two plaits.

A feather or plume stuck in the hair was called piki, but my informants had never heard that red was objected to or disliked in the hair by the ancient Maoris (as Tregear states), indeed they were of opinion red was sought after.

The father of one used to say the men like to wear a piki-kaka of the very red feathers from under the kaka's wings. The men wore it, anyway, but she was not positive if the women did so, too.

Strings of small shells or twisted flax were sometimes worn round the wrists and were called tauri, a name now bestowed on bracelets. Strings of small shells strung together were called toitoi.

SECTION V

PAINTS, DYES, AND SCENTS

Maukoroa or Red paint — Kokowai or Red paint — Horn or Blue paint — Kura, etc. or Colours — Hinutuhi or Perfumes — etc.

PAINTS AND DYES

*Maukoroa was burnt and to burn it the only wood employed was hinahina as this wood leaves a very white pungarehu or ash. It was thought this ash purified the color of the maukoroa. The maukoroa was then pounded down into a dry powder and to use it oil was added and compound was called kokowai. To paint the human body bird oil was added to the maukoroa and to paint a house or canoe, etc., fish oil was used instead. The paint so made would stick better to rocks and exposed surfaces than Pakeha paint and it is said that the red paint which Mantell in 1849 got the Maoris to put on the rocks at Koukourarata (Port Levy) to mark the rohe (boundary) of the Native Reserve in that vicinity is said to still adhere to the rocks there. Horn was like kokowai but was a different color, being blue. Maukoroa was got on Bank's Peninsula and was the start or basis of horu but he did not know what it was mixed with to produce latter. They got oneone a blue soil in the creek – it was not pukepoto which was a North Island clay – to mix with maukoroa but he forgot the name of the compound. [It has been stated in print that Otakou, or Otago Heads, was named because the Maoris got 'takou', a kind of ochre there, so the collector asked re this. His informant had never heard of 'takou', and moreover said that the name Otakou was brought from Hawaiki. H.B.] In the old days [unlike the present time. H.B.] the men painted more than women. They thought it made their tattooing look nice. Men going to fight painted themselves – maybe to keep the cold out when they stripped for the fray. They used not to mind snow or frost in those times but all the same the paint would protect the skin a bit. The paint being oily made the skin soft and kept it from cracking. It was only used by the higher people and there was no particular style of decoration. Kokowai was hard to get off unless washed with horu and then the latter could be washed off with water. It was put on from the hair and face to the feet and toes. It was kept on a week or so and, unless washed off before, gradually wore off, and in summer sweat would wash it faint. (Sweat is variously called kakawa, tota or werawera.)**

As to dyes the old people would put flax or whitau in a kumete (bowl) of maukoroa to dye it red. This red (or maukoroa) dye would not wash out but would fade in time. Another dye was got by using pokaka bark and mud. The bark of the pokaka was beaten with a patu (club) to soften it. It was the only tree he knew that was so used. The bark was then steeped in water and put in a bowl with the whitau to soak in it for some days. The whitau turned black but not a stable black so to 'firm' it, it was further soaked in 'dead water' with parapara mud from the swamps. This name was parapara, he said, not paruparu [as the collector put in his Murihiku notes. H.B.]. After soaking a week in the black earth the whitau is found to be dyed a permanent black.

A lady in the Kaiapoi district said she had seen her grandmother dye flax in a kohua (boiler or pot) with bark and black clay but she had not taken notice of the process. The only other color she knew in flaxwork was pao. [Pao is a natural freak in coloring of some blades of the flax. H.B.]

COLORS

The principal informant said that kura was a deep red like that of a kaka's wing; whero was a red also; pakaka was a yellow; kakariki was green, and he thought pukepoto stood for a blue but he was not sure of this color. Ma was white but a white or pale skin was kiritea and grey hair was called hina. It was a subject he had heard very little about

At the Temuka tangi an old man told the collector that the Maoris had very few definite names for colors and often just used expressions to define what meaning they intended to convey. For instance, 'Kai te pouri te moana' drew attention to the dark color of the sea at a given time, and so on.

Add to Dyes and Paints

The collector saw it stated in print that a yellow clay called maraki was got at Waikouaiti and was used to seam canoes. His principal informant (Canterbury) said he had never heard of maraki clay but a kind of dried fish was called maraki. Probably maraki should be maukoroa. *There was a yellow clay burnt in the fire (hinahina wood was used as its ash is as white as flour) and this clay (mixed with ashes) was further mixed with oil. It gets hard but use oil and it gets soft. He has seen it used to daub the body from hair to feet and to paint canoes. It is called maukoroa when dry and kokowai when wet. It was also called horu. Pani is no color but means to rub paint on things = to paint. The maukoroa came on the Araiteuru, Takitimu, and other canoes and was a valuable thing to the Maoris. The people used blue clay as a soap – its name was horu(?). He thought that the blue clay called pukepoto in Taranaki was found here also. The blue clay here if crumbled in water glistened and shone (evidently phosphorescent). It was procured in lagoons and in streams near Kaiapoi and Kaikoura and other places, but he forgot its Maori name.** For dye pokaka bark was steeped in water, beaten, and soaked with parapara (black mud) as a black dye. The toatoa was used for dye elsewhere – it did not grow in Canterbury. He had not heard name kiakia as a tree from which dye came but there was a tree called kiekie on West Coast.

A Maori said that maukoroa could be got on the Peninsula but if used it was better to put finish on with Waikouaiti clay which was very superior. This clay and oil = kokowai. He did not know about blue paint but black could be got from kapara (resinous heart of pines) burning, the soot being caught in muka (flax fibre). A yellow dye was got from karamu tree.

COLOURS

*When the collector asked re colors the principal informant took it as meaning the color of the skin or pigment and made the following statement: He knew four colors among the Maoris. 1 Kiripako – dark hair and skin. 2 Urumawhatu – dark skin and curly hair; not to be confused with mangumangu, the negro. 3 Kiritea – light brown skin and dark hair. 4 Brown or copper skin and ginger hair – urukehu. That was the four shades of the Maori Race, but in addition there was an abnormal coloring in the korakorako – the albino with white hair. The four shades were all in the South Island once but are all mixed now.**

In regard to ordinary colors pango was black; whero was red; pakaka was light red; blue was mangu; ma was white; kakariki was green; yellow was pakaka; pink, etc. came under the term purepure, a word really meaning speckled, or mixed colours; whakaporoporo is piebald black and white. Clouds were called paiao and pukeao and things might be compared to their color. The colors of the sea were tai-tonga (very blue color) and tai-koehu (a dirty, greyish shade). Moana-uri (not uri uri) is out in the deep sea – a dark blue – the word means 'deep ocean'. 'Ka pua te kohai' was to say 'yellow flowers' as the kohai is yellow. He had never heard any names given to the various colors of the bush. Kikorangi does not mean the blue of the sky – kiko means the centre of the arched dome of heaven, but the name kikorangi as referring to the sky has been much more extensively used since the missionaries came to New Zealand. The word tihore means a cloudless sky and and tihorehore denotes a clear sky. The Maori had not many definite color names – he usually referred to a thing as like something near, or some well-known object.

A Maori said 'Anything yellow is puakohai and anything green is kakariki.'

SCENTS

To make scent, said the principal informant, you could use mokimoki, taramea, hakeke, tarata and other trees. In the evening place dry, inflammable stuff against a taramea (speargrass) plant and fire it and next morning collect the ware (gum) from the scorched leaves. Take an ipu with weka, tui, pigeon or kiore hinu (fat) and put in the gum – do not put raw leaves in fat. You do mokimoki the same. Mokimoki grows in the North Island. The oil must be hot before you put the ware in. Some leaves could be put in hot oil without any scorching. You did not scorch tarata leaves. The gum of this tree was sometimes used without mixing with oil. The mountain musk (whose Maori name he forgot) has a beautiful scent naturally. The scents were used on the body and the fine ones in the hair. They were sometimes mixed with kokowai or maukoroa. A pawa shell was sometimes taken, the holes blocked, and filled with scented fat. It was put in a whitau bag (kopaki) and carried on the body suspended from the neck.

A Rapaki Maori said that the word piapia meant sticky or slimy but pia was the gum from trees. The pia from tarata had a kakara (nice smell). Scent could be got from taramea also.

At Tuahiwi the collector was told there were two species of speargrass, the big being taramea, the small papaii. Only the former was used for scent and a nice scent it made. If you used it lavishly the girls would like it (and presumably like you, too). The plant was cut to let the pia (gum) collect and this exudation was mixed with oil. It was cut in the evening and the gum was gathered in the morning. When working the taramea it is said the workers slept in a crouching position as superstition asserted that should they sleep in the ordinary way the wax of the plant would never rise but would sink into the roots. So the old people said. The tarata tree could also be cut and its gum collected and mixed with oil. These were the only two scents they knew – taramea and tarata.

Add to Scents and Oils

The titoki seeds, said the principal informant, could be cooked and put in a flax bag and twisted and an oil extracted. This was good for hair oil but it was not much procured in Canterbury, He had never heard of miro berries being used to get oil from, but, of course, there was not much miro in this district.

Another Maori said the red titoki berries provided good eating and there was a black stone in each. These stones or seeds were collected and were crushed for oil but he did not know how this was done or what the oil was used for – he had simply heard the old people said it was done long ago.

Another referred to scents and said the taramea was burnt and the people, after sleeping in a traditional posture all night to ensure the success of the process, would collect the gum next morning. This could be mixed with titi kakata (muttonbird oil) to make hinu-tuhi to rub on the head. The people would get the titoki berries, which are red like strawberries, and dry them in sun until hard. They are then put in a kumete or bowl and pounded with a stone pestle. The people would put taramea or tarata gum in a flax bag before the fire to drip into an ipu (basin). The titoki could be treated the same. Scent was called hinutuhi. Miro berries, some of which are as big as plums, could also be pounded for oil. The scent from taramea was called taramea, and from tarata the name of tarata, but the word titoki was not used in this connection.

SECTION VI

TATTOOING AND WOOD-CARVING

Moko or Tattoo — Uki or Tattooing Needles — Whakairo or Carving — Whakaupoko or Figureheads — etc.

TATTOOING

*The principal informant said that tattooing (ta ki te moki) took a long time and was very painful. The person being done was laid on his back. The tools were an uhi, small sharp bone points tied together in the shape of a matarau with four or five prongs, hit with a hammer of wood called a whao. The points were arranged in a straight line for tattooing. An expert operator (tohuka ta moko) could do it much more quickly than a beginner or one who was new to the work. It was done in the wharekura or wharemaire. The tohuka who was doing the tattooing would take the man to the tuahu for karakia (invocations) and then to the wharekura. Tattooing was done in instalments. It destroyed the beard as a rule, what hair remained being pulled out. [See Customs section, H.B.]**

An old Rapaki Maori said he reckoned tattooing became neater and the patterns better defined after European tools came in. In the olden days, he thought tattooing was mostly on the face and not so much on the body until the Maoris saw the tattooed arms of Pakeha sailors. He had seen some old people bearing tattoo (moko) and heard that wee, sharp points of whalebone were employed before British needles came in. The karehu (tattooing ink) was soot from the chimney mixed with tree juice but he did not know much about it. The old people never gave much information about some of those things.

An Old Kaiapoi Native said some of the old people (when he was young) had tattooed faces. They were mostly men who had fought in the Kaiapoi Pa against Te Rauparaha and most of the tattooing was in circles but some was in straight lines. He had seldom seen a woman tattooed. It was rare but one or two like the late Mrs Tikini Pahau, of Puketiraki, were done in straight lines. He had been in the Kaiapoi district for over sixty years but he had never heard how moko (tattooing) was done.

Two Tuahiwi Maoris said they considered the circles in tattooing was an idea from lines on thumbs. Circular tattoo was moko and straight was haehae. This latter style came into fashion [it was revived. H.B.] sixty years ago in the South as Maiharoa's followers adopted it. It was also called tuhi.

Note: Some of the Maoris referred to tattooing as 'face-carving'. One said: 'The tohunga was the man who could do the whakairo on the face or on wood'.

Add to Tattooing

*The principal informant said that the chin-tattooing of North Island women was called puakauae but was never done in South. This chin and mouth tattoo he thought was recent – about sixty or seventy years perhaps. His grandmother was tattooed all over the face like some other South Island women – the name of that tattooing was moko-pokere. The thigh tattoo the rape was not done in South as far as he knew.** He had never heard the names puhoro, rauru, hotiki nor takitaki [vide Tregear. H.B.] but hopehope was an old North Island name for tattooing round a woman's hips. *An uncle of his who went Home in the whaling days to England was tattooed on one side of his face only in a curved design. Being only on one side was moko-tahatahi or sometimes called kawetahi. The scroll pattern of moko came from Hawaiki and about twelve generations ago was brought south with the Kaitahu. The tohunga Terehaka, who did his (narrator's) grandmother Hakeke, was very good at tattooing. The women down here were tattooed like men often. In old days he understood, women were not tattooed at all in the North Island and he thought it was fairly recently since it started in South Island, but he was not sure of this. He forgot the names of the various portions of face tattoo save that on the rae (forehead) was tiwhana.** The straight lines and dots between was a South Island mode and people so done were termed jocularly 'Te hipi o John Topi' (the sheep of Topi) because it was said to be a whaling idea. In Stack's book 'South Island Maoris' [[1898]] is shown a portrait of Pita te Hori but it does not show much 'face carving' or moko. The collector was shown an enlargement of his likeness depicting tattooing much more clearly than the book illustration gives any idea of.

CARVING

The principal informant said he had never seen anyone carving in the old way, but they used a mata (flint) tied to a piece of wood which was hollowed to receive it (like a tomahawk, he added) and struck with a heavy club or whao. Not much carving was done on stone but mostly on hardwoods. *Carving was called

Pita Te Hori of Kaiapoi, whose tattoo is discussed by Beattie on page 250.
J.W. Allen photographer. Archdeacon Cholmondeley Collection, Canterbury Museum, 1946.94.1.

whakairo and he considered the whorls and scrolls originated from the lines on the thumb, or that was what he was told long ago, and also that it started in Hawaiki.** The tuahu was built of stones with carved wood above and there samples of the best carving of the tribe could be seen, executed by the most skilled tohukas for that sacred place. A Rapaki Maori thought that carving became much neater after European tools came in. Old taiahas were roughly carved, newer ones were finely executed. Of course you could not expect stones and bones to make as neat a job as steel. You see tokotoko (walking-sticks) carved splendidly nowadays. [The collector saw a beauty at Temuka. H.B.]

A Kaiapoi Native said that when he was a boy you could see good whakairo work on a lot of whakaupoko (figureheads) of the wakas still used. Some of those carvings were swept to sea by floods and the rest had, no doubt, rotted long ago. Some fifty or sixty years ago old Patea Tura-katahi did some carvings representing Turakautahi and other Kaitahu ancestors and these were now lying beside the Tuahiwi Hall. It was a shame to see them lying rotting there and the collector should endeavor to see the Upoko-runaka (Mayor) and Council (Maori) and have the carvings removed to a place of safety. They might not be of great value but still they were the last carvings done in Kaiapoi district.

Note by collector – I saw five big carved boards lying exposed to weather at side of hall and under drip of roof. They were long and of good weight but I shifted two further out from drip (frost on roof). Four had outlines carved on them but the other had a human figure at its base and was carved deeper up the sides than the others. One or two seem as if marked out in outlines for carving which has not been gone on with or completed. I told several of the Maoris I would inform Christchurch Museum *re* this lot. H.B.

Add to Carving

The principal informant said he did not know of any rakau-whakapapa (notched sticks) in Canterbury but he had heard it was sometimes done in North Island to help the owner recall details. The people (in South Island at any rate) usually trusted to their memories without such unnecessary aids. Tekoteko were carved to remember ancestors and could be made on pou (posts) inside houses or put on porch outside. The figure was named after person whom it represented. He had seen an excellent carved house at Gisborne, the boards of which were whakairo'd (carved) to depict Maui pulling up the land and his brothers rowing; and other scenes. This was all done to keep the minds of the people strong and their memories clear as to the great deeds of old. Carved slabs were sometimes put up in memory of chiefs – these slabs were mostly in pa walls. They could scarcely erect carved slabs or posts over the 'graves' in old days, in South Island at least, as so few were buried, nearly all being heke (slid into water) or tahu (cremated). [In the Christchurch Museum there is to be seen an elaborate 'tomb' carved over a grave in North Island so 'tis said. H.B.]

SECTION VII

GAMES AND MUSIC

Kotaha or Slings — Manutukutuku or Kites — Karere or Hoops — Omawhakataetae or Foot-races — Niti or Teka or Throwing-darts — Pakete or Boys' Archery — Whai or Cats' Cradle — Mamau or Wrestling — Moari or Giants' Stride — Morere or Swinging — Piu or Skipping — Pouturu or Stilts — Puharu or Water-Sports — Mu or Draughts — Makamaka or Riddles — Kau or Swimming — Rangi or Tunes — Whakatuwaewae or War-Dances — etc.

GAMES

The principal informant took rather a pessimistic view of ancient Maori games and amusements. Their chief object, he considered, was to train people in expertness for fighting and moreover they often led to disputes, brawls and fights. Niti was the game of throwing a dart or teka > of wood with a stick ten feet long with a bent top and a whitau string wound round and round it. The dart might go ten chains. An underhand throw was called teka. Kotaha was to sling a stone from a flax sling. Teka and kotaha could be used in fighting although really meant for play. Karere te tono [See *Journal of the Polynesian Society* in articles by H.B.] – he had never heard of this exactly but on sandy beaches the children made karere (messengers) of karetu leaves. These were made circular (like a boy's hoop) with a diameter of a few inches. It ran like a hoop along the beach driven by the wind. It kept on the sand and was not blown along up in the air. You could have contests at it – it was just a game – but if those beaten got angry it might lead to fighting. The white down of the puha (thistle) could also be chased along by children. Another game was for the young people to throw a stick from hand to hand. It was good training for quickness of eye and accuracy of hand but he forgot its name. Whai, a string game on fingers, was only played to train the eye and hand. [He had a 'go' at collector's whai string for a while but could not remember what he saw when a boy. H.B.] As for draughts he thought that was started after the Pakeha came. Tops (potaka) was an old amusement. The marae of the village would be swept and cleaned and the tops would be run about over it. This would sometimes lead to fighting. Wrestling was 'he takaro' (a sport) and was called mamau – a sort of catch-as-catch-can. A cross-buttock is called raka. [Note: In Tregear's *Dictionary* under 'Rakahu' it is stated that in Samoa Rakaraka is a tutelary deity of wrestlers. H.B.] Oma-whakataetae was a footrace – not for a prize but through challenges – and would usually end in a fight. [Oma – to run. Whakataetae – a trial of strength.]

Waikakahi was a very extensive pa and was said to be a great place for all kinds of games and sports. Ruke, a pebble game, is started by one movement, which is then doubled, followed by the koruru movement. Raraki figure comes in it. It is really a baby game but often adults joined in and this often led to rows and fighting – not the real whawhai (warfare) but sometimes someone would get killed. Kites, called manu because shaped on bird pattern, were made of raupo. Their full name was manutukutuku. Some were very big and the taura or string of flax that held them was sometimes plaited. They looked like great hawks [See Mythology Section, H.B.] soaring about in the sky. Rivalry between different owners often led to kaitatawhaiaka [Tatawhainga – to vie, to compete. H.B.] or contests to decide who had the best kite. This often led to a fight – fighting was the aim and object of the olden Maori.

A Rapaki Maori (aged seventy) said that whai, ruke, manu, potaka, etc., were all before his time. When he was a lad he used pakeha tops. He never heard of a Maori form of draughts.

An old man said he knew no old-fashioned games but a middle-aged man (who was standing by listening) said that in the North Island he saw 'matemate' a game where you work the hands but do the opposite to your opponent. If you do the same you are 'out' and quit playing.

A lady at Tuahiwi said Tapu was a game where one stone was not to touch another. If two came together you were out. She had also seen ruke. Huri was to throw up stones and catch on the back of the hand. Poi was throwing up and catching pebbles in various orders.

Whai – In regard to whai the collector had no luck. En route North he called in at Temuka where oldest woman tried it but could not recollect girlhood's moves. At Rapaki a man and a woman did part of a double one they had seen in North Island, and a man did two Wairarapa ones. He remarked that the old folk at Wairarapa would hit you if they saw you at whai as they said it brought bad storms. The collector found no one at Tuahiwi who had seen the game except an old woman (a visitor from Henley, Otago) who stumbled through Tawhititara. She said another was called raramai and others represented a rat trap and building a whare. After some trying she gave it up and returned the string with the words: 'Na, tou whai, E ta' (Behold, your string, O son – the collector was told the 'ta' in this case was short for 'tama' (son).) From this it appears the string was called whai as well as the game. At the tangi at Temuka four old women and two old men answered they had heard there was such a game but they had not seen it. A young woman said she had seen it in the North Island and finally a Maori clergyman dextrously executed four or five whai he had learnt at Hokianga in North Island. The game seems forgotten in the South Island. A Temuka woman said her father used to whai but all she learnt of it was the figure eight. She was a duffer at it and had even forgotten the little she knew. [Note: Kurupohatu said he knew two whai so there is still a chance to get a genuine South Island sample of game when we get hold of him again. H.B.]

An old Maori told the collector he had never heard of a Maori swing in Canterbury.

Add to Games, Amusements, Sports and Pastimes

The principal informant had a dim remembrance of having heard of bullroarers being swung overhead as a pastime [but he knew not the names purerehua nor mamae. H.B.]. In skipping two men would turn the rope and skippers hopped in centre; its name was piu or piu-rangi. Sometimes two ropes would go in opposite directions requiring quick jumping. A long pole with a cross-piece with perhaps six holes in it and a rope (taura) attached to each hole would be erected near water, on a bank for preference. The persons who held the ropes took a run and swung out over water, and let go, landing with a plop in the water. It required practice to enter water by head or feet as in a dive, as otherwise you could be stunned by unskilful impact. The name of this swing or giant's stride was moari and it was done in both islands. The kai-morere was to tie a loop in a rope, sit in it and swing; or you could have rope doubled ◊ sitting on the bend of the bare rope – he thought the Pakeha brought the wood seat idea in. You could tie a rope to other rope above (or below) seater and a person on the ground pulled this and soon 'worked' the swing up high. The ropes were made of whitau or ti.

The seesaw was made in ancient days. The wood was solid and was carved (whakairo) on each side in many cases. All the pas like Kaiapoi, Onawe, etc. had these seesaws and they were a great amusement but the name had completely eluded him.

He had heard of hoops but also forgot the name. Potaka was the Maori top and when a boy he had spent hours and raced miles at whipping these tops along.

Kai-panukunuku was to slide on toboggans. Cut the head of the ti (cabbage tree) and sit on the leaves and hang on. The leaves are slippery and slide fast down steep hills. Some twisted leaves in hands to guide, but mishaps would happen and some got hurt. (Some years ago the Maori boys, after a heavy rain when hillsides wet, misappropriated a ladder and were tobogganing. The schoolmaster joined their sport with a sledge but ran into a clump of gorse and narrator had job of picking the pricks out of the Pakeha's skin and rubbing vaseline over him. This was painful but was a minor mishap to some experienced in the days of old.)

Jumping was indulged in in pre-Pakeha times and was practised so that when a speaker was orating [or gyrating] in whaikorero welcomes he could gracefully jump over the takitaki (fence) of the marae. Akoako ki te tupeke was 'learning to jump'. They used to jump over korari sticks but not for prizes as Pakeha does. It was to make the young men active for war. That was the high jump or leap but he forgot name of the long jump. Rere was another name for tupeke and expressed any kind of jump or leap.

Somersaults were perhaps rere-titaha or possibly rere-aronui but he was not sure. Standing on the head was rere-tupo and was done to make people laugh. He did not know about hide-and-seek at all, or that it was played in old days.

Matemate was a 'ti' to make your opponent's hand go wrong in doing the opposite to your hands. It was a practice for expertness in war and ti was the correct name.

As for tutukai (Tregear says 'hunt the pebble') he had heard the name somewhere or other but no details. As for childish games of lacing fingers he had never heard the Maori names.

An arrow (pakete) was used by the children before the Pakeha came. It was made of pukakaho reed with wet flax tied round tightly at one end to give weight (and perhaps to keep from splitting). The bow was made of supplejack with a string of flax or whitau. The whole sport was called pakete and children played it for fun to see how far the arrow could go. [The collector once thought the arrow was introduced by whalers but he is now inclined to think it was ancient. Wohlers found the pakete in use in 1844 in Southland. The Maoris regard it as very old form of play but never used in warfare. It may have been a survival of the ideas of Moriori or tangata-whenua people but not adopted by the conquering Maori although relegated to boys; or it may have been chanced on by boys. H.B.]

For teka or niti get a stick of wood six feet long with a weight at one end and further get a manuka stick and burn in the fire and bend. Twist string round it and it will send the teka about two hundred yards. The teka is a straight rod but the niti is shaped ⌒ and is projected the same way, going from fifty to one hundred yards. The men used to join the boys at it for a bit of fun 'when they were feeling jolly'. They would sometimes stick up a papa (board) at which to aim. Tuahuriri hit the spiral (maihi) of a whare when others could not do so. This is mentioned in the history and shows the sport was an ancient one.

Pouturu was the name of two sticks [Stilts. H.B.]; you put the feet in flax or whitau and held the tops – one in each hand. This was not a Pakeha idea but was very old – a sort of game. You could go up and down hills as well as over flats and go a long way and much faster than walking as you took such long steps. He had never heard how the idea started. They were useful to ford rivers if the current was not too swift nor the bottom too rough.

Puharu was to sport in water and to put other fellow down in it until he gave in. Rumaki was another name of this ducking. To dive was called ruku and manawa-roa was to see who could remain under water the longest period. The people of old were great at water sports and used to swim across Lyttelton Harbor at one time.

*Another amusement of the people of old was asking riddles (makamaka). There was another name for this but he could not recall it. They were simply asked to puzzle the people. When he was at a gathering in a hall in Hawke's

Bay someone proposed makamaka to vary the proceedings and impart a little pleasurable guessing. Several were asked and the answers were forthcoming quickly. Finally he asked one of local interest which no one could answer so he gave them a week to think over it but it was still unsolved so he elucidated the mystery. The makamaka was 'Taku pounamu pia, he mahia no tona' and the answer is Napier and Mahia. Pia stands for Napier. If he had 'said it plainer' or asked it more simply and plainly it would have been soon found out and answered.

Mu was the old Maori game of draughts. At a Maori gathering at which he was present in North Island a game of draughts on a gigantic scale was carried out.** Squares were marked out on the ground and the men were living men who stood in the squares, a king being represented by two men. Major Kemp and he controlled the destinies of the game at first but later he relinquished his position to Henare Tomoana. It was played in the Spanish style and in almost his first move he 'killed' three men. It interested and amused the people immensely. In the old mu the moves were different to Pakeha draughts, the last and winning move being in a circle or dot in the centre of the board. The men were kai-some-thing-or-other (he forgot name). When he was young they used Indian Corn for men. The Maoris soon picked up English and Spanish methods; in the latter the men come back as well as go forward. He learnt all three styles at Akaroa: The Maoris could usually beat the Pakeha at draughts. When he was nineteen years old he played and won a challenge game (English moves) against a Pakeha, the admission to hall being one shilling.

The collector's whai string was not used this trip. The Hokianga clergyman who used it on previous trip remarked it would have been better to have been a bit longer for the more intricate figures. An old woman whom the collector met this trip said she had seen whai at Moeraki when a girl but she never learned it.

A Peninsula Maori said that the olden Maoris used to fly kites on Marokura Hill (known to settlers as Devil's Knob). These kites were called pakau and were made of toetoe. This name pakau for kites was common all over New Zealand he said when collector queried it. [Note: He spent some years in North Island. H.B.]

SWIMMING AND WATER SPORTS

The principal informant was of opinion the olden Maori people were fond of swimming, diving and sporting in the sea as well as in fresh water. They would get a flat board and go out in the surf. He never saw this but he had heard about it. The name of the sport was kaukau and the board was called paparewa. If it was a big board it might hold two or three people and this increased the fun. Another thing was to get the shell of a hue or anything for a poito (float) and tie one to each side of you by a whitau belt (tatua) round you. This was a good thing to support anyone learning to kaukau or kautahoe and it is also a fine thing to bring you through the surf. The boards were taken out three or four chains as a rule and came in with a rush. Kautitaha is swimming on side; kautahoe is a crab-like paddling when lying on stomach; kauaronui is the breast stroke; kaupou is standing with the elbows on the water and working with the feet (kau = swim; pou = post) and kautuara is swimming on the back. He was not sure but that kauaronui and kaupou were the same. There is also the crawl stroke = kaupiroha. Kautitaha, he considered, was the fastest style of swimming. Many of the Maoris were excellent swimmers.

A Rapaki Maori said that the upright style of swimming (kaukau) was still done and some pakehas could do it. When swimming to turn over and rest on the back was called whakata.

A Tuahiwi Maori said he had never heard of surfing on the beach near Kaiapoi, but it might have been done long ago on some parts of the coast. Kautu was the old-fashioned treadwater, upright style of swimming. He had never seen it but had heard of it. (He named several old men whom report said swam this way.) He forgot the name of the crawl stroke but the breast stroke was called kaupapa and the side stroke, kautira. To float or swim on the back was kautuara while diving was called ruku.

MUSICAL INSTRUMENTS

The principal informant said he could not say much on this subject as the old people never said much about it. [They apparently dropped their own instruments for pakeha violins, accordions, Jew's harps, etc. at a very early stage of European colonisation of New Zealand. H.B.] He had not heard of a gong or wooden drum unless perhaps two pieces of wood were banged together to alarm a pa or kaika in war time. A pukaea or trumpet was blown. He did not know the name of banging wood (or wooden drum) to make a noise. It was very little used, he thought. He had heard of a wooden drum called a pahu being used in the Pacific Islands. To alarm a pa a trumpet was blown. He never knew of a proper shell horn being used by the Maoris but the end of some shells could be knocked off and the shell blown through. Such a thing was called a pu. A pukaea or flax trumpet was often blown. It did not last long but made plenty of noise. Once some Oamaru people went on to Pukeuri Hill and blew a pukaea on it and the sound was heard at Waitaki Mouth about ten miles away – so tradition said. The putorino was made of poroporo wood from which the soft pith had been extracted. It was a nose flute with three holes for the fingers. The player blocked one nostril with a finger and blew with the other nostril. The koauau was made of wood and had three holes too and was blown with mouth, as was also the porutu, a bigger instrument nearly as long as the pakeha flute. It had half-dozen rua or puta (holes). He forgot the name players were called. Only boys made kelp flutes.

The flute started at Rotorua where Tutanekai played at Mokoia. Hinemoa, a puhi or carefully kept, high-blood girl swam to where flute was playing so that lets us know it started there although perhaps earlier races (in New Zealand) had it. It was played in the South Island but no fuss was made over it like Hinemoa did, but nevertheless it was an amusement in every pa to hear skilful players.

A Rapaki Native said he had seen a tame kaka play a koauau flute which was made of tuturakau (a wood like elderberry). It had three holes, viz ruarahi (big), ruaiti (small), and ruaitirawa (very small hole).

A Kaiapoi Maori said he had seen a porutu which was made of tuturakau. It had four holes but he never heard anyone play it. Flax pukaea (trumpets) were blown as a game – they made a noise like a foghorn. They might last a day or two with care but were only temporary instruments.

Add to Musical

The air or tune of a song was rangi, said the principal informant. To sing out of tune was called rangirua ('two tunes'), but 'Kia rite te whakahua i te waiata' is to sing together correctly in exact time and unison. In the days before the white people came four kinds of voices were recognised = thin and deep-pitched women's voices and men's ditto. Reotakiri was highest of lot, reomaru next, but he forgot the names of the other two. The one who led a party singing was called kai-whaka-riterite and gave the signal to start and the time. Most songs were short but sometimes you would get a long one.

Pakuru was to hit light piece of wood out of which the pith (forgot name) had been extracted. This hollow tube was blocked at both ends. It might be three or four feet long and thick – like a Pakeha drum only longer. It was hit with a stick about two feet long; an aruhe, shark or whitau beater would do; and the noise called the people together. It could also be used at tangis and koreros. There was no music in it – simply a noise. Hitting two sticks together was merely a boy's game, a device sometimes used to accompany juvenile singing.

The roria was a small harp made of split supplejack and held between the teeth and struck. He had done it – it was just a child's amusement and the 'music' was merely of a very rattling character. It was not taken from the Jew's harp of the whalers; it was used long before then.

The trumpet with flax lining inside [See Tregear's [[1904]] *Maori Race*. H.B.] he had a vague idea of having heard about, but he could not say why the flax was used – it may have been a child's play, even as the pakete (bow and arrow) was [See Section re Games, H.B.]. The putorino and koauau were not much used in Canterbury. The koauau was played by the nose in the North Island. The porutu was chief musical instrument in South Island. It was made of tutu wood usually and had six holes in it by which the musician produced the rangi (tune).

An old woman had often seen the toitoi shell about Akaroa. In the olden days the Maoris knocked the end off and used it as a koauau (flute). It was a sort of shell trumpet.

POI AND DANCES

The collector has so far collected very little information about the two subjects classed under above heading. The principal informant said that in the old days poi was played with long strings and usually standing except in those depicting boat rowing (waka-poi) and kindred things, these latter being done while sitting. Te Whiti and Tohu brought in the latest style – that now generally used – when the old poi had almost fallen into disuse. This was at Parihaka [In Murihiku this name is called Parihanga. H.B.] about the year 1890 and it was at first associated with some religious idea they had.

*The haka was not a war-dance. It was a kind of powhiri or one part of the dance of welcome accorded visitors. As well as the men, girls used to dance hakas and sometimes both sexes would dance in unison. The time was kept by singers and was called whakatoitoi. This name was also applied to a haka to keep time for the rowers in canoes.** [Tregear's [[1891]] *Dictionary* has: Toitoi – to rehearse canoe songs. H.B.]

*The war-dance was called whaka-tuwaewae. Peruperu was a name sometimes used for it but it was really only the beginning, or opening movement, of the war-dance proper. As the dancers got worked up and the dance got stronger it became a whaka-tuwaewae. A part of it was also known as whaka-tutu-ngarehu.** [Tregear's [[1891]] *Dictionary* gives a name of the wardance as ngarahu-taua. H.B.]

The puha was a form of wardance, a familiar start being 'ka mate', etc., and means to make the blood go strong. Some pakehas objected to the noise. At the war the Germans would throw a bomb if they heard a noise but the Maoris would catch it and throw it back. The puha is a lively dance and once at Gallipoli when the New Zealanders fought against the 'Turkeys' for thirty hours without food and were very jaded the Maoris who had fought beside them under an equal strain sang a puha to cheer themselves up and this had the effect of inspiriting the whole lot. So returned soldiers say.

SECTION VIII

MEDICAL LORE

Tahutahu or Salving Wounds — Wairukahu or Medicine — Puhipuhi or Gout — Mare or Coughs — Hakihaki or Skin-Troubles — Paepae or Syphilis — Torohi or Diarrhoea — Tutaki or Costiveness — Kaupapa-atua or Body-Healer — Whakawhanau or Child-Birth — Hori or Tutu Poisoning — etc.

MEDICINAL LORE

On this trip the collector heard of two or three cases of gout among the older Maoris. He had never heard of this in South and asked its name and was told it was puhipuhi, a word which means 'swelling'. One of the sufferers is the principal informant. In speaking of bodily ailments and Maori ideas of curing same he made following statements: The olden Maoris had a form of consumption but there was no mare (coughing) nor spitting and it was cured by patient sitting in a running stream to let water into the private parts. There was no pneumonia then. The worst thing in those days and most dreaded was makutu (witchcraft) which could bring illness. Consumption is called matekohi or tarai. The fat of seals was a good food and a good medicine. It was good for babies (after it was cooked) and a sick child would be given a piece to suck if it was thought the case demanded it. Roriki is a water-plant like cress but would burn skin or burn you inside if eaten. If eaten raw it was poisonous but boiled as a medicine (known as wairukahu or waikahu) it was good for any illness. It could be taken internally or the water from boiling could be rubbed on externally and would cure skin diseases such as hakihaki. If a warrior got a severe wound a cure was to put hot oil (hinu) in the wound. This was called tahutahu. *The Maori brought very few diseases from Hawaiki. Even the well-known hakihaki (itch) which doctors say is a Maori complaint he reckoned was pakeha and brought in by whalers. The doctors asked him why it hung on among the people but he maintained it was pakeha like lung troubles, etc., which still keep on. Paepae (syphilis or pox) was another bad disease brought in by whalers as was also the mitara (measles) which killed very many Maoris.** There is a leaf found in the mountains – it is green on one side and white on the other – it is not the tikumu but he forgot its name. Boil it and apply as poultice for gout and it is very good. It is a modern cure. His father had gout too and tried this cure on the advice of old Roro from Wairewa. Once his mother had breaking sores on her legs and karakia was no good nor the English doctor either. A North Island Maori was down at Akaroa and went into the bush and got the barks and leaves of all trees and ferns. He boiled these and the water cured his mother in a week after five years illness. Narrator forgot some cures of old but kohai bark boiled was good for colds; karamu bark (looked like beer when boiled) was ditto. Ko-ro-miko (koromiko) was excellent in cases of stubborn diarrhoea (torohi). An epidemic of this thirty years ago filled the Christchurch Hospital and the doctors could not cope with it until the Maori remedy was used. The Maoris got twelve soft leaves (over that number was too strong) and chewed the koromiko raw.

Burn hinahina and put all kinds of leaves on fire and mix pork oil with ashes into balls. These dry hard like pills. Scratch the side ('a sort of vaccination') or place where pain is and rub the 'powdered pill' in it. This relieves pain and cure is called pungarehu (ashes). It must be a modern cure since the pakehas brought most kinds of diseases in. Costiveness or tutaki (a word which means 'closing door') is cured by flax root (putake-harakeke – the very bottom of the root is called pakiaka). The root is roasted in fire until properly cooked and when cool is chewed. It is sweet like sugar but extremely effective, being probably one of the best cures for costiveness known anywhere. Flax-gum (piaharakeke) will cure pakewakewa (ring-worm). Runa is said to be another remedy. There are two kinds of this water-plant – the runa has broader leaves than the rekareka, while the runa is on one stalk and the other branches out. The runa is good for worms in horses. It is boiled and the water drunk lukewarm and applied very hot to mane and back. When children have worms (noke) they can be cured by runa but of course do not make so strong as for cattle. The root of the toetoe is good for some sicknesses. The soft part of ti leaves were chewed to secure regularity of the bowels.

From this point the narrator passed into a more personal discourse: The mata-titiro is a seer of visions and if your child is ill he will dream what is best for it or tell by looking at the sufferer. He (or she) is not the same as a tohunga as the latter among many branches of knowledge goes in for makutu and whaiwhaia, etc. The law stops the tohunga with his witchcraft and putting the body in cold water, but the Matatitiro and Kaupapa-Atua although vaguely called tohungas are sometimes not only not so, but are quite different. A tohunga-nana-tupapaku tried to cure narrator's gout and was fined five pounds by Maori Council. Narrator wrote to head Council explaining the man was not a tohunga but a Kaupapa-kikokiko-atua and asking for a refund of the fine. The Council said 'Let the Government decide', with a result the money was returned, it being decided the man was not a tohunga but merely a healer of the body. Once narrator suffered from a very serious stoppage of the bowels and three doctors attended him. They said he was blocked inside at five places but could give no relief and wished to operate. A Maori kaupapa came and said 'If they operate you will die'. He recommended an enema of starch, turpentine and salt but said 'Ask the doctor first!' The latter said it was an undoubtedly clever suggestion and to use it. He did and his puku (stomach) swelled worse than ever. The kaupapa gave him castor-oil and next day the five blockages came out as the kaupapa foretold. Some time later when doctors attending him, water began to spurt from his pito (navel) and they got nearly a bucketful. It was sent (a sample) to Wellington and analysed and said to be pure water, probably caused by sweat stopping in his body. The doctors who attended him asked what he was going to do next – 'the first time he produced ambergris like a sperm whale and the next time he was like a camel with its hump full of water.' He had never been ill since but it left the gout with him and he uses rimu (red pine) decoction – a pakeha drink put up in Taranaki.

An old man said if your belly was sore or you felt bad inside boil the puha (sow thistle) and drink the waipuha or water wrung out of it. The olden people were wont to use various leaves and barks as remedies but he did not know the particulars of these as the Maoris for many years past had neglected their own medicines and cures and sought the chemist's shop instead. They had done this for the past fifty or sixty years at any rate.

An elderly halfcaste woman (a capable nurse and a believer in Professor Kirk's very efficacious home treatment such as hot and cold fomentations, bran poultices, olive oil, etc.) told me these facts: Her first baby was extremely ill and was costive a week and nothing doctor could prescribe seemed to help him. An old (Maori) woman told her to give the baby a drop or two of its mother's urine (mimi) – not the first water but when it began to run clear. She thought it a queer cure but in desperation did so and the child's bowel's moved and he lived (and is now wedded with a big, fat baby boy of his own. H.B.). The Maoris still use the mimi cure for sore throats. It is warm and seems to scald throat they say (if swallowed it may cause diarrhoea). During the 'flu epidemic a white woman lay very ill in Christchurch Hospital. The doctors gave her up and she lamented sorely about her poor children in Invercargill. The next bed was occupied by a Maori woman who confided to her the mimi cure (her throat was very bad, etc.). She surreptitiously tried it and to the intense surprise of the medical men and her own great joy recovered and took train to her family in Southland. The collector further heard of the use of this cure quite recently but to a young Maori woman whose throat was sore and voice very husky (but who did not like to try such a drastic remedy) he recommended a gargle of salt and water with beneficial results. Next day her korokoro (throat) was much better. Speaking to two Maoris they told the collector that for certain internal ills the ramarama (pepper tree) leaves could be chewed or you could boil them and drink the water. Kaio or kohai or karamu leaves could also be steeped with it with good results. The kokomuka (koromiko) leaves were highly beneficial for torohi (diarrhoea) but one man said he knew a far better and more certain cure for this complaint. This was the seeds of the manuka – te hua o te manuka – which had to be chewed and juice swallowed. He did not care if all the doctors in New Zealand could not cure a bad case of diarrhoea just let the sufferer get the juice of these small berries into his system and the complaint would stop in half-an-hour. There was no cure like it.

The collector has read that litters, stretchers or hammocks called amo were sometimes used to carry sick persons. Whether such was the case in Canterbury he does not know but he met a little girl called Amo after an aunt of hers. He was told the word meant 'a stretcher' but was given no reason for its employment as a personal name.

Burn toadstools and the ashes are good for the sore backs of horses – Modern Maori Surgery!

To boil the puha (sowthistle) and eat it as greens [See Tregear's [[1891]] *Dictionary* under 'puwha'. H.B.] is a vegetable food but the Maoris say it has a medicinal quality by being a blood-purifier.

*The principal informant had a touch of nihotuka (toothache) one day the collector was there. He said it was a rare complaint among the olden Maoris. In the ancient times they might eat food warm in the morning but it was eaten cold at other times – hence their good teeth. Now they have hot food or hot liquids at every meal and it is bad for the teeth.**

Remnants of tohungaism still linger and the collector heard one person scathingly condemned as 'too fond of jimmy-work with its cold water'. [For meaning of 'jimmy' see Murihiku Notes, H.B.]

Add to Medical Lore

*The principal informant said he reckoned close intermarriage and inbreeding was decimating the race.** [His first wife a relative and the children died; his next distant and some of the children survived.] *He lectured in North Island on this and quoted case of Queen Victoria and Prince Albert as example to follow. He told the people to marry 'wide apart' and so beget and rear healthier children. In the old day the Maori practically ran naked and was so hardy you could have struck a match on his skin. They were fighting constantly and yet increased plentifully. They ate anything, much of it raw, but throve. Now hot food is ruining the teeth. Although the food is better now, or of much more variety and nutriment, the race is not nearly so healthy. So many died of the measles, the remainder could not bury them. The complaint rewharewha worked havoc. It was a mare (cough) and started in a bad cold. It was he mate-uruta (an epidemic). It was called maremare in South Island and was 'a strong sickness' in both islands.** The old form of consumption or matekohi did not spread. When a sick person ate, the remaining food was thrown to the dogs and not given to others to handle. It could be cured by sitting in the coldest water possible. It was now a different consumption – ngaene he called it. In the old days fat was poured in wounds to heal. Some doctors said that the habit of giving birth to children in a creek or of putting the little ones straight away in water [See Childbirth, H.B.] left the Maoris with weak chests. For a person to be mentally deranged through excitement or worry is poraki; for the 'head to go round' or be dizzy is haurakiraki. This latter word is now applied to drunkenness. A good medicine for haha (thrush in baby's mouths) is to beat karetu grass soft, strain in water and rub on affected parts. It is a speedy cure. A woman said that blindness was pohe ka kanohi and a hunchback was kunu. Madness is called porangi now, but the old Canterbury name was karakiraki or karaki. She knew a person with six toes (he ono taotao) on each foot but knew no name for such an uncommon person.

Add to Medical Lore

The principal informant said he did not think you could tell Pakeha from Maori footprints in sand. The foot of the latter was not flat but toes were a different shape. European toes were longer, especially the big toe – perhaps generations of boot-wearing had squeezed them. Maori toes were compact and evenly-shaped. His own foot was symmetrical and two Highlanders once sincerely complimented him on his feet; they said that chasing sheep over the mountains when boys had ruined their feet and hence their ugly shape. (He showed his bare foot to collector and it was certainly compact; the second toe was slightly longer than his big toe and rest ran very evenly.) To have six toes (or fingers) was called waewaepiri or, jocularly, hauhaua (cripple). In the old days cold streams were used to cure sicknesses such as the old form of consumption. This was not a galloping consumption but a person attacked could live a very long time but became very thin. The Maoris never used hot water in the old days – it was all cold. He had seen one or two cases of Maori albinos in Canterbury, (Leah Hari being one). He knew one in Westland, a man with an ure like a horse – altogether abnormal – but they could not beget children. The women used to bring home from the bush a beautiful soft moss to keep babies cool or to put in their maro during menstruation (mate-wahine). It was a very fine moss – not the scented kopuru. Papapuni is a blockage of bowels but he did not know what old cure was – 'it was too far from him'. Katirehe is quinsy. He had heard the pupil of the eye called karupango, but this would be kanohipango or konohipango in Canterbury. A wart used to be called tona, and ira is a spot or mole usually to be found on the face of any beautiful woman.

An old man at Kaiapoi felt very ill, 'E kore au e mate wawe mea pea taihoa' – if he did not die soon he would do so some day perhaps – he said to collector. It was only 'te mahana o te ra' (warmth of the sun) that was keeping him alive, he explained. (A neighbouring woman said he was consumptive.) He said he had never heard of a cure for papapuni.

A woman at Akaroa mentioned that a complaint, 'water running from mouth', of children was called ware.

CHILDBIRTH AND INFANCY

Mention of Tura brought the principal informant to this subject, but he had to be pressed to speak of it, evidently considering it more within woman's province, and furthermore that anything he would say on it would not be suitable for any popular publication such as a Museum would care to issue. Tura reached that portion of Hawaiki where the people opened the stomach to take the child and the mother died. Tura said this was not right; 'we can push the child out'; and they replied, 'do so then'. He took his wife's stomach between his knees and pressed and the child was born. She cried with the pain and said, 'Use our method', but Tura would not and she was soon all right. Thus that people were taught the correct way of accouchement. A white man had told the narrator that the Kapuhi (Auckland) Maori women experienced very easy childbirth and this was true of most parts of New Zealand in the old days. In Canterbury they would get a tohuka and the woman would crouch on her heels with her hands on her knees. Sometimes the husband or another woman would do the assistance necessary, or sometimes the woman would go to a creek by herself and come back with the baby. When in the house Tura's method was employed as a rule. The woman and assistant on their heels would face one another and the latter would put his (or her) arms round woman to hold her back and press two knees into her sides and the child would be born on to space between them. To start the birth the man would put his hand on the woman's head and give it a good bang with his other fist. This usually had desired effect if well-timed. An English doctor to whom he told this said, 'You might as well hit the head of the blooming woman on the wall.' That was his exact words and he went on to advocate stomach massage. In cases where Maori women went to creeks the doctors said this was very wrong too, and tended to produce weak chests because the child came from its warm environment into the cold water. The child should be left awhile before it is washed, the washing being with lukewarm water.

After the child was born (whaka-whanau) the umbilical cord (iho, he thought) was cut near the pito (navel) by a woman (or tohunga for leading people, he thought) with a shell and tied with whitau. The afterbirth was called whenua.

There was no whare-kohanga or birth-house here – he reckoned that was 'only North Island talk to look big'. After the child was born the tohunga would karakia the mother to make her noa. He (narrator) hoped that was the end of the questions as he did not feel qualified to expatiate on it and subject was distasteful to him.

At a later date the collector casually asked him at what age women ceased bearing children. Narrator replied that he knew a case where a woman had a baby and it was twenty two years later before she had another, but he knew of no cases where old women had had babies. He considered that even after a woman ceased bearing she was affected (in temper at least) by the moon at the time of her former periods. He knew no Maori name for 'change of life', nor any details about it.

Tohi is the ceremony of taking the baby to the tohunga who takes it to the waitapu. He did not know if this ceremony was more to preserve the life of the child or to give it a name. Tohi was also part of karakia over warfare. *Iriiri is present baptism since the Pakeha came but tohi was the old style. He could not give the details of the ceremony.**

An old Maori man told the collector that when a child was born motu-pakake (seal fat) was given it to 'clean it out' before feeding it for the first time – there was no castor-oil then, he added. At a later stage of development the old women would sometimes give baby a pipi mussel to suck as a dummy if it was bad for crying. Motu-pakake (seal fat) was also used for that purpose.

For (haha) thrush the mother would tawhiri-te-karetu (twist this grass) and put the juice in sufferer's mouth. Pouaka grass was also soaked in water and wrung out the liquid being used as a mouth-wash. The stem of a small or very young ti (cabbage tree), or rather the heart or centre shoot of it, was also got and the juice squeezed out as a third remedy for this infantile trouble.

Add to Childbirth

*When a child is born, said the principal informant, the Pakeha usually burns the afterbirth or placenta but the Maori would on no account do such a thing as it would injure or destroy the mauri of the new arrival. [See section on Mana, H.B.] The afterbirth (whenua) was carefully committed to the whenua (ground) and the mauri and mana of the child was thus preserved. [Even to this day the objection to burning the whenua continues and if a Maori woman is attended by a European doctor or nurse she usually tries to arrange that one of her own race will bury the whenua.]**

'Taukiri e Tura' is a cry of pain given by women in the pangs of childbirth. The word is not 'takiri' meaning to start or move back suddenly but taukiri [also taikiri. H.B.] an exclamation of surprise or alarm and it is a traditional saying arising from the historic childbirth superintended by Tura. This famous ancestor married a woman of the Rapuwai or Maeroero breed on a strange island where the people had no fires but ate their food raw. The women were good-looking but were delivered of children by the Caesarian operation (causing death). Tura would not let the old women treat his wife so and held her while the child was born, hence her cry of surprise and pain has been echoed by women undergoing the ordeal of accouchement many generations later.

The Maori women used to search the deep recesses of the forest for a beautiful, soft, green, filmy moss to place inside their maro when the periodical mate-wa-hine came. They also used this moss to lay young babies on as it is said to be not only soft but cool, and refreshing in touch to the skin.

POISONS

*The principal informant mentioned a strange fact about tutu. At the river Rangitata [Rakitata in old documents. H.B.] in Canterbury tutu berries could be eaten with impunity but they were poisonous [unless seeds taken out. H.B.] elsewhere. If a child (or adult) was poisoned eating tutu berries the remedy was to burn a rag, etc., and run the smoke up the sufferer's nostrils, but he did not know the name of that cure. He had never heard of a cure for karaka poisoning [which causes convulsions. H.B.]. A plant named Roriki, like cress in the water, was poisonous if eaten raw but if boiled the water could be taken internally for blood disorders. The katipo spider was in Canterbury and its bite was poisonous. The remedy was to rub puha (sowthistle) on and do so frequently, when the place would not swell. That was the only cure for this bite he had heard of.**

A Rapaki Maori said that fortunately the katipo was not so plentiful as of yore. It was a black spider with red markings. If you were unlucky enough to be bitten by it the best plan was to at once put some puha on, heat the puha at the fire and keep applying it for a time. The longer the delay the more the danger – it was indeed 'paitinitia a mea' – a poisonous thing. [Paitini is word from 'poison'. H.B.]

Two Tuahiwi Maoris said that tutu poisoning was called rori-te-tutu or hori [Note. The Polynesian comparatives of rori and hori are interesting. H.B.]. It would distort the face and cramp the jaw. A rag was put in the patient's mouth so he would not bite his arero (tongue). Smoke was driven up his nose to make him vomit (whakaruaki is attempting to vomit but ruaki is throwing-up in reality) . Some would recover but some died. Katipo poisoning was called katia-te-katipo. The place bitten swells up (pupuhi). If bitten get puha and heat it at a fire and rub the juice on. This would cure if done in time. Katipos are still on beach near Kaiapoi. They knew a woman who was bitten by one of these venomous spiders and drank saltwater straightaway and rubbed puha on the wound and she recovered.

Add to Poisons

A Taumutu Maori said he had killed a katipo on the beach that morning. In winter the katipo lies dormant and 'half-dead', but in summer it is venomous. If a person is bit, a swelling comes, and the old remedy was to rub puha (sowthistles) on, but now mustard or nicotine can be used; and any or all these things 'kill the strength of the poison'.

A Peninsula Maori said that at Waipuna, near Wairewa, there was plenty of tutu and his grandmother when young got 'tutued'. The people flogged her round to keep her moving fast, smacked her lustily, and got the sweat running freely and she recovered. If you ate raw karaka berries you would get 'hori or paralysed', he said, 'as also from kiekie or too much tiori.' The only attempted remedy he had heard of was to bury the patient in sand to stop their 'antics' from injuring them.

SECTION IX

DISPOSAL OF THE DEAD

Whakaheke or Water-Burial — Huna or Cave Burial — Tahu or Cremation — Whakamomori or Suicide — Haehae or Ripa — or Mourning Gashes — etc.

BURIAL AND MOURNING

*The disposal of the dead was undertaken in a number of ways according to the principal informant. In wartime they were cremated or placed in deep springs or hapua (lagoons). At Taumutu is a place where the dead were buried in deep water with stones attached to sink the body and prevent it rising again. The spring was called Waiwhakaheketupapaku and was said to be bottomless. He did not know what this burial was called [whakaheke. H.B.] but the spring was tapu. In the old days many tupapaku (corpses) were burnt (tahu), the ashes being buried. He had never heard of the ashes or bones of deceased persons being put in burial chests or receptacles of any kind. Others were buried or placed away in caves with their knees tied under their chins.** No food was ever buried with or placed near dead people. Cemeteries or present-day burying-grounds are called urupa. In the old days the dead were sometimes preserved, the head, or body in some cases, being 'cured' (whakatamiro). The whole body when done would not keep very long but the head could be kept for thirty to fifty years or more. He could not say how this 'curing' was done. *In regard to the scraping of the bones of the dead he fancied it was called ahu. It was done up at the Bay of Islands but he did not think it was done in Canterbury or Otago.** When a chief died his widow or widows made great lamentations. Sometimes the head-wife would kill herself – kohuru or really whakamomori (suicide). *Those who came to the tangihanga (burial) would wear a parepare (head band) of green leaves.** If the dead person was of high rank the tangi party would cut their skins with sharp mataa (flints) or with pipi shells – men as well as women doing this. As a tohu-mamae (sign of mourning) the bereaved would cut their hair with a mata or pipi. *Teketaupuhi was to cut a swathe of hair from ear to ear leaving a tuft in front.** The custom of cutting hair as mourning for the dead still survives and when his son died during the influenza epidemic the whole family (including women and girls too) cut their hair short. *In the old days when farewelling the dead the tangi party bade the soul of the deceased to go to Hawaiki-roa, Hawaiki-nui, Hawaiki-pamamao and on to Te Hono-ki-Wairua. This was sometimes rendered as Tawhiti-roa, Tawhiti-nui, etc., but Hawaiki was the proper name to use, as it was the correct name of those places. 'Tawhiti' means distance and is only a substitute name or nickname for those places and was given because the olden Maoris could not specify the exact location of those countries or islands.**

Two Tuahiwi Maoris said that to cut the skin in mourning was called haehae or ripa. Any sharp thing such as a mata or a pipi was used. If you saw a widow frantically rushing round streaming with blood the best thing to do was to get out of the road unless you were looking for trouble.

While the collector was on his northern trip he had the melancholy duty of attending two Maori funerals. At Tuahiwi a girl was buried. At the house the doleful wailing took place. There was no clergyman there and the takiaue or wailing lasted half an hour reaching its climax as the coffin was borne away. An Anglican service (High Church) was held in Saint Stephen's Church Reverend Frese [[Frere, according to Beattie 1920 diary entries]] officiating, and at the graveside he read the burial service in the liquid Maori tongue and the Maoris sang their beautiful burial hymn very effectively. Afterwards the collector saw men laughing and smoking in the urupa (cemetery) and was assured the 'old superstition' (about using tobacco there) had died out except among the unduly fanciful crowd 'down South'. [Where the collector attended three Maori funerals and heard no wailing whatever. H.B.] At Temuka where a prominent halfcaste, James Rickus, was buried there was a noticeable gathering of representative men from all over the South Island, the body being kept a week, enabling some to come from a distance. A special carriage was put on the express at Christchurch 'Reserved for Maoris' travelling to the tangi at Temuka. The deceased died in Wellington and when the corpse arrived at Temuka the men of that Kaik met it wearing macrocarpa twigs in their hats. The manuhiri (visitors) from Tuahiwi arrived at the Hall (where the body lay) wearing green wreaths. When most of the prominent visitors had arrived and been welcomed, and returned thanks therefore, an animated discussion took place as to where the body should be interred. Deceased has expressed a dying wish to be buried in the Pakeha cemetery of Temuka where his two dead daughters were laid, but the elders in council assembled wished him to be laid to rest with the kaumatua in the urupa in the Kaik, where, it may be added, a grandson was buried. After considerable argument it was decided to accede to deceased's request and relatives' wishes and he was accordingly buried in the Cemetery at Temuka. [This was an opposite decision to that when Maiharoa was buried (about 1886). His relatives wished him to be buried at Temuka and his followers at Waitaki Mouth. After protracted negotiations the latter won and he was interred at Korotuaheka – where now only one Maori family lives. H.B.]

Speaking to various people during the tangi the collector gleaned a little information. A prominent Kaiapoi Maori said he had never seen widows gash themselves although he had heard of it but he had seen the hair cut as a sign of grief. He forgot the name of this haircutting. It was maybe taua, as parepare-taua was a mourning cap. As long as the cap was worn it was a tohu or memorial of mourning, but when a widow took it off she became whakanoa (made common or freed from tapu). In the old days during a tangi she sat in state on a wharetaua – a widow's stage – while the corpse was laid in common view on a whata built in the marae of the village. Burial was not common in those days (earth-burial that is) but the body was hid in some secluded spot while the head was often preserved by a secret tamiro process.

Another man, who spent some years in the North Island, told the collector that while contracting for some settlers at Tolaga Bay and Tokomaru he inadvertently dug up four corpses. Nothing was known about them by the district residents so the bones were interred elsewhere but what had struck him as strange was that each figure was in a sitting position with knees under chin. [This corroborates a statement made in another portion of this section. H.B.]

The principal informant said that in the old days after a tangi a tohunga would get on the taumata (probably the height of the marae) and deliver a speech about where death came from. [As his children and the young people do not know these things he gave a speech of this nature after the burial recently of an aged woman at Rapaki. Some who heard it told the collector it was a very good speech and informative of ancient lore on the subject. H.B.]

Note: The collector wrote a brief account of Temuka tangi for the local paper 'Temuka Leader' and a copy of this is herewith appended. H.B.]. [[It was not.]]

Add to Death and Disposal of Dead

*When a leading man died in the old days, said the principal informant, slaves were killed and a tangi party often felt bound to kill someone.** They would particularly seek to patu (kill) a relative and these used to clear out till the coast was clear if they suspected such a design. The Maoris used to fight month after month and death was ever-familiar so a relative more or less did not matter. *The tangi parties would cut the skin also and let the blood run = tangihaehae. Widows used to strangle (kaehere) themselves when grief and love was too strong and they could not control the mind. Sometimes a father or mother would commit suicide if a favorite child died, or a child would do so on the death of a greatly-loved parent, but these instances were not common. All these customs came from Hawaiki. In regard to men killed in war he had never heard of burial in a circle, feet to the centre. Bones found in sandhills were those slain (and often eaten) in battle. This occurred before Whites came – the corpses were not buried, but were simply left lying and the sand drifted over them.

Kaihuanga (eat relatives) was a recent war and the bones of those slain were left lying too and no doubt are some of those unearthed by the wind and the Pakeha.** Death in a building rendered it tapu but it could be freed by the tohuka doing the whakahorohoro ceremony and saying karakia to make it noa (common).

After a certain time of mourning arrangements would be made to dispose of the corpse. (In Tregear we read of kai tango atua the despised persons who handled the dead and so were outcast but my informant had never heard of such a class in the South Island). The tohukas buried the dead using appropriate karakia. They did not carry the body but they went with the party. The latter were usually sons, brothers or relatives. If there were no close relations available, ones up to fourth cousins would do. A man without relations or posterity would probably be thrown on a fire and reduced to ashes without any ceremony but this would be very rare. It was usual for high-born people to leave instructions about the mode and place of burial. Such people were often deposited in caves, *but burial in water and cremation were also common methods.**

Tanu means to dig the ground and cover the body but it was seldom done in the old days. *He had never heard of letting the dead drift out to sea on canoes or rafts.**

Waro is a big hole through which water was running once but now dry. *Such a hole would be used to deposit the dead in. This was not called tanu but kua huna tia he thought. A cave (ana) was a desired sepulchre and one on a cliff facing the sea or a deep gorge was reckoned secure.** The body had the knees doubled under the chin and was strapped on a kawe borne by one man on his back, the kawe being subsequently burnt. Narrator forgot the name of this posture, 'if it had one, but perhaps it had none'. *The body was tied in a rope and lowered down cliff-face to its destination, the men who set it in the ana being than hauled up.** Kua tukua te tinana o te tupapaku ki roto ki te ana i roto i te pari (the words 'te pari' can be read also 'te rua i te maunga'). There was a name for that burial and also for the men doing it but he had forgotten them.

He had known bodies were put in ana (caves) and one was found at Waipuna Hill on the Peninsula. He did not know about this orua or rua (hole) until the Pakeha found it. A Russian Finn (a 'Square Jaw') found a small hole and crept in and found bones, one being those of a man of gigantic stature. The Maoris consider this was Te Rakiwhakaputa, the 'biggest man of his day', who is stated to have been seven feet high. 'He was not a good man – he was as bad as Tutekawa for killing people.' The Finn brought out a jawbone which went completely over his own jaw and obscured the lower half of his face. The fame of it went abroad and George Robertson, a halfcaste, made him take and put it back. George looked in hole and saw a very big cavern in the rock. He was afraid to go in, however, so wrote to narrator, who was busy and wrote to police to attend to matter. A constable with George and a party (and a plentiful supply of beer) went up and covered the hole with a big stone and put soil over and around it. It was a whole day's work. They also put up a notice warning trespassers. The constable penetrated the cave and said it was two and a half or three chains long and that there were numerous bones in it. They would be deposited there from Te Pa-o-Te-Rangiwhakaputa and from the Little River district.

*Other common methods of disposing of the dead were heke (water) and tahu (cremation). Near Taumutu a deep hole was used to heke the weighted corpses in and near Kaiapoi another deep-water hole was used also. The idea was so that nobody would get the body up. They were very careful in those days as they did not want bodies to roast in hangi or the bones to furnish fishhooks to foes. He had never heard of aerial sepulture on trees, nor on stages or canoes in the bush.** [See Tregear's [[1904]] *Maori Race* – in which work it is also stated that in the South Island burial is nehunga, exhumation is rukutanga tupapaku and scraping is hahunga. The collector asked *re* these. H.B.] Nehunga is to bury corpses. Nehu is a new word since Christianity came in to express the rite of burial but it was never used in the old days. Nehu as a word means the body is soft like pungarehu (ashes).

Rukutanga cannot be right. It means 'diving'. To dig a body up would be huakanga tupapaku. Ahunga tupapaku is to dig up a corpse at the Bay of Islands, scrape the bones and put them away. Hahu (or 'ahu) means scraping to take the fat and stink away. *The Ngapuhi do that – it was not done here. If it was done in Canterbury it must be modern as how could you scrape the bones of those who had been burnt to ashes or dropped into the unfathomable pools? It was not a South Island mode at all.**

Whakatamiro [He said this was formerly pronounced Faka ta miro – the collector noted it was called Waka-tau-miro in South. H.B.] is to cut the head of a corpse and preserve it and put it on a little kaupapa (stage) outside a pa wall. The head was sometimes stuck up inside a house where people were living. It would last for years. The hair would be tied up (koukou) and kotuku or other feathers put in as a pare or taupare, and a pohe would be inserted in each ear and through the poke (hole) in the nose (ihu). After this adornment the head would be treasured. At each corner of a pa stood a puhara (stage) and on a pole on it was a little 'monkey-house' (atamiro) to hold the head. *Moki left instructions for Hikatutae to bury him. When latter reached the body it was too decayed to carry so he burnt it and carried the head (he carried it himself as it was too high rank (and therefore sacred) for common men to handle) down to Kaiapoi. Here he left the head at a spot called Pekapeka in a little house on the top of a long pole.**

Rara was a way of preserving heads different to tamiro. This way the head was heated by fire and would last for years also. The ordinary rara to cook eels was embers laid along and a manuka stage made along each side like / \ and the eels being fixed on it. The rara for heads was not the same but it dried the fat and oil out of the head – a sort of smoke-drying perhaps. The heads were put in boxes on poles at intervals round a pa but were never very numerous. He did not know how the tamiro process was done. He knew no meaning for makura – it was not burning the dead which was called tahu.

Speaking to a Maori at Kaiapoi he said the Tuahiwi urupa (cemetery) was the site of an old pa. The Maoris did not now bury clothing with the dead – they burnt it – but they still continued to bury greenstone and mats with the departed if these were people of influence who had possessed such articles.

*The principal informant said the wairua (soul) of dead went to Reinga via North Cape of New Zealand. Here there is a place Morianuku where there is a rock whose name he forgot and on this rock the spirits cut off each other's hair prior to entry of spirit world. There was lamentation there, and as well as hair, the hupe (phlegm) of the nose and roimata (tears) of the eye had to be left on that rock before the spirits jumped into the water. He did not think souls went to Hawaiki although such is stated in tradition; and honoki wairua is simply a term meaning the soul has left the body and gone on. He had never heard of Haumu; but he had heard about Tawhaitiri and Tuapiko but that was merely a fanciful yarn, and not proper history.**

Add to Burial

A statement made to the collector that a man's body was burnt and the ashes collected in a box and forwarded to his relatives two hundred miles away [See H.B.'s [[1918]] paper – page 92 in *Journal of the Polynesian Society*. H.B.] caused the collector to ask his informants if such was a custom. The replies all negatived such a conclusion. The principal informant had never heard of the ashes of the dead being put in boxes – they were buried. Another old man said: 'I never heard of such a thing at all; ashes were not kept.' And these opinions were corroborated everywhere the collector asked the question.

In speaking to the people at Akaroa the collector found that water-burial bore no part in their recollections. Near Onuku stands the site of the old pa of Otehore (called Paradise by the Pakeha so 'tis said). People who died here were carried uphill through the bush in a kawe on a man's back. The corpse was put in a hole in the hilltop, a crack or crevice between two rocks, being probably lowered by cords of aka vine. Such is traditional account but the collector was told the cavity could not longer be seen or identified. The man who bore the corpse became tapu, or, at least, his back did, and to free it he was taken to the creek, where the tohuka splashed (tauhi) water on his back. My informants could not say if the tohuka used the branch of a tree to spray water over man, but they knew he repeated karakia during ceremony.

In latter years it was revealed (by a landslip probably) that a burial cave existed at Parakakariki (Sleepy Cove near Long Bay). The cave was up a cliff and men must have been lowered to it. Skeletons, as well as patu, tiki, heru, tattooing needles, etc., etc., [now in the possession it is said of Mr Vangioni of Akaroa – Professor Benham has twice seen his collection. H.B.] were found, showing it had been a sacred burial ana (cave) of the old people.

SECTION X

CUSTOMS

Tapui or Betrothal — Muru or Raiding of Unfortunates — Unu-unu or Pulling Beard Out — Tehe or Circumcision — Tautohe or Debate re genealogies — Putao or Disposal of Widows — Tapatapa or Dividing property — Tapikitara or Girl's 'Coming Out' — Kauamo or Stretcher-bearing — etc.

CUSTOMS

*Tapui, said the principal informant [who supplied all the information under this Section. H.B.], was the custom of betrothing children when they were small. The girls would often be wed at the ages of thirteen and fourteen. The marriage was called moe or noho but there was no ceremony.

Whakapapa (genealogies) could be recited from either end – from top or from bottom. The former is more usual. You say the name of the earliest ancestor you wish to quote and then say 'tana ko' and name the son and so on down the list. In the other method you say your own name (or that of the person whose ancestry you wish to trace or illustrate) first and then say 'ko ia ta' and mention father's name and so on upward.

Coming from semi-tropical islands to New Zealand the Maoris felt the cold. Down in the South Island they made a practice of eating as much fat as they could assimilate. This was no doubt a good custom but sometimes individuals overdid it. To eat too much fat was to be moreha.

Muru. This custom was observed on Banks Peninsula at least (if not over all South Island). Tapui, a son of Whiua, was taken a prisoner to the North Island by Rauparaha where he married a Ngatiawa wahine. They came down to Akaroa at the time of the rongopai (peace being made and Christianity coming in). He died and a North Island man at Akaroa took her to wife. She was a putao and this was not according to etiquette so the people felt they must muru him or kill someone. So the people went there and muru'd him (but there was not much to take, gravely added the narrator). The woman died soon after. In the old days a muru party took goods and burnt the house. [Note: Some of these people were related to the narrator. H.B.]

Tamatama was to reverence or show deference to a superior. Maiharanui was the upoko-ariki of Ngai-Tahu [prior to Rauparaha's raid, 1831. H.B.] but narrator said his ancestors never did tamatama to Maiharanui as they considered they were his equals. [A case of family pride. H.B.]

Tuku-a-ihu (though often called tukuihu, he considered this name should have an 'a' in it), hongi or hoki is the name of the old Maori salutation (commonly called rubbing noses.) The custom came from Hawaiki. While pressing the nose gently, you hold the other's hand and each states his or her relationship to the other. The name tuhuaihu is for the farewell salute. He did not think it was mentioned in the history and he knew no account of its origin. [Although the collector saw plenty of hoki on the streets of Bluff when the muttonbirders returned from their annual trip, he could not help noticing how little of it was done when the people were bidding each other farewell at Temuka tangi. There was abundance of 'smoojing' – good hearty kisses on the mouth usually – young fellows even gallantly kissing old wrinkled dames, but as for the more healthful hoki it was left for a few old-fashioned people. H.B.]**

It was a custom of the olden Maoris to people most hilly localities with fairies or wild men of the woods (maeroero) but the principal informant told the collector he knew no tales of such beings inhabiting any of the numerous hills round Banks Peninsula.

*Tattooing destroyed most of the beard but what grew was cut (tapatapahi) with the pipi, or a bivalve would be used as pincers and each hair pulled out (unu or unuunu). It is said that the old Waikakahi pa was three miles long and a jocular allusion to it was that by the time a man walked from end to end he could grow a beard (pahau). The hair of the head was sometimes cut (with the pipi too).**

An old Maori said that in olden times the Maoris in each district only had one name for each thing and where there are more names now, the extra ones have been brought in from elsewhere.

Add to Customs

Abstinence from Certain Foods: A woman told the collector that her father would not eat koau (shags) because the name was in his whakapapa and it would be like eating an ancestor. [Tregear's [[1904]] *Maori Race* says such a person is a wainamu. H.B.] *The principal informant did not know the word wainamu at all and although he knew custom did not know name of not eating food named after an ancestor.

Patatara – This said the principal informant meant the 'highest place' of the native. It was a tapu place (and from description given the collector takes it to be a racial division or boundary defining hapus) and the people who held such a position were the tino-momo-rakatira (very high-blood chiefs).**

Hair-cutting – The principal informant had never heard of hair being cut at puberty [*vide* Tregear. H.B.] but it was cut at mourning. The hair and the head were both sacred but he never heard any particular reason for this.

Teeth-Filing – The principal informant had never heard of this foolish idea before.

Circumcision – Tehe was seldom done. It was done more, he thought, in the South Sea Islands. He had had no one to discuss these things with long ago and so had missed many ceremonies and names and so could only speak of what he knew.

*Spitting – Had heard old people did not spit much as spittle could be bewitched.

Whistling – Was whio or kowhio and he thought the old people objected to it. This objection was probably owing to the idea of spirits but he was not positive about it.**

Etiquette – He had always understood it was considered to be against proper rules of conduct for a rakatira (gentleman) to abuse an inferior.

Cannibalism – The Maoris of old were a bad people because they ate human flesh. He could not say if women ate such flesh or not.

*Tautohe – This name is applied to an argument over whakapapa. (Tom Green and he had done some tautohe to the evident enjoyment of the late chief Taituha.) Hutihuti – Was to pluck the beard out. Tuangi (or tuaki) shells were used to pull the hairs out. [See Previous Notes, H.B.] Moko (tattooing) cut roots of beard and destroyed it or most of it. Now beards and moustaches (both called pahau) grow abundantly.

Tapui – is the custom when a girl or boy is promised in marriage. This is the correct and proper way. Other ways cause rows, but this was the calm and quiet way. It was a meeting of parents sometimes, at others relatives were invited to hear the negotiations. Elopement was kai-te-tuhera-te-ritenga and usually led to wars.

Putao – is when a man dies and his family has 'the say' over the widow. If she fancies some other choice than that selected for her and goes contrary to the family's wishes this will probably lead to a muru to pay for the infringement of the putao. When the woman is married again she is no longer a putao.**

Dissent – In Tregear's [[1904]] *Maori Race* it is stated that silence implied dissent and raising the eyebrows acquiescence. The collector asked the principal informant about this but did not get 'much furrader'. Dissent may have been implied by silence once but now it is expressed by 'kaore' (no!). Raising the eyebrows is whaka-timo (really means 'winking') and in a gathering was a 'signal to a young man to get a girl'.

*Tapatapa – is a name-giving, a public pronouncement, or a division of goods or land, etc. In one way it might be naming engagements to marry. The tohunga did it and it was a tapu thing as a rule. Then suppose there was a heap of gifts – food or clothes – and the tohunga tapa'd it. He would cut boundaries in it and divide into portions naming each one after a person as for his or her use. Being a tapu observance and there being a likelihood of makutu hanging round the tohunga would perform whakahorohoro to free the gifts for the use of the allotted owners. When tapa'ing couples, objectors could come forward and if their objections were sustained the tapatapa was taken off or abolished in that case. This has been known to have been done occasionally.

Tapikitara – this was a custom of some consequence to a young woman. It was like the 'coming-out' of a Pakeha damsel. The decoration of the girl was very elaborate. Her hair was done in first-class style and high-class mats adorned her. It was a 'rig-out' for the house and not for outside. If it was thought a girl would not live she would be made tapikitara for the tohunga to come and karakia her. Otherwise it was a 'bit of swank', for 'showing-off purposes', 'an eye-opener', concluded the principal informant.

Kaihaukai – is the Southern name for feast-giving. Platforms were made to hold the food and these might go up to thirty feet in height. The staging was called whata or tirewa, and the various platforms kaho. The staging might be built like ⌗ at each end and boards run across to provide tiers to place food on in baskets. A different kind of food would be placed on each platform. There would be two of these erections – the kaihaukai and the paremata (not paaraamata = parliament), the latter taller or bigger than the former – built close together and food would be heaped on both at same time. Maybe the home people would make the kaihaukai and visitors the paremata but the correct way was for visitors to make the former and residents the latter as a return compliment. There was more food here than in North Island and nothing was stinted to create a good effect. The people would send word of a projected kaihaukai some weeks before. The people from Kaiapoi might go to Rapaki carrying tuna, kiore, kauru, aruhe, kuri, kumera, etc., and the home people would prepare pipi or kuku, shark, maraki and sea products as a return gift. The food was not eaten as an exchange at time, but some of the Rapaki people would assist the Kaiapoians to carry their share to that place for subsequent enjoyment. The stuff taken to Rapaki was stored there till their people came back from helping the Kaiapoians. In two or three years time Rapaki would carry food to a kaihaukai at Kaiapoi and bring back inland food. It was an act of courtesy to enable people to vary foods a bit. It was not etiquette for food-carriers to walk across marae before visitors or chiefs but to come from behind or go round the back. A man doing so might be killed as 'the Maoris were the worst people in the world for killing offenders against the rules' or for breaches of etiquette.**

Offerings to Gods – The principal informant had never heard of kai-popoa [See Tregear] nor of offerings of any kind to the gods. He considered that as language to say kai-poapoa would be more correct than kaipopoa.

*Tohi – This is a name of karakia when going to war. The tohuka would go to the same pool as to tohi (baptise) children. If the sign was bad the people would not go to war. The tohuka did not use branches as far as he knew, and he had never heard that the tohuka shook or waved branches or that he put anything in the water.**

CUSTOMS

Kaikaiwaiu (a word which means 'suckling two breasts') is the custom to warn relatives to flee when danger threatens them. A tip from a relation in many a case saved lives otherwise forfeit.

*Maoris were advised not to snore. It was said that snoring was an invitation to lizards to come and hang on to the snorer's nostrils.

Hanihani is to insult a girl. (Let us hope this was not a Maori custom although here presented under that heading.) The famous chief Moki hanihani'd two women and died from makutu over it.

In the old days chiefs were very particular how they ate. In some instances, the collector was told, they did not touch food but were fed.

If a man was sitting with his legs stretched out before him a maid was told she must not step over them as they were tapu, but she could walk round the front of them (or behind him) with impunity.**

In regard to things that were tapu at one time the following customs are still observed. The Maoris will not wash their faces or hands in basins that have been used for cooking or for holding food (such as potatoes to be peeled, etc.). The hair having been tapu, no combings or clippings must be burnt (but buried) and scissors which have cut the hair must not be used to cut threads or materials, and vice versa. In the wharepuni you can hang your hat on the wall at the head of the bed; but the rest of the clothes must be put at the foot of the bed.

*Tapatapa was to name a thing in advance so that when the person whom it was named for came along he or she could seize it. An historical example of one form of this custom was given the collector. When Tamakino and Kaiapu escaped from the disastrous fight at Mokamoka near Bluff they made their way through hostile Waitaha-Kati-Mamoe country to Kaikoura. En route they noted that Waihora (Lake Ellesmere) was full of inaka, patiki and tuna and at Otawiri, near Wairewa (Lake Forsyth), they found excellent aruhe (fernroot). They then went over the Ka Mokaikoi Saddle to Akaroa. This was before Tutekawa's death. When they got to Kaikoura, Te Ruahikihiki asked about Waihora and being satisfied with the answer said 'Taku kaika, ko Orariki', and so tapatapa'd that place. Mako asked what was at Wairewa and being answered, 'Tuna, inaka, paraki and aruhe', he said, 'Taku kaika, ko Otawiri'. Te Ake asked what was at Akaroa and was told 'kuku, pipi and mako', and he said 'Taki kaika, ko___'. [Here narrator's memory failed him for this name. H.B.] Wheke asked and was told that the Lyttelton Harbor could also supply kuku and shark and he said 'Taku kaika, ko Whakaraupo'. This was the origin of those names. They were given at Kaikoura and those men came down and claimed the localities so designated and lived there and their descendants lived there until the Kaihuaka feud. [Taunaha is another name for this custom of bespeaking. H.B.]

The Maori would go to any length to return with interest any slight or fancied slight and they had (to us) some queer ideas of retaliatory methods. A man named Whakatohe journeying one moonlit night came to Waikakahi (later than he intended) to his brother's place. The brother (according to my informant) said 'E te pai o te po nei haere noa te takata ki te parore tae no atu ki te wahi haere ana ia te pai o te po nei te atamarama.' (Informant said parore meant 'wonderment' and he boiled the statement, as a translation, down to 'If you go to a place by moonlight you will get there'.) These innocent (apparently) words were taken by Whakatohe as a slight and he went outside and exhumed a recently-interred corpse from under a ti (cabbage-palm). This he bore to Onawe and laying it down went inside. His wife said 'Ka nui te hauka' (great is the stench) and he explained matters. He then washed the corpse and it was cooked and eaten as a return slight to the one he felt was implied in the words given above.** Once or twice the collector noticed the custom of wailing when two persons met after not having seen each other for some time. In each case the persons were elderly women. The wailing is in memory (or honour) of those who have died since the 'mourners' last met. The collector could get no name for this custom. Even the principal informant knew no name for this 'tangi'.

CARRYING LOADS OR THE BURDEN-BEARERS

The collector asked the principal informant regarding the porters mentioned by Stack. He had heard of the kawe (shoulder-straps) ┼┉┼ to which the kete was attached. The kauru was packed in kete, the weight being say forty pounds on average. A strong person would carry two kete and a very strong man three = one hundred and twenty pounds roughly. Carrying = whakawaha. A staff was borne in the hand and for a rest the kawe would be slipped off. When carrying poha-titi a stool was carried behind and the load would rest on it at stops. He could not remember the name of these two sticks forming the stool as it was about one hundred years since it was used. He forgot the name of the 'porters', but carrying food was 'poi', hence name Kaiapoi. Kaiapohia was only a recent form of this name – it was an enemy name bestowed by Rauparaha's people. It had the same meaning as Kaiapoi, only it was a different dialect, the North Island people putting on more flourish than the South Island with their plain, matter-of-fact Kaiapoi. In carrying burdens of food to it, everybody, men and women, shared the work, even chiefs assisting – the only ones being exempt were tapu men. In kaihaukai [See Customs, H.B.] everyone shared the burdens too.

The amo or kauamo was an affair of two sticks, a bit longer than the human body, with flax tied between to form a hammock on which to carry sick persons or the dead. Amo was a term which might mean carrying a man on the back or two men carrying another but the word kauamo usually implied four men carrying a litter, although both terms could be used for carriers. It was not a common thing like whakawaha (carrying anything on shoulder-straps).

A well-informed Maori said he had never heard of porters' stools but the name of the porters might be pononga – a slave or servant made to work. The word 'amo' means to carry on shoulders and so perhaps was the name of the litter used in ancient times to carry influential sick people. He did not know the word kauamo at all. An old man over seventy said he had heard of porters or load-carriers in olden days but not their name nor yet the name of their stools.

SECTION XI

WEAPONS

Tokotoko or short spear — Tao or long spear — Maipi or the taiaha — Paiaka or the tewhatewha — Panehe or adze (complete) — Patu or the mere — Pukahu or thick stave — Ron or long stave — etc.

WEAPONS

*Weapons came under notice several times in conversation with the principal informant. The tokotoko, he said, was a spear about six feet long while the tao was about twelve feet long.** He knew little of the toki but when adze was completed it was a panehe. Toki-titaha would be a straight axe – perhaps the kakau (handle) had a slit through it to put greenstone toki through to lash on. Patu and mere were the same thing but former name mostly used. *A patu of black stone was called an uri. Taiaha and maipi were the same weapon and the paiaka was sometimes called tewhatewha, its North Island name. He had heard the name pou whenua but did not know the weapon.** In the maipi the tongue was arero, the bunch of feathers uru [huru. H.B.] and the blade rapa. *'Te-uru-o-te-patu' was to kill two (or three) with one blow of the taiaha. It was said a skilled exponent could kill two men and stun a third man with one hit.** He had never heard of toki-poutangata but the toki could be used to fight with on occasions. Teka was a game of projecting darts but the kotaha was different. It is to get a stone in a flax loop and whirl round and let stone go. It was like the sling David used to kill Goliath. You could use teka and kotaha in fighting but they were really for play. Maori proper fighting was at close quarters. *He had heard of wood with sharpened point like knife.** You could hang it to your body or place in tatua (belt) and if chance offered stick it into your foe. It was seldom used. *He forgot its name but fancied it might have been called a tia.** He had heard of hoe (paddles) being used as weapons, and history mentioned one disastrous instance. *When Rauparaha's men were chased south of Blenheim and Rauparaha cleared out and left them to their fate, a tall Northern chief Te Rangiangaanganui had a paddle in his hand – his only weapon at time. He hit a Kaikoura man with it but it broke. A woman, Tauwhare by name, downed him with a maipi and he lay laughing that a woman should disable him. Smilingly he said 'Kill me as payment for you' and she obligingly slew him with the taiaha she held. The oar was no good in that instance. He did not know what sign a tohuka required to send out a warband. If the sign was bad he would ask the warriors to await a more auspicious occasion. Each taua, whakaariki or whawhai band consulted its own tohuka. The latter would take a pukahu, paiaka, taiaha or tao in his hand and do karakia to ascertain the signs. The pukahu was a thick stick used to hit an opponent across the neck, head or body.** It is not much of a weapon. At the Christchurch Exhibition (1906) the Fijians were using thick waddies in their demonstrations and he told them those pukahu were no good and would not kill a flea, let alone a man. They took his jest in good part but laughed at idea of weapon's harmlessness as they reckoned it quite efficient. The celebrated weapon of Tarewai was a mere of pounamu but he forgot its name [See Manuscript of T.E. Green copied by me and sent to Museum. H.B.] [The collector has always heard this famous weapon called a patu-paraoa (or whalebone mere). H.B.]

An elderly Maori showed the collector a fine greenstone mere called Kahotea – it was an ancestral possession and highly valued. He reckoned the maipi was a spear with shark-teeth on it at one end. The paiaka was like this ⌐ , (he drew one roughly). The taiaha was made of goai, manuka or ake (hard woods) and there was a whakatauki (proverbial saying) about that weapon which he forgot but which he would ascertain against the collector's next visit.

The collector was also told of the poho-taupa (chest protection) worn to protect warriors when fighting. These were generally made of pikao (pingao in North Island) and as far as my informants knew were probably held by a string round the neck and there may have sometimes been two such shields, one for the front and one for the back. The pikao leaf is tough and the shields were intended to ward off thrusts of the huata or tao (spears) or deaden the blow of the taiaha.

*The principal informant further said there was once a weapon called rou used in fights. It was shaped something like a hockey stick and was held with both hands. It would kill a man all right but was not much used. [In Tregear's Dictionary, rou = a pole. H.B.] The kaheru (a weeding stick) was also used in fighting and sometimes the hoe (canoe-paddle) if it happened to be handy.

Add to Weapons

The commonest weapons of old, said the principal informant, were the taiaha, tokotoko and huata. The paiaka and tewhatewha were seldom used. The mere pounamu and toki-uri (black mere) were also used a good deal. The kurutai was in South Island but was not much used. The tao was a spear – long, not short.** Perhaps the tokotoko was called tao in North [Tregear says tao was short. H.B.] and no spines were on it. He had never heard of puraka (like a matarau with three or four points) nor koikoi (double-point) being used in South Island. Neither had they a tete (a short spear with break-off point) but they had a short, heavy stick (made of maire or kohai or heart of manuka) the tukituki, which was like a beater for stunning on the head – not for stabbing. *The mere and uri were both used on the head too, with a thrusting motion. The tokotoko was the 'smartest stick of the lot' and could be used to karo (ward-off) spears. One end of it was sharp – the other not so sharp. The ripi was used to patu (kill or stun) the tuna (eel).** It was of wood, was like a sword somewhat, but shorter being usually about three feet long. It was rarely used in warfare and when used was for hitting – not stabbing. He had never heard of the hohoupu [greenstone adze sacred to cutting human heart out – see Tregear's list. H.B.]. If a man in the South Island wished to cut out an enemy's (or anybody's) heart he would use a flint (mataa) or a greenstone point or pipi shell. *No kotiate nor kokoti was used here while patu was another name for the mere-pounamu.** The wahaika had been seen in Canterbury, he thought, but was very rare. It was a seldom-used weapon anywhere. He had not heard of the onewa or okewa but the kurutai was used in the South Island. It was perhaps made of black stone or of wood. *The kurutai, he understood, was usually a beater for aruhe, kauru and whitau** and was not really a weapon although like other things it could be used as such. The patuki of the North Island was evidently the tukituki of the South. He had never heard of the mira-tuatini (or mata-tuatini) in Canterbury, nor of a knife of shark's teeth, nor of the kautete, nor of mata knives. They may have been used by the old people of long ago, however, without his having heard of these things or names.

They used to take manuka sticks, six feet long or so, tie round like a matakokiri or niti and whana (project) it over the walls of pas to set fire, if possible, to houses inside. The stick had burning stuff attached. This idea was common to both islands.

He had never heard of the reti, but the hoeroa was a North Island weapon, very seldom, if ever, used in the South Island. He had never heard of meres being thrown at a near enemy and recovered by a cord, although as a general rule meres had cords attached to them. This cord was wound round wrist and was used so that the owner of a mere would not lose it if it became slippery with blood or perspiration and slipped out of his hand. He had never heard name korepa but the idea of a sharp stone held by a cord being swung round to strike anyone was no good and it 'would not kill a cat'.

The kotaha was not for war – it was merely pastime. Even in play it might kill a man by chance (or mischance) but it was too uncertain for use in war. *Of all the Maori weapons the taiaha was perhaps the most deadly and in the hands of a strong expert man it could do wonders. For instance if four men would stand side by side and a taiaha exponent brought his weapon round he would knock the whole four out with one blow. One would be killed, if not two, and the others so stunned as to be incapacitated. He had offered to 'lay out' simultaneously four white 'men of standing' who had been rather dubious of his statement about a taiaha he was showing them, but they would not have a trial.**

At Tuahiwi the collector saw a fine mere (of kawakawa pounemu) – [an heirloom of the Tainui family. H.B.] – but he could not ascertain its name or history [the custodian being ignorant of both. H.B.]. It is said to have been exhibited with pride to various notabilities visiting New Zealand.

SECTION XII

GREENSTONE

Tangiwai or a kind of greenstone — Koko-tangiwai or a kind of tangiwai — Kuru-tonga-rerewa or a kind of tangiwai — Aotea or a kind of greenstone —Auhunga or a kind of greenstone — Inanga or a kind of greenstone — Kawakawa or a kind of greenstone — Kahurangi or a kind of greenstone — Marakamu or the mother of greenstone — etc.

GREENSTONE

Contrary to expectations considering their ancestors explored the Southern Alps to find passes or routes to the West to procure the coveted pounemu the present Canterbury Natives had little to say about nephrite. In some old documents written by Canterbury Maoris some thirty or forty years ago the South Island is always called Te-Wai-Pounemu and the southern pronunciation is more like 'ponemu' than pounamu. *This is a mere dialectial variation, however.**

The principal informant had a nice piece of greenstone on his watch-chain. He said it was of the kawakawa variety. *This kind was called after Kawakawa a chief on the Tairea canoe which came to New Zealand under command of Tama. All the crew are now greenstone and the various varieties were named after them. Tangiwai was a woman on that canoe and Inanga was also on board. Aotea is the name of a kind but Kahotea is not the name of a kind but of a patu (mere) made of the kawakawa variety. Tutaekoka is not the name of a kind, but (like Kahotea, he added) is the name of a piece. Koko-tangiwai is the same as Tangiwai – it is clear like glass. Kuru-tonga-rerewa is a form of tangiwai. All forms of the greenstone were got on the West Coast. Greenstone had a human origin – all the kinds you find were originally a people, or a number of persons, turned into stone. This was only on the West Coast – on the East Coast the Araiteuru's crew were turned into other kinds of stone.** [Note: The Tourist Department's publication *The Wonders of Western Otago* gives some extremely interesting legends about tangiwai and greenstone generally. It was published about 1905. H.B.] A Rapaki Maori dismissed the subject briefly: 'There were a lot of Maori names for the different kinds of pounemu, but I do not know them.' [Stack [[1893]] in his *Kaiapohia* (page 30) mentions that the greenstone was broken off with stone hammers. The collector could find no one who knew about these hammers, or its Maori name. H.B.]

Add to Greenstone

*The pounemu or greenstone was originally a race of people and being frightened that the mata would cut it and the hoaka grind it, it cleared out (from Hawaiki presumably) in the Tairea canoe and came to this South Island and the mata and hoanga came after it on the Araiteuru and later canoes. The hoaka (grindstone) which was here in New Zealand before that latter event was too soft to affect the greenstone but the hoaka introduced by the later canoes was hard and could tackle the pounemu and vanquish it. Some of the old soft hoaka is still to be found on Bank's Peninsula.

It was the Tairea canoe which left the greenstone and the various kinds are named after the crew, such as Kawakawa, Inanga, Kahurangi, Auhunga and others. (He considered that Tuapaka and Totoweka, etc., were North Island names introduced in later days and were not after the crew of the greenstone canoe.) The crew became greenstone and took refuge under waterfalls and in river-beds. They were afraid of the hoaka (grindstone) and mata (flints) people in Hawaiki and fled, but when they got to the South Island their karakia went wrong or they forgot it and they were turned to the familiar greenstone. Kahukura, the rainbow god, led them safely to New Zealand but was powerless to avert disaster on the land when their karakia went wrong. For this fault the crew became the prey of their old enemies Mata and Hoaka when the latter two arrived in New Zealand and the Maoris use these two to help them subdue the stubborn pounemu.**

A good number of greenstone articles have been unearthed round the southern shores of Waihora (Lake Ellesmere) in recent years. The Maoris say tradition states that plenty of curios were buried here at the time of Te Rauparaha's raids.

*In speaking briefly of the pounemu (greenstone) the principal informant said that kokotakiwai or kokotangiwai was a woman who came on board the Tairea and matakirikiri (a small kind of pounemu) is, or are her children. They stayed down about Piopiotahi (Milford Sound). The kurutongarerewa of the

North Island is the takiwai of the South Island. Kawakawa and Inaka were men on board the canoe Tairea and Aotea was also on that waka. The Tairea was one of the canoes that safely crossed the stormy ocean, but got wrecked on the coast of the land they had reached. When she was lost a great wave carried her with a rush up the Arahura River, where at a place called Ohonu there it lies turned into a big block of pounemu which no one can lift or shift away. There is a waiata or song mentions the above names. Tama the captain of the Tairea was not turned to stone but went to the North Island. Tutekoropaka (or as he rendered it once – Tukorotepaka) and Kupe are also mentioned in that song but narrator was sorry he did not know the song well enough to repeat so that it could be taken down at his dictation. [See Mythology Section also, H.B.]**

'Marakamu,' said a woman to the collector, 'is the mother of greenstone. If you find the marakamu you will have the luck to find its child, the proper pounemu. It is said you cannot find the latter without finding the former first.'

SECTION XIII

CANOES, ETC.

Ama or Outriggers — Unua or Double Canoes — Kaupapa or Deck, Hua or Masts — Ra or Sails — Pora or Body of canoe — Pakokori or Cabin on canoe — Mokihi or Rafts — Turama or Torches — Ko or hapara or Spades — Kaheru or Weeders — Takoko or Scoops — etc.

CANOES AND RAFTS

*The principal informant said that in double canoes the bigger one was waka the other unua. The poles connecting them were rahoraho.** Holes were made in the taha (sides) of the wakas and the poles were lashed with aka (vine) and whitau, this lashing being rori. The deck of canoes was kaupapa. *The hua (mast) was usually put in centre of the deck.** The sail (ra) was often made of the bark of trees like houi and sewed with ti as flax was not strong enough. *There was more than one shape of sail; some were square and some 'leg-of-mutton'. They were hauled up by a rope to mast.** There was a stick across top of sail but he did not know its name. The tauihu (bow) and taurapa (stern) were carved in spirals and after likeness of tipuna. The outrigger was a thing used in the islands of Polynesia but the mokihi was a New Zealand device. *It was made of raupo and light wood as it was only for temporary use on rivers. It was made large enough to carry from ten to twenty people as wanted. It was seldom used again.

The people would walk inland to the lakes and mountains and come down rivers on mokihis. It was made very large and broad as a raft but boat-shaped and was generally all of korari, a foot or so thick, and raupo on top to be soft for passengers. Toko (poles) were used to guide it down the current and over rere (rapids) where small ones would capsize but big ones kept right. Mokihi were not used on Waimakariri River but mostly on the Waitaki.** In Akaroa the waka used to race the whaleboats. The timekeeper is the first paddler and he is pakihiwitahi as one shoulder is up. The kaiwhakahauhau shouts orders and some big canoes have two of these men – one near front and one near rear. They watch to see that all pull together. In old days the war canoes used to race one another out to sea. They only put out in fine weather and this rivalry to get first was a sort of 'racing the weather' matter.

*Referring to canoes again he continued: 'You could put sails on single canoes. There were usually two masts on a single canoe but only one on an unua (double canoe). These masts were joined by a spar between them but I forget its name but rahoraho was the name of the decking on either double or single canoes. Some canoes could carry three hundred people. Double canoes were shorter than big, single ones. On some double canoes no people were carried on the ama, the small canoe attached to the bigger one, but in fine weather the crew could walk across the poles joining them.** There was no decking except on the body of the main canoe – there was none on the ama. These double canoes could be rowed slowly but the crews liked to use sail. *They never went out in head winds or side winds as they could do no tacking,** but used to wait for fair winds. *On the unua the sail as a rule was square = ra-aronui but on the waka it was triangular with the sharp point uppermost = ra-titahi. Some wakas had two of these sails.** The sails were made of ti and the manner of their making was whiri-parahalaha (paraharaha). The "joins" on a tiaka on the floor are called morua but I forget the name the "joins" on a sail were called'.

An old Maori said he had seen hoe (paddles) but they were very ordinary and just made plain of common wood. He had also seen waka – logs hollowed out for fishing. Some had boards added to make their sides higher but he did not know the name of this addition. 'They had made holes and used whitau for nails,' in making these additions. Some of the old-time canoes could carry two hundred men and used a sail. Raupo could be used for making ra = sails. The sails were square as a rule and had a pole across the top and were hauled up the mast. He had heard, however, of some sails being like a pakeha jib-sail.

Add to Canoes

*Taitaiarimu, said the principal informant, is the rite of killing a slave when launching a canoe, or after having a first trip on which no fish were caught. If fish were caught on that trip a fish would be offered as a sacrifice or offering for the success of the ensuing trip. Such an offering ensures a good trip. If prior to launching an important canoe slaves were killed and used as skids for the launching this was also called taitaiarimu. When the canoe had run off the sand into the water the punga (anchor) was let down. Then the crew would return to the land to put the body of the slave into the kapa-maori to be cooked, and eaten later.**

On a canoe the whakahauhau is the time beater and the pakihiwitahi is the 'stroke' the man who gives the rest the rangi (stroke). Rangi also means the tune of a song.

*The pakokori was a room on the staging of canoe with two, three, or four tatau (doors) for the sake of convenience in passing to and fro. It was only for higher people. The staging was kaupapa or rahoraho. Single canoes (pora) had it. The body of a canoe is called pora. Amalialia are poles between a canoe and an ama (small canoe). The people are on big canoe but the ama makes it safer. The whole is a waka-unua. Stones were carried to light fires on to cook food. The sails were almost square as no tacking was done – they simply ran before the wind.** The mast was hua but he forgot names of sticks at top and bottom of sail. The sail was not tianga matting but was of plaited ti and houi bark as flax was not strong enough. It was in strips as wide as the ti leaves allowed and was sewed (tuitui) with whitau he thought. Sewing was easier and stronger than morua joinings. When sailing you would see the sail a long way off and see it like a cloud white in the sunlight, hence (he reckoned) its name of ra. You cannot see the body of the canoe at a distance but only the white sail. The more valuable canoes were often housed in rough sheds (whare-takotoranga-waka).

A very old woman said she had never heard of pakokori nor amatiatia, and an old man said he had never seen an outrigger from collector's description of it.

TORCHES

To make torches, said an old Maori, get some dry flax. Let this be koka (flax dried on bushes, not harakeke maroke – flax dried after it has been cut). Split the koka stems lengthwise and tie in tight bundles. This is lit as a torch and gives a good light if there is no wind, and light reaches a good distance. Another torch is made from kahika – te iho o te rakau – or the heart of white pine, called mapara. This is split thin and tied in suitable bundles. Both these torches are called rama or turama, and concluded my informant, these were the only two kinds of torches he knew.

*The collector's principal informant said very little about torches except that they could be made of dry manuka or pirita (supplejack) split and tied in suitable bundles or of white pine (mapara). He said these torches were sometimes used for eeling and such purposes.**

Another Maori in speaking of spearing flounders at night said the rama (torches) were made of toetoe, of flax koka, or of bark, but he did not mention them further.

SPADES AND DIGGING

The principal informant had not much to say on this subject. He mentioned that the ko was used both in planting and in digging the kumera in the old days. This ko was a long, stout stick made out of hard wood and with a sharpened end to push into the ground. About a foot or so from the ground a tuke (footrest), a block of wood, was tied on to the ko by means of aka (vine) or fine pirita (supplejack) stems of a flexible nature. What might be called 'the Maori shovel' – the takoko – was usually made of maire wood. It had a handle above and was used as a scoop to make ditches round forts (pa), drains to drain water away, channels to catch tuna (eels) in, etc. The kaheru, like the ko, was made of manuka, kohai, maire, or other hard wood. It was sharpened to a point and was used mainly for weeding. It was about three feet long and had no footrest on it.

A Rapaki Maori said the old wooden spade was called hapara [See Tregear's [[1891]] *Dictionary*. H.B.]. The ko was a long stick and there was a wahia (piece of wood) tied to one side of it to push the foot against. The hapara was not the exact shape of a Pakeha spade but had a stick tied on (here te rakau) to push the foot on when digging. The hapara was the best to use. The kaheru was nearly the same as the ko, only shorter and smaller. The ko was for rough ground, although the hapara was better, and the kaheru for finer soil. The old people used to fell (tuawaereka) [Tua = to cut trees. Waereka = a clearing. H.B.] a piece of bush, burn (tau ki ahi, or = tahu ki ahi) it and leave a clear space (watea). The kaheru, which was no good in hard ground, was used to root among the soft bush soil and the ashes round the stumps. 'A clearing like this,' concluded the old man, 'was the place for the spuds (or taewa) and the pumpkins'. [See section re Introduced Plants, etc. H.B.]

SECTION XIV

DOMESTIC SCIENCE

Tao or One way of cooking — Whena or One way of cooking — Kohiku or One way of cooking — Komuka or One way of cooking — Murumuru or One way of cooking — Rara or One way of cooking — Ipu or basins — Rourou or plates — Puna or big umu ovens — Hika or fire-making — etc.

COOKING

In regard to the different methods of preparing food for human use the principal informant briefly described four of them. If one had caught inanga, mata or tuna and wanted to eat them right then while fresh the fish were placed in a flax roll (whena) next the fire and cooked. One part of the flax is sour (the inside side) but the outer side is all right and care was taken to place the sour side so as not to taint or taste the fish. He did not know the names of these sides of the flax. The kohiku was a stick stuck in ground alongside the fire and it might be threaded with twenty smaller birds such as makomako and kakariki, or ten or twelve of the size of the tui but usually only one weka, kereru or kaka was allotted to each stick. One way was to push the stick through the bodies of the birds another way was to put the bird (or birds) in a fork or cleft of the kohiku. If the wood burns up keep the sticks up but as it dies down slant the stick over it until the birds are almost on the embers. The hardest feathers handy were tied up into a bunch (urupuu: uru = a broom and puu = to hold oil, he explained), and this was held under the bird to catch the fat as the Maori never wasted the oil or fat of anything cooking. The umu, puna, hangi or kopa-maori was too well known to need describing. He reckoned the puna was bigger than the umu, which in turn was bigger than the hangi. To cover things in the umu a kona, papaki or tapora mat was made of ti, harakeke or toetoe and the same plant materials could be used to make rourou or 'plates' to eat from. The kohatu-umu (oven stones) were usually of kala (kara) a hard stone. Another way of cooking food was to use a taha, kumete or ipu and boil the birds in their fat. In some cases where an extensive boiling had to be done small canoes (waka) have been used. The birds were plucked of feathers but down (hukahuka) was left on. The birds were placed in ipu and hot stones placed on top or in the middle and the ipu covered with a tapora of tii or harakeke leaves. The birds were not singed by process. When they were adjudged cooked they were left till cold and then the kohatu-umu (stones) were lifted out. Get another cooking bowl (ipu) and cook more birds and so on until you have the required number of ipu full of birds in hinu (fat). Then cover each ipu with totara bark firmly lashed down with aka vine to keep the air out and they will keep for years. If you saw a fungoid growth or mildew (puruheka) on the bark you would know that mould (puru) would be on the contents beneath and that it had better be used at once. [Mildew on posts is called kohukohu. H.B.] The old people also used Rimu-poha (kelp bags) to preserve rats and birds in but these would not keep so long as the ipu's contents would although the poha was handier to carry on the back.

A Rapaki Maori said there were just five ways of cooking food in the old days, viz, 1 tao in umu, 2 karehu (embers), 3 kohiku, 4 rara, 5 ipu. The rara was a stage about eight or twelve inches above the embers and the heat cooked the food which was occasionally turned over. No fat was kept this way but the fat made the fire burn better. A ropu was a bunch of feathers tied together to catch fat from birds on kohiku. The fat could be wiped off into bowls (ipu) or feather could be licked by anyone desiring such a diet. It was just a fancy and was often not done except when fat was needed for some purpose such as preserving (Whakaputu-kai). [In Tregear's [[1891]] *Dictionary* under 'putu' the Samoan 'putu' and Tahitian 'putua' are interesting here. H.B.] The poha of kelp was sometimes used for preserving but the ipu was used oftener. The titi was preserved from year to year but the mainland birds could be got almost any time so there was not much need to keep them long. If they were sending a gift of preserved birds a distance the rimu-poha was used. He was an old man and had lived in Canterbury all his life but he never heard any term but ipu for a wood bowl, and the only name for an earth-oven he knew was umu.

A woman whom the collector met at the tangi at Temuka said she knew these ways of cooking: 1 tao in umu. 2 kohiku. 3 whena beside fire. 4 rara. 5 komuka in ashes. 6 murumuru on embers. 7 boil in ipu. The collector was not able to enter into details, but later an old man said that komuka was just making damper in the ashes or cooking in the ashes of the fires and he reckoned the whalers brought it in. Whena was lengths of flax laid along eels or potatoes, etc., and tied round here and there. It was not put in umu but laid by fire and as soon as flax was soft top and bottom you knew the contents were cooked. The flax kept the steam in and this made the food delicious to eat.

One old man remarked 'Kapa-Maori is just a Pakeha name for umu.'

Add to Cooking (and Preparation of Food)

Cooked food, said the principal informant, was called kai-maoa, uncooked was kai-mata while food hanging up raw was hei-kai. Paka is to cook the titi and as you hand it out say to each person 'There is a paka for you'. Can also use term for wekas and other preserved birds but not for fish nor for birds done in umu. It is when they are boiled in oil and put in ipu or poha the word is used – not for whole contents but as you pull the food out you call each item a paka.

Cooking was not done at an ahi (fire) inside a house but outside at an umu or at a fire in a detached kitchen or a rude cooking shed (wharekauti). There were no chimneys – the smoke got out as best it could. To cook the kiore after if is cleaned [See Kiore section, H.B.] place them in a totara bowl (a taha or kumete) with stones hot from the fire with them. Then put the taha and its contents in an umu and steam them. The rats are never burnt with the hot stones – it is good, careful work. The people would also pluck the weka and take out the backbone (iwitu-ara) and lay these birds with hot stones in a taha and into kapa-maori with it. The kiore or weka, etc., were then put in ipu made of totara bark very carefully made. These ipu were covered with raupo on top and bark until airtight and would last for years. After these kinds of food had been so put away – practically preserved in fat – the ipu were carried to wherever wanted.

Speaking to two Maoris they said the umu of the South Island was different to the hangi of the North Island. The umu was buried but the hangi was not buried but covered with wet sacks. Umu stones were not called ahi-pohatu (that was a term not known to them) but pohatu-umu; the wood used for burning was wahia; and tapora was the matting covering the puha, cress, flax, etc., which lay over the food, and then earth was heaped over.

One Maori in chatting to the collector said that after you had killed the tuna ['First catch your hare'. H.B.] you could whatu (or weave) round it koareare or pohue (or other edible roots and plants) and put it (so bound or clothed) in the umu. This was something like the whena [See Murihiku Notes, H.B.] and was called a tapaki and it is said this vegetation flavored the eel agreeably and that the juice from the eels soaked into the roots and plants adding to their natural flavors. Be that as it may the eel was soon disposed of and all the 'trappings' were eaten as a kinaki (relish).

The collector was curious to know where the Maoris got the idea of steeping Pakeha foods such as maize and potatoes and was told it was in consonance with ancient Maori ideas of steeping koura (crayfish) and kina ('sea-eggs') in fresh water until rotten (and that also in the North Island shark was hung up until rotten – a custom from time immemorial).

A Peninsula Maori told the collector that koko-te-rimu meant opening up kelp to insert food inside so that it could be cooked by the murumuru process. [Note: See Murihiku Notes for murumuru-te-poha cooking, H.B.]

FIRE-MAKING

The idea of cooking [in those parts of New Zealand not blessed – or cursed according to the point of view – with hot springs] pre-supposes the fire to cook with. The principal informant said that fire-making was called hika and that the bottom fire-stick was the kauati and the top, or rubbing, one karimarima. The wood commonly used was the kaikomako. The holding of the kauati rigid was not necessarily done by a woman or girl – anyone handy could hold it, but it took a strong, deft man to achieve quick results. The holding of the stick was called kai-pupuri-o-te-kauati and the action of rubbing was hika. The tindery stuff in which spark caught was called kaurehu and when it caught fire the expression to signify this was kua-tu-te-ahi.

Add to cooking

The collector asked the principal informant where the word kohua came from. He replied that it was a North Island name but he understood it applied to a small hole in the ground into which heated stones were put for cooking. The hole was a round shape and when the Maoris saw pots (Pakeha) they named them kohua after it. The word kapa-Maori (or kopa-Maori) is a Pakeha name for the earth oven. The hangi of the North Island and the umu of the South Island could be big ovens but the puna (or puna-ti) was the biggest of the lot. It was a great, long, squared umu perhaps a chain long and was used to cook the kauru [See Earlier description in these Notes, H.B.]. The umu to cook barracouta was also big.

The collector asked his informants regarding the remark of an early European settler that he had seen the Maoris bake kiore (rats) in mud, the mud bringing the skin and hair off. There was a diversity of opinion about this matter. The principal informant knew little about it. Rolling a thing, birds principally he thought, in clay to cook was called muru. It took the feathers off clean enough but was not much used. The next informant dismissed the matter curtly, saying it was learnt from the whalers. The next man said that birds would be rolled in clay and roasted same way as the whena – it was known as whena-paruparu. It was not learnt from the Pakeha. An older man than any of foregoing said he never saw clay or mud used in cooking and he doubted if Maori ever did so. A woman said she had heard of birds being cooked in clay and thought it was called kopaki, but she was not sure.

An old lady and her daughter gave the following description of some forms of the culinary art in old Maoridom, concluding with a modern note or two:

The word kohua was not used in Canterbury for the hollow excavated for the umu. If an umu was to be made the old people would say 'Karia te rua mo te umu' (Dig the hole for the oven). They understood that some North Islanders say 'keri' for 'kari' (to dig). Then 'ka pohatu mo te umu' (the stones for the oven) were collected and placed in the rua. Then an ahi (fire) was made on top of the stones. Any inflammable wood could be used but there was a superstition against kotukutuku (North Island = konini) because its use was said to bring on illness. They thought it affected some people but not others, for they had seen it used without ill effect, but a male relative got watery scabs and a peculiar break-out of the skin through using that wood. This was the only timber they knew whose use was regarded as evil or hazardous. It would probably take three or four hours burning to properly heat the stones. Then the charred stuff was picked out (kapekape is plural, kape singular) with a stick (rakau-kapekape) as well as possible and swept clean. The stones were pushed apart to let the unswept ashes fall to the earth, this loosening being called 'Paratiti-tia ka pohatu'. Water is then poured on to cool the stones = 'Whakamakariritia ka pohatu'. (They said that 'makariritia' could also be 'makaririhia' but former was commoner usage in South Island.) This not only cools the stones but washes the remaining ashes off them. Then puha (thistles) or raupola (pora leaves) were put in on stones i mua (formerly), but now watercress is used, and a tapora was put over this. A tapora is a form of big rourou (flax or ti plate) and the food is laid on it and leaves spread over it. Sometimes herehere (flax strings) are fastened to rourou and tied across top to hold the food tight in position. A layer of patiti (tussock) was then spread over it, but now bags are used. Then a closely-woven flax-mat (the tipaki – sometimes called a papaki but this is more a North Island name for a floor-covering) is laid over this and covered with oneone (earth) and your umu is complete. It would be left some hours until it was properly steamed or cooked (tao). You could tell by the tokoahu (steam) issuing through the earth when the food was sufficiently cooked for the umu to be opened and the contents extracted. Food so-cooked was, in the old days, left until it was cold and was then eaten. The collector was assured it had a splendid taste – a taste far superior to that of food cooked in European utensils in these degenerate days. One of the informants said that when she was a girl, the children sometimes made small umu to cook things for themselves, being so-encouraged to do by the elder people. They were told to pull eyelashes (kamo) out to tell if the umu was sufficiently cooked. If no eyelash came out at one tug the food was not cooked; if one came out the food was nearly cooked; if two or more came out the food was ready to be removed. She had actually done this but she could not recollect the old-time jingle it was customary to say when doing the performance. Now (except on special occasions – such as New Year festivities) the umu is a work relegated to the past. The Maori matron or cook looks at the utensils on her Orion or Champion or other range, or at the ironware suspended over the fire in the big open chimney and says 'Ko pupu te pata' (the pot is boiling) or 'Ko pupu te wai' (the water is boiling). She may dream of umu – but now 'all the same the Pakeha'.

The collector has been surprised in Maori homes to see the quick way a fire is re-created. It may appear to be out, or almost so, with a few charred remnants of stick at each side of the hearth. These are drawn together point to point (not laid across ashes as Pakeha does) and soon smoke appears at apex and this is followed by flame. When such a thing is necessary you will hear the remark 'Tukutu tia mai te ahi' (Draw together the fire). [This is called tungutungutu in North Island. H.B.]

HOUSEHOLD UTENSILS

The principal informant mentioned vessels to hold liquids. The shell of the gourd (hue) was used to hold rat oil, weka oil, etc., or water. The hue grew on Banks Peninsula and he reckoned it was brought south from Gisborne by the Ngaitahu Tribe about ten generations ago. The people also used a taha or kumete [This latter word is North Island I think. H.B.] made of wood to put fat in and to cook birds by dropping hot stones from the hangi into the fat (huahua) and so cooking birds. [See Cooking section, H.B.] The 'household club' or beater (patu) was made of kohai, maire, manuka, or other hard wood, and was shape of mere only round-bodied. Stone beaters were not much used as too heavy. The wood patu was often carved and was usually tapu to one use such as beating aruhe or kauru. You could not (properly) take a patu of this description to sea but might beat shark, barracouta or groper with it on land if the necessity arose. You could patu tuna (eel), hapuku (groper) with a club of wood also – fish were not hit or beaten with stone clubs. He had never heard of a stone hammer among the Maoris.

A Rapaki Maori said the best wood to make ipu (basins) was mako as it was soft and easy-worked. Totara was not so bad but other woods were rather hard. As a rule ipu ran from eighteen inches to three feet long. You could lay two sticks across a big one and strap flax round and carry it like a hammock. There were no

Rourou (flax food bowl) from Temuka, purchased through Herries Beattie. Tūhura Otago Museum Collection, D20.128. With kind permission of Te Rūnanga o Arowhenua.

handles on the old-fashioned ones as they were seldom carried about. Some of the more fancy ones may have been carved. In olden days the ipu had a square bottom to sit flat and did not have legs. The ones in Museum with legs he reckoned were copying the Pakeha idea of whaling trypots. As for the hitter or patu he had heard of bone patu but never of a stone hammer.

In the Christchurch Museum is to be seen (in the Maori Section) a 'stone oil lamp'. (A stone with a circular depression where oil had been burnt. H.B.) The collector asked two old Maoris at the Temuka tangi re this and one said she thought stone oil lamps was a whalers' idea, and the other said he had never seen a 'stone oil lamp' but he had seen whale oil with a wick burning in it.

The principal informant said bowls (ipu) had legs (waewae) and handles (maunga-a-ringa or katau). The legs, as well as the bowls, were often carved as fancy work. Bowls were usually made of strong wood, such as kohai, manuka, maire, etc. An Akaroa woman has an ipu-wai used by an ancestor. It is a small hue (gourd) with a narrow mouth and as name implies was used for drinking purposes.

SECTION XV

VEGETABLE FOODS

Aruhe or Fernroot — Kauru or Cabbage-tree — Koareare or Raupo root — Pitau or Raupo shoot — Purau or Edible Root — Tutuna or Edible Root — Pohue or Edible Root — Titoi or Edible Root — Nikau or Edible Palm — Kumera or Sweet Potato — Karaka or Edible Berry — Rehia or Edible Jelly — Rimupuku or Kelp — Karengo or Edible Seaweed — Kau-puha or Sowthistle Gum — Kauri or A Masticatory — Poketara or Edible Fungi — etc.

FERNROOT AND CABBAGE-TREE

Ferns, said the principal informant, grew all the year round but aruhe or fernroot was only got at certain times. It was dug with the ko and kaheru [digging implements – see Section re them, H.B.]. It was bundled up, carried home and dried in the sun and stored away. When you wished to eat it, it was soaked in water to soften it and then roasted on the fire. It was then beaten on a papa-kohatu (flat stone) with a patu [See Household Utensils section, H.B.] and eaten. Good places for fernroot were eagerly sought for and jealously guarded and such a section was a koutu-aruhe.

A good section of ti (cabbage trees) was called a para-kauru. While the soft part of ti leaves could be cooked at any time and chewed and eaten to ensure regularity of the bowels [See Medicinal section, H.B.] the kauru, or proper food from the ti, was got at a regular season. It was a work of magnitude and a start was made from November to January according to the season. The big ti were not cut down but the ones about four feet high. They were not cut flush with the ground but about a foot up. They were cut (tapahi) with a toki (axe) and the leaves were cut off leaving a log from which the rough surface was chipped (tarai). After these were cleaned they were left standing a month to dry. The trunks, as a rule, were about four feet long and these were cut in two and put in baskets (kete) made of ti leaves. The kete were made big and perhaps fifty or sixty of the slender trunks could be put in one, which was then laced (ruru) at the top. A very big hangi [North Island name for umu. H.B.], about one chain long and of a square shape, was made and a lot of firewood (wahia) and stones (kohatu) were gathered in readiness. When the morning star (he forgot its name in summer) rose the fire was set alight. The pit was later cleaned out, water poured in and stones placed on the bottom. Long poles were laid across in two or three rows. On each row kete were piled up perhaps to three tiers. The whole was then covered with earth so that no steam would get out and steamed (komaoa) for twenty four hours. The contents were then taken out and piled up in a dry place. This was the first lot of kauru cut probably in November and cooked at the end of December or early in January. As soon as it was disposed of another batch of kauru was cut to be cooked in March. The name Kaiapoi means that 'kai' was carried there, and the carrying of the kauru was one of the facts that originated the name. While the second lot of kauru was drying the first lot was being carried to Kaiapoi, perhaps a distance of ten or twelve miles. It was carried in baskets on men's backs. Although heavy before cooking it became lighter in the oven and a strong man could carry two baskets of cooked stuff. It was generally left a month near where it was cooked before it was taken to Kaiapoi or other settlements. To render it palatable for food it was beaten (patu) on a flat stone. One man would be hitting it and another stringing (here) every two kauru together with ti leaves. The beating softened it but it hung together and being in pairs was to enable it to be easily suspended on lines in (or rather under) an open whata with a roof on it. After being in the drying whata it was stacked in baskets and placed in store whatas. It must not get wet. To be eaten it was soaked and twisted (whakawhiri) when the fibre (para) came out, leaving a soft 'porridge' called waitau. It was sweet to taste and Bishop Selwyn liked it. The Bishop had a habit of carrying a bit of aruhe (fernroot) with him. The second and last instalment of the work (mahi) of the kauru was carried out in March. The ti tree grows from the stump and can be cut again after four years. In regard to moreti (ti root) it could be dug at any time but the tree died. When dug it was cooked and eaten at once as a rule. It was roasted, scraped, opened and laid on a papaki (a mat of harakeke handy to carry) and flax juice (waikorari) was shaken (ruirui) into it.

The more could then be chewed and the juice swallowed and also the softer parts of more [[swallowed]], the remainder being spat out. Another way was to let the waikorari soak into and mingle with the juice of the more and then wring or twist the ti root over an ipu. The resultant liquid (compound of juice of flax and ti) was sweet and was called waireka. The korari was ripe in November and that was the only month the moreti was eaten (or chewed). When they were cooking tuna (eels) the old people used sometimes to put moreti in a rourou (flax plate) to hold the oil of the eel. The North Islanders talked a good deal of moreti but it was not much spoken of down here because it was only a work of one month and then of very minor importance to the kauru.

[*Note: For description of kauru see Stack's [[1891]] *Kaiapohia* pp. 26, 27; also Shortland's [[1851]] *Southern Districts of New Zealand* – H.B.**]

Add to Vegetable Foods; and Fruits and Berries

*Aruhe, or fernroot to eat, was sought after, says the principal informant, and the principal hapus had wakawaka (sections) of it. Bishop Selwyn said that he thought the South Island product tasted better than the North Island aruhe. Near Taumutu there used to be good fernroot – excellent taste, big and sweet, and with little string. The narrator thought personally that aruhe should be better in the warmer north but perhaps Bishop Selwyn** disliked the shark flavor with which many North Islanders tainted their fernroot. In the *old days the Maoris used to mash fernroot and mata (whitebait) up into a kohere-aruhe.

The people at Kaiapoi used to eat hinau berries – cooked into a sort of bread or mash whose Maori name he did not know.** The titoki berries were red and could be eaten. *[He remarked he had sent Mr Elsdon Best an account of fish, kauru, pora and foods.** Mr Philips of Dominion Museum had also written to narrator (J.C. Tikao) asking about whitebait *but he did not know him or his standing and so had never answered the letter. H.B.]** At Rakitata the people could eat tutu berries without straining (pukoro) but these were strained elsewhere and the juice (waitutu) drunk. *The people used to make rehia, a jelly composed of kelp and waitutu.** The kiekie the tawhara part of which was eaten did not grow in Canterbury but on the West Coast. The pakeha, he understood, called it gigi. In regard to rengarenga, perei, pohue, parareka (horseshoe fern) and ririwaka (sedge) – the roots of which are eaten in the North Island – he did not think any of these grew in Canterbury. [The collector got these names from Tregear's book. H.B.]

An old Maori said that the word pitau [mentioned as a weed in *Kaiapohia* by Stack [[1893]]. H.B.] did not mean weeds but was the shoot at top of the koareare or raupo root. It was soft and sweet and was easy to chew but was not nearly so well liked or so much eaten as the koareare part. He was fond of both, especially the latter, and they were not bad for loosening the bowels as some people said. The pollen of the raupo was a yellow flour but he knew no particular name for it. His wife was very fond of eating it raw and just as gathered, by the handful. Neither of them had seen bread made of it.

The fern is called rarauhe and its root aruhe but he had never heard of its being mashed with whitebait. There was no whitebait at many places where fernroot was got and he thought such a yarn was only nonsense. He had never heard of hinau berries being on the Peninsula but they might be away back in remote corners. There was only one kind of tutu he knew, or if there was more than one kind he had heard no name but tutu for them. The people used to whakawiri-te-tutu (twist the berries in wee bags) to get the juice to drink and waitutu made a good refreshing drink. Miro berries are eaten by birds but he had not heard of people eating them although the red titoki berries make good eating.

An intelligent Maori said that when you kuru (crushed) the aruhe you had made a kohere or mash ready to go into eel fat, rat oil, titi fat as well as mata (whitebait). Kelp was cut and dried, soaked in fresh water to get the salt out and kept until the tutu berries were ripe, when the juice of these was mixed with it to make rehia. He had seen this done at Little River. There was no mamaku (the edible Treefern) on the Peninsula. Hinau berries never come to anything in Canterbury but he saw (in 1891) bread made of them at Whanganui. The matai berries, however, were eaten here raw. He had seen miro berries as big as plums. They were pounded for oil and you could eat one or two of them (raw) as a flavor in the mouth. The tutuna a grass with triangular leaves grows in swamps and the roots were eaten. If you see the leaf brown it shows it is a year old; black leaf shows plant is ancient. The pohue grows here and its roots can be eaten, as can those of the koareare.

He (informant) said that koareare had not much taste to him although there was a thick white juice in it. It was as tasteless as the kawakawa which the Fijians made at the Christchurch Exhibition and which was like oatmeal water. In old days the people made a bread called punga from raupo dust. The stump of the titoi makes a good substitute for kauru and is quite as edible and nutritious.

Add to Vegetable Foods

A woman said: 'When I was a girl we ate rohutu berries, and the titoki berries, which are red with a black eye. We also ate the berries of the popohue – not the clematis or climber known as popohue, but the shrub of that name. We ate the poroporo or "native gooseberry" also, but the berry I liked best of the whole lot was the konini or fuchsia. I have heard that Maoris ate the berries of the bush lawyer but I have not done so myself, nor seen it done, so I cannot speak as to that being a food of old.'

*To his former information the principal informant added: 'The pitau is the young part of the koareare or root of the raupo and was eaten of old.** The purau is a plant which grows on the land and the roots are sweet to taste and were put in with tuna (eels) to tao (cook) in umu. They are nice to eat; the plant is something like shallots in height and has round balls of roots like marbles. Purau Bay, near Lyttelton, is named after it. The berries of the popohue are sweet but the seeds are bitter. It makes birds fat but these berries were only eaten by boys for mischief or fun. One kind of popohue with white flowers was called poanaka by the olden people.'

An old man said: 'If you drank tutu wine on very hot days you would go hori and stagger about, but it was good on cool days. Both mikimiki and miki bear berries that people can eat. Take a kakahu or mat, spread it on the ground, and ruru (shake) the tree. Soak the berries in water and the leaves and bad berries will float, and the good berries sink. Do this until they are cleaned right and then put them in a rourou and eat them at your leisure. The rohutu has a black berry and you can break a limb of the tree and eat till you are tired. You can do the same with the konini. The mako berry is good but rimu berries are bitter. The berries of the kahika (white pine) would bind you so it was not eaten but matai (black pine) berries are right enough. You can momimomi (suck) the berries and spit out the skins and seeds. The tataraheka (which I think is called tataramoa in North Island) berries could also be eaten. The plant called purau could be found at Waikouaiti; the roots were cooked and eaten. The pora or Maori cabbage ate better than the Pakeha cabbage. I have seen the young koareare but I never heard it called pitau.'

Our scientific men say the root of the speargrass belongs to the carrot family. Rats and wild pigs are very fond of it. The collector asked Maoris why they did not eat it!

The principal informant replied: 'I have never heard of our people eating speargrass roots. This is strange as they would eat anything as a rule – even leaves – as a relish to other foods.' An old man said there were two kinds of speargrass – the taramea has a wide leaf, and the papaii a narrow leaf – but he never heard of the roots of either having been eaten. Another man, usually well informed, said the Maoris never ate the roots of taramea or papaii. The former is red and is bigger than the latter which is white. [Note: Two old Murihiku Natives gave a different opinion – see Murihiku Section. Pitau seems to me to be a Canterbury name for young koareare and not known down South, whereas the eating of papaii seems to be familiar to Southerners and unknown in Canterbury. H.B.]

A Maori referred to the excellent aruhe (fernroot) found at Otawiri (now known as Buchanan's, near Wairewa). He knew two kinds of aruhe: one has no kaka (pronounced kucka) or strings in it, and the other has strings; but he forgot their names. It was the former superior kind which made the name and fame of Otawiri and some of it lingers there to this day.

The collector was told that Akaroa was the furthest south place in New Zealand where the nikau grew naturally. A part of the tree, a sort of lump where the leaves branch out, was eaten. It required more steam to cook it than merely being rolled in a whena by the fire, so it was always tao (cooked) in umu. The tree died when this part was taken. (The collector was told that Maoris chewed naupiro (anise) in Murihiku; but in Canterbury he was told it was too strong.)

'Kawakawa is the root of the best kind of Maori turnip,' said an old woman, 'but pora has only leaves. A kind of pora is called pohata, or sometimes paritea.'

The principal informant said: 'Aruhe is the root of the rauaruhe fern – the only kind that was eaten.'

KUMERA AND KARAKA

*These two foods are not found in Murihiku but the collector heard a little of them in North Canterbury. The principal informant said the kumera (or kumara in North) came from Hawaiki. It was originally a man named Hapu-matua but when the Horouta and Manuka canoes went back (from New Zealand to Hawaiki) the crews did not catch him but brought back other seed and it proved to be only the small size. Hapu is the proper kumera. There were different kinds of kumera such as Te-roa-mahoi, etc. A big kind had been introduced comparatively lately, but the old kinds – the descendants of those brought over twenty generations ago – were smaller and sweeter.** They were planted in September, October and November with much ceremony but he forgot the name. Like the potato, the kumera was dug about April – before the leaves were 'eaten' by frosts. The ko was used in both the planting and digging. He did not know much about the kumera.

A Rapaki Maori said the kumera did well for a time and then dies out. A warm and sandy soil was needed. The taro and hue had never grown here. At Kaiapoi the kumera did well for a short time and then went off and would die out. He did not think it throve at Kaikoura even, but only in North Island.

Two Tuahiwi Maoris said the gravel pits and mounds near St Stephen's Church (Tuahiwi) and at Pou-a-moko (Woodend) were a sign of the ancient kumera mara (cultivations). None had been grown for forty years in Canterbury. The kumera-maori is the old Native sweet potato and is to be distinguished from the waina or introduced American sweet potato. My informants did not know any names for sorts of kumera and stated the olden Maoris were afraid to call any foods after persons or with personal names so were chary of bestowing nomenclature on such an esteemed food as the kumera. The purapura or seed kumera were sowed by laying them on surface of ground and covering with fine soil, sand and grit. When the leaves came through the Maoris broke the shoots off and laid the tubers down and covered in puke (hillocks). They ate the kopura or seed after the leaves were off or they had been put by. They were dug up when ripe – probably told by leaves drying up – in April. Their place was usurped by the present Pakeha potatoes. [Only one of these two men had seen kumera growing and then only a few, and their statements were vague and hard to follow so had better be verified from published accounts of kumera cultivation in Gisborne district. H.B.]

The old man who has been sixty years in Kaiapoi district said he only knew of one kind of kumera. It was planted in October like seed potatoes and heaped up in the sand and fine gravel. This gravel was riddled through kete (baskets) and the big stones thrown to one side, but he never heard the name of this performance. A man wishing to plant would invite his friends to help and give him a day's labour, he providing the kai (food) of course, and there might be two or three dozen stout fellows roll up to assist him in the laborious task. The tubers were carefully gathered in the Autumn before the cold could hurt them. They have long been a thing of the past – the hardier and easier reared potato having ousted them.

KARAKA

*Karaka berries could be eaten, said the principal informant, after they had been prepared by steaming for twenty-four hours in a Maori oven and then dried. This converts them into 'Maori nuts'. Another way was to put them in water to cure like rotten corn, leaving them steeping for months.** If eaten raw they were poisonous and he knew of nothing to counteract this poisoning. *The Kai-Tahu brought this tree from the North Island to Kaikoura and it flourishes there but very few trees of it are further South.**

A Rapaki Maori said that karaka berries were gathered and cooked (tao) in umu and then dried in the sun. Then they were stored away in baskets and (if left) would keep from two to five years but as a rule they were soon eaten. They were like nuts and were up to two inches long. They tasted well or, at least, he thought they did. You took off the kiri (skin or husk) and ate the kernel.

Two Tuahiwi Maoris said the karaka was not much in evidence in Canterbury but grew at Kaikoura. [Also a few on Banks Peninsula. H.B.] It was cooked in umu but they did not know the details. Neither of them cared much for these berries – did not like the taste. If eaten hot from the umu the eater would get kopeke (cramp) in the waewae (legs) and peke (arms) and this could not be stopped – it had to run its course and sometimes its after effects were visible for a lifetime in attacks of cramp. It was also said that if eaten raw the berries were poisonous but they had no details of this.

*The principal informant was of opinion the hue (gourd) was grown on Banks Peninsula at one time. Note: A description of kumera-planting is in Stack's [[1893]] *Kaiapohia*, pp. 24–26. H.B.]**

Add to Kumera, Taro, Hue and Uhi

The principal informant said he did not know if the hue, taro and uhi were grown on Banks Peninsula in pre-pakeha days but he had himself grown the taro until tired of it – a period of about four years. There was not much in it – the result was not worth the labor. At Wairewa the people grew the hue and he learnt to swim on the shell of one. They made good eating when young, but were not extensively grown. The kumera was grown. At Taumutu the collector was shown where the kumera was grown in patches. [Shortland [[1851]] in *Southern Districts of New Zealand* writing in 1844 said Taumutu was most southerly place in New Zealand where kumera grew. H.B A Taumutu Maori said he had never heard of hue nor taro being grown there although the kumera had been planted round south end of Waihora (Lake Ellesmere). The kumera preferred a sandy loam and required much care, labor and attention to grow successfully. The people planted the kumera the day before or day after full moon according to the rising of the appropriate stars. After potatoes came these were planted when moon full and this is still done. His father did so and he (narrator) did so too. He knew no reason for this planting by the seasons of the moon but the old people here had been very superstitious and everything had to be done by ancestral lore. The collector would notice the heaps of fine gravel where the kumera grew. Shingle was the Maori manure – they never used the stuff from the village paepae (latrine). He had never heard a reason for this, but he understood it was because it was unclean. [This may be so – Tregear's book gives it as reason; but an old Maori told me it was because they thought manure was no good – what the body had rejected could be no good for the ground, hence they nearly always let it float away on water from the paepae. I have never seen this question (as to why they did not use manure) raised before! H.B.] [Probably it is too late to get real genuine old reason now. H.B.]

A Peninsula Maori said the kumera and hue, but not the taro or the uhi, had been grown at Wairewa. The hue had seeds of a light grey color with two grooves at the propagating end. If the calabash was not broken the seed would last probably one thousand years but if taken out the seed soon became useless if not sown within a reasonable time. He had heard of one (unopened) being used as a 'buoy' to teach children swimming and four generations later it was opened and the seed planted and they produced 'bashes. The calabash has a hook on top, being very handy to carry water. To grow, it had to be nursed till November, being covered with kona or rourou (of flax usually) until warm weather came. There were two kinds – one long and one flat. The former was called kapitana (captain) from its size probably, and the latter hue. The kumera was grown in an arai (shelter) of manuka – both the old kumera-Maori and the later kumera-moutere (Island = South Sea Island). The rows were directed towards the sunrise so as to get the morning warmth first to dry the ground and later in the day the direct heat. They were planted in November and gathered in May – the frost instead of hurting them after they had matured, sweetened them. The kumera was planted at full moon or within time between three nights after first quarter and three nights before last quarter. The same times were observed for hue and taro and in whaling days for marrows and potatoes but no one bothered to keep those times now.

When the collector was talking at one place a boy came to borrow the 'tukituki'. He was asked which one and he replied 'mo te kari' (for the digging). It proved to be a broom-shaped clod breaker and was said to be based on an old idea of breaking clods when ground had been dug with the ko.

SEAWEEDS (EDIBLE)

The principal informant had very little to say about edible seaweeds. Karengo was eaten in Canterbury. It was cleaned and fried with oil. Down here seaweeds were not so much eaten as in the North Island where the people ate all kinds boiled in fat and declared they were good.

A Rapaki Maori said the people used to (and could now if they liked) eat kelp (rimu). A round piece like your wrist and hard like wood would be taken home, put in the fire and roasted, then scraped and eaten. It was called 'he rimu', and was not very pleasant. Karengo, which is fine seaweed of red, pink and green colors, is still eaten here boiled and dried or fried in fat – it is very good. In the old days they used to dry it a bit and put it in a rourou basket and into the umu with it. He did not know what carrageen was. He had heard that rehia [See Murihiku Notes, H.B.] was made by the old people but he had never seen it and they had never described it to him.

Add to Seaweeds

At Akaroa the collector was told that the Maoris of old used to eat rimu (kelp) and kareko (a short, glutinous kind of seaweed). Other kinds of seaweeds which the collector cannot positively identify but which were mentioned are the paru-o-te-moana (or more shortly parumoana) said to be a spongy stuff, and a slippery kind of weed called rimurimu which the fish called moki and marare are said to be fond of and to live on. This last may be the tangled mass of shining red, yellow, green and other colored seaweed oft cast up on our shores. When the tide runs out at Akaroa you can see patches of bright green stuff covering the rocks. The collector did not examine it (and probably would be no wiser if he had) but it is known to the local Maoris as pati [See Shellfish Section, H.B.].

The big flat blades of kelp used to be called rimurapa while rimupuku is thick and round. The puku part was eaten of old. It might be so old that it had become as dry as rhinoceros hide and as hard as wood but it could be tackled. It might be so old that the rapa portion had crinkled up, withered, and crumbled to pieces but the puku could still be dealt with. It was put in the fire and charred (murumuru). It was then soaked in the creek until you could uhu (scrape) the char off with your fingers. When you had the blackened parts wiped off, you rinsed it and 'ate it like a piece of licorice'. Children were warned not to put kelp in the fire on days when the men were fishing as it was said to cause winds to blow.

CHEWING-GUMS

*The principal informant said that one form of chewing gum was the puha (bush thistle). The gum of it forms white and hard. Like the stem of the plant the gum is bitter, especially at first, but in half-an-hour it gets all right.** It makes a crackling noise and lasts a long time. *Another kind of gum was mimiha [A North Island word. H.B.].** It was a kind of fish or marine black stuff which drifts ashore and is picked up and chewed. Like the puha it is good to clean the teeth. If it is too hard use a little hinu (lard) with it. It is like ambergris in substance but has no smell. The people of old hid it in the bush to keep it – it was too extremely popular to leave lying about. It is also called kauri. [Tregear's [[1891]] *Dictionary* gives this name as kauritawhiti but all Southerners simply say kauri. H.B.] *The pikirangi [pikiraki further south. H.B.] berry is good to chew. It is small and yellow and sweet, and can be chewed for a long time.**

A Rapaki Maori (about seventy) said he had never seen nor heard of mimiha or kauri. Two Tuahiwi Maoris said that kauri was black like coal but chewed well. At one time the pakehas thought it was ambergris *or* pitch; but they could not explain where it came from [[Charles Heaphy, 27 March 1846 (Taylor 1959: 207) refers to pakaki, or pitch, as a chewing substance obtained between Cape Farewell and West Wanganui, Northwest Nelson]]. Had chewed it but it had not much taste. It was passed from one to another in old days and they thought this must have spread disease. The puha was white and tasted bitter at the commencement but soon got all right. You could chew a piece almost all day. Nowadays they sometimes chewed the down of the Scotch thistle but it did not last anything like the juice of the puha.

At the tangi at Temuka an old man said he had seen and chewed kauri. It might be a fish as the old people said but he did not believe that, as there was too much kerosene in it. Another foolish suggestion was that it was tutae-wera (whale dung) but it was not likely. He reckoned it looked like the lava from 'springs' in the sea. The old people used to hang it on makomako trees as they said ti would grow and thrive there. Another thing he remembered chewing was kau-puha, [Kau or ngau = to chew. H.B.] the gum of the sowthistle.

Add to Chewing-gum

While speaking about bush flowers the principal informant mentioned the pikiraki, and added that the children used the berries of it as chewing-gum. The berries are sweet and go into a pulp that can be chewed for a long time. The oldest man at Tuahiwi also casually mentioned this masticatory. The pikiraki, he said, has red flowers and yellow berries and the latter could be chewed as a gum until the chewer was tired of it when the pulp was usually thrown away. The taste was pleasant enough while it lasted.

MUSHROOMS AND FUNGI

There were different kinds of fungi here before the Pakeha came, said the principal informant, but they were in the bush. Harore was the name and they were not fancied as edibles. Whareatua, he thought, was white outside, round like a ball and with a net inside. You could eat the whareatua mushroom. The weho and poketara were about the same. The poketara came from thunder, so the Maoris said, but all grew from the land. The poketara was eaten. Ordinary mushrooms, he understood, could only come from animal manure. The toadstools were now gathered by the Maoris and burnt as the ashes were good for sore backs in horses. This was quite modern. The porotata sprang from the ground but he had only heard about it. It grew big and broke out and there was a net and ware (viscous jelly) inside it. Some people roast it on the fire and say it is good but he had never tasted it himself, although he would eat the ordinary mushrooms of the field.

A Rapaki Maori said that mushrooms were called mataruna [a la Pakeha]. He liked to eat ones white outside and red inside. Whareatua is thin, and white on both sides and is no good to eat. He never heard of weho. Poketara is round like a ball and sticks to the ground. It was not eaten as far as he knew as they were simply puffballs. He knew nothing about the bush fungi.

A Tuahiwi Maori said tree fungi was hakekakeka. The olden Maoris did not know about the mushrooms. Whareatua is a big round white mushroom; they did not like it as it might be poisonous. It was a 'taipo house' and they would not eat it. During thunder the poketara drops down and it is thus known as tutae-whaitiri. It was not eaten. He tried one once, a new one. He put it in fire to cook but it went into water and left a funny smell. The weho grows on the trees and is eaten. It is the color of tapioca when cooked and is glutinous. You put it in the fire and when done take the skin off and eat the slimy interior.

Another Tuahiwi-ite said there were several kinds of mushrooms but he did not know if they were in New Zealand before the Pakeha came. He had heard the Maori ate one kind of whareatua. A taua invaded Banks Peninsula and landed near Rakaia and ate whareatua and some died thereof. Other authorities say they did not die but were very ill. This was three hundred or four hundred years ago and he could not say if it was the present common mushroom. He did not eat poketara. He does not know about weho – never heard the name even. He had never heard of Maoris eating tree fungi – as far as he knew they took no notice of such growths.

Add to Fungi

The collector did not get much about this subject. The Principal informant said that a fungus called hakekakeka grew like mushrooms on trees but he did not know if it had ever been eaten in Canterbury. A Rapaki Maori said he had never heard of hakekakeka being eaten. A Taumutu Maori said that the Maoris at Otaki in the North Island used to gather tree fungi (of which he, on his visit, never heard the name) and sell it to the Chinese in that locality. A Wairewa (Little River) Maori said that on Banks Peninsula the kind of tree fungus known as harore was eaten in the old days but that the kind known as hakekakeka was not, although the Chinese used to buy it. They gave six pound for it and he thought they used it to make varnish but he was not sure. The whareatua on the Peninsula was a peculiar thing – it was a sort of mushroom framework with a jelly inside to trap unwary insects. Poketara was a mushroom growth which 'got a fright' when the thunder rolled and came out of the ground. It grows rapidly, grows round and grows very big, but it was regarded as no good for kai (food) as far as he had ever heard. It may have been eaten elsewhere although not here. A Maori, who was listening to the last speaker, chipped in and said he had heard toadstools called whareatua.

SECTION XVI

ICHTHYOLOGY

Ika or Fish — Hi-ika or Fishing — Rapu or Guddling — Rauiri or Reserves — Kupenga or Big Nets — Kaka or Small Nets — Koko or Small Nets — Tata or Small Nets — Patiki or Flounders — Mata or Whitebait — Kahawai or A Fish — Kokopu or Native Trout — Tuna or Eels — Patuna or Eel-weirs — Hinaki or Eel-pots — Matarau or Eel-spears — Kuku or Mussels — Tio or Oysters — Kaio or Sea-nuts — Kina or Sea-eggs — Mako or Sharks — Paikea or 'Big Fish' — Pakake or Seals — etc.

FISH AND FISHING

The collector asked his principal informant if he knew of fish gorges. *He did not but he had heard of one kind of 'fish-gorging' called whakapuku. It was made of flax or whitau with a big bait tied round. The koiro (conger eel) would bolt it and not being able to disgorge would be caught.** No bone or hook was in the bait. Pawa shell had been used on hooks for kahawai at Akaroa. *To catch makaa (barracouta) a pa (jigger) of wood was used, and this spun in water and attracted fish. The rod was matere, the line was aho and he thought the hook was called niho in this instance.** The barb on a hook is naku and was discovered by Maui (see Mythology section). *On Oruapaeroa (New Brighton Beach) in summer the Maori used to go swimming, and catching horihori (the sole – it has another name which he forgot). The flounder is patotara, the dark flounder is mohoao, the dotted one, raututu is almost the same as the patotara while another kind is whawhai. The people would wade out with kaka nets, one going out as deep as he could, and they would catch many fish. The mohoao was only found in Lake Ellesmere (as its home). Other patiki were found all over the world. When the lake broke out the black flounders would go out to sea and up other creeks and rivers in New Zealand but it spawned in Ellesmere. Although the lake has been continuously netted for forty years it had never exhausted the fish – they seem as numerous as ever. The sea mohoao got thin but the lake ones were thicker-bodied and always in good condition.** The inanga (inaka further south) goes up the rivers and comes down to sea again and leaves its eggs (hua). You never see its spawn but (mata) whitebait come up from the sea. The inanga can be and is caught in hinaki occasionally but the main catch is in flax kaka in March. The mata is caught in August and September in a kohao of very close weave and called kaka. *It is put in side of river and when full of whitebait, the string round mouth is pulled, the kaka is taken out and contents emptied into a basket.** They are usually sundried. To eat fresh they are put in a whena next to the fire and cooked. The collector has Shortland's account of a kupenga (seine); and this informant gave the following names: karihi was the bottom line; the sinkers were of kohatu (stone) and were called mahia (mahi is a fishing line sinker); the floats were poito; the top line was kaharunga; posts at ends = pou; ends next poles were matakeke. In regard to Shortland's nomenclature he considered tuara-matakeke was the centre of net where fish are caught while he thought the heketanga was in centre too. The kupenga was not used the same as a pakeha net. *He saw it used on Ellesmere when it was taken out with a canoe. He considered his tribe (Ngai-Tahu) had brought the kupenga down from the East Coast of North Island with them.**

Speaking to two Maoris they told the collector pawa shell was put in hooks 'for flashness'. It was only done for kahawai fishing but very little of that was done in the South Island although it was said this fish could be taken down as far as the mouth of the Rakitata River.

An old man said the only fish caught with a matere (rod) was the barracouta and you used a pa or jigger for it. Put pawa shell on the hook and the shine attracts the fish. He had never heard of kahawai fishing. Any fishing line was an aho. The matau (hook) to catch hapuku (groper) was of whalebone. Other fish were caught with hooks too. After the makaa was caught it was opened up (tuaki or pawhera) and dried (paku) and then eaten. The groper was also cut open and dried (then becoming maraki). These fish could also be eaten from the umu

Riki Te Mairaki Taiaroa, photographed in Taumutu by W.A. Taylor in 1936. With his mother he provided Beattie with information about fisheries. He is wearing the Kāti Māmoe mat mentioned in the text on p. 570. W.A. Taylor Collection, Canterbury Museum, 1968.213.6322.

(earth-oven). The kupeka was a net to catch fish. Even sharks could be caught in it. It was made of flax and was made till recently. It was made in different meshes.

A Tuahiwi Maori said he had never seen a kupeka but he had seen a kaka used in the Waimakariri for catching flounders, aua (mullet), paraki (smelt), inaka (minnow), puataata (young minnow or silverbait) and other fish. The kaka is made all of flax and lines run down and others across in close formation. For whitebait (mata) a length is doubled and sewn up edges leaving a waha (mouth) using pirita (supplejack) as a stiffener. The whole net is then known as a koko and a pole (forgets name) is attached to lift it handily. In the bottom an opening (kumu) about nine inches long is made and attached to koko is a flax bag (te kotore or te kumu). It is said that the presence of this bag is of advantage when turning the koko over to empty contents. The whitebait slip through the hole and down to the waha steadier than if no kumu was attached and pour out better (the collector was told). This is the only set net allowed now and if placed right in stream the tiny fish won't come out of it, 'unless you are unlucky or illfated', the narrator added. It is only for mata (whitebait) [which is, of course, the young of the minnow. H.B.]. The inaka (minnow), like the eel, goes down on a heke to the sea, the first starting in January and others continuing to April usually, but to May in a late season. It spawns in the deep sea and he never saw it do so at river mouths. Lake Ellesmere is sometimes closed for two or three years so the Natives there should know how the inaka in it spawns at such periods. As the tiny fish rush to the sea the Maori fisher gathers them in with the kaka, a closely woven net (or mat) of four to five feet in depth and up to fifteen and twenty feet in length. It has a pou (stick) at each end and the two men wade out into water shallow enough for purpose and scoop them out on to shore. The narrator remarked that he had never heard fish sex mentioned by the Maoris, but he could say from his experience that in the vast numbers taken by the fishers, one and all were full of roe (hua). What is caught is only a small proportion of heke and rest continue to sea, returning up the rivers about one or two weeks after spawning. The inaka is then known as matua-a-iwi and they are left alone by Maoris as they are not (in Native estimation) fit to eat – they are lean and 'full of grit they have taken in as ballast'. For catching them on their seaward journey the koko was sometimes used but it was not so good for the purpose as the kaka. The first lots of mata begin dribbling up the rivers in July but these are only pioneers or forerunners of the main body which arrives about October although in some years November is also a good month and sometimes December too and then arrives the tail-end. In the height of the season there appears to be endless chains of them. They come in shoals (potiritiri – one shoal is called potiri). A good place to catch them is any dam or obstruction in river and you might get up to five quarts a night at springtide in full-moon. In the old days the Maoris made dams (pa) at the sides of rivers to catch fish and although these were not made with any set purpose of catching matait was a handy place to get them as a rule.

The koko up to seven or eight feet long could be set in three or four feet depth of water and lifted out when necessary but a koko attached to a pole could be used in deep water. In regard to the kaka, he added, it was used the same as pakehas use the net for flounders now. Besides inaka the Maoris caught other fish in the kaka. One of these fish was the paraki but it seems to have died out in recent years up this way. He had never seen kokopu or kokopara here nor heard of them being caught here in his time but he understood they were netted; at least one kind, the panako, he had heard was caught in nets. The panako had a better taste than the kokopu. These fish were far too bony – they had too many iwi to suit the Maori. The trout had eaten the 'bullies' (kokopu and kokopara) out up this way. He had heard the grayling (upokororo) was in this district but he had never seen it. In regard to patiki (flounders) they were speared by torchlight as a rule. He had never seen the old Maori spear (the matarau) with several prongs, but you could spear them quite well with a rod or stick of sharpened manuka and called a patia. He forgot the name of the yellow-belly flounder and the brill but the sole was called kutuhori while the mohoao was a black flounder – a patiki-wai-maori, a freshwater flounder – and the whawhai was a sea flounder – a patiki-wai-tai. Flounder spearing by torchlight was good sport as a rule.

An elderly Maori showed the collector a notebook with some whakapapas in it and on two or three pages were diagrams showing the best fishing grounds off Moeraki. These were worked out to points by dotted lines from prominent landmarks and were well executed.

Add to Fish and Fishing

The principal informant said he had never heard of a houka or hauka net but of a tata one. (Tataa is a bailer.) Tata is a small net, two or three feet across and round. Some were put in deep water to get tuere ['slime fish' he called it too the 'blind eel' I think is another name. H.B.] and another kind of tata was used to carry eels, etc. To catch tuere it was let down with a rope into deep water with a bait inside and left an hour or two before being pulled up. The Pakeha does not like the slime on the tuere but the Maori found it good eating it made him grow strong. He cleaned it in fresh water, put the inside out, dried the fish and cooked it at the fire. For the tuere the tata was like a basket with a bait in it but there was a different tata made. Its mouth was open as it is set but as it is pulled up the mouth closes together (like the mouth of a carpet bag or a portmanteau). [This will be the net known as the tuakitata because it is built on tuaki (cockleshell) principles. Murihiku Notes. H.B.] *To catch the koiro (conger-eel) the whakapuku is to make a mass of whitau tangled round a bait of fish or meat and throw it in the sea. It can be left all day or night. The only fish to tackle it is the koiro as others cannot eat it but koiro bolts it over and finds he cannot digest it nor spew it out so he is held a prisoner until fisherman comes.**

The mullet (kanae = North Island) is not found in Canterbury waters but *the herring (aua) comes up from the sea into fresh water, and is caught in kaka nets like very close netting.** A man holds this net on shore and other wades out with other end up to a depth of water to his neck and drags the net. This can be done in rivers everywhere and on sea-beaches. The mata (whitebait) was caught in koko net and dried in the sun. *Its mother, the inanga, was not allowed to be taken on its way to spawn in the old days,** [This, it seems to me, is a quite erroneous statement. H.B.] but could be caught in small creeks as they returned from the sea. The Maori made runways and the small fish swarm into these and are scooped out on to mats laid alongside, and are left to dry. The Te Ikamaru was, he thought, first caught by Maru and was called after him but he did not know what kind of fish it was. *The patete is a small freshwater fish and the waharoa is a little bigger.** Another name for the patete is paraki. It is small and white, is scooped in with the kaka net and sun-dried. It has plenty of oil in it and dries hard and if broken snaps with a crackling sound – hence its name patete. It tastes excellently. The paraki and inaka are different kinds of wee fish – the former is not so big or so flat as latter. The paraki is rather like the marakuha (sprat) which keeps to the sea – they are of the same shape and about the same length – but the latter is bony while the paraki is not. He had heard the legend that the octopus known as the tapairu was only eaten by men and tapairu women. The tapairu is a female and is first-born in chiefly descent. [Probably a North Island tradition. H.B.] The octopus known as wheke is eaten. The warehou was not in Canterbury. He had once thought the trevally (komutumutu) was a young warehou but his father said it was of same race but distinct from warehou of North Island. The puaiwhakarua is a smallish fish, reddish and is found off both Islands. When caught its teeth can be extracted like those of the dogfish. He had never heard of whakahoki = cooking fish twice [vide Tregear. H.B.].

*Fishing was called hi-ika, and the big nets were kupenga. The mataa (mesh) in these was the same all along the net but the centre or belly of the net was made a little wider than towards the ends.** After they had been used they were whaka-maroke (dried) and pokai (rolled) and stored (often in caves on beaches) for next year or season. Often the kupenga were broken [See section re Sharks, H.B.] in first season but others would last a year or two. The saltwater did not seem to rot the flax – the nets broke through the struggles of the fish. The striving of the more strenouous fish was called pakuku and when such had rendered the mesh broken, rotten or useless the net was cast away. Flounders were caught during May, June, July and August and did not knock the nets about much. Those months constituted the proper season although the flounders could be caught all the year round if one wished. Mohoao were principally taken in May and June. Sometimes the raututu, patotara and whawhai varieties of patiki were taken at the same time – the horihori (sole) was also caught in nets.

A Rapaki Maori said the inaka spawned in Lake Ellesmere when the lake was blocked but even then salt spray came across the sand-dunes at high tides and storms. In rivers whose mouths are not open in spawning season the inaka comes up to shingle bar and spawns there – the water is white like milk. The sea oozes through the shingle and gives them a taste of saltwater. Then the inaka proceeds up the rivers to under falls or rapids where the gravel is clean. They could be caught then but best time was before spawning as they proceeded down-stream. The river would be black with them before spawning – you could not see one after, wherever they went, although they might wait about to see if mouth opened so they could get to sea. If not they spawned in shingle and this spawn was there until bar broke when it was swept to sea to grow until it came up rivers next season. He did not know patete or waharoa; but paraki is the smelt but he did not know about its spawning although no whitebait came from it. It favored some rivers more than others – very few in Waihao but numerous in Waitaki. The aua runs up the rivers but he did not know why. It is caught about same time as the whitebait (September) in South Canterbury. Two men would use a kaka net and scoop them out. They were nice when fat but were usually a bony fish and not much sought after. He did not know of any other sea fish running up the rivers that he could think of, nor had he heard of tata or houka fishnets. The warehou was not off Canterbury. The trevally – he did not know its Maori name – he thought it was only prominent recently. The tarakihi was another fish and so was the koekohe (trumpeter). The puaihakarua at Otago Heads and Moeraki is a sort of perch and is called Soldier Fish. The moki is like a trumpeter but not so big. Rari is the ling. The octopus or wheke was not eaten, so far as he knew, but the koiro (conger) and Tuere (blind eel) were. The whai was name of two kinds of skate or stingray which were eaten. They were caught on hooks on fishing lines.

A Kaiapoi Maori said the aua was not the mullet but was the herring. There were three stages in the development of the smelt. The first stage the smelt had white underneath and this is the first formation of its spawn. The spawn develop into little fish called puatata and these increase into paraki or the waharoa stage of smelt. [Note: The talk was in his garden as he would not consent to an interview and notes I hurriedly made do not clearly state whether he considered the smelt further developed into the herring. H.B.] The aua came up the rivers after the whitebait and were then good fat fish. The kahawai came up the rivers but was not much caught or eaten – too dry to relish and there were too many other good food fishes. He had never heard that inaka spawned in rivers but that they went out to sea but how far was 'a conundrum'. Lake Ellesmere was sometimes blocked for two or three years and he had heard it was full of inaka ready to spawn and that these had gone up the little creeks and came back without their spawn. He thought flounders mostly spawned in freshwater. His father used to say he would hear the Ellesmere bar had broken and in a month's time the rivers would swarm with patiki. He did not know exactly when the bar broke but usually Autumn or Spring as a result of the February or August rains as far as he knew.

The Natives at Taumutu (one said he thought this meant 'end of landing' – it is at south end of Ellesmere) have fished for centuries and following are their remarks; or rather the lore of the present remnant of the race: In the first full moon of January or February they used to prepare for inaka. Funny (they thought) inaka work was in full moon-light (and they would send eight or nine tons of inaka away) and the tuna (eel) work which followed was in hinapouri (dark of the moon). The people used to ohu (work together) with hoe (paddles) to scoop sand away if lake was so high as to threaten the fronts of the the waterside whares (houses). The kupeka-kohao is the net to catch the inaka. If you laid this on land with fish in it the oil from them caked it so that you could not use net again. [This seems doubtful. H.B.] Drains or awa were made to whakaheke the inaka. The end of these awa was blocked with sand and the inaka were scooped out wholesale in kohao baskets and emptied on to a flax mat – name forgotten. It takes days to dry them as turned and returned and then they are put in baskets on whata stage. The inaka's spawn must be thousands of eggs. The males are also caught but have a whitish paste and are more bitter to eat than the female with its brownish roe like very wee sago. Perhaps a quarter of those caught have white and three quarters brown roe. Trout roe is like barley and is on same system. If the olden Maoris had plenty of inaka they would put out the males as these were bitterer and as they shrivelled up flatter when dried. (This particular informant considered the white milk, seen in water sometimes, is from males and covers the eggs laid by females to propagate them like trout spawn.) He had known Ellesmere to be closed for eighteen months and inaka in it all the time. You could see them one moon with spawn and the next thin and bony. The old Maoris used to say the inaka took in gravel as ballast to keep them down from floating on top of the water after spawning. The roe of the male inaka is called huaparu. Another said he had known Wairewa (Lake Forsyth) to be closed for seven years – it is freshwater not brackish like Waihora (Ellesmere). It was opened prior to this in a September and the inaka came in but had died out in two years so they cannot spawn in fresh water and keep healthy. He was positive the inaka (minnow) was the mother of the mata (whitebait).

Patiki (flounders) – Ellesmere is famous for its flounders – it has been fished constantly for many years without exhaustion. There is said to be a deep hole in centre of lake, said one Maori, but he had not seen it. The Waiwhio (Irwell), Kuaowhitu (Hart's River) and Waikirikiri (Selwyn) all run into the lake and it has no outlet to sea save when the wide bar of sand breaks. He had seen in lake flounders from the size of a fly to big whoppers and he did not know what they fed on but sometimes grass seeds and green pulp is found inside them. The trout eat the small flounders. The fishermen here say the flounders live in tiers one on top of the other after spawning and live on their own slime until a certain size, and that they do not go out to sea save when swept out. Seine nets work all the time with marked and uniform success. When lake goes out it appears not to lose its own denizens to any extent or if it does it gains a corresponding number of sea flounders – which are not so fat as the lake ones but soon fatten up. The ordinary flounder is called patiki, the mohoao is a black, freshwater one and the patotara (yellow belly) were all in lake. The kutuhori had not died out here but is rare; the koihi had died out here but was still caught in Dunedin Harbor, he understood. The sole is here called raututu (he continued) and if the lake was open in summer for two or three months you could catch a few. It is really a freshwater fish. [Name not correct. H.B.] If the lake opened now (September) you would catch hoka (red cod) in winter – short, thick fellows much better than sea ones. They must come in as small ones. Herrings (aua) grow as big as trout almost. The sea fish must come in young and often must breed in the lake. He had heard the name waharoa but forgot what it was. He never heard of the patete but the paraki is the smelt and has a smell like a cucumber. He had heard of the puaihakarua but not of the ikamaru. The warehou and kahawai are caught in the lake at times by anglers with lines, but are rare. He would prefer to eat the former as it is the nicer fish. Another Maori (who had just come in from fishing) said the yellow-belly in the lake was whaiwhai. The sole (horihori) is also a yellowbelly. The raututu is here called 'Three Corners' by the Pakeha from its shape [He showed collector one. H.B.] while the mohoao is very dark. The male inaka had huaparu as a sort of roe but he did not know what male flounders had in this line particularly, yet every flounder caught has roe of some sort. The sole has inohi (scales) and can be skinned but the flounder has no scales. He had caught far more fish at night time than in the daytime. Fishing is hi-ika. To catch makaa on the Peninsula jiggers (pa) of New Zealand cedar (a kind of totara) and tawai (birch) were used. The hook was matau. The old people said they learnt fishing from the maeroero, but he did not know details of this.

One man said the old people went by stars for fishing, but he could give no particulars.

Add to Fish and Fishing

A Rapaki Maori referred to the inaka (minnow) and said he had been at Waihao (South Canterbury) when the inaka on their heke to sea met the bank of shingle which often closes the mouths of that (and other) East Coast rivers. The saltwater oozes through the shingle and the inaka spawn in the shingle. He reckoned that the inaka did not straightway proceed up rivers after spawning but wriggled through the sand and shingle into sea for a taste of genuine sea-water first.

A Kaiapoi Maori told me he had seen the inaka spawning in Saltwater Creek at highwater mark. You could see them racing about and the water turns milky round about the rushes growing there. They then hang about the mouth of the river a day or two before returning up-river. They go back upcountry very thin. He was willing to take anyone, Pakeha or Maori, to this spot in January and show them the truth of his remarks.

A Wairewa Maori, who gave me information about the inaka before, merely said this time that the way to tell the sex was to examine the roe, that of the female being called hua and that of male huaparu, the latter being darker than former. Although the females preponderated, on several occasions he had seen catches in which the sexes seemed to be very equally divided. The female fish were more prized for taste usually.

An Akaroa Maori said a slippery seaweed was called rimurimu and you would find bits of it in moki, and marare (butterfish) as those fish lived on it. Kahawai was caught at Akaroa and wrapped in patiti (tussock) was put in umu. The flesh (if I understood right) was then hung up and dried in sun, forming the luxury known as paku. Children were warned not to put kelp [See Seaweeds, H.B.] on the fire on days when the men were going fishing as it would cause winds to spring up. The jellyfish is called reperepe-tautini at Akaroa.

'The kanakana is called piharau in the North Island', said a Peninsula Maori. Killing fish is called tairo; Kupe is said to have introduced nets into New Zealand. [See Mythology Section, H.B.]

EELS AND EELING

*The principal informant said that ancient eel spears (matarau) were made of** akeake or kohai or akerautaki (a tree which grows on Banks Peninsula and is of strong wood to make spears and matarau). Some eel spears had seven mata (prongs) and others less. The handle was kakau. The spear was wero'd into mud crosswise to where eel was supposed to lie, the left hand never being used. Sometimes you would feel eel with your feet but again you would see the raupo and reeds moving and judge where eel was threading its way through them. Another little spear or big needle = au with string (taura) attached was carried and was stuck through tail of eel to thread it on to line. After you threaded it on you remove matarau giving eel's head a 'biff' on matarau to kill or stun it. The eels were then to (dragged or towed behind). A spear with a single point was patia (and is now made by tying an iron spike to a long stick) and it could be held as matarau and thrust or it could be thrown at eels. Eeling canals or drains were made at Lake Ellesmere (Waihola) up to three chains long. The awa (drain) was made with a takoko (scoop). When the tide is going out the current in the awa is fast and the eels come to taste the saltwater and are caught in thousands. You could block the drain with a stone. The kohao is a net with a mouth of pirita (supplejack; karewao is its berry) and a long stick for a handle. With this go into water and scoop the eels out. Kohao-tu is the receptacle to hold them when they are secured. The tuna (eels) are split (pawhera) and then hung on whata to dry. At Lake Forsyth (Wairewa) short awa were made and pahuri (shelters). These pahuri were roughly made of sticks and popohue (a vine that grows on Birdling Flat) and patiti (tussock) was spread to lie on. Put white stones in awa and see the tuna passing. The hole at end of awa is called kotore. A parua or (dry) hole is made in shingle and as eels taken they are hit on head to kill or stun and put in it as temporary store. Kohao the tuna till you are sleepy and then put in hinaki in awa and retire to your pahuri for the night. The hole where hinaki is set is called parua also. The hinaki is made of aka vine; its mouth is called kutu; it has a puraki or kohao of flax and the rohe is part of this kohao; its end is called kotore. You can catch kanakana in exactly the same hinaki. The kaitara is an eelpot with bait in it. It is made of akatea vine held out by hoops (no name for these) and then totara bark tied round while a moenu (bait) is hung inside. Te-waha-o-te-kaitara (its mouth) is a hoop of pirita (supplejack), while a puraki of flax leads into it and a kotore of flax is at other end (where you take eels out of trap). You could make hinaki or kaitara of all flax but this was not often done as it would not support a big weight of eels. He could not say where eels spawned. There was a very deep spring in Ellesmere which the fishermen can't bottom and he thought eels spawned there. They like the taste of the froth of the sea waves so migrate. As to patuna; *in the Waiwhio (near Ellesmere) the Maori made a fence like a sheepyard and made it so they could put a trap at either end according to the way the eels were going in season. At Waikirikiri (Selwyn) and other rivers pa were set also.** These pa were usually set at the sides of the rivers as sufficient eels could be caught there. The pakanakana was almost the same as the patuna. It was not used at Ellesmere but further down Canterbury at Temuka and Ohapi; and also up at Kaiapoi he thought.

An intelligent and reliable old halfcaste who has been in Kaiapoi district sixty years told the collector he had seen a patuna in the Whakahume (Cam River) but he never knew any in the Waimakariri. The work of catching eels was called mahingatuna or sometimes mahingakai. The eels would 'flow' (heke) out of the swamps (hapua) into the river and here the pa was set. The fence was of sticks (usually manuka) about one inch apart. The sticks were about one inch through and ten or twelve feet long as the water was four and a half to five feet deep. As soon as the season was over these sticks would be pulled up, rolled in bundles and put away. By so doing they lasted for years. Behind these sticks were several pou (posts) here and there to strengthen fence. Battens formed a sort of tirewa (frame) and the sticks were lashed to them with flax. In the centre of the stream were one, two or three hinaki and these were emptied as occasion required. Take a canoe (a log waka) out and untie fastenings and drag hinaki ashore. Near the bank a hole (parua) had been made and hinaki was emptied into it and then towed back to centre of pa and replaced. He had seen hao caught in thousands. The heke is generally in the rainy season and the water is dirty. When the eels hoki (return) from the sea reverse the fence downstream by lifting sections (it is made so) of fence and put them in new position. The country is drained now and the swamps are now farms and the pa-tuna or pa-mahinga-kai is a thing of the past. The pa was in rivers not in swamps. The only one he saw, and so the only one he can speak with authority about, had the hinakis in the centre. These were pulled out two or three times a day, but were left all night till early morning. A big one would take three hundred to four hundred eels. He has seen one ten to twelve feet long and about three foot six inches high. Hinaki were just used in heke and stored till next season. They were carefully dried in sun before storing away. They were made of big vines lashed with small flexible vines and would last for ten or twelve years as a rule. The heke was generally August and September and mostly hao eels were caught but also ordinary eels such as papaka, horihoriwai, kirirua and tunarakau as they 'flow' too. He never heard of arokehe eels here. He used to werotuna (spear eels) with a matarau with iron prongs. (Old matarau had prongs of hard wood.) When spearing if water is muddy feel eels with the feet and spear on chance. He pulls foot back and lets drive and sometimes was lucky enough to get eel, although sometimes got none and often only a few. The matarau has more chance than a spear with a single point. He also caught eels with a bob (puti-noke = bundle of worms) and this is still used in the Cam. He showed me a kaitara he uses. It is netting (wire) with sacking around. The front is of string mesh and the opening is pulled by a string going right through to kumu or lid of netting tied on to end. The eels are emptied through here. The bait was a dead hen somewhat roasted. Bait is always toasted on fire to create smell. Shag birds makes good bait for eels. He did not rightly know why bag was tied round netting but it was customary. It must be to exclude light as the eels at dawn usually make great attempts to get out. He had had the kaitara (the collector was looking at) so full of eels he could not lift it but had to roll it out on to bank.

A Tuahiwi Maori said he had never seen a patuna but heard it was made in a V shape both ways but mostly downstream during heke in February and March. The fence forming the V was called taupa. The hinaki was made of vine – a kind of clematis – popohue was suitable. The puraki and rohe were of flax. The kumu was of vine also. The potaka (hoops) were of stout vine or supplejack laced with fine vine. Some were very expert at making the hinaki but none had been made here for many years – he saw one when he was a child. In a heke they would be examined several times in a good night but sometimes were left all night. The kumu was taken off and they were emptied and replaced in river. At a narrow part of the hapua (lagoon) Tutaipatu at Woodend he saw stakes (poupa of an old patuna decayed to stumps). He did not know about the big rivers but it was said there had been a patuna at Ohapuku on the north branch of the Waimakariri but he never saw it. He has known eels go down to sea in September but does not know if this is usual. The hao (mainly a lagoon eel) goes down in November and December in creeks and in February and March from lagoons, and back in

February and March and April and May respectively. The tunarakau goes at the same times in many cases. Horihoriwai he cannot make out. They are always in river; he has never known them to heke but they do – they had him raru-raru (puzzled). He could not tell male from female eels and never heard the old Maoris speak of sexes of fish. The horepara leaves the holes and springs in August and works downstream and is still going in January, returning from the end of January onward. He does not definitely know how long eels remain in the sea. Up to January if disturbed they always make downstream but after that if disturbed they won't go down but always upstream. He has opened eels and seen spawn not in main stomach but in bag alongside which is full of matter. The spawn is about length and thickness of a fine darning needle and colored red. He thought they were called pua. They were all red. He has seen them out of the eel – they can be got in mud as far as tide goes up Waimakariri and also in tidal creeks. They are then of a darkish color and he could not distinguish breed nor had he heard any name for them at that stage. They were found making downstream but he could not base any theory on that.

The manawa was an eel he did not know about but it was found further inland. The arokehe, he fancied, was a lake eel. Some eels had small heads and big tails and long fins and some had big heads, small tails and short fins and thus you could distinguish them. The papaka lived on mudflats in salty water and very seldom in rivers. They are good to eat but tackle you quick if you dab spear into them. They are the worst of all eels for this, especially if the tide is coming in. The other eels are not so vicious. Some eels grow to great size and a horepara got in a drain at Ohapuku (Eyre) weighed thirty two pounds. The kaitara is often made of flax like tiaka, stiff and straight, and has a puraki, rohe and kumu like the hinaki. It has a bait (moenu) inside it. The sport of bobbing is called hi. The bob or putinoke is made of whitau or frayed flax with red or white worms threaded on wiwi rushes and looped up. You could use a bit of weka (woodhen) if worms were not handy. It was an easy way to catch eels and a good bit of it is still done by Maori and pakeha.

Rapu was groping for eels. You got right into the water and feel for them in the ruatuna (eel-holes). Eels sometimes lie in the cress (kuta) and are thus hard to get. The bigger eels make fair-sized holes but the small ones lie handy to the eeler. If you stick your fingers in one's mouth don't pull back or it will strip your fingers – get someone to cut its head off. It is a tax on the nerves but he did it once with a twenty pound eel and waited till a boy used knife, but as a rule if eel touches palm of hand it backs. (His fingers bear marks of his encounter yet.) Work the fingers into the eel's pihapiha (gills), get it on the run and sling out on bank with continuous action or it will elude you. Use forefinger of each hand – one in each gill – and sling it out before it can wriggle. (He thought forefinger was called korua, but was not sure.) Sometimes you got an eel in such a position you could balance it on both hands and heave it out without delay or trouble. Playing an eel with the hand is kaipara. (English call it 'tickling'; Scots name is 'guddling'.) He understood they made awa awa (channels or drains) at Little River and got eels. At end of channel dig a big parua (hole). Halfway place white stones and sit by when eels pass in do not wait till they return but rush and puru (block) opening of drain. The water filters away and leaves the tuna stranded. This was done at night he thought but he never saw it done, only he heard about it. He had never heard of channels to catch eels being in the Kaiapoi district. Kanakana used to be taken in this district. They threw out a fence into the water with fern between and the kanakana groped through and remained hanging to inside offence and people took them off with their hands. Pepehi is name of this way of securing them and was followed at Kaiapoi until fifty years ago. Then the fish disappeared. A chief named Te Muru was said to be angry at some local women and said a makutu against the kanakana. That is the explanation of why they failed to appear, but though they are not now at Kaiapoi the kanakana can still be caught at Temuka. In regard to the words 'whakapuni tuna', he thought that was just another expression for pa-tuna. When the collector revisited him he would say more re eels.

An old man said 'eeling sprang from Maui', but when pressed for details of this statement he said he had not learnt the history of eels, and then he told the tale of Maui fishing up the North Island.

A Rapaki Maori said patuna used to be 'built' in streams around Canterbury. They were not made right across big rivers but just enough to guide the fish into the hinaki. The fence that did this was called a pa. The place where such was built was selected with care avoiding kohio (whirlpools). Eels could also be caught in paakaatuna (commonly shortened to paakaa) a kind of hinaki set in the awa (rivers) with a bait inside it. This paka was also called a kaitara but the former name was used more as it was quicker to say. Besides, kaitara was not a polite name to use. The Maoris had not two names for one thing but only one name, although another place might have a different name.

In researching his voluminous notes the collector has come across additional remarks by the principal informant and they are herewith appended: At Kuauwhiti, near Leeston, where the Hart? River [[Hart's Creek]] runs into Lake Ellesmere there is a vast spring with 'no bottom' and he thought the eels in that district spawned there. In answer to a question by the collector he said he had heard the name 'whakapuni-tuna' but he fancied it was in the North Island. As far as he knew it was nearly the same as the patuna which was the only term used in Canterbury for eelweirs that he knew of. There were more eels in the South than in the North Island. Lake Taupo had not many eels – nothing like so many as Waihora (Lake Ellesmere). *Another way (besides those discussed) of catching eels was by a bob (moenu) tied on a rod (matere). It was an ancient method of catching tuna. The people used to dig nokewaiu (big white worms) for the bob. They got flax and split it fine; they got wiwi (rushes), hooked it on to the flax and put the wiwi through the worm and then doubled up the lot in loops and there is your bob.** A different matere was used to that used for maka and kahawai. A popular rod to use was houi (ribbonwood) as it was supple. It was held with its point in the water as the bait was tied on to its extremity. *The tuna came along and fastened his teeth in the bob and was swished to land in double-quick time.**

Also herewith diagrams of hinaki for kanakana. Copies of drawings by W. Rehu (Tuahiwi). Notes by H. Beattie: The kanakana are going up-country to spawn. The fern is tied round posts as a means to encourage fish to enter the trap. Rehu reckoned fern leaves enticed them (but I think it is merely a disguise). The tiu is a swinging flax net out on the river side and swings as aka frame comes back against the current. The main current is further out in river as pa-kanakana is at one side.

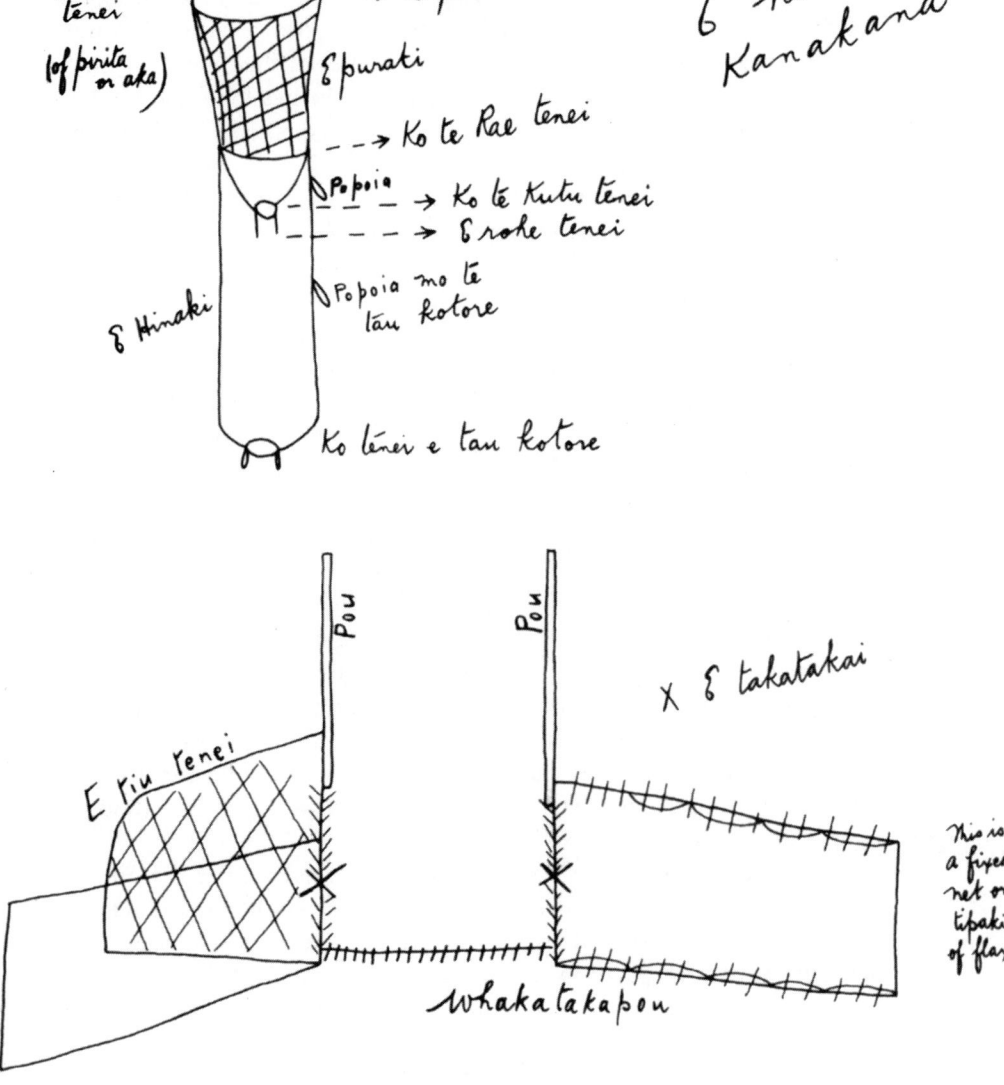

Add to Eels and Eel-catching

To the information given last trip the principal informant answered two questions. He had never heard of eels being caught by Maoris by a hook tied to the wrist and held in palm of hand. He reckoned such would break but he had heard of sticking a hook in an eel and pulling it out with string attached to hook. This was a form of rapu [See previous Notes re, H.B.]. Nor had he ever heard of a Maori dying of a surfeit of lamprey [See Tregear. H.B.] or of any food.

A Rapaki Maori said he had never heard of eeling with a hook tied to the wrist but with bare hands. Eel holes in the banks were called he rua-tuna. He used to accept the Pakeha superstition that eels came from horsehair but last year about October when he was whitebaiting in Waihao River he, with others present, saw millions of young eels (of the hao variety) in the gravel. They saw them moving in banks of gravel that had been tramped down at sides. They were about a foot down from surface. They took two bottles of them home to show people but the eels soon died. They were about two inches long and thick as darning needles, the same color as whitebait and yet you could distinguish shape of eel – head, mouth, eyes and all.

A Tuahiwi Maori said that at certain times a white stuff called pua shows under the tuna (eel). It disappears; and forms into young eels he thought. This pua could be seen on other fish too. The kanakana would not travel in the moonlight but came up the rivers in the hinapouri ('dark o' the moon'). He thought it must live 'by suction' as it is gutless. It can be got in holes in the banks. Whakatoremu means 'away at the back' and can be applied as an expression to eel-holes. Some eels spawned up the rivers but he did not know about the kanakana. Last week's rain would bring lots of eels down as it was good travelling in floods and it was near their time. You could now get plenty of good eels in the streams but in March and April you can get none.

A Taumutu Maori said that for the tuna they used to make awa (drains) and block with hinaki, or put white stones in bottom and club them as they passed over when they would drift dead or stunned into hole at end of drain. Otherwise they would have to be killed in hole. Clubbing was rare and only done when a few were coming in. The hao, the horepara (silver) and mairehe (large black) were three principal eels in Ellesmere. The eel was a bit of a mystery. It would eat fish of any kind or any dead thing. Some Maoris said there was no roe or spawn in eels but that a bluish bag carried its young and shot them out alive into gravel. The shark and the dogfish carry their young in this way and he thought, personally, that eel did same.

A Wairewa Maori whom the collector met at Taumutu differed from last man's view and said eels spawn. He had seen the hao spawn. It crawled over the sand and if the sea was smooth lets its spawn go and you will see the surface of the water oily. Most fish spawn in July but the eel in January February March to May according to kind and condition. The horihori-wai (its old name, now called 'tuna-Pakeha' – the silver eel) and the tuna-kai-noke comes in January. The 'stockwhip' (weko) and the Tunaheke in February. The tunatai and tunahau in March. The mairehe and the big eels in April and May. The tunahau is faster than the tunatai and if it gets a fright can 'scoot' along very fast on surface of the water. The kaio is the little red curly things – a sort of worm – found in eels. The pua is a fatty roe – not like sago. The eel goes over the bank into the sea and leaves the pua on sea. When it returns to the lake its skin is white after its sea-bathing. He had opened hundreds and never yet found a bag with young in it. He had opened about two thousand seven hundred last season and never found one. [Previous informant said he had seen one or two but it was so rare he had offered one pound and a bottle of whisky to anyone lucky enough to get such an eel. H.B.] From this he concluded breeding was from oily pua he had seen, but he knew the old people said it was from bag. Eels can spawn in freshwater too. In old days a man securing a good bag of eels carried them home in kawe (shoulder straps of flax). In 1903 when up the Selwyn River with some mates he had got a monster eel in a blind creek. He speared it through both ears and gave a big heave [he is a big, powerful man. H.B.] on to bank. The eel was short and thick, its length would be about five foot six inches but it was of enormous girth. He took it to a woolshed near by and the runholder weighed it for him. Its weight was fifty seven and a half pounds. It was a horepara eel and as he had to leave just then his mates ate it. He had always regretted he had not taken it to Christchurch (Museum or private person) and sold it as a curiosity or monstrosity. [The collector thinks the heaviest eel he has heard of was one of one hundred and six pounds caught in 1863 at Queenstown and taken to Dunedin. H.B.] The eel-drain or channel (awa) at Wairewa and Okiri (Little River) is boarded forming a permanent rauiri (reserve). [The collector is to see it next trip. H.B.] In the heke the eels were usually caught by kohao net, the mouth (kaututu) being of pirita (supplejack) or akatea (vine). You could use two of these kohaos (on poles) to do a drain and empty the catch into a parua (hole) to let die. Don't patu (kill or hit) them as bruises the flesh, but touch the tail with a knife and it bleeds away – a painless and a cleanly death. The kanakana (or piharau) goes up falls by plaiting itself up. Some hold on to rocks with their sucker mouths and others mount higher and hold on and so on till whole face of rock is covered and then remainder worked their way up this living ladder by twisting and plaiting. The pepehi is one way of catching the kanakana. It is done by placing bundles of fern in the sides of rivers and the kanakana plait themselves into it and when it is lifted out they are caught, or they can be pulled off by inserting the hand among them.

One Maori said the people used to go by stars, puaka in particular, for eeling. As for any Maori dying of a surfeit of lampreys [See Tregear's [[1904]] *Maori Race*. H.B.] he did not think it was possible. He had known a Maori who could eat twentyfour big kanakana at one meal. He would eat more than rest at table put together. He was a very big man and had a big mouth. He would take six of the lampreys in his hand at a time (like a bundle of leeks) and chew away with his strong teeth and enjoy them. This was at Waikanae (in North Island), and the repasts never seemed to do him any harm.

Add to Eels and Eeling

[Newspaper clipping] November 1920. 'Mystery of the eels. The mystery of the eels was referred to by the president of the British Association (Dr William A. Herdman, Professor of Oceanography at Liverpool University). The eels, he said, live and feed and grow under our eyes without reproducing their kind – no spawning eel has ever been seen. After living for years in immaturity, at last near the end of their lives, the large male and female yellow eels undergo a change in appearance and in nature. They acquire a silvery colour and their eyes enlarge, and in this bridal attire they begin the long journey which ends in maturity, reproduction and death. From all the fresh waters they migrate in the autumn to the coast, from the inshore seas to the open ocean, and still westward and south to the mid-Atlantic, and we know not how much further – for the exact locality and manner of spawning has still to be discovered.'

The collector read the above newspaper clipping to a number of Maoris and, needless to add, they were much interested, for it is a question they debate among themselves. One middle-aged man said that while he and one or two other Maoris were cleaning out a spring up under the summit of Monument Hill (so-called from its formation) they found a small eel, a horihoriwai or 'silver belly', in it. They were surprised to find an eel there four hundred yards above the creek and with precipitous rocky faces all around. As a tribute to its 'pluck' (in getting there) they put it back in the water. He had seen the white spawn stuff underneath hao eels but he could not speak for other kinds. All the same he was in favor of the theory of spawning as against that of propagation of young eels alive from old eels. Another Maori said he had seen a mairehe eel thirty five pounds weight caught near site of old Kaiapoi Pa. It was the biggest eel he knew about. Some people said it took two years for an eel to grow to eighteen or twenty pounds but he considered it would take far longer. He had caught eels when netting in saltwater at the mouth of Ashley River. Some years ago the Honourable James Carroll gave a very fine address on eels to the members of the Kaiapoi Debating Club (Maori).

The Tuahiwi Maori who gave me so much information about eels on a former trip said the white stuff found in eels was not hua or spawn but was a white fat or substance that turned into the reddish-colored 'pins' which emerge alive from the parent like young sharks do. The little ones in conger eels are not reddish but white. The white stuff in eels is not found in the windbag but in paunch. All the same he could not tell a male from a female eel. He had seen the young inside the horepara eel and he considered the hao would be the same but he could not say as to the lamprey or kanakana. The old eels did not die when they spawned but returned up the rivers. They were very long-lived and of very slow growth, taking years to reach any considerable size. The biggest eel he had seen personally was one of twenty eight pounds weight.

A Little River Maori who has devoted much time to the catching (and also the habits) of eels differs from the opinion just quoted. He has opened thousands of eels and never found the young in any one of this large number. He reckoned they deposited their spawn and he would argue that point with anyone. All breeding eels come down to the saltwater, but you would find hardly any roe in the big eels such as the horepara and matamoi – perhaps they were males. In the other eels the spawn is like fat and covers the paunch and is called pua-o-te-tuna. The eels turn a whitey color after they spawn – probably the absence of the roe and the action of the saltwater do this to them. After they spawn and have a taste of the sea they come into the grass and eat worms and in the creeks eat paraki, kokopu and (now) frogs. They sleep in winter although he had seen the horepara bite in July. He had never found a dead eel.

An old dame who has often caught the kanakana (lamprey) said they took a run up the rivers in Spring and return back to the sea to spawn. The young ones are known as wairaki or kanakana-wairaki and she reckoned they came forth from parent fish alive. If the Ohapi River bar was closed the young kanakana could be found in the sand.

An old man referred to the fact that eels were dried on lines, or tirewa made of manuka or other suitable poles. An uhi or shelter made of patiti (tussock) wiwi (rushes) or flax would be erected over them to keep the dew of nights or rain off them. This uhi was removed on fine days, he concluded. When on his recent trip the collector visited the awa-tuna at the broad sand-bar which separates end of Wairewa (Lake Forsyth) from the sea. Leaving his bike at Birdling's Flat siding he took his way over the stony, sparsely-grassed, tumatakuru-covered flat, amid startled sheep and vagrant seabirds until he arrived at the place. The lake carried plenty of waterfowl, principally black swans, ducks and pukaki. The first thing that attracted notice was a framework of stout manuka ⌐┬─┐ on which to hang the captured eels. There were two short blind canals leading into the sand for about ten yards or so. At mouth of each was set a sheet of galvanised iron boarded at top and bottom. A stake ran into the centre of the awa and the sheet was attached to this. The sheet evidently was placed lengthwise in stream so that eels could pass on both sides and then when the eelers decided, it could be swivelled round across mouth and so block exit while the trapped eels would be scooped out to 'terra firma'. A hoop of fencing wire to which was attached a kohao of wire-netting lay battered, derelict, and half-buried in sand by the side of one of the awa. The collector could see no trace of the awa made of wood he had been told about and came to the conclusion that the stake and wooden sides of sheet of corrugated iron were meant. These sheets are a simple, but no doubt highly effective, expedient to pen the eels up when they are making their annual heke to the ocean.

A Maori said to me: 'Waikakahi was a great place for eels, and so was Wairewa, but Akaroa was the greatest place of the Maori in the olden days. It was noted for its fish.'

SHELLFISH AND CRABS

*The principal informant said there was not many tio (oysters) round Banks' Peninsula, but a lot of pawa, kuku, tuaki, pupu, toritori, kopakopa, karuru, taiwhatiwhati roroa and other shellfish, as well as kaio. The pawa was eaten raw after being soaked in freshwater; it was also boiled and dried.** It is beaten soft and boiled in oil now as a delicacy. The kuku [This is simply the North Island name for southern pipi. H.B.] was boiled and the meat extracted in old days and it was strung (tuitui) on an aho (line) and dried. It was also soaked in fresh water and eaten raw. It is now stewed but he prefers the old way. The roroa and tuaki were eaten raw after freshwater soaking, but are now boiled. The taiwhatiwhati is found plentifully on Oruapaeroa (New Brighton) beach and is boiled. *It once used to be roasted in embers, as well as all the other shellfish. Mataitai is the salty taste of fish or shellfish when from the sea and the ancient Maori always tried to get rid of this, hence the soaking in fresh water.** The kaio [See Murihiku Notes, H.B.] was not plentiful as a rule but some grew big like those in the South. When found they are boiled and eaten even to this day.

A Rapaki Maori said there were two kinds of oysters — tio-kohatu (rock oysters) and tio-pati (mud oysters). The latter drifted ashore sometimes but the former are the sweeter although not so big as the latter. They were eaten raw and could be roasted also as well as pipi, tuaki, karuru, etc., by being placed in rows on hot embers. Put karehu (embers) on top and they are soon done. The pawa was soaked in freshwater for two days and eaten raw. It could be roasted also but this was not so often done. The koura-waitai or sea crawfish boiled red as is commonly known but the koura-waimaori (inland crawfish) although smaller and blacker comes red also. The sea ones when caught are put in fresh water (waimaori) for some days and in the old times were put in umu or eaten raw, but now they are boiled. It was caught on the rocks by hand or in a trap (poraka) made of flax. This was just a flax net shaped and made all of flax with a mouth of supplejack and with a bait inside. Pakeha twine is no good to make this trap and the white fishermen come to the Maoris to get them to make flax ones, frankly admitting that the poraka-Maori is better than the poraka-Pakeha. The freshwater koura are caught by hand and are usually treated the same as their sea-brethren – viz. eaten raw, roasted, or put in the umu. Koura are all sweet, but the Waimaori ones are sweeter than the Waitai ones he considered.

Crabs were called papaka and the little ones seen on the shore are known as papaka-kokoriki. The kakahi-wai-maori (freshwater mussels) are as good as the kakahi-wai-tai and can be found a long way inland. They could be eaten raw or roasted in the karehu (embers). This informant's advice to collector was that if he put pipi, or other shellfish, in an umu not to leave them too long.

Speaking to a Rapaki matron about shells she said the shellfish the collector called koruru (as in the South) she had always heard spoken of as kar-uru. [She gave the collector the names of a number of shells which he labelled and which will be given in with these notes. H.B.] The big crab, the papaka, was eatable and she was fond of them. The papaka-tuatini has a white shell with dots on it but she quite forgot the name of the little crab. [Given above 'kokoriki'. H.B.]

A Tuahiwi Maori said he used to ruku (dive) for pawa and koura. The latter was caught by a head to tail grasp to avoid the pricks, but once when he was ruku-koura he pricked his hand badly and painfully through grabbing a big crayfish the other way and it was a lesson to him.

Two of the shells named by 'a Rapaki matron' and labelled in Māori by Beattie. Exterior views: (top) tuaki, Rāpaki, Temuka, *Protothaca crassicosta* (Deshayes, 1835), D63.23; (bottom) tuaki, Rāpaki, *Ruditapes largillierti* (Philippi, 1848), D63.24.
Tūhura Otago Museum Collection; scientific identifications by Graeme Mason.

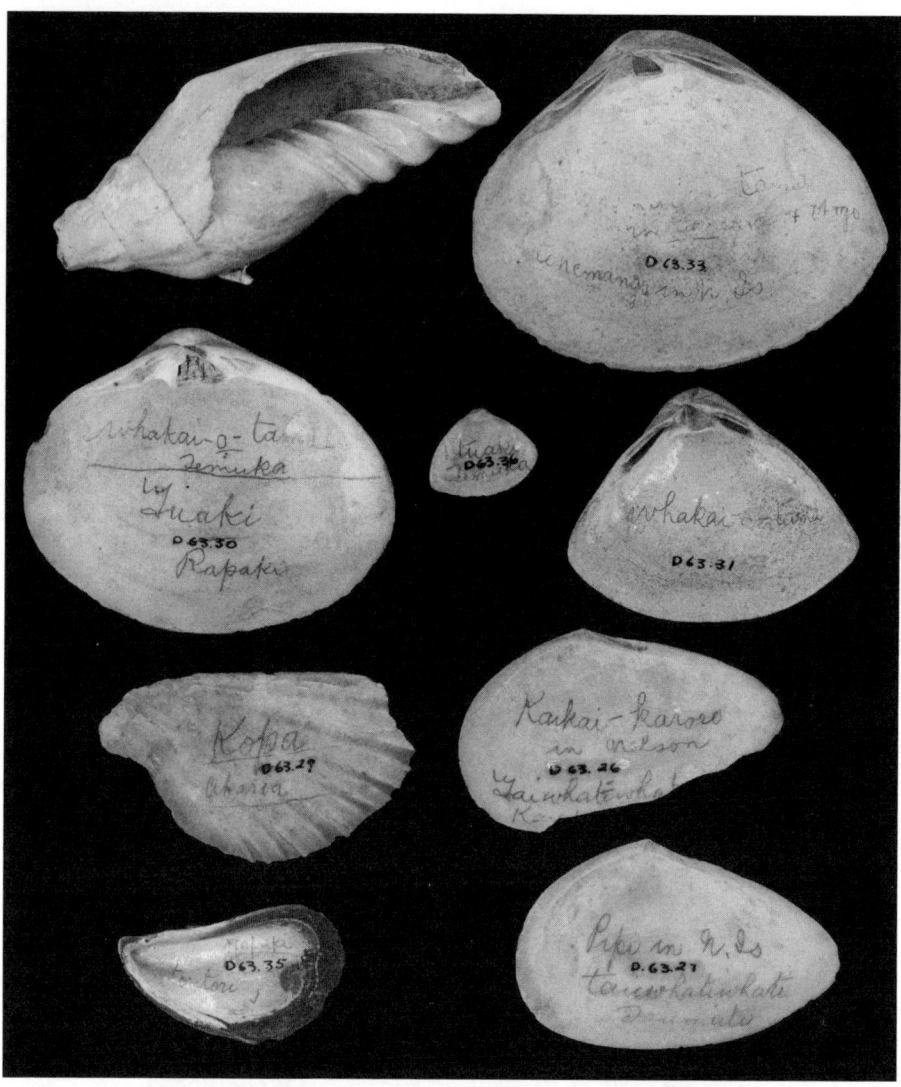

Interior views of shells labelled by Beattie, reading left to right, top to bottom: *Alcithoe swainsoni* (Marwick, 1926), D63.38; whakai-a-tama in Nelson and Otago, tohemango in North Island, *Mactra murchisoni* (Deshayes, 1854), D63.33; whakai-o-tama, Temuka, tuaki, Rāpaki, *Mactra ovata* (Gray, 1843), D63.30; tuaki, Temuka, *Spisula aequilateralis* (Deshayes, 1854), D63.36; whakai-o-tama, *Spisula aequilateralis* (Deshayes, 1854), D63.31; kopa, Akaroa, *Pecten novaezelandiae* (Reeve, 1853), D63.29; kaikai-karoro in Nelson, taiwhatiwhati, Kaiapoi[?], *Tellina gaimardi* (Iredale, 1915), D63.26; toritori, Rāpaki, *Mytilus edulis* (Linnaeus, 1758), D63.35; pipi in North Island, taiwhatiwhati, Taumutu, *Tellina gaimardi* (Iredale, 1915), D63.27. Tūhura Otago Museum; scientific identifications by Graeme Mason.

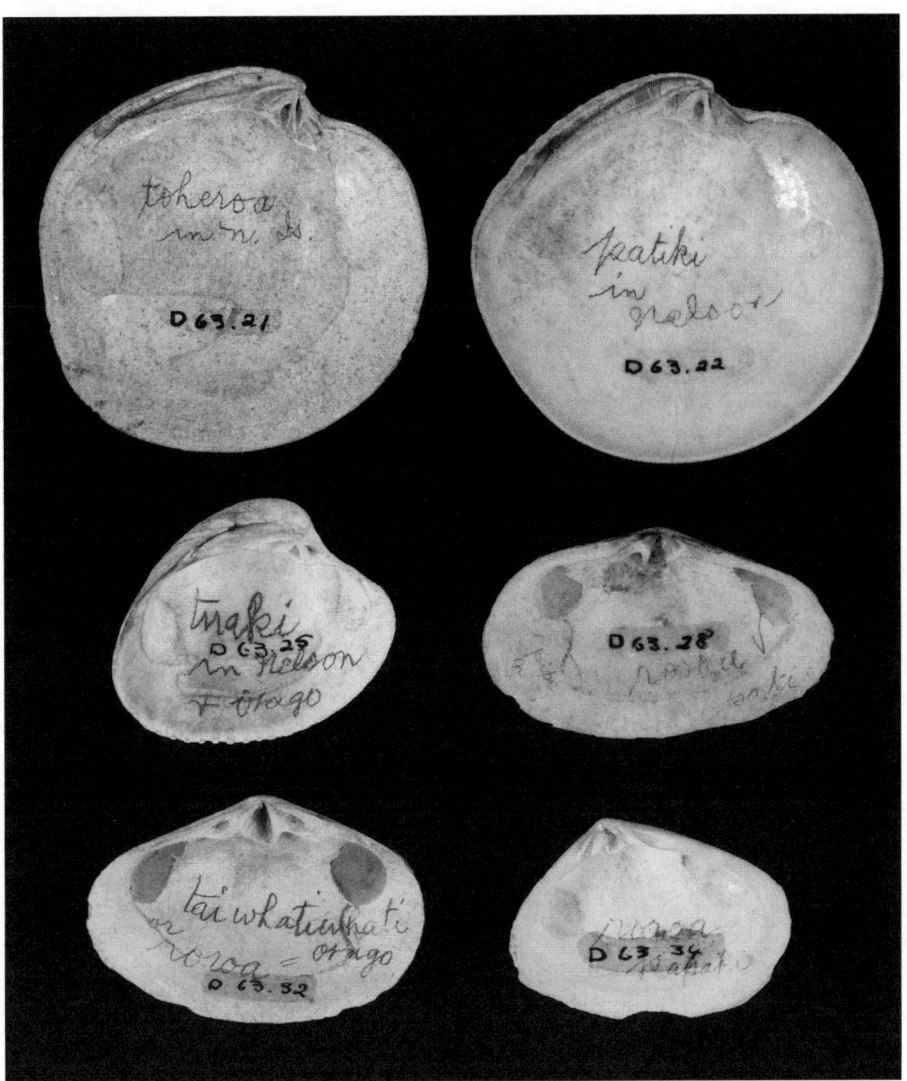

Interior views of shells labelled by Beattie, reading left to right, top to bottom: toheroa in North Island, *Dosinia anus* (Philippi, 1848), D63.21; patiki in Nelson, *Dosinia anus* (Philippi, 1848), D63.22; tuaki, Rāpaki and Temuka, *Chione stutchburyi* (Wood, 1828), D63.25; roroa, Rāpaki, pipi, North Island, *Paphies australis* (Gmelin, 1790), D63.28; taiwhatiwhati or roroa = Otago, *Paphies australis* (Gmelin, 1790), D63.32; roroa, Rāpaki, *Paphies donacina* (Spengler, 1793), D63.34. Tūhura Otago Museum; scientific identifications by Graeme Mason.

The collector asked the principal informant if he had ever heard of the Canterbury Maoris using the rou-kakahi (or rake to rake in mussels in lakes or streams). He had not heard of such a thing and further added that the kakahi had never been extensively eaten in the South Island and what quantity was eaten was gathered by hand.

Add to Shellfish and Crabs

This subject scarcely came up when with the principal informant but he said he had never heard any name particularly for the bone or wood needles used to pick shellfish (the pupu) out of the shells. The 'Maori pin' was called au and this was a general name. As for the koura it was from the saltwater and did not live in fresh water. The people had got the plan from the North Island and soak koura in creeks for some days. There was no need to tie them as they were dead. They get soft in the creek and could be eaten raw or *could be cooked in the kapa-maori as the owner wished. The kaio was cut with a knife** and soaked in the fresh-water if got fresh; but if it was two or three days old when *got it was put in the freshwater without cutting. It was eaten raw but he had seen** Pakehas boil and stew them. [See Murihiku Notes re kaio, H.B.]

An intelligent middle-aged Maori said the kaio or 'sea nut' was cut open, then soaked in freshwater and eaten raw. It tasted like oysters and he could recommend Pakehas to use vinegar with the kaio – they were very good. The koura was also soaked in fresh water before eating. The only shellfish that was picked out with a pin that he knew was the pupu – it was probably a wood or bone picker but he did not know its name. There were a number of kinds of karuru – it was like a big pupu – but he did not know the different names of them. The kakihi is a shellfish like the pawa only small. It adheres to the rocks in the same manner – if you touch it it fastens on tight so pull it off suddenly or you will have to work it off with a knife. The shell is silvery inside and stone color outside. The whetiki is a small pupu – its shell is lighter colored than the pupu. The pipi and the kuku are the same. The toritori and pukanikani forms of pipi are found on Banks Peninsula. A fan-shaped shellfish [new to the collector and which his Nelson and Otago informants did not know as it was unfamiliar to them. H.B.] was identified as kopa. It is found on the Peninsula and although its contents are small they are good eating. The roroa has a hinge at the side; the taiwhatiwhati is rounder and bigger. My informant had never heard of the tupehukura [found in Murihiku. H.B.] but a very big pipi which he had seen at Akaroa is called pati. The tuaki is a cockle with a fluted shell; the plain smooth cockle is called tetehe. [A new name to me; as also is pati – perhaps the latter is a form of the hoe-moana described in Murihiku Notes. H.B.] The rori is a form of pawa without a shell – it adheres to the rocks and is not eaten in Canterbury [nor in Otago. H.B.]. The kina or 'sea-egg' was soaked for three days in freshwater and was eaten raw, but can be roasted or boiled now. My informant concluded by saying that the seahorse was not eaten – he did not know its Maori name; nor the names of ordinary shells.

A woman stated that the kaio was washed ashore, picked up, cut open, soaked in fresh water, and eaten raw. A man showed me some big fossil shells he had picked up in the Southern Alps. He added that up the Rakaia Gorge in a cliff could be seen the fossilised skeleton of a fish ninety feet long.

*The principal informant said that to catch crayfish the taruke was like a basket or rat cage with a bait inside and the koura could not get out so that it could be left a long time. The poraka was made of supplejack on top, round shape mouth with flax net below.** Four stones, one at each corner, were used as sinkers and the poraka would be pulled up in half hour. A bait of paua would be tied in centre and as the crayfish are feasting at this, the poraka is hauled up like a bucket with perhaps forty koura in it. The mouth of the net does not close.

A Peninsula Maori mentioned four shellfish to the collector and these were kokoto, whetiko, karuru and tuangi.

Add to Shellfish

A woman told the collector she vaguely remembered the old people telling a story about the kakahi and kakihi kinds of shellfish. She thought the karoro (seagull) had something to do with it but might be able to pick the story up somewhere. The collector tried a number of his informants but without success until he met the mine of information [See Murihiku Notes, H.B.]. An old Tuahiwi Maori said he had never heard the folk-tale. The kakahi is found in inland streams and the kakihi by the sea but he knew no yarns about them except that a representation of Maui's fishing-line is said to be curled up in the kakihi [See Mythology Murihiku Section, H.B.]. A Maori in speaking to the collector mentioned that toheroa and tohemango were names in different parts of the North Island for the same shellfish, but he failed to supply the South Island equivalent for name.

The collector was told at Akaroa that the ancient people there ate pauua, pupu, kuku (this was said to be the main name for mussels), tuaki, pipi, tio, roroa, toretore, kopakopa, kakihi, rori, toitoi, whetiko, kakahi and other shellfish. In addition they ate such sea-products as the kaio, kotoremoana, kina, and patakaroa, etc. The patangaroa is a sort of a starfish with very long yellow legs and it could be cooked. The informant forgot the name of the starfish itself but kina is the sea-egg. The kotoremoana is striped and is reddish inside. If touched it draws itself up together, hence its name. In regard to kuku being general name for shellfish informant's grandfather used to say 'Tikina e kuku' (Fetch shellfish) not 'Tikina e pipi'. She could not say if rori was eaten as she never saw it eaten. The kopakopa is purplish colored and ridgy, while the whetiko is the 'pennywinkle' and feeds on the sand. They used to be placed in packets and sold at Lyttelton; they were got in great quantities. The hoemoana is at Akaroa called pati, or kukupati, or patikuku, as it lives and grows among the green slimy weed called pati. She found one with small pearls (which she showed to collector) in it. An old man said there was no such shellfish as toheroa in South Island.

SHARKS AND BIG FISH

*Kupeka from ten to fifteen chains long (said the principal informant) were once used to catch sharks – karaerae and tutahuna [[Further down paragraph is tutauna, which appears to be the same creature. Both forms occur in the Nelson volume.]] (this is a small form of former shark) and huarau. The ururoa, a strong fighting 'fish', was caught on fishing lines.** The root of the manuka made a hook 'strong enough to hold a whale' and a bait was tied to it. *Taniwha is a big shark, so is the kaupane and another (whose name he forgot) with a big head, could be caught with lines.** The taniwha teeth made earrings, makotaniwha. The sharks, opened and split (pawhera) were hung up to dry; or you could hang them up with offal out but not split (puku). The North Island folk especially like this as it has 'a nice smell'. Here (Canterbury) after being split and dried the shark flesh was eaten without cooking. Mango is a general name for sharks and mango-maroke = dried shark. In November on the springtide at Rapaki the people used to get numerous karaerae and tutauna but not now. The huarau gets very fat but not much used. Nets were used for these sharks at the springtide in each month of November December January February and March. It was hard on nets and some got 'played out' quickly but some would survive and be rolled up and 'carried forward to next season'. Now the young men wait till the young sharks come into shallow bays and spear them with matarau (eel spears) or gorse-knives, and they get enough for a change of food. Shark oil was got from the ate (livers) which were cut out and the surrounding offal scraped off. Then the stomach of the shark was cleaned out and the liver was put inside it and hung on a whata for some weeks in the sun and the oil was 'burnt out' or sweated from the liver into the 'guts' of the sharks. In three weeks boil or cook the lot and the oil comes out readily. The oil can be eaten with potatoes by those who like a tasty dish of strong flavor, or it can be put in a basin with a wick in it as it burns well and good. In the old days it was used to mix with red maukoroa clay to form kokowai or red paint.

A Rapaki Maori said that the karaerae was the only shark he knew that was eaten in old days round Lyttelton Harbor. It was not found in the South he thought. It is two or three feet long, the size of a good hapuku. It was sun-dried (tauraki) and stored and eaten as required. It was called makoo when dried – indeed, mako-karaerae was its full name. Other sharks are too greasy so it was only one that was dried. They are now killed with gorse knives as they swarm into shallow water inshore in January and February. The repe or elephant fish is a sort of shark which in the 'War Days' scarcity of fish (and since) is sold in the shops as 'white fish'. It is good eating [but it amuses my Maori friends to think the Pakeha is now eating under a fictitious name food he had scorned the Maori for eating. H.B.]. It has a skin like a makaa (barracouta) and a trunk like unto an elephant's. These were the only two edible sharks to be found in Lyttelton Harbor, the ururoa being a big shark out in the open sea. He did not know the names of other kinds of sharks.

Shark oil (hinu-mako) is very rich and the Pakeha now seeks it to rub on 'lousy' cattle. He also used porpoise oil (if he can get it) for the same, or similar, purposes.

The collector asked the principal informant what he called the porpoise and he answered popoti. The collector said terehu and he instantly agreed that was right Maori name. [His use of Pakeha-Maori name, however, shows the insidious corruption of language going on when one so particular about correct language is caught napping. H.B.] He further added that paikea was a general name 'for all big fish which escape from the deep sea'.

SEALS AND SEALING

*The principal informant said the Canterbury natives used to kill seals on Banks Peninsula, notably round Akaroa. The seals were killed with clubs (patu) made of manuka or kohai as a rule.** The skin of the seal was not used by the ancient Maoris and the mammals were cooked in their skins. *The pakake and popoiakore were the kinds found round Akaroa. The fat of the seal was good food and being oily was as good as malt extract for colds.** Babies would be given a piece of seal fat (cooked) to suck as a medicine. *When the Christchurch Exhibition was held (about 1907) the Committee asked him about seals but he knew so little about them that he considered the Committee would have to provide saltwater for those got for the exhibition. A Pakeha knew more and the seals sported in fresh water for months. After the exhibition was over the seals were let go in the sea and provided amusement for visitors to New Brighton and Sumner for some weeks until they betook themselves out to sea.**

A Rapaki Maori said he did not know about the industry of sealing but pakake came up on the sands and were killed by being hit on the ihu (nose) with a club of wood or bone. It was cut up, put in umu to cook, and eaten. The flesh kept a long time and was not so rich as one would think. It is dark flesh and tastes something like the titi – very nice. The popoti [This is word porpoise Maorified. H.B.] was harpooned sometimes but he did not think it was eaten. He did not know the names for the different whales the word 'wera' (whale) covering the lot. It was sometimes washed ashore and he never heard of its being eaten as there was abundance of hapuku, etc., to eat. When the whalers were 'trying-out' the Maoris would eat a little of the flesh of newly-killed 'fish' but this was 'only as a taste – not as a practice'.

One old man told the collector he remembered when a boy seeing whares illuminated by whale oil with a 'wick' burning in it – a pakeha idea. Another in mentioning (casually) fishhooks said that ones made of whalebone were called 'iwi-wera-matau' – they were not called matau-paraoa as paraoa was a weapon. [This distinction between whalebone used for weapons and other purposes is new to me – doubtful. H.B.]

SECTION XVII

ORNITHOLOGY

Manu or Birds — Kaha or Snares — Pihere or Nooses — Karumahaka or Snares — Tuke or Bird-perch-trap — Paruru or Catching Woodhens — Turutu or Imi-tating Woodhens — Whakapepe or Calling Birds — Aru or Driving Ducks — Kotuku or White Herons—Koau or Shags — Korora or Penguins — Pipiwharauroa or Shining Cuckoos — Makomako or Bellbirds — Kakariki or Parrokeets — Parera or Ducks — Maunu or Moulting Birds — Whakataki or Calling Birds — Mokai or Decoy Birds — etc.

BIRDS AND BIRD-CATCHING

*The principal informant said the kotuku (heron) used to come round once a year and he thought it flew from other countries. He whakatauki (a proverb) about it was 'Kotuku rerenga tahi' (the heron of one flight) referring to the infrequency of its appearances. The pipiwharauroa was not a New Zealand bird but flew across from the islands. It flies across every year when it is time to sow the kumera, the potato and the pohata seeds. When you heard its kowhio (whistle) you knew it was time to start planting. The karoro was always here – it never went away. These birds (seagulls) sing out every morning. The torea (redbill) whistles 'torea' in great style at certain times. He had seen a pipiwharauroa *egg* in a riroriro's nest once and wondered how it got there. This nest is the only one of its kind in New Zealand. [It has a sort of porch. H.B.] but he never heard any name for it but kohanga (nest) [Kohaka further South. H.B.]. He thought the cuckoo *egg* had perhaps been laid in the warbler's nest before the latter bird had put the roof on its nest – that was his conclusion.** Ringeyes are now called titiripounamu but this name rightly belongs to a very diminutive green bird, formerly fairly common in the bush. Popokotea is the native canary, now very rare. *The kakaruai (robin) is a fair-sized bird and very easily killed but he never heard it was caught especially by olden Maoris. It lives on insects, worms and grubs, etc., and its flesh would not be very choice nor comparable to that of larger birds which fed on honey, and on berries principally. **He had never heard how the Maoris caught the koka (native crow) or the tieke [often called 'the jack' by young Maoris as Tieke is southern form of pakeha name Jack. H.B.] (saddleback) but he presumed they did so. *Birds were usually called after their cry or whistle. In regard to edible birds the weka (which was usually got in March and April), the pigeon, and the tui boiled down in their fat very well but the kaka did not preserve near so well. The tui, kaka and pigeon were not opened out (if eaten right away) but were put in the umu 'guts and all'. The kaka has a crop like the fowl, but the pigeon is not like that, so the Maori ate all, including the berries inside. The berries were not chewed but simply swallowed and although some might taste bitter they never seemed to harm the eater. You caught the tui at one pool and the pigeon at another.** There were two differing seasons for them. In the winter the birds were eating fruit and in summer drinking water, and they could be caught accordingly. *Snares called kaha were set, the nooses being karumahanga. The kaha had steps on it and nooses hung all round and as bird drinks its head goes through a noose and it is caught.** The birder would go in afternoon and get the quarry. *You could also make mahanga up in trees and catch birds.** Select trees with good fruit (huareka) and make arawhata Gadders) up to snares. You could make snares another way also in the trees. *Build a tutu, or stage, up in rimu, kahikatea or totara trees and sit on it with pole to which is attached tuke snare. When bird caught you pull pole down and reset snare. You also have a mokai (tame bird) to lure wild birds. This is for kakas and another way to catch them is the pouwhenua method with a tuke from under a 'maimai' near the ground. A variation of this was maukuku where the hands were covered with leaves to deceive the bird and when it settled on stick (called by the mokai) one of these camouflaged fists caught its legs. The kaka was the only bird to catch by this pouwhenua style.** In summer you used the kaha snare to get tuis and pigeons at drinking pools. In re catching tuis with clusters of piripiri (bidibidi) he fancied he had heard of this dodge being used in the North Island. Down here he had heard of birds being clubbed with poles in winter. Even in summer you could hit some birds from a pae (rail) with sticks. *You called (whakapepe) the tui by holding patete leaf in mouth and when they settled on pae you clubbed them with a stick. The makomako (bellbird) could be killed the same way. (This bird was sometimes called koparapara as in South). The kakariki (parrokeet) was eaten and could be killed on the pae like the tui and makomako.** The hunter would hide in a ponga house, or shelter made of leaves of ponga (ferntree) with a mokai (pet bird) to call others and he would sweep the pae or perch when required. This bird ate the flower of the puha (bush thistle) and while it was intent on this the wily Maori dropped a kakaho snare over its head as it was eating. *This snare was made of a long kakaho reed the flexible end of which was utilised to make a suitable running loop,** but the pae was a better method to secure big results. It could be put in a kapa maori [this word, 'kopa' in dictionary, he often used for an 'umu', pronouncing it as koppa (like copper) and adding 'maori' after it. I have never heard it before – is it genuine or merely pakeha-Maori lingo like kohua for 'go-ashore', the whaler's cooking pot. H.B.] but usually was cooked kohiku fashion in a rapa (split stick) as was the custom of roasting small birds. *The pioioi (lark) was eaten although the Maori did not like birds that ate worms, etc., so much. The children used to drive these larks towards a kaha snare and when bird saw** opening it would go through and be caught by neck. The kaha was adapted to bird's size and was made on its tracks. The children would aru or drive it towards the snare and the bird walked into the mahanga. He did not know the koreke (or quail) but perhaps it was caught in same way in the days when it existed. *The pakura, which was called pukeko in the North Island, was a big swamp bird. When there was a strong wind blowing from north west or south west, either dry or with rain would do, the people beat the swamps and drove these birds, which flew against the wind. After half-hour or so it gets tired and drops. It is a good runner but there were people waiting, and dogs too, and many were secured. It could also be caught in kaha snares. It was not nearly so much eaten as some other birds – it was not highly esteemed as it was too stringy and very bony. Its feathers, although bright, were not much used. The pakura was the mokai bird of Mahuika [see Mythology section, H.B.]. The koukou, or rurukoukou (morepork) was a bird he knew little about. In daytime they hid in the darkest places – in ponga and in thick bush, but at night they sallied forth to catch moths and bats flying about and, since the pakeha came, mice on the ground. He did not think they caught the kiore (rat) in the olden days, as it would be too strong for them. The mata (fernbird) was a bird in the swamp-growth which could run very fast through the pukio (niggerheads). It called out a good deal. The totokipio (dabchick or diver) was sometimes caught in the creeks – it didn't fly. He did not know much about them as it was not much sought after, although eaten. The cranky flight of the titakataka or titaiwaka (fantail) was caused by Maui [see Mythology Section, H.B.].** The kakapo was one of the finest birds in New Zealand. If you travel through bush you cannot see the bird but its mark is visible in bits of gnawed fernroot. Where such evidences exist man can find the best of fernroot near. The birds eat the inside of the aruhe and leave the stringy portions. The kakapo and the kiwi live only in the 'back country' and he never heard the old people say how they were caught but they had remarked about the fernroot. The kiwi was not very good to eat as its skin was thick and its flesh very tough, but the kakapo was good to eat, but was unfortunately scarce. There were a lot of kiwi in North Island, but he thought the kakapo was mainly on this island.

*The putakitaki (paradise duck) was a good edible bird. Its big feathers drop from December–January to March and while moulting (maunu) it was slaughtered. On Lake Ellesmere the Maori in canoes drove the birds right round the lake. Each kaika facing the lake made fences into the lake like sheepyards and the birds (which cannot fly) were driven into these and the gate shut. Those which did not go in were driven along to next fencing (taiepa or raihe) [Tregear's [[1891]] *Dictionary* gives raihi as a pen or small enclosure. H.B.] and 'so many cut off like sheep when yarding' said narrator. And so on right round the lake so that each kainga would get its respective share. When the last one was served the remainder of the birds were let go, while the occupants of the canoes and dug-outs came ashore and joined in clubbing the birds or 'screwing their necks like fowls are done now.' The game is then put in the 'koppa-maori' to cook. Some took the bones out to cook and put in ipu to preserve.** If wanted to eat them at once they were put in umu as it was not usual to kohiku them – they were not fat enough probably. *The parera (grey duck), a blue bird called kukupako (black teal), the tataa (brown duck or shoveller?) and the pateke (teal) also moult and were all caught in the same way at the same time. These were the kinds of ducks on Ellesmere.**

An old Maori at Rapaki also gave particulars about some of the birds. Haere tao te wero was to go birdspearing. Your spear might be an eighteen foot length of manuka, akeake or goai hardened in the fire. Sometimes a tara (point) of bone was tied on – there were no barbs. It was said a plain wood point would pierce into bird better than a bone one. The spear was called tao and you speared kuku (also sometimes called kereru), kaka, tui and other birds. You aimed at the chest or the best place you could and if you had any strength the spear would go through. Another spear was made of pieces (weheka) joined (tuhono) together. It was made of mako wood which was not heavy. He once saw one at Koukourarata (Port Levy). One of the simplest ways to get birds is to go into the bush and make a 'maimai' and sit on the ground under it and whistle (kowhio or whakapi) or call on a leaf (whakapepe) and bring the tuis (some call them koko), and mako-mako and other birds to settle on a horizontal whakapae (perch) you have fixed up. Then hakuku (sweep) the whakapae with a rakau (stick) called a huakau and gather up the slain birds. You could not whakapi (call) the kuku, but you could the kaka. The kuku is sometimes caught with karu-mahaka (snares) set round its drinking place and you can also catch the tui the same way. [He made a loop or two to show the collector and these will be submitted with these notes. H.B.] [The knots holding these loops he called tuhono and said they were made in the proper old style. H.B.] To catch kaka with tuke build a maimai with four pou (posts) sticking up and to each pou affix a tuke. Tie (houia) the tuke to a pou and run the string through a koroputa (hole). When the birds settle pull the string tight and it holds them tight to the post. Hang on to string or bird will get away, untie the fastening, secure bird and replace the tuke. The bush weka was easily caught with two sticks and a red rag. The longer one has a karu-mahaka (noose) on it and the shorter one the rag. Turutu or call birds on a piece of flax and when they come paruru (shake) the rag and they are soon victims of their curiosity. Although there are several kinds of woodhen they only have one name – weka.

The kaha was the same snare as the karu-mahaka. Put a taura across a river to pou on each bank. If the water is wide a pou or two may be put in river to prevent taura from sagging too much in centre. To this taura are tied a large number of loops each being lashed on side by side. Then a double line (one on each side if the collector understood rightly) is run along about the middle of the loop and above where the duck's head will take the lower line of loop and pull it taut and strangle itself. This double line of thin flax is to prevent the loops going all over the place in wind. It is called pupuri-te-kaha. This snare will catch putakitaki, parera and other ducks, kamana (grebe) totokipio and other water birds. He had never heard of any bird called kurupatu nor of koreke (quail) but the matuku (bittern) could be caught with a moenu (bait) and hauled in. The bait was tied to the rushes and held a bone shaped like a hook and it held the bird. The Maori caught the kotuku (white heron) in the lakes around Banks Peninsula in the same way. The pakura or pukaki was caught in the ordinary way by hanging snares around its nesting place here and there and snares were suspended on sticks. Another way of catching the weka was to spread a net (mahaka) on the ground and when the bird stepped in pull the noose taut. You could also catch wekas with kuri (dogs). He had never heard how the old people caught the kiwi and kakapo. The putakitaki moults in November-December and while in this state (maunu) is driven ashore (arutia ki uta) as you can't catch them on water but on land they can be patua te rakau (hit with a stick) or caught by dogs. Then pluck them and into umu with them. The Maori could pluck the pukaki and it was easy enough if done right but the pakeha had not mastered the art [And usually skins the bird. H.B.]. The titi is a hard bird to pluck too. The feathers were useful for kakahu and bedding. The pioioi (lark) could be caught in nooses. They are tame birds and the children snared them. The kakariki (parrokeet) was easily caught. Take a puka-kaho and strip the fluff or tassel off and make a loop in the flexible end and slip over kakariki's head and pull. This was a pihere and sometimes you could make a harakeke (flax) loop at the end of a long stick and bag kuku, kaka, tui, etc. The kakariwai (robin) was a very quiet bird and you could kill it with a stick (patua te rakau or huakautia) or slip a pihere loop over its head. The tatariki (Native Canary) could be caught with the pihere also, but none of these small birds were much caught – there were plenty of fine big birds.

The only other Rapaki informant only mentioned birds briefly. The tara was a manuka spear to kill birds. You could get the point off the whai or stinger eel. Tara was really the name of the point; the spear itself was wero or timata. Long spears were joined in sections but he did not know the name of sections although he had seen one. You could use the short spear in all one wood and cut a barb in end. Different names for this barb were taratara and kaniwha. The pigeon (kereru or kuku) and the kaka were speared. The latter bird was also caught on a tuke snare. The tuke was a stick with a branch inclining out and up from its side like ⌴ and a string went through it and down to the 'maimai' beneath. The string was called katau, the loop mahaka, and the seat for the bird was named peka. A decoy bird (mokai) was employed to entice others on to perch where snare operated. These mokai birds were clever and could be trained to do many things and he once saw, and heard, a tame kaka play a koauau flute. Tamahua (Quail Island in Lyttelton Harbor) had titi burrows (rua) on it and thirty years ago the Maoris got thirty or forty birds yearly but now they get none as the pakeha spoilt the holes digging up rabbits (and titi also) but they can still get from fifty to one hundred titi near Akaroa. The pi (young birds) are pulled out of the ruas and hit on head. Being so few they are not preserved but are cooked and eaten at once.

Two Tuahiwi Maoris gave the following particulars about birds: Kiwi and kakapo could be caught on ranges at Oxford. Latter used to be hunted with dogs (kuri-maori) as it fossicked about on moonlit nights. The bird sings out at night. If the dog knows its job, well and good, if it doesn't the kakapo can kick like a horse and 'ka kiki te waewae' is a serious matter for the dog. The kiwi is a night bird too and is caught in atamarama (moonlight) with dogs. The kiwi and kakapo were mostly caught for their feathers and not so much for food.

Pakura or pukaki – Make a karumahaka of harareke (flax) and place a snare in its tracks in raupo and can catch a good few. The kuri (dog) was trained to grab pakuras in swamps. Dogs were also trained to catch maunu (moulting birds) at the edge of lakes and lagoons.

Matuku – One man said the Maoris did not catch the bittern much as they did not care for it. 'Kai-te-taki-te-matuku' was how they referred to its booming cry when it caught tuna (eels). It was not snared at all. The other man said the matuku was fat in November and December but he did not know much about it as it was only recently that he heard the olden Maoris ate it. He shot one as an experiment and found it quite momona (fat) and it tasted all right too.

Kotuku – This, said one informant, was really a seabird although found inland on the lakes. It could be snared in lagoon swamps with flax snares. Put a moenu (bait) of patiki or fish in centre of mahaka (snare) and the bird would be caught by legs. It dies at a certain time and if at sea it is washed ashore. When caught on back-country lagoons it was used for kai (food). The inaka, the whitebait's mother, was a favorite food of this bird and it patiently fished for them.

Takahe – This bird was too rare to catch; they never heard the old people speak of catching it. (My informants said name was 'takahe' not 'takahea' as Murihiku Natives maintain).

Koreke – Neither of my informants had heard of the New Zealand quail.

Ducks – The parera and the teal were caught in kaha (or karumahaka) snares in creeks, the whio in the mountains was also snared. The putakitaki was caught in snares until it moulted (maunu) in February. There was once plenty of these big ducks in the swamps round the Tutaipatu Lagoon at Woodend and the Maoris made mokihis and drove the maunu ashore to watchers hidden in wiwi (rushes) who promptly caught the birds and whakawhiri te kaki (wrung their necks). My informants said the only bird whose head or neck was bitten was the titi.

Wekas – These birds were called (whakapi or whakataki) the hunter using kakaha grass, ti leaf or young flax doubled. You could use the butt-end (putake) of flax-root not doubled. One informant saw a Kanaka in Westland (New Zealand) use a button and call successfully. He had seen old Maoris call the birds with flax-root but he could not do it himself. Turutu is imitating bird's call. The hunter twisted flax round finger and answered bird. This was done at night when using kuri (dogs). The dog was held in leash and let go at right moment, but others let their dogs go loose and chanced it. The bird if alarmed says ke-O, ke-O and warns others and this is called whakakeokeo. Once escaped dog or net the bird is shy and wary. My informants never heard of puhuka; male and female calling each other being called putahi. When they keep in pairs just before laying season they are called wharetaka and after laying purua. The male bird is toa and female uha although terms manutane and manuwahine were also used. The old people did not seem particular about this although it was not proper language to use. There were two distinct kinds of wekas – the smaller, darker, bush ones and the larger, greyer plains ones and their seasons varied a bit but they all had the one name – weka. The season for taking them ran from April to August – it was useless to take them at any other time. They were fit to take here at the end of April but further south the season was later. The plains ones were taken April May and June and the bush ones (their food was later) in June, July and August. The former lay their hua (eggs) in July and the latter in September. They did not know if both birds sat on nest but after hatching the male takes charge – perhaps he is in better condition to do so. From this on they are too poor and lean to catch till next winter. A lean bird is called pakikore or (more commonly) maiki. One bird out of one hundred clutches might be white or have white 'wing'. Such a bird was a toa-tuatahi and was a bad omen to hunter – it portended misfortune or death to a relative. The chief food of the bush wekas was tapuku, takapo, patotara, miki and mikimiki berries [See Plants section of these notes, H.B.]. Some berries were shaken down by the wind. The birds got very fat on the snowberries. The plains birds lived on insects, worms, karara – lizards, of which they are very fond, and my informants believed it was this food which made weka oil so rich and penetrating – and berries (mostly miki). Besides enticing the birds by turutu so that dogs could grab them the hunter took them by whakaki method. He had a long stick with a noose (pihere) and a shorter stick = paruru. On this paruru he tied any bright or noticeable object. A most effective thing was to tie on the pakihau (wing) of a defunct weka and the bird seeing this would think it a young bird being ill treated and advance. When its head was in the pihere the hunter gave a thrust forward of stick to tighten noose and then a jerk back but they never heard a name for this, nor had they heard of the bird being taken in a set snare. After the weka was caught its legs were doubled in (whakapeke) to body to keep body compact and to keep fat in place. The Maori idea was that if the legs were stretched out it stretched the fat in body and the bird becomes maiki and looks thin and ugly. Sometimes the heads were tied to flax (whakatautau) if there was no kete (basket) handy and this flax was strung round the shoulders and the man might return to camp with ten birds – five on each side to balance. They were generally carried in kete, however, and a strong man might carry from forty to eighty birds in a big, strongly-made kete securely fixed on and carried by shoulder straps (whakakawe).

The kahu (hawk) was a taipo bird. The Maoris would not eat it – Maui was in one perhaps. It is all string also. If a kahu sees a fire it circles over it, screeching 'piu', 'piu', in a loud voice. My informants had heard that at Patea and Wanganui (North Island) a goddess Tutakakino was in the form of a hawk and that the people at those places said the fantail was a taipo bird too; they had heard it was called pari there although titiwaka in rest of North Island and titakataka in South Island. It was said to be in the form of a goddess too.

The ruru (morepork) was a taipo bird but they had heard that some would eat it, although they knew no cases of this. One of my informants added he would tackle one as a novelty if he had the chance. Karoro (seagull) – Take the young birds from nest and patumanu (hit them on head) them. The tarapuke is smaller and is better eating – it is taken in the same manner. Torea (redbill or oyster-catcher) – They had never heard of its being caught by Maoris – it was not oily. Poaka is the black torea but some people called it kuaka. Neither of my informants had heard of the kamana (grebe) or totokipio (dabchick).

Korora is the little blue penguin while tawake is the big penguin. The korora breeds on Banks Peninsula in holes near the sea. It is nesting now (July and August) and it gets very fat. The hunter puts his hand in and pulls out both old bird and young one. It is the only time you can get them and the sport is called patukorora. On one occasion one of my informants got birds near Lyttelton. They are very hard to pluck and can be cooked by kohiku in umu. They are somewhat greasy but eat very well, said my informants.

Toroa (albatross) – can be got on Campbell Island where you can take young birds out of the nest. Round New Zealand you have to catch the old birds when out fishing. Take a makaa (barracouta) and kokotia (push a stick) inside it. This is thrown over with line to it and when toroa swallows it he is 'nabbed'. Poapoa is the name of throwing the bait to the bird and so enticing it but they had never heard any name for the sport. The bird was valued more for its feathers than its flesh. It was eaten but was very tough and consequently was not much caught.

Karae – They had heard the name of this bird of ill-omen but knew nothing further about it.

Koau is a general name for shags. The kahia has a crest and the big, black shags are named mapua. *The mapua has its home in cliffs but if a wind (like a sou-wester) blows hard into his home he betakes himself to the patiti (tussocks) and camps there for the time being. This was the olden Maori's chance and he took it – if it was moonlight. The hunters crept stealthily up to the vicinity and one reconnoitred the position. He crawled forward to see if the sentry bird (tutei – a human scout is tutoro) is watchful, and ready to give the oho or alarm call. If it is he must wait patiently, or crawl back to others and have a nap, but if it is asleep or nodding he sneaks on it and grabs it so that its wings won't flap and then twists its neck. Then the men would creep on the sleeping birds in turn and might get a good haul if skilfully done. The bird sleeps with its head under its wing (nearly all webfooted birds do – added my informants) and if any man's hand slips or is awkward or fumbling the bird soon lets out a squawk (which one informant imitated) and then good-bye to the rest of the flock.** They did not know any special name for that hunting but 'haere mai ki te mahi koau', or 'haere mai ki te patu koau' would be the wording *of an invitation given by one man (who knew where birds were) to come and assist him.**

Not many of the North Canterbury Natives go South for the Muttonbirding season but one old Kaiapoi resident said he had been going for years past. He noticed that Putauhinu or Hidden Island was supposed to be worthless so he took it up in 1911 and did all right. Then the Crown stepped in and collared it but now he was petitioning for it to be allotted to his soldier sons.

Add to Birds and Bird-Catching

The principal informant said he did not know the word 'uhu' [Stated in Tregear's works to be name of mode of catching tuis when feet numb with frost, and stick to branch. H.B.] for catching birds during frosts but the tui and kaka got very fat and would try to shuffle higher out of hunter's way. Shake the smaller trees and the birds drop off and are caught. The meaning of word 'uhu' is 'to scrape down' and it is also the North Island name [huhu. H.B.] of a grub in soft timber but which is called tuka in Canterbury. He had never heard of catching kiwi by patete (wood rattle) or kuri. The patete is a leaf here and you could blow on it and call birds. He had done so when sitting in a ponga-whare (shelter) and the tui and *makomako had settled on pae and been killed with a stick. Usually one or two birds were on** pae when you hit their heads or bodies – the hunter did not wait till too many settled as if hit on legs or wounded they would flutter away. He thought that Tregear's remark that the kakapos were caught with dogs when sentinel birds fed was perhaps right but he had not heard of sentinel birds and knew little of this bird. They cannot fly and are caught with dogs on West Coast, being fat and good to eat. They stay in holes at the roots of trees. These birds eat the best of the aruhe (fernroot) and reject the fibre. If you see this refuse lying about you can search locality as good aruhe is near at hand.

He had never heard names of tutelary deities of birds. The tohukas used to carve birds in whakairo work and also (he believed) in shape of bird but he had not any details of latter performance. He had heard that the miromiro (tomtit) carried love messages but it was a trifling thing not worth recording. He had heard of the hakuai at the Titi Islands and thought it was a big bird although some argued it was small but with strong wings. (His son said he thought the 'tutaki thrush' and kuruti were the same bird.)

*A decoy bird was a mokai (he had never heard the North Island name = timori). A ring round a bird's leg was poria and was made of bone and sometimes of whitau. He had never heard of the kotuku (white heron) as a pet. This bird goes round once a year and when it becomes hungry it drops down to a lake and gets a 'bellyful of fish' and continues its flight over New Zealand. Each year it comes to exactly the same spot as on its previous visit so the Maori would place a mahanga (snare) there to catch Kotuku by the legs. It is a 'knowing bird' so the snare is covered with light grass and baited with kai (small fish – 'bully', inaka, etc.) and once caught the bird was killed at once. The plumes made a taupare or pare-kotuku for the head. The Maori used to remove skin (kiri) of the bird and dry it and cut suitable piece off and stick this on head with a kopare (band or circlet). He had never heard of the bird being eaten but if it was fat no doubt it went into the umu. If one was killed another would come down at the same spot next year. This was wonderful and it must be the smelling of its nose which enabled it to do this.

Seagulls (karoro) provided pets, the young dark ones (known as pohio) being kept but they would all eventually get away. They were not tied after the first few weeks as they were so tame and Nature always called them in the long run. The Maoris ate seagulls and even yet eat them boiled in stew or soup. The torea (oyster-catcher) is very wild and he had not heard of them as pets, but the putakitaki was kept at Little River in his day and fed on wheat, bread, etc. They would breed in captivity. The wing is cut at first but they get very tame. They fly away and come back and so on, but at last they go for good. All wild birds would do so if allowed any freedom. The kakariki (parrokeet) were good pets. There were three kinds of them – the porete was the one with no red on top of its head but he forgot names of other two. (Powhaitere was a North Island name and some North Island people said kawariki for kakariki – both forms were nicknames perhaps.) The parrokeet would learn to talk Maori well and could live twenty years. He had one for ten years – a very fine pet. The kaka and tui were kept as mokai. The kaka would whistle and speak a little but the tui was wonderful. They would live about seven years and learnt to talk excellently. They were taught old songs and whakapapas and one tui he once had could recite fluently the Rarotimu whakapapa [See Mythology Section, H.B.]. He became greatly attached to this bird and when it died he felt its loss severely. He covered it with a silk handkerchief and buried it with a very sad feeling. Re the cleverness of tuis Major Tupe Turoa told him that Ngati tukoro a te awa (of Whakatane) visited Whanganui. Latter did not know where visitors came from but a pet tui said to them: 'Uia te manuhiri memea ko wai? Te kuti, te wera, te rapa, te haua – moi e ko Apanui'. It then repeated the words to the visitors and added 'moi e haeremai', so whaikorero'ing the visitors to everyone's amazement. The chief of the visitors was Apanui and he had been scalded (wera) and it had left a mark (kuti). Rapa means the skin was doubled up and haua is to be lame and crippled. How the bird knew his name and of his accident no one knew. To know strangers was an unaccountable thing. It belonged to the wisdom of the bird.**

A Maori told me he had heard his father say that he thought the kea ate the seed of the 'vegetable sheep' plant and from this had tackled living sheep. The kea is a parrot but was no good for food as it was too maieke (lean). The kaka is a parrot too but eats berries and got so fat it could be shaken out of trees. He had never heard the name 'uhu' for numbed feet – the word used here was peke, the same word as for the convulsions caused by karaka poisoning. The bird's feet would be drawn up with cold. The waxeye he had always called titiripounamu and when a boy he caught them under a tin dish. [A familiar ruse with Pakeha children. He did not know if waxeye was a Native bird. H.B.]

Another Canterbury Maori said there was a little bird in the swamps that was called moeriki, but he had never heard name mohoperuru [These are two Rails. H.B.]. The moeriki was not so big as a thrush. He had never seen it caught but it may have been eaten at one time for all he knew. It was the only bird of that kind he knew and lives and stays in the raupo all the time. Another water-bird the powaka had long legs and long beak. It was black and white. The torea had long legs and beak too but was a bigger bird. The totokipio (diver) lived here but he had never heard of the kamana (grebe).

A Peninsula Maori said that the shag with a white head and of small size was the koauteko. The kaha was of mapua species but has a plume.

Another Maori referring to Lake Ellesmere said that moulting ducks (maunu not mounu which means a bait) were driven ashore (arutia te manu) by men on wakas (canoes) and kopapa (boards lashed with flax) on to pakihi (flats) where men and boys hit them on head with koradi sticks. The birds were preserved but did not do so well as titi as not so fat. Where possible pohas of rimu (kelp) would be used to hold them. Parera and putakitaki ducks were driven; also a rare brown or spoonbill. The only brown (he thought its Maori name was tata) he had seen on a drive was so uncommon that its possessor had it stuffed. He thought the spoonbill was called pateke as it says 'patek', patek", at night. He had never seen a teal in a drive. The pakura (swamp turkey) was at Ellesmere but was not much used. It was snared as were ducks in the rivers. Putakitaki (Paradise Ducks) were not caught (in these snares) so far as he was aware as it eats grass and vegetation like a goose and keeps on dry flats and not in the waterways.

A woman said that she knew shags were caught near Temuka and eaten. Her father would not eat shags (koau) as name was in his whakapapa. [See Customs, H.B.]

The principal informant said that a bird which lived in the haumata grass in swamps was called haumata in Canterbury but matata elsewhere. [Mata in Murihiku. H.B.] *Bird preserves in old days were kept in hapus and trespassing was a grievous offence. Hapus had certain boundaries in forests and these divisions were called rauiri, as were also preserves for eels in the rivers. The boundaries were called wakawaka. There were no wakawakas for wekas nor for ordinary bush birds. He thought that rats and wekas were more hunted in South Island; and the tui, pigeon and kaka in the North Island. Owing to the vast number of birds and the small population these three birds in South Island did not need to be chased nor sought for with the elaborate preparations used in North Island.**

Add to Birds and Birding

An old man (at the collector's request) made a number of the hono (knots) the old Maori birder used in making nooses for snares. On his own initiative he proceeded to make a section of a karumahaka for catching parera (ducks). [The knots and the three loops of the duck snare have been handed in by me to the Museum. H.B.]

*The principal informant said he thought the moa was almost killed out by a great flood about the time, or some time after, the first people came to the South Island. The few that were left were gradually extirpated. These birds were once numerous in the South Island but from the Maori traditions he had heard it appeared there were never many of them in the North Island.**

From the description given the collector concludes that the kuruti [See Birds under Nelson Section, H.B.] is a sort of swamp rail. A few are said to still survive in the marshy ground at Woodend near the old Kaiapoi Pa. It lives in the raupo, etc., and its 'squeaky crow' (not a loud sound – it may perhaps carry forty or fifty yards, I was told) can still be heard there.

An Akaroa Maori matron said she had seen the kakariki (parrokeet) snared with a loop at the end of a pukakaho stem. The birder would pepe (call) on a hinahina leaf to attract them and they were caught alive. To kill them make a pae (perch) and under it a hiding-place (pahuri or whakaruru) of poka (treefern) leaves from which to whakapepe (call birds) and strike birds off pae with a rod. The birders used to bring home kaka, kereru, tui (usually called koko), makomako (bellbird) i mua (formerly) but now there are no Native birds, not even the friendly kakaruai (robin). She occasionally heard the pipiwharauroa (shining cuckoo) yet. It is a funny bird as the ringeye, the riroriro (grey warbler) feeds its young. This riroriro is the only bird she knew which makes its nest with the opening to one side, not on top, but she never heard a Maori name for this freak nest. The ringeye (also known as whiteeye, silvereye, waxeye and blightbird) was called (at Akaroa) pihipihi. [This is a new name to collector. H.B.]

SECTION XVIII

ENTOMOLOGY

Mokarakara or Butterflies — Popokorua or Ants — Kihikihi or Crickets — Tuka or White Pine Grubs — Noke or Worms — Toropakihi or Lizards — Mokopapa or Tree Lizards — etc.

INSECTS, BATS, ETC.

The principal informant said that the toroku (or torongu) the caterpillar which used, in pre-pakeha days, to put holes through the flax is now transferring its affections and tackling the pakeha's grain. He forgot the name of the centipede but the snail was kata. He had heard of the whe and the ro (latter was very long) but did not know about them. The long-legged grasshopper is called pakau and a small size is kowhitiwhiti (kofitifiti). There were two kinds of crickets – one sings 'in the holes in its sides' by flapping its wings in and out. It is nice singing and in summer it makes a big volume of sound. Its name is kihikihi or kikiawaru (a shortening of kihikihiwaru, he considered). He had heard it said that it commenced singing just at the sowing time for potatoes. This was in the eighth month, waru, hence part of the cricket's appellative. There was another kind, a black one, he had seen around the street lamps at Napier, where it was called piharenga. To return to the South, in the banks an insect has its home. It comes out white and the sun gets at it and then it flies away. He forgot its name. *There is another creature, a tiny, black one, which has a rua (nest) running either into banks or down in sand.** It stops in its hole as its home but it gathers food for the winter. Its name is popokorua and there is 'more history' about it than the other insects because it collects for winter while the rest simply die away. *There was a lot of talk about it and the old people would tell lazy persons, 'Hohonu kaki, papaku awa' (deep neck, shallow water). In the summer they would say to the young people to work industriously like the popokorua and so not be in shallow water during the winter months of scarcity. The activities of this tiny creature 'touches both land and water', and it was a great favorite with the old people.** The pekapeka (bat) lived in thick bush or cliffs or caves and slept in the daytime hanging on to one another in strings and it came out at night and flew about. Although it had been said the Maori would eat anything and everything he would not eat bats and he had never heard even the faintest suggestion of such a thing. He knew no tradition whatever about the pekapeka. The collector asked him regarding the controversy whether the flea was brought to New Zealand by whaling-ships what his opinion was and he said he thought both the tuiau (flea) and the kutu (louse) had been brought by the Maori from Hawaiki.

Another Rapaki Maori said spiders were called pukawerewere and their webs were whare-pukawerewere. He thought the only fly in New Zealand in pre-pakeha days was the rako (blowfly). He did not know when the tuiau (flea) came to New Zealand. The Maori name of the sandfly is namu and caterpillars were called toroku. Mokarakara was a general name for all kinds of butterflies. The name he knew for the daddy-long-legs was kohitihiti. Ro is the stick insect and the whe is like the ro but is not so long. Wetaa is the name of several ugly insects which the Maori would not eat. The tuka, or tukarakau, is a fat white grub out of white and black pine trees. He had not eaten them raw but they were grand when fried. [Some Maori and halfcaste boys still eat them raw. H.B.] He never saw ants but he caught the pekapeka (bat) for fun to examine it. Some people were frightened of it. He had never heard of them being eaten.

A Rapaki lady said the big stick insect was ro and a small kind whe and to see the former in certain ways meant death to an adult relative and if it was the whe you saw it meant death to a juvenile relative [See Omens section, H.B.]. The daddy-long-legs was waeroa, the mosquito was keeroa and there was an ugly thing in the bush called weta.

The principal informant said the red and black butterflies (which were then flying round his garden) were called mokarakara. There was a sort of moth called wairua-tangata (men's souls) but he did not know the reason why such a name was bestowed on it. The collector did not quite follow his further remark that 'the wairua-tangata was the moth of the purehurehu' – perhaps it is an earlier form of the latter insect.

Add to Insects

The principal informant said the mosquito was called keroa and the sandfly namu. As a flying machine passed over he and the collector yarning in his garden he said the shape reminded him that its shape was forestalled centuries ago by the insect which the Maoris call Te-Tatau-o-te-whare-o-Maui. This insect must have been known in Maui's time so the idea of the flying machine must have evolved from it ages after. He did not know its Pakeha name or the history of this interesting insect. The centipede was called waerau not waeroa as sometimes stated. The kekerengu is a small insect and if you handle it with your fingers it leaves a very bad smell. It is not sharp on nose but its behind is round and the smell of it is awful. The Maori bug lives in the boards of old houses and in beds like fleas and they bite you and this bite leaves lumps. He forgot their name but thought they lived more in warmer North.

An intelligent Maori told the collector that the awheto was not found in Canterbury but it was very bad in the North Island where on a visit he once saw a train pull up through the rails becoming too slippery by reason of hordes of these insects. The cricket or kikiawaru was also called terakihi in Canterbury. The kekerengu is not to be found in Canterbury but in North Island. It has an abominable smell and you cannot stay in a house with it. He knew the centipede but not its Maori name nor had he heard the name of the beetle that lives in the manuka. There is a small shield-shaped insect which lives on the Peninsula. It stinks badly but he did not know either its Maori or English name.

While the collector was talking to one aged Maori a ladybird came along and the collector asked the Maori name of it – a question he has asked in vain hitherto. The old man said the only name he knew for them was hakopa [but whether this is a genuine old name the collector has doubts. H.B.].

An Akaroa woman told the collector that the Maoris ate the tuka (white-pine grub) roasted on the embers, when she was a girl.

WORMS

The principal informant said that big white worms were called noke-waiu and red ones, noke-tuatara. There was also a dark worm with sharp nose and 'tail' – its name he forgot. They ate the waiu ones in the North Island. Down here they caught the waiu for 'bobs' for eel-fishing.

A Rapaki Maori said that black worms were called noke-pako and white ones noke-ma. These latter were used on bobs (puti) tied to a matere (rod) and this puti-noke bait was very good for catching eels in the creeks. Worms were not eaten in Canterbury.

An Akaroa woman had heard the old people say the Maoris would whena worms (noke) by the fire and then eat them, but she was not sure if the information referred to the North Island or Canterbury.

LIZARDS AND TUATARA

The principal informant said he knew several kinds of lizards. There was the mokohuruhuru, black and hairy; the mokomoko on the plains, very fast; and the mokokakariki, a green lizard, a sign of the death of a friend if you see it anywhere. Karara is the general name and Motukarara in Lake Ellesmere is so-called because the lizards are there when the waters are out. A big lizard, the tuatara, is found on the islands but not here. A big lizard was found at Lyttelton and the people thought it had come off a ship but he saw it and said it was a mokopapa. It was seen in an apple tree and the children who saw it were afraid but a man caught it. It was about four feet long [sic. H.B.]. It died and was taken to the Christchurch Museum. He never knew lizards to be eaten and never heard of the big kind once to be seen on the plains [And described by Stack in *Transactions of the New Zealand Institute*. H.B. [[This probably refers to discussion about large lizards and similar monsters by Haast (1878) and Stack's comment on the mythical tuna tuoro in appendix 3 to

Haast's paper]]]. A Rapaki Maori said there was only one kind of lizard there now – it was a small, dark karara. He had heard there were big ones on the Titi Islands. He had never heard that lizards were eaten. Some people were afraid of them but some were not and would nestle them against their skins. It was said that in the old times some men would have killed you if you had brought a lizard near them. The tuatara was not here. The moko-kakariki was in the bush but was scarce. It was a sign of death. The mokotuahuruhutu, which he thought was called mokopapa in the South, was found in rotten wood. It was black and very ugly and was once plentiful. A Rapaki woman said the tu-atara was not in Canterbury. Karara was a general name but toropakihi was the small lizard, mokopapa the ugly tree lizard and mokohuruhuru the hairy one. To hear the taki (cry) or squeak of the big mokokakariki presaged the death of a relative. [See Omens section, H.B.] A tuatara had escaped from captivity at Lyttelton. [See above, H.B.]

At Tuahiwi the collector heard that tradition said a big karara-tuatara had lived at Takitu (Belfast). The tuatara never lived at Kaiapoi but was said to have been at Motunau. The mokokakariki is green but since the bush had gone they had disappeared. They could go up trees and you would see them on the houi, etc., perhaps eating the leaves. The mokopapa and the mokotuahuruhuru had been here formerly. The last name is now jokingly applied to hairy men. On the plains the commonest lizard is the small toropakihi.

Add to Lizards

According to the principal informant the big lizard caught in a garden at Lyttelton [Note: See previous Canterbury Notes, H.B.] was a mokopapa – it was not a tuatara which has a ridgey spine and is of an ugly shape. He saw it and would say it was about three feet long and about twenty five pounds weight. It did not matter which sex it belonged to its mate was expected to come round seeking for it, but if so no other similar lizard was ever seen or captured. He said it would live on flies, mud and water but it did not thrive in captivity and died, and as far as he knew its stuffed carcase was now in the Christchurch Museum. *The mokopapa looks ugly – as ugly as Ruaimoko. Mokopapa is from the same family as Ruaimoko but is not a god. If a child is 'as black as the ace of spades' [like one lad he pointed out. H.B.] he is called a mokopapa or sometimes a mokote. If anyone's eyes look dark, wild or fierce such an expression is called mokote.** (The collector has never heard mokomoko as a lizard name and asked after it.) He understood that the karara-mokomoko was the same lizard as the toropakihi. He had never heard of a name like karara-papani [used in South. H.B.] nor had he heard of any cases of lizards being kept as pets.

A native of the Peninsula said he had pulled a lizard apart [in 'the interests of scientific investigation' – he is a keen observer. H.B.] and that it rejoined itself but strange to relate the two halves did not match, one being bottom side uppermost, and it went off in this strange conjunction. If the tail is pulled off the lizard will return searching for it. If a cat eats a lizard or two it will die as the scales are alive. Lizard blood is a stain, scanty and brownish. Nicotine from a pipe dropped in a lizard's mouth will kill it in five minutes. The tuatara was (or is) to be found near Whakamoa (Island Bay) on Banks Peninsula. He had seen them there. The mokopapa (tree lizard) and toropakihi (grass lizard) are also on the Peninsula. He had seen the mokotuahuruhuru in Taranaki where it is called pirirewa after the tree it mostly frequents. They are about seven inches long and if you see them in a tree and poke them with a stick they will turn their heads and set sail for the next tree on a long slant, their tails going 'eighteen to the dozen'. They can change color to that of the tree they are on. If they light on a mahoe (hinahina in South Island – the whitewood) they will assume a shade to match it in the course of a few minutes. He had seen the big green mokokakariki in the bush on the Peninsula. In the spring you could see them going round in flocks or crowds – after that in pairs. One day he was bushfelling he laid his coat on the ground and when having lunch he noticed eight mokokakariki in single file cross the coat in an undeviating line. The sight interested him as he had not seen such a thing before. The mokokakariki lives on the konini, manuka and other trees and in the old days of superstition its appearance was regarded as a bad omen to the spectator or to his friends. [See previous Canterbury Notes re lizards and omens, H.B.]

Karara, said an old woman, is the common name for all lizards. The two best-known species in Canterbury were, she considered, the toropakihi, the little lizard so common on the plain, and the mokokakariki, the green lizard usually found in trees and shrubs, probably the prettiest one of the lot.

An Akaroa woman said she had never seen, nor heard of, the old people catching, handling, or eating lizards.

SECTION XIX

ZOOLOGY

Kuri-Maori or Maori Dog — Kuri-Kowao or Maori Dog run wild — Kiore or New Zealand Rat — Tawhiti or Trap — Kaurehe or A Fabulous 'Animal' — etc.

DOGS AND DOG-CATCHING

The kuri-maori (the Maori dog), said the principal informant was of medium size and carried a 'lot of wool', which was valuable in making kakahu – an ihupuni, or dogskin mat, being highly treasured. Not only was its skin valued but its carcase was in demand by Maori epicures as toothsome food. The Takitimu and other canoes brought dogs from Hawaiki. Kopuwai on the Araiteuru brought two dogs which were later drowned in the Waitaki, and being turned to stone can still be seen in the water of that river. The people of old could breed the kuri-maori and many were kept in a tame state. Some ran wild and were trapped occasionally but he had heard nothing of the kuri-tawhiti (dog-trap) save the name. He had heard of the stone-trap for them but he thought it was a yarn.

A Rapaki Maori said he had never seen a kuri (and he was seventy years old) but he had heard it was sharper in the ihu (nose) than ordinary dogs. He had never heard how wild dogs were caught.

A Tuahiwi Maori said he had heard the old men speaking of the kuri. Some were kept tame in the villages as pets, for their skins, for food and to chase and catch birds. The kuri-kowao (wild dog) was caught in a tawhiti (trap) set in its tracks or where it was likely to be. A manu (bird) was used as a bait. When the rope went off 'ping' the dog was hung up in air where he could not bite the rope and he was soon strangled. He was skinned so that his coat would go towards an ihupuni, or dogskin mat, his piro (entrails) were taken out and his body was put in the umu. They were often nice and fat, and 'kapai kai te kuri', the flesh was good to eat. He had never heard of the method of killing or stunning them with a trap loaded with big stones and reckoned it was 'he korero tito' (a fable or romantic invention). He had personally heard the old men say the tawhiti was set on a track with manu as a bait, being set in the morning, and at night the dog would come and being enticed by the skilfully arranged and tempting bait would be caught.

Another Tuahiwi Maori added that the olden Maori trained the kuri to assist him in catching weka, kiwi and kakapo and also in assisting to catch maunu at lake edges.

Add to Dogs and Dog-Catching

The kuri had just one name, said the principal informant. In the North Island they may have had fancy names like mohorangi and ruarangi but in the South Island only kuri-maori. In color they were not piebald but were a shade not quite brown and not quite white. The kuri had a stout body; legs not long but long hair. Old pas were full of them – each rangatira had perhaps twenty or thirty of them. They were bred for their woolly skins for ihupuni mats and for meat like the Pakeha does mutton. Castrating was called whakapoka but he did not think it was an ancient custom. Pigs and calves are done now so as not to spoil the meat but the kuri was not like that – it ate well even if not operated on. It was not a savage dog by any means. He did not know nor had he ever heard in his travels that tattooing soot and fat was fed to dogs and the faeces used as tattooing ink [as is stated in Tregear's [[1904]] *Maori Race*. H.B.]. These kuri were kept in captivity

– they did not run wild. If they strayed someone would probably meet them and spear or otherwise kill them for kai (food). He had never heard of kuri being caught in tawhiti – that style of trap was only for kiore (rats). The old native kuri used to howl. You would hear someone say Kai te kaitau te kuri to express that one was howling but now the noise made by dogs is called pari – an adaptation of word 'bark'.

An old woman said she had never seen a native Kuri nor had she heard how it was caught, but she had heard the old people speak of its being cooked in the umu and that it provided good eating.

RATS AND RAT-CATCHING

The kiore, the principal informant stated, was (unfortunately we must speak in the past tense – many people sixty years old have never seen this rat) a dark grey color and it had a woolly fur and was long tailed. He thought it had been killed out by the destruction of the bush and the consequent loss of its food – mainly berries. It was very fond of the tawai (birch) berries. It did not live in an earth rua (hole) like the pakeha rats but was migratory, and made hekes following the fruit as it ripened in various localities. It ate no filth and was quite suitable for human food. In the season (April or May) it gets very fat and the Canterbury Natives went to Oxford (Tawera) and the back-country to trap it. The trap (tawhiti) was set in the animal's tracks or paths and no bait was set in it but the rat touched a string and was caught and choked. It stepped on a stick and this slipped and released the noose which closed round its neck. At night you could take the rats out several times and re-set the trap. The rats came after berries and were caught in thousands. The wekas were caught in March and April, the rats immediately following and the bush birds in winter. The rats were cleaned and put in a taha or kumete (North Island name. H.B.] and boiled down like weka, tui, etc. and so preserved. On its hekes the kiore crossed big rivers by the whirituamanga plan. 'Whiri', means 'to plait', and 'tuamanga' is name of the style. [Note Tregear's [[1891]] *Dictionary* says: Whiri-tuamaka, to plait with eight strands. H.B.] Sometimes the rivers were waipuke (flooded) and the rats would swim (perhaps a chain or two of them) right across, the ones first over pulling the rest across. If the chain broke a lot were drowned. It was not head to tail but the tails only and these were looped to each other in a way he could not exactly describe. *The Maoris had noted rats crossing swift rivers and so when they wished to cross a rapid but wadeable stream they joined poles and a chain of strong men held these against current while old men, women and children crossed below them. They broke the current for the weaker ones. This was a lesson man had learnt from the rats. He had not seen these things but had heard the old people discussing them.**

A Tuahiwi Maori said the kiore was caught in a tawhiti set on its track, no bait being used. The traps were all over the place and caught hundreds of rats.

Each trap only caught one kiore at a time. The bent stick was a whana and the noose a karumahaka. This was at Oxford. They were not skinned but the fur was plucked (Uhutia ka huruhuru) [Huhutia. H.B.]. Take the piro out (kotia te puku) and put carcase in an ipu (trough) dropping in pohatu (stones) hot from the umu to cook. Put in kelp bags and these poha-kiore would keep a long time.

An Akaroa woman said the Maoris ate the kiore-tawai or Native Rat. It is a whitey grey color and lives largely on tawai (beech) berries – hence its distinguishing title.

Add to Rats and Rat-Catching

The principal informant said the kiore came to Tawera (Mount Oxford) in June to eat the tawai (birch) berries. The district was divided among hapus into wak-awaka (sections) named after the tipunas, even as were the titi wakawaka on Titi Islands. The trapping was a particular and careful work as traps were set all over likely spots and by the time a man got to the end of them on a trip and reset them they were all full again so he went over them again and again. Each trap caught only one rat at a time. This was done at nights and the rats were not seen in daytime. The defunct rats were singed and plucked (huhuti). They were not plucked like a bird but the fur was rubbed off and then animals cleaned and cooked [See Cooking Section, H.B.]. The rat season was from June to August. When they migrated away they crossed rivers by plaiting tails [See previous Canterbury Notes, H.B.]. They knew by instinct when the berries were ripe. They bred in the mountains – not in earth-holes like the present rat but in holes in trees and dry places in tree roots. Such a hole was called a kohanga he thought. Perhaps they also made nests in moss. He did not know the number in a litter. One kind was kiore-tawai and were called kiore-maori simply to distinguish them from Pakeha rats. The expression 'koroke' [See Tregear's works. H.B.] means mischief or evil man or 'that fellow' – but was not used here for the rat nor was a poa bait used – both of these customs were North Island. A bait was not needed here as traps were set on defined tracks. Rats were more common in the South Island than in the North. The native rats never came into pas nor kaikas nor near whatas – it always kept to the bush away from man.

A Maori said he saw native rats (in 1891) cross the Waimarino River in North Island. He and seventeen men stood on bridge and watched. Three rats held on bank – two facing bank and one facing river – and rest across river holding tail of preceding one in teeth. The long line of them walked up bank and then into water and were swung across the river by the current to the opposite bank. A lot ran across this living bridge and then the three on bank released their position of twisted tail and the bridge swung downstream to other bank. The gorge was so precipitous the men could not get down but all voted it a great spectacle.

A woman said that Tawera and a place near Waimate were only places she knew kiore were caught. When a girl at Moeraki she saw whata but never heard the name of the niches round posts to keep rats from getting up to the food stored there.

THE KAUREHE

*[At the back of Hocken's [[1898]] *History of Otago* is an appendix giving Monro's account of Otago in 1844 and at the end of that account it is stated that the Maoris told the white investigators that aquatic animals lived at Lake Wanaka and from the description the white men surmised them to be beavers. This always puzzled the collector and the Southern Maoris could throw no light on the mystery. Recently, however, he happened to see this in Tregear's [[1891]] *Dictionary*: 'Kaurehe, the name of an animal said to live in New Zealand, and whose existence is not yet to be considered proven. It is supposed to resemble the beaver, or otter'. This gave a clue] and the collector asked the principal informant what a kaurehe was. He replied: The kaurehe is a kind of pukutuara and is sometimes given as another name for it. The kaurehe is also like a lizard – perhaps it is just a big one (lizard). It can go on the land or swim in a lake. It lives in the caves and gullies in the mountains, and if it got the chance would hurt men and tear them to pieces and eat them. The pukutuara could stretch itself like a concertina. It was between a lizard and a fish and the kaurehe was similar. They were found in the back country but were never plentiful and some might be there yet. [I hope not. H.B.] The kaurehe was like a sort of crocodile but it had no shell on. The pukutuara would eat and then lie down, stretch itself and go to sleep. It must be a sort of snake he thought. He had heard it could swallow a man whole but the kaurehe would tear its food into bits before eating it. The pukutuara was more lazy than the kaurehe.

A Tuahiwi Maori mentioned it casually: He was eelspearing and saw a big hole in the riverbank and stuck his spear in.** There was a terrified squeak and he thought it must be a giant lizard or a kaurehe and he left hurriedly. A karara-tuatara was said to have lived at Belfast while a huge double-headed lizard haunted the bank of the Waimakariri and was said to have been seen in olden days.

*Meeting the 'mine of information' at Temuka the collector asked him the question with this result: The kaurehe is a big lizard or reptile sometimes on the land and sometimes in the water.** Some were said to be of great size. He had not seen any of them although he had heard of them. He knew no stories nor traditions connected with them.

*[This, the collector considers, is the origin of the 'beaver story'.]**

SECTION XX

BOTANY

Naupiro or Anise — Pukio or Niggerheads — Paku or Moss (on Beech-trees) — Kuta or Watercress — Tapuku or Snowberries — Taramea or Speargrass Papaii or Speargrass — Horoeka or Grasstree — Tarutaru or Grass — Akerautaki or a kind of tree — Kawakawa or a kind of tree — Rohutu or a kind of tree — Rautawhiri or Kaiwhiria (in North Island) — Hinahina or Mahoe (in North Island) — etc.

TREES AND PLANTS

The principal informant said very little on this subject. He said the tree called rautawhiri in South Island was also known as poroporo-tauwhiri but in the North Island it was called kaiwhiria. The name piripiri means 'sticking' and was applied to both the plant and its burr. One variety of popohue has nice white flowers which serve to beautify the bush. The hinahina here was mahoe in North Island.

A Rapaki Maori said 'cutty-grass' was matirewa, 'wild Irishman' was tumatakuru, while the only speargrass he knew was the taramea. The only treefern on Banks Peninsula that he knew was the poka which could not be eaten. Some tikumu grew here – it had been brought from West Coast mountains, but another plant with big leaves which grew on mountains had a name which always eluded him. He had never heard the Maori name of the plant which the pakeha called 'vegetable sheep'. At Tuahiwi the collector was told that one kind of watercress was called kuta. None of his informants here had heard of 'vegetable sheep' and they could not recall the name of the big lily on the mountains. In the back-country grew the purau, a plant with yellow flowers. The Maoris ate the roots. The collector was told it also grew in the hills behind Puketiraki in Otago. His informants did not know how the word tumatakuru was corrupted into matagouri but after seeing and hearing some pakeha mispronunciations of Maori they could believe anything. Tumatakuru has largely vanished through cultivation but the name is now applied by the present Maoris to gorse or whino. The big kind of manuka is called kaikaatoa but they had not heard of a kind called kirimoko, but kirimuka meant the skin and leaves of a tree and was applied to manuka when it was steeped in boiling water to make 'backblocks tea' (in absence of proper tea). The kawakawa and piripiri leaves were also called by this name when used to make tea so they did not think this was the name of a variety of manuka. [The fact that 'muka' means leaves is interesting. 'Rau' is the usual Maori name of a leaf but Tregear's [[1891]] *Dictionary* says that in Tonga the young leaves of the coconut and other trees are called 'muka'. H.B.] They knew two species of speargrass – the big one being taramea and the smaller one papaii but only the former was used to extract scent from. [See Scents section, H.B.] The grass tree is here called horoeka. [In *Pioneer Recollections* Volume II [[Beattie 1911]] page 60 Mantell calls the grasstree, 'nei', and says it forms a constant part of 'mosses' that latter are called nei too. H.B.] Asking about this the collector was informed that nei was a 'swamp' or boggy patch in mountain gullies but that the ordinary swamp on flats was called re [This is synonymous with repo of North Island. H.B.] At the same time they thought a tree on the Chatham Islands was called neinei. The tapuku was the snowberry, the white berry growing so close to the ground. [How I did enjoy them when a boy! H.B.] The takapo is the same kind of berry with a reddish tinge and growing higher off the ground. The woodhens (weka) used to get very fat gorging itself on these luscious berries. The patotara, some bearing white and some red berries, is another species of the snowberry.

A plant esteemed by the olden Maoris for its medicinal and food qualities was the puha (bush thistle – commonly called 'sowthistle'). The principal informant said the wind increased this plant. Its white down (whose Maori name he forgot) was blown away by hau (wind) and spread the seeds broadcast. Its stems are very good to eat – they are better for the blood than Pakeha cabbage – the puha is a blood-purifier. Returned Soldiers (Maori) said it was found in France. They gathered all they could and ate them as greens to the surprise of the Pakeha soldiers. The Maori boys taught their neighbours to eat it too and the white men soon relished it as much as the brown did.

When he learnt what country the collector's people came from the principal informant jokingly said the kotimana (Scots Thistle) was the collector's tarutaru (grass). In his grounds he has a number of South Sea Island plants which he takes great pride in. The mildew which comes on top of fencing posts of Native timber he called kohukohu. It comes through bad weather.

Add to Trees and Plants

The principal informant said he did not know the vegetable sheep plant or its name. Some people brought Mountain daisies and mountain musk from the Southern Alps to Banks Peninsula some years ago, but does not know their Maori names. The haumata is a grass in swamps. It is like toetoe but small, the leaves growing high and about as thick as a cigarette. He did not know upoko-takata or rerewa as names for plants but pukio is the niggerhead. The nettle is onga-onga; lawyer = tarataheka; bramble = tataramoa; he thought these names were common to both islands. Ordinary native grass, mauku uku, is like a tussock but small and soft; the strong tussock is patiti; the pouaka is a plains grass of which he had heard the name only; karetu is a grass like the 'bell flower' – it is long and bends at the top [See Medicinal Lore section, H.B.]. In the big bush at Te Ahupatiki (Mount Herbert) the ponga and wheki ferntrees abound, but he did not know if mamaku or katote were there, nor regarding ferntrees as food. The Maoris used to say some trees were male and female but he had never learnt that lore [See Murihiku Notes, H.B.].

An old Maori said he had never heard of the vegetable sheep plant. The pouaka is like rushes only whiter. The karetu is a long grass which grows by the lakesides. The only ferntree round the Peninsula he knew was the poka and he had been all over the place. It is no good to eat and no good for permanent use as the leaves dry up in no time – it is only good to make maimais or temporary shelters. Kawakawa is a tree in the bush; the berries are not eaten but the green leaves could be made into tea in an emergency. Manuka leaves and bidibidi could also be used for tea.

Another Maori said he had heard of the vegetable sheep plant but did not know its name. The mountain daisy was called tikumu but he forgot the name of the mountain lily – it was not rengarenga at any rate. The lily had bigger leaves than the tikumu.

Speaking to two Maoris they stated they did not think the mountain musk and the anise were native. One had seen snowgrass at Lake Takapo that was six feet high at least. It was like marram-grass to look at. He knew no name for it but patiti (tussock). Kopuru is rare – a sort of moss found on rocks in the bush.

Two other Maoris said that matagouri should be tumatakura. There were two kinds of speargrass – taramea and papaii – the former (from which scent is got) is yellow and the latter more whitish. Papakoura is a prickly weed, small, but can not walk over it barefoot. It was here before the Pakeha came. The musk was a native but they did not know its Maori name. They did not know regarding anise (or aniseed). Kopuru is a kind of moss. If you take ordinary moss from a wet spot and transplant it to a dry or rocky spot it will turn into kopuru. It has a pleasant scent. The edible ferntrees do not grow on Banks Peninsula. The wheki is a form of poka and is as hard as iron. The titoki has leaves like the rautawhiri and grows as big as the houi (ribbonwood) and its berries are eaten and used for oil also. [See sections Vegetable Food; and Scents and Oils, H.B.] The pohue grows at Lake Ellesmere. It has pink and white flowers and its roots can be eaten.

Professor Wild [[probably LJ. Wild, lecturer 1915–1920]] of Lincoln College had told one Maori there were no fewer than seven hundred Native Grasses in North Canterbury and had asked him if he could identify a few of them, but informant considered he would be lucky if he could name half-a-dozen of them.

A Maori said he had never heard of the vegetable sheep plant but up on the Peninsula hills there was a plant with a flower like a cup and with leaves which would hold water as they were round-shaped; he had never heard the Maori name ot it.

There was no shrub in South Island called rangiora – it was a North Island plant.

Add to Plants, Trees, Ferns, Grasses, etc.

The pikiraki, said the principal informant, is a parasite plant growing up on trees and bearing yellow flowers. He never heard the name pikiarero used in South Island. Puaawai is any flower of any tree as well as name of rata flower. It is also called puaitu in Canterbury when budding and then when buds open comes the puawai. Akerautaki and akeake are two kinds of same tree. The former is hard and was used to make spear and huata. Both bear nice flowers but these have no smell. It was said the ake on Takitimu Mountains had a nice perfume but this was a somewhat different species he thought. He had tried to grow shrubs from the Titi Islands at Rapaki but they died. Mauku uku is a sort of soft tussock with a small stem. It used to grow on Banks Peninsula but there is none visible now probably the cattle ate it out. He had never heard of anise, or a shrub called korokio, nor a tree called kauheke. The thorny Wild Irishman was called tumatakuru and there was not a word in the Maori language anything like 'matagouri'. Kohuwai is of two sorts – a grass or moss in water and a green moss on wet rocks in bush. There is still another kind of moss in the bush – not the paku that grows on the tawai (beech) – a beautiful, soft, green moss used to keep babies cool, or used by women in their maros during menses. The kopuru is a different thing. Moss is also called kohukohu. The mokimoki grew in Canterbury as far as he knew. There was a shrub called miki but he did not know meaning of place-name Mikioe. There was a fern called turukio (not turokio as collector was told in South). It is a hard leaf shaped like a poka (treefern) leaf and makes good covering for a whare or shelter against rain. He had heard of piupiu fern but was not familiar with it. It might be like paretao, another kind of fern found in Canterbury.

The rohutu was a tree, said a woman to the collector, which grew on Banks Peninsula and was much prized by the old people as tops made of its timber made a hum or whistling sound. They ate the rohutu berries [See Vegetable Foods, H.B.]. An old man at Tuahiwi said a plant which grew near water and on cliffs and had leaves like parsnip and a white flower was naupiro. [This is the anise. H.B.] The Maoris used to gather it to feed to horses. He knew no Maori name for musk. The kopuni grows on rocks and has a nice scent. Korokio he had heard of but not seen and he had not heard tree name turukio or turokio before. He had heard name pikiarero somewhere or other but knew nothing of it. The pikiraki has no father or mother as it has no root. It has red flowers and yellow berries. He never heard name mikioe or mikihoe. The mikimiki has a blue berry and the miki a yellow flower, and a berry like the pikiraki had. The rohutu has a black berry. Hinau grows up at Oxford but he did not know its uses. The makamaka is a fern and the turukio is ditto. Puawai was the flower of rata or any tree. The akerautaki is a tree and in the South it was used to make good taiaha. He could not say why rohutu wood should make 'te aue o te potaka' (the hum of the top) more than other timber. He had never heard of kopata grass but mauku uku was a name for any grass. As far as he knew kohuwai was not in the water but crept over wet tree-boles.

A Wairewa Maori said the piupiu fern of the South Island was called mouku in the North Island. Two other Canterbury ferns are the turukio and the mata, the latter having a long single stalk. There were numerous bush ferns but he forgot most of the names.

An aged Temuka woman said that anise was called naupiro, but the matika (a rendering of word musk) was not known in Canterbury in old days. The makihikihi is a plant with a nice smell (she could not describe it further but said it could not be eaten). The kopata is a sort of weed with a nice flower. The akerautaki, she thought, grew in North Island. The kohuai grew in rivers and creeks and also in the bush.

SECTION XXI

METEOROLOGY AND ASTRONOMY

Matakokiri or Meteors — Kapo or Lightning — Umu or Ring round Sun — Tahupokai or Red Horizon — Marama or The Moon — Aniwaniwa or Rainbows — Te Ika-a-Raki or The Milky Way — Hau or The Wind — Hautane or A Strong Wind — Hauwahine or A Gentle Wind — Hautuwhenua or An Inland Wind — etc.

WINDS AND WEATHER

*In regard to winds the principal informant said that the hau (wind) from the north-east was called whakarua; north-west = mauru; west = ta; south-west = toka, and east was marakai or marangai. They now called the south-east wind tautehi which is its Pakeha name Maoricised. Haumatua is a wind between north-west and north-east. A strong wind is called hautane, a soft one, hauwahine, but he forgot the other names. At a later stage he said marangai was the east, whakarua the north-east, wahanui the north north-east (this was a strong wind), mauru the nor-west, taa the west, tonga the sou-west, but he could not remember the old Maori name of the south-east wind. The names of these winds were taken as being directions because the Maoris had no compass like the white man had. [Some very interesting information he gave about the various goddesses who control the different winds will be found in the Mythology section. H.B.]**

A Rapaki Maori said that toka was south-west wind; mauru was the north-west one; whakarua the north-east one; taa the westerly one, while paia was an easterly wind which if it kept coming up for a week would bring rain. Hautuwhenua is a breath of wind from inland and if you get up in the morning early you will feel it. It comes like a draught of cold air but is soon gone. He had not heard much lore about winds or weather among the Maoris but remembered paretao was a south-east wind of variable character.

Another old man at Rapaki speaking of the weather said ra-kino was a bad day, ra-tamaru a dull day, while ra-paki was 'kai te marino' – calm and peaceful – meaning (divided thus) 'a fine, fair day'.

Two Tuahiwi Maoris said mauru was the nor-wester, ta a westerly wind, toka the sou-wester, wahanui was north-east and whakarua an easterly wind, but they could not recollect the name of the south-east wind. Waihora was a southerly wind from direction of Lake Waihora (Ellesmere) and Tawera from Mount Tawera (Oxford) in a nor-westerly direction and they reckoned those two winds derived their names from that fact. [Those names are used in Murihiku too. H.B.] Rawhiti te ra or rawhiti = the east; hauauru or mauru = north-west; and toka the south in speaking of directions. Some old Maoris were very expert at foretelling weather by observing clouds and streaks in the sky but this lore is lost. These tohu or signs were more necessary at seaside villages. Old Kaiapoi was a mile from the sea but at the nearest canoe anchorage, the Ashley River (Rakahuri) the bar was very rough and canoes were not much used.

Add to Winds and Weather

*The principal informant said that matakokiri (meteors) were a sign of wind, so were kapo (flashes of lightning). If these kapo came all round the horizon the side on which they were strongest would send the wind. An umu, or ring round the sun or moon was sometimes a sign of wind, sometimes indicated fine weather and when right round forecasted a heavy fog. The Southern Lights (for which Ka-tara-tokai is not the right name) is also a sign of weather but he did not know what it signified. One weather sign of the old people was if the torino (ear-drum) rang it was a warning of rain. His ears had rung alternately twice the evening previous to yesterday's rain and hence his forecast of rain had been verified. One way to foretell the weather by young people was to hold two bits of flax in the hand and let another draw – if they pulled the long piece it would be wet, if the short it would be fine. In regard to the winds he thought the name marangai was bestowed on the east wind in the North Island in fairly recent generations. He thought paoa was old name but that about ten generations ago it came to be known as marangai. A strong east-nor-easter is still called paoa and a weak one whakarua in Canterbury and wahanui is also north-easterly.

Frost which is called hukapapa in North Island is kopaka in Canterbury where both ice and snow are called huka.** To a query by the collector if there was any traditions about floods in Canterbury rivers, he said he could call to mind none said to have occurred in *more recent centuries but that legend said a great flood destroyed Tutewaimate, Moko (who was said to be one hundred feet high or tall) and the moas. He reckoned that story was true.** This flood was not the Parawhenuamea one – it happened in Hawaiki.

A Canterbury Maori said that winter was called makariri; summer = raumati; autumn = kahuru; and spring = kana as far as he recollected old names.

A Peninsula Native said the east wind was called waihora; the north-east was whakarua; the north-west = mauru; the south-west = ta; and the south wind was called toka. If a fog came down in a tongue-shape on Oteoka Hill at Wairewa it was a sure sign of south-west wind and rain but if the fog spread out and descended level you could expect fine weather. If the sun rose over Hikuika (Mount Sinclair) and you could see it preceded by red streaks round that peak, this was a tohu (sign) of rain, but if the streaks were gray this was a good sign, forecasting a fine day. Tahupokai (a red sky all round horizon) was a tohu of fine weather, but ata-a-wai (a light bluish light out to sea due south) was a forewarning of bad southerly weather. Ata-a-mauru, however, was a good tohu; it is a peculiar light-colored shade in the atmosphere to the west, inland over Canterbury plains viewed from the Peninsula. The people of old used to go largely on the profusion or scarcity of bloom on trees and plants for their lore of the weather for the season as a whole. They would take special notice of flax, toetoe, and other plants. On the Peninsula the kohai is usually the first tree to flower and an indication of what it will do in this line can be got as early as July. If it has some bloom up and some down it indicates a mixed season; if all are drooping or there is a noticeable lack or no bloom it foretells a dead, bad season. This year all the trees were blooming in their best style so this was the sign of a good season. If there are plenty of koradi it is a good year for fish; kakaho is the same; but little notice was taken of moss, etc. In regard to floods it was said the Waimakariri had changed its course a great deal as a result of these but he knew of no definite traditions about floods or weather in pre-pakeha days.

*The principal informant remarked that the season could be foretold by observing the trees flowering and such like but he had never been taught that lore.

Add to Winds and Weather

The principal informant said that if the new moon came in upright or almost so and with its face bent north (it denoted fine weather but if it came in 'belly up' like ⌣ it was said to be full of water and a sign of bad weather. In parts of the North Island he found that if the moon came in facing North it was regarded as a bad sign, but each place had to go on their own lore. It was often rain in North Island when fine in Canterbury and vice versa, but the moon showed the sign to each place. If the moon came in half-and-half (half on its end and half on its side) like ⌒ , it was a sign of mixed weather. The climate, he thought, used to be more severe than now. In 1861 he saw snowdrifts on the Peninsula about twelve (12) feet deep, and there has never been a big fall of snow since. The bush used to be wet and attracted rain and snow but it is now nearly all cleared. Creeks which used to run merrily all the year round now only run intermittently. This, he considered, was probably caused by clearing the bush and draining the swamps and marshes.**

Another intelligent Maori concurred that the climate was not now wetter than it used to be, but on the reverse it was drier than of yore.

*A woman remarked that 'ka heia te kopaka' was a saying of the old people when they arose of a morning to find a heavy frost coating the trees and ground.**

MONTHS AND SEASONS

This is a very difficult subject to get information about at this late date when the Maoris have been using European chronology and reckoning for at least seventy years but the principal informant remembered a few items that have been traditionally preserved.

*The seasons were three in number, viz., Ngahuru = Autumn; Takurua = Winter and this division embraced springtime also; and Raumati = Summer.

There are thirteen moons in the year, continued the principal informant, although the Maori only had ten names for them, as ngahuru has the meaning of being only ten in number but it really means 'more than ten' and here implies that twelve of thirteen moons have only ten names; or in other words that twelve English months are crowded into ten Maori ones. [That is, if the collector rightly understood his mentor. H.B.] The Maori New Year was in May and from this month commenced their yearly calendar or calculation of time. The months were as follows: 1. Matahi (May) 2. Maruaroa (June) 3. Matoru (July) 4. Wha (August) 5. Rima (September) 6. Ono (October) 7. Whitu (November) 8. Waru (December) 9. Iwa (January) 10. Ngahuru (February, March and April – apparently). Ngahuru was a harvest time and the Maori was happy then because there was abundance of good things to eat. At some times of the year he would get one meal a day, at others two, working up to Ngahuru when he got ten a day if he wished them or could eat them. [No wonder he wanted to spin it out as long as he could. H.B.]

He had heard the nights of the moon named many years ago. Ari was the eleventh night but he forgot the others although some might come back to his memory. A new moon was now called marama-hou but that was not the olden name. He also forgot the old names of full moon and the moon's phases.

In the springtime the Maoris like to feel the sun's ray on their skin as it is not too warm and the old people would lie against a takitaki (fence) and repeat the old whakatauki 'Ae! Nga ra o torn whitu' (Yes! the sun from third to seventh months = July to November.) When the sun was going down the old people used to say, 'Ka to te ra', and when it had gone down or set, 'Ko to te ra.'**

STARS AND GENERAL SKY LORE

*The principal informant said that the sky lore of the ancient Maoris had been forgotten, except a few fragments. Puaka, he thought rises about June 6. Matariki, a group of stars, rises two or three weeks earlier. Puaka is a star which flickers and changes color. Ngakapa, a group of stars in a straight line, shows the near approach of Puaka as they rise two or three days before. Puaka has a great history and is mentioned in the song about Tane. Takurua comes in winter to which it gives its name. [Winter is usually called Makariri in the South. H.B.] Then Mirimiri rises and then comes Aotahi-ma-Rehua. He did not know the origin of this name but Rehua was the father of the sun. These were the principal stars but there were others also.** The Wero stars mentioned in old songs were names of heat and indicated heat of summer advancing, culminating in Mahana-nei. *He considered the stars were somewhere about the top of the Ten Heavens. [See Mythology section, H.B.] Rainbows were called aniwaniwa. They were a sign of good weather or clearing up. You could tell if good (tohu pai) or bad (tohu kino) by the color. If there were two arches either the top or lower one was called Kahukura, the other was Rokomai perhaps. When sailing, rainbows showed the canoe men their directions in the migrations. The name of the axe Awhiorangi is another name for the aniwaniwa or rainbow. It is a sign of the track one canoe took in coming to New Zealand. [See History section, H.B.] He had heard a Maori name for the Aurora Australis but forgot it.**

Two Tuahiwi Maoris said star Puaka was Rigel. Autahi, Meremere and Takurua were other stars. Puaka appears as a morning star in the beginning of May and the Maori used to tell the seasons by this star. Te-ika-o-te-raki is the Milky Way. Rainbows are called Aniwaniwa or Kahukura or another name they forgot. Kahukura was a goddess who directed Tura on his voyages by making rainbows appear for his benefit. [See History section, H.B.] Neither informant knew the name of the Southern Lights – one remarked that he 'never knew until lately such a phenomena was visible'. Clouds were called paiau or pukeau but they did not know names of the different kinds. They never heard the old people refer to sky lore.

Add to Sky Lore

*The Maori, said the principal informant, did not hold the idea that the earth revolved round every day, and that it went round sun. That was a Pakeha idea and he would contradict it. The world is flat and the sun comes up one side of it, over the top of it and down under it, to come up on the same side every morning and sink down under the opposite side each evening, travelling underneath during the night. [Note: This is different to North Island legends and to the cosmogony drawn at the front of J.C. Andersen's [[1907]] book *Maori Life in Aotea*. H.B.] The sun's course is pikopiko-i-rangi; that is its name he thought and means that it curves in an arch through the heavens. Some stars follow the course of the sun and moon. The sun and moon do not take the same track across the sky day after day all the year round but vary the course a bit. They work back and forwards on a wide road, their track being higher in summer and lower in winter. The moon possesses big mana and does a lot of work although not so important as the sun. It has the power to look out over the sea at high tide, and to see that the sea does its work. Full moon was called ohua and so spring tides were known as tai-ohua. Although the moon is usually named Marama its full name is Maramahuakea, the last half of this word meaning 'fullness'. The moon is a half-brother of the sun, being the second son of Maku by a different wife than Mahora-nui-a-tea, but narrator could not recall the lady's name. [Huareare is her name. He recalled it subsequently. H.B.] The two brothers disagreed. The elder brother, the sun wished both to go together on their journey, but the younger brother, (evidently thinking he would be too much overshadowed), did not want this. He said to the sun, 'You can go by day, I will go by night'. The sun agreed to this and hence the two keep their separate ways as man can see to this day. The moon has power over the weather to a large extent. At sunrise the sun looks big and near as you can tell by standing on a sea-cliff and looking over the waters and watching it dawn; or as it appears over a mountain range. But as it mounts in the sky it gets smaller because it gets higher in the heavens in its curve over the earth. It still travels very fast (if not so fast as in Maui's time) but it is visible only in the daytime whereas the moon can often be observed in the day as well as the night. 'Ko mate to marama' is a saying when the moon disappears away and it is not really dead. It will come again very small and grow quickly till full size and then waste away again. Narrator forgot the name of eclipses but 'Whatutaki te marama ki te ra' is a way of expressing the meeting of the sun and moon when one blinds the other from your sight.

Some stars were said to rise in the evening, travel all night, and set in the morning. They would set a little higher each morning. An ancient waiata (song) said stars moved so that was how he knew the old people considered they journeyed. Puaka, or Puanga, who comes up in June is the principal star of the Southern Maori and if it came up on the south side it was a sign of bad weather and if up on the north side it was a good tohu (omen). Takurua, another important star, carries the same signs. These two, with Autahi (also called Autahi-ma-rehua), Ngakapa, Matariki, Tawera and Meremere are seven of the twelve principal stars, but he could not recollect the names of the other five just then. Although the stars in the crown of the vault of the sky were said to be in the tenth heaven, he did not know exactly what position could be assigned to stars all round the horizon as he never heard the old people say. Te Ika-a-Raki (The Milky Way) with a myriad other stars were at the top. These stars come out at night and some move like the sun and moon – that was all he remembered the ancient folk saying.

As for navigation the Maori did not steer by stars although he mentioned them in his** sea-going karakia [See Section re Tohukas, H.B.]. Matakokiri are shooting stars – those that 'glit' (glitter). *[For further remarks regarding stars see Mythological Section. H.B.]** [Note: Full moon being called ohua in South Island is interesting. In Tregear's [[1891]] *Dictionary* the table giving days of moon's age has no ohua or hua in Maori but there is ohua in the Moriori and hua (or ua) in all the remaining tables. H.B.]

SECTION XXII

RELIGION

Wharekura or Maori College — Wharepurakau or Maori College — Wharemaire or Maori College — Wharewanaka or Maori College — Wharemata or Maori College — Tohuka or Priests — Akoako or Pupils — Matakite or Seers — Tuahu or Altars — Karakia or Invocations — Tapu or Sacred etc.

THE OLDEN MAORI COLLEGES AND THEIR PROFESSORS

The Wharekura

*The wharekura, said the principal informant, was an important thing in ancient Maori life. It was where the tohukas, or learned men of the tribe, taught the youths the different subjects of Maori education and about tribal history and whakapapa (genealogies). It was a big house and was a tapu (sacred) building. The teaching in it was done in the night time, starting about eleven p.m. and finishing about two a.m. or three a.m. The light necessary was supplied by torches [See Torches section, H.B.]. The tohunga who was going to impart knowledge went to the tuahu (an altar in a sacred spot) first and there said appropriate karakia (invocations). From there he proceeded to the wharekura and taught the selected youths of the community when the rest of the people were asleep, the average length of the lessons being about four hours. This was regarded as particularly tapu work and not lightly to be undertaken. The doings of the wharekura were invested with ceremony and solemnity and hedged in with secrecy. The highest branches of the tohukas' art or knowledge were taught in it, such as religion, mythology and makutu (wizardry). There were three divisions of learning or rather three colleges or schools, viz. the wharepurakau to teach the use of weapons, the wharemaire to dispense general instruction and the wharekura to perpetuate religious and metaphysical knowledge. A youth would go to the tuahu, then to the wharepurakau, wharemaire and wharekura and then back to the tuahu to complete his course. By the time he had gone through all these processes fully he was as well equipped (if his mentality was good) intellectually, as Maoridom could make him. But alas, this teaching was left many decades since – about eight generations ago. It stopped in the time of Hateatea as there has been no more fighting since (on a big scale). There was still continued on, but only partially, wharekura instruction but not the proper old Hawaiki learning, and even these wharekura terminated in the whaling era. Narrator's father was not through the wharekura – the last of the men who were died many years ago. The wharekura was often known as wharepurakau in later years and is often so-called to this day although not a strictly correct proceeding or designation.

The Wharemaire

This was the school for general instruction but like the other two schools it was not open to the general public, being hedged in with tapu restrictions. Each of the three houses was separate with a different tohunga as professor or master. The teaching in the wharemaire and wharekura was necessarily of much the same character inasmuch as it was mostly oral repetition but the wharepurakau differed somewhat in that in teaching fighting the uses of the various weapons were ocularly demonstrated. In the wharemaire there was one teacher, in the wharekura another teacher but each went to the tuahu before teaching and after. The teaching in the wharemaire was general. [The only things narrator mentioned here were carving and tattooing; but probably agriculture, astronomy, treatment of diseases, etc., were included. H.B.]

The Wharepurakau

This was where warfare, tactics, strategy and the use of weapons was taught. It was tapu too but not, of course, to the peculiarly deep extent the other two houses were. It was taught in the daytime and whereas the scholars in the wharekura and wharemaire were mainly youths, the course of training in physical prowess and handling weapons extended from twelve to fifty years of age. (Its teaching may have been more honored in the breach than in the observance during long spells of peace but in troublous times it was imperative that every able-bodied man should be in a state of training and in physical fitness to meet possible contingencies.) Weapons were kept in this building. [Stack [[1898]] in *South Island Maoris*, p. 10 divides the word up as whare-pu-rakau which may be 'pu – a skilled person or a bundle; rakau – a weapon'. Tregear gives wharepurakau as 'a temple'. Purakau is also stated to be the god of witchcraft. Be that as it may it is evident that in later years wharekura and wharepurakau became interchangeable terms (see *Kaiapohia*, [[1893]] p. 50.] When** the collector was at Tuahiwi he spent some time chasing after manuscripts left by the late *T.E. Green, an intelligent halfcaste who took a deep interest in history. Some of this he copied and sent to** the Hocken Library, Dunedin. Green got much of his material from Natanahira Waruwaru Tu, a *tohuka who had been through the Wharekura learning. He also got some from Taiororua, the last tohuka-o-te-Wharepurakau, Taumutu. [He is mentioned in *Kaiapohia*, [[1893]] p. 49. H.B.] This tohuka's very** valuable description of the Wharepurakau and its teachings is appended to this section.

Two Kaiapoi Maoris mentioned the Wharepurakau in passing. In the old days, they stated, the wharepurakau was run at night to teach karakias and history and here the wise old men of the tribe handed down the knowledge of the past.

Herewith follows Maori Manuscript with rough translation. H.B.
Copy [[of]] part of T.E. Green's book

Te Whare Pu-Rakau

Ka tona riteka o te Whare Purakau, he whakaako i ka tamariki rakatira ki maatau ki te tako 'Tuaahuu', ki te karakia mo ruka i ka Taumata, Whaka-Ariki, karakia Ruruku Manawa me te Tupaapaku ki te mea ka hemo,
Karakia whakanoho Manawa kia ora te Turoro,
Karakia Taahuu mo waho i te moana ki te mea ka rere te waka ka puta te hau nui.
Karakia haumanu mo te tupapaku mo te mea ka mate rawa.
Karakia mo te tupapaku ina tuhia raakaitia.
Karakia Taputapu Ariki mo te tupapaku ina whaka-taamirotia.
Karakia Whaka-Tauira mo te takata whakaako ki te patu takata.
Karakia Tako Taahuu mo te mea katata te taua ki the hoariri.
Karakia tohi i te taua.
Karakia Naanaa tupapaku kia ora mai.
Karakia mo te karukaru o te takata a te takata whakatauira ki te patu takata.
Karakia Tuaa tamariki ki te whanau, ka mahu te Pito, ka Tuaatia.
Karakia Tohi i te upoko of the takata ina whawhai raua ko tetahi takata ka kawhaa, ka haere raua ki te wai tohi ai.
Karakia Tapuae mo te takata kia tere te haere.
Karakia Tupe i te takata kia kore e tere te haere.
Karakia mo ka matiti, mo ka kaamo, mo ka waihaka a te takata
Karakia mo ka kiri mamae.
Karakia mo ka tino Rakatira.
Karakia puru i te waho o te Tupapaku.

Karakia whakai i ka tamariki rakatira kia kaitapu.
Karakia Whaiwhaia i te takata kia mate
Karakia Whaiwhaia kereke.
Karakia Whaiwhaia i te raki kia ua, kia taki te whaititiri.
Karakia Tua i te raki kia pai kia kore te ua.
Karakia Taumaaha mo ka umu taapu he nui.
Ka Karakia e whaka akona ana i roto i te whare Purakau, me ka Tako Taahuu mo te takata — tiimata mai ia 'Te Pooo Kouatipu taemai kia te 'Poo Puakahuru' taemai kia 'Te Ao Maarama' tae mai kia 'Te Kare Tuatahi' taemai kia 'Te Aka Matua'; kia 'Te Kore-Te Whiwhia', tae mai kia 'Raki nui e tu nei'; tiimata mai ia 'Raki' tae mai kia 'Io', raua ko 'Tiki', ka haere mai tenei ki ka take o te takata. Ko ka korero tenei o roto i te Whare Purakau; otira he nui ka korero o roto; aua whare. E kore e taea e au i naia ne engari Pea kei muru atu, te oti ai ki te tiakina au e te Atua kei reira au te aata whakaoti ai i etahi wahi o enei korero kua mahue iho nei i au.
Ka tae atu maua ko te Tohuka ki te whare ka kua atu te Tohuka ki te nuika.
Kaore aku korero kia koutou, ko taku korero, i tenei poo he tiimataka whakaako naaku ki te Taiti nei he 'Tauira' tenei ma koutou hoki e whakaroko mai ki taku korero kia ia. Ka tiimata tonu mai tona korero koia tenei. Te korero a Taiororua — Te Tohuka o te Whare Puurakau; Taumutu.

Hakahaka te Raki i ruka nei, ko te Poo Kouatupu, taana ko Rarotimu, taana ko Rarotake, taana ko: Te Poo tuatahi, Poo tuarua, Poo tuatoru, Poo tuawhaa, Poo tuarima, Poo tuaono, Poo tuawhitu, Poo tuawaru, Poo tuaiwa, Poo tuakahuru.
Na te Poo tuakahuru ko Te Matahi Te Poo, tana ko Te Ao, a ha Te Ao Turoa, ko te Ao Maarama, taana ko Te Kare tuatahi, Te Kare tuarua, Te Kare tuatoru, Te Kare IV. Te Kare V. Te Kare VI. Te Kare VII. Te Kare IX. Te Kare X. na te Kare tuakahuru ko Te Aka Matua te Tama ko Te Kore Te Wiwhia te taina.

Ka wehea a Te Aka Matua hei Atua ko Te Kore Te Wiwhia hei takata na Te Kore Te Wiwhia. Te Kore Te Rawea ko taana ko Te Kore Te Taamaua Te kou Matua Te Maku.

Raki =1 Pokoharua Te Poo
Uru Te Maaha, Rakamaomao

Uru Te Maaha = Tawhirimaatea = Te Mauru e taki nei

Rakamaomao = Tiu

Te Operuaraki

Te Haakuetipu

Te Operuaraki = Pe Puuaitaha

Te Haakuetipu = Puunui o Toka

Raki = 2 Papatuanuku
Rehua, Hakina, Taane, Paia, Wehinuiamamao, Tutakahinahina, Te Aaki, Whatina

Raki = 3 Whanakeipapa
Tu Mataueka, Roko Maraeroa, Ru, Uako, Hua, Tea, Weri, Tama nui Te Raa, Puna, Wherei Uru, Kakana

Raki = 4 Hekeheke ipapa (not filled in)

Ko te whanau mahaka tenei o Raki. (Here writing concludes. H.B.)

Rough Translation: The Maori College

The custom of the Wharepurakau was the teaching of the children of the upper class the knowledge of the common tuahu, the prayers for use on the taumata, in making chiefs, in binding the heart (?), and for corpses. Some of the karakaia were:
Karakia to strengthen the lives of those in sickness,
Karakia and ceremony that canoes may be swift on the ocean and winds favorable,
Karakia giving or restoring life to those apparently dead or almost dead,
Karakia for the smearing of the dead with red paint,
Karakia for chiefs whose bodies are to be preserved,
Karakia for initiating pupils in the arts of killing men,
Karakia and common ceremony for men going to meet the foe,
Karakia and sacred ceremony for men going to war, Karakia for health to those tending the sick,
Karakia for stopping the flow of blood when wounded, Karakia for children being born, for the healing of the navel, and for the 'baptism', Karakia and ceremony (evidently branch and water) on the head of each man going to fight so that his skull will not be cracked (?),
Karakia that the footsteps of travellers may be swift,
Karakia that nothing may disable or prevent a man from travelling,
Karakia for the —, for the eyelashes (?) and for the making of the man(?),
Karakia for pain in the skin,
Karakia for the highest chiefs,
Karakia for blocking the mouth of the corpse (?),

Karakia for feeding the children of chiefs with sacred food,
Karakia to bewitch a man to death,
Karakia to bewitch a man so that leprosy overtakes him,
Karakia to bewitch the sky to bring rain and the rolling of thunder,
Karakia that the sky may remain fair and without rain,
Karakia that offerings (thank-offerings) in the sacred ovens may be numerous.

These were the karakia that were taught in the College and in the common religious house for the young men. The teaching began at Te Po ko Matipu and went on to Te Po Tua Kahuru (the tenth po), and on to Te Ao marama, and on to Te Kare Tua Tahi, and on to Te Aka Matua, to Te Kore and Te Whiwhia, arriving at the standing up of the Great Sky. Beginning at Raki (Sky-Father) we come to Io and Tiki the start of mankind. This was the teaching and talk within the college; great was the amount of teaching that went on in these buildings. The one who desired to learn would go with the narrator, who was the guardian of the god at that place, in the early morning to complete some part of the addresses necessary for the occasion. On the arrival back of the pupil and the tohuka at the College the tohuka would address the assembled scholars telling them this was a pupil and he was not going to speak to them but they could listen to his talk to the new pupil on the Po.

[He concludes this portion by adding it is the talk of Taiororua, the tohuka of the Wharepurakau (College) at Taumutu, Lake Ellesmere. Then begins genealogies from Te Po – it is evidently what he starts to teach the new pupil – and of the children of the different wives of Raki the Sky-Father – and here the Manuscript ends. H.B.]

The Pupil

*The sons of the upper classes attended the colleges of learning and the most diligent, or those best able to master the requisite knowledge, became the great masters (or tohukas) of the next generation or the one succeeding that. When a bright boy proved an adept at acquiring the matauranga (knowledge) of his teachers he advanced till he reached the highest stage. Then if he wished to prove his possession of the deepest understanding and skill he had to makutu his teacher so that the latter died. 'That was the worst part of the ancient education of the Maori – if your incantations did not kill your instructor you were not firm in the lessons given.' Before a youth could be admitted to the Wharekura he had to prove his desire by undergoing some trying initiatory tests [See *Kaiapohia* [[1893]], pp. 48–50. H.B.]. The father of the narrator wished him to learn some of the ancient lore of his people and got two tohukas, Koroko and Tuauau by name, to teach the lad who was then only eight years of age (about 1858). This was at Akaroa and they put him through the first stages of pupilship. They took him to the tuahu and said karakia and then took him to water to remove the tapu created by visiting the tuahu. This removal of the tapu is called whakahorohoro. He could see his own shadow in the water. Then they took him a little way from the water and gave him a nasty thing to eat. This was tutae of three kinds, that of takata, kuri and poaka (man, dog and pig) mixed and wrapped in leaves. After this he was free to learn and was taught some karakia. By the time he was sixteen he was to have learnt all or most they could teach him, but alas! the two old men died soon after this.

The Professor

The men who taught in the wharekura were the most erudite of their kind, men with comprehensive minds and trained in verbal accuracy. Some were not only intellectual, and clever mind-readers, but skilled with the hands in doing tattooing and wood-carving. Some excelled in witchcraft and in doing apparently supernatural feats and all were masters of karakia.** He mentioned the name of Tipua-tawhirowhiro as that of a great tohunga in the North Island (Some of the feats of Maiharoa have already been described). *Matiaha-Tiramorehu of Moeraki was a great man of knowledge, chiefly on mythological lines. After the narrator was initiated as a pupil he lived with old Koroko. One morning he got up and the old man was motionless. He touched him and then knew he was dead. The lad then ran down the hill to where Tuauau lived. Tuauau told narrator he knew Koroko was dead because he had seen a ruru (morepork) with its wing stretched out. This is a very bad sign. (It is said the ruru lives there yet.) Tuauau died a year or two after so narrator had not time to acquire much knowledge.

One of the works of the tohunga was to perform the tua, a sort of baptism over small boys and girls. The narrator had not seen the ceremony but the tohunga took the child first to heat – to the ahitapu (sacred fire) at the tuahu – and then to cold – to water (waitapu) perhaps a spring. The tohunga would sprinkle water with a branch of a tree over the baby. It was given a name. After this ceremony the baby was freed from tapu and was free thereafter. Another work of the tohunga was to predict when to go to war and to sprinkle water on warriors going to fight.**

An old man said: 'The tohungas used to tattoo, to carve, to teach the youths, and to recite history but now they pretend to doctor. A man who could carve was a kaupapa-tohunga while the man who had a knowledge of healing was a kaupapa-nana. [Is this word nana short for 'tinana'? H.B.] The tohungas, as a body, had excellent memories.'

The Tuahu

*The tuahu, continued the principal informant, was an extremely tapu spot. To bluntly define it, it was a heap of stones which had been made tapu and here the tohukas adjourned to say their most solemn karakia (invocations) and here they took the sons of the high chiefs to teach them karakia too. No offerings were taken to this sacred spot. The tuahu often had wood about it. The foundation was stones and carved wood would be placed above the pile of stones. Here you could see the best whakairo (carving) of the tohungas – the masters of the art. When a pupil was taken there the professor put him through some preliminary paces to ascertain his adaptability for acquiring and retaining knowledge and then 'when the karakia was firm in him he was taken to the houses of learning and taught the course of instruction.'

Speaking of the tuahu reminded the narrator of the story of one of the most famous progenitors of the Kai-Tahu tribe and as the story centres round the tuahu as well as illustrates Maori customs it will be given here. Tumaro married Rakaitekura and then went from Turanga (Gisborne) to Nelson in the South Island where he built the pa Matangiawhia. The number of his taua (warband) was hokowhitu (seventy) doubled (140). He then went back to Turanga and found his wife 'in the family way' and was suspicious of adultery. When the confinement came on the child was a long time in being born and this confirmed his belief his wife had been false to him. Karakia were said and still the child was not born. Finally the tohunga began to whakapae (name men who might be the father of the child) and just when he named the man whom Tumaro suspected, the child, a boy, was born. Tumaro gave his wife and infant son to Te Ahuhikuraki (or Aohikuraki) and departed to Nelson to live. The boy was called Te Hikutawatawa. One day when playing niti or teka [See Games section, H.B.] the boys tried to hit the maihi (gable) of a house but Te Hiku was the only one who achieved the feat, and the other lads cried 'This bastard is strong'. The boy felt ashamed at such an epithet being applied to him and asked his mother and she said it was true. She also told him he would find his father towards the sunset. When the lad grew big enough he and his party journeyed from Turanga to Nelson on the canoe Makawhiu. When he arrived at Matangiawhia he sat down and cried bitterly. Kahukura-te-paku, his grandfather, told the manuhiri (visitors) to come in. He did not know who the lad was and the latter did not know him of course. At the same time while ostensibly welcoming the visitors the old man gave secret instructions to his men to heat the stones in the hangis (umu) to roast the said visitors. Te Hiku was conducted to a large whare, where reclining on his back he admired the heke and kaho (rafters) of the building. Then he recited a whakatauki or saying about a famous house in Turanga (Gisborne). His grandfather's name was mentioned in this saying and when the old man heard it, he called out to the young man 'Unutai?' (An obsolete term meaning 'Who are you?') The young man told his parent's names and the old man feeling ashamed of his conduct over the oven secretly despatched other orders regarding them. The tohungas, Tautini and Iriraki by name, took the lad ['and pushed him through the window'. H.B.] and put him through the matapihi or matao (window) in the tuaroko (back) of this big carved house and carried him to the tuahu to karakia him. They then put him back through the window and in the whare a tangi (cry) and whaikorero (exchange of oratory) took place. After this it was ascertained that the lad was not learned in the lore of the wharekura and the two tohungas taught him for six months. Before he had properly completed his course a girl told him about the fire that had been made to cook him and his companions. He went to the tuahu and gave way to a fit of temper – hence was his name altered from Te Hikutawatawa to Tuahu-riri (angry tuahu). After this ebullition of passion and resentment he told the people of that place he was going back to the North Island. His grandfather tried to persuade him to stop and learn the rest of the karakia and sacred lore but he set out for Wellington Province. Here he gathered together a taua of kinsmen and friends and returning to pa Matangiawhia took it, killing his grandfather, father, and others. Some of the inmates who escaped fled down the West Coast towards Westland. [Note: In the genealogies Tuahuriri is always given as the son of Aohikuraki.** He was the father of Turakautahi, the reputed founder of Kaiapoi. An influential section of the Ngai-Tahu Tribe – the Ngati-Tuahuriri, to wit – is named after him. This is the first time I have heard the origin of his name. H.B.] This is all the principal informant said about the tuahu but another old man mentioned it in a manner showing the veneration still attached to such places:

'I do not know exactly what the tuahu was but it was very tapu. It might be in a tree, a rock or a house but I do not know that any of those places could be tuahu although its mana might be there. It was a place to be avoided at any time and certainly not to be desecrated in any way. Above Lyttelton there is a place where we Maoris and halfcastes went shearing. One year one poor chap had torohi (diarrhoea) very bad and being unable to shear went to a stump of totara and sat for a while smoking. Then he went to bed and became very ill. That night he dreamt an old man was hitting him on the chest with a stick and the pain of the dream woke him up delirious. It took four or five of us to hold him down. He spewed blood and screamed "Look at the old man! Look at the old man!" and next morning he was dead. Then we found out from an old learned man that that stump was a tuahu where the Tauhinu-korokiu pa had been. The Pakeha won't believe it but it was the mana of that place killed that man and which will kill others if they go there too.'

[Mention of carved figures and carved boxes to hold them and of the ceremony of consulting the god Kahukura is given in Stack's [[1893]] *Kaiapohia*, pages 58–62. H.B.]

Add to Tuahu

*The tuahu was the greatest karakia place of the Maori, the most tapu or inviolate spot, the most religious or sacred spot, the most dread and venerated spot, the most potent in preserving the mana of the race. To those able to worship (or invoke the gods) there with confidence and yet with due reverence it gave the command of the powers of the earth, air, fire and water. By the sacred fire by its side the tohuka would know who had the power of that particular shrine's mana and he would karakia to that power. The Maori did not worship fire, continued the principal informant, but he recognised the power behind that sacred fire and its ability to take away sickness, to counteract makutu and to avert evil from dwellers on the earth. The power or god above the fire was able to protect those who were below it or within the radius of its influence. If the tohuka using that fire, however, was (in prestige, authority or priestly attributes) inferior to the tohuka whose makutu he was trying to thwart, he would fail – the mana of his fire would be no good. These sacred fires were always to be found in close connection with the tuahu. They were not built on a stone or on stones but in a hole in the earth over which a flat stone could be laid to keep in the ashes. Stones were always to be found at the tuahu. Why? Because stone is the strongest thing in the world. Earth can be washed away by floods but stone stands fast. The mountains are made of it – it is an enduring thing.** His son who was at the Great War saw the Pyramids standing in the shifting sand of Egypt and wondered where the great stones came from and how they were placed as they stand. Narrator understood those great stone monuments were a puzzle to white scientists. In the same way he believed that if the very ancient history of the Maori had been preserved, including the origin of the tuahu, the Pakeha would marvel at it and scarcely credit it.

KARAKIA

*The principal informant had little to say regarding karakia (invocations or prayers in one sense, or incantations or charms in another). He mentioned that at Blenheim one of Rauparaha's men Tumatataa had two pups which nosed out the hiding Southerners, who then rushed toward him. He retreated karakia'ing with a stone in his hand and then threw the stone behind him to stop his pursuers. They never shot at him – the karakia saved him, and he warned the Northerners and Te Rauparaha escaped like an eel in the water although a spear struck his pokeka before he dived.**

An old man said to the collector: 'The Maoris never had idols although they said prayers to the gods. It needed a good memory to say karakia successfully, especially the kaupapa-atua or sacred ones. The old-time Maori said karakia before he went to fish, to catch birds, to eel, to dig or do any work. These were ordinary karakia but some of the other karakia were very powerful. That called tapuae-takuhia would enable a man to travel great distances in very little time. A young fellow would be sent from Kaiapoi to Temuka (one hundred and ten miles) and he would be back in an hour or less. An umu could be started when he left Kaiapoi and the food in it would just be ready as he got back again.'

In T.E. Green's writings occurs this: 'Nga Karakia Maori. Tapuai. A te Maiwerohia i whai ia Tu te Maakohu. Hikihiki taku tapuai, Rakaraka taku tapuai,

Te whetu ka hikoia, te marama ka naua, homai he Toroa. Nanau ana te po ia wai? (koe). Whiti ana te Ra ia ia (iau) Tupea.' [This was said by Te Maiwerohia when chasing Tu te Makohu on the West Dome. It is an invocation asking that his footsteps would move quickly and be urged on; and it refers to the stars and the moon, the albatross, to night and to the sun but it would need one skilled in the niceties of such figurative expressions, or familiar with the references here implied, to give an adequate interpretation. H.B.]

THE POWER OF KARAKIA

*The karakia used by the tohuka, said the principal informant, all depended on the occasion, or on what was wanted at the time. If it was the seed-planting season the tohuka would karakia the gods concerned to give a propitious year and a good yield. He could karakia to the sun to restrain or increase its heat as desired. He could karakia to the moon, which it was thought sent cold and storms and minimised the heat of the sun to a certain extent, and ask it to restrain the storms or to decrease the rainfall, etc. The karakias used on sea differed to those used on land and vice versa – the environment being so different. Great care and diligence was needed for successful karakia. Tuahuriri was an accomplished tohuka but he was caught napping and paid the penalty. With Hamua and a crew of hoko whitu (seventy double) he was drowned when the canoe Te Hauwai was lost in Cook Strait. He was anxious to cross and was perhaps careless, for despite his knowledge he did not know a storm was coming. If he did his karakia was ineffective.

Karakia, rightly used, was then all-powerful to bring rain, smooth seas, quell wind, calm storms, dispel darkness at night, etc., although its mana has gone now. The karakia for fair weather would bring good days and nights and favorable breezes but karakia that went wrong would act the reverse way and bring storms. It had to be done extremely carefully as it was easy to 'step over the line' as my informant termed it. All the time-honoured rites and observances had to be rigidly enacted and a word-perfect rendition of ancestral invocations given with the necessary gravity and exact reverence due to the occasion. 'Some of the navigators were wrecked, or turned to stone even as the wife of Lot was turned to a salt pillar,' said my informant, and he went on to explain this was because they had not obeyed to the minutest detail the obligations imposed by repetition of the karakia if it was to be successful.** [Even the ancient Jew under his 'Schoolmaster, the Law' was not a greater stickler for 'exact obedience'. H.B.]

*The Araiteuru and Takitimu, he continued, came together [I do not think this is correct, although he stoutly maintains it is. H.B.]. At Matau-a-Maui (Hawke's Bay) they ran into rough weather and both canoes' crews said karakia. The Araiteuru was only a 'food boat' (she had kumera and seeds on board) and had no one on board who was much good at karakia, consequently she sank when she reached Matakaea (Shag Point) and her crew were turned to stone. The Takitimu was the most tapu canoe which ever came to New Zealand. She had more tohungas on board than any other waka which came from Hawaiki, but even this did not prevent her being wrecked. In the stress of the great storm or in their haste some error must have marred the karakia for safety. When the Araiteuru sank at Matakaea the Takitimu staggered on to Foveaux Strait, where she ran ashore. Despite the karakia of her 'most sacred tohukas', said the informant, she did not land right, but although the waka was lost, the people were all saved and were not turned to stone (like their less-favoured brethren of the Araiteuru canoe).

When a storm arose on a sea-voyage the tohuka (or tohukas) on board would karakia to quell the violence of the karu (waves). He would appeal to sea-monsters to come and protect the waka (canoe) and these (if the karakia was correct) would come and range alongside the canoe and protect it from the fury of the storm and escort it safe to port. The tohuka would pull a hair from his head and offer it to the whale or taniwha. The narrator knew no special name for this observance – it was a part of the karakia, he added. Throwing a human hair to the taniwha was a recognition of its help – it was a way of thanking the big fish for its timely aid.**

Add to Wharekura, etc.

*On this trip my principal informant said that the term whare-maire was a North Island name and he did not know its meaning. This school of learning was, in the South Island at least, usually called whare-mauri – a name with some meaning, mauri being the hau or wind or spirit from inside a person. He did not know any wharekura save that at Kaiapoi which was destroyed with pa in 1831 and he did not even know its name. The first wharekura of all was built in the heavens. The Maoris brought these wharekura knowledge with them to New Zealand and the Ngaitahu wharekura and wharemauri learning came from the North Island with them to the South Island. The door of a wharekura faced east but so did that of every Maori house – either east or north – not to the west or south. This was to avoid the souls of the dead flying through the air on their way to the Reinga. If a building faced the sun ghosts (wairua) nor devils (atua) would not go in it. [See Sections re Mythology, and Death, H.B.]

The wharekura was held at night and no one left the building during the four hours it lasted each night of the season. If they went out they would be killed at once by mana [See Mana section, H.B.] and some had died thus. In opening the wharekura for the season he had heard it said a high-born woman helped in the ceremony but he did not know what she did nor what she was called. There had been very little wharekura in Canterbury so not many details were preserved. The pupils in the wharekura were called akoako or ako – (the word tauira now used for a pupil or scholar simply meant an imitator) – and were tapu during the course of instruction. They were made noa (or common) again by a ceremony called whakahorohoro. The tohuka (priest) would say appropriate karakia and touch the lips with food. The tohukas would do each other first and then the akoako. Many pupils learnt in the wharemauri, the whare-wanaka (where debating speeches were made) and the whare-purakau (where the use of the taiaha, paiaka, tewhatewha, and other weapons was taught) but few became tohukas. The really great ones turned back the karakia on to their teachers whom they thus killed so this kept the number down.

In the wharekura he understood the pupils chewed toetoe, etc., to avert the evils of tapu. To touch the mouth of each with food was called horohoro. He had never heard that this chewing was done to strengthen the memory.

The whare-mata was the building where the tohukas taught the cutting of greenstone; where they cut the navels of babies; or where they cut the skin and hair of men and women who were mourning for deceased relatives.

Astronomy could be taught outside the wharekura as it was not tapu, but the proper teaching was under a roof and no one was allowed to go out. For astronomy, however, they could go out and the tohukas pointed out the stars and gave instruction. One reason why the learning was given inside may have been that it was said the atuas (evil spirits) were worse at night – but such a reason is only superstition.**

TAPU

*The tapu on the wharekura was very sacred – almost as great as that on tuahu. No one could go out or he would die. The mana of the tapu would kill all who violated the karakia or rules. A different tapu went on fishing canoes. You could take food in these canoes except the aruhe which was tapu because it was 'top food' of Maori and also because the fish would flee from the fernroot and the trip would be resultless. For birdhunting, as far as he knew, cooked food was tapu in some forests and not in others – he thought it depended on historic associations.**

A woman told the collector that when she was a girl she was warned from trespassing into the niu (guest-house) of the kaika as it was tapu (to her).

Add to Tohukas

*The principal informant made frequent allusions to tohukas during his nine-days korero with the collector on latter's second trip and collected together they read: He considered that in the old days for a pupil to kill his master to prove his possession of the highest tohuka powers was very wrong. He (narrator) never killed the tohunga who taught him but of course he was only nine or eight years old. Some of the learning put in his mouth still remained with him. His father was a lay reader in Church and never learnt the old Native lore but had no objection to his son learning. Good ways of proving that a pupil was an adept was for him to say a karakia that would make the side of a hill fall, or shift, or slip; or for him to turn the course of a river or cut away a bank. There were not many tohukas in the Kaitahu tribe – only five in recent times. They were frightened, perhaps, to teach others as they might be killed by their pupils as an exhibition of latter's powers.

In regard to recent tohukas, Karaki, Tuauau and Koroko came from the great Hateatea; Waruwarutu from Tuahuriri but not via Hateatea; and Taiarorua from another branch of the family. Tuahuriri [see Tuahu Section in previous Canterbury Notes] left his learning to his son Turakautahi who transmitted it to his son Pokeka who handed it on to his son Hateatea who left it to Te Paho whose brother Paka was a grandfather of the learned man Tiramorehu of Moeraki. [Father of latter was Karaki, the tohuka. H.B.]

The proper old wharekura seems to have weakened after Hateatea's time but Te Paho the third son of Hateatea's five sons (and sixth child of his family of eight) did his best to have knowledge perpetuated. Karaki married a niece of Te Paho and acquiring some lore transmitted it to Tiramorehu. Tuauau and Koroko were grandsons of Te Paho, Tupakihi being father of the former and his brother Potaura was father of Koroko. Te Maiaki (a word which means 'shifting') was another tohuka of the same period as Tuauau and also descended from Hateatea. It was these men who taught the late Natanahira Waruwarutu what he knew. [Note: Waruwarutu's account of Kaiapoi Pa and its downfall was copied by me and sent in to Hocken Library. H.B.]

Some people would not believe him when he said that the matakite (seer) was 'top of the lot' – that is greater than the tohuka. The latter could do makutu, whaiwhaia, whakairo and healing and although the matakite was not a real tohunga he could 'beat the lot', as he saw beyond ordinary vision. The matakite could see everything over both islands in his or her eye. If a thing was lost a matakite could tell you where to find it. The seer could look in pools and see the faces of others at certain times and tell what would happen. Some tohukas were bad men and destroyed wantonly by makutu, but the matakite could best such men. The matakite would watch and would take the tohuka's tokotoko (staff) unknown to him and would perhaps rub handle in tutae of tohuka and replace staff. The tohuka would dirty his hand and angrily would curse and say makutu against the man whose excrement had defiled his stick. He would thus makutu himself unknowingly and he had not the power to undo his own curse. After pronouncing his angry makutu he would probably go to the water and seeing naught but his own image as the 'guilty party' he would find it was himself and would succumb to his own makutu. If a theft, etc., had been committed the tohuka might makutu the footmark to ascertain who the culprit was. One makutu killed quick, another kind slow. If people heard a rustling or thought spirits were about he had heard that smoked food would scare atuas (spirits) but he really knew nothing on this subject from South Island lore. The tohukas of old knew when spirits were about and why!

When travelling about people were afraid of makutu and to make part of the protective karakia, put something in the mouth but he forgot the name of this ceremony. If your karakia was 'firm' nothing could touch you – sickness, makutu, whaiwhaia, etc. If you missed a word 'kua whati te karakia' it was a bad omen, or to break (ko whati) a song was bad also. If words in karakia or speech go wrong (ko tapepa) it was a bad sign – it meant the tohuka was going to die soon. He thought that every tribe in New Zealand considered tapepa a really ominous happening. Ko heke might also mean an omission or slip in enumerating names, etc. ('Ka heke tatau ki ko' means to shift to another place, and heke is to shift a word out of its order. He considered that the terms whati, heke and tapepa denoted practically the same thing, and all were bad.) When he had made the mistake, if he could go back and repeat it right there would be no aitua in it, but if he could not do this he was doomed to speedy death. Aitua meant death or sudden misfortune and was all over the world. There was no need to kill a tohuka if he made a mistake (and could not immediately correct it) in karakia, whakapapa or history recital as he would die in any case, but if a tohuka began to desert the ancient lore and teach his own ideas he would be put to death as otherwise his conduct and the promulgation of false teaching or erroneous ideas or heretical doctrines would destroy the tribe. He fancied he had heard of such a case in the South Island – something about Te Wera killing an unorthodox teacher, plugging every orifice of the body with clay and putting same in umu, but he had forgotten the names and details.

The mauri might be called the knowledge that was held within the wairua (soul) of man or the animating principle of anything – it was very hard to describe in English. He could not say how far this principle went. The tohungas gave its interpretation in the wharemauri – the chief school of learning, the seat of the highest education of the Maori. The mauri could proceed anywhere – its karakias could touch the bush, hills, deep sea, rocks, rivers, mountains and anything. Karakia was all over the world. Besides invoking the mauri of anything, the proficient tohunga could take it away from anything. He could take it from a man – the man would die; he could take it from a forest – the bush would die; he could take it from a mountain – the mountain would fall. If he took the mauri of the sky, nature would rain, snow or storm tempests. The knowledge of mauri started from the heart of man and went through everything. Speaking generally, makutu was to take the mauri of anything from it. [In answer to questions narrator stated:]

Kehua is a devil, a ghost, a spirit left the human body. It is a North Island name, a common or slang name. Not used in South Island. The real name is wairua.

Ahua is the likeness of the face of a person or a thing; its resemblance. Take a photo of a man or woman or of a place and you have his or her or its ahua. Aria is no language at all as far as he knew. Never heard word. Probably means ahua.

Mauri is like unto the wairua, only the latter comes out from the body, but the former remains within a person in the soul or seat of intelligence. You might call it spiritual knowledge, mental education or the accumulated experience which comes from observation and instruction. It was an invisible essence in the composition of the spirit or soul, and if taken away or it departed the person died. When a person was sick the tohunga would recite karakia to preserve the mauri of the patient, but if it died or departed no words that the tohunga could utter were fit or able to enter the dead person.

Hau means wind is like the mauri – as far as he knew it practically meant the same.**

The accounts preserved by the tohukas in the wharekura were, to his idea, very like Pakeha ideas of creation, etc. God made everything in six days, but the ancient Maori made this a long time nevertheless it was not far from the Bible account in essentials. *Some tohukas varied from others but some of them must be right and no single one of them could give and explain the whole lot. Some people might say that narrator was born at too late a day or was too young to give the ancient histories but he would do his best.**

Add to Tohukas

*The subject of tohukas and their work cropped up ever and anon during conversation with the principal informant. The tohukas could bring on rain and thunder, he knew, but to say one brought down tukarakau grubs in rain [H.B.'s articles *Journal of the Polynesian Society* [[Vol. 26, 1917]] p. 76]** was only 'a rubbish yarn' although the old tapu people believed in it. *The tohuka could not only bring on rain but he could stop it when required urgently. At Akaroa the tohuka got the people to sit down and he said karakia and the rain stopped. This is not the end of the story, however. The people were grass-seeding and Te Kakau, the tohuka, got water out of the centre of a big flat stone. It came with such a gush it spurted up into his eye, and it formed a spring they could not bottom. This spring was the result of that tohuka stopping the downpour of rain. The South Island tohukas had no use for water in their karakia save that they used a sheltered pool with a surface clear as crystal for whakaata. When they said a makutu against some unknown person's footmark, etc., they would see the shadow or reflection of that person in the pool – hence the name whakaata (a mirror or reflector). A common use (not by tohukas only) of streams was to cure sickness [See Medical Lore, H.B.]. They never used hot water in old days – it was all cold. The tohuka, as a sacred personage, did not drink in the usual way, but the water was poured into his hands held so as to guide it to his mouth. In the old voyaging days the tohukas were responsible for the navigation of the canoes. They did not steer by the stars at night but would mark a particular spot (called a kahukura) in the sky and steer by it. In the daytime they would steer by what the Pakeha calls 'sundogs' (called kahukura, also, by the old Maoris).

They did not steer by the stars, although the names of these are mentioned in maritime karakia.**

Another Maori said: 'The tohuka was to give turakau, or strength in battle; to make a youth into a toa-taua or warrior; and for other tribal purposes.'

Add to Tapu

*The ramifications of the tapu are so widespread throughout the old Maori system it is hard to say where its influence begins or ends, but the following few items have been sorted out under this heading from a mass of correlated facts concerning mythological data, former religious beliefs, ancient wizardry, present-day remnants of superstition, and evidence concerning the curricula and procedure of the Wharekura together with the prestige and powers of the higher class of tohuka.

The principal informant mentioned tapu a few times. He was once with old Te Maiharoa at Lake Wairewa near where Little River runs into it, and lit a pipe to smoke but he did not enjoy it in customary way – the tobacco seemed to have a funny taste. The old tohuka said 'No wonder' (or words to that effect) and told him that he was tasting a relative who died there long before. It appeared that some sixty years or more before this a body was found floating in the lake together with an upset canoe. The body was pulled ashore and placed on the rock beside them to await someone to identify it and then for the relatives to take away and burn it. Maiharoa said the man's name was Tapui and that he was a relative of narrator, hence the strange taste of the pipe. The rock was bare of vegetation but the old tohuka lit a match and put it to the top of the rock and it flared up into a blaze for several minutes. Narrator said it must have been the oil out of the dead body but Maiharoa said that that had been washed off long before. The tapu was still there, however, and he had now destroyed its power.

Going to Taumutu with the old tohuka they passed a locality which witnessed some fighting in the Kaihuaka ('Eat Relatives') War [See [[Jacobson and Stack 1914]] *Tales of Banks Peninsula*. H.B.]. Maiharoa told narrator latter's ancestors were 'looking at them' as 'they wanted him.' They came to a clump of tumatakuru and he told narrator to stand in the centre of the patch as Tawha and another chief had been killed there. He would try to get the spirit of the place and warned narrator to keep a sharp lookout and catch hold of anything which came along. He said 'Here it comes!' and grabbed at it but could not hold it although he stooped and got down to it. It was a karara about two feet long but it had no head or tail. Narrator grabbed it by one end and held tightly. He never let go but it simply vanished, leaving him looking at his clenched hand. It was a 'miracle work of the tohuka to kill the tapu'.

Then again he was with Te Maiharoa crossing the Peninsula and on Waipuna Hill saw another exhibition of the powers of this old tohuka who was endeavouring to destroy the tapu of places so that the modern Maori need have no fear of them but could dwell in peace and security. He saw the old man jump from the ground to the top of a stone twelve feet high. This was to end and destroy the mana of Tahununu who was killed near there. Narrator called out in astonishment 'What have you got there!' and Maiharoa held up a lizard of which he was ordinarily very frightened. He dropped the lizard and narrator caught it and tramped on it. Simultaneously the old man fell off the high stone and landing on his head lay as one dead. For a long time those present did not know if he was dead or alive but they put cooked food on his head to 'take away the force of the spirit'. They looked at Lake Wairewa and could see the fish playing in shoals. When Maiharoa recovered, he sat up and said the fish would depart and sure enough they migrated then. The old tohuka then burnt the lizard to kill the tapu of that place. This was in 1872. Tahununu, who was an uncle of narrator's grandfather, was a great chief of his day.

To remove the tapu from a house the tohuka said karakia = 'whakahorohoro'. To remove the tapu from a person they did not pour or sprinkle water over him, but said appropriate karakia. The only use for water, he knew of, as far as tohuka work was concerned was for whakaata at pools and even this was accompanied by karakia.

Taowhakamoe is one way of removing tapu. You make a fire and put the stones in a kapa-Maori and the heat from the umu comes up and takes the tapu away. This method was, as usual, accompanied with karakia and is mentioned several times in South Island lore. [See Fairies, H.B.]

The korero-tipuna (talk of ancestors) used to be tapu once and a man would not eat till it was finished, but now that the mana of the Maori is broken and the tapu gone, the narrator remarked, here he was telling the collector the things of old, many of them of a tapu nature, and smoking as he talked and breaking off for meals just as if such a thing had never existed. This was a sure sign the tapu had lifted.

[Note: The collector would remark here that his principal informant is alone in saying that water was not used in ceremonies. He had said that the tohuka would go to the tuahu and karakia and then to the water and karakia, but he will not have it that water was laved over people. Either he had forgotten this (which is unlikely), or he sees the greater significance of spirit over matter (of karakia to an invisible god to [[the performance of]] a visible act), or (what is more likely) his instructors laid particular emphasis on the importance of fire in perpetuating mana and tapu. H.B.]**

Two matrons (one aged and one middle-aged) at Temuka said: 'To relieve the tapu off a person, put that person in the water and say karakia. The name of this we forget, but tuku-ki-te-wai is to go into the water. Such a ceremony was done to enable pupils to remember whakapapa and karakia, and also at the naming of children. It was the karakias used which made these ceremonies differ from one another. No fire was used at any of those ceremonies that we know of – only water.' [Note: It is possible that expression tuku-ki-te-wai may be derived from New Testament concerning John the Baptist. H.B.]

A rock near French Farm, Akaroa, is of a red color and is said to have been made so by the blood of people slain on it. [Was it sacrificial?] It is tapu.

*The head of a man is his most tapu part and the hair is sacred also. Hairs of the head were used in certain rites but were not to be burnt and the principal informant had never heard of such being done. If it had been, he added, the tohuka would have died or been killed for interfering with such a tapu thing.**

SECTION XXIII

MYTHOLOGY

Maui's Exploits — Tane and Heavens — The Sun and Moon — Kahukura — etc. — The Work of the Gods — etc. (Note: Most of this information is printed in the book Tikao Talks [[Beattie 1939]]. H.B.).

MYTHOLOGY

*The principal informant did not set out to give the collector an exhaustive view of what Reverend J.F.H. Wohlers (Porora is his Maori cognomen) called the 'sublime mythology of the Maori', as the stories relating thereto have been put into print** time and again but in the course of his extensive descriptions of ancient Maori life and customs he now and then referred to the higher lore of the Polynesian people and these scattered fragments have been pieced together and are herewith presented:

THE TEN HEAVENS

*When the children of Te Rangi (the Sky-Father) and Papatuanuku (the Earth-Mother) determined to push them apart the question was how was it to be done? Finally Tane lifted his father Rangi with a great pole called Poututorangi. This is the pole that now props up the ten heavens. It rests on Papatuanuku and although the Pakeha with all his wisdom cannot see the pole the old tohungas could. There were only ten heavens and they extend beyond the stars and are suspended one from another, the bottom one being propped up from the earth. When Tane finished his great work he laid the pole across the last floor from north to south and hung the heavens below. Whaka-tarewa is not the real name of this suspension but each world or heaven hangs to the one above – he did not know if by ropes or something else. The stars were somewhere at or near the top he thought. There might even be a 'floor' beneath the earth. He was sorry he forgot the name of these ten heavens. He even forgot the name of the god or people who lived on the first floor, but on the highest floor the head of that place was Te Rangi-whaka-upoko-i-runga – a great deity.

THE REINGA

Besides ten heavens there were said to be ten po or underworlds but the principal informant said he did not know where they were. From this floor (the po) the soul went on to Ta Anu-Matao (freezing cold) but he did not know where that was. The reinga is at one side of this floor (the earth) and the soul leaves this world and goes into the reinga (also called reika). The soul leaves New Zealand at Moreanuku [See Tregear's [[1891]] *Dictionary* – 'Morianuku'. H.B.] – it is the Rerenga-wairua. A big tree, perhaps a puriri, hangs down its roots there and it was said the soul went down under the water but he did not think so as the Reinga is practically next door to us. In the history the soul lives in the body on one side, then the body dies and the soul passes on to the other side. [He used his hand to illustrate – palm equalling the living side and back of hand the dead side, the soul apparently going through at death. This was to show what a thin division divided life and death – this world and the next one. His explanation of Maori ideas of Death, etc., were very hard to follow. H.B.] The collected [[i.e. collector]] asked what and where Honokiwairua was and was answered that Honokiwairua is the last of life – it is death itself and the name of Death, after which the wairua (soul) slips through to Te Reinga. In the great dispute between Tane and Hinetitama over the question of life or death Tane unfortunately let Hinetitama go, hence it is that she draws men to the region of shades and that death pulls all human beings from the world of the living.

This was the native history and he thought in its essentials it did not differ very much from Pakeha ideas as to the Soul and Death.

THE GREAT WORKS OF MAUI

Work Number 1. His Arrival

To get back to the beginning of the story, according to the principal informant, we must consider his (Maui's) immediate ancestry. Mahuika (which was his name on land but he was called Murirakawhenua at sea) married Hinepunuiotoka and they had a family of five girls, viz., 1. Hinearoraki, 2. Hinearoaropari, 3. Hinehauone, 4. Hineroriki, 5. Hinerotia. The eldest of these girls married a man named Te Ranga or Te Raka and was the mother of Maui. 'I know,' said the narrator, 'it is asserted that Mahuika was the father of Te Raka, but I am telling you the proper story as told to me many years ago.'

Te Raka and Hinearoraki had five sons, viz., 1. Mauimua, 2. Mauiroto, 3. Mauiwaho, 4. Mauitaha, 5. Mauipae. Then the mother had a miscarriage (whanau karukaru) and the napkin was thrown away into the sea. Maui's grandmother and her four daughters (without including Maui's mother, that is) were then living out at sea and Hinehauone got hold of the premature child and nursed it to life. On warm days she would put Maui ashore on the sand for the sun to develop him; then she would take him into the health-giving sea and nurse him. Soon he grew into a fine child and then into a robust boy. When this stage of development was achieved the grandmother and aunts decided that Maui could leave the sea which had cradled him and go and visit his mother and live on land. But when Maui was put ashore on the sunlit beach he was covered with marine creatures and growths and he got rid of these before proceeding on his travels. He stood on the sand and told them to go back to their home or environment but three of them still clung to him tenaciously, so he unwound the rimu (kelp) and tossed it out on the rocks in the sea and there it waves, and rises and falls with the tides, to this day. The pawa he pulled off his body and clamped it on to the rocks where it adheres to this day. The wheke (octopus) hung to him so he pushed the pu (hollow) seen in it, tugged it off and threw it into the rocky pools where it now lives. Then he went to his mother. At first she would not accept him as a son but eventually she acknowledged him.

Work Number 2. The Barb on the Fishhook

Some time after Maui arrived at his mother's home he went out fishing with his brothers. These latter were very jealous of Maui's prowess in most matters and would not let him fish but he looked on instead, noticing everything as usual. At that time 'matau kaore hi naku' – the fishhooks were without barbs – so many fish slipped off the hooks and consequently not nearly so many were caught as should have been. This the quick glance of Maui noticed and he drew his elder brothers' attention to it but they calmly paid no heed to his words. It was their policy to ignore Maui-tikitiki-o-Te-Ranga ('Maui on top of his father's head' – a title he had acquired) as they were afraid he would by reason of his supernatural cleverness rise to be 'he upoko', a man greater than any of them. When Maui got home he found his mother alone and told her about the need of improvement in fish-hooks. He said that if a barb or something was fixed near the point the fish would not escape so readily and he asked his mother where he could get an idea for a suitable barb. The mother sympathised with the youth and said she would show him. She slipped off her mats and told him to 'look at her tara and take notice of the** sharp bit at the bottom and made a barb of that shape'. [The narrator here digressed to say that woman's sexual organ had one hundred and seventy Maori names, of which he had heard about fifty – but he only mentioned three – tara, hi, and rapa (see Hawaiian). The penis, on the other hand, had very few names attached to it.] *So Maui made a barb of bone as near the shape of the model as he could devise and tied it on to a fishhook near the point. Of course the brothers were not satisfied with such a newfangled idea and would have nothing to do with it until they found that Maui could go out and catch fish in abundance while they caught almost nothing, so then they adopted the idea. 'This,' said the narrator, 'is a very long story but I have cut it short.' [He said that since Maui called the barb 'naku' that has been its name. It is new to me. H.B.]

Work Number 3. Turns a Man into a Dog.

As Maui grew up he married (and not content with one wife for a start) he took unto himself Hineturepo and Hinetakahere, the sisters of Irawaru. After this Maui (as a householder, no doubt) made a garden separate from that of his brothers and worked hard to make it a success. Irawaru was supposed to help him clearing ground and sowing seeds but he was a very lazy man and did very little. He would often lie down and go to sleep. Maui spoke to him but it made no improvement and he bore with it as long as he could. Then he said 'This is no good to me', and finding Irawaru stretched out snoring he lost patience altogether and he pulled the sleeping man's ear, nose, tuara (spine) etc. into the shape of a dog. Then to complete his work and show his utter disgust at the conduct of the man whom he had changed into a kuri (dog) he did a tutae on its nose. In the evening he went home leaving the dog still sleeping. His wives noticed that Irawaru was not with him as usual and they asked Maui 'Where is your taokete?' (brother-in-law). Maui kept silent at first and they got anxious as they knew he was a strange man to cross. He finally said call 'Moi! Moi! Moi!' and they did so. The dog answered with a kaitau (howl) and came running up. 'That's not him' said the sisters. 'Yes,' replied Maui. The sisters were very sorry and wished the dog changed back into human shape as their brother but no one, not even Maui himself, could re-transform the dog so thus it remains to this day. And that was the beginning of the dog's nose, of its shape and color, of its power of smelling things and of its habit of eating filth. It ate the tutae off its nose and dogs continue to eat such stuff to this day.

Work Number 4. Turns Himself into a Pigeon.

Maui wanted to know why the fire his mother used lasted so long each day and then faded away leaving no ash or refuse to carry over till next day. The other brothers took this fire for granted but Maui pondered over it a long time. Finally he asked his mother why the fire behaved in such a manner and she answered that his father brought it in quantities just sufficient to do each day. 'He brings it from your tipuna, Mahuika, down below there in Raroheka.' 'Can I go there?'

'No! No! You cannot.' 'Where is the road?' 'I do not know.' He then asked how his father travelled and she replied he could fly like a bird through the power of his maro (loin-cloth). Maui said 'Make me a maro, too,' and his mother whatu'd (wove) one like the shape of a kahu (hawk). Maui got into it and could fly all over the place and that is why ancient kites (Polynesian) were made as like hawks as possible and were called manu (bird) or sometimes kahu (hawk). [See Tregear's [[1891]] *Dictionary* – 'Kahu'. H.B.] Maui's mother said, 'I will now make you a maro in the shape of a kereru (pigeon),' and he tried it also and found he now had the power of the kahu and the kereru. The father noticed Maui flying about and was suspicious of pranks but his suspicions gradually lulled. One night while all the rest slept the wakeful Maui hid his father's maro and blocked up every hole in the whare through which daylight could filter. His father invariably awoke at the first glimmer of dawn and was away before anyone else stirred but this morning he was deceived by the absence of light and slept in. At last Te Raka jumped up and a glance outside revealed how late it was. He frantically looked for his maro but could not find it. He even awoke Maui who declared he did not know where it was, so the father reluctantly went off without it. Maui (who was sleeping with one eye open, to use an English phrase) saw his father shift the poutokomanawa and disappear down the hole. That night Maui quietly handed his father the latter's maro and said 'I know where you go.' His father sadly remarked, 'I did not want to show you as you might do something to my friends or me, even as you did to Irawaru.' Maui explained he was anxious to know the mystery about fire and asked could he not go to get it but his father said that was impossible. This answer did not satisfy Maui, so early next morning he slipped down the hole through which his father had already gone and set out to find him. Maui, who was in the shape of a kereru, saw men working in plantations as it was the time for sowing the purapura (seed) kumera. He sat on a tree and looked on. The people tried to snare this plump pigeon but Maui dodged all the attempts. Finally he settled on the ko (spade) of his father, who was suspicious all the time who it was. After a little talk between them Maui changed his shape from a pigeon back into a man. He then asked his father where Mahuika lived, but Te Raka, at first, refused to tell. At length, however, after considerable persuasion, he said it was in a great cave away off in a certain direction.

Work Number 5. Maui Obtains Fire

Maui set off to visit his grandfather who lived in the cave. When he arrived there he saw a pakura which was the mokai (pet bird) of Mahuika. [The pakura or the swampturkey of settlers; pukeko in North Island. H.B.] He asked the pakura if Mahuika was inside and on receiving an affirmative reply he told the mokai his name and lineage. The bird thereupon went in and informed its master who said he was glad his mokopuna (grandson) was there and to bring him in. Maui was then ushered into the presence of Mahuika who was a giant. After some talk Maui explained his errand and asked if he could carry up some fire to the world above where it could be all the time and not have to be procured every day from this country (known as Raroheka or Rarohenga). The giant gave Maui a blazing finger and Maui went off with it, but only to return and say it had gone out. He got another and this he blew out also and so on until he had got nearly all the giant's fingers extinguished. Then the pakura sang out to his master, 'He puts the fire out purposely.' Maui was angry and caught the bird and jammed down on its head a spark (of the last finger) which was still lingering. Hence it is that that bird (which is a blue color) has the red patch on the crown of its head to this day. The giant, enraged at the trick, threw fire out of the cave to consume Maui and the whole country round went alight and blazed up. Well was it for Maui that his mother Hinearoraki, [Hine = girl; aroraki = 'the flight of birds like the hawk' (or soaring) c.f. aroarowhaki in Tregear's [[1891]] *Dictionary*. Hinearoraki is now the goddess controlling the flight of birds. H.B.] and that she had taught him to fly. He changed himself into a kahu and soared up and up till he got beyond the reach of the flames but not of the smoke which turned his feathers into that dingy brown livery that hawks wear to this day. He said karakia all the time and a storm came on but the wind only fanned the flames although the rain deadened the fire a little. Even hail did not check, to any extent, the conflagration but then the soft snow came and fell and fell until it completely put out the fire. Then Maui came down and passing the mokai at the mouth of the cave he went in to find that Mahuika was dead – killed by the power of Maui's mana. Maui asked the (bird) titakataka (fantail) where Mahuika kept fire hidden. The fantail refused to tell so Maui took it and placing his thumb on its head and his index finger on its stern he gave it a good squeeze. That is why that little bird's eye is so prominent – it nearly bulged out – and why its tail projects so far out beyond its body; and further, why it flies 'so cranky' ever since (too much pressure on its brain, evidently). This drastic treatment, however, made the fantail reveal the secret. In case of eventualities Mahuika had stored plenty of fire away. He had put a certain small quantity in every tree in the bush and then finding that after this distribution there was a considerable quantity over he had placed the remainder in the kahikomako, or kaikomako, tree. Hence it is hard to get fire from most trees; but easiest of all is the kaikomako. The fantail got a kauati and karimarima and holding the former, directed Maui to rub (hika) with the latter and he got fire. (The narrator said both pieces were kaikomako.) Maui then cut off Mahuika's head and extracted from it the kauwae (jawbone) which he named Omurirakawhenua (after Mahuika's other name). Then he changed himself into a hawk and flew back to his mother. When he got there he explained how he could get fire from two pieces of wood his brothers sneered at the idea. (In their country they had never seen any fires save what their father brought.) But the mother believed in her youngest son and held the kauati while Maui rubbed the karimarima and procured fire. 'No one can take it from us now,' he exultantly cried, and his brothers reluctantly agreed it might prove a very good thing.

Work Number 6. Maui Secures More Daylight

In those days the sun went round its daily journey far too quickly to please Maui, or indeed any of the rest for they all felt the nights were too long and the days too short, but they did not know how to alter this state of affairs. The morning meal (about ten a.m.) was eaten in daylight but by the time the women could get the afternoon meal ready it was dark and the food had to be eaten in darkness. This did not suit Maui at all and he gave a deal of earnest thought to the problem. Finally he said to his mother: 'It is not right we should eat in the dark. You put food in the umu and every day by the time it is ready darkness comes on. The sun is going too quick so I will go and fight it.' His mother said, 'It will burn you,' but this did not discourage Maui for he went on making ropes. What these ropes were made of I do not know but Maui took them to the place where the sun rises and put a snare over the hole. Next morning when the sun rose the noose caught it round the neck and threatened to strangle it. Maui, who was by himself, was holding on to the noose prepared for a grim struggle. 'Let me go,' roared the sun, as well as it could for the strangling cord, 'Let me go.' 'I will if you will make the day longer,' replied Maui. The sun demurred but finding Maui obdurate and that it could not escape, it finally agreed and hence we have the present length of day. The rising of the sun (before it took the longer journey Maui imposed on it) was at Te One-ki-pikopiko-i-whiti which was a sandbank on the back of Maui's aunt, Hinehauone, and the narrator thought this lady helped Maui to hold the sun. 'The sun was hot and gave off such a strong heat that Maui jumped into the sea to keep himself cool, and I think Hinehauone assisted him, although it is not so stated in the history,' said narrator.

Maui was a god. Some Pakehas think Maui could not stop or alter the sun but it is quite true as he was a god. He was angry because he had to eat cooked food after the sun went down. After his fight with the sun Maui went back to his mother and said 'Watch the days now.' She did and found the days were long – there was no more eating at night.

Work Number 7. Maui Fishes The Land Up

Maui's next great work was to fish the land up, to accomplish which he used the jawbone of his tipuna Mahuika or Murirakawhenua as a hook, adding a naku (barb) to it. The brothers refused to allow him on their canoe, the 'Mahunui', so he went out in the early morn and hid under the rahoraho (planking). It was a single canoe to hold seventy double (one hundred and forty) and the brothers sailed quite unwitting that Maui was on board. When a long way out from land

Maui showed up, and the brothers growled, 'We did not want you. You are in too much mischief.' One brother said, 'We are out far enough,' but Maui exclaimed, 'No! Not at all! Go further out into the deep sea.' The people on board argued the matter some saying Maui was right and some saying they were out far enough but finally they went on. Then they came to a stop and put the anchor down. Maui had a line and hook which he had brought, but the brothers would give him no bait. He got angry and hit his nose and it bled. Blood when cold is karu-karu, clotted, and he tied some of this to hook with a little string. 'Kai mai e waro, kai mai e waro, ko waro uri e waro,' said Maui when his sinker touched ground. ('Waro is a part of Mahuika – it is on the sea and latter is on the land. He had two bodies, had the giant tipua called Mahuika,' said the narrator, but the collector frankly admits he could not understand this explanation). 'Ko waro tia e waro,' repeated Maui three times as the fish took the hook (or vice versa). The brothers sang out 'Maui, let that fish go!' but all Maui's reply was addressed to the fish, 'Ka whanake, ka whanake' (Come out, come up). The brothers screamed, 'Let it go; it is a devil,' but Maui commanded them to pull the anchor up and paddle for their lives. By this time the stern of the canoe was so far down the people were afraid. Maui shouted 'Keep rowing,' and doing so held the fish up. Thus was the North Island of New Zealand exposed to view. The South Island is Mahunui and is the canoe Maui was in. When he saw Te Ika-a-Maui he wished to join it to the South Island by pulling it up to the canoe and shouted 'Kumea, Kumea, Kumea' (pull, pull, pull) but when the brothers saw solid land they were so relieved (after their fright) that they jumped on to it and left the canoe to fend for itself. It was through their disobedience (when Maui requested them to keep on the canoe as he wanted to pull the 'fish' close up) that the North and South Island are separate to this day. Then Maui had time to have a look at the fish he had hauled out of the depths. He saw the long tail (the Auckland Peninsula) and he saw its head (at the Wellington end), the tip of its upoko being ORokoRoko; He saw the two eyes – Wairarapa (Lake) the eye which emerged first being freshwater, while the other eye Whanganui-a-Tara (Wellington Harbor) is still salt. The hook Maui took out of the fish's mouth and laid it alongside the fish where it now forms Matau-a-Maui (Hawke's Bay). 'That was the finish of that fight,' said the narrator, but he had a few ideas and surmises of his own to add. He considered that not only did Maui pull up the North Island of New Zealand but he pulled up all the other Pacific Islands at the one and same time. There was no other history touching those islands he knew, but that each island knew the history of Maui seemed certain. He did not know if it had been said before or not but he considered Maui pulled up Polynesia all together at one time. How could the island people all know the story of Maui unless they had all been pulled up by him. Perhaps Melanesia was pulled up by him too. He had heard of an Anglican Bishop sailing in Melanesia saying [to] his Polynesian crew 'Ko whea tenei moutere?' (What island is this?) and the black people on shore knew his meaning, 'so they must be like us and perhaps Maui pulled them up too.' He reckoned that Wahu and Oahu in Hawaii was mentioned away back in Maori tale and history.

[As the next page sees the end of the principal informant's account of Maui it may be well here for the collector to say that though he has divided the story into eight sections the narrator only divided it into six, viz. 1. Finding the barb. 2. Irawaru 3. Finding Fire 4. Fighting the Sun 5. Fishing up Land 6. Fighting Hinenuiotepo. He called them 'fights' not works. The collector made an extra division at the beginning, and divided the one on 'Fire' into two – hence his eight sections. The concluding section brings in so much food for reflection, and is so different from any account the collector has seen, that he gives it in the narrator's own language as near as possible and leaves commentators to draw their own conclusions. The material is clearly very ancient. H.B.]

Work Number 8. Maui's Last Great Fight. He Meets Death but is Vanquished.

Maui's next 'battle' and his last was with Hinenuiotepo (Great Lady of the Night, or Underworld). She was 'atua mo te mate' (the deity of death). 'Maui's conflict with her did not happen in New Zealand for after he had pulled up this land he went back to Hawaiki-nui or Hawaiki-roa – I think it was the latter. I think Hine was a big wave of the sea or a sort of depression between two big waves at sea or two hills on land. Maui said to his brothers, "Now when you see me go through this wave – this woman – remember not to wake or disturb her – let me struggle through." To this they agreed. Maui crept into the tara, wriggled his shoulders in, squirmed his body in until only the legs were out. Then he began to push harder and the little kick his feet gave made his brothers laugh. The birds joined in and the united laugh awoke the giant lady, the tara closed on Maui and he never appeared again. If Maui had got through to her mouth people would not die; they would grow so old and then renew their youth time after time, but since Maui failed everyone dies. If Hinetitama had come back with Tane after their big argument, death would not have entered the world and there would have been no need for Maui's attempt to overcome it many, many generations later. Maui was smothered. A line of an ancient song says, "Nana i kome mai Maui ka mate i te karu whakapuke ra" – he met his death in a wave (karu) heaped high, but whether this death was on land or sea I know not. I think it was on land as he died at a place called Te One-ki-pikopiko-i-whiti and Hinehauone could not help him on land although she holds the sands at Pikopiko-i-whiti which is a very ancient name, afterwards brought to Rarotonga I believe. She is in the sea yet and her mother and sisters (the grandmother and aunts of Maui) hold important positions in connection with the world. They are in the points of the wind. They stand at points round the world and hold the principal winds. The mother, Hinepunuiotetoka, is in the South-West holding "te pu o te toka (tonga)" – the beginning (origin) of the south west. Hinearoaropari holds the echo of the parikalakalaka (parikarangaranga) on all sea cliffs and land cliffs. Hinehauone besides holding the sands at Pikopiko-i-whiti holds the easterly to north-easterly winds Hineroriki holds part of the northerly winds – the powerful ones. Hinerotia, I think, holds the north to westerly winds – all these women are on the water yet. The only one of that family on land is Hinearoraki who controls the flight of birds. She was the mother of Maui.'**

[Here endeth the principal informant's account of Maui.]

More About Maui

An old man told the collector what he remembered about Maui. The collector was looking for other information but the old man would not be denied. The information may not be of much value but is interesting as showing a version of the olden tales as told by an illiterate man – 'the man on the street' a la Maori.

Maui had three brothers and also one without any life in him – a lifeless character not taken into account – so there was five of them. His father was married to two sisters – one wife had four sons but Maui was the only son of his mother. I forget their names. There was no marriage in those days – they just lived together. The three brothers had a 'set' against Maui. They went fishing and caught good fish such as moki, trumpeter and groper for their mother, while poor fish such as ling and mako they gave to Maui's mother. This did not suit Maui so he decided to go fishing too. He made a dummy (whakapakoko) in his bed and slipped out early and stowed himself in the canoe. The brothers got up, lit a torch, and looked at Maui's bed in passing where they could see him, as they thought, sleeping. Then they went down and to (launched) the canoe and put out to sea. About one hundred miles out to sea they were astonished to see Maui appear. 'How did you get here?' they asked. 'Where are all the fish?' replied Maui. The bravest brother answered, 'On all other days we get fish in plenty but to-day we have none.' 'You can't fish,' said Maui, 'Give me a line.' But they wouldn't until the oldest one said 'Here's a short, broken line to play with.' Maui had no hook and they wouldn't give him one so Maui took out a jawbone he had in his mat. It was the jawbone of Murirakawhenua I think but I am not sure. The brothers said, 'Look at that hook!' Maui was in the peak of the canoe and smacked his nose and let the blood drip on the bone, and rubbed it over it. His nose stopped bleeding without the brothers having noticed it and they wondered how the bone which Maui was going to use for a fishhook turned so suddenly from white to red. They were still wondering when a nibble shook the waka and the sea became rough. When Maui was dribbling his blood on the jawbone he said the right words and also when he let the line over but I forget those prayers he said. They were strong prayers and acted at once. When the sea became rough (agitated) the brothers asked 'What is there?' 'Just a nibble,' replied Maui. The waves by now were mountains high and the brothers called out 'Let go!' At the third bite the fish made off with the line and the sea became rougher, the canoe bucking. 'O Maui let go,' yelled the brothers, 'Let go – it is a taipo.' 'No fear,' replied Maui. Then he hauled in the line and hauled up the North Island. There it was – houses and gardens, fires burning, smoke going up and people talking. Maui hauled it up. His god was the jawbone – kauwae-o-te-tipuna. Maui was always great. When he was a boy he could give any bigger boy a hiding and people used to taunt him with being a poriro (bastard) and a tiraimoko – this is a slang word to say you are a ghost. [Tregear gives Tiraumoko – illegitimate. H.B.] The first name Maui had was Hikutauataua [See Tuahu section, H.B.]. He could catch eels by karakia. He wore a raukura on his head. This was the pikimanu of some bird. When it is on the bird, feathers like that are called pikimanu but when cut off and put on a man it is called raukura. [This struck me as interesting and I notice Tregear says the Moriori meaning of 'piki' is a feather. H.B.] It was through wearing a raukura he could turn himself into a bird at any time. Tikitiki-o-te-raki is the name of the prayer he said to ascend the sky. The jawbone was to fight with and he fought fire, the air, the sun, rain and wind, the sea and all dangers, but death got him at last.'

[So ended the breezy narrative of this old man and it is just such narrations that give zest to the remark of the sage in the 'Lore of the Whare-Wananga', when he dismisses the Maui stories as a lot of 'idle tales'. Yet when we heard them told as the principal informant told them we recognise that there is a world of meaning hidden away in these tales if we could but unlock the gate of folklore with the key of science.

*Stack [[1898]] at p. 100 of *South Island Maoris* names seven labours of Maui.**]

Add to Mythology

* Rarotimu
Rarotake
Raropoiho
Raropoake
Ko taku
Ko takeo
Io io whenua
Tipu kerekere
Tipu anana
Kai a hawaiki
Ko Matiti
Matititua

Matitiaku
Matitiaro
Ko tekehu
Te Wharepatahi
E hui te rangiora
E rongo ki waho

matatahi mai te ara o tu
manuhiri tuarangi kei tawhiti
te kai; kai te waro te kai
e kainga tu ko ko ko itu ha

Io whatata
Io whatamai
Ko Hekeheke-i-nuku
Ko Hekeheke-i-papa

Te Po ko Uatipu
Te Po tuatahi
Te Po tuarua
Te Po tuatoru
Te Po tuawha
Te Po tuarima
Te Po tuaono
Te Po tuawhitu
Te Po tuawaru
Te Po tuaiwa
Te Po tuakahuru

These, said Tikao, are the great whakapapas of creation if anyone living could unravel their mysteries or unveil the full meanings. No Tohunga living could whakapapa from Rangi (the sky) to the present time. All details of Maori belief were bound up in main whakapapa above but he could only explain a little – not much. This was where the teachings of the whare-mauri would have been invaluable. According to what he had learnt there were four main roots in the story of creation. 1. Starts from the water, from Rarotimu in the ocean. 2. Starts from Te Po ko uatipu and begins the po and the kore. 3. Another root is Io – the Supreme God – the greatest root of the lot. 4. The fourth root is Tiki and from this comes man, fishes and birds.

Firstly – dealing with the whakapapa given he was sorry that though he had learnt it [He could recite it fluently. H.B.] he had been unable to obtain so little information. Only the old people could have given the exact details but he would say what little he knew. The word 'raro' in that whakapapa meant beneath the sea. At that time the ocean was very prominent, and the first life in the universe began in the water; then the fish came and then the human body – all from the water. The words Rarotimu and Rarotake both mean 'roots'. Raropouiho is to dig a hole and put a post in and Raropouake is to turn the post or pole up. This might refer to Tane raising Rangi up. Taku means to make the land firm (as like putting a pile under a house). Tipukerekere is thick, dark clouds and Kai Hawaiki is the land coming up. He did not know the meanings of Matiti and Rangiora – whether they were houses or what, but waro is the deep sea fish from which Maui pulled up the land. Waro is part of Murirakawhenua at sea and Mahuika was his fire on land. He had never heard the least explanation how the ocean came into existence but it was the start of life in the universe. He believed this root was correct – that everything came from the water. The whakapapa starts in the water and the details of rain, hail, snow, frost, dew, fog, thunder, lightning and other manifestations of nature are all bound up in it and other very ancient whakapapas but he was 'too young to catch this learning', but the one (given previously) starts in the sea and proceeds from the deep water to Hawaiki (the cradle of the Maori Race). In that whakapapa the words ma tatahi might mean the people along the seacoast or beach but he did not think so. The manuhiri-tuaraki referred to means a visitor (like recent visit of Prince of Wales – this title was applied to him by the Maoris) – a baby from the sky or from a great distance – it really means the birth of very high-class people – a distinguished event. Old Henare Matua, the last tohunga in Hawkes Bay; knew one form of this whakapapa, but whether he left an explanation of it, my informant did not know.

Secondly – He knew even less about the Po than about the Rarotimu whakapapa. The po were the ages preceding the beginning of creation. It was never said in any Maori history or song which he had ever heard that there were worlds under this one – under Papatuanuku the earth. [The collector read him the names of the ten Po or underworlds as recorded in Tregear. H.B.] This, he said, was simply the North Island people trying to explain the Reinga. He did not know where the Reinga was, nor did any Maori whom he had met, but it was not underground – old legends stated it was near us or beside us, practically next door. The Po that were referred to in the whakapapa he recited to me had nothing to do with any Hereafter or Underworlds but were the long ages of darkness before the earth came out of the ocean and the sky was heaved up. The Kore were also long ages of Nothingness but he did not know the details of this lore. At the end of the Po whakapapa Te Maku married Mahoranuiatea and begot Rehua, the sun, now commonly called Ra.

Thirdly – Io was the greatest root of all. He was the Supreme God. The Pakeha has Father, Son and Holy Ghost as supreme but the old Maori made Io the god over all. In the short whakapapa given (of four names) Io Whatata goes one way and Io Whatamai goes another way. They were on top of the water – there was no ground to stand on but when the dry land appeared Hekehekeinuku was called

Rangi, and Hekehekeipapa became Papatuanuku. These two married and had only one child – Tane. The whakapapas which started in the water from Rarotimu and Tiki did not continue on Papatuanuku when she appeared but went upward and continued in space – hence they do not come down to present mankind. Before this time all life or creations were from and in the ocean but after Papatuanuku came up and Rangi was raised they had places to stand on and space to go up into. The word Hekehekeinuku means hanging upright and shifting and Hekehekeipapa means hanging horizontal or flat. He considered that Io was the beginning of both Rangi and Papa, and that Tangaroa or Takaroa (now known as a god of the ocean) came long after these two. He must explain, however, that he knew very little about Takaroa. It was said he was from an old race turned to atua or taniwha, a race of sea-beings such as brought the Maori from Hawaiki (original) to New Zealand. Takaroa was a great fish or sea-monster, but he had heard very little about him. He would cut the waves for canoes migrating. The ocean was Moana-nui-a-Kiwa but he did not know who Kiwa was. The old people said that in the middle of the sea was a vast rua (hole) and this caused tides – when the water went in there it ebbed from land – taitimu; when it came out it flowed up the beaches – taipari. Taipana is beginning of ebb or flow – kua pana te tai. Te Waha-a-Parata is the name of the rua and Parata spits water out and swallows it back but he did not know who Parata was – he was not a whale although so-called; sometimes Parata is given as a figurative name for death, it means a swallower. How the ocean came before the sky and land he had never heard explained but Io the great god brought the sky (Rangi) and land (Papa) into being.

Fourthly – The position of Tiki was also hard to explain and he had not heard as much information about it as he would like, but he had been told that Tikitohua was the start of human beings; that Tikikapakapa was the start of the fish in the sea and that Tikiauaha was the start of birds. He believed this root was given because we all started from the water, but we had come higher and left the fish in the water. When fish are ashore their tails kapakapa (flap) on ground but in the ocean these tails guide them. Birds come from Tikiauaha – the word auaha means that when birds fly about their mouths are open. Man comes from Tikitohua. The term tohua means the same as ahua – built up. Rangi ahu'd his wife from the oneone (soil – onepu means sand). He wished he had learned the history of Tikitohua – the start of mankind.

CONCERNING TANE AND TEN HEAVENS

In regard to the detailed story of Rangi, etc., 'he had left that behind', except some details about Tane. There were no whakapapas from Tane nor from any of the gods of that time. Tane was the son of Rangi and Papa and Rangi said to him that he (Tane) had better push both Rangi and Papa up, but Tane said he could not do that. Then Tane got the pole Poututarangi which had ten hono (joints), which afterwards constituted the ten heavens, but he forgot the names except that this great pou was called Poututerangi. Narrator was prepared to uphold this fact against anyone. [The collector read a list of the ten heavens as recorded in Tregear. H.B.] He considered these names were not correct with what he had heard – he was familiar with none of them. Tiramorehu had composed a song about Rangi and the heavens and the right story was in it, but narrator could not recall it. It stated that Rangi was pushed up and formed top one of ten and after he was pushed up Tane came down to see how Papa, his mother, was faring and she told him to go up again, so he went to first floor (heaven) and left twenty children there and so on to each floor, his progeny equalling two hundred. He left Te Maiwaho as the leading god on the first floor, Rehua on the ninth and Te Rangi-whaka-upoko-i-runga on the tenth. This is probably Rangi himself. No one knows the song now and narrator forgot the remainder. When Tane went down to Papa he found all the heavens were firmly fixed so when he went back up he said to Rangi he would change the position of the pole from upright to horizontal across roof of sky from North to South. This he did and then returned down to earth, leaving his big canoe Tutepawharangi (the canoe of Ruatapu many centuries later was named after it) to the family of Tamarereti and it can still be seen, renamed as Te-Waka-a-Tamarereti, among the stars that adorn the heavens. This Tamarereti people were lifted by Tane when he lifted Rangi, and they are there yet as they don't die like mortals. Narrator would like to 'catch hold of Tiramorehu's song re creation. He had 'caught' the gods of three floors but seven remained beyond his recollection. Some North Islanders had told him Tane had one hundred and eighty children but he replied it was two hundred. He did not know the ladder Tane came down – perhaps it was his mana. When Tane returned down again his mother was alone and there was no one on earth, so Rangi thinking that Tane would be lonely sent down the wairua of Tane's own daughter Hinetitama to be company for him. Tane heaped up soil and put the spirit in it and it became Hinetitama in the flesh, and bore him two daughters named Tahu-kumea and Tahu-whakairo. Soon after Tane went away for a while and during this time, two of his heavenly sons, Te Ahuhu and Te Amaruraki by name, came down to earth from one of the heavens. Hinetitama questioned them about Tane and to her horror and dismay found he was her father as well as her husband and she fled. When Tane came back these sons told him Hinetitama had gone away. Tane sprang up into the wind and sniffed and so knew direction Hine was going and hurried after her. When he overtook her they had a spirited argument but he could not prevail on her to return – hence death came into world. She went to Te Reinga where her name was changed to Hinenuiotepo and from where she drags the souls of men and women to her abode. When Tane lifted Rangi everything went up and left Papa bare. Te Maiwaho was one who went up and who stayed on the first floor, from whence comes all the rain, snow, hail and wind that beats on the earth. When Tane saw his mother was so bare he sent down a lot of his offspring from the heavens. These are now the totara (a son of Tane), matai (belonged to Titikura, a son of Tane), kohai (of Mautakitaki a grandson of Tane), houi (a daughter of Tiriwa a female), rata (a son of Tane's son Mumuhako) and others. The bush is now called Te Wao-Nui-a-Tane and there are nearly two hundred trees in it. Above the first floor there is no wind or air, but these things come from that floor to the earth. If no rain came no vegetation could live and if no wind blew we could not live – that was the Native history. Maui's aunts have tawhiriwhiri (fans) to create winds but he could not say what these fans were made of. The sun shines through the heavens from the second top floor and the stars were higher – on the very top one just beneath the pou of Tane. He did not believe that the souls of the dead went up to these heavens as Hinetitama pulls them to Te Reinga. Tane returned from his controversy with her to upbuild and rear mankind and for this purpose he apparently remains at or near the lake Waiora-a-Tane in the heavens creating fresh human souls to endow each newly-born baby with. If Tane had prevailed on Hinetitama to return to earth with him Death would not have entered the world and man's soul would not be doomed to pass into Te Reinga. If Maui had vanquished Hinenuiotepo he would have regained the advantage lost by Tane. If he had done so all people then living would have renewed their lives and never died. There would have been no married life or at least no more children, hence no overpopulating of the world. The demigods in the heavens have never bred since immortality was conferred on them so there is no overpopulation up there and this state is what Tane lost to men and Maui failed to regain. There was no sickness in the heavens – at least in the nine top ones – as dew, rain, snow and frost were absent from them. These things bring sickness on earth. He did not know how people breathed before Maui's time but Maui's grandmother, Hinepunuiotonga and his aunts began to fan (tawhiriwhiri) the air so that mortals could breathe. Since then if the winds stopped altogether the sun would prove too strong and we could not live. The winds just blow between the first floor and the earth – he had heard the name of Ururangi applied to that wind but he knew nothing about it. The wind does not blow higher than the lowest floor as there is no air up there. He does not know how the gods live up there – they must be very different to the human race.

In regard to Maui's family some said that Maui had three brothers, thus making four sons; while others said he had five brothers making a total of six sons; but narrator considered that there were five sons. The Maui pae given by adherents of the theory of Maui having five brothers was really Maui himself, who besides the title of Maui-Tikitiki-a-Te-Raka was also called Mauipae because he drifted ashore. After his treatment of the titaiwaka and pakura (as recorded in former Canterbury Notes) these birds were extremely angry and when Maui was trying to conquer the Great Lady of Death the former bird tickled her nose and wakened her up to Maui's destruction.

CONCERNING THE SUN AND THE MOON

Rehua the sun dwells in the ninth heaven and comes up over the back of Hinehauone who holds (how he (narrator) does not know) the sands at Pikopikoiwhiti. Rehua means fire. (Mahuika means the same – Murirakawhenua lives on the water but his other body (he has two) lives on shore as fire). Marama the moon lives on third or fourth floor above earth and is from the same whakapapa as the sun. Marama dies and comes to life again each month. He had never heard much history about it. It was said that Tererewa was thirsty one night and sent her servant Rona with a taha (or calabash) to get some water to drink. (Tererewa was a woman and Rona a man – perhaps he was her husband but is generally stated as her servant). It was a cloudy night and he had difficulty in finding his way through a clump of bushes to the spring and cursed the moon for hiding its light. The moon heard and came down and whisked Rona up and now every full moon if you look at it you can see Rona with his calabash and also the clump of trees. This was a common yarn and narrator first heard it at Akaroa many years ago. In the old days the Maoris used to count thirteen moons to the year.

The sun has more mana than the moon – it is Rehua the fire but he had not heard that the moon was fire. The old Maoris seemed to have no details re the moon. In karakia, ra (the sun) was mentioned and marama (the moon) was mentioned also. One could not say definitely and exactly the sun was worshipped or prayed to, but karakia were said asking it to confer favors re seasons. Rehua was the sun. If it did not shine grass, vegetation and life would cease.

THE FORCES OF NATURE

The collector asked the principal narrator what he knew about Ruaimoko** [It is said in Tregear that earthquakes are caused by Ruaimoko turning. H.B.] but he simply laughed *over the Ruaimoko idea. Ru, he said, was an earthquake and he had never heard the old people explain. [It may be explained it is a custom of the old man to go over old waiatas, etc., at night-time and a day or two later he informed the collector he had come across Ruaimoko. H.B.] It was in an old puha (war-song) referring to the banging of thunder and the flashing of lightning which, he added, come together. The reference to Ruaimoko was in the line, 'O Ruaimoko puritia tawhia kia i ta i ta e,' and this is asking Ruaimoko to hold fast (puritia tawhia) amid the fury of the storm. Ruaimoko is here seen as the chief, or god, holding the power of both thunder and lightning. Whatitiri in North Island talk is the thunder but Whatitiri is correct and is so mentioned in the whakapapas. Perhaps he is a minor god controlling thunder. Tawhirimatea and Tupai are also mentioned as powers of the air. As for lightning (uira) or zigzag flashes (kohara) he had never heard much about it. He did not know its reputed origin nor its god. [Next day he said he had picked up part of a song about lightning and this had brought a few things to his mind. H.B.] There were three kinds of lightning – ouria, kohara and kapo. The latter name is applied to a flash here and there all round the horizon or sky and it is a tohu, or sign, of wind. Tawhirimatea sends it, and lightning generally. Hinenuiotetoka holds te-pu-o-te-hau (the power of the wind) and Tawhirimatea (or Tawhiriwhiri as he is also known) is the fan the wind-goddesses use to disperse the winds over the world. Narrator did not know if Tawhirimatea was in existence before the time of great Maui, but since that time he has acted as a fan to the winds. The song says lightning is a fire. If the full force of the wind was let loose on man the result would be disastrous so the lightning and clouds are put in being to retard the winds or we would be blown away. Then if the full force of the lightning was let go man would be burnt up, but Ruaimoko and Tawhirimatea hold back its full power and just send enough to help control the elements. [Next day the old man resumed the subject. H.B.] The song said that not only was lightning a fire but that ru (earthquakes) were also fires. The lightning shows up but the fire of the earthquake does not; yet if the ru burst the hills fire would show up or come out. Tawhirimatea and Ruaimoko hold these great forces even as the Goddesses hold the strong winds. He could not say what good they were for, like he could the winds, but the world would be destroyed but for those two retarding gods. All these things were in the whakapapa from Rarotimu if one could just elucidate them. Io io whenua was the power given to the various gods who control the elements and the manifestations of nature. Tipukerekere's mana or power was given to Ruaimoko and if he liked to be 'a bad brute' he could do a lot of mischief. So could the other gods but there were usually restraining or minimising influences; but he did not know the details.

He had never heard the origin of snow nor the name of its god. In an eclipse of the sun or moon they were said to meet together. The details necessary to give an explanation of this were hidden in the Rarotimu whakapapa but he had not the key to it. He never even heard the old people give a name to an eclipse of either sun or moon. Eclipses, even partial eclipses, did not occur very often.

'Tiwhanawhana ai Kahukura i te rangi', is a line of a song referring to the arch of light in the sky. The name kahukura is applied to night rainbows and the Aurora Australis, although another name of latter is tutumaiao. Kahukura was also the name given to ordinary rainbows, but a more common and perhaps a better name for ordinary use was aniwaniwa – a name which refers to the beautiful colors in the bow. A ring round the sun or moon was called umu, and a meteor or shooting star was called matakokiri.

SOME MYTHOLOGICAL NAMES

Kahukura – When the people navigated the Moana-Nui-a-Kiwa, Kahukura assisted them in the form of a rainbow. Narrator never heard origin of this lovely phenomena of Nature, but it was like a sign or compass pointing the road into unknown seas to the bold, venturesome navigators. Kahukura's sign was the rainbow – either double or single. Aniwaniwa is the ordinary name of the rainbow, alluding to its beautiful shades. Awhioraki (or Awhiorangi) is a personal name bestowed on rainbows. Awhioraki goes in a circle from ground to ground round the sky; but the proper (mythological) name of all rainbows is Kahukura. After the main beginning of the world and when people began to spread, Kahukura became the main god of the migrators. He would separate the good from the bad weather; he would protect the frail canoes on the heaving ocean; he would send fair winds to waft the canoes over favorable seas. Kahukura is very high in Gaitahu (Ngaitahu) estimation generally – they do not all claim him as their god but certainly some of the principal hapus do so.

Takaroa – Tangaroa (as called in North Island) was like Tinirau one of the chief fish in the sea but narrator did not know their relationship. There was an ancient saying, 'Te Whatu-Kura a Takaroa', which was now a figurative allusion to a-highborn girl. He did not know its primary meaning – 'whatu' means 'weaving', not 'a stone' as collector thought, although a leaden bullet is now called whatu. Anyway, whatever its original signification, if you now see a bevy of chief's daughters and wish to refer to them in proverbial or complimentary strain you would call them 'Kahui-kura-a-Takaroa', or more briefly, 'Kahui-a-Takaroa'.

Maru – This was the name of a god he thought, but it was merely a name to him as the old people had never explained it to him.

Tawhaki and Karihi – went to heaven for something very important, but he never learnt the whole history of it so would not speak about them.

Kaikaiawaru – Was some sort of god – he was a bird in one shape, a dog in another and yet a pig in another. [The collector reminded him that Captain Cook introduced pigs and he agreed to this. He did not know how the Maori called the pig poaka when he saw it – but puaka was a star from the beginning of creation.] The meaning of Kaikaiawaru was all kinds of birds from big to little. [Does this mean he was the tutelary deity of feathered creatures? H.B.] Kaikaiawaru was a wairua (god) of Gaitahu. The old name of Kaiapoi Pa was Te-Kohaka (kohanga)-a-Kaikaiawaru.

Mu and Weka – He thought these were people from heaven but he did not know much about them. They were said to have given different languages to the different races of men. The word 'pakeha' once meant an enemy in a fight and also denoted a person with a white skin. In the days before Europeans came if a Maori had a big family and one was an albino (korakorako) such an one would be called a pakeha. The eyeball of such people were white. He did not know where albinoism started – probably in Hawaiki. There was a race of people or spirits called patupaiarehe and one might come of a night and sleep with a Maori woman and the resultant child would be whitish, even though all her other children were brown. If such a thing had gone on very much and for long the Maoris would have become white, but albinos don't breed. The turehu was another race of spirits like the patupaiarehe and maeroero, but hakaturi and ponaturi were terms not used in South Island – must be North Island words. The Tini-o-te-para-rakau was a race – the race of Wahieroa the father of Rata.**

Add to Mythology

*The principal informant recurred to the question of the origin of the universe on several occasions. Once there was nothing but water. The only whakapapa which did not come from the water was that of Io. There was no sun then, but only darkness. This continued for ages and ages. Io then brought the two Hek-ehekes (Rangi and Papa) out of the waste of water. Io-whatata went to one side and Io-tatamai to the other side and the sky (Raki) and earth (Papa) emerged from the vast ocean of water. The pair were very close together, Papa underneath and Raki on top. When Tane pushed the sky up the earth was level, but narrator could not say what had made the mountains and valleys. Some Maoris say that the earth was soft then and went up and down in mounds through the gods or people stamping on it but he could not accept this explanation although he had no ancient theory to account for the long ridges and sharp peaks. The people of old said the world was flat (not a globe) but they never said how thick it was. Ancient songs say the world is round [i.e. circular – like a plate. H.B.] and that the sand lies round it like a rim and outside and beyond this is space. It may be compared to a basin of water – the sea lies round the big Hawaikis and beyond the water is the fringe of plain – its general name being Pikopiko-i-whiti. [The idea of the basin of water, as the collector understands it, is that the world to the ancient Maori was chiefly sea with a sprinkling of islands on it and also the big ancestral land in part of it. If a basin was filled with water and a number of tiny floats anchored in it – that would give the Maori conception, as far as I can see, the rim being the encircling fringe of sand. H.B.] It was from this fringe of sand that Maui noosed the sun as it came up in the morning. The sun goes up high through the heavens and then sinks down west side of space, under the earth during the night, and up east side each morn. Maui was not born in Hawaiki but at Nuku-tawhangawhanga. It is a plain near where the sun rises in the morning. It is near Pikopiko-i-whiti. Another place, Hui-o-Rangiora, mentioned in the Rarotimu whakapapa he gave me on last trip, is also near Pikopiko-i-whiti at the end of the world near where Maui was born. Two other names were Pikopiko-i-rangi and Pikopiko-i-nuku and he thought they denoted the sun's course in its circle round the earth – the former being its course through the heavens and the latter its course through space.

He had told me last trip that Tane had no brothers – this was a mistake on his part for he had recalled old songs and recitals that named several brothers. Takaroa, or Tangaroa, was one brother, as, like Tane, he was a son of Raki, or Rangi, and Papa. Rangi's proper name is Rangi-nui and he is also sometimes called Rangi-roa. Papa's full name is Papa-tua-nuku. Tanemahuta and Tane-nui-a-Rangi are also names of Tane. It was Tane who raised Rangi up and who named him Rangi nui and for answer Rangi named his powerful son Tane-nui-a-Rangi. An old song says that Tane had brothers and narrator understood he raised his brothers up also when he raised Rangi. Tane made the form of a woman and his father Rangi sent down a spirit from the heavens to put in the form and this Tane did, naming her Hinetitama and taking her to wife. When Tane was away, Te Ahuhu and Te Amarurangi, sons of Rangi, came on a visit to Hinetitama with disastrous results to mankind. This first-created woman [with the natural curiosity of the sex, eh!] was very curious to know where she came from but Tane evaded her queries adroitly. The day and night had no answer to her query, so she asked the 'poupou o te whare' (posts of her house) but no answer came from its mouth. She asked 'te pakitara o te whare' (the wall) but no answer came from its mouth. She asked 'te tahu o te whare' (the roof) but no answer came from its mouth. She asked 'te maihi o te whare' (the veranda) [Tikao said the maihi was the 'spire' or apex of the two facing-boards. H.B.] but no answer came from its mouth. Then she asked the two celestial visitors (named above) and they told her she was in reality a daughter of Tane up above, whose spirit came down to the form of the woman Tane formed. [This myth recognises the spirit is the real person – not the body, evidently. H.B.] The woman was dismayed when she heard this and fled with her three daughters, viz., Hinenuiotepo, Tahukumea and Tahu-whakairo. Since then she has pulled souls to the world below. This world is like a compass on the balance and there is one beneath us. [See Later. H.B.] [This statement was too obscure for me – I could not grasp his halting, involved, meaningless explanation. H.B.] Tane pursued her and argued with Hinetitama, but he was ashamed and hence she won the argument. Finally she said 'You go back and rear our children and I will proceed and drag them down to me' – hence death entered the world. Te Whare-o-Pohutukawa is the house from whence the three girls (Morehu, of Moeraki, mentions two in his waiata) watch the souls passing from the world of life to the Reika, or Reinga, the region of shades. The four or five brothers (of Tane?) look after the world and keep it going. Ruaimoko is the worst of the four and Tawhirimatea is the best. All Tane's children came down from the heavens to dwell on the earth and most of them are trees; Te Whanau a Punga is a family of fish which jumped right from the heavens down into the sea when Ruaimoko first banged his thunder (whaitiri). They were afraid of the noise and although the thunder made the sea rough the fish took refuge in it. The family of Tanemahuta came down about same time as that of Punga, near the beginning of the world. The family of Rautu or Tama-Rautu (whoever he may be) is mentioned in an ancient waiata dealing with creation. Some of that family dwell above in the heavens and some on earth, but he (narrator) could not explain what they were or are. Tawhiti and Torikiriki are mentioned in it as children of Rangi but their particular history he knew not.

The people of old Maoridom said karakia to Rehua, the Sun. This luminary is a son of Maku and Mahora-nui-a-tea and they named him Rehua, but Tane called him Tama-nui-te-ra, hence he is usually known by the abbreviated title of Ra. An expression in an old song, 'Te ra o tu waru,' means the heat of the sun for eight months in the year. (The other four are cold.)

Maku by his second wife Huareare had another son Maramahuakea, now known as Marama, the Moon. [See Sky-Lore Section, H.B.] The word Huareare is applied to spittle but also means the phlegm or mucus inside a person. [Note: These names are interesting. Maku is rendered as Moisture by John White but is much more likely to be the South Island rendering of Mangu = blackness, a state of being one could expect to rank in Maori conception at the conclusion of Te Po or ages of Night or Darkness. From the marriage or cohabitation of Darkness with Great Expanse of Whiteness (Mahora-nui-a-tea) comes the Sun. From the union of Darkness and Spittle comes the sun's lesser brother, the Moon. There may be nothing in these names, or again they may put us on the track of how the old Maori considered that these great cosmic forces came into being. H.B.]

An expression in an old song – 'Ko nga tupuni a Wehi-nui-a-Maomao' the narrator considered to be a mythological allusion to the heavenly bodies, (the sun, moon, and stars), but he could not (or did not) explain it further. The song calls the stars 'nga kanohi o te rangi' (the eyes of the sky). Stars mentioned in these old waiatas are such as Hirauta, Hiratai, Te Parinuku, Te Pariraki, Te Kahui-whetu, Puaka, Takurua, Meremere, Aotahimarehua, Pungarehu, Maki-motumotu; Wero-te-ninihi, Wero-te-kokota, Were-te-Au-maria, Te Ahuru, Te Wewera, Te Mahana, Te Ika-o-te-Raki, Whitikaupeka, Manako-uri, Te Kore, and Manako-tea. [See Sky-Lore.]

The narrator went on to say he had not referred to Maui killing Tuna when he was giving me his abbreviated account of the doings of that celebrated hero. Takaroa, a son of Raki and Papa, was the root from which Tuna sprang. It was through this killing that Maui originated eels and also the hinaki method of catching them, thus adding to the list of useful labours accomplished by him as narrated in these notes on previous occasions. Tuna was a kind of taniwha who lived in a stream and got himself into bad odour with Maui because he frightened Maui's two wives – Hineturepo and Hine-te-ngahere who were tuahine (sisters) of Irawaru. The name of the place where this very big eel, or taniwha, lived was Papakura-a-Takaroa and he was descended from Takaroa. After the scaring of his wives Maui asked a man called Haere to make a trap, noose, net or snare or other thing to catch the monster. Haere gathered the tororaro vine which was spread out over the pakihi (plain) of Nuku-ta-whanga-whanga and he made the first recorded hinaki (eel-trap). It was a very big, strong eelpot and was put in the stream where Tuna lived and caught him. It took a lot of people to drag the hinaki, with its heavy captive, ashore. Maui cut the great fish in two and the head part jumped by its own power into the sea where it formed the koiro or conger-eel and the tail half jumped into a river and there originated the tuna or ordinary eel. The head flew off to the sunrise, or east, and landed in the sea in the vicinity of Pikopiko-i-whiti and Pikopiko-i-rangi, while the tail did a dive into the river known as Muriwaihoata. The collector asked the narrator if he had heard the name Rohe as the name of a beautiful wife of Maui whose face Maui stole by duplicity. He replied he had heard a smattering of such a fairy-tale but it was only fanciful embroidery inserted to make the story more wonderful than it really was and to make it longer in narration. Other fictitious yarns were sometimes inserted in the history, but instead of making it attractive they only made it strange or ridiculous. Rohe is the part of the hinaki which leads the eel into the pot.

Maui fished up the land and he (narrator) was of opinion that at that one mighty pull Maui not only heaved up the whole of New Zealand but also Oceania as well. The name of the canoe from which he did this was Mahunui. If Maui had not been cruel to the pitakataka (fantail) and other birds he might have escaped death but these feathered creatures remembered his unkind behaviour to them and they did not obey his injunctions when he tried to creep through the Great Lady of Night. The pitakataka instead of keeping well back came fluttering over her face and its long tail tickled her nose and made her stir a little in her sleep. This made the fantail snigger and the other birds laughed and the sound awoke her with dire results to Maui.

It was Tutekoropaka who brought the okaoka (nettle), tataraheka (lawyer), and tumatakuru (Wild Irishman), etc., to New Zealand and who planted them round his whare to elude pursuit. [See Mythology in previous Notes, H.B.] Tama who tore up and down the West Coast in his frantic search for his fugitive wives is also credited with introducing what my informant called 'rough seeds' (i.e. prickly, jaggy plants and coarse vegetation), and he thought that Kupe was also sometimes included in the category of those bringing plants which were not a blessing. It was said that these very early explorers wanted to block other people from spying out the country and landing, so they left rough, impenetrable-like vegetation round the coasts but narrator thought this was not a 'true yarn' about those men. Kupe was also said to bring the first nets to New Zealand. Killing fish is called tairo and Kupe started it here. 'It is to drag fish ashore and is a good work; but taramanuka and tumatakuru are bad works.' Taramanuka is to set a fire through manuka and then when the blackened remains dry they are hard and jaggy and you cannot get through them. This, and planting prickly shrubs to tear men's feet and legs, are works of an evil nature.

Mentioning the name Matamata to the narrator elicited these details: Matamata, a 'ghost', came originally from Hawaiki. There is a race known as Kati-Matamata in the South Island but he is not sure if any descendants still survive.** Mrs Pirini Ruru, at Koukourarata (Port Levy) is probably of this descent and *there is probably another at Kaiapoi. Rakitauneke, the famous

Katimamoe warrior, was one of this branch. Matamata was the god of war in Canterbury, and in some parts of the North Island too, but he knew no karakia nor waiata about him.

The collector asked the principal informant if there had ever been any 'winged people' in Canterbury or the South Island. He repudiated the idea that there had ever been any people of this kind anywhere in New Zealand. It was all moonshine and nonsense by a section of the North Island people and had no real historical backing. The Kahuirere, whom they state were people who could fly, was a family of the kumera and the true meaning of the phrase is that the people who were guardians and growers of this tuber fled with it – hence came the story which has been magnified into a statement they flew away.**

Another Maori said there was a people in South Taranaki called Kahuirere. Another people there was the Kahuimatangi. He was descended on one side from the former people. Their name was derived not from flying but from running swiftly. They had no wings at all but were merely speedy of foot.

Additional

*Since writing above the collector has again seen Mr Tikao and asked several questions relative to above. His answers state: Hinenuiotepo was a daughter of Hinetitama. The two other daughters of latter woman were called Tahukumea and Tahuwhakairo. Some Maoris say that Hinenuiotepo was a sister of Rehua but he said No! to this suggestion or statement. Hinetitama lives at the same place as her famous daughter Hinenuiotepo and like her watches the gateway of the dead but narrator could not say where this place was or is. The other two daughters see spirits going to Te Reika – he thought this was below this world. Perhaps some spirits went to heavens and some below but he could not say which spirits went up and which down or whether they all went up or down. Those two women direct the spirits where to go. They say to some 'you go there' and to others 'you go that way', but he did not know the names of any of the places save Te Reika was the general name. Raroheka was a different place altogether and Maui went there to see his grandfather. It was perhaps near Pikopiko-i-whiti.

When Maui cut Tuna in two the first piece flew (it was not thrown) to the rising place of the moon, to Pikopiko-i-whiti; the other part flew to the rising of the sun, to Pikopiko-i-rangi. The first portion was the head and had the eyes in it; the second portion had the heart in it. The pieces were both extremely heavy and came down to earth with a good thump ('like boulders' explained the narrator) and made marua (hollows). Pikopiko-i-whiti, as far as he knew, was one long sandbar round the earth, but the different parts of it had different names which he did not know as he could recall no ancient songs which named them. The moon in going through the sky journeys through the second heaven and the sun through the heaven above that. They do not rise at same place but both come round from underneath the earth [where the ancient songs say that space is cold. He believed the winds came from down there too and came up over the rim of the earth, but he could not state this definitely. The moon has more work than the sun in looking out our weather. When he was a boy at Akaroa he never heard the old tohukas explain how the moon waxed and waned but it was commonly said that when the moon was small the tide (of the sea) was small and that each increased with the other. The sun travels very fast – he could not believe the Pakeha idea that it was stationary. [Note: Further Mythology Notes will be given in Book Number 14. H.B.]**

Add to Mythology

The following is additional information given by the principal informant during a flying visit paid to Rapaki by the collector:

*According to an old song he took it that Marua-i-nuku was a land below ours, but he had no particulars of it whatsoever.

The people on top of the earth are like the balance (needle) of a compass. The earth is flat and the people on it move about like what the 'balance of the compass' does. [Note: This is the explanation he gave me when asked regarding an obscure portion of his information already quoted. H.B.]

Maku married Mahoranuiatea at the conclusion of the long ages called Po. All the po were maku (black or dark or nightlike) and so Maku was named because he came out of the thick darkness of space or because he emerged from the dark waters of the sea while darkness covered them.

In the Rarotimu whakapapa (given previously) the words Rongo-ki-waho means a good way out in space and the sun comes up a good way out from the earth. Before Maui slowed it down the sun travelled very fast.

The word 'Maori' as a name for the race did not come from Hawaiki. It was evidently applied in New Zealand but how or why he knew not.

Hawaiki as a country dates from the beginning of the world. It was the first country the Maori race lived in. They have lived in many lands since. He did not know where Poroporo-Huariki was originally but the name was brought to Gisborne. Turanga was a name brought from Hawaiki and so was Aorangi, Tapuaenuku, and many others. Tawhiti-a-Rua was one of the Hawaikis although some Maoris erroneously say it is on West Coast of North Island. He had heard the name of other old lands but forgot most of them. Wawau is a home of 'kanakas' now and Rarotonga was visited by some canoes coming to New Zealand.**

Whakaamoa, on Banks Peninsula, was a Katimamoe pa, where that people was defeated and fled. You can see the earthworks yet.

*Birdling's Flat district was once a great centre of the Maori people. The flat was called Te Marokura and two miles nearer Christchurch is Waikakahi** and Te Puia. Te Puia was the pa and Waikakahi the district. The hill now adorned with a powder magazine is Mautaurua and was an old-time fishing camp. From *Te Marokura you can see the saddle called Puwaitaha or Ka Mokaikai. This is the most direct way to Akaroa and the saddle must be six or seven [[miles]] off as the crow flies, yet you can see a man crossing it very clearly. It has an extremely clear skyline and one noted in Maori lore. It is said that the tohukas of old karakia'd and tapu'd the place so that the people at Marokura could see enemies approaching via that route. Be that as it may its visibility is a matter of pride to local natives.

As to landholding, hapus held pieces here and there for cultivation and they would taunaha or claim land according to results of fighting. Waitai was great at claiming land and through his pushing ahead to south, large tracts were claimed subsequently. He had no children like the other tipunas had, but his tribe claimed through him. He was largely of Katikuri descent but had Kaitara blood also.**

At the recent wedding at Rapaki the principal informant read the bride's whakapapa from Rakaihautu (as well as one from Uenuku) and as the collector was afterwards chatting with him, the clergyman Joughin (formerly of Hokianga and who speaks Maori fluently) came to say adieu and asked Tikao where he got his whakapapas. Tikao tapped his head and the clergyman said he knew an old man who could recite the genealogies by the hour – he could even go back to Kupe. Tikao said one of his was older than Kupe and the interlocutor smiled and incredulously asked, 'Where can you get older than Kupe?' He then said farewell. [Note: This is a good sample of Northern belief that Kupe discovered New Zealand. H.B.]

SECTION XXIV

SUPERSTITION

Omens and Dreams — Visions — Fairies — Enchanted Trees — Wizardry — Spiritism — etc.

WAIRUA-ATUA

The collector has now written up all the information given him by the Maoris in North Canterbury, except one small item which refers to the subject indicated by above heading.

*In conversation with the principal informant the word 'taipo' came up.** [It is a handy word to express the works of spirits or powers of evil – although it is not much used by the younger generation, who seem to prefer the Pakeha term 'Jimmy' to express the ideas of ghosts, spirits, or supernatural manifestations. H.B.] *The narrator said the word was certainly taipo (and not taepo) and that it was not correct Maori. When the early whalers were learning Maori they said taipo was an easy term for anything they thought was connected with the devil or with spirits. It was not a true Maori name, the correct word being atua.** Wairua and atua were about the same – both mean a spirit. The word atua is now used for God. [He is out in saying meaning of wairua and atua is similar – all my other well-informed informants draw a distinction – See Murihiku and Nelson Notes, H.B.]

OMENS

In regard to omens always a fruitful source of trouble to the olden Maoris and still a bugbear of superstition to their descendants, the principal informant had little to say.

*The karoro, or seagull, has a habit of calling out every morning, he remarked, but if these birds spoke to one another in a nice voice it was a bad sign. This happened frequently at Akaroa and now all the old people there have died. The torea (redbill) was also a bird that foretold evil that would befall human beings, especially when it would repeatedly whistle the call that gives it its name 'Torea! Torea!' He had heard of the karae and had heard its cry but he had never seen the bird itself so could not describe it. It was a night bird and its cry was regarded as particularly ominous. The conduct of the koukou (morepork) was also an indication of approaching events. If it repeated one cry through the night it was a sign of bad weather. If two or more of them answered each other for a certain time during the night it was a signal of storms coming. To see a ruru (morepork) with its wing stretched out presaged the death of someone (a friend or relative probably) very soon after, or it let the person who saw it know a friend had just died.

The collector asked if sneezing was an omen and was answered that sneezing (matihe) was the start of a cold. There was a lot of it since the Europeans came – before that the Maoris did not sneeze much.**

At Tuahiwi the collector was told that to see (or catch) a white weka (albino) or one with white patch was an unfortunate occurrence for it portended misfortune or death in the family of the one who saw it.

To hear the taki or squeak of the bush lizard, the mokokakariki, was an evil augury. A young man and an old one were chopping bush and heard a lizard call several times. They were puzzled where it was but the young man persisted till he found it. It was the most beautiful lizard either had ever seen and was big in the puku (belly). The old man said it must mean the death of a woman and child and with a sudden presentiment of evil they hurried home to find a telegram saying that the young man's sister had died in giving birth to twins and that the latter were dead also. Thus was the premonition given by the lizard mokokakariki confirmed.

A halfcaste lady esteemed by both races told the collector another instance of an omen forecasting bad tidings. She knew the Maori superstition that to see a ro (big stick insect) or whe (small stick insect) foreshadowed the death of an adult or juvenile respectively. She had swept her sitting-room (her home is always a picture of tidiness) and immediately after she saw a whe on the middle of the floor. She looked at the roof, the walls, and carefully round the room but could see nothing to account for the uncommon visitant. She was puzzled then, and to this day the mysterious appearance has been unaccounted for. She remembered the Maori belief and a foreboding of ill swept over her only to be too unhappily verified when she received word her little niece had died.

DREAMS

*In dreams, said the principal informant, you see what you will do when awake in some cases. In other dreams (moemoea) your mind is enlightened about things you are wondering over. Some dreams can be proved. One kind of moemoea is for the tohunga class; the other kind is for the general public. A seer of visions, or seeing visions, is called matatitiro (mata – a medium; titiro – to look). A matatitiro could be either male or female and although sometimes referred to as tohungas were not really so. If you had lost anything you could go to a matatitiro who would dream about it and tell you where to find it. If a relative was ill you could ask the seer what was best to do and he (or she) would dream over it and tell you what to do. He did not know any lore about ordinary dreams.**

An old man at Kaiapoi happened to mention Te Puaho's raid on Tuturau (1836) and recalled the fact that Puaho invited Niho, a Westland chief, to accompany him, but Niho had a dream which was regarded as a warning not to go. According to my informant (who said Niho was a tipuna of his on his mother's side) Niho dreamt a hill was falling on him. [Southland accounts say he dreamt of a shark. H.B.]

A VISION OF THE NIGHT

When the collector visited the principal informant this trip he found him in bed and interviewed him by his bedside. The old gentleman would tell the following narration and although it is not in line with the rest of the information collected, it may prove interesting as it shows a strange blending of the ancient beliefs of the race largely intermixed with Christian beliefs.

His son died on November 16, 1918 (during the Influenza Epidemic of dread memory) and on the night of June 20, 1919 while narrator was sick he heard a step on the verandah. He thought the 'flap, flap', of the foot was the tread of his dead son and so he lit the candle. A knock came at the door and narrator called out 'Come in' and door opened and his son came in and advanced to the foot of the bed. The narrator opened the conversation:

'Hallo! It is my man again!'

'Well father! how are you doing?'

'Sickly. I've gout all over.'

'You ought to be where we are,' he said, raising a bright arm and pointing upward, 'There is no sickness there and you should be there now.' The narrator noticed that he could see a glass mirror as if it was shining through the raised hand. 'You had better agree and come with me!'

'I am in bed and have nothing on – no clothes to travel in. Besides I don't want to leave your mother and the grandchildren. There is no hurry as my life is getting short. Have you seen your brothers and sister up there?'

'Yes! I've met them. We are a very happy family.' Then he continued. 'You can have a look in my room,' and narrator saw a bridge like a gigantic water-chute stretching from Rapaki over the bay (Lyttelton Harbor) to the top of Monument Hill. Then narrator felt his bed shift and he in it followed his son as latter flew off. As they went through space he looked at his watch and it was twelve o'clock, midnight. He soon saw thousands of people and a lovely tile floor of glass stretching for miles and miles and people sitting around on beautiful seats.

'This is a beautiful land – the land of glory. But where are the houses?' He asked.

'Houses are not needed here, for there is no rain, snow, frost, hail, wind, cold or death!' answered his son.

Narrator saw a woman coming towards him wearing a long gown. He saw she bore the facial likeness of a relative of his – she was that relative. She came to within six yards of him and then passed on to a seat. What a beautiful face she had.

'Is there not marriage here?' he asked and his son replied, 'No! It is not allowed.' He saw the people flying about like a mob of geese. [No disrespect intended. H.B.] They were in white and renewed their youth every thirty or forty years.

'Is there any farming here?' 'No!'

'How do you feed all the people then?' For answer his son took a photo of a sack of flour and said that even looking at photos kept life going. He gave him a bit of bread, however, red-colored and sweet-tasted and narrator ate it. It ate well – it was soft and filmy and seemed like cream inside.

'Do you get the dark races here?'

'No! None darker than the Maori.' He went on to say that the place where they were was a first-class place; the South was a second-class place and the North a third-class place. He pointed out Te Waka-a-Tamarereti [a canoe of stars. H.B.] – a name the young man had never known before; he certainly never knew it on earth. He said it could travel two hundred miles an hour and carry three thousand passengers. It would travel south till it came to the end of the trip in three months' time and then back in three months. Then it flew north for three months getting back to the starting-point just at the expiry of a year or twelve months. The highway was a great pole, three thousand miles round in circumference and as solid as rock. It stretched from the extreme North to the extreme South and was hooked at both ends. Narrator did not ask concerning it but in his mind he thought it was the great pole of Rangi [See Mythology Section, H.B.].

His son said that Christ came round sometimes; He was not proud; He was of man's stature; He was in colour like a Maori and he spoke good Maori. Questions would come from all sides and Christ answered all these in the different languages of the askers. He wore long garb when worship was on. The organ sounded magnificent and majestic. The peoples of the South and North lived in great cities of steel houses. The young man said that God was dwelling away to the East in a truly beautiful land. He further said that Christ had given him the glass he wore in his hand and that not many wore such a thing. It had strong power and could shift a mountain if needed.

Narrator then found himself back (with his bed) in his room. The young man bade him farewell and narrator told him he would soon follow him to the beautiful land where he now was. Narrator looked at his watch and it was 12.15 a.m. The candle was burning strongly all the time and narrator was positive he was not asleep when his son came to him and departed from him. The only time he slept was when borne aloft on his bed into the regions above.

He might add that his son had a craft called the Toitoi and some time after his death he was seen (in broad daylight) aboard it, being seen by the crew to their great astonishment. What these visions portended the narrator could not say. Before this he used to wonder if some spirits went 'up' or some 'down' or if families were united, but his son said that he and his seven brothers and sisters (who had finished their earthly careers) were all living in a happy family together.

SUPERSTITION

The old people were very superstitious, said an intelligent Maori, and so are their predecessors. A lot of elderly people died one after the other at a populous Canterbury centre a generation ago and word went round that makutu was at work. A reason had to be found and it was said that a present of eels sent to Otaki (North Island) had dissatisfied the people there and the priests (tohunga) there had pronounced makutu against the donors, but narrator reckoned the people were dying of pneumonia. Some of the houses were declared tapu and stood desolate for years until a match was put to them by narrator. A wind was blowing and some of the ashes were carried into the lake and since then the young

Maoris left won't take fish from its waters but go miles to spear eels in lagoons. 'They are as bad as the old people for superstition, although they are a drinking lot,' concluded my informant.

In speaking of old men who have gone it is quite common for present Maoris to attribute marvellous powers to them. Thus the collector heard of Paori Taki who lived at Rapaki. He was tattooed a little on the cheeks and was 'an old soldier of Kai-Tahu', getting a military funeral. He loved to tell old tales but alas! they did not listen much. In his old whaleboat 'Manawatu' he did feats of great seamanship, although it had 'a half-moon bow'. The old man would go out when others dare not – he was a fearless seaman – and moreover would get no water in his boat. He could do wonderful healing. A boy hurt his leg so he could not walk, was carried to Taki who karakia'd it and the boy ran home. All present knew of this and considered it a miraculous thing.

In one long house thatched with reeds and which stood at Rapaki till thirty years ago 'Jimmy-work' was said to go on. 'This was just tohungaism' – but none of those present could say how name 'Jimmy' originated in this connection. They considered it probable, however, that those who first used the term did so because it was uncanny to say the real name.

Add to Supernatural Things

FAIRIES

*The patupaiarehe were on Bank's Peninsula in pre-Pakeha days and the people of old would see the gleam of distant fires and hear the sound faintly** of flutes played afar. It was the Pakeha [an intrusive, inquisitive and unimaginative *race] who caused the fairies to vanish. Sometimes of a night the ancient Maori would see the torches the fairy people used in lighting them when spearing fish and would be near enough to hear the children crying and the guttural tones of the adults 'growling at one another'. He did not know if these fairies ate cooked food but he thought they went away into the bush to cook the fish – these fairies were a kind of people very long ago. [See also Some Mythological Names book 8. Canterbury Notes, H.B.] My principal informant had never heard the name Nukumaitore – it must be a North Island term he thought.** Another informant mentioned that the people of old used to hear the fairy music of porutu or koauau played by the patupaearehe on Te-Poho-o-Te-Mahaki (a hill near Little River).

*As for the maeroero the collector could hear nothing of these in Canterbury.**

The children used to be warned to look out for patupaiarehe if they went to Taukahara bush on Mahuraki near Lyttelton.

ENCHANTED TREES

*In Tregear's [[1904]] *Maori Race* it is mentioned that there are clumps of magical trees on Banks Peninsula called Te Aitanga-a-Hinemateroa, Ti-a-Tauwhetuku, and Te Papatua-mau-heke and the collector asked the principal informant about these with very little success. Hinemateroa (also known as Hineroa) was a wife of Tahumutu as was also her sister Rongokohuwai; but Tahumutu and his two wives were buried in the North Island. They were before the time of Tuahuriri and latter was drowned in Cook Strait so Hinemateroa never in South Island. A clump of trees at Akaroa may have been called Hinemateroa and the spirits may have gone there and been talking to one another and originated the idea of talking trees, or the name of that woman may have been put to a tree which had thus become endowed with a spirit and been able to talk to other trees. It may be there yet but would have, 'no mouth to talk now all the ancient people are gone'.** After Moki killed the Ngatimamoe on the Peninsula his tribe came and narrator and family are the aitaka of that woman. By Rokokohuai (the first wife) came the Kaiapoi people and narrator; by Hineroa (the second wife) came the Akaroa people and narrator. *He did not know about Te Papatua-a-Mauheke but the name Ti-a-Tauwhetuku should evidently be Te Ao-tauwhetuku whose family came** down from Rangitakapumaro, but there are not many descendants now, the principal *being Miss Mutu, Taiaroa and narrator. The names of tipunas were transferred to trees, rocks, lakes, etc. in those days but are now used for racehorses, cows, pigs, dogs, etc. He objected to this strongly as it was not proper to use rakatira names for animals. He wished people to call their children after tipunas as his own tamariki and mokopuna were.

As for ti-haere (trees walking about) he knew of no instances of such but had heard dim rumors about it. The branches spreading and waving about in wind in dull lights may be origin of tale, or it may have been spirits moving in the locality and people thought it was the trees. Such an idea was only possible in times when spirits were common.

TANIWHA

The principal informant said he had heard a story of two taniwha in Canterbury. Once upon a time Te Ake and his daughter Hineao travelled from Akaroa to Ohikuparuparu (Sumner) the chief of which place was Turakipo. The latter asked Te Ake for his daughter in marriage and was refused. Turakipo, who was a real tohunga, makutu'd that girl and when she returned to Akaroa she fell ill and died. Te Ake was angry and with his nephew Te Ruahikihiki went to the Patea (West Coast). They went via Kaikoura and Nelson and both stayed long enough to have wives and children there. They saw the great Tohungas, Irirangi and Tautini, and Te Ake learnt the karakias and makutu and other lore. When he had got all he required he returned to Akaroa and karakia'd his daughter, who had been cremated, into a fish, a taniwha. This fish went to Sumner and drifted ashore and the people cut its flesh for kai (food) bringing it home in canoes and placing it in the umu. Turakipo as an expert tohunga had a premonition and before the fish-eating occurred he went to the Poho-areare pa at Opawa. The people ate the big fish and slept and in the morning no one wakened save one named Hinerotu, the daughter of Wheke. The name of the death of those people is tuawera. Te Ake made that taniwha as a payment for his daughter's death. Its spirit destroyed a lot of people in after years. It is an atua or harmful spirit still existent and supposed to bring sickness. The karakia said to avert its evil mentions the taniwha as Te Rangiorahina (or perhaps more accurately Te Rangi hora hina) and some die and some recover. Its work even extends to the North Island where it is known as Hinewera – visitors took its reputation from here back to there. Its influence is good some-times and sometimes bad. It took Te Ake years to learn the karakia. His nephew left progeny among Katikuia, Rakitane and Kaitara and some descendants are still existent from these lines. At a later stage narrator said that Hineao's name as a taniwha is Te Wahine maru kore and that a male relative Te Rangiorahina is also a taniwha. They go together and if the sea turns like blood the fishers know that the pair are under the water. If a storm comes on and the fishers karakia (invoke) these fish the latter will lead the canoe safely and guide it to the shore. He had never heard of the ultimate fate of these fish but both had ruas (holes – said to be bottomless) in Akaroa near Mairaki Point near the Opukutahi Reserve. Te Ake eventually left those fish to safeguard friendly people on the sea. Narrator did not know if the story was true in every detail but the tohukas of old had found these matters out and had told the story.

OMENS AND DREAMS

A tohu, said the principal informant, is a sign or omen, and it is well to heed its warning. If you have a bad dream of a person at a place warn them to leave. If they do not go they are bound to be killed or meet very grave disaster. Tohu means a pointing to a mountain, hill or thing. A kind of lightning showing time after time at the same place is a tohu – a sign of death at a distance. There may be good and bad tohu – tohu no te ora and tohu no te mate respectively. The former might mean a boat capsize or motor accident and person lucky to escape; the latter they are unlucky enough to be killed. To sleep and the head to go forward (takiri) is a sign of death not far from you – such as a wife or child; putting out the arm (takiri ki waho) and bringing it back is a bad sign; turning over was scarcely a sign; if you put a leg out, he forgot name and sign. Old songs tell the signs. Dreams had meanings. If you dream of a houseful of visitors and go fishing you will get a boatful of fish; if of an empty house you will catch nothing. If you dreamt you were arm-in-arm with a woman you would get a fat fish, a toki (a fat strong fish, a hapuku say). There were numerous other interpretations of dreams if he could think of them. (In 1875 a woman dreamt she saw narrator climb a tall pole and in 1891 the North Island made him Chairman of the Maori Parliament. If he had dreamt this himself it would probably have come to nothing.)

There is a point at Birdling's Flat (Waikakahi) where a shag sits. If it sat to one side a good sign, if to other side a bad omen. It is said to be still there. The kind of lightning known as kapo if repeated again and again is a sign a rakatira will die.

Add to Fairies and Maeroero

In the South the collector was told of warning voices [See *Journal of the Polynesian Society* [[Vol. 28, 1919]] p. 213 of H.B.'s articles] – voices from the bush that asked the Maoris to desist from cutting more flax or catching more fish. The collector asked after this in Canterbury.

The principal informant said that warning voices were a tohu from the maeroero. His wife once saw one. One old man called out 'The Devil! The Devil' and everyone rushed out, including some Pakehas. They could see a fire on a point across a bay, but if you go to where you see the fairy fires you will find no ashes. Akaroa and Banks Peninsula were something like Murihiku in possessing maeroero. These people (maeroero) lived in the bush and would go out on the mud-flats and spear fish with their finger-nails. They would sometimes sing out in the Maori tongue to warn people not to come too near and not to interfere with their belongings. The maeroero used to play the flute near Akaroa – these maeroero were Rapuwai people. The maeroero as a rule were tall; they were called turehu in the North Island. The Kahuitipua were a branch of the maeroero people.

Kaiheraki was a daughter of a man (forgets name) on Takitimu canoe and was to wed Kahukunu (a son of Tamatea). She landed with the people of that canoe in Murihiku, but somewhere near the Takitimu Mountains she strayed a little apart from the rest and was caught and carried off by 'wild ghosts' or maeroero. A maeroero ran away with her – hence she was separated from her people. She still roams those mountains. Some generations ago a Maori caught her and tried to taowhakamoe her but she escaped. She may be there yet if the Pakeha fires have not scared her. The maeroero who abducted her probably died long ago. The maeroero were a great Rapuai race and were good flute-players. It was in this race that Tura wed his second wife. They were good-looking women but the race had no fires and ate their food raw.**

An old man said to the collector that he did not know about warning voices, but the maeroero were devils; he knew no stories about them.

TAPU TREES

*The principal informant said he had heard of rakau-tapu (sacred trees) and he thought Stack mentioned one or two. There is a tapu tree near Acland's run between the Rakaia and Rakitata Rivers. It might be a rata or a tawai – he was not sure – but it stands by itself. Abner Robertson told narrator his father was at Mount Somers run when the Pakeha cut down that tree for posts but next morning on returning they found it up again. They cut it down another time but it was up again on returning, so they gave the matter up as a bad job and put a fence round it to protect it from further assaults. It was said Turakautahi and a big tohuka went there on some hunting trips and that karakia was said at its base giving it mana and rendering the tree tapu.

The collector said he had heard that tree called Hinepaaka but principal informant said he had not heard that name for it, but it might be as she was the wife of Maru. Narrator was descended from that family who had always owned the land from Tawera (Mount Oxford) to Te Umukaha (Temuka) and that tree stands in midst of that strip.

A place called Te Whata-a-rama was on north side of Rakaia (and was perhaps the Otarama of the Pakeha) and narrator's ancestors used to go there to hunt pigeons, kaka and weka. They also went to Mairaki (up Coast way) for wekas and kauru. He thought that tapu trees existed at both those places but he could give no particulars.

He had never heard that the karamu and kawakawa were regarded as sacred shrubs [Tregear's [[1904]] *Maori Race* makes the statement. H.B.] or were used in rites.

As for uru uru-whenua (the act of placing gifts at the foot of a tree to placate the spirits of the land through which travellers are passing) he had never heard of such a proceeding.** He thought that viewed as a name merely the term should be huruhuru-whenua (hair of the land) because uru-uru meant 'something like poking the fire' and did not seem to fit in very well in such a connection – but he was not sure of this.

WITCHCRAFT

*The principal informant several times made references which come under this heading although some of the information is given under the section about wharekuras and tohungas. The tohungas were taught witchcraft (makutu) as a part of their education. Makutu could bring death either sudden or slow. Makutu could be pronounced against man, beast, bird or fish; against land or sea, and could only be averted or exorcised by more powerful makutu being brought against it. As for rotua he reckoned it was only a name, and whawhaia was a kind of leprosy produced by incantations against an enemy or one who had slighted you or done you an injury. He had once had a charge of makutu laid against him. This was in 1895 when he was touring the North Island re Maori land claims. In Hawkes Bay he and Henare Matua, a tohunga, had an argument. The old man karakia'd but forgot twice and his opponent (narrator) gave him the cue. Going away from that place he shook hands with the old man saying 'I may never see you again'. Matua died soon after and in a crowded hall narrator was charged in no uncertain terms of having caused the old man to die by having makutu'd him. He cleared himself of the charge but things were very warm for a while and he threatened if ever a whisper of such an accusation reached him he would haul the leading people of that place up for defamation of character and let a Pakeha Judge decide the matter.

The narrator resumed: Te Maiharoa (who died an old man in 1886) was a man without education until he went in for the study of Maori lore. He seemed to grasp it readily and became a proficient tohunga. He was a miracle worker. [Two instances of his prowess are recorded in *Journal of the Polynesian Society* [[Vol. 29, 1920, p. 133]] by H.B.] Narrator saw him in a crowded hall at Temuka take a boy by the arm and throw him from the stage to the door. The boy sailed over the heads of the people and, landing unharmed on his feet, walked back to the stage where Maiharoa seized him by the leg and whirling him over his head sent the boy over the heads of the people a second time. The boy landed on his feet, unhurt, at the door and walked out. Then he said that only one man in the building had a watch which was exactly right to the minute and that was narrator's. He said not to look for a minute or so till he gave the word. They heard the Temuka Town Clock chime eight and all pulled out their timepieces and sure enough the only one that tallied to the minute with the Town Clock was narrator's. Then he waved a fowl about and said it would sleep exactly three minutes and so it did. For the last twelve years of his life Te Maiharoa worked hard to uphold Maori mana. He was often called Patu-whenua because the people said his work was even as one hitting the ground. But all his attempts to stay the decay of Maori mana were futile. Yet he could bring on or 'lay' taipo (narrator explained that 'taipo' should really be 'atua'). Once up near the top end of Ninety-Mile Beach some of the men were sitting sheltered under a clump of tumatakura having a korero over things Maori. In the course of it Maiharoa said a 'taipo' was coming and would visit narrator (Tikao). He warned him to be ready and said 'Here it is' (or words to that effect) and a big karara (lizard) dropped (from the clouds to all outward seeming) on to narrator's lap – but that was enough of that sort of talk.**

A Tuahiwi Maori mentioned that it was said a chief (and tohuka) pronounced makutu against the kanakana fifty years ago and that lamprey has ever since ceased to come to the streams in that district (as it had previously done from time immemorial).

A woman told the collector that Te Rakiihia, a Kati-Mamoe chief, had such a powerful voice he could call at Kaitakata (Kaitangata) and be heard at Wharepa (Warepa). This chief came to Kaiapoi to 'hoi-te-roko' (make peace). Going back he found his sister cooking and enraged killed a servant. Another man speared him and as he was recovering he made a whakapepeha (boast) that if it had been his arm drove the spear the man speared would have been dead. This whakapepeha was told to the man who did the deed and angered him. He looked at his spear point and there was some of the dried blood (of Rakiihia) on it. He makutu'd that blood and the famous Kati-Mamoe chief died of madness.

WIZARDRY AND SPIRITISM

The principal informant said he had not heard of divination by sticks being tossed in the air – which the collector remarked was called niu in the North Island and rotarota (he thought) in South Island. *This latter name was familiar to the old man and he explained it. If someone did an evil deed such as theft, etc., you would call everyone who could possibly be implicated. Wiwi (rushes) were cut into varying lengths – one for each person. The one who pulled the longest was adjudged guilty and in the old days was killed. If they were on board a boat the 'guilty' person was cast overboard. It was a bad thing was rotarota and it was well to forget such foolish and wicked conduct. [Note: The collector soothed the old gentleman by telling him of the Anglo-Saxon 'trial by ordeal' and he came to the conclusion the Maori was not so bad after all. H.B.]

The principal informant once passed some eerie experiences in the company of Keama, a tohuka of sorts. The tohuka Te Kakau [See Section re Tohukas, H.B.] lived at his home Manukatahi near Otehore hill and after his decease his 'taipo' or spirit was said to haunt the district for years, often in the shape of a ruru, or morepork. In his (narrator's) sojournings with Keama, the pair lived in a hut together for a time. One day the narrator hit a ruru a good clout with the broom, but after lying as if dead for some time the bird miraculously revived and flew away apparently quite unconcerned. It was a spirit of Te Kakau. The bird came back to the hut again and narrator angry at its intrusion hit it a hard whack that seemingly 'laid it out' properly this time. To make sure, however, he had got it this time he took a lot of flax and tied the bird up in as many knots as he could devise and then went to bed. Next morning they got up to find the flax lying unbroken and unbitten on the floor and the bird gone. Shortly after on a dark night narrator saw a 'ghost' sitting by a stream near the hut. It was in the shape of a man and its head was shining as if kokowai (red ochre) had been rubbed on it. Narrator slipped into the hut and got some cooked potatoes and threw them at the ghost. Two of the missiles found their mark and it slipped away into the darkness. The narrator knew enough even then in his young days to know that you could not hit a spirit with stones or sticks, so he used cooked food and this proved quite effective. Keama reproved him for his impetuosity, and prophesied evil from this manifestation of spirit activity, saying it boded no good that such a ghost should appear. Next year Keama's wife and two children died so his forecast of impending ill came true.

On another occasion the narrator carelessly emptied the potato-boiling scraps into a spring nearby. Keama was horrified at his act and said it would kill the spirit of the spot and that the spring would soon cease to run.** Soon after, somewhat to the narrator's astonishment be it said, the 'blooming spring dried-up'.

*The collector asked the principal informant what truth there was in the statement (page 71 H.B.'s articles in *Journal of the Polynesian Society* [[Vol.26, 1917]]) that guardian spirits or lizards would hang from the nostrils of magicians or wizards. He replied that the ancient Maori had a custom of boring a hole through the ihu (nose) and sticking a feather or greenstone pin through. This accustomed the race to the idea of having the nose decorated. A saying of the old people was that if a person snored lizards would come and hang on to his or her nostrils. The snoring, according to the tradition, was an invitation for the lizards to come to that particular person. [As lizards were usually held in a sort of abhorrence or shuddering antipathy this tradition would imply that snoring was as unpopular among the Maoris as among us. H.B.] In regard to Matamata [who was said to sleep with two lizards hanging to his nostrils – they were guardian spirits of his. H.B.] he had never heard of such a legend in connection with him. Matamata was a famous ghost who came originally from Hawaiki and in later times was a guardian god of Rakitauneke, the famous Kati-Mamoe warrior. A yarn said that Matamata was such a powerful magic-worker that he could restore a dead man to life, but the narrator was not familiar with his alleged exploits.**

An old Maori told the collector he had heard of divination by whakaata (pool-gazing) but he knew no details. It was just makutu (wizardry or witchcraft).

The old people, said one Maori, were, as a general rule, afraid of meeting atua (evil spirits) but I remember one who boasted that he was not frightened of atua and if such a thing appeared he would 'have a go at it'. The people were at Puharakekenui (Styx) at the time engaged in hi [bobbing for eels in this case – usually means fishing. H.B.]. The kaumatua (old man) (who was not scared of spirits) was out in a canoe which he had tied to the bank and was busily engaged hauling the captured tuna into the waka. As dusk descended a young man slipped into the river (the water was pleasantly warm at that season) and sneaked up to the canoe. He silently dived and caught hold of the bob and gave it a vigorous tug. The kaumatua thought he had secured a giant eel, but when the head of an 'atua' appeared in the indistinct light, he gave a gasp, dropped the rod, grabbed the paddle, raced the canoe to the landing, hopped out, ran home without his eels and lay down on a bed panting and quaking. The young man slipped ashore, put on his clothes, gathered the eels the bobber had left behind and went up to the house with others who were in the 'joke'. When they saw the state the old fellow was in their hearts misgave them and they explained the affair. 'All's well that ends well', but the old man was very angry over it and 'cut' the perpetrators for many a day.

HYPNOTISM, VENTRILOQUISM AND MENTAL TELEPATHY

The collector inquired about these things on his recent trip but did not get much information. It is 'too late in the day' for such inquiry now. [The question was brought up by collector's papers to *Journal of the Polynesian Society* which see in this connection.]

*The collector had an opinion that 'rotua' might be hypnotism and asked the principal informant what 'rotua' was. Rotua, he replied, is to feel sleepy. 'Kai te rotua koe e te hia moe' (You are overcome by the desire to sleep) is said to a dozing or sleepy person. It means to feel so sleepy one cannot keep awake. He had never heard of the tohukas doing such a thing, i.e. making people sleep against their wills.

As to ventriloquism he had never heard of such a thing among the Maoris. Once near Akaroa as he and some others were in a field a white man came along the road. The Maoris [with characteristic hospitality. H.B.] gave the stranger dinner. After it they heard a voice from the hillside. They were considerably mystified until Bob Paurini's father found out it was the Pakeha who was throwing his voice up the hill. It appeared he was a ventriloquist, but such were unknown among the Maoris. Of course, in the olden days, the tohuka could make a 'taipo' speak from the top of a house, or the roof, to the people below, but calling up a spirit to speak was not ventriloquism. It was an exhibition of the wonderful powers of those men of mana.

The matakite (seers) were the mediums through whom lost things could be discovered. They far excelled the tohukas at this particular thing and 'could discover anything'.

The collector further asked the principal informant what Maiharoa did to get the attention of the people at his notable meeting at Arowhenua (Temuka). The reply was that he did no physical actions, hand-waving, arm-motions, finger-pointing, etc. His power had come to him (explained narrator), not by instruction when he was young nor by hereditary descent, but direct from the heavens. It was a gift and came in middle life. All narrator remembered of the meeting to be described was that Maiharoa stood on the platform and the hall was full of people. He asked the people if they had all washed their faces that morning – he wanted them all clean. He said that it would soon be eight o'clock and that when that hour struck only one watch in the building would be exactly right to the minute – and so it proved. He took a rooster, put its head under its wing, swayed it about and said it would sleep exactly three minutes. At the expiry of that period the rooster unburied his head and sat up. [Note: The collector saw a European boy do this trick twenty years ago. H.B.] Maiharoa then took a boy on the stage and seizing the boy's arms whirled him round over his head and let go. The boy's body went through the air, performing revolutions meanwhile, and passing over the heads of the audience, it came to the back of the hall where in a clear space the boy landed on his feet, unhurt. He was apparently somewhat dazed but made his way to the stage. Maiharoa asked him how he felt and the boy replied he was giddy. Maiharoa asked would he like another trip but he said he would rather not as it made his head so giddy. The tohuka, however, took the boy again and holding him by the feet whirled him aloft again. When momentum was gathered he let go and body went hurtling and gyrating to the door where boy landed on his feet and walked outside. [The hall is a long one and the people were amazed at the doings of the 'man of mystery' (as Pakeha advertisements term such performers) H.B.] Maiharoa, concluded narrator, was a religious man. He was sometimes characterised as a Hauhau but this was not correct. He was not an orthodox Christian but a sort of Israelite.**

An intelligent Maori of whom the collector asked an opinion as to what the word 'rotua' meant, gave an interesting reply. The word was not 'rotua', he said, but 'rotu' and he had heard the old people speaking of it. His own opinion (he is a man of middle age – about fifty years old) was that rotu was simply hypnotism. [This opinion given without hesitation and without prompting interested the collector as it coincided with the opinion of a younger man who spoke to the collector at a place two hundred miles further south. H.B.] Only some tohukas, he continued, had the power to do rotu, but he could not say how it was done – it was different to the Pakeha style of hypnotising. A worse thing than rotu was atahu as it was often put to a sinister use. Atahu, as he understood it, was a form of mental suggestion which could be transmitted over a great distance. A person with this power could make another person far away think the same thought. It was done by mana. The doer could say (mentally) to the distant person to do such an action and he (or she) would do it; he could say to look at such and such a thing and the recipient of the suggestion would look at it. Most of this power, he was sorry to add, was used by bad men wishing to gain their own evil ends and much of it was directed against women. He had heard of this power being used to influence women many miles away and [like a bird fascinated by a snake. H.B.] they were unable to successfully resist its appeal and had unwillingly journeyed to the source from which the imperative mental summons had emanated.

A Peninsula Maori said he had never heard of matakite on the Peninsula but he had heard of atahu. He had heard a case of a woman who was made to travel ninety miles against her will to see the man; but he never heard any details how the thing was done.

An old man said he had never heard of hypnotism nor ventriloquism among the Maoris.

The tohuka could put a person to sleep by karakia, said a woman, but she did not know how it was accomplished. Another woman said that there was a form of hypnotism in karakia – it exercised a sway over the mind. She also knew a woman who would go into trances from which she emerged deadly fagged. She would prophesy the death of people, see visions of heaven, name thieves, reveal wrongdoers, etc. The thing became too much for her strength and its baleful power over her was finally vanished by karakia said over her by an old man. The power (of revealing unseen things) left her. [The karakia said were Christian prayers the collector understands. H.B.]

SECTION XXV

FOLK TALES AND PROVERBS

A STORY OF TINIRAU PROVERBIAL SAYINGS

NOTE: A number of Folk-Tales from Canterbury were published in the *Journal of the Polynesian Society*. H.B.

A STORY OF TINIRAU

An elderly lady told the collector she had a dim remembrance of a story she had heard when a girl. She would tell me what she could and I could ask for the full and correct story elsewhere. This is her tale: 'Tinirau had lost her whale and set out to find it. She asked the kutu-hori (sole) the road and this fish refused to tell so she stamped her foot on its nose and bent it (as seen in these fish to this day). The full name of that fish is patiki-kutu-horihori. The elephant fish also refused to tell so she chased it but it was swift so she slipped off her maro – it was time of her monthly period – and threw it at that fish. The cloth struck its head and stuck to its nose and now forms its trunk, whence comes its Pakeha name. The Maori calls that fish repe. The Maori calls the little crab tautini and the moeanu is a fish with a big mouth. It lies in the sand and can be dug up but she had not heard of its being eaten. Both tautini and moeanu and others whom she forgot were mentioned in this old time tale. The jellyfish is now called reperepe-o-Tautini and is described in story as the house one of the characters lived in. Perhaps Tinirau was a man for Hineiteiwaiwa was in the story and she may have been Tinirau's wife.' The narrator concluded by expressing the wish the collector would get the full story somewhere.

*On being appealed to the principal informant said the jellyfish was called reperepe-o-Tautini but how it got this name he knew not.** In one whakapapa the name Tautini occurs three times and then you come to Tautini the big tohunga of the Ngaitara. Some names recur frequently in genealogies and also at intervals.

*Tinirau is a god something like Ruaimoko – he thought he was a man once, but later a great fish or monster (taniwha). Tinirau, a male fish, was one of those who guided the people from Hawaiki. He had heard it said that Tinirau shaped the kutuhori's nose but that was only a trifling matter and he had learnt no history of it.**

The nose of the repe (elephant fish) is the napkin of Hineteiwaiwa, who was a *sister of the other celebrated 'Hines' and an aunt of great Maui. He did not know how** the fish got the napkin – perhaps it ran off with it. She chased it and did not catch it. (He did not wonder at this for when young and fleet he chased one on a mud flat at Napier and it got away as it is very fast.) He did not know meaning of word repe *but a fancy name for that fish was Te Maro-o-Hineteiwaiwa. He did not know which wind this lady held but she was in circle. She is the Hine whose name he** could not recollect on collector's previous visit. [See former Canterbury Notes, H.B.]

Add to Proverbs and Sayings

*The Maoris like reciting genealogies and disputations sometimes arise. After one bout of recitation to prove who belonged to the older branch of the family the principal informant after giving some hitherto unknown lines of descent, remarked to his vanquished opponents the old saying 'You did not know where the wind came from!'

Another saying to people of lesser breed was 'Our ancestors drank waiu-pai (good milk) – yours didn't'. Needless to say such an allusion would not have a soothing effect on its hearers.

'O te parara' was a remark jocularly made to halfcastes. The parara is the iron hoops round casks and the inward meaning of the saying was that the mother had been paid for with whaler's casks (or that for gifts bestowed by a whaler the tribe had given him a wife). The principal informant laughingly said this remark to an aged and influential halfcaste in the North Island and received the unexpected reply: 'You are wrong! My mother was not paid for with whalers' casks at all – she was paid for with guns and powder!'

When a stranger goes to a place the saying may come up, 'When the fire gets more ashes,' referring to the fact that the longer the visitor stops the more ashes the fire accumulates and inferring that he is getting more used to the ways of the place and also to know the people better.

When the sun goes down the old people will sometimes exclaim, 'Hallo! The blanket is away!' The sun is presumably called a kakahu (blanket) because of its warmth.

If a person comes into a room or hut where a fire is burning giving a grateful heat, he may exclaim, 'Te hauka te ahi!' (the smell of the fire). Here the word hauka (or haunga) does not mean 'stink or bad smell' which is its usual meaning.

'Ko te kete ika a Tutekawa' (the fish basket of Tutekawa) is a proverbial allusion to Lake Forsyth (Wairewa) because Tutekawa was the first Kai-Tahu chief to settle by its fish-teeming waters. The collector is now informed the saying also embraces Waihora (Lake Ellesmere).** The district between the two lakes was called Kaitorete by the olden Maoris but what occcasioned the name the collector was not told.

Add to Proverbs

'Ma ka hutawa hoki e haere ai te takata' (the legs are what make man go). This old saying shows us that 'hutawa' was an old name for the legs. The saying was used something like what the Pakeha uses his expression, 'Shanks' pony'.

Add to Maeroero

A Maori said that he had heard the old people say that in Canterbury in the olden days when the people had done enough eeling a gruff voice would say Kati ra! (Stop!). The people would cease operations and next day would return and find plenty of eels lying dead on the bank. That was maeroero or patupaiarehe work.

SECTION XXVI

HISTORY

Arrival of Canoes — Historical Jottings — Various Fights — Rauparaha Raids — Origin of Place-Names — Some Men of Old — Moriori People — etc.

THE CANOES

The earliest to the South Island

The principal informant was less informative (and also less reliable) on this section than any of the numerous ones he dealt with. *He considered six peoples had inhabited the South Island viz., the Hawea, Rapuwai, Waitaha, Ngatimamoe, the people now (i.e. the present Maoris) and the Pakeha. The Wakahurumanu, he thought, was not the proper name of that canoe but Kapakitua and Taiehu was the captain. The axe that cut the Cape of Good Hope off was Te Awhioraki. Later on he said: 'The Wakahurumanu came from the Cape of Good Hope. To cut the waves is only figurative language – I think they were parted by taniwha. The toki or axe was Awhiorangi – a name meaning an aniwaniwa or rainbow.

The rainbow it left is a sign of the track from South Africa to Australia and then to New Zealand. Some say the name he gives the canoe is the axe. Te waka-a-rangi canoe was at the beginning of the world as Tane took it to the sky and left it with Tamarereti. After the canoe brought here by Taiehu, the next canoe, I think, was Tairea, the commander being Tama. These canoes found people in the South Island. One of these people was Tutewaimate who was here about one hundred generations ago. This man stayed at Kaikoura and caught fish. He cooked these fish, put them on a rourou (plate) and took them to his brother Moko who lived in a cave in the Rakaia Gorge. He would arrive with the fish still hot – the pakeha cannot travel so fast. Footsteps have been found in the rock at Takahaka (Cheviot) about four feet long so he must have been about one hundred feet high. This is true – there were great giants in those days. He was not killed by Moko [as stated in Stack's [[1898]] history] but like the rest of those people, and the moas also, was drowned by The Flood.'

THE ARAI-TE-URU

The principal informant had not much to say regarding this celebrated canoe which he spoke of as coming about or at the same time as the Takitimu. The Araiteuru was wrecked on a reef off Matakaea which he** thought was alongside or near to Oamaru [It is thirty three miles south of it. H.B.]. The crew landed safely *but after various more or less prolonged wanderings were turned to stone. Some got as far inland as the Lakes and into the Southern Alps beyond Takapo where there are two mountains named after a man and his wife – Kirikiri and Arokaihe, and other heights are named further south. This canoe brought out from Hawaiki a cargo of stuff, including ipu, utensils and seeds of all descriptions. Strange as it may seem these seeds included those of the kumera and wheat. If the Pakeha doubts this last statement he had just got to carefully examine the boulders at Moeraki and he will see the wheat seeds embedded in the stone that is a perpetual reminder of the cargo of that pilgrim canoe. The likeness is so real that some Maoris with visions of easy money broke up some stones and mixed the 'stone wheat' with real wheat and sold it to a mill. It could be heard ripping and grinding away in the machinery and the imposture was soon discovered. The Moeraki boulders are known as Hinaki (he considered that Te-kai-hinaki was adding to the old name) and are also a reminder that the Araiteuru brought out hinaki (baskets or eelpots) from Hawaiki. These were turned to stone when the canoe was upset but they were not needed on shore for the crew found that they could get aka-toropapa – or akatea is even better – in the South Island of New Zealand which would make better hinaki than they could make in Hawaiki.

THE TAKITIMU

The Takitimu, continued the principal informant, came from Hawaiki and landed at Ahuahu (Mercury Bay). The marangai (east wind) was blowing at the time and made the people very cold. It was warm on the sunny side of the sandhills and they scooped sand over their bodies, hence the origin of the name Ahuahu. The canoe continued on and landed at Whangaparaoa but he did not know if it left people there but it continued on to Matau-a-Maui (Napier). The Araiteuru was then on the coast too. The marangai and a cold rain came on and both canoes were in a sinking condition so they ran before the north east wind down the South Island and the Araiteuru pulled up on a reef near Oamaru. He forgot the name of the rocks but the people had not far to walk to shore. The Takitimu ran on to the south and round to Mussel Beach where the people landed just before the canoe upset and broke. Tamatea, the great chief, and his three nephews Tamatea-nui, Tamatea-roa, and Tamatea-kaimatamua were on board this canoe. Nukuroa had married Tamatea's sister Tekotu and begotten those three young men. The Takitimu had left the Aotea, Arawa, Tainui and other canoes up in the North Island and her crew wished to rejoin those people so they set out to walk back. There was a fire on the canoe and they brought it with them as far as Oamaru where it went into the hill. It was then only a piece of charred stick but it was sufficient to start a fire Te-ahi-a-ue in those hills which lasted in the hill from that time till when the narrator was a boy. The fire burnt a lot of stone there and that is now the famous Oamaru building stone. That was the end of Tamatea's fire and the name of that place is O-amaru (O = a place; amaru to shelter from burning stone, or to cover a fire down). The party went on without fire and sometimes felt cold. When they got to Banks Peninsula Tamatea climbed the steep peak called Te Poho-o-Tamatea. (It is now called Mahuraki. In 1849 old Mahuraki told the Commissioner to call hill after him so he put it on map 'Te Upoko-o-Mahuraki'.)

From this height Tamatea sent a karakia to the famous old tohunga Ngatoro-i-rangi in the North Island and the latter sent volcanic fire from Ruapehu etc. to warm Tamatea. The fire burnt out the channel the Whanganui River now follows and crossed the sea and on via Parnassus to the hill above Rapaki where Tamatea got it. A piece got detached from the rest and formed the hot springs at Hanmer. Another piece ploughed a black mark along the whole ridge round the head of Lyttelton Harbor as far as Kaituna Hill.

This ridge is called 'Te Whakatakanga-o-te-ngarehu-o-te-ahi-a-Tamatea' (the falling of the embers of the fire of Tamatea). The fire so sent warmed the party to Nelson from whence they walked over the sea to the North Island and up the course now taken by the Whanganui River (which was dry then) and on to their meeting with Ngatoro. The heat he had sent ended at Rotorua and here Tamatea received his title Tamatea-pokai-whenua because he had traversed both islands. This was twenty generations ago. Tamatea did not name Oamaru – it was named afterwards in memory of he and his party – nor did he bestow any place-names that the narrator knew of. When the Rarotongans were at the Christchurch Exhibition, Makea of that party and the narrator could understand one another and they had some interesting chats on matters of mutual interest. Makea said the Takitimu was named 'pull up stump' because the stump of the tree from which the canoe was made was pulled up. The narrator although he knew that to pull flax up is still called 'taki' did not think that was correct meaning – he thought it was only a name.**

THE TRAVELLING OF TURA

Tura is a celebrated ancestor of the Maori people. Many Southern Maori genealogies begin from him and the name is well-known in the South. The story is told of him and the fairy people, and of his wife and the Caesarian operation, of his grey hairs, etc. but no one ever seems to know the name of his canoe. Two Tuahiwi Maoris in speaking to the collector about rainbows said that Kahukura the goddess of rainbows was an ancestress of Tura and when he migrated to New Zealand [? H.B.] she directed him by appearing as rainbows. She was his chart – the names of his two canoes were – (after some cogitation they gave it up). He was an old man when he came here and spent a good deal of his time in thinking of his son in Hawaiki. He often thought he would like to see him again and the son 'had a similar sensation' (so quoth my Maori friend) and simultaneously they 'chanted karakias' to bring this to pass. Some say the mana of the chant was in his taiaha for when he laid it down a rainbow appeared and the son came sliding over it to New Zealand where he gathered his aged parent to his arms and took him 'back home' to Hawaiki. The names of the rainbows are forgotten also. [See story of Tura in Murihiku Notes, H.B.]

HISTORICAL JOTTINGS

While the collector was gathering information from the Natives of Canterbury he dropped across odd scraps of historical lore which while not of much value in themselves may eventually fit in with other information either previously procured or yet to be acquired. These items herewith follow:

DEATH OF TUTEKAWA

*Tutekawa was one of the earliest Kai-Tahu chiefs to come to the South Island – some say the very first. Over in the Wellington Province he killed Rakihikaia and took his wife Tukorero. He also killed two women called Tuarawhati and Hinekaitaki and it was owing to this he met his own death (by violence). When Moki captured the pa of Tutekawa (Waikakahi near Lake Ellesmere) he would have spared the life of the old man but Whakuku, a brother of the two murdered women, knowing Moki's intention forestalled it by casting his tao (spear) into the aged Tutekawa.

TUHAITARA

Tuhaitara, a great ancestress of the Kai-Tahu people, married Marukore a chief of the Katimamoe and of the Kahea people in the North Island. Some say she had twelve children but the principal informant considered it was eleven that is the number given in most genealogies, and some give ten. A section of the Kai-Tahu and Kati-Mamoe tribe is named after her and other sections after some of her children, notably Huirapa.**

A WESTLAND EPISODE

The Kai-Tahu early in their conquest of the South Island sent a war expedition to Westland. This came to disaster at Lake Mahinapua where the Chiefs Tanetiki, Tutepiriraki and Tutaemaro were killed. Their heads were severed from their bodies and it is said Hikatutae, a surviving chief, swam the lake with the three heads held by the hair with his teeth. A lady at Tuahiwi was most careful to impress on the collector the fact that this could not be correct. He might possibly have done so with the last-named two dead chiefs but Tanetiki although his nephew was really of higher blood and Hikatutae could not have desecrated the hair of this highborn head by placing it in his mouth and arrived safe at the other side. He would have been seized by avenging spirits and dragged down to death – at least he would have been in accordance with ancient Maori ideas as to what was tika (correct). She added that Hokitika river was named 'Return Straight' because Hikatutae brought the heads straight back to Kaiapoi and that Arahura was named because of the paths (ara) he cleared (hura) through the bush on this expedition. [Note: In the *Journal of the Polynesian Society* [[Vol. 29, 1920, p. 192]] these names have been given as of much greater antiquity than the above. H.B.]

MOKIS BURIAL

*When Hikatutae arrived back from Westland he found that Moki was dead and had left instructions for Hikatutae to bury him. The collector has heard varying accounts of this incident, and here is that of the principal informant. Moki, he said, wished to be buried on Tapuaenuku (one of the highest peaks of the great Kaikoura chain) so that he could look northward over the rippling waters of Raukawa (Cook Strait) towards his old home at Turanga (Poverty Bay–Gisborne) where he had been born. He had been dead some time when Hikatutae set out to fulfil his dying wishes. Soon after the party started the 'stink' was so pronounced that they removed the 'offal' (piro) and burnt this part. Before they reached their destination the rest of the remains were so offensive that they burned these at the foot of the mountain and buried the ashes. The head was carried back to Pekapeka (a name meaning 'the branch of a tree') at Woodend near Kaiapoi where it was properly whakatamiro'd (preserved).

THE FIGHT AT MOERAKI

In speaking of other things warfare was sometimes introduced into the trend of the conversation and the principal informant mentioned the old fighting pa at Katiki, near Moeraki. The collector has written of this Te-Raka-a-Hineatea pa several times** but he has never met anyone who had the slightest idea (as far as he could ascertain) *of how the name was given or what the words mean in this connection. The principal informant was almost equally at fault. He said the name was Te-raka-a-Hinaatea and that Te Raka means a cross-buttock at wrestling while Hinaatea means that the hair of anyone is gray and white but he had never heard the origin of the name. His tipuna, Ruapapa, went down to fight there, the rest of the taua being Kati-Kuri. (He then told the story of Ruapapa and the eels as recorded by H.B. in *Journal of the Polynesian Society* [[Vol. 29, 1920, p.193]].) Ruapapa fought later and proved he could fight well as he fought the Kati-Mamoe and beat them back to Otakou. He reckoned that Te Raka-a-Hinaatea was a Kati-Mamoe pa. [Not so. H.B.] At any-rate the people were all so mixed by that time it was hard to distinguish them. The intermixture commenced in the North Island (Kati-Mamoe and Kai-Tahu).**

RAUPARAHAS RAIDS

After Rauparaha and his men had demolished Kaiapohia pa they went to Akaroa to attack the Onawe pa. There were only eight firearms in this pa and yet Te Rauparaha feared to take it by assault so made up his mind to take it by treachery. Of the eight guns, two belonged to a chief named Wharaki (Whalagi of the whalers), one being an old big-mouthed blunderbuss and the other a flint-fire gun. Momo, a brother of Te Maiharanui, had been taken prisoner and was shoved forward with other prisoners to say there would be no killing by the Northerners. While this act of taware (cajolery) was going on some of Rauparaha's men had sneaked into the pa and began killing the inhabitants. Some of these had wished no parley with the Northerners as they suspected duplicity and these had trained the eight guns on selected marks among the Kati-Toa. When the murder began they fired and seven bullets found their mark but the eighth one intended for Rauparaha unfortunately missed its mark through the gun being knocked to one side.

The Southerners went up to Marlborough to make things even with Rauparaha. Hempleman, a whaler on Banks' Peninsula, gave Tuhawaiki (Bloody Jack) a big two-masted boat and it may have been in this a number of the Murihiku men went north, but their well-meant intentions miscarried and Te Rauparaha again escaped by the skin of his teeth. When the narrator was up at Otaki in the nineties he saw the old Native Church done with kakaho reeds. The people were building a monument or a memorial to Te Rauparaha and he chanced to see the wording intended for it. This was most insulting to the Ngai-Tahu tribe and to the South Island generally so at a public meeting he put in a strong protest against such a gross violation of the spirit of the old rongo-pai (peace) between the two tribes. The leading men acknowledged the justice of his contention and the obnoxious wording was altered for a less offensive rendering [although this is bad enough according to the average South Island Maori. H.B.].

ORIGIN OF SOME PLACE-NAMES

*The principal informant said that quite a number of South Island names of places had been imported from Hawaiki. Otakou (Otago) he considered was a name from Hawaiki. He also mentioned Te Ahupatiki in Lyttelton Harbor and Rapanui, a rock in the sea near Sumner (?), as being from Hawaiki.

Whakaraupo. The name Wakaraupo (properly Whakaraupo) is sometimes given, as the Maori name of Port Cooper (or Lyttelton Harbor as it is now called), but it is really only the name of the head of the harbour. It is said the name was bestowed by the Kai-Tahu chief Te Rakiwhakaputa (or Te Rangi-whaka-puta) who came from the North Island and settled there, or at least he lived there for some time. The name means whaka = harbor (whanga in north); raupo = a water plant.** An old Maori said the correct name of Lyttelton Harbor was Owhaka (harbor).

*Hitawerewere is a name of evil repute among the old people familiar with the history (often one of barbarity and ferocity) of the olden times. It was the name of a pa which stood 'imua' (formerly) near the Little River and a runholder unsuspectingly almost put it over the doorway of his fine mansion but an old halfcaste warned him in time. He was expecting friends from Home and it was a name he could scarcely take a pride in or explain in polite society. It records an episode in local Maori history somewhat similar to that in Jewish history recorded in Judges XIX, verse 25, although the Maori story does not state that the girl died, as far as the collector knows.

Hokanui, the name of the well-known range of hills near Gore in Southland, was mentioned by the principal informant. He considered this name was merely a dialectial variation or version of Hukanui, a word meaning 'Big Snow'. The collector told him this was a libel on Southland's good climate.

The principal informant mentioned the difficulty of giving a Pakeha an adequate conception of some Maori names which the intelligent class of Maori seemed to understand by instinct. He often found it very hard to express the right meaning of Maori in English and many intelligent English people quite misunderstood Maori idiom. For instance he once had quite an argument in a gathering comprising some of the leading men of Christchurch. The subject had come round to both Pakeha and Maori place-names and a barrister said the name Hurunui should be deleted off the map as it was immoral. The narrator was appealed to and said 'hurunui' had many meanings and none of them evil. It might mean a woolly dog with fine long hair for the ihupuni (the dogskin mat); it might mean that the kakano or purapura (seeds) of the maanuka had been brought down by floods in the river and been deposited on the lower banks and flat and had grown very thick together (brushwood); it might also mean the rays of the rising sun – the rays dispersed by the waewae (feet) of the sun just before dawn. 'Hum' might mean 'our children' – not one but all of them. Dog begets dog, hairy man begets hairy offspring, plants beget plants and all trees beget their like. He did not know how to make it any clearer but the proper meaning of the place-name Hurunui was 'plant'. Babies were just like young plants – they were the offspring of their parents. [It must be confessed this was not quite crystal-clear to the collector. When he searched Tregear's *Dictionary* the mystery was elucidated. In the midst of a great array of comparisons only one small one met the case, viz., Paumotan – 'hum', color; (b) species or kind; (c) height, figure, shape. The second of these meanings seems to fit the present case. H.B.]

THE STORY OF RATA

Wahieroa and Matukutangotango had a fight. The latter were giants and killed people of former. Matuku cooked Wahieroa and used his bones to go in a fence of men's bones he was making. He thought Wahieroa's bones might complete fence but they did not so he kept some of the slaves in his cave to use one by one. Rata came to kill that big bird. He came to a river and his atua Pungawerewere (a spider) told him to leave his men behind and come on with him. They came to a river where was no boat so the Spider made a cobweb and let the strand blow over the deep river. (The name of this web and of cobwebs generally narrator forgot.) Then the spider ran across and tied the strand to a tree and called out 'Come on' but Rata said, 'Too small, twist it,' so the Spider plaited it to a taura or rope. Then Rata crossed and the Spider undid its rope at end from which they had come and swung across the chasm on it. Rata told Spider to get a big log and tied the web rope round it and let the rope dangle over the cliff where Matuku had his cave. Then Rata went to near the mouth of the cave and Matuku said 'Your bones will finish the fence.' It slapped its wings at Rata and as its head was up Spider dropped the noose at end of rope over its head. It tried to fly but could not break the rope. Spider called to Rata, 'coil the rope quick' and Rata obeyed and Matuku was hanged. Spider laughed and said 'Ka mau koe i au te here ka mate koe' and the bird died. They lowered the body down, cut off the head, made a kapa-maori (oven) and put the body in. Soon after the 'guts burst, and blew off like a cannon'.

Spider laughed again and recovered the umu. Then Rata liberated the captives. Matuku had no assistants but had killed many, many people. Rata and his friends ate the body and used the bones to finish the fence. The cave had some name like Waro-nuku. This event happened near the time when the people were preparing to leave one of the Hawaikis – which one he could not say – perhaps it was Hawaiki-pamamao.

STORY OF RUATAPU

When the Maori people lived in the last Hawaiki (before New Zealand) said the principal informant, Uenuku married two wives and had two children by one and five by the other. One son Ruatapu angered him and he told him he was a poriro (or bastard) but that Kahutia-te-Rangi was born 'from my body' but you are from 'moenga rau kawakawa' = you are a 'tamaiti meamea' – a common child from a common bed. Ruatapu was enraged and when he went out in the canoe Tutepawharangi with 'seventy double' (one hundred and forty) sons of high-born chiefs he determined on a signal revenge. He said to go, 'out till the mountains come down to the sea' (looking back at land) and then let down punga (anchor). He was sitting with his rekereke (heel) on ma (hole) as a puru (plug) and removed it. He speared them with tokotoko spears of which he had made and secreted one hundred and forty under the rahoraho (deck). He used one spear on each man. All were killed save Paikea who floated off on the tata (bailer). He had a similar power to Ruatapu in sea and latter called out, 'You will be safe and when you get ashore tell the people I will send a flood to drown all save those who take refuge on the hills Te Pukekihikurangi and Te Pukehapopo. My great wave will be sent in Takuma (winter).' Paikea answered he would bear the message ashore and he called two taniwha – one male (perhaps this was Tinirau) and one female – to aid him to the far distant shore. When he got to Hawaiki he told Ruatapu's message. The people were very angry at the drowning and this led to a fight in which Uenuku was killed. At the appointed time Paikea and his two sons (Whatiua te Ramarama and Tahupotiki) and a few, very few, friends ascended the hills and were saved, the rest of the people being overwhelmed by Te Tai-a-Ruatapu. Another name for this flood was Parawhenuamea.** The escape of those people when 'te karu (ngam) o te moana' swept over the land was 'something like Noah building the ark in the back country and escaping' but it was true Maori history. *The late Tom Green had reckoned this flood of Parawhenuamea had happened in New Zealand but narrator argued it was in Hawaiki.** He (former) reckoned Nga-toko-ono-a-Hemo was drowned here but this was not so as the names had been brought from Hawaiki to Turanga (Gisborne) and then down here. *The son of Paikea, Whatiua, married a woman called Hamo in North Island or Hemo in South Island whakapapa and had Porourangi, a girl Matiherangi and another child. When Whatiua died his widow was married by Tahupotiki and bore to him three sons and one daughter. This girl married Porourangi, her half-brother. One of the sons Iratahu married his half-sister Matiherangi and had a son Rakatehurumanu who married a daughter of Porourangi named Huiarei. The narrator added 'They married close to make the race go high in birth as the custom was,' (but the collector also thinks the flood already described may have made eligible partners scarce). [From this point the narrator went on to trace** lines of descent from Paikea to the present day and spent two days giving the collector a wealth of detail genealogically. There was no gainsaying this. H.B.]

VARIOUS LEGENDS

A Maori lady told the collector two fragments of ancient stories she had heard when a girl. One concerned the origin of lizards. When the great giant Kararahuarau was burnt two inohi (scales) flew out from his funeral pyre and one formed the karara in the sea (a kind of shark) and the other landing on the earth formed the karara on the land (lizards).

She had heard the old people talk in the niu (guest-house) and do whai (the game of cat's-cradle but she learnt none of it) and tell old yarns. One was about echoes but she scarcely remembered it. *A man named Tama or Rona – she thought latter name was right – fled from his wife (whose name she forgot). He threw his two children in a cave and tried himself to take refuge in the sun but it was too hot so he tried the moon with success. His wife not finding him on earth returned to the cliff and tried to get at the children by scratching the cliff but 'kia whakiwhaki maikuku' she broke her fingernails, so went away disgusted and left the children sealed up in the cliff and now they answer the Maoris as echoes. [See this story in *Journal of the Polynesian Society* [[Vol. 27, 1918, p. 103]] by H.B.]**

A young man told the collector he had heard an old man tell a tale about three boys who wished to make canoes. The father told each of them to walk in bush until a leaf fell on his forehead and then to make a canoe of that tree. The two elder did so and felled trees. They went back to find the trees standing again. They reported this to their father who, after some thought, said not to hit the lizards (in bush) away but to feed them. Next day when they ate they coaxed the lizards and gave them the remains of the food. The king of the lizards in gratitude said his people would finish the canoes and so they did and the two sailed proudly away, followed later by their youngest brother (who had made his own canoe). This lad came to where the sky then met the sea and here he found one brother turned into stone on one side of this curtain (?) and one on the other side. (He apparently got through safely himself.) *This was all of this story that informant knew, but he continued by saying that the old man also told of a fabulous giant who was so mighty he could kill from five hundred to five thousand Maoris with a sweep of one arm and from five hundred to five thou sand with a sweep of the other arm. On one occasion he killed so many the corpses not only filled up a gully but changed it into a hill.** [The collector met the old man and asked for names of above-recorded celebrities but the old man said he had forgotten them. He may have; but he has the reputation of being a pakeha-scorner! H.B.]

The collector was privileged to hear a brief discussion between two intelligent Maoris (aged between fifty and sixty) concerning the whence of Hawaiki. One said he had always been of opinion that the South Island of New Zealand was Hawaiki because the canoes of totara were said to be hewn with pounemu. In support of this view he quoted that the Rarotongans who came to Christchurch Exhibition (in 1907) said that Hawaiki was on New Zealand. He added, however, that he was not so sure of this idea now – in fact he was very doubtful of it. The other said that when on a visit to Taranaki he there saw the famous axe Awhiorangi which traditionally was declared to have carved out the celebrated Aotea canoe. It was made of a hard slate. This, to his mind, showed that the Maoris came from a land where there was no pounemu (greenstone) and hence Hawaiki must be such a land – but it would have slate similar to the axe.

*The principal informant said he remembered a smouldering fire in the Waitaki hills 'Te-ahi-a-Ue' and history said it came from Hawaiki on the Araiteuru canoe but he forgot the name of the person who brought it. Ue was perhaps an abbreviation of name Uenuku (father of Paikea). The fire Tamatea brought in Takitimu to Murihiku went out at Oamaru (the ashes of it form the white stone of that locality).

The principal informant considered that giant Kopuwai lived on the Waitaki River as his petrified dogs are there still. [See Murihiku Notes, H.B.] He had heard of Kararahuarau but did not know his locality – it was in Hawaiki perhaps.

(He continued: In regard to The Canoes, Tairea's karakia was not right and the crew was turned to pounemu [See Greenstone, H.B.]. Takitimu's karakia was right so the people landed safely. Araiteuru came to Matakaea, Otago, but its karakia was not correct so the crew was turned to stone. Pakihiwitahi was turned to stone. Kirikirikatata and his wife Kirikirikaehe [This should be Aroaroakaehe. H.B.] walked inland and became mountains, and so on. This canoe brought 'Pakeha things' such as frying-pans, saucepans, wheat and food and if it had not been turned to stone owing to that bad karakia the Maori would have forestalled Pakeha ways by many generations!)

When Ngatoroirangi [See Previous Canterbury Notes, H.B.] sent fire from the Volcanic Region of North Island to Tamatea the latter walked on it to keep his feet warm and also to guide his footsteps.**

Add to History

In regard to a legend (quoted by Tregear) that after Maui raised the South Island he gave it to the people called Kui who were dispossessed by Tutumaiao people, the collector asked the principal informant who thereupon gave the following information: *He had heard of Kui and Tutumaiao but very little. The latter was mentioned in an old song. 'That story was a detail of Ngatimamoe.' Maiharoa's mother came from Kahea and that ancient race and he could perhaps have told something about it. The Ngatimamoe were only a family, the Kahea were a race. Personally he thought that the word Kui should be kae, but he was not sure – it was so long ago. A fragment of a song he recollected was: 'Tutumaiao haehae one nei ka tau ra ia na rangi ahuru nei'. The words 'haehae one' did not mean 'to rip up the sand' but that a battle had been fought on the sands and the dead left lying there, but he had no details about it. He did not even know the name of the battle on the beach. Hoani Matiu (Southland) was the only man who might possibly know. Tutumaiao had three meanings he knew. To start to make a pa, a house, etc. and to leave it unfinished was tutumaiao (and was a bad omen, it may be added). Tutumaiao was a name applied to the Southern Lights dancing up and down in streamers in the southward sky, and the name was also given to a heat haze shimmering in the sun on a hot day, but perhaps the most correct interpretation and proper meaning was to get up at night or in the early morning and see an unusual light or uncommon radiance touching the sky. These names, such as Tutumaiao, were given long, long ago and were very dim and shadowy now, details being lost.

He did not even know the meaning and origin of word Maori, but he considered it was bestowed some time in their history as it was not a name coming from the beginning of mankind. He did not know if it started when the pakeha came, or if it came from Hawaiki.

The Kapuhi (Auckland Peninsula) people brought their whakapapa from stones. At a big gathering in North Island the question came up. Some said the name Nga-Puhi came from the puhi (plumes) of canoes – Arawa, Aotea, Tainui and Takitimu but the Kapuhi would not have it so. They claimed it was from ancestors Puhikaiariki, Puhimanawanawa and Puhi-o-Rakaiora but they would not explain. So narrator said that 'puhi' meant a highborn woman, Manawanawa is thinking important thoughts and heart beating when near a loved woman; Kaiariki means 'Descended from chiefs' and Rakaiora is a tipuna of the Waikato people – he thought a female. These ancestors were long before any of the canoes mentioned and he told the Ngapuhi they did not bring their name from Hawaiki but put it on in New Zealand and tacked it on to various ancestors picked at random – the Puhi ones. The Ngapuhi are dunces at whakapapa and he used to say to them 'There is no doubt you people are descended from boulders.'

Ngaitahu brought their name from Hawaiki and Ngatimamoe from a different part of it.** He could not explain the latter as they were out long before the former, but the Hawea, he thought, came from South Africa and the Cape of Good Hope. *These Hawea people had dark skins and curly hair and spoke a different language to the present Maoris. The Waitaha were not so dark and had long straight hair and they came from the West. Te Rapuai, the third race to inhabit the South Island were, he thought, copper colored and with ginger hair (like the Fijians whom he had seen at the Christchurch Exhibition and perhaps they came from that country). The Katimamoe, the fourth South Island people, were Polynesians like the Kaitahu, the fifth and present Maori inhabitants. Narrator was from most lines of descent in South Island being connected with twenty one hapus.

Canon Stack had whawhai (fights) correct in his history, but he had missed out all the whakapapas from his book. It was not Stack's fault he was so extremely meagre in recording some of the more important battles – it was the fault of his informants for not saying more.**

Narrator considered that Uenuku, the famous Kaitahu ancestor in Hawaiki was about same time as Wahieroa, father of Rata, and that Tura lived about then too.

Tamatea the famous captain of Takitimu had a son Kahungunu who was born in Hawaiki and came to New Zealand as a child. *Seeing the Ngaitahu, Ngatiporou and Ngati Kahungunu come from same stock, the people of those tribes had difficulty in welcoming narrator but finally called him 'taina'. In his replies he whakapapa'd [He is admittedly one of the finest genealogists in New Zealand. He has no written memoranda but relies wholly on memory for his fluent and full recital of numerous whakapapa. H.B.] to the astonishment of his hosts and proved he was 'tuakana' to them. They freely admitted he was correct and he said to them the old proverb, 'You did not know where the wind came from,' suitable to the occasion. Again he proved to them Kahungunu got his second wife by blackguardism (tinihanga). He took a fancy to the wife of Tamatakutai, one Hinekakara, so-called because her skin smelt like scent.** On a visit to that pa he sent his people for pawa (at Napier) and he purposely ate so many it gave him 'bellyache' and in the night his 'puku began to boil' and he had diarrhoea. He slipped along to bed of Tama and his wife and quietly 'did diarrhoea in it'. She woke first and saying smell was bad put her hand in the result of Kahu's blackguardly trick. She blamed her husband for putrifying the bed and was so furious she would not accept his denial. The result was she left Tama and eventually Kahu got her. *When the people said to narrator 'haeremai taina' he asked who he was young brother to, and set to work and proved beyond doubt he was tuakana from Tupurupuru.

After Moki came over from North Island he defeated Tutekawa at Waikakahi as is well-known. Moki told Tutekawa's son Rakitamau to go to Te Kohanga (now Kaiapoi) and dig fernroot so that when Moki returned South they would undertake an expedition to Westland. Instead Rakitamau went to the Plains and built the pa of Paturiki (Longbeach, near Ashburton) and dwelt there till he went over to fight the Ngatiwairangi, the Ngaitara and Ngatiwairua on West Coast. The ostensible reason the war-parties went there was to get greenstone but a matakite (seer) there saw a vision of them coming and warned the people.

The tohukas Tautini and Irirangi who had fled from Nelson when Tuahuriri took the pa there [See Previous Canterbury Notes, H.B.] and gone with the Patea people from Nelson to Westland were then there and it was one of them who foresaw the taua's approach in two divisions and who took means to thwart their intentions. Rakitamau's party went via Rakaia Gorge and the tohukas stopped them with rain, and the party camped. Rakitamau did not like look of weather and said to one of his leading men, Takawa by name, to come into the shelter when retiring to rest. Takawa replied, 'E mahana pu werawera tenei te ahuru te taka nei,' meaning that he would keep warm in any circumstances. He had a kahukuri, ihupuni or kirikuri (dogskin mat) which he prided himself on to keep cold and wet out. In the morning the place was piled four feet deep with snow and Rakitamau called Takawa but received no answer. They dug him up frozen stiff and dead. This was in the mountains near the other side and as the weather continued bad the party returned without fighting and without meeting the other party, which was more unlucky than they had been. This lot went via Waitui (up Hanmer way) and were met by the steady downpour brought on by the tohukas. The Mahinaapua was much swollen but some of the party ruru (made) mokihi (rafts) and although it was raining hard set out downstream. Some steered badly through the rapids and were upset and drowned and swept to sea. Hikatutae was not in the disaster and waited two days by the coast to see if the sea would return the dead. Some were washed ashore, among them being Tanetiki, Tutepirirangi and Tutaemaro. Hikatutae burnt the bodies and taking these three heads, one in his teeth and two in his hand (held by the hair) swam the river or a branch of the lake. He did not hold Tanetiki's hair in his teeth as that chief was higher and consequently tapu but one of the others. The rain stopping the party returned without fighting. The whole expedition is called Tawiri-o-te-mako (heaping of the sharks) in allusion to the sea washing up dead in a heap on the beach. It was a disastrous campaign as so many chiefs were dead.

While this was going on Moki slandered Moruka and Te Kahukura as a joke. In public he mentioned a fault of each jokingly but the ladies took it seriously. This was somewhere near the West as the tohungas Tautini and Irirangi were up repairing a whare whakairo (carved house) and heard Moki cursing when the women reproved him. They said the tohungas were there and Moki cursed again, and died soon after by makutu. Moki's kanga (curse) against the tohunga invoked the latter's makutu and he died suddenly.

When the news of Moki's death reached the North Island another batch of Kaitahu came across. In crossing Cook Strait the canoe Te Hauwai was upset in a storm and Hamua and Tuahuriri were drowned. They were coming from Hataitai and Hamua left a wife up in Wairarapa. The other canoe, Makawhiu, with Turakautahi and his party got safely across. Hamua's widow was a putao to Turakautahi, but latter had a bumblefoot (waewaehape) and she refused to marry him as she said his foot or toe would tear her clothes, and she married

Rangitawhanga instead. Turakautahi was wounded in fight at Pariwhakatau and was carried from there to Te Kohanga-a-Kaikaiawaru (the first name of Kaiapoi) where he lay feeling very ill. He hung his war gear up and addressing it said there was no more fighting for him. He was so near death that his family gathered round. It was felt that the only cure was hinu-tangata (men's fat) and word was sent North to where fighting was proceeding and some men were cooked and the oil collected in a taha and sent to Kaiapoi. This oil was poured in the wounds (spear holes) and cured the wounded man but he never fought again, although he either built a new pa called Kaiapoi or re-modelled and strengthened the old one (Te Kohanga) and renamed it Kaiapoi. 'It was only in Rauparaha's time pa was called Kaiapohia and that by North Island people.'

The Kaitahu fought the Katimamoe for four generations in the South Island and then all were fused into one race through killings and by intermarriage. Tutepopoarangi welcomed Te Rakitaurewa to Waipapa but his visitor asked him what kind of food he had to eat – had he any tangata (man). Tu was insulted and in a duel killed his visitor. Ruahikihiki was a nephew of Mako, Maru, Te Ake and Te Rakitaurewa, but no one vindicated Te Rakitaurewa's breach of etiquette nor avenged his death. The great Kaitahu chief Te Rakaitauheke eventually was killed by Katimamoe but narrator would not say where. It was Wheke who killed Matauira at Moeraki and he was sorry as the slain man proved to be one of his own tribe.

Narrator had tipuna (ancestors) who lived up Geraldine River at Opuaha, and Tuteurutira and Kahore were killed up there. The former chief was an uncle of latter.** [From an extremely confused account the collector made out following but does not vouch for its accuracy. When descriptions of warfare are so vague and puzzling there is always a grave suspicion that the narrator is hiding details – perhaps the killing of ancestors, etc. H.B.] Kahore and Tuteuretira were up at Opuaha and the former brought his granddaughter Ruaitawhaki there, together with Tamahoru and Kapu, brother and sister of Tuteruretira. Puaka, the father of Kahore, lived at Kaiapoi and made hunting trips to Tawera but his brothers and sister lived at Opuaha. *Then a woman called Hinekato made some 'untrue details' about them and Kahore and Tu murdered two chiefs (whose names narrator forgot) through these lying reports. This made a taua come and murder Kahore and Tu.** Tamahoru and Kapu heard the noise in their sleep and arose and escaped, as did others, including Ruaitawhaki. They fled to Manahune in the Mackenzie Country. *From the pa Waiteruati (near Temuka) Wahakai and his men went up-country to see about these murders and they found the two old chiefs lying dead and they buried them. They sent word to Kaiapoi and a taua from there came round base of mountains (Alps) hunting the enemy [Whoever this was. H.B.]. They met some and killed them including a woman** (whose name narrator forgot). They reached Opuaha where they killed the fugitives who had come back, including the untruthful Hinekato, whose lies were the cause of the whole trouble. Wahakai then** appeared and stopped the taua from killing

Ruaitawhaki (who although a tapu girl forbidden to carry loads and work was forced to catch tuna (eels) for the taua) and also Kapa her mother and Tamahoru. Ruaitawhaki then married Tukarekare (and their descendants are in among the collector's whakapapa).

*Hikaiti, a wife of Ruahikihiki, drowned herself (whakamomori) by jumping off pari (cliff) into sea at Whakamoa, near Akaroa, because she was jealous of her sister, Te Aotarewa, who had married Ruahikihiki after her former husband Te Rakitaurewa had been killed by his second cousin Tutepopoarangi in a fight or duel at Waipapa.

Add to History

The Rapuwai people were in a big battle in Hawaiki, the name of it being Pohatu-parimurimu. Kakakaiamio was a later fight and Te Aruhe-taratara a still later one. He (principal informant) did not know which Hawaiki it was as this name Hawaiki was a general name for all big islands the Maoris passed (in their migrations). Te Rapuwai (or Rapuai as it is often shortened to) was a tribe before they came to New Zealand. That tribe could fight on land or on the water and in one sea fight some of their canoes were upset and occupants had to swim about – hence the origin of their tribal name. (The Kati-Ira and other South Island tribes also came from Hawaiki.) It was from this race that Tura got his second wife. They were fond of canoe fights and it was through being capsized and having to swim they were called Rapu-wai. At the time Tura knew them they had no fires and ate their food raw. They had good-looking women and Tura's wife was beautiful. [See Section re Childbirth, H.B.]

Narrator considered (from his teaching) that Hawea was the first tribe who came to New Zealand. They were under Taiehu (a name which means 'rough sea') and the canoe was Kapakitua and his axe Awhioraki – which is really another name for Kahukura. He was sure Kapakitua was the canoe and not the axe and this seemed to be Maiharoa's only error in the account H.B. published in *Journal of the Polynesian Society* [[Vol. 27, 1918, p. 83]]. The Hawea, he reckoned from his reading, came from Zululand in South Africa. They were a very dark people with thick mops of hair and strong white teeth.

The Rapu-wai were a clumsy race and, like the Hawea, were 'not much good', but the Waitaha people were a bit better. The Kahea were another Hawaiki race and merged into the Waitaha. The whakapapas given by Maiharoa (and two of which are published in *Journal of the Polynesian Society* [[Vol. 24, 1915, pp. 8–9]] by H.B.) are the best genealogies of any in either North or South Islands to connect the present Maoris with those old emigrants to New Zealand and moreover their accuracy is such that they cannot be challenged or disputed.

The Waitaha people were led by Rakaihautu and descendants still survive. The hapu name Kati-Rakai is merely a shortening of Kati-Rakaihautu, and Kokiro, the mother of Te Maiharoa belonged to this hapu. Akaroa was once a great Waitaha centre and the hill Tuhiraki perpetuates the name of the ko (spade) of Rakaihautu.

Asked about the Kahui-Tipua people the narrator said that they came from Hawaiki but he was sorry he knew practically nothing about them.

Asked about Tukete (whom Stack says was a great navigation-man) the principal informant said he had heard a little about him. He was an 'early settler' somewhere between Hawea and Waitaha. 'He probably stopped in New Zealand. I can not say which was his canoe – there is no whakapapa from him. The Huruhurumanu was only an imitation canoe but the Uruao was a real waka. Te Waka-a-Rangi is only another name for the Uruao.'** [Note: We can scarcely accept the rendering of the narrator – an acknowledged champion of Kai-Tahu, the last tribe to come to the South Island as against that of Te Maiharoa (who died an old man in 1885) of Waitaha-Kati-Mamoe descent. H.B.]

*Narrator resumed: 'Hawaiki-pamamao, Hawaiki-nui, and Hawaiki-roa were all big countries. Honokiwairua means that the soul leaves the body here (and presumably goes back to those lands). The name Hawaiki was given by the Maori to those great countries. It embraces America, Africa, and Asia and was the name of those places before the Pakeha named them. Then as the Maori travelled among the islands he called some of them Hawaiki too.'

An early man to come to New Zealand was Toi-te-Uatahi, went on the narrator, and he was a son of Hinerautu. He came from the stock of Whaitiri-paku and latter may have married Hinerautu, but he was not quite sure of this. A son of Toi-te-Huatahi was Rauru and a tribe in Taranaki, Nga-rauru, comes from him.

Some said that Rokoitua came from Hawaiki on the bird Manu-nui-a-Tane in five days. Toi was in New Zealand then and gave Rokoitua some mamaku (ferntree) to eat. Rokoitua did not think much of such a food. He had brought cooked kumera in his tatua (belt) and he got the loan of a bowl and soaked the food in water and gave it to his hosts to eat. Toi and his people did not know what kumera was before this time and they liked it and determined to get some from where it grew.

(At another time the narrator remarked that the genealogy of Rokoitua given in the *Journal of the Polynesian Society* [[Vol. 24, 1915, p. 20]] by H.B. was 'a good whakapapa' and he went on: 'He lived in the time of Tura and other famous men in Hawaiki. He came out to New Zealand and reported it was a good country to settle in. In the North Island he met Toi-ua-tahi who gave him mamaku and aruhe to eat. He went back to Hawaiki on a big bird with a name something like Te Manu-a-Tane'.)

Rata set adrift in Hawaiki a big log which floated to New Zealand where it was found and split, the canoes Horouta and Manuka being made from it. These canoes went back to bring kumera, but narrator knew very little about them.

Kahuiroko is the name of a race who held the kumera in Hawaiki. The

Kahuimatua also held kumera seeds in Hawaiki, but narrator did not think they ever came to New Zealand. These people did not want to part with the kumeras and ran away. The crews of the Horouta and Manuka gave chase and tried to overtake them but only succeeded in catching a few kumera and bringing them to New Zealand. Those were the races holding the kumera at that time. This vegetable was not all over Hawaiki but only some parts of it. What race they were he knew not.** An Anglican Bishop, who had been a missionary, told narrator that when he was sailing about in Melanesia he came to an island inhabited by a big-made, tall people. The Bishop is a tall man but he said these dark savages were taller than he. He said to one of his Polynesian companions 'Ko whea atu tera whenua' (What land is that) and one of the barbarians answered the question showing they knew Maori. The Bishop landed and they had a hakari (feast) and whaikorero (welcome) over it. This showed that the knowledge of Polynesian races was widespread, and *narrator said he did not know what were those races who held the kumera.

The Araiteuru canoe also tried to bring kumera to New Zealand. Te Heni was the captain and Hekuru the tohuka but the vessel was wrecked at Shag Point.

In regard to the origin of New Zealand tribes the Nga-Puhi start from three women named Puhi-manawanawa, Puhi-kaiariki and Puhi-rere. The tribe Kati Ira is from Ira-turoto, the eldest son of Tura, a well-known Hawaiki chief. The Kati-Mamoe tribe is older than the chief called Hotu-Mamoe (or Whatu-Mamoe) in the North Island. It is a very old race from Hawaiki.

The Takitimu canoe had more tohukas on it than any waka (canoe) that came to New Zealand. It was the most sacred canoe of the lot and the men of knowledge on it knew their own history thoroughly.** [Note: This claim by a South Islander is interesting and is borne out by the history from Takitimu sources secured by the Polynesian Society [[Smith, 1913, 1915]] and published in two volumes of their Memoirs. The narrator was quite unaware of the work of this Society or of its objects. H.B.] *The men descended from other canoes start their whakapapas from men on board those canoes, but the descendants of Takitimu migrants start their whakapapas away back in Hawaiki. He had heard old Mrs Gilroy at the Bluff sing a waiata (song) called Te Tere o Takitimu (The Voyage of Takitimu). It is a long song of the South Island but narrator had not picked it up. It was like a karakia and he advised the collector to endeavour to secure it. He understood that Mr Wi Parata once copied it down from dictation.

Some time before the Takitimu left Hawaiki there were battles there called Ui and Ua, and Tutakahinahina had something to do with them. Tutakahinahina came on the Takitimu, the captain of which was Tamatea. Tamatea was a good skipper and could karakia, 'te pu o te toi', and quell the winds. [Note: Exactly what 'toi' means the collector cannot say but it has something to do with the efficacy of the karakia. H.B.] The Takitimu left Tutakahinahina behind somewhere about the Bay of Plenty. He was a bad man and Tamatea did not like him; in fact, was glad to be rid of him, as he had not been in favor of his coming at all and wished to leave him at some islands en route. This was not done and Tutaka reached New Zealand but was left in the North while the canoe ran down to Foveaux Strait. The North Island tohukas at one time knew very little about Tamatea and why he acquired the name Tamatea-pokai-whenua, but listening to what the South Island tohukas said about him and picking up a little here and a little there and putting two and two together they were finally able to make a fairly complete history of the man, his ancestors and his family. All the same, Tamatea did not die peacefully at Hokianga as some of the histories stated, but he was killed fighting in a battle at another part of the island whose particular name eluded him.

Speaking of history recorded in books he would deny the accuracy of Stack's statement that Moko killed Tutewaimate (in Waitaha times in South Island). Both of these chiefs were drowned in a big flood.

In regard to Kai-Tahu doings in the South Island the name of the fight at Matangi-awhia pa at Nelson when Tuahuriri took it = Whakamarama.

The tohukas Tautini and Iriraki mentioned were of Kati-Ira descent.

Tu-te-kawa killed two women Tuarawhati and Hinekaitangi (who were sisters of Whakuku) in North Island and fled to South Island. Years after a taua under Moki went to Tutekawa's home at Waikakahi (Birdling's Flat) and found the aged man sitting alone in a whare lying with his back to the fire. All the people of the place, save his daughter-in-law Punahikoia and her children, were away eeling at Taumutu. Tutekawa was killed by Whakuku throwing a spear through the window in the tuaroko-o-te-whare (back wall of the house). Punahikoia lit a fire and her husband Te Rakitamau saw the smoke and came over to see what was the matter. Moki told the Kai-Tuhaitara to keep awake but they said the enemy would be afraid to come and they slept in the heat of the fires. When Rakitamau reached the sleeping camp and saw the strange warriors there he sat down to weep, thinking his wife and family were dead but Punahikoia went out and cheered him up. Then she went back and awoke Moki and told him and at his bidding she brought Rakitamau to Moki and the two cousins cried together. Then Moki awoke the people. The account in *Journal of the Polynesian Society* [[Vol. 26, 1917, p. 68]] by the collector (H.B.) was not correct. There is a custom [see Customs H.B.] called Kaikai-waiu to warn relatives if danger threatens so Moki told Rakitamau to take his wife and children away as their lives were in jeopardy. Rakitamau took the timely advice and with his family hid in the clump of manuka at Otutohea (near the site of the present cemetery at Koukourarata or Port Levy). [Last time narrator was there the Pakeha was unnecessarily destroying the small patch that had sheltered the refugees and he felt sad and angry over it.] When Te Rakitamau could not be found the taua was angry and killed a mokai (slave) of Moki in revenge for his warning his kinsman.

The collector asked who Waitai was but did not get much information in reply, nor any whakapapas to place him in the scheme of South Island history. Waitai, said principal informant, came in the first batch or contingent of Kai-Tahu to the South Island. He was of mixed Kati-Kuri and Kati-Ira blood. This latter tribe joined Kai-Tahu when Irakehu married Rakawahakura. Poho was a brother of Waitai and both were probably sons of Rokotaitawhi, but he did not know much about him, as he was not joined to many influential families as was Tuahuriri the biggest Kai-Tahu chief of that period. [Waitai was killed at Mokamoka near the Bluff.]

The collector asked about the Ripapa pa on an island in Lyttelton Harbour but the reply was that Ripapa was not much of a pa at any time and there was scarcely any fighting at it. Rakiwhakaputa, went on the principal informant, made a number of pas round Lyttelton Harbour with the intention of clearing the Kati-Mamoe out of that part of the country altogether. He killed the Kati-Mamoe chief Mawete (or Mawiti) who owned the old Moriori pa of Te Manuka at Halswell. Omawete (or Omawiti) in Governor's Bay is named after the spot where that chief was slain, but narrator had given an account of the affair to Mr James Cowan who had published it (in among others) in a series of articles he contributed to the Christchurch 'Star'. Rakiwhakaputa, a man of gigantic stature, was a father-in-law of Turakautahi and was a Kati-Kuri, of which sub-branch of the Kai-Tahu tribe narrator said he was the present head.

Narrator has a long account in Maori of Te Rauparaha's attempt to conquer the South Island. He got the narrative from Paora Taki and wrote it down. Te Mautai, narrator's uncle, tried to burn the canoes of Te Rauparaha drawn up at Akaroa but dampness foiled the attempt. The last fight of series was at Tuturau where Puaho (not Puoho) was met and killed. That was down in Murihiku, a name which narrator considered was quite recently bestowed – it is not nearly so old as name Rakiura (the name of Stewart Island).** The Tukete who was killed at Rakiura should be called Tukete-te-rua to distinguish him from the former Tukete.

A Maori said to the collector: 'Te Waipuna was Rakiwhakaputa's pa and the urupa (burial-ground) of his people was found in a cave there. [See previous Disposal of the Dead notes, H.B.] His leg-bone from his foot to his knee came up to my thigh so you can tell he was a giant. [Narrator is a big, tall man and was at Cave the day it was blocked. H.B.] It is said he built his pa on Waipuna Hill so that he could look down to Wairewa where his daughter lived and back to Kaikoura where his son, or some other relative, was. There is a splendid water supply in that pa site. The Pakehas have condemned the Onawe pa at Akaroa because they say there is no water there, but there is water at that place inside the old pa walls if you know where to look for it.'

Additional

*Having seen principal informant again he added: Kaka kai amio was a big war in Hawaiki. The name means a bird (kaka) looking for food all round the world.

It finds berries here and eats them and goes on and finds berries elsewhere and eats them and so on. The people fought like that in that war in Hawaiki, but he did not know the name of the race they fought. That was how it came that Rakaihaitu came to New Zealand. Two other wars were fought in Hawaiki, Pohatu-parimurimu and Aruhe-taratara. The former word means that the oven stones had been put in the umu or kapa-Maori, time after time until they had become slippery with the oil and grease out of cooked persons' bodies. Aruhe-taratara is to put fern leaves in the umu when cooking, or to spread them nearby to lay the cooked bodies on. Kakakaiamio, as a name, can be applied to the whole series of wars and Pohatu-parimurimu (slippery, oily stones) and Aruhe-taratara (long coarse fern-leaves spread out) to the feasts which followed each fight.** [This explanation places cannibalism very far back in the history. H.B.]

*Through that long series of wars the Hawea (?), Rapuwai, Waitaha and Katimamoe people left Hawaiki and other lands and came to New Zealand. The fighting was a 'ki mokai' to put down the taurekareka or inferior people. They were branches of the Maori races but not similar to the last Maoris to come to New Zealand. After these last-named people had driven the former tribes out of Hawaiki and elsewhere, they 'renewed their race' and when they came to New Zealand carried all before them, and in about two hundred years or eight generations, he thought, they destroyed the former immigrants to New Zealand and had Aotearoa to themselves. As for Rakaihautu he was a Waitaha chief but his wife belonged to a different race. Her name was Riki-o-waio and she came from the Hawea people. The Takitimu 'lost' no people on her voyage, but most of the other canoes left food (taro) and people at various islands, such as Rarotonga, etc., before they finally arrived at New Zealand. The Government should have got Thomas Green, John Mark and he to write South Island history ere it was too late.**

An old man said he had never heard of Tukete as a sailor, but as a Katimamoe chief. Another informant said that Ruahikihiki was in trouble in the North Island and was starved so he swam to South Island where he got plenty to eat.

The hall at Rapaki is called Wheke after a son of the Kaitahu chief, Te Raki whakaputa, by latter's second wife. This man is said to have slept out on an adjacent hilltop in the troublous days of old.

MAORIORI (MORIORI)

*[The principal informant had something to say about this celebrated people.** He pronounced the name different to what the collector had previously heard, just saying the name 'Maori' as customarily pronounced, and adding 'ori' – as 'Maori-ori'. H.B.]

*The Maori-ori are a part of the Kati-Mamoe people and narrator had heard some of their history. Te Karaka a Maoriori from the Chathams wanted narrator to take a case in Native Land Court against some North Island Maoris over the ownership of one of the Chatham Islands. This was forty years ago and he learned some history over the matter. Te Karaka said the old Maoriori stock on the Chathams came from the South Island of New Zealand whence they fled to escape their enemies. They were one of the old peoples inhabiting the South Island and were part Ngai-Tara and part Ngati-Mamoe. One of their chief settlements was at Halswell where they had a pa called Manuka. The Ngati-Kuri [The collector thinks this name erroneous here as Kati-Kuri came to the South Island ten generations ago. H.B.] fought against the Maoriori and captured the pa at Manuka. The fugitives from here fled to Ohikaparuparu (Sumner) and put out to sea in a number of canoes (whose names narrator did not memorise). All the voyagers landed safe on the Chathams, no canoe being lost, and here their descendants dwelt until some North Islanders went across in a Pakeha ship and killed the Maoriori like dogs or pigs. Some of these invaders, thinking there was not enough room for them, left the Chathams and sailed to the Auckland Islands under a chief named Matioro. Here some children were born and narrator had met a woman who was one of those born down there. The place was too cold for cultivation so the wanderers left and eventually returned to the North Island. Not all the Maoriori people left the South Island at that migration long ago. Some remained drifting down to Murihiku intermarried with other people. He had heard one lived at Colac; and Whaitiri's daughter married a pure Maoriori from the Chathams, Rita by name and their son Henry married a daughter of Rickus [Whose tangi at Temuka the collector attended. H.B.].**

Add to Moriori

*The Maoriori or Moriori people, said the principal informant, came to New Zealand with the Katimamoe but he could not name the canoe. They called themselves by the name Moriori and this name was not applied to them by the Maoris until the latter found the former so denominating themselves as a race. He did not know what the name meant – in fact, he could add, he did not know who gave the name Maori nor its original meaning, nor did he know when it was first given or in what circumstances. It was the god Kahukura who enabled those Hawea people and subsequent migrations to find New Zealand. He sent rainbows and these resting on the waves, smoothed the sea and let the canoes find a way through southward. They would not have found this land at all but for the beneficent actions of that god.

When the Katimamoe people came to the South Island and spread about trouble sometimes arose and it was through a fight at the Manuka pa (near Taitapu) that a portion of the Moriori people fled to sea in canoes and their god directed them to the Chatham Islands.

He remembered hearing long ago, people who had visited the Chathams say the Morioris were good singers. Two Maoris who visited Wairewa (Little River) used to sing Moriori songs they had picked up when at the Chathams but narrator could not understand the lingo. These men said the Morioris would sometimes continue singing all night and even when they got accustomed to this procedure of singing straight on, they were often puzzled to know where a song began or ended and this was always a source of bewilderment to them while at the Chathams. Narrator considered from what he heard of it that the language was quite different to Ngaitahu talk, but was allied to the Ngatimamoe speech as far as he knew.**

Add to Morioris

The principal informant briefly referred to the Moriori people in his remarks on various topics to the collector on the latter's third trip although it cannot be said he added anything much to what he had previously said on the subject.

*These Moriori people used to live at the pa called Te Manuka near what is now Halswell** (This pa subsequently belonged to the Kati-Mamoe and a chief called Mawete was killed there by the Kai-Tahu.) *It was from this place the Moriori people fled for safety to the Chathams. Their atua told them there was land over there and they went and peopled it. The Moriori were partly of Kai-Tara blood and their language was like that of the Kati-Kuia and Kati-Rakai people of the South Island.**

This was all that the principal informant had to say about the Moriori or Maoriori people but the collector has a further note on this topic. When speaking to a woman he noticed that in pronouncing a name T --- (something or other – the collector forgets the name she was quoting as that of a person who had done some recent act) she said the Te as if it was Tche. (This may have been because of front top teeth missing, but she is ordinarily a clear speaker). The collector remarked to her that she said 'Te' like the Moriori were reputed to do. She laughed and said she could not say as to that, for she knew scarcely anything about the Moriori language except she had heard those people never used 'h' when it was in a conspicuous place, saying 'omai' for 'homai' and so on.

SECTION XXVII

TABLE GIVING NAMES OF RELATIONSHIPS AT RAPAKI, TAUMUTU AND TUAHIWI [CANTERBURY] AND ALSO UP IN THE PROVINCE OF NELSON

[[A gap in this table means that the information was the same for both settlements in each pair, ms = man speaking, ws = woman speaking.]]

RELATIONSHIPS		RAPAKI	TUAHIWI
Father		Hakoro tou matua = your father	Tou matua
Mother		Hakui tou whaea (mama) (koka on East Coast North Island by Katiporou)	Tou Whaea
son		tama	
daughter		tamahine	
Elder Brother	ms	tuakana	
Younger Brother	ms	taina or teina	taina
Elder Brother	ws	tukane	tungane, tukane
Younger Brother	ws	tukane	tungane, tukane
Elder Sister	ms	tuahine	
Younger Sister	ms	tuahine	
Elder Sister	ws	tuakana	
Younger Sister	ws	taina	teina
Father's brother		hakoro	papa keke
Father's brother's child		tuakana if older brother	
		taina if younger brother	teina if younger brother
Father's brother's wife		hakui	matua whakai
Father's Sister		hakui	whaea keke
Father's Sister's husband		hakoro	matua whakai
Father's Sister's child		tuakana if older sister	tuakana
		taina if younger sister	taina
Mother's brother		hakaro	papa keke
Mother's brother's wife		hakui or matua whakai	matua whakai
Mother's brother's child		tuakana, taina	
Mother's sister		haku	whaea keke
Mother's sister's husband		hakoro or matua whakai	matua whakai
Mother's sister's child		tuakana, taina usually (also teina)	
Mother or Father's father		poua	
Mother or Father's mother		taua or (kuia)	taua
Husband		taku tane	tane

RELATIONSHIPS		RAPAKI	TUAHIWI
Wife		taku wahine	wahine
Brother's child	ms, ws	iramutu	
husband's b's child		iramutu	tamaiti whakai
wife's b's child		iramutu	tamaiti whakai
Sister's child	ms, ws	iramutu	
husband's s's child		iramutu	tamaiti whakai
wife's sister's child		iramutu	tamaiti whakai
Son's child	ms, ws	mokopuna	
Daughter's child	ms, ws	mokopuna	
Son's wife	ms, ws	hunoka wahine	hunoka
Daughter's husband	ms, ws	hunoka tane	hunoka
Sister's husband	ms	taokete	
Sister's husband	ws	whaitane (or intimately	
	ms	tukane)	
Brother's wife	ws	wai wahine	
Brother's wife		taokete	
Wife's father		matua-hukoi or poupou	matua hukoi
Wife's mother		matua-hukoi or poupou	matua hukoi
husband's father		matua-hukoi or poupou	matua hukoi tane
husband's mother		matua-hukoi or poupou	matua hukoi wahine
wife's brother		taokete	
wife's sister		wai wahine	
Husband's brother		whaitane	
Husband's sister		taokete	
wife's sister's husband		hoatane	
husband's brother's wife		hoawahine	
Son's wife's parents		not known	not recognised
great-grandfather		poua	tupuna or tipuna
great-grandmother		taua or (kuia)	tupuna or tipuna
great-grandchildren		mokopuna tuatahi	
widowers and widows		poueru tane, poueru wahine	poueru wahine or putao
bachelors and spinsters		takakau tane, takakau wahine	poueru tane, poueru wahine or putao
sweethearts and betrothed		taku nopa, tapui	tapui
Father		matua-hukoi or poupou	Hakoro
Mother		whaea	Hakui
Son		tama	
Daughter		Tamahine	
Elder Brother	ms	Tuakana	
Elder Brother	ws	Tungane	tukane
Elder Sister	ms	Tuahine Matua or Tuahine Matamua	

RELATIONSHIPS		NELSON	TAUMUTU
Elder Sister	ws	Tuakana	
Younger Brother	ms	Taina	
Younger Brother	ws	Tungane Iti or Taina	Tukane
Younger Sister	ms	Tuahine Muringa	Tuahine
Younger Sister	ws	Taina	
Father's brother		Hakoro	
Father's brother's wife		Hakui	
Father's brother's child		Tuakana (if older brother)	
		Taina (if younger brother)	
Father's sister		Hakui	
Father's sister's husband		Papa	Matua whakai
Father's sister's child		(either) Tuakana or Taina	
Mother's brother		Hakoro	
Mother's brother's wife		Hakui	Hakui or matua whakai
Mother's brother's child		(either) Tuakana or Taina	
Mother's sister		Hakui	
Mother's sister's husband		Hakoro	Matua whakai
Mother's sister's child		(either) Tuakana or Taina	
Father's father		Tipuna	Poua
Father's mother		Tipuna Wahine	Taua
Mother's father		Tipuna	Poua
Mother's mother		Tipuna Wahine	Taua
Brother's child		Iramutu	
Sister's child		Iramutu	
husband's brother's child		Iramutu	Tamaiti whakai
		(Note: Tamaiti-Whakai is an adopted child)	
wife's b's child		Iramutu	Tamaiti whakai
husband's sister's child		Iramutu	Tamaiti whakai
wife's s's child		Iramutu	Tamaiti whakai
Son's child		Mokopuna	
Daughter's child		Mokopuna	
Husband		Tane	
Wife		Wahine	
Husband's father		Hungarei or Poupou	Poupou
Husband's Mother		Hungarei or Poupou	Poupou
wife's father		Hungarei or Poupou	Poupou
wife's Mother		Hungarei or Poupou	Poupou
Son's wife		Hunonga	Hunoka
Daughter's husband		Hunonga	Hunoka
husband's brother		Whaitane	

RELATIONSHIPS		NELSON	TUAMUTU
Husband's sister		Taokete	
Wife's brother		Taokete	
Wife's sister		Wai wahine	
Wife's s's husband		Hoatane	
husband's b's wife		Hoawahine	
Sister's husband	ms	Taokete	
Sister's husband	ws	Whaitane	
Brother's wife	ms	Wai wahine	
Brother's wife	ws	Taokete	
Spinster or bachelor –		takakau	
Widow, Widower –		poueru	
Childless wife –		pukupa	
Wife one child –		hua tahi	
Wife (with family) –		whaiereere	

SECTION XXVIII

INFORMATION RELATING TO NAMES OF THINGS, ETC.

Contact with Pakehas — Some Interesting Words — Introduced Animals — Introduced Plants — Parts of the Human Body Named in Nelson — Canterbury and Murihiku.

NAMES OF THINGS

In the course of long conversations with the principal informant many side-issues were raised and from these the collector gleaned a large number of jottings which although disjointed are worthy of being noted down under above heading:

Rakai means to comb the hair or decorate the head with finery.

Kaupehi means 'don't interfere' and 'aitia' means 'married'. Mania means 'a hollow' and tukinga is 'karakia'. Roiroi-whenua is a heat-mist coming out of land like a fog and ata means the early morning or dawn.

*In regard to 'kai' this word is used on East Coast of North Island while 'kei' is used on West Coast. Rakaihikuroa of South Island is Rakeihikuroa up Gisborne way and Rakaunui in Canterbury genealogies is rendered Rakeinui up on East Coast of North Island. There is quite a change in vowels between the different parts and kauati may be rendered kaueti elsewhere; [also pounamu and pounemu; and kumara and kumera, etc.].** Kai te pai is quite correct as a phrase whereas 'e pai' is not usually so. You can say kai te mahana, kai te nui, kai te ora and many similar phrases, and all are correct. Kai = Kei.

Wetaweta means to go to pieces but he did not know what wetoweto meant. Weto in North Island language means to put the fire out. *He had never heard the origin of place-name Otepoti (the name of Dunedin). Any bend is called poti and whaka-poti is each corner of a kete or rourou. Perhaps the people had been making flax baskets there and this had suggested the name.

Taiari is sometimes pronounced Taieri and is named after tipuna of that name. The word means 'to throw a man down', to cross-buttock him while wrestling or struggling. Mount Cook was called Aoraki but he did not know how name originated. The word means 'cloud' and there is always a cloud on it, and perhaps this had to do with the naming.

The place-name Puketeraki, he thought, should be Puketiraki but he did not know the meaning. Kakanui should be Kakaunui and this latter word might mean crossing a river or swimming. It might be named after an ancestor.

The 'South Island language was no good and some of the North Island speech was worser,' said the narrator emphatically and he had had a large experience of both. In the collector's papers published in *Journal of the Polynesian Society* [[Vol. 28, 1919, p. 44]] the words** of the song or karakia about the axe Aumapu was not right language at all. [Note: It is an old karakia at least thirty nine generations old. H.B.] The language in the brief song about Takitimu is also a bit shaky – down South the people might not pronounce the words right. Hateatea's descendants are the only correct speakers in the South Island. He could not recollect the song Te Tere o Takitimu but I might get it in Southland but I would have to be careful regarding their idiom. *Murihiku is a comparatively new name for that part of the South Island, but Rakiura is a much older name.**

Kopae means 'heaped up alongside a house', and 'kawei' the shoot of a plant.

*Fires of lignite underground are called Te-ahi-a-Ue because Ngatoro of Arawa canoe brought underground fire from Uenuku in Hawaiki to New Zealand.

Wanaka is to learn speeches or debates or how to whakapapa. The lake of that name he did not think was called after a person but after an act.

As for Whakatipu he considered Whakatipu-waitai was one part of lake and Whakatipu-waimaori another. The name Whakatipu means 'to rear' and was so bestowed because the broken tribes of old retired there to rear fresh hapus. Many names in South Island came from Hawaiki but he did not think that Whakatipu came under this category. The olden Maoris used to say it was so deep its bottom was on a level with that of the deep sea.**

The collector asked if the principal informant had ever heard of a chaplet for the head called kauheke, or of a tree of that name. He replied that kauheke was not a Kaitahu word at all but a North Island one and that it meant a great grandparent, a tipuna. [A Southern name for an old man is koroheke. H.B.] The chaplet for the head had the name of kopare and he had never heard of kauheke being so applied nor of a tree called kauheke. [In Murihiku Notes the 'Mine of information' described the kauheke as a species of ribbonwood and said that kopare were made from it. H.B.]

The collector asked the principal informant if latter had ever heard an ocean ogre (or taniwha) described as a puka-atua. He had not, and furthermore said that pukaatua (or in North Island form punga-atua) was not correct language. He thought it should perhaps be Puke-atua (hill of demons) as there was a place called by that name (on the Peninsula).

In regard to the pronunciation of word 'Rarotonga' the young Maoris now follow the Pakeha example (as if it was spelt Rarotanga) and not the old way of Rarotoonga. [In same way they say Rot-orua instead of Ro-to-rua. H.B.] Totara is pronounced by some Pakeha as To-tara and by others as Toot-a-ra but the old Maori pronunciation was about halfway between these two extremes and was said (trippingly) as To-tar-a. Manuka should be maanuka, giving about equal emphasis to each syllable and kaapuka is similarly dealt with. The place-name Motukarara is very seldom pronounced right by the Pakeha. It is a piece of higher ground surrounded by water at high floods and lizards took refuge there; hence its name (not mo-chew-ka-rara but mo-tu-kara-ra).

Speaking to an old man he told the collector it was a 'lazy day'. 'Lazy' was called tukeke in Canterbury although the North Island word makere (mangere) might occasionally be used. The old man had a fence made of manuka sticks ▭ and knotted across it transversely were rows of flax ▭. It was for the Pakeha sweetpea to grow up, but the old man said it was a patatara. [This is a new name to the collector. In Tregear's [[1891]] *Dictionary* patatara is given on Wohlers' authority as 'an old house'. H.B.]

A Maori told the collector that 'o' meant 'shaken by the wind'.

Another old man said that wetoweto meant 'drops' or 'small bits'. The place-name Waikouaiti, he said, meant 'trickling water'.

The principal informant had not heard of word 'whakapepepa', and neither had the oldest man at Tuahiwi who added: 'Whakapepepa must be a North Island word; or perhaps it has been "put on" by the Pakeha as I do not think it is a correct Maori name.' This ancient man gave some very good information about a number of subjects but I see my notes concerning his talk say: He had never heard of pitau, not of the wharetako, nor kopata, nor tawhakamoe, nor kauheke, nor Maori ventriloquism, nor toropenepene, nor putara, nor pukaatua. The old man was very good on nature lore, however, and much of the Canterbury information incorporated in former Notes was given by him.

Add to Names of Things

Kumi is measure from fingertips to centre of chest, but, said principal informant, he did not know names of other measurements – the North Island people were good at that sort of thing. Another man said he forgot the names of hand-spans, fathoms, etc., but a stride was called a whiti.

*Apiti is a tight squeeze in fighting at close-quarters. The call apitia! apitia! is shouted to give encouragement and strength to those endeavoring to force a position in a mass.**

Tara and hika are the two commonest titles out of the alleged one hundred and seventy names of the tara.

In Tregear's [[1904]] *Maori Race* it states that in South Island tangatahara means men without lands. Principal informant had never heard this. According to him tangatahara is a bad or mischievous man. Present meaning is a man in gaol. Synonymous with Tangata-kino. It can also mean 'ugly man'.

*Rahui in one way means a reserve; in another to gather your family in your arms; and in another to taunaha (proclaim a certain thing or place is yours).** Kimi is common term to search for anything, but rapa and rakahau mean the same thing also. To these the principal informant added poraki – to search in a frantic, hasty, distracted manner, such as when one has lost a child and is feverishly looking for it.

*Maori in South Island, principal informant thought, was harder to learn than in North Island and it was quite possible for a man who knew it well here colloquially to fail to pass quite a simple test in North Island.** [A Riverton Maori told the collector the same thing. H.B.]

Tokoahi is name of steam and tokopa is when it comes belching out in force.

Whakatu means to imitate. Matamata means sharp at both ends.

Wakawaka, said a Maori, means a boundary; rahui means a reserve; while rauiri is a reserve for the cultivation of pora, etc. (The man who said this is a South Island Maori, who speaks Maori fluently. He used to be an interpreter up at Gisborne for a year or two.)

Mokimoki means solitary or alone.

PARTS OF THE HUMAN BODY

ENGLISH NAME	CANTERBURY	NELSON	MURIHIKU
Head	upoko	mahunga	upoko
Crown of head	te akaaka o te upoko	timuaki	mahuka
Hair of head	huruhuru	makawe	huruhuru
Back of head	hamo or 'emihemi	kohamo	hamo (?)
Sides of head	aka aka	paroparo	aka aka
Face	konohi	kanohi	konohi

ENGLISH NAME	CANTERBURY	NELSON	MURIHIKU
Brow	rae	rae	rae
Eyebrows	tutemata	tutemata	tutemata
Eyelashes	kamo	kamo	kamo
Eyelids	kamo	kamo tukemata	kamo
Eyeballs	whatu o te konohi taka o te konohi	whatu	taka
Eyesockets	koroputa o te konohi rua o te konohi	rua o te karu	rua o te konohi
Eye-pupils	taka o te konohi	tinana	
Eye-whites		koma	
Temples		te ngakau	
Wrinkles (brow)	kurehe	rangatawhaki	kurehe
Wrinkles (cheek)	putere		
Nose	ihu	ihu	ihu
Nostrils	pokaihu	koropihaka	pokaihu
Bridge of nose	moremore		
Division in nose		tiriwa	
Upper lip	kutu o ruka	ngutu o runga	kutu
Lower Lip	kutu o raro	ngutu o raro	kutu
Mouth	waha	waha	waha
Upper teeth	niho o ruka	niho o runga	niho
Lower teeth	niho o raro	niho o raro	niho
Eye teeth		niho kanohi (?)	
Double teeth		niho kaupapa nihopu	
Front teeth		niho takatahi	
Tongue	arero	arero	arero
Palate	tapawaha	korunga o te waha	tapawaha
Tonsils	weri	tohetohe	weri
Cheeks	paparika	paparinga	paparika
Cheek-bones			
Chin	kauae	kauwae	kauae
Jawbone	kauae	kauwae	kauae
Ear	tarika	taringa	tarika
Ear orifice	koroputa o te tarika	rua o te taringa	rore-o-tarika
Ear lobes		papaki	rore
Glands			

ENGLISH NAME	CANTERBURY	NELSON	MURIHIKU
Throat	korokoro	korokoro	korokoro
Neck	kaki	kaki	kaki
Back of neck	kaki	hemihemi	poro-o-te-kaki
Adam's Apple	tohetohe (o te korokoro)		pukorokoro
Shoulders	pakihiwi	pakihiwi	pakihiwi
Shoulder-blades	papakai	koko	papakai
Chest	uma or poho	uma	upper = poho lower = uma
Breasts	u	u	u
Waist	hope	hope	hope
Ribs	rara or kaokao	rara	kaokao
Collarbone		te-iwiroa-o-nga-pakihiwi	
Belly	puku	puku	puku
Navel	pito	pito	pito
Back	tuara	iwi tuara tuaroa	iwi tuara
Spine	pokotuahiwi	paparoa iwiroa	tuara
Spinal cord			kakau
Small of back	hope	hope	hope
Posterior	kumu	kumu	kumu
End of spine			timu-o-tuara
Anus	kotore	kotore	kotore
Ring of anus	kotore	kotore	kotore
Lungs	pukapuka	pungapunga	pukapuka
Heart	manawa	manawa	manawa
Kidneys	kini(?) or takihi	whatukuhu	takihi
Liver	ate	ate	ate
Stomach	puku-takoto-kai	pukurahi	ateroriki
Bronchial Tubes			kaoho
Blood Vessels	uaua	uaua	uaua
Intestines	piro	piro	piro
Arms	peke or rikarika	ringaringa	rikarika
Armpits	kaokao or keke	keke	keke
Arm Muscle		hono-pakihiwi	
Elbow	Tuke	tuketuke	tuke
Crook in arm		whatianga	
Forearm	hono-tuketuke		
Wrist	tauri	kaoiti	tauri

ENGLISH NAME	CANTERBURY	NELSON	MURIHIKU
Wristbone	pona o te rika		
Hand	rikarika	ringa	rikarika
Palm of hand	Kapu	kapu	kapu
Back of hand	tuara-rika(?)	muri o te ringa	
Fingers	taotao	taotao	taotao
Thumb	konui	koromatua	konui
First Finger	koroa	koro-ringa	koroa
Second Finger	mapere	kororoa	mapere
Third Finger	manawa	korotau	manawa
Little Finger	koiti	koroiti	koiti
Knuckles	ka pona o te rika	ponapona	pona
Finger-joints	ponapona	ponapona	ponapona
Finger-tips	matamata o taotao		matamata
Finger-nails	matikuku ka rika	matikuku	matikuku
Lines on hands and fingers		(no names)	
Notch hand to Thumb			
Penis	ure	ure	ure
Foreskin		kiri-matamata	uretehe
Glans-penis		upoko-o-te-ure	urepakuru
Testicles	raho	raho	raho
Hair (on body)	huruhuru	huruhuru	huruhuru
Pudendum	tara	tara	tara
Clitoris		tara	
Womb	kai te whanau o te tamaiti	Whare-takotoranga-tamariki	
Peritoneum			
Hips	remu or papa	papa	papa
Whole leg	kuha	waewae	kuha
Thigh or upper leg	front part = io inside part = tumukeke	papa	kuha
Knee	turi	turi	turi
back of Knee	(forgotten)		
Lower leg			
Calf of leg	ateate	ateatenga	atiati
Ankle	pona o te waewae	ateatenga	pona
Foot	waewae	kaurapa	waewae
Top of foot			
Sole of foot	papanui	kaurapa	papanui
Instep			
Heel	rekereke	rekereke	rekereke

ENGLISH NAME	CANTERBURY	NELSON	MURIHIKU
Toes	taotao	matimati-waewae	taotao
Toe-Joints			
Big Toe	Konui	Koromatua	konui
Little Toe	Koiti	koroiti	koiti
Toenails	maikuku or matikuku	matikuku	matikuku
Trunk of body	takata	tinana	
Limbs	peke (see notes)	waewae	
		nga ringaringa	

[[A gap in this table means no information was provided.]]

NOTES

The above answers were got at Kaiapoi for Canterbury; from my Nelson informant; and from the 'mine of information' for Murihiku; and I checked them over at Temuka for Canterbury. Nelson approximates to North Island – Canterbury and Murihiku are mostly in agreement. The collector was told positively not to write tautau for taotao (toes and fingers) as taotao was correct. At Kaiapoi he was told that peke meant 'limbs generally' and quarters of beef or mutton are called peke now; but at Temuka he was told that peke meant 'drawn up' and was only applied to the arms, legs being called kuha. An old saying [See Proverbs, H.B.] showed that hutawa was an old name for the leg, although now seldom used. The 'mine of information' said he had never heard other names for the fingers than those given. [It was difficult to get above list as present Maoris say heti for head, kini for kidney and so on. Further information bearing slightly on above list may be sought in sections devoted to Medical Lore and Names of Things. H.B.]

SOME INTERESTING WORDS

While the collector was looking up Tregear's [[1891]] *Dictionary* for various words mentioned in these papers he noticed others which he made a note of. They all bear on Southern Maori linguistics and are worth following up: Hamua – This word bears on relationships of the South Island. Hinga – Is South Island dialect for hika. [See Hika and hinga in *Dictionary*.] Hungoi – Bears on South Island relationships. Huti – A South Island name for fishing. Kainamu – A South Island name for early morn. Kamoa – bears on story of Maui. Kaniwha – South Island name for barb on fish-hook. Kaueti and kauwati – South Island forms of word kauati. Kohu and Kohua – The latter word is used in collector's notes re cooking. Korapa – evidently identical with Southern 'rara'. Korohe – A

Murihiku word but new to the collector. Mahau – A Murihiku word form of mau. Mahaku for maku, etc. Makuare and Makuware – words used in Murihiku dialect. Mataotao and matautau – words used in Murihiku dialect. Ngungurakau – a mat shield, (c.f. with Southern 'Taupa-Poho'.) Pakete – a bow (see notes by collector). Pataka-tawhiti – c.f. this with collector's notes. Patatara – a new (Murihiku) word to the collector. Puruhia – a new (Murihiku) word to the collector. Taitai – ceremony of launching canoes – see notes. Tako – a house for young men – none of my informants knew re it. Tungane – See the interesting notes regarding relationships. Tupuni – leggings. This is given as 'taupa' in Murihiku now.

A QUESTION OF LANGUAGE, DETACHED JOTTINGS

The word sweat, or more politely in these days of refinement, perspiration, was mentioned while the principal informant was discoursing on the habit of the ancient Maoris of painting themselves. In the South sweating is called tota but the narrator asserted that this was 'only a nickname', the proper name being kaakaawa. The young people nowadays, he continued, (with the disregard for the ancient ways and proper Maori language that is a characteristic of the age) simply say werawera (hot) to indicate perspiration and he was prepared to say no young person could tell the collector the correct Maori name for it. [Note: He pronounced the name kakawa the first time (no doubt for collector's convenience) but as kau-kau-wa the second time. H.B.] Continuing he said that many of the children and young people were too 'whakahihi' to speak or learn Maori [The collector noticed that all the children knew the meaning of Maori when spoken by their elders and grandparents, but when addressed in Maori by the old people they invariably answered in English. H.B.] The collector thought the word 'whakahihi' meant 'proud', and that it was synonymous with 'Whakatekateka' the southern word meaning 'proud', conceited, vain, 'stuck-up' or 'flash,' but on consulting Tregear's [[1891]] *Dictionary* he finds the old man was hitting hard as 'whakahihi' means 'supercilious, arrogant, contemptuous or defiant'.

The Maoris are speaking a debased form of the language now. So many Pakeha words have crept in, even where unnecessary and where old Native terms would have suited equally well. The collector has not studied this aspect of the matter enough to institute comparisons but he noticed several instances and is looking further into the question. The use of the word 'kai' is very frequent now but how it came about the collector has not heard. It is put into all sorts of phrases as 'Kai te aha koe' (how are you?) and 'kai te pai' for 'good'. A lady told the collector that the last phrase should be 'E pai' simply and warned him not to accept current talk as good Maori.

Some Pakeha pronunciations of Maori words amuse the Maoris intensely and they tell some rather good stories of instances and some nature. One prominent white man had a very unfortunate knack of mispronunciation and as he was associated with them in various functions this gave rise to some ludicrous jests. He would call the Native Member Mr Ure instead of Uru and one day at a gathering he looked round and asked where he was. Then he espied him talking to another Maori and loudly exclaimed 'O! there's Ure and Raho.' (The last name should have been Rehu.) The Maoris with their usual politeness gave no sign that anything unusual had occurred but the incident was well canvassed when they got home.

T.E. GREEN'S WORKS

At the beginning of one of the late Mr Green's Manuscript books he had drawn a map of New Zealand with nothing but a few Maori names on it. The North Island is marked AOTEAROA, the South Island TAIREA, and Stewart Island RAKIURA, while Chatham Islands to one side are WHAREKAURI.

The few names round the South Island are Kaikoura, Kaiapoi, Akaroa, Te Taumutu, Tiimaru, Otakou on East side while only name on West side is Kawatiri.

Round the North Island are Whakaari (White Island), Turanga, Ahuriri (Napier), Whanganui, Taranaki, Manukau and Te Rerenga-Wairua. Cook Strait is Raukawa and Foveaux Strait is marked KAKAUTAWA.

Unfortunately it proved to be true (as the collector was told in the South) that the Manuscript of the late T.E. Green had got scattered about. He saw four books [as recorded elsewhere. H.B.] and was promised to see one or two others when he came back. One of these is said to contain the names of trees, plants, fish and 'such things' (as well as the names of hills and rivers) so the collector is looking forward to making its acquaintance.

PAKEHA-MAORI NAMES OF INTRODUCED BIRDS, ANIMALS AND THINGS

Rabbits = rapiti. Ferrets = fereti. Dogs = kuri. Bees = pi. A swarm of bees = hekepi. Flies = rako. Sheep = hipi. Rats = pohowaiki. Donkeys = taaki (kaihe = ass in North Island). Goats = naninani (Koati in North Island). Hares = hea. Weasels = witara. Cats = puhi and naki (pronounced 'nucky' – called tori and ngeru in North Island). Goose = kuuhi. Gosling = pikuhi (plural pipikuhi). Skylark = kairaka (or pakeha pioioi to distinguish it from Maori pioioi).

This informant did not know what Maoris called stoats, hedgehogs or frogs (= poraka, North Island). She had made a sort of white syrup of flour, sugar and water. The collector asked what this was and she said rerepi. [The Maoris loved this in whaling days. H.B.]

Another aged lady added a few further names: Cats = puhihi or puti (or keru in North Island she understood). Hens = tikoko; and eggs were hua-o-tikoko. Sparrows = manukino (bad bird) or kai witi (eat wheat). Thrushes =

manu-kai-hua-rakau (the bird that eats fruit). Turkeys = takitaki (pronounced 'tucky tucky'). Hedgehogs = kiore or kina.

From other sources the collector gathered: Butter = pata (putta) also called hinu-kau (cow-fat). Bread = papa (flat) – also said to be occasionally called paraharaha (flat). A loaf is called rohe in North Island and often loofi in South. Jam = tiami. Knife = mikara throughout South Island generally, but also called maripi and naifi. An old Maori using an adze (European) called it heti to the collector.

INTRODUCED PLANTS AND ANIMALS

The only item (that would come under above heading) that was mentioned by the principal informant was that the kamukamu (marrow) was introduced by the white people. [He reckoned the hue, brought south from Gisborne ten generations before, grew on Banks Peninsula. Perhaps it was an introduced gourd, etc., that the Maoris christened the olden name. H.B.]

A Rapaki Maori said the kamukamu (which he said was the English pumpkin) did well in his district. The merene (water-melon) did not thrive there, but kanga (maize or Indian corn) grew well. This corn was formerly steeped in water and kept a long time before being eaten but it was now sold as soon as gathered or it was eaten when fresh. [The collector saw some corncobs hanging on a clothes line at Rapaki and asked about them. The woman said it grew well in the garden. It was not now kept till it was rotten. It was called kaak – this is a contraction of kaka the southern form of kanga. H.B.]

At Tuahiwi the collector was told of the following names for potatoes: hopa, karaponia (Californian), koura (with red skin), katotee, noinoiraki, papaka, patiti, raramu, repe and waitaha and ropi. The general name for potatoes in Canterbury is taewa, further south, mahetau.

Some of the Canterbury Maoris drew the collector's attention to the difference between the names of domesticated animals, etc., in their district and further south and in some cases further north. He was told that hoiho was a horse in Canterbury and haata in Murihiku, that a bull in Canterbury is puru and in Southland paala; that a rooster was heihei in North Island, and manutane or tikaakaa (pronounced to him as te kaw kaw) in Canterbury; that a cat is ngeru in the North Island, puhi (pussy) in Canterbury and naki in Southland; that a mouse is kiore (the old name of extinct native rat) in Canterbury and hinerata in Murihiku; that a rat is pohowaiki in Canterbury and pouhawaiki in Southland, while an apple is apora in Canterbury and hapura in Murihiku.

Add to Introduced Plants

The pumpkin (paukene) and marrow (kamukamu) were once grown a lot on the Peninsula, said the principal informant, as were also potatoes (taewa). The chief kind of potato grown, the parareka, had perhaps been brought with the kumera on the canoes. A comprehensive nickname for all the other kinds was kikopu (bellyful). A garden or cultivation was called mara and would be divided into wakawaka. One wakawaka might have kumera, the next pora, and so on. The pora was here before Captain Cook. The Pakeha calls it 'Maori Cabbage' but it is near a turnip in species. The roots grew to a fair size and were cooked in the umu. The kumera and the pora were both dried into kao. Kawakawa and paritea are kinds of pola (pora) but he did not know what kind of kawakawa would produce a skin you could carry water in [As stated to me in Murihiku. H.B.]. The paritea when split looked white inside like a cliff formation. Pohata, another form, had a pora root but the top which grew on a stalk could be cooked with eels and fish as a relish. This top (waikoti) was green and was where the seeds were. If the seeds ripened they had a nice yellow flower called puaitu. When ripe the pohata had a long stem like peas and the seeds could be gathered for next season. They were planted like turnips in straight rows. None of these were ever manured but were watered until the pakiaka (roots) had a firm hold in ground and then watering ceased. Any kumera, potato, or pora which lay long in a koropu (storehouse) and became soft would be called a maimai.

A Rapaki Maori said that the pora was a wild cabbage or turnip but he did not know the kawakawa. Taewa was the general name for all potatoes, but the Derwent was called raramu and white kidneys a name he forgot. Other kinds were kopara, papaka (very black inside) and kariparaoa (white one). Kotoro is potatoes steeped in water and kopi is another name for this – such treatment made them taste well. The old Maoris never manured the land – they thought it useless and scorned the Pakeha's way as stupid. They would make a waereka (clearing) and work it until exhausted and then go elsewhere. This explained their inability to farm well on European lines.

A Tuahiwi Maori said his mother used to put wild turnips (pora), which had fair roots, in umu and then dry in the sun and keep stored – they ate well. She did parsnips the same and they were known as 'Maori figs' by the children and tasted well.

A man said that steeped maize was said to be very easy to digest. If dry corn was hung up it would last for years. It could be put in bags and placed in springs and when properly steeped was ready to eat and tasted remarkably good.

The Maoris at Kaiapoi said the river there was being blocked up with some weed introduced to give food to the trout. It was an American plant and would prove a disastrous and costly experiment.

Most Maoris whom the collector met seem very fond of flowers and one or two had nice flower-gardens.

At Kaiapoi some of the older Natives are farming their land with diligence but a number merely let it to Europeans. At Rapaki the young Maoris were fencing, wire-netting, ploughing, etc. They seemed to work hard enough but they lack the continuity of effort which the Pakeha has acquired through centuries of experience. The tendency of all Maoris, however, to exhaust the ground through lack of liming and manuring, is a drawback which even the most 'modernised' Maoris find it hard to overcome. The young men told me this several times; so being aware of the fault there is a chance it will be remedied in time.

MAORI AND PAKEHA

Contact with Pakeha Ways

*The principal informant said there was a tradition among the South Island Maoris that when they saw Captain Cook and his crew they called these white strangers 'korakorako', (a word which means an albino). Smoking filled the Maoris with awe, and tradition asserted that Te Ihutakaru, father of Karetai (Otago Heads) doused Captain Cook with water to see if his head was burning as smoke was issuing from it. He told the other Maoris what he was going to do saying if the water put the fire out the white chief was a man but if it did not he was an atua or devil and should be killed. The water put the pipe out all right so the Captain was a man. The Narrator reckoned that was why Captain Cook was killed at Hawaii – not with any ill will or murderous intent of the people of that place but simply to ascertain if he was a god or a man.**

A ship is called kaipuke in Canterbury but pora in Murihiku. [This is an interesting fact – particularly the latter name as Tregear says that in Samoan 'pola' is a flat-built canoe while in Tahitian 'farepora' is a small house on a double-canoe and the Moriori name for a ship is poro. H.B.]

The reasons that actuated the Maori in naming European articles are always interesting and (talk about going from home to hear news) the collector was told up in Canterbury the reason the Southlanders named bread and potatoes papa and mahetau respectively. Up North bread is called piraua a word signifying flour but in the South the first bread the Maoris saw was damper and they called it papa = flat. Up North the general name for potatoes is taewa, but in the South it is mahetau (mahe means a fishing sinker and tau is a string). When the plant was pulled up the cluster of potatoes struck the Southerners as like a bunch of sinkers, hence the apposite name.

*The principal informant said that years ago he strongly urged Mr Ell the politician to get the Government to make an adequate grant and appoint Maoris to co-operate in producing a standard series of volumes on the Maori Race. Nothing was done however. He reckoned it would take the collector years to collect the Maori lore of the South Island.

The principal informant said that when he was born in 1850 measles (mitara) were decimating Akaroa, Port Levy, etc. down to Otakou. The people thought cold water was a cure and many perished. At Akaroa the Roman Catholic priest saved a number by saying not to go near the water but to keep near the fire. The narrator had the measles at that early period of his history.

Canon Stack was the best Pakeha speaker of Maori he knew. The Canon originally learnt in the Waikato as a boy. Then he went to England and nearly forgot the Maori tongue, but when he returned it came back to him. [Quite a number of Maoris have praised Stack's beautiful pronunciation. H.B.]

The narrator's father taught a school for Maoris at Wairewa in 1861 and supplied the flour and sugar for forty 'kids'. The parents supplied fish and pork. [This word 'kids' for children is in very common use among the Maoris and is even interlarded when addressing them in Maori sometimes. H.B.]**

Some of the children have great names such as 'Operation', etc. The collector met a boy called Transvaal in memory of an uncle who died during the Boer War – the word has no Maori equivalent. There are plenty other instances of queer naming if the collector could recall them.

Maori orators can wax eloquent when descanting on their grievances under the Treaty of *Waitangi and through various land purchases, etc. At a meeting in the North Island the narrator spoke for eight hours. He was asked to assist in presenting a petition to Parliament but felt compelled to decline.**

The collector was told that the word hine although meaning a girl was only used when addressing a girl. Girls were called kera in Canterbury but kotiro was the name in the North Island. The collector surmised that kera was just the English word 'girl' turned into Maori. They acquiesced but said it was the only word they had ever used in that connection.

The Maoris feel very sore over the fact that they were not allowed to travel at all during the influenza epidemic while pakehas could use the trains; and also that now they can not travel by rail without a doctor's certificate certifying that they have been vaccinated while there is no such restriction on Europeans. They feel these regulations should apply equally to both races.

A full-blooded Maori showed the collector his engine-driver's certificate of competency dated 14.11.96. It is said that only three Maoris in the South Island hold such a certificate, the other two being his brothers. To see Maoris taking an interest in machinery is refreshing.

From the splendidly compiled whakapapa (genealogy) books of the late T.E. Green the collector culled the following two items as having interest relative to the Pakeha-Maori days:

'Pokene and Hinetaumai had a son Tu te Rakipaoa who slew a — and was arrested by whalers to take to Sydney, New South Wales. It is supposed the sentinel placed over him here gave or allowed a gun by which the young chief committed suicide by shooting himself.'

'Tai te Kiteraki and Toi te Uatahi. These two boys went to sea and never returned; supposed to have settled in New South Wales.'

*During the Christchurch Exhibition a party of Rarotongans were one of the attractions and needless to say the Canterbury Maoris looked with great interest on their brethren from the Pacific Isles. They could converse with one another in the Polynesian language of which both speak dialects but the collector was told there was one rather strange difference. The Rarotongans could stand by the Maoris who were talking among themselves and understand them at any time, but the Maoris could not pick up what was said by the Rarotongans speaking in their own idiom among themselves but only what was said when the visitors directly addressed them.**

An old Maori shrugged his shoulders and said that at one time they thought they could understand English but since the War the language was changing so fast they could not keep pace with it. He was referring to expressions brought back by the Maori soldiers (such as 'getting the wind up', etc.).

The collector saw two albums of photos taken and developed by a Maori – quite creditable. Two of the groups of Maoris distinctly reminded him of pictures he had seen in magazines of groups of Tunguses or Siberian Natives. One middle-aged, buxom woman the collector meets at Temuka often wears a balaclava over her head and with this Arctic-looking headwear on and with her dark brown, oval face, jet black eyebrows and hair, straight nose and smallish dark eyes irresistibly reminds him of an Eskimo woman as depicted in illustrations. The collector once witnessed a moving picture showing the Alaskan Indians salmon-fishing and some of the old women would have passed for Maori women and vice versa.

One veteran Maori expressed great sadness at the amount of drink at takis (tangis) and the ruin it was spreading among the young men. This is true, but the Reverend Rakena told the collector it was nothing like so bad in the South Island as in the North Island. How the Maoris would vote on the question the collector can not say. A 'trade' emissary before the last Vote expressed regret that the Maoris could not vote on the Drink question but was bluntly informed by a Maori woman that they did not wish to vote – the Pakeha had brought the drink, let the Pakeha take it away. [The Maoris had no intoxicating drink before the white man came. It is said they were one of the few peoples of the world who had no form of intoxicant. H.B.]

The race is getting a decided intermixture of Pakeha blood. In years past white men used to marry Maori women but the collector came across two or three cases where Maori men had married white women. The latter seemed contented and no doubt had done better for themselves than they would have done with lots of Europeans. The collector also saw an English girl of good type, the bride of a tall, handsome Maori soldier.

Add to Contact with Pakehas

Some white men who were roadmaking at Cheviot, said a peppery old Maori veteran to the collector, would not eat wild pigs as they said the animals 'ate grass', nor would they eat wekas as they said the birds 'ate worms', and they poured good-natured contempt on narrator and another Maori who freely ate of both. But what 'a change in their tune' when long-continued floods prevented the baker and butcher from delivering any supplies for over a week. Hunger drove them to the Maoris' hut and the smell of pig and woodhen cooking was too much for them and they succumbed to the inner pangs prompting them to eat despised 'Maori tucker'. After the first taste or two they fell to with a will and then praised the food and moreover ate it whenever they got the chance thereafter. That was why native birds are so scarce, continued the narrator, the Pakeha found them good and shot and ate them.

The Pakeha had (or has) no 'gumption' about the matter of bush shelters, went on the same old fellow in his racy style. He had gone pighunting with them on Banks Peninsula and he knew. Once two white men and two Maoris (narrator and another) were out in the bush after pigs. The Pakehas got back to camp first – a tent – and threw a few leaves on the ground and said that would do for a bed for them. (The tent was pitched in most convenient spot they could find but even that was unsuitable, being on a hillside.) When they got back the Maoris pointed out that rain was coming and that the Pakehas had placed their 'bed' in the most likely spot to get wet, but the superior white man would take no advice. The Maoris got two logs laid saplings across, strewed fern over and so kept dry and comfortable. In the night the Pakehas found they were in the midst of a stream of water passing through the tent and they got wet and had no peace nor comfort till they lit the lantern and made a bed a la Maori fashion.

To make damper in the ashes was called komuka, continued the same old man. While the collector was there, the old man's wife put some scones she was making into a flat iron pot hung over the fire and then heaped hot embers and ashes over the lid. They knew no Maori name for this style of cooking but the iron vessel was called a kohua in the North Island, and a pata (pot) in Canterbury, they added.

After the introduction of Christianity, said one man, the Maoris kept Sunday very rigidly as a day of rest and worship. They used to cook the food on Saturday to be eaten on the Sabbath. Now, he was afraid, the Maori was a drinking, swearing, horse-racing, card-playing, picture-going, dance-indulging sort of heathen.

*The Maoris went in greatly for cricket at one time forty or fifty years ago, said the principal informant, and he once won a prize of six pound for throwing a cricket-ball one hundred and three yards at a Sports Gathering open to allcomers. The Maoris had a cricket team at Kaiapoi and were often coached by Reverend Harrison (who when he departed for England many years ago is said to have taken fifty or sixty pounds worth of Maori curios – at then values** – as gifts from the Native people). – The collector may add that he was told by a middle-aged Maori that latter once made thirty four runs in one over at Rangiora! He was opposed to a bowler whom he disliked and hit him for five sixes and one four in the over, anger lending strength to his arm!! The young Maoris at Rapaki still play in cricket matches.

*The principal informant told a white man who was very doleful about his son having to go to Europe to the war (in the 46th Reinforcements) that he should feel proud and elated instead of sad and gloomy. He also told all the young Maoris who asked for his advice that they had better go to Europe and fight the Germans than let the enemy come here to New Zealand where we had only one or two puny warships to protect us (Narrator's son was a captain in Maori Forces in France).**

Add to Pakeha Contact

An old North Canterbury settler tells me that when he went to Rangiora District in 1861 as a boy the Kaiapoi and Tuahiwi Natives were very loyal to the British. The Maori War was raging and they thought it well to be prepared. As he drove the cows out in the evening he could hear the Maoris rehearsing war-dances in the distance. In the stillness of the evening the rhythmic thud of the bare feet as they stamped the earth in unison, and the vigorous barks as the 'hoos' and 'ahs' were exploded from their lips, could be heard coming with peculiar distinctness, and impressed his boyish mind.

The Maoris near Akaroa told the collector of Mr Vangioni's big collection of curios. He, unfortunately, was unable to inspect it but Mr Vangioni said that Professor Benham had seen it at least twice and had got two or three items on loan to take casts from. Mr Vangioni said that he had at least 'four hundred axeheads', including some splendid greenstone.

Quite a number of Maoris now own separators and treated the collector to cream. At one place a woman was instructing another where to put the skim milk: 'mo te kuri' (for the dog); 'mo te poaka' (for the pig); 'mo ka tikaka' (for the fowls) and so on.

*There is a clump of manuka (mentioned in Maori history) at Otutohea (near Port Levy – Koukourarata). Last time the principal informant was there (two months ago) he was both saddened and angered to see the regardless Pakeha destroying that historic clump.**

On December 15, 1920 the collector attended a Maori wedding at Rapaki. The little Maori Church was crowded and the service was conducted both in Maori and English. Rev Joughin who officiated was formerly at Hokianga (Wesleyan) and speaks Maori fluently. By a strange coincidence he baptised the bridegroom (in 1890), ordained him as a Native Clergyman (in 1918) and now he married him to the girl of his choice. After the ceremony a photographer took several photos [Note: the collector asked him to take a front and side view of Tikao but unfortunately he had no slides left. H.B.]. An excellent repast was served in Wheke meeting-house. Two old women welcomed the couple to the Hall. Most of the speeches were in Maori and 'For They are Jolly, Good Fellows' was sung in Maori and a haka or two was given. Otherwise the proceedings were the same as at Pakeha wedding-breakfasts.

Some of the white settlers near Maori kaiks take a great interest in their brown neighbours, and are always willing to discuss their ways (some favorably but many unfavourably). But even where the intention is good, the information is usually only partially accurate. A white man who thought kindly of the people of the 'pa' volunteered some information to the collector. The hall (the wedding was in) was called 'Weeky' (Wheke) after a man who once slept on a hilltop near informant's farm. The bay at Freezing-Works was called Motu-kauiti. There was once a bush there and the name meant 'warm inside but cold outside'. Corsair Bay was called Tapoa = 'the wind swirling round'. A halfcaste had told him these items. [Note: This white man did not know the collector's mission but was willing to impart to anyone what little he knew of the Maoris. H.B.]

The present owner of T.E. Green's manuscript book of South Island Maori history is not adverse to selling it, as otherwise it might get burnt or lost.

MEMO – CANTERBURY MUSEUM EXHIBITS

While in this Museum the collector noticed the following items which he had not observed in the Otago Museum: A long Wooden Flageolet, Carved Box for Huia Feathers, Maori Tops (with whip), A shell, War Trumpet, Dried Fernroot, Prepared Flax, Bread from pollen of Raupo, Hinau Bark for Dyeing, Matting for covering food in Umu, Flax Leggings or Parengarenga, Potae-Taua (Widow's Mourning Cap), Canoe Outrigger (from Monck's Cave), Paint and red Kokowai, Model pas, Stone Oil Lamp, Bull-Roarer (purerehua or mamae), Spinning Toy (of wood like) _[string of wood]_ , Moriori carved tree-bark, rafts, weapons, etc. Patu-ngaro (like a toy tennis racquet of wood and string ❧), Woman's belt (Karetu one of ten strands), Woman's belt, (Muka one of ⎮ twelve strands), Bird Snares.

NELSON

CONTENTS

Section		
I	Habitations	**471**
II, III	Clothing and Flaxwork	**475**
IV, V, VI, VII	Personal Adornment, Paints, Dyes and Scents, Tattooing and Carving, Games and Music	**478**
VIII, IX, X	Medical Lore, Disposal of the Dead, Customs	**485**
XI, XII	Weapons, Greenstone	**491**
XIII, XIV, XV	Canoes, etc., Domestic Science, Vegetable Foods	**494**
XVI, XVII	Ichthyology, Ornithology	**500**
XVIII, XIX, XX	Entomology, Zoology, Botany	**508**
XXI, XXII, XXIV, XXVII	Meteorology, On Religion, Superstition, Table (see Canterbury Notes)	**513**

SECTION 1

HABITATIONS

Whare or Houses — Whare-potae or Round Houses — Whare-puni or Communal Houses — Whare-harakoa or Amusement Houses — Pahuri or Temporary Shelters — Moenga or Beds — Pa-kakari or Fortifications etc.

Note: Except a rare sentence at odd intervals all this Nelson information was got from one man Te Kahupuku (known to Pakehas as Peter Roberts) at Kaiapoi in 1920. He was born at Whakapuaka, Nelson, and lived there the first twenty five years of his life, before shifting to Canterbury. Taare Teone Tikao strongly recommended me to visit Peter, saying he was one of the best informed and most reliable Maoris he knew – and so I found him in four interviews totalling seventeen hours. If he could not answer my numerous questions (my query book started with five hundred questions and ended with over one thousand) he admitted the fact at once and we went on without loss of time. I have a very high opinion of Peter. H.B.

HOUSES AND BUILDINGS

Houses were called whare and were generally made of wood or of ponga (tree-ferns) with kakaho reeds inside and roofs of nikau, or rushes, or toetoe. For effect, inside the houses, the kakaho reeds were sometimes previously steeped in mud and made black and these were used alternately with the white (natural) reeds.

In addition to the ordinary ∧ whare, round houses called whare-potae were made. These were only sleeping-huts, a fire being in the centre and sleepers lying round circle with their feet to it. These huts went up to a peak like a bell-tent. No smoke-hole was made as the takuahi (fire-place or hearth) only held embers as a rule. These were brought from hangi (ovens) outside when required. The walls were branches made into framework on which toetoe reeds were sometimes bound and thatched outside with flax or raupo. While not elaborate these round huts were good enough to sleep in.

The wharepuni was a sleeping-house too, for visitors or residents. It was the familiar ∧ shape and was made into the ground for warmth. Perhaps two feet of the walls might show above the ground.

Other buildings in a Nelson pa or kainga would be the whare-korero (house for meetings or assemblies). It could also be called a whare-purakau or whare-runanga. For the young people a whare-harakoa was erected as a concert house. The posts and over the doorways in these assembly houses were usually carved.

In making a meeting house or a rangatira's big whare, shears (tokorangi) would be used to raise heavy timbers and a kaupapa (platform) built to handle the logs. The main posts were large wood pillars (poutahuhu) the ridgepole (tahuhu) being further supported by two or three poutokomanawa, these latter being carved to represent male and female tipunas (ancestors). The walls (pakitara) had large carved slabs (poupou) kakaho reeds being fastened to cross laths (kaho-tarai) making a sort of latticing (taniko). The wall-plate (maiangi) supported rafters (heke) to which battens (kaho-tukutuku) were lashed (tawhiri) with akatea vines. Layers (tuahuri) of thatch (nati) were then put on to complete the roof (tuaroko). The top layer was often of toetoe-pukio [see Plants section. H.B.] but double thatching of toetoe and raupo was called arawhiuwhiu. The roof projected beyond front of building forming a sort of veranda the common Nelson name for which was mataihi although some North Island people there settled called it whakamahau. The barge-boards (taurapa) were supported by slabs (amo) and if surmounted at the apex with a plain board this was called a kurapa but if by a figurehead, a tekoteko. (The koruru board of North Island was not used, he stated.) The veranda sill or fence was paepaeroa and the threshold of the door was paepae. The doorway was maihi and a board (papa) slid in a groove as a door (tatau, or sometimes matahihi). A sliding board also covered the window opening (ihi or matahihi). In some buildings there was a hole (pihanga) above door or window to let smoke out. Two side-jambs (papawai) supported a piece of wood (tuapoki) on which rested a carved lintel (korupe). The whole front of the house was called roro, or sometimes mataihi. The back was called tuaroko, the same as the roof, and supporting a board (heketipi) were a number of slabs (pahiwa) ranged from ridgepole to corner post (poutuaroko). The eaves were called whakaheke. Inside the house the skirting-boards were called papatarai, the hearth was takuahi, and the bed separating boards, pahuru. Knotted cords (aho) were sometimes used to fasten door and window shutters.

In opening a chief's or gentleman's dwelling when everything was ready a tohunga would creep through the window and open the door when three women of rank would cross the threshold thus rendering the house fit for entry and occupation. This ceremony was called takahi-te-paepae (tread the doorstep).

In opening a meeting-house or assembly-hall more elaborate rites were indulged in. A man, presumably a slave or lesser freeman, was killed, his heart was eaten by the officiating tohungas and his body was buried either at the base of the poupou-tuaroko or a poutokomanawa, but generally the latter. This body was called a whatu and was supposed to impart a sort of invisible essence or spiritual influence called whare-mana to the building. This body was usually dug up after the lapse of a requisite time and the remains interred elsewhere.

Besides dwelling-houses and meeting-halls and guest-houses, pas and kaingas would have storehouses called whata and pataka, store-pits for kumera and potatoes, etc., called rua (some of these had carved wooden fronts), and cooking-sheds called kauta. Outside a pa there would often be a wahi-tapu containing a tuahu or altar, and away to one side (and not near the tuahu) a burial-ground. Some pas may have had these places inside according to situation of ground or extent of pa.

A fort or village generally (or we may say, invariably) had public latrines, called in olden times paepae, but my informant had never heard of urinals in old Maori settlements. Since European influences began to be felt latrines or water-closets have been called whare-nohoanga or whare-hamuti.

In concluding his remarks on the subject of ancient Maori dwellings and halls my informant said he had never heard of the old people making buildings of stone or using stones in pa construction.

Add to Buildings

My informant had never heard of a wharetako up in Nelson, but the wharehaka was a building in which the young people could amuse themselves. The niu, or whare-niu, in Nelson was a popular place of assembly. The word means 'a gathering', he thought, and the building was used for korero (speeches), haka (dances), or at times as a sleeping-place.

Although it is not a building in the ordinary sense of the term the people would spend nights sleeping in a pahuri at some periods of the year when out eeling or birding. This was made of scrub and constituted a breakwind, but it would not keep out a heavy, continuous rain. When no flax was handy the scrub was laced with aka vine which is nearly always procurable in the New Zealand forest. The pahuri was only a temporary erection and it answered the purpose for which it was constructed.

BEDS AND BEDDING

In the old days Maori beds were mostly made on the ground. One of the commonest things to put down for the sleeper to lie softly on was kohungahunga which was the tow which came out when flax was well dressed. (Dressed flax was called muka in Nelson, not whitau as in rest of South Island.) Other things were laid on the ground also, vegetation such as patiti (tussock), rauaruhe (fern leaves), toetoe and raukiokio. (The raukiokio is a large-sized fern with very big leaves something like ponga or treefern leaves.) When the prospective sleeper had spread what he or she regarded as a proper allowance of soft, springy stuff to make a comfortable mattress they spread over it a taka or whariki [Known as a tiaka in Murihiku and also in Canterbury, where, however, the use of whariki is increasing. H.B.] This is made of flax and was often used to spread over earthern floors like Europeans lay down carpets – they are still used as floor mats in the dwellings belonging to the Maoris. On this taka a kakahu (mat made of muka or dressed flax) of the big, or bed, size would be laid and there was the bed ready to be used. The different beds (moenga) were marked off by ponga (treefern) trunks, so much space being allotted the sleepers as circumstances decided and as these divisions kept the ferns and leaves and downy grasses in place, the result was a very comfortable bed. The rara was a moenga (bed) raised off the floor. It was made of karewao (supplejack) 'something like wickerwork or coal baskets' and might be called a stretcher. Perhaps it was a Pakeha idea brought by the early whalers but as to that he was not prepared to say as he was not certain about it. All the same he knew that the old people mostly slept on the ground, although the rara might have been kept for special visitors as a mark of honor.

FORTIFICATIONS

In the old days it was highly necessary to have a strong defensive place to live in, or in other cases to retire to, when the tide of war swept through the land and the narrator considered the Natives of Nelson Province were not a whit behind their brethren in the rest of New Zealand in their search for strong, natural positions and their utilisation of such when found. There were usually two 'fences' or lines of palisading round the pa. The outer one was usually called watawata and the inner one karewa. The poupourahi or big posts that supported this palisading at frequent intervals were called after toa (warrior) ancestors of renown. The gateway into the pa was called kuaha while the ditch round it was awarua and the embankment that was thrown up was known as the parepare. An ordinary kainga or village often had a watawata (fence) round it but all the same it was not fortified. The real pa-kakari (fighting forts) had the two palisades, the bank and the ditch. They also had a kaurangi or look-out station built up in a position commanding a good view. The tower that held the look-out platform might be thirty feet high and in fighting days a man, or men, were stationed here to view the surrounding country and report suspicious signs. These sentinels were called matai [Note: See the Hawaiian meaning under word 'Matai' in Tregear's [[1891]] *Dictionary*. H.B.].

SECTIONS II AND III

CLOTHING AND FLAXWORK

Kakahu or Clothing — Whatu or Weaving — Muka or Dressed Flax Fibre — Paraerae or Sandals, Harakeke or Flax etc.

CLOTHING AND MATS

Of kakahu (mats) in Nelson my informant had heard of pokeka, korowai, torotoro, parawai, ihupuini and taniko; this was all that came to memory. In old days the tohunga taught the girls how to weave in the whare-whakaako. The weaving (whatu) was done on poupou (sticks) and the first thread was called the aho-tuatahi. A thread or strand was an aho or whenu. Miro means to roll on knee.

The korowai and parawai were alike but of a different weave. Korowai is a miro partially but parawai is a miro all through.

In Nelson the dressed flax fibre is called muka (not whitau as further South). The refuse over from muka is called tika; and flax merely scraped = haro harakeke.

The taniko mat is made of muka but is distinguished by its border (taniko).

The ihupuni was made of muka and dog's hair (huruhuru) and must be differentiated from the kahukuri which was of dogskins sewn together.

The torotoro is like a pokeka but was made of pure muka mixed with tika. The pokeka was made of tika or flax from which the muka had been dressed out. Pokeka could also be made of toi, and of wharariki (mountain flax), and of koka (flax dried on bush). He had only seen koka ones. He had never heard of tussock ones. The idea of the pokeka was to shed rain and keep a person dry.

All the mats named were full-length ones but shoulder mats (or 'short capes') were also made and worn. They were mostly ihupuni in Nelson.

Of half-length garments, or 'petticoats', or 'kilts', or 'waist-mats' there were piupiu, pakipaki, rapaki, and kinikini. The piupiu was made of muka; the pakipaki of scraped flax = haroharakeke. 'It was a girdle and rapaki was another name for it.' Kahukuri, of dogskin, could be made for the waist too, if the maker so desired. The kinikini was made of dried flax quills, which was 'pinched' at regular intervals and colored with dye. It rattled when wearer walked.

These waist garments were fastened with a tatua (belt) attached to their top end like a string round an apron. Both men and women wore maro but the men wore a different make to the women. Men's maros had shoulder straps (pakawe) and were worn at all times. My informant had never heard of maro being worn only on war expeditions nor of special war maros but he thought that warriors wore a special tatua or belt for active service. The women's maro had belts (tatua) attached and these were made of muka. [There is a woman's belt of karetu in Christchurch Museum, but karetu does not grow in Nelson. H.B.] Maros were made of fine muka.

The ribbonwood (whauhi in Nelson) was also used for clothing. Kakahu-whauhi were light for hot weather wear, but as the material was more fragile than any other enumerated, great care had to be taken of such mats to preserve them for a reasonable time. The whauhi was also used for lining pokeka made of koka, and to make kopare or head-bands. It is now used to make poi balls and ornamental nick-nacks.

Add to Clothing

My informant had never heard of sealskins being put to any use by the Maoris. Dogskins were used as cloaks, however, as well as garments of flax fibre. The latter were by far and away the commonest clothing worn, and girls were taught how to work the flax. They were taught weaving in the whare-whakaako by a tohunga, the latter being sometimes a man and sometimes a kui (old woman), for it must be remembered there were female as well as male tohungas. A single strand of flax fibre was called aho and if three or four of these were twisted together, the cord so-formed was also called aho. (He had never heard term 'whenu' until he came to Canterbury.) These strands were miro'ed (rolled) on the knee. Raranga is the name given to plaiting harakeke (flax), but weaving the muka or prepared fibre was called whatu; he had never heard the names of the different weaves. He had never heard of bird quills or feathers (huruhuru) being used as needles in Nelson, but bone needles (kaka) were used, holes, or eyes, having been neatly drilled through them. Bone pins (iwi) were sometimes used to fasten the kakahu mats over the chest but as far as he knew aho (strings) were attached to the mats and this mode of fastening was more commonly used.

FOOTWEAR

You could have paraerae-harakeke, paraerae-ti, paraerae-toi, or paraerae-muka according to the materials these sandals were made from. A whakapuru of flax could be tied round the legs as a sort of leggings as a protection against thorns. These whakapuru could also be made of ti-whanake (cabbage tree) ti-tohea (dwarf cabbage tree or plant) and toi leaves. Paraerae were common but leggings were uncommon.

Add to Footwear

My informant had not heard of a combined sandal and legging (called rohe in North Island says Tregear) in Nelson, where these things were used separately; that is if used at same time they were not joined together.

Sandals were called paraerae and were very generally used. Taupa, or leggings, were not near so commonly used – in fact, in Nelson, their use was somewhat rare. They were made of ti (cabbagetree leaves), harakeke (flax), and muka (whitau is Southern name) and were usually made for rangatira. They had aho (strings) which had been miro'ed (rolled) and which were used to bind the taupa round the legs. Paraerae also had strings to bind round ankles or feet.

Sometimes when no leggings were used and there was a likelihood of scratching the legs on thorns, mauku (patiti or tussock) would be put under feet in sandals to hold them firm at end and then this tussock grass would be swathed up legs as far as it would go and then bound round with flax. This protection was called a whakapuru. The sandals did not cramp the feet like boots and to this the Maori attributes the fact that (to him) his feet are better shaped than the average European foot.

FLAX

The fact that the North Island Maori has *Phormium tenax* divided into quite a number of varieties was mentioned to my Nelson informant without result. He had only heard of harakeke, the ordinary flax; wharariki, the mountain flax; and pao a browny-yellowish, variegated kind of harakeke. [In this classification he agrees with both the Canterbury and Murihiku Natives. H.B.] The haumatangi, which grows in Nelson, is a kind of small toetoe with leaves like harakeke. It is a dwarfish plant and the leaves are good for nothing, in fact the only use the Maori found for the whole plant was that he could whakapi (call) wekas by putting the root in his mouth and blowing.

SECTIONS IV, V, VI, AND VII

PERSONAL ADORNMENT; PAINTS, DYES AND SCENTS; TATTOOING AND CARVING; GAMES AND MUSIC

Heitiki or Jade Ornament — Kopare or Head-band — Whakaheke or Dyes — Kokowai or Paint — Moko or Tattooing — Whakairo or Carving — Panukunuku or Tobogganing — Haka or Dance of Welcome — Tupeke or War-dance — Kau or Swimming —Waiata or Singing etc.

HEITIKIS AND ORNAMENTS

The heitiki is nearly always of greenstone and commemorates an event which happened very long ago. It is made after the likeness of a woman named Hinepoupou who was deserted by her husband and who was turned into rock. Her husband cleared out in the only canoe that was at that place and left her stranded there. She sat down and pined over him day by day but he never came back. Friends went to see her and they found her there ko mate (dead) and turned into stone in the position she had most adopted in her grief and despair. Some of her whalaunga (wharaunga = relatives) could carve and one carved a stone tiki of her and that was the start of that style. Both sexes could wear the hei-tiki – only they must be of rangatira rank.

Besides the heitiki (often called the shorter name of tiki merely) there were other forms of hei or ornaments used to suspend round the neck. He knew two other names of hei made of pounamu (greenstone). One was the hei-kohunga which was just a straight piece of greenstone (of various kinds) of no particular length (they varied considerably according to the ideas or affluence of the wearer). The hei-matau was the shape of a half-moon circle – contrary to the opinion that might be engendered by its name it was not based on a fish-hook idea nor was it the shape of a fish-hook.

The collector asked him about the headless figure in the Otago Museum. He replied he had never heard of such a thing, ornament or carving among the Maoris but he was sure it must have some meaning.

Add to Personal Adornments and Ornaments

In regard to hair-dressing my informant had heard of tikitiki (rings) being made near front of head, but not of the koukou style. Mahora is to comb the hair straight out to back of head and then put a kopare round head. In Nelson kopare were made of nikau, houi, muka, etc. Plaits (whiriwhiri) is modern innovation in Maori hairdressing, my informant considered. He had never heard of anklets. Parepare is a war-plume of feathers, those of the toroa (albatross) mostly being used. In the old days people put kokowai (ochre) and akakohia on their faces. This plant has red berries which made a pronounced red stain and this was daubed on cheeks. Girls would go into bush and come out with their faces playfully streaked with kohia, but the 'clowns' in hakas and amusements would be liberally plastered all over face. He had never heard of the seahorse being used as an ornament to hang round the person. The sea-cat or sea-elephant is similar to the seahorse but he does not know their Maori names.

DYES AND PAINTS

The name for dyes was whakaheke and the colors were red, yellow and black. Red was obtained out of the bark of the toatoa tree. The bark was beaten (kurukuru); and steeped (tutu kiro wai) until the strength of the bark was into the steeping water. This was held in a taha (calabash) and constituted a permanent dye. Tawai bark could be treated the same way but the result was a brownish dye, and like the former it was permanent. The bark of the hinau (called pokaka in South) could be treated the same and gave a colour much the same as tawai did, but it was not permanent, so after the muka or kakahu had been soaked in it, the fibre or garment was further treated by being placed in the paruparu-pango (black mud) of any handy swamp. This double treatment rendered the black dye permanent. Yellow dye could be got out of the bark of the karamu tree. The wharangi tree (its leaves are called raurekau in Nelson) also yielded a dye of the same color as the karamu – a yellow.

In regard to paints my informant said he had never heard of blue paint being used by the Maoris of Nelson district but they had two kinds of red paint – a light-red and a dark-red procured from differing shades of earth or clay. This was mixed with shark-oil and the resultant paint was known as kokowai. It was used to paint canoes, carvings or woodwork; for smearing on the face and body; for decorative or any other purposes as required by the owners.

At another time in speaking of daubing canoes he said that horu was a red paint, as was kokowai, but the former was darker than the latter.

COLOURS

This was a subject he knew very little about, he said. He never heard the old people refer to the subject. There only seemed to be three or four well-defined names for colors among them. [Time did not permit us to go further along this line. H.B.]

SCENTS

In common with his brethren throughout New Zealand the Nelson Native had a keen appreciation of the perfumes (often sweet and delicate) provided by Mother Nature in the foliage and garbing of some of Her lowliest offspring.

A statement that some North Island tribes used the piripiri (bidibidi) for scenting purposes called forth the remark that my informant had never heard of that plant (called hutuwai in Nelson) being used in such a manner, but, he added, the kopuru, a sort of musk, was used and was much esteemed for its sweet smell. The taramea, so much used in other parts of New Zealand, does not grow in Nelson (and my informant added it did not come into evidence until you reached Kaikoura coming southward), but scent was made from mokimoki and tarata.

The mokimoki is a sort of fern which has a pleasant scent. It is finer than maidenhair (whose Maori name he could not recall) and its fine tendrils or leaves are boiled in hinu-weka (woodhen oil) as a perfume.

The tarata is often called lemonwood by the settlers, and the tree is bled (my informant knew no Maori name for this operation) for its ware (gum). This gum is gathered into a pawa or kuku shell or in an oko (wooden basin) and is mixed with hinu-weka (like the mokimoki was).

These scents could be put in tiny taha (small pieces of wood hollowed out) which could be worn on the chest suspended to a cord hung round the neck (and from this position a grateful odour would (presumably) rise into the nostrils of the (envied) wearer). [The last statement, in parenthesis, is added by the collector who has heard very old Maori women wax rapturous over the lovely scents of bygone years. H.B.]

TATTOOING

The Nelson Maori was not a whit behind his confreres in other parts of New Zealand in wishing his countenance (and often his body, or portions of it) to be skilfully and elaborately 'decorated with skin-carving'. Tattooing was called moko and it was the sign of the rangatira, or 'upper class' to be well and faithfully tattooed. The tattooing ink was called mamangu and was made of ngarehu (charcoal or soot) mixed with hinu-weka (woodhen oil) or with hinu-mango (shark oil). [He had never heard of this mixture being eaten by kuri (dogs) and faeces used, as stated in Tregear's works. H.B.] The best tree to burn to get the soot was the tuturakau – the ngarehu or soot of this wood provided an indelible ink. The mahoe tree gave a good charcoal and soot also. The ink was put in an oko (basin).

The tohunga did the moko and the modus operandi was to dip the needles in the ink, apply them to required spot and tap with a wood mallet (kurukuru). The needle was usually of albatross bone and so was called iwi-toroa. Generally three or four points were arranged in a line to get quicker results with each tap.

Matatahi was one point, matarua two points, but perhaps matatoru (three points) was the most common number. The operation was very painful.

The moko on the rae (forehead) was called tiwhana; from rae to taringa (ear) huritua; full scroll all over face, taniko; on the cheek, whakairo; lip and chin on both sexes was called kauwae-tehe. In tattooing on the body a design running from hip to knee was called rape, while on the hips or thighs it was puhoro.

CARVING

To carve wood, said the narrator, the old people used to use a kohua made of pounamu (greenstone) or kororariki (a very hard, black stone which if cracked was like glass – he thought it was called mata-tuhua in the North Island). 'This kohua was made like a cross-cut chisel with a crook in the point. It was not called a whao. Up in Nelson a whao is a boring point.' The kohua or chisel was tapered to a sharp edge = whakaheke. The operator or wood-carver puts the kohua to the slab he is carving and taps it with a tukituki of akeake, a hard, heavy wood. This tukituki (mallet) was shaped like the handle of an adze. The knob or striker was called pane (and if a toki was attached to it, it became a panehe) and the handle was a kakau. The only things used in old carving were those two things – the kohua and the tukituki. Modern carving with steel tools makes a better job, of course. He said he did not know much about the origin of the designs that were carved but he had heard that the figures with three fingers originated in a man (whose name he had heard but had forgotten) who had only three fingers. When there was two or three Poutokomanawa in a whare one of them would always be carved to represent a wahine. All would be called after tipunas. Plain carving was called whakairo but the carving of a human figure was called tewhatewha. (He understood that in the rest of the South Island such a figure would be called whakapakoko or tiki.) Canoes were often carved. [See Canoes section. H.B.]

Add to Carving

If a man had a mokai (pet) bird and became very fond of it, he might, on its death, carve a figure or representation of it out of wood. Manuka wood was commonly used for such a purpose, as well as for most carving. The mokai-whakairo would be done as skilfully as possible and they were valued as keepsakes. Such figures were called by the name of the bird they represented, these names being usually after tipuna (ancestors). The narrator had seen a good example of such workmanship owned by Rora Pukekohatu at Wairau. It was nicely carved and the manu (bird) it depicted was a kaka called Pukekohatu after the ancestor who owned it. It was well done and one could say at a glance 'Hullo! There's a wooden kaka'. In his journeyings the narrator had seen one or two other 'wooden birds' lying around discarded because children had broken off a wing or perhaps both wings, etc., but he could not say if any of these objects were still in existence. He had never seen them in Canterbury or Otago, but only round the Northern end of the South Island. He had never seen nor heard of rakau-whakapapa (carved genealogical sticks) in Nelson, however.

GAMES AND SPORTS

In Nelson in olden times the people played plenty of games, etc. A swing or giant's stride which let you go into water was called moari and a swing in the bush was morere. The swinger sat in a loop in the morere and a friend pulled a rope attached to it. My informant had never heard of seesaw among the old people. A skipping rope was tarapekepeke or tupekepeke but he never heard of the 'double skip' – all plain. The potaka was a top and a whip (rauraka) was used to ta (lash) it along. A teetotum was called potaka-whaka-whiri and if made right would hum. It was made of kapuka, totara, ramarama and also matai.

Stilts were called poutoko or tamatekapua. This secondary name is after a tipuna who used stilts to steal fruit from Uenuku's whakamarumaru in Hawaiki as per the well-known tradition. [This interesting fact (re name) is new to me. H.B.] Hoops were called porotaka or porowhiti and were hit with a stick (pakipaki). A game where the players toss sticks from hand to hand, a miss counting a player out, was called makamaka. Jumping jacks (tarapihia) were made. Darts were made of fern or pukakaho and were called niu. Skipping stones on water = whakatipi. The Maori boys of old used to amuse themselves by standing on their craniums but my informant never heard the name of this sport, but somersaults were called tupopori. Leaping was tarapeke and the long jump was pekeroa. Hide-and-seek was hunahuna or whaimomoka. Wrestling was turakiraki or mamau and was a sort of catch-as-catch-can under go-as-you-please rules. Cats' cradle or whai was indulged in by old people and he had forgotten all about it, except that each figure had names such as kapukapu, tawhititara, and others which he could not recollect. Making your fingers do the opposite to those of your opponent was usually called mama, but sometimes matemate. Little windmills were manufactured of flax or raupo and were called porotiti. A game of hunt the pebble held in someone's hand in a circle or row was known as tutukai.

Riddles were called maka and were often asked of a winter's evening, while a childish game of counting-out was named tatao. Some of these simple games used to cause hilarious gaiety among the smaller fry and sometimes among the grave seniors, too. Toboggan was an exhiliarating pastime and was called panukunuku (slipping down). A steep hillside was chosen and the tobogganer sat on a mamaku or a nikau – the former for preference as it was the faster. The player sat on the leaves of the treefern or palm and held the trunk up between his legs and, 'let her go, Gallagher'. On steep, grass-covered hillsides a great speed could be attained and it was a decidedly stirring (and sometimes dangerous) sport.

Another but quieter pastime was mu (draughts) and my informant had seen the older people play it when he was a boy, but he forgot the names of the men and also the 'King' or principal man. The moves were called manihi and you could 'kill' your opponent's men from one end of board to other if in a straight line. He had seen the old people play all day by the roadside on boards of wood marked out. Often they were not able to beat one another being too equally matched and so could not finish the game, hence many draws but sometimes they made direct wins.

My informant had not heard of toy canoes having been made in old days for chiefs' sons to hold miniature sailing races on lagoons (as is stated by Southern natives).

SWIMMING AND WATER SPORTS

The natives up Nelson way went in for plenty of exercise in the water and were mostly expert swimmers and divers. They were fond of sports in the water and a band of young people would extract considerable fun from trying to duck one another (kaurukuruku or kaurumaki). Some would swim out beyond the breakers with a papa (board) or log and come in floating back through the surf with a rush, but my informant had never heard of small canoes or poha floats being used in this connection. A similar mode to the 'poha' was used to teach swimming or as sport. Take two taha or hue-Maori (gourds) and couple them with harakeke (flax) or with a pakipaki (flax mat) and this coupling was placed under the poho or uma (chest) of the would-be swimmer, the buoyant gourds preventing sinking.

A number of different styles of progression through the water were practised and were named as follows (as far as my informant could recall): Kautu or haeretu (treadwater style), Kautapapa (breast stroke), Kautitaha (side stroke), Kauwhiu (the crawl stroke) and Kautira (swimming on the back). He had never heard of 'dog-paddling' being done by Maoris, but diving was called ruku, and some would get very proficient at under-water swimming.

MUSICAL INSTRUMENTS AND SINGING

In answer to a question my informant said he had never heard of a gong or wooden drum having been used by the Nelson Maoris.

One of the commonest musical instruments was the koauau, a flute made of tuturakau wood, or sometimes of kelp [whence perhaps its name. H.B.]. It had koroputa e toru (three holes) but he had not seen anyone playing by nose-blowing, nor had he heard of such a method. The putorino had three koroputa also, but was quite small, not being so long as the koauau. The porutu might be called a large flute. It was usually made of tutu wood and had five or six holes. The pukaea was a trumpet made of harakeke (flax) and could sound like a foghorn when blown vigorously by a 'musician' with good lung capacity. It was more a boyish pastime than a proper instrument.

My informant had never heard of the pakuru [where a resonant stick is held in teeth and tapped with another stick, with sounding properties, to keep time to poi or singing – a North Island practice. H.B.]; nor did he think the roria (a kind of Jew's harp) came into Nelson until after the Pakeha sailors came round these coasts.

A song was called a waiata and singing was also called this name as a general rule, but the playing or singing of a tune was called whakatakitaki. The tune or air of a song was called rangi.

My informant had never heard of a musical instrument called the putara, nor of a trumpet in the South Island with a flax tubing inside it.

DANCING AND POI

The Maori dance most known to Europeans is the haka. It is generally, although erroneously, supposed to be a war-dance but (in Nelson at any rate) it was danced as an amusement. A woman or girl or boy might haka or sing for entertainment. Hakas would be danced in competition against different parties in one kainga or when they met people from other kaingas, and it was often done to interest and amuse visitors. The wardance (tupeke) was another matter altogether. It was danced when the tohunga or chiefs decided to start a war against another tribe or even against a hostile division of their own tribe. It would start in its first phases as a haka and then the warriors would drift into pairs and begin fencing with their weapons to let the chiefs select the best warriors at the different weapons. Some might be poor at one weapon but good at another. Some might be poor at all. Some in consequence would be rejected while the rest would be let *go* on the warpath. That was when the tupeke (war-dance) was danced in the olden times – it was really a test of courage, ability and endurance. Then the party would set out and if they came home victors the people would turn out and give them a rousing welcome (powhiri). The haka, he repeated, was the ordinary dance at any time.

Poi – The present style of poi was modern. The old kind was played with a poi ball on a long string. It was something like boxing. The players would sit or stand facing each other and while others sat or stood by singing they threw the balls from one another to see who would hit the most. The old method was only done to singing but now the new kind of poi can be performed to the music of any instrument.

SECTIONS VIII, IX AND X

MEDICAL LORE; DISPOSAL OF THE DEAD; CUSTOMS

Wairakau or Medicine — Rori or Paralysis — Kohepiro = a Deadly Poison — Tanu or Burial — Hongi or Nose-pressing — Kauamo or a Hammock — Tuha or Spitting — etc.

MEDICINAL LORE

Up in Nelson, said my informant, wairakau (water from steeping tree barks) was drunk for internal troubles; and raurakau (leaves of trees) were used for external troubles, wounds, etc. Waitapu, he added, means medicine now.

Some of the old bark and leaf remedies used to cure quickly, but with the advent of Pakeha medicine – shops and drug-stores and chemist's premises the old knowledge has largely died out, but he still remembered a few things he had been told.

The leaves of the kawakawa (pepper-tree) and of the kopakopa (a weed) were very good for cuts and wounds, as was also rata bark. The punitanita (Scots thistle – called kotimana further South) is now used for cuts, wounds and bruises. The vine called aka-puatawhiwhi was used to stop bleeding in the old days.

Taki-harakeke (flaxroot) was chewed and swallowed to relieve costiveness (tutaki) and was very effective; and koromiko (not kokomuka as this is called in the South) was used to stop dysentery (torohi) and was equally efficacious.

Hakihaki is now known as Maori itch – it breaks out, the skin trouble called titi is only pimples – and was treated with kawakawa leaves.

The only name he knew for rheumatism was rumatiki – he did not think it was a pre-pakeha complaint, at least he had never heard any Maori name for it. All such troubles or pains were treated with hinuweka (woodhen oil).

He had never heard of the rewharewha epidemic sweeping through Maoridom when the whalers came, but this name was applied to whooping-cough at Takaka and Nelson when he was a boy. Consumption (mate huhu pungaroto) was here before the Whites came but he did not know the cure used. The present tuberculosis is called matekohi (wasting sickness).

Add to Medical Lore

The kawakawa tree growing in Nelson, said my informant, was useful to the old-time Maori as he used its leaves to cure skin diseases.

In Nelson sore throat was called korokoro-mamae or korokoro-mate.

With regard to physical attributes he considered that the feet of Maoris were flatter than those of Europeans. You could tell the difference if you saw the footprints in wet sand. Pakeha toes are usually longer and more unequal in length than Maori toes, the latter being shorter and more of a uniform shape and size. [Note: The Nelson names for various parts of the body as given by him will be found (together with the Canterbury and Murihiki names) in a separate sheet, at end of Canterbury Book, number 14. H.B.]

POISONS

To eat the karaka berries, when these had not undergone the necessary preparation as food, brought on a paralysis (rori). The cure was to drink the water of the puha (sowthistle) to induce vomiting (ruaki). They also sat the patient in cold water till the blood almost stopped circulating through numbness. 'This was to kill the heated part of the body where the poison was working'. In tutu poisoning (hori) the same remedies were tried – waipuha and cold water. For katipo bites the puha was rubbed on spot affected. This was the commonest cure but sometimes those handy would attempt bleeding by 'lancing' the spot and one would suck place with the lips. This was called momi-nga-toto (sucking the blood) but it was only efficacious if done at once. My informant had heard of deaths from katipo bites through inattention or through leaving the sufferer too long before attempting to relieve the affected part.

The whaoriki is a weed with flowers like wee white violets. The wild bees are fond of these flowers and much of it in a place renders the honey poisonous. It also has a poisonous berry. This is like the kupenga berry (which is a light-blue) but it is a darker blue. A few of them would not hurt a child but many act as a poison. The tohu (sign) of this is that the child moans and cries, and the cure is to give puha to create vomiting. The child can be cured if this is done in time.

If you chew the leaf of the kohepiro it is a deadly poison. Children were warned against it. It caused you to sleep – there was no cure. Cattle which ate tutu could be saved if found in time and bled but there was no cure for cattle which ate kohepiro – even if bled, etc. They simply go mad and charge about till they fall exhausted and die. His father once lost twenty head of cattle through kohepiro.

DISPOSAL OF THE DEAD

There were various methods in Nelson, (in common with the rest of the South Island although the details may have differed somewhat) of disposing of the dead. Some bodies were put in holes and caves – this was waro-tangata. Some bodies were put in springs of water – this was waiwhakaheke. Some bodies were put in sandhills, etc., – this was tanu. Some bodies were burnt in special fires – this was tahu te tupapaku.

The narrator made no comment on the burial (or placing) of bodies in dark caves (waro); nor on letting the bodies whakaheke (descend or slip downwards) into deep pools or apparently-bottomless springs, but he said that when bodies were committed to the earth (usually deposited in sandhills as these were easily dug) the deceased person was tanu'd (buried) lying flat [And not in a crouching posture as recorded of some localities. H.B.]. As to the burning (tahu) of the dead it was usually chiefs who were thus treated (or honored). It was done with ceremony and the plant called Koromiko [not kokomuka as in Murihiku] was the one used to provide the fire. The tribal tohunga performed the obsequies and after the body was burnt, the ashes were gathered and were either buried in some selected spot or taken to a waro (cave) and deposited there. He was not sure if koromiko wood was always used but he had heard that was the kind of wood that composed the blazing pyre of two chiefs who were cremated about the time the Pakeha began to live in Nelson. He had never heard of bone-scraping in that district but at Picton a chief's bones were made into fish-hooks and this led to a long and bitter war. [See Stack's [[1898]] *South Island Maoris* p. 42–3. This is a poor account and does not mention the fact that the Kai-Tahu found the cave where Ao-marere's bones were by noticing that the Kai-Tara made pilgrimages to it. H.B.]

The narrator had never heard whakatamiro (preserving the dead) described, but he had listened to the old people saying that the tohungas could karakia a chief's body and so preserve it. Perhaps this was only a myth.

Add to Burial

The people would put the dead on a kaupapa (platform) for some considerable time on occasions. Particularly was this done if the dead person was a rangatira who had died some distance from his usual home. This was to give his relatives time to arrive and then a united tangi would be held over the corpse. The dead so kept were whakatamiro'ed and would keep a long time if the tohungas saw to them every now and again. Sometimes the body was burnt and the head preserved and kept. He had never heard of bone scraping in Nelson, nor of the ashes of cremated people being kept as mementoes of them, nor being sent to near-relations at a distance. The ashes were buried. Cremation was the rangatira way as it prevented the corpse being disturbed and the bones used as fishhooks.

My informant had heard of people being buried in, or with, canoes. On this (south) side of Kaikoura near to Cheviot was a cave called Papataipuhi which had a canoe with the remains of a long-ago rangatira woman called Hinerauwharangi in it. The name of the canoe was the Makawhiu and she was buried with it. It is said you could see the cave until some generations ago, when the old people blocked it up. Up in Nelson Province at Maitahi (Brightwater) the traditions record that a chief was buried in a canoe called Pukekohe. This was probably about Captain Cook's time, narrator thought. The people pulled up the river and went into a cave there ultimately leaving the body quietly resting in the canoe in the ana (cave). In narrator's youth some old Maoris went to see if they could find the spot, but owing to the forest having been cut down and the changes made by the Pakehas, they were unable to locate the place.

My informant had never heard of burial chests in Nelson, nor that such a thing had ever been used by Maoris anywhere.

CUSTOMS

Hongi – This ancient custom of nose-pressing, he had heard the old people say, originated in Hawaiki and was brought to New Zealand. It was said to have been started by a man whose name he forgot. Before that those meeting or parting had shaken hands. This was called ru-ringaringa although ru is a word that might mean an earthquake let alone such a minor operation as shaking another person's hand. This man when shaking hands 'introduced some affection into it', and pressed his nose against those of his friends. The custom (called hongi) caught on and became popular. To state the relationship to the person whom you are thus engaged in saluting is known as whakahua-whanaunga.

Muru – This peculiar custom apparently occurred in Nelson as in most parts of New Zealand. The narrator said he had heard of two or three cases in the South Island. [He only mentioned one case and that was the one on Banks Peninsula (at Akaroa) which has already been detailed in the Canterbury Notes. H.B.]

Add to Customs

The Eating of Human Flesh – The collector asked if women could eat kai-tangata, and if not, why not? [Tregear's [[1904]] *Maori Race* says they were not allowed to indulge in this luxury – that was a privilege reserved for the sterner sex. H.B.] My informant said that women could eat it if they wished and told the following story to uphold this contention. His great-grandmother ate kiko-tangata (man flesh – the word kiko is now applied to beef and meat). A woman named Hine-putauhinu went out to where the rat-runs were in bush and set a tawhiti or snare. Going back to see how it was faring she came across a parua or ruawhenua [See Section on Rat-Catching. H.B.] and sat down and watched it in curiosity for a time. A mokai (slave) had made it to a chief's order and he noted the woman looking at it but said nothing about it just then. When he went to collect the victims he found someone had stolen them and naturally he blamed the woman whom he had seen inspecting the trap. He told his master who instructed him to set taraponga [See bird-spears in Birds Section. H.B.] in the ground round the trap. Next day the woman in passing to her own tawhiti quite unsuspectingly stepped over to see if there was a good haul in the parua and she trod on a taraponga which lamed her so she could not walk. The chief, the owner of the trap, killed her as a thief, took her to his kainga and preserved (huahua) her flesh like that of the manu (birds). The woman was missed for days and people wondered where she had gone but the mystery was not elucidated till some time after. It so happened that a woman who was pregnant (hapu) had a vehement hiakai (desire for food) as sometimes occurs in such cases, and the food she hankered after was kiko-tangata. Her husband was desirous of placating this craving and set out on a tour of the district, not, however, to kill the first man he met or any such violent conduct, but to ask if anyone had any human legs, arms, sides or hams in their larders. Things were fairly peaceful at the time and his quest was unsuccessful until he came to the kainga of the chief who had killed the missing woman. 'O, Yes! He had kiko-tangata!' So straightway he produced his huahua and gave his inquiring friend a thigh (papa or kuha) out of it. When the friend departed and had time to inspect the gift minutely, the moko (tattooing) on the hip struck him as strangely familiar and on examination proved to be the rape [In the North Island a woman's hip tattooing is said to have been called hopehope but my informant stated that a woman's tattooing on hip had the same name in South Island as that of a man – rape. H.B.] of his sister – the missing woman. He kept his discovery to himself and on reaching home and finding his wife's inordinate craving still unsubdued he handed over the flesh and hence his wife partook of the flesh of her sister-in-law. When her child was whanau (born) it was named Maru-kaitangata in memory of the appetite recorded above. These people are ancestors of many South Island Maoris but my informant had not his book of whakapapas to refresh his memory as to their names and relationships. He remembered that the well-known chief Puraho was connected with them. [Note – It has often occurred to the collector in the course of his researches that the position of women in relation to that of men was very different in the South to the North Island. The same strictness is not observable for greater freedom and latitude were allowed. Thus women in the South were sometimes adorned with a man's tattoo; thus women in the South sometimes taught the girls weaving, whereas the tohunga usually taught it; thus dog's flesh and octopi reserved for chiefs in the North are said to have been eaten by women as well as men in the South; and so on. The question requires more investigation however. H.B.]

In regard to other customs such as filing the teeth and the custom of tehe (circumcision) said to have been done in various parts of New Zealand, my informant stated he had never heard of either of these rather unusual ceremonies ever having been done in Nelson.

Kauamo – People of old were sometimes carried in kauamo (a sort of hammock, stretcher or litter). In Nelson this was made of muka (dressed flax fibre) or kareao (supplejacks) knitted on to two long sticks. It could be carried by two or four bearers according to the weight of the occupant, the roughness of the country or the length of the journey.

Add to Customs

Hakari was a return gift of food after an original gift. One party would send a karere (message) and ask another party along. The home folk made a platform (or series of them) called pataka and shaped like a bell-tent, and stacked this with fernroot, with bread made from hinau berries, with tuna, or the delicacies common to the district. After the first introduction they would hand over the kai (food) to the manuhiri (visitors). These would remove it and fill the place up with food they had brought from the hills, or from the sea, as the case might be, and they would ceremoniously present this to their hosts. The first presentation is called wero the second or return one whakahoki. It is simply a method of 'swopping diet'.

My informant had never heard of teeth being filed, nor circumcision performed, in Nelson.

The old people up Nelson way objected to kowhiowhio (whistling) and boys used to be reprimanded for doing so; but he never heard the reason of the objection.

The old people at Nelson used to warn the young people against the act of tuha (spitting) as the huare (spittle) could be makutu'ed by enemies and so harm them.

A North Island book stating that bait was used to catch kiore (rats), and that on rat-hunts kiore was called koroke (that fellow!) was quoted to informant, but as far as he knew neither of these customs were observed at Nelson.

Cooking rats or birds in clay put on embers is called pokepoke. Clay is better than mud which does not hold together so well. He thought it was an old method.

SECTIONS XI AND XII

WEAPONS; GREENSTONE

Paiaka or a Kind of Weapon — Huata or a Plain Spear — Pouwhenua or A Projectile — Kawakawa or Kind of Greenstone —Auhunga or Kind of Greenstone — Parihi or a Hard Cutting Stone — etc.

WEAPONS

Mere – The mere was made of pounamu (greenstone) and some were not only effective as mankillers but were beautiful to look at. There was a weapon made the same shape as the mere but of the black stone called kororariki. A weapon of this was as hard as one of greenstone and was called kurutai. As to a mere being made of bone the patuparaoa was not really a bone mere as it was a different shape – in Nelson at least. [Note: He thereupon drew representations of two shapes of patuparaoa and these drawings are attached. H.B.]

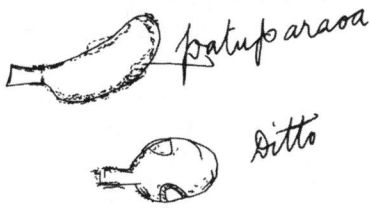

Taiaha – As far as he knew the taiaha up in Nelson was the same as the ones in Canterbury and Murihiku. The tongue was called the arero, the blade being known as the kauringa and the end of the blade was called rapa. To ward-off a blow of the taiaha was called karo and he had a list of the names of these karo up in his house (some seven miles away and then untenanted) but if the collector would advise him when he was paying a return visit he would have the information available.

Paiaka – The 'blade' of this weapon was called rapahoe [This name practically means 'the flat part of an oar'. H.B.], and the feathers which usually dangled round it formed a taupuhi. The handle was called kauringa and the point of it, mata. The weapon called tewhatewha is the same shape as the paiaka but not so long, its handle being about three feet in length whereas the paika has one about five feet long. [Note: He made a rough drawing of a paiaka. H.B.]

Huata – This was a plain spear, usually made of ake wood, and sharp at both ends which were called mata. The Maoris never threw their spears – the huata was for close fighting.

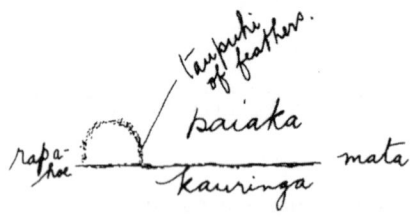

Pouwhenua – The pouwhenua had a kauringa and rapa like the taiaha and went to a sharp end called the mata. It was a much used weapon. One kind of pouwhenua was for throwing a long distance – it could then be called a kauamo. It was thrown with a kotaha. You took a stick shaped like ⌒‿‿ and tied muka (whitau), which had been miro'd (rolled or twisted) into strong cords, on to the end. A koromahanga (loop) was put in a hole in the ground and the spear or pouwhenua was placed on it. This hole was only two or three inches deep – just sufficient in depth to hold the projectile with an upward incline when its base rested in the hole. This projectile could be a suitable rod, a spear, but was often a pouwhenua. The man had to amo or project the spear, hence the name kauamo. The pouwhenua when flying through the air was known as a kotaha. It would rise perhaps one hundred feet in its flight, and cover a distance of about one hundred and fifty yards. [The collector did not grasp the explanation how the man sent the missile away. H.B.] It went with considerable force. It was mainly used against the people in pas or forts.

Toki – The toki was not primarily a weapon although it could be so used. Since the Pakeha came in the trading days the Maori has used a tomahawk (patiti) in fighting. This name patiti is an old name transferred to a European article. It was an old name of pounamu or flint (mata) axes. The toki-titaha is straight – it is not a panehe. You made a groove down the side near the end of the handle and fastened the toki-titaha in with muka (whitau in South). It was for felling trees while the adzes were for tarai or chipping it out into wakas or canoes or into anything desired. The part of the handle to which the adze-head was attached was called pane (the head) and a small adze was panehe. The big adze was kapukapu. It was a double-hand tool but the panehe was a one-hand adze.

Hoe – this was the canoe paddle. It might be used as a temporary weapon but very seldom. Other things such as heavy clubs might possibly be used, – but here the narrator quit the subject and spoke of greenstone.

Drawings of weapons by Te Kahupuku a native of Whakapuaka, Nelson. (P. Roberts 28.7.1920.)

Add to Weapons

My informant had never heard of the toki-poutangata (man-killing adze).

He had heard of the poike – it was a sort of whao (chisel).

He had never heard of a dagger among the Maoris but in close fighting you could use the mata-tuhua or flake knife. One form of this was a number of mata (flakes) set in wood. The mata were fitted into the side of a piece of wood and lashed with muka.

Add to Weapons

My informant had never heard of flaming arrows being shot into pas in the old fighting days in Nelson. Boys used to use bows and arrows. The bow was sometimes called a kotaha although that name designates the whiplash projector usually. The bow was made of kareao (supplejack) and the arrows (mata) of toetoe or fern stalks (some of these rauaruhe are five to six feet long). It was only a boyish sport and too weak and uncertain for warfare. The miratuatini was a sort of saw made of the jawbone of the tuatini shark. This jaw was straightened and lashed on to a stick and used as a saw to cut up tangata (man) for cannibal feasts, etc. The proper old Nelson knife was the mata-tuhua. Pieces of flint, or sometimes only one piece, would be fastened to a stick and used for cutting. The ripi was a wooden club or stick made like a boomerang so that when killing eels its end would not hit ground and so foil the blow. It was made of akerautangi or manuka-pouri (black manuka) and although meant for killing or stunning eels could be used on occasion for close-quarter fighting. He had never heard of a wooden sword among the Maoris but the taiaha was straight and some Pakeha may have thought it was a kind of sword. He had never heard of a four-sided wooden club nor a dagger among Maoris. The tarawhai is to put a stingray's 'stinger' on to the point of a tara (spear) and it would break off into person pierced by giving spear a wrench or twist. He had never heard of flax or dogskin cloaks being put over each other to form several thicknesses and so being used as armour against spear thrusts.

GREENSTONE

The pounamu came from the West Coast of the South Island and there were a number of varieties recognised by the old people. The tangiwai which came from Milford Sound could be used to make mere or hei – he had only seen one patu of it. [This is exactly what he said – the collector took it that although he knew that meres could be made of tangiwai it was rare as he had only seen one. H.B.] Kawakawa a dark variety was used for making meres or tikis; the inanga was a brighter kind than the last; while auhunga was the top-notch kind of the lot. Kahotea was not the name of a variety but of a block of greenstone. When hunting for the pounamu if you dreamt of a person you named the next piece you found after that person. Thus when Ihaia Tainui of Arahura dreamt of Canon Stack he named the piece he found Taka and bits of it are now scattered all over the South Island. Kahotea was a block which was found and was manufactured and distributed much the same way. Te Taka weighed about one hundred and fifty pounds when found. In the old days parties used to go from Nelson and from other parts to hunt for pounamu. When they got a heavy piece up the river they would build a mokihi for it and float it down the river to the kaingas at the sea-coast. The block would be split with a piece of parihi held in the hand and rubbed up and down in a groove. There are two very hard kinds of stone found on the West Coast – the kororariki [See Carving section. H.B.] and the parihi. The latter is used for cutting greenstone – it is the only material you can cut it with. When rubbing the groove with the parihi dry sand was used. This sand was like cut glass; he had seen it but forgot its name. The pounamu is then ground down on the hoanga (grindstone). A coarse hoanga is used at this stage and water is used with it. The kororariki could be used in the process of transforming the rough block into manufactured articles but not to cut. It could be used to mark out the shape of the mere (or other item) on the stone, the cutting being done with a parihi. A fine hoanga was used to polish the article. It was then hung in the sea or in running water to wash all the dust off it and out of the crevices. It was so washed for a day or two and was then taken and rubbed up for its final polish and there was your smooth, shining mere-pounamu or hei.

SECTIONS XIII, XIV, AND XV

CANOES, ETC.; DOMESTIC SCIENCE; VEGETABLE FOODS

Waka or Canoes — Poutuhua or Masts — Ra or Sails — Rama or Torches — Mokihi or Rafts — Tunupapa or Ember Cooking — Oko or Small Calabashes — Tutuhaupo or Preserving Birds — Kono or Flax Plates — Kurukuru or Stone Pounders — Kumera or Sweet Potatoes — Ngau or Chewing Gum — Mimiha or Chewing Gum — Harori or Tree Fungi — etc.

CANOES

In the olden days waka (canoes) had sails (ra) of a triangular shape and set with the point up. The mast was called poutuhua. It had a hole (rua) at top and taura (rope of whitau or keikei) was used for hauling the sail up. The sails were usually made of toitoi-pakau – this is not pukakaho but is a plant not seen in Canterbury. This plant is broader than toitoi (and like flax but with blades one and a half inches wide) and narrower than kiekie. The sail was made of these leaves (which can also be whatu'd into tiaka [see Beds]) raranga (woven) and the binding was called raureka. There was no boom on the sail which was fastened to a stick (tutoko) projecting from the gunwale over the water, the outside end of the sail being tied to it and the inside end to the mast. Sails were only used when the canoe had a fair wind – they could not sail broadside to a breeze. At other times hoe (paddles) were used. These paddles were often made of manuka and akerautangi. The one for the chief and the hoe-whakatere, the steering-paddle, would be carved as a rule, the rest being plain. Sometimes the kaiwhakahauhau, the man keeping time for the rowers, might use a tiny paddle as his baton of office but he could also use a paiaka or a rod, etc. Some of the canoes had rather elaborate carving (whakairo) on them. A carved bow was called tauihu-whakairo and a plain one adorned with tufts of feathers was known as puhipuhi. There was no whakairo on the stern which was often called ke although its real name was taurapa. On some canoes the gunwale or haumi was carved, this work being known as haumi-whakairo. If an extra plank was added to the side of the canoe to raise the height it was also called a haumi.

Add to Canoes and Sails

The sails (ra) of canoes were made of muka and of toetoe-pakau in Nelson and both square and triangular sails were made. The square sail was for heavy canoes and the triangular for lighter canoes. The mast was called hua. A sail might be five feet across at its narrower end and a stick across it there was called tiaha while the pole across the bottom of sail was called rara and its length varied according to the size of the canoe. The carved spirals at bow were called tekoteko or whakapakoko and the taurapa or ke (stern piece) was frequently carved also.

He had never heard of outriggers but had seen 'double canoes' in Nelson. This was a long, single canoe made out of two trees and joined together in the middle. One half of the length of the canoe was cut out of one tree and the other half out of another and the two open ends were pushed up against each other and lashed (honohono) and caulked with raupo stalks and painted with kokowai. This caulking was called puarere in Nelson and tahuka in Canterbury but a general name for caulking as usually done was purupuru. A 'double canoe' of this description might be over sixty feet long and was quite seaworthy. The length might not seem much considering the height of trees and perhaps you could get single trees longer than this but without the beam (riu) of about six to eight feet required in a rough sea-way. For valued canoes, sheds or shelters would be built to protect them from sun and weather and so developing cracks. These sheds were known as whare-takotoranga-waka (house where the canoe lies).

My informant had never heard of toy canoes being made in olden days; in Nelson at anyrate.

In concluding our long three nights (7pm to 11.30pm) korero (talk) my Nelson informant said he had answered my patai (questions) to the best of his ability.

Add to Canoes

My informant had nothing further to add to what he said about canoes on the collector's former visits but he mentioned the rafts which the old people used to cross rivers and lakes on inland journeys and these craft may be included under above heading.

The mokihi (or raft) used in Nelson was generally made of korari (flax-sticks) or raupo (a species of flag). The bigger rafts were made of the former material and had raised sides. They were poled along. Mokihi made of raupo were smaller. The raupo was tied in bundles easy to handle (small, tightly-bound bundles) and it might take five or six bundles to make one wall of the moki and a similar number for the bottom. It was a rough canoe and was rowed. A quick, rough-and-ready expedient to cross a deep or a rapid river was to make a bundle of either korari or raupo and sit astride it and paddle with the legs. [The white pioneers were wont to cross rivers this way. H.B.] This method of paddling was called takopi.

TORCHES

Torches (called rama) were made of korari (flax-sticks) or kakaho (reeds) tied (ruru) in bundles and set alight. You needed no oil on these materials – a twelve foot torch would take half-an-hour to burn and would give a good light during the process.

DIGGING AND CULTIVATION

The old Maori 'spade' was called ko and had a tuke or footrest tied on to it about a foot from the business end to enable the digger to push it into the ground. The kaheru was not a spade but was simply a plain stick sharpened, or with a pointed end. It was used for weeding purposes.

Clearings (waerenga) were made in the bush and were worked until the soil got weak and exhausted when another spot would be utilised for four or five years then the agriculturist could go back and work up the original clearing again.

As in other parts of New Zealand the Nelsonians never used animal manure on the land. My informant gave no reason for this fact.

The Maori would never plant anything unless the moon was right. From new moon to full moon, whether wet or dry, [See Weather Lore Section. H.B.] was said to be the correct planting time [See Canterbury Notes also. H.B.] by the Natives up Nelson way. The rising of certain stars also played a great part in planting lore. Puaka, Tawera, Ngaputahi, Teka, Matariki, etc. were stars consulted in estimating when to commence cultivating the ground. [See Sky Lore Section re these stars. H.B.] The principal ones studied were probably Tawera (Morning Star) and Puaka or Puanga (Evening Star or Venus (?)) as they are watched carefully even yet by the older Maoris who plant potatoes, etc., in accordance with the movements of these two stars, in conjunction with the correct quarters of the moon.

In regard to crops grown in pre-pakeha days my informant said he had not heard of the uhi (yam) being grown there, but the kumera (sweet potato), taro and hue (gourd) all grew in the fertile soil and sunny climate of Nelson. [This fact was elicited just as we were parting, so the collector cannot give further details of these crops. H.B.]

COOKING

The earth-oven was usually called hangi in Nelson, and to cook in it was tao. My informant said he knew of five ways of cooking food employed in the olden days by the people of those times, viz., 1 Tao in hangi (this is too familiar to require description). 2 Kohiku – this was to impale the fish or bird on a stick which was stuck into ground alongside fire acting as a spit. 3 Mataa method – Get a whakapuku or firestone (called ahipohatu in some parts of South Island) and place it when heated in centre of food which is tightly wrapped round (takai) with harakeke to make it airtight to keep the steam (mamaoa) in and so cook the food. 4 Whena mode – This is to take the food which is to be baked or cooked and wrap it in harakeke roll. This whena is then placed alongside the fire or on the embers and turned frequently until the food is done. 5 Tunupapa way – This is to take the eel, fish or bird and place it bare in the embers, watching it to see it is not scorched too much.

He knew no other ways of cooking in the olden times than the above, but of course there might be ways of which he had not heard. A closely-woven mat (like a floor whariki) was used as a big plate to serve cooked food on or as a mat to cover food in a hangi. When used thus it was called a tapora.

HOUSEHOLD UTENSILS

Basins – The taha was a large size calabash and the oko was a small size ditto. Both were got from the hue or gourd formerly grown in Nelson. The people could also make ipu basins or troughs of manuka, ake or totara woods. All these would hold water. They used the kiri (bark) of the totara or hinau mostly, but other trees could be used on emergency, to make tutuhaupo to put birds preserved in their fat in. A lid (popoki) of bark would also be made to fit these utensils to keep them airtight and keep the contents good. My informant said he had never heard the Maori name of mildew, but mould coming on preserved food was kopuru or purua.

Flax plates to hand round food on were used and were called rourou or kono.

My informant had never heard of stone hammers (like that in Otago Museum) being used by the Maoris of Nelson.

Kits or baskets – These were an indispensable article in ancient Maoridom and were called kete generally. My informant named five materials of which they could be made, the resultant kits being called respectively – Kete-harakeke, kete-wharariki, kete-toi, keteti, and kete-keikei, and perhaps there were others he had forgotten. Of these baskets, those made of harakeke are commonest as flax is so easily got and worked. Fancy baskets were made of muka in different designs and colorings. The whakataratara was a fancy kit, and so was the kete-taniko, but he forgot the names of the remainder.

Fernroot was a common food in Nelson. He knew two kinds – the aruhe and the rarauhe, the former being the better. They were beaten or mashed with pounders. As far as he remembered wood pounders were called tukituki, and stone ones kurukuru.

Add to Vegetable Foods

The Maoris grew kumera, taro and hue in Nelson in old days and uhi (yams) brought from Pacific Islands in later years. You could always tell how many taro tubers there would be to each plant by the number of leaves, but it was hard work to cultivate it. A hole would be dug six inches in diameter and filled with sand and the purapura (seed) planted. Breakwinds of manuka were erected to shelter tender plants. The leaves were plucked off as they formed and a tuber would grow for each leaf. Otherwise there might be a dozen leaves, and no roots but the seed one. If five leaves were left they were spread out and tramped (whakareke) apart, the more that was done the better they grew. Leave them to grow until the tops died off and then dig out, when you would find a taro for each leaf. They were then sunned for two or three days and pitted (whakaahu) in mauku (tussock) to keep dry. They were more work to grow than kumera – his father grew half acre of taro and he knew. You could chew the kumera raw but the taro is bitter raw although it is sweet after tao (steaming) in hangi or roasting at the fire. He did not know if taro was still grown in Nelson but kumera was. Kumera planting was once main work of Maori cultivation, although now potato is. They were grown heaped up, and their runners (kawei) like marrow-runners were kept cut as the cultivators said there would be no crop otherwise.

The Maoris in Nelson or elsewhere, as far as he knew, never ate taramea nor papaii (two kinds of speargrass) roots although he had noticed that wild pigs ate same in backblocks. He had never heard of purau (edible plant) growing in Nelson, and the young shoots of koareare (raupo) called pitau in Canterbury were called karito in Nelson. The only treeferns he knew there were the ponga and mamaku and of course only the latter was eaten. They ate the nikau where it branches to form leaves, calling it rito – it was like kauru. The kiekie grows from Kaikoura round to West Coast and the people ate the first fruit, the tawhara, the leaves continuing, and later the 'banana part', the tiori. A sort of bread was made from hinau berries. In planting kumera, etc., the people used a piece of ground until it was exhausted and then they picked a new waerenga (clearing). They never used manure and he never heard any reason for this; in any case manure was scarce.

SEAWEEDS

Kelp, generally, was called rimu in Nelson – this name rimu seems common all over New Zealand. Rimurapa was the kind used to make pohas to put preserved birds in. Koauau is the narrow part of the rimurapa and only use he knew for it was that it was made into flutes. The masses of very fine and tangled seaweeds found along seashores were called rimurimu. Karengo was one form of this. As for edible seaweeds karengo was eaten but he never ate it himself and knew practically nothing about it.

CHEWING-GUMS

Two chewing-gums exercised the masticatory functions of Maori Nelsonians, the first being the white sap or wax of the puha thistle and was called ngau. The other was a blackish substance picked up on the seacoast and called mimiha and also pakake. The mimiha, it may be explained, is a seal and so is the pakake and according to my informant tradition reckoned the black gum was seals' tutae (dung). He had never heard of mimiha being taken into the bush and tied to a certain kind of tree [as narrated by Murihiku natives. H.B.] – It was merely picked up and chewed.

FUNGI

Up in Nelson the harori (tree fungi) was eaten by the Maoris. My informant had never heard a Maori name for the ordinary ground mushrooms, so he concluded from this that they had never eaten these mushrooms. Whether the ordinary edible mushroom was in New Zealand in pre-Pakeha days he could not say, but the supposition was that it had not been.

The harori or tree mushroom is edible but the hakekakeka is not. The former is like a mushroom in appearance, but the latter is widespreading and flat.

SECTIONS XVI AND XVII

ICHTHYOLOGY; ORNITHOLOGY

Hi-ika or Fishing — Katire or Fishing Rod — Matire or Fishing Jigger — Ngehe or Kelp Fish — Haku or King Fish — Hature or Mackerel — Pua-ata-ata or Silvery — Matawha or Kind of Shark — Korakiraki or Kind of Eel — Papaka-rerere or Big Crab — Manu or Birds — Kura or King of the Birds — Pa-manu or Bird-Rookery — Koau-pateketeke or King Shag — etc.

FISH AND FISHING

Fishing in Nelson was called hi-ika. My informant had never heard of bone gorges. In fishing for kahawai in Nelson the hooks (matau) were adorned with paua or pawa shell. One kind of pawa used was inaka, the other wharangi; they were differently colored; the former was the better of the two for fishing purposes. The pa was usually made canoe-shaped and the pawa was let in and an iwi (bone) barb attached to pa near end. The pa (jigger) for the mangaa (barracouta) was of plain wood – tawai (birch) is almost invariably used. Tradition said the matuhi a very small bird which lives in the rocks [See Birds Section. H.B.] at certain times would feed on the tawai and would break wee branches into the sea and it was noticed the mangaa came to and bit these branches so that wood is now used for pa. This was a Maori korero (tale), but there is no doubt the tawai answers the purpose best. The mangaa is voracious and would chew through most kinds of wood in a month but the tawai is hard and tough. It sinks its teeth into the pa and many fish are caught without being near the hook (matau). My informant concluded this part of his remarks by saying the rod was called katire and the pa often matire.

He had seen in Nelson a kupenga seventy five yards long and about five feet wide. The poles at each end were called kauringa; the top line was kaharunga and the bottom one, kahapopou; and the floats pungapunga. The mesh of the net was mata. The belly of the net was called waenganui-o-te-kupenga while the heketanga was the narrowest part – at each end. The matakeke and tuara-matakeke were respective parts between the waenganui and the heketanga.

SEALS

Sealing was never carried on in Nelson, stated my informant, so he did not know re seals. He had heard of sealing down Westland way.

Add to Fish

The warehou is found in Nelson and in Kaikoura, said my informant. The gurnet is called kumukumu in Nelson and was rarely eaten but was used as bait. The rawaru is the blue cod, the pakirikiri (rock cod) being the rawaru on a smaller scale. The patangatanga (Red Jacket) was not used in Nelson. The trumpeter (kohekohe), moki and tarakihi are all eaten at Nelson. A fish found stranded on sandy beaches at Nelson was the Ring Fish or kukupa. It is shiny like a mangaa (barracouta) but has two black rings round it. The butterfish was called marare and the kelp fish, ngehe. The Nelson kingfish (haku) is different to that of Canterbury, the fish called kingfish at latter place being called maka-taharaki or maka-tikati at Nelson. The kelp fish of Canterbury is the Blue-bone of Nelson and may be the Green-bone of Southland. The mackerel was called hature but he forgot the Maori name of the trevally. The upokororo (grayling), kanae (mullet) and aua (herring) are all found in Nelson Rivers. The kanae is hard to catch – they are shyer than the upokororo and a net would be set in river below where they were and they would be caught returning by same tide, or you could go above them and hit water and they would dart downstream into net. They eat better than the aua. The upokororo eats well too and could be done in hangi (earth-oven) or on rara (grid). The kokirikiri or Leather Jacket is good to eat if skinned. He had never heard of wheke (octopi) being eaten but it was used as bait. He had never heard of a fish called ikamaru. The patete is a form of 'bullhead' (kokopu) but is flat. The paraki and waharoa are much alike, the latter being the bigger, and the Pakeha 'silvery' was called pua-ata-ata (usually abbreviated to puatata – with macrons). The puaataata is a shade bigger than the whitebait and my informant thought it was the young of the smelt (waharoa). The mesh of a net is mata but he had never heard of names of different meshes. The kupenga (nets) were stored in smoke-houses (kaute) to preserve, as it was said the smoke preserved the flax. Nets were not made of fresh flax but of stuff which had been smoked. He had never heard that cooked food could not be carried on fishing trips, nor any similar superstitions or traditions.

Add to Sharks

There were (or are) a number of sharks about Nelson, said my informant. The tutaahuna, mangatara, huanga and ururoa were all eaten, but the tuatini, takapani, papaki and matawha (this last-named is ten or twelve feet long as a rule) were not eaten. The tutahuna (or dogfish of the Pakeha) was caught in nets along the beaches, but the other three edible sharks were taken with lines baited with ika (fish). The sharks were sun-dried before being eaten and were often kept a considerable time hanging up. The mangotara and huanga were very fat and oily. These edible kinds all ate well except the ururoa which was usually only caught for the sake of its liver from which shark-oil (hinumango) was extracted. The ate (liver) was hung up where the heat of the fire would get at it on a rara (or gridiron) and a kohua (pot) or taha (calabash) was placed underneath, the oil dripping into this utensil.

EELS AND EELING

Nelson eels, as remembered by my informant, were mairehe, hao, korakiraki, horihoriwai (this is the horepara of Canterbury, he added), matamoi and take-harakeke. The former three heke (migrate), the latter three don't.

The eelspear (matarau) was of wood, had several points (mata) and a long kakau (handle). It was usually made of akerautangi or manuka and was much used in old days.

There are no kanakana in Nelson but eel-weirs (pa-tuna) were made on the streams. They were made from banks \ / of posts with flax nets stretched between and were called pa-tu. The gap was filled with hinaki made of aka vine. Leading into this was a flax puraki joined to a flax te-rohe through which the eel made its way but could not find its way back. At rear of hinaki was the popoki made of aka and detachable to pour eels out. At the heke time these hinaki had a busy session bagging the migrating eels.

Eel canals (awa-whaka-heke, or often simply awa) were made from Lake Kaiaua (at Croixelles) at heke times too. These ditches were shallow and were dug with ko (spades), and a poupa (hole) made at end. They could only be used (in daytime) when the water was muddy. There would be enough water in awa to carry eels along to poupa where men would catch the eels. The awa was mainly used at night and white shells were placed on its bottom so that could see if eels moving. A kairere (made like a puraki or like a whiuwhiu or crawfish pot) was set in awa at poupa and when the eelers considered it full enough they could remove and replace, or leave it all night at their option. Eelpots of the variety known as paka or kaitara and made of flax and the bark of totara, miro, hinau or such trees, could be set all the year round. A bait was placed inside to attract the eels.

Add to Eels

The collector told his informant of the two theories of eel propagation viz., that the eel deposits ova like the trout and fish generally, or that its young come forth alive, and asked him what the old Maoris of Nelson had said. He replied that they said the eel carried its young inside like the shark and that they had seen evidence of this, but narrator had never seen an eel with either young or eggs, although he had seen young eels, two to three inches long, coming up creeks from sea. They were silvery-colored and not so thick as a stout darning needle but were proper eels nevertheless. These young he thought were called kuao in Nelson and punuatuna in Canterbury. You could not tell one kind of eel from another when so little. They breed out at sea. Whakapipi is damming a creek to form a pa-tuna. It is packing a dam with manuka and rarauhe (fern leaves). In drying eels a shelter (uhi) was made of kiekie leaves or wiwi rushes to keep off dew. The largest eel he had seen was a mairehe weighing thirty five pounds, and he had never heard of a heavier one, although such were no doubt caught at odd times.

SHELLFISH AND CRABS

The collector took some shells he picked up on Kairaki Beach at Kaiapoi to his informant who gave the Nelson names which the collector checked off with an old woman from Otago. The tohemango of the North Island is in Nelson called whakai-o-tama [Also in Otago. H.B.]. The next shell neither the old lady nor the collector had seen before but it is called patiki in Nelson. What is called pipi in the North Island is called kaikai-karoro in Nelson and taiwhatiwhati in Canterbury and Otago. The name kaikai-karoro was given because the seagull likes to carry this (as well as other) shellfish up in air and drop them on rocks to open them. In Nelson the term pipi was applied to all shellfish as a general name and the blue mussel was there called kuku the same as in North Island. [It is called pipi in Canterbury and Otago although the term kuku has crept in during the past forty years until now both terms are regarded as synonymous by the younger Maoris. The old dame said the name kuku was unknown when she was a girl. The blue mussel was pipi. In this she corroborates all my Southern informants. H.B.] The tuaki or tuangi (a sort of cockle) is the same in Nelson, Canterbury and Otago and appears to be one of the few shells with identical names all over New Zealand (?) H.B.]. A flat shell called roroa in South my informant forgot its Nelson name; and he did not know a fan-shaped shellfish I had picked up (neither did the Otago woman). He knew no legends regarding seagulls breaking shellfish on rocks to get the contents.

At a later stage he enumerated some of the edible shellfish eaten in Nelson viz. – Tio (rock oysters); paua; kuku mussel; rori had a small shell, the rori was sometimes eaten; kakihi is a sea shellfish, the inland shellfish is kakahi; roroa; tuaki; kina – the 'sea-egg' or sea-urchin; kaikai-haroro, also called taiwhatiwhati; karuru; pupu at least three kinds – pupu, pupu-korama (known in Canterbury as Kanohi-o-Tawhaki; it has the 'cats-eye' beloved of children) and the pupu-kari-kawa which is smaller and of a different shape; toheroa; patiki, also called pipi-poro; whakai-o-tama, also called the North Island name of tohemango. In Nelson, he concluded his remarks, pipi was the general name for all shellfish.

The koura (crayfish) and crabs (papaka) were sought after in Nelson as in the rest of New Zealand as a palatable food. The papaka-rerere is the big crab and was caught in a tata made of harakeke (flax) held out by kareao (supplejack) stiffeners and using stones as sinkers (mahea). The mouth of the trap was called waha and inside was a maunu [[elsewhere in ms181 moenu is the word for bait]] (bait) usually of paua of which the big crab is fond. Many were caught in these tata by the olden Maoris.

Two other species of crabs, the papaka-roharoha and papaka-taniko were not eaten but were caught to use as bait in fishing. Fishgut (pukuika) would be tied to a pole stuck in the sand where the tide washed over and the crabs would adhere to it to eat it and could be taken by hand.

The collector has a further observation that crawfish or lobster pots made by Nelson Natives were known by them as whiuwhiu. The rou-kakahi or shellfish rake (as described by North Island writers) was not used in Nelson.

Two kinds of paua or pawa were called inaka and wharangi – they had differently colored shells.

Toheroa (or Tohemango) was a North Island name for the shellfish called whakai-a-tama in Canterbury. (He had seen them on a visit he paid to Moeraki.)

BIRDS AND BIRD-CATCHING

Kaka – This big brown parrot was once common. The people of old would find a kohanga (nest) and take a young bird home and rear and train it as a mokai (decoy bird). My informant had not heard of these birds being speared in Nelson but had heard the old people speak of two ways of snaring them. The tahi-tahi method was to make a papakaurewa (shelter) with posts (pou) projecting to which was fastened the hike. The noose was koromahanga, the string aho but he forgot the name of the hole through which it ran. On the same principle the kaka could be snared in the trees where it ate the berries. The snarer would run a stick (kauwhata) from a suitable branch to another branch and would hook the tuke to it. The tuke had a kairoro (hook) at its top for this purpose. The snarer would build a small platform (terapu) to sit on and make a canopy of leaves over it and thus ensconced would manipulate the tuke to the destruction of 'Brer Kaka'.

Kereru – the fat-fleshed, handsome-plumaged, sleepy-headed pigeon provided many an epicurean repast in ancient Nelson. This bird was speared and snared. If a big branch had a hollow for water to gather snares could be put round this natural drinking trough or they could be placed round holes in creeks. You could put two snares – the one for the head being koromahanga, the one for the feet was called tawhiwhi. My informant had seen spears fifteen feet long. They had points of bone, or ponga. In latter case you took the ponga (treefern) and when soft inside rotted (pirau) you extracted the hard streaks and used as spear points. These wiry threads were as hard as flint and were called mata as were also bone points. Another point was of the whai-uku species of stingray, which has a whip-tail, the point five inches long being used. (My informant had speared whai with a manuka spear.) The whai point has natural barbs and if driven in well is worse to pull out as tears bird up. The spear points

↟ for birds were usually notched, this being called whakataratara or kaniwha; the spears were called whakarewa.

Tui – This sweet-throated and sweet-fleshed bird could be taken in several ways. They could be snared on tuke the same as kaka, but in their case the tuke was decorated with suitable flowers or berries to entice them. The rata vine flowers (puatawhiwhi) whose juice they sucked was used, or in the poroporo season poroporo berries would be used as they ate them. The tui is fond of korari but he had never seen this used. The tui could also be caught in snares round waterholes. Another method was the pae. A karewa (stick) was tied to two trees or branches and a maimai or whareponga (of leaves) was built under it and in this the hunter sat and whakapehe (called) the birds by blowing on a raurakau (leaf) of mahoe [This tree is called hinahina in Murihiku. H.B.]. The tui hears the call and settles on the karewa and is 'settled' by hunter striking it with a patu (heavy stick) brought round sidewise. Users of the pae method get very expert and informant said his uncle could drop one or two tuis from the karewa as fast as they like to come. The makomako (bellbird) could also be killed by this method, or the tuke or noose for that matter, but he had never heard of tuis being caught with piripiri (bidibidi) at waterholes, or on frosty mornings when too numb to fly. Neither had he heard of the Nelsonians catching kakariki (parrokeets) or small birds – there were far too many good birds of larger size .

Ducks – For these birds a koromahanga called a paeke was made and stretched across lagoons (roto). Pegs or stakes were put in water and held the snare at a height to catch birds' heads as they swam along. The ducks caught were the parera (grey duck), putangitangi (paradise duck) and parera-kowhio (blue mountain duck). A small grey teal was also sometimes caught but it was very rare and he never heard its name mentioned. At the Otu lagoon putangitangi were formerly very numerous and when moulting was on the hunters would place snares round the shores and drive (aru) the moulting (maunu) birds [[See different meaning of maunu in section on Fishing]] into them.

Matuku – The grey and blue bittern were both in Nelson and were both called matuku. He had never heard of their being caught.

Kotuku – He had not heard how the white heron was caught. It was a very scarce bird – one might go for years and never see one.

Pukeko – The swamphen was snared with head-snares (mahanga) which were suspended from a stick over its tracks. Several loops would be hung down to make capture more certain. It was not hunted with dogs.

Shags – He knew two shags in Nelson. The King shag (koau-pateketeke) was captured on cliffs by tukutuku method. Men, with kete (bags) on backs, were lowered over cliffs, sitting in a noose or loop in a rope (taura-tukutuku) made of muka or of harakeke or of kiekie and often thirty to forty fathoms (whanganga = a span of six feet). This was the only shag caught, the other, koau-pango (the black shag) the residents of Nelsonian Maoridom not bothering with.

Seabirds – In Nelson the Maoris used to eat young karoro (seagulls) which were found in nests on beaches and riverbeds. The people used to eat the eggs of the tarapunga (sea-martin), the karoro, the torea and ducks. These eggs were put in ashes of fires or in hangi (ovens) – he had never heard of them being eaten raw. Long ago the Maoris went to a little rock island (about two acres extent) near Nelson to get the tarapunga eggs. There was no place to catch toroa (albatross) in Nelson – these big birds were away out at sea, but the Maoris ate young torea (redbills) when they got them. The kuaka was eaten at Nelson. The Maoris made rama (torches) and went to rookery (pa-manu) and the birds were dazzled by light and caught. This was the only bird he knew that was 'torched'. The titi (muttonbird) had come to Nelson in the last sixty years and could now be caught in rua (holes) on Takaporewa (Stephens Island). The birds were caught (nanao) in daytime and were hung on whata and then put up in poha (kelp bags) covered with the kiri (bark) of totara or manuka. Only a few poha-fulls were caught.

Weka – Only way he knew they were caught was by mahanga noose held on a long stick (poutari). A shorter stick (paruru) held the wing of a defunct weka and this was shaken to attract the attention of the ever-inquisitive bird and it was noosed. The Nelson wekas were the big grey ones, not the small dark birds found in the South. At a later stage he said the weka could be called (whakapi) by blowing on young flax or mata (a small kind of toetoe) held in mouth. In the daytime a kuri (dog) would be kept handy on a taura (leash) and let go at the birds when within striking distance. At night the kuri was let range free. In old days very few people had kuri so was not a common sport. He had never heard of hunting kiwi with kuri.

Kiwi – He knew two kinds of kiwi – the ordinary kiwi, also called the totoweka, and a whitish kind, the kiwi-ma. He had never heard the name moho for them. They were snared with harakeke snares – koromahanga – put over their rua (holes). Sometimes the birds would have their rua under a big tree and the hunters would block every exit but one and over this one would suspend the noose.

Kuruti – This is a bird the collector cannot identify. It is the size of a pigeon, the shape of a weka, the color (grey) of a lark, lives in swampy places and can fly. It lives about Maunga-a-whiu (Blue Mountain) between Nelson and the Southern Alps, so my informant said. He had not heard its English name but only the Maori name kuruti.

Other Birds – The tieke (saddleback) and koka (crow) were in Nelson but he had not heard of their being caught and eaten. The kakapo was not found in the district round Nelson town, and as far as he knew the kea and the Native Quail had not been there either. The ruru (morepork) was unmolested and he had never heard of Maoris eating hawks. The koekoea (long-tail cuckoo) and pipiwharauroa (shining cuckoo) both came in summer. Besides the harrier (kahu) were found the bush hawk (karewarewa) and its less shaggy mate, the sparrowhawk (kaeaea).

The kotare (kingfisher) frequented streams, and there was a bird called matuhi – it was bigger than a lark but was not a dottrell of which there was none in Nelson.

Small Bush Birds – The yellowheads or Native Canaries were known as popokotea; the robin was totoara; the fantail, hiwaiwaka; the grey warbler, riroriro; the tomtit, pimiromiro; the rifleman, titiripounamu; while the 'glass-eye' had a Maori name in Nelson but he could not recall it. [This 'glass-eye' is variously called white-eye, ringeye, waxeye and blight-bird and is said to have come to New Zealand in 1856. H.B.] My informant had never heard the legend that the pimiromiro carried love messages. He was afraid he did not attach much importance to such lore when he was a boy.

Pets – The only mokai (pets) he had known to be kept in Nelson were tui and kaka. He had never heard of other birds being kept as pets in old days.

Notes – The bird called matuhi (see head of this page) must be wrong name here as at another place the informant [See Fishing Section. H.B.] described the matuhi as 'very much smaller than the sandlark or whioioi, which it is like in color. It lives in the rocks' – and the collector noted 'This is probably the rock-wren.'

In regard to titi on Stephen's Island he added later that he thought the reason the old Maoris had not gone there for muttonbirds was because of their horror of the tuatara, but when whalers came and half-castes appeared these latter went to that island and had done so for last sixty years.

Add to Birds

My informant had never heard of a rail called the mohoperuru (North Island name) but the mata (fernbird) lived in swamps, as also did the kuruti. The latter bird was the color of a weka and could fly and was perhaps as big as a thrush. His short tail stands up perkily like that of a weka. [The description is like that of a rail. H.B.] The rerewaka is a water bird in Nelson – it has a very long beak. He had never heard the old people speak of the moa, nor had he ever heard that the tomtit was supposed to carry love messages. Decoy birds were called mokai. He never saw bone or greenstone rings on birds' legs but rings (parekereke) of whatu' muka (woven flax fibre) to tie them to pae (perches). If a mokai (pet) died and the owner was very fond of it he might carve a figure of it [See Carvings. H.B.]. The usual pets kept were parrokeets, tui and kaka, the last two as decoy birds (mokai). He had never heard of white cranes (kotuku), seagulls, or putangitangi (paradise ducks) as pets in Nelson. The parrokeets were called kakariki generally, the yellow-headed ones being called porere and the red-topped ones parewaka. The old Maoris reckoned the former were the young of latter species and that they would eventually turn red as they aged.

My informant had not heard of the tutelary deities of the various sorts of birds, but remembered the old people said the kura was the rangatira of all the birds – some said of the kaka only. The kura was the king of birds and could never have been very plentiful as it died out long ago. He had never heard that cooked food could not be carried by bird-hunters for fear of polluting the sanctity of the forest.

SECTIONS XVIII, XIX, AND XX

ENTOMOLOGY; ZOOLOGY; BOTANY

Naeroa or Mosquitoes — Ngaro or a reddish fly — Mahitihiti or Grasshoppers — Were or Centipedes — Rongarongaro or Midges — Karara = any insect or lizard — Noke or Worms — Mokopapa or Tree Lizards — Whakaroro = Howl of Wild Dog — Ruawhenua = A way of Catching Rats — Kupenga or An Edible Plains Berry — Horopito or Pepper Tree — Penemauroa or Maidenhair Fern — Tupakihi or Kidney Fern — etc.

INSECTS AND BATS

In regard to the Nelsonian names of insects the informant said that mosquitoes were called naeroa [keroa in Murihiku and waeroa in North Island. H.B.]. The daddy-long-legs was there in Nelson called keroa. He had no recollection of ever hearing the old people mention the kinds or names of butterflies. Ants were upokorua and the mata was a sort of 'wasp' – a red fly which stung badly. He only knew one kind of cricket and that was the piharenga. The blowfly was rango. This was the ordinary bluebottle but there was another kind called ngaro – a reddish-yellowish fly which carried live 'blows' (iro) whereas the rango deposited its eggs. He considered both these flies were native, but that the small house fly was imported. Grasshoppers were mahitihiti. He had forgotten the names of the dragon flies, and the mason flies. These latter 'were good lads for building sod houses'. The ugly but harmless weta were found in Nelson as were also the ro and whe (two kinds of stick insects). Caterpillars were called torongu or toroku, and centipedes were were. He never knew the kekerengu to be in Nelson, but the kekerewai or manu-a-Rehua was found on the manuka but he never heard it was ever eaten as food [As stated in Tregear's works. H.B.]. The first of its names is applied before it flies. It then 'goes away in mobs' and never reappears – hence its second name. Fleas were called tuiau but he did not know if native or introduced; but the kutu (louse) was mentioned in history of ancient days. Bats were called pekapeka. The old Maoris did not seem afraid of them but did not eat them. The informant made the interesting remark that 'any lizard or insect was a karara in Nelson'.

Mosquitoes were called naeroa in Nelson (not waeroa as in North Island, nor keroa as in Murihiku) and the little gnats or midges which fly about at dusk were called pongarongaro.

WORMS AND GRUBS

In Nelson, as in South Island generally, worms are chiefly considered as in relation to bob-fishing (hi). This bobbing for eels is called hi and the bob is called punoke (bundle of worms). The huhu grub can also be utilised for bobs. To make the bob strip flax very fine, or use muka, and string the worms, or the huhu, on. Wiwi (rushes) or fine manuka twigs are used to thread (kotui) the worms on and the whole is looped up with flax into a bundle, that seems toothsome to Tuna and he sets his teeth into it and is yanked out before he knows what has happened. The bob is much used in Nelson and is a good way to secure eels. The bob is tied on to a stick (matire) and the art lies in rushing the eel out before he can relinquish his hold. The worm usually used on bobs is the big white one, called rua-whenua in Nelson. The red worms = nokewhero and the 'black ones', somewhat darker and larger = nokepango are also found in Nelson but my informant had never heard that any of them were eaten [as is stated to have been the case in certain parts of the North Island. H.B.].

The huhu is the big, fat, white grub found in pine trees. It is called tuka in Canterbury but huhu in Nelson. It was eaten both raw and cooked but my informant 'could not come at it', so cannot pass an opinion as to its edible qualities.

LIZARDS AND TUATARA

The tree lizard was found in Nelson where it was called mokopapa the same as in the rest of the South Island. A common lizard in the grass regions of Nelson was there called tupakihi (but toropakihi is its Canterbury name). The hairy lizard mokohuruhuru (often known as mokotuahuruhuru in Canterbury) and the bush lizard, the handsome green mokakariki (usually called mokokakariki in Canterbury) were also found in Nelson. He had never heard of lizards being eaten, nor that they had ever been kept for pets – the old people seemed to be afraid of them. The general name for them was ngarara or karara. 'Any lizard or insect was called a karara in Nelson,' added my informant.

The tuatara lived in Takaporewa (Stephens Island) and that was why the ancient Maori was afraid to go there for titi (muttonbirds) but now modern half-castes go there. The tuatara lived in rua (burrows) and laid eggs he thought, but he had forgotten the little history he had ever heard about them. It was said that if you took the eggs and the mother tuatara returned to the rua and found them gone, she could scent them and would follow you for miles. As far as he knew the tuatara was not found on the mainland.

With the exception of the tuatara he had seen no lizards in Nelson which were not common to the rest of the South Island. He had never heard of the Maoris keeping them as pets.

THE NATIVE DOG

My informant did not consider the kuri had ever been very plentiful in Nelson, stating that very few Maoris had owned them from what he had heard so that hunting birds with them was not so extensively indulged in as it apparently had been in some other parts where the dogs were more common property. The male dog was called a kuri-toa, or a kuri-tane sometimes, while a bitch was kuri-uhi and a pup kuri-kuaoa. He understood the dog ran wild and people acquired it as follows. If a man came across a bitch which he thought had pups he would hunt for latter, there being e rua to e wha (two to four) in a litter. One or all or as many as wanted he would take to kainga to rear and train. Male pups would be whaka-poka (castrated) sometimes so as to fatten them for food, such food being highly esteemed. Women could eat this food [notwithstanding a contrary statement in Tregear's works. H.B.]. He had heard that in old times kuri of the mohorangi breed were found in Nelson. The kuri had a habit of howling (whakaroro). Kuri hair and kuri skins were greatly valued for mats but very few of these seem to have been kept. A piebald dog, that is a black and white one, was a whakaporo-poro. He had seen one kiri-kuri (dogskin) with black and white on the same skin – it was said to be the only one in Nelson.

My informant had never heard of the kuri-tawhiti nor the 'stone-trap' nor of any other method of catching the wild dogs save as pups (kuri-kuaoa).

RATS AND RAT-CATCHING

The kiore, or native rat, was mostly black in Nelson but some of the light-grey kind used to be found in the Blenheim district. As far as he knew the grey ones were called kiore-maori and the black ones kiore-tawai. He had heard the old people speak of the whirituamanga [See Canterbury Notes re Kiore. H.B.] method of crossing rivers but he could scarcely credit it. The kiore was a forest-dweller and made its hole (rua-kiore) in trees. He had dug into one rotten tree and found a nest with three young in it. It lived on bush berries and on the patotara berry of the flats and was good to eat. It was caught by two methods – the tawhiti trap and the rua-whenua trap. (The former has been described in Murihiku and Canterbury Notes but the latter style was new to the collector and his informant described it.) A hole was made on the kiore's track (which it may be explained the rodent traverses at night) the bottom being made so that the rat won't get out, thus

A stick called a tirapu was put partly across this hole, balanced so that when kiore walks out on it, it tips up depositing him in the pit from which he cannot climb out. The other end of the stick or board resting on the bank is slightly weighted so that when the rat slides off the other end, the board resumes its former position ready for another victim. Often a stick or tirapu would be projected from both sides of the pit (rua whenua) to catch the rats going either way and some very good hauls where made on nights when the rats were actively moving about in the berry season. It is a migratory creature following its food in the various districts through the rotation of the seasons. My informant had never heard of bait being used in catching rats, nor of the kiore being called 'koroke' (that fellow) during the ratting season. [Both these facts are stated in Tregear's Works re North Island. H.B.]

TREES, SHRUBS AND PLANTS AND BERRIES

In regard to trees my informant considered that the hinau of Nelson was called pokaka in Canterbury and Murihiku but he was not quite sure of this. In speaking later of dyes he said that the pokaka of the South was called hinau up in Nelson [See Dyes Section. H.B.]. In regard to forest trees in the course of his information he mentioned the totara, tawai, matai, kapuka, miro, and other trees common to the South Island if not to all New Zealand. He mentioned a ramarama tree – this, he explained, was not the ramarama, or pepper-tree, of Murihiku, but was a tree like the rohutu, bearing black berries like the konini (fuchsia). He had seen trees in Nelson which he had not noticed in the rest of the South Island (although that did not say they did not grow in bush there which he had not penetrated). Of such trees were the tawa, puriri, pukatea (called bukatea by the Pakeha), poporokaiwhiria (which grows to a good height but not of thick girth, and bears red berries), kowhiuwhiu (a shrub-like tree) and the nikau palm.

Tawa, hinau and matai berries were eaten raw when ripe; the berries of the miro, kahikatea and titoki were also eaten, as were also patotara and kupenga berries out on the plains or flats. The patotara is a pinkish color and the kupenga a light-blue.

With regard to plants, in Nelson there were several varieties of toetoe, such as toetoe-pukio, toetoe-pakau, toetoe-mata, toetoe-matai and toetoe-herekau, the common kind. The first of these was often used for whare-thatching, the second for sail-making, while the mata is a small form of toetoe. My informant had seen a grass called tataki round pohas (kelp bags) from the Titi Islands but this grass is not found in Nelson, neither is the karetu grass. The rengarenga in Nelson is like the ice-plant or edelweiss but grows on low country. He forgot the name of the Mountain Lily and had never heard of the 'vegetable sheep' plant. When he visited the King Country he saw the beautiful horseshoe fern (paratawhiti) but he had never seen it in South Island.

Add to Plants, Trees, Ferns

There are two kinds of manuka, viz. manuka-pouri (black manuka) and a 'white manuka' the kiripapa (known as kirimoko further South). My informant thought it was called kiripapa because the black tree lizard [mokopapa. H.B.] is often found in its kiri (bark). The patiti (ordinary tussock) of Canterbury is called mauku in Nelson. The leaves of the kawakawa tree in Nelson were good for skin diseases. The pepper-tree [ramarama in Murihiku. H.B.] is horopito in Nelson. The karamu there is used for dye purposes. The titoki also grows there. My informant had never heard of anise plant or korokio shrub. There were two kinds of tumatakuru (Wild Irishman) in Nelson but he forgot the name of the finer sort. He had never heard of any berry or plant called 'oe'. Puawai was a general name for all flowers; the pikiraki grows on tawai (beech) and is a red mistletoe; puatawhiwhi is the red flower on the rata (ironwood) while the pikiarero is the white clematis. The kohuwai is a moss on the banks of creeks or on old trees, although the latter is really kohukohu and the kohuwai is the water moss. He forgot the name of the Native grass – he thought a little patch of it still grew at Oxford, Canterbury. Nelson ferns were piupiu, turakiao, kawakawa, paretao, pikopiko, penemauroa (maidenhair), tupakihi (kidney fern), toromiro (True Lovers's Knot), kiokio, and others whose names he could not recall. The mountain musk grew in backblocks but he forgot its Maori name. The popohue of Nelson was called miki in Canterbury. The mingi of Nelson is very small; spreading; and with whitey-blue edible berries.

The rakau-toa (male tree) has not flowers the same as the rakau-uha (female tree) – so the old people said. The kahika (white pine) and rimu (red pine) male tree bears bloom but has no berry like its female companion.

The titoki tree is found in Nelson (and a few grow on Banks Peninsula, Canterbury) and it has a red berry with a black head which could be eaten or be used to extract oil from. The miro berries could be eaten if wished, and you could also (like titoki) squeeze an oil from them.

SECTIONS XXI TO XXVIII:
XXI METEOROLOGY, XXII ON RELIGION, XXIII NIL (MYTHOLOGY), XXIV SUPERSTITION, XXV NIL (FOLK-TALES), XXVI NIL (HISTORY), XXVII TABLE (SEE CANTERBURY NOTES), XXVIII NIL (PAKEHA)

Teka or Southern Cross — Ika-whetu or comets — Whetu-rere or Meteors — Tawharepapa or West Wind — Haukopata or Frost — Aio or Fine Weather at Sea — Matakite or Second Sight — Makutu or Wizardry — etc.

SKY LORE

Phenomena – The Aurora Australis is called Te Rama-o-Tawhaki in Nelson because when Tawhaki went from the earth back to the sky darkness came on and he called for a torch and the Southern lights were sent. That has been his sign since as it lighted him back. Some said that Tama sent this torch and some said that Tane sent it. Comets are called ika-whetu; meteors are wheturere and falling stars are called whetutaka.

Rainbows – Called puaniwaniwa and double ones purua. Sometimes the top one of double ones was called Kahukura and lower one Rokomai but usually they were known as purua-puaniwaniwa. He had never seen nor heard of incomplete rainbows. Kahukura was held as a god all over South Island and Rakaiora was said to be a son of his and was regarded as a second atua of the rainbows. In Nelson it was said he appeared in the wee rainbows. If he appeared before a person contemplating travelling he was a warning. If he appeared across the projected route 'stay at home', but if he came lengthwise to it, 'go'. He was in the very small bows and was said to only appear as a tohu (omen) to his descendants.

Stars – were called whetu but he could only recall very few names. The Milky Way was called Ika-o-te-Rangi. Ngaputahi was a group of stars arranged something like this, three being in a row and two out from each side. Matariki was also a group, there being six in the bunch, and Teka was the Southern Cross group. Besides these groups Tawere (Morning Star) and Puanga (Evening Star) were studied to reveal the propitious times for planting [See Cultivation Section. H.B.].

Tuhinapo is a black streak in sky, and is shape of a flounder at its head. It has stars all round it, but he did not know its European name.

Lightning – The only name for this he had heard in Nelson was uira [See Canterbury Notes for other names. H.B.].

Add to Sky-Lore

One informant had never heard the Maori names of comets, meteors, or eclipses of sun or moon, but ordinary falling stars, he said, were called whetu-taka. [It is doubtful if this is an ancient name. H.B.]

Rainbows were called puaniwaniwa in Nelson and the only lore he had heard about them was that they were said to be waewae-ua (footsteps of the rain). He did not know the name of double rainbows.

Earthquakes (ru) used to be fairly frequent in Nelson and some of the tohungas could tell when these disturbances were coming within a week. Narrator had never heard these men account for the origin or cause of earthquakes, but one old man, he knew, on two occasions foretold earthquakes which duly came to pass several days after the prognostication. This old man was very good at weather lore and studied the sky in the mornings and evenings. He scanned the heavens and observed the clouds and the winds (which may vary in Nelson three or four ways in one day). The old man, he thought, attached importance to the cloud strata of the sky. The traditional name of a wavy sky with ridgey strata is Ranga-Tawhaki and has some allusion to Tawhaki climbing the heavens to find his wife. [Note: A wrinkled brow is also called rangatawhaki according to informant. H.B.]

WINDS, AND WEATHER LORE

Up in Nelson the East wind is called marangai; pounui is a northerly wind; mauru is a nor-west wind; tamauru is somewhat more to the west; tawharepapa is westerly; ta is south-west wind; tatonga is southerly; and tonga is a south-east wind. These eight winds were all my informant could recollect when speaking to me. Pounui and tonga are the two rainy winds, he continued, and tonga is the strongest. There are several mountains which acted as weather indicators to the olden Maoris in Nelson. The first fog (kohu) on one or other always foretold whether rain could be expected or what wind would blow the next day. The following was the Maori weather chart: A fog on Karororangi was a sure sign of tonga (south-east wind) with rain following. A fog on Mahipuku was a sure sign of mauru (north-west wind). A fog on Timingi was a sure sign of ta (southwest wind). A fog on Tapuaenuku was a sure sign of pounui (north wind) with rain following. A fog on Pukeone in the evening is a sign of paki (fine weather). If you see uira (lightning) on Matau (or Matauu) at night you will have squally weather. My informant closed his interesting meteorological remarks by saying that in Nelson rain was called ua, snow huka, and frost haukopata. They did not often get these latter as the climate was good.

If the new moon came in lying thus ⌣ facing the sky the olden Maori said it was a wet moon or a sign of wet weather, but if it came in thus ⦙ standing up it was a tohu (sign) of dry weather. 'This is exactly opposite to what the Pakeha says, but I reckon the old Maoris were correct in what they said on this matter,' added my informant.

Add to Winds and Weather

Fine weather on the sea was called aio and rough weather tupuhi, fine weather on land being paki. The mahunga (head) was the most tapu part of man and a hair was pulled out and the tohunga said 'karakia mo te paki' for a fine spell. When narrator was a lad at Nelson a great storm arose and the tohunga karakia'd. The narrator was an unbeliever but next day a profound aio came. The hair used was thrown into the sea – it was never burnt. The tide coming in was known as taipari and going out taiheke (or taitimu). The old people said the puhi (or taipuhi) made the sea roll. You would see the sea rise before a storm came and this was said to be the puhi (currents) fighting each other. The strongest would win and the storm would come from that quarter. Nga au o te moana kei te whaiwhai (the ocean currents are fighting) was said of the ground swells heaving (and apparently struggling). He had never heard the Maoris say what caused the tides. He had never heard of a great fish swallowing and ejecting it. Te Waha o Parata (in Nelson) is the name of the Southern wind. It is the fiercest hau (wind) which blows there. Taikopo is a certain tide there and it sometimes runs in so strongly and far that at three quarter tide it is in further than ordinary high tide and you are puzzled to tell high-tide and then it recedes perhaps an hour before usual highwater. The Nelson climate was said to be warmer long ago than now. This is said to be caused by cutting the bush down and letting the frosts into the ground. They get more rain now than they once did. The old Maoris used to say Nelson was the best climate in the South Island.

THE TUAHU

When the Tuahu was mentioned the narrator said it was a subject he did not know much about as the old people among whom he was brought up had said very little about it. All the same he had seen several places up round Whakapuaka and Nelson which were said to be the sites of ancient tuahu. Of the ones he had seen one or two seemed like mounds of natural earth, over which, he understood, the people of old had built a kaupapa (platform) made of wood. Some spots must have been just the bare ground – he had seen two of this description. When in use the spot must have been marked by a post or a stone. Only the tohunga went there and then just to karakia. It was a more sacred place than the urupa (burial-ground) or wharekura (school of teaching). It was very tapu. Other spots could, however, acquire tapu of a more or less permanent character but he only knew one such spot from personal observation. It was in the water. The story ran that a boy was drowned there by some people in the bad old days and that his grandfather said karakia over the spot and thus rendered it tapu. But the most tapu place of the lot was the tuahu.

THE WHAREKURA

The narrator very briefly dismissed this important institution of ancient Maoridom: 'The wharekura,' he remarked, 'was the same thing as the wharepurakau, and karakia, history, and whakapapa-korero were taught there.'

Add to Tohungas

My informant said there were male and female tohungas as well as male and female matakite (seers). Matakite was really second-sight he thought. He had never heard of any form of hypnotism or ventriloquism among the Maoris of Nelson or elsewhere. Rotua is to go to sleep naturally in your chair or dozing by the fire; but the word is also applied to being made to go to sleep by makutu. He did not know how this compulsory sleep was brought on but the skilled tohunga could do it. It was a form of makutu. He could recall just then two cases of matakite. Once Mr Robertson, of Little River, was in the Kaiapoi district and lost a pocketbook containing sixty pound. He was naturally much disturbed at the loss and told the old tohunga, Poihipi, about it. The old kaumatua told him where to go to find it and he went straight to the spot and picked up the missing pocket book with its contents intact. 'That was matakite or second-sight.' Another case was that of an old lady who had missed a valued brooch for eighteen months or two years and who finally consulted old Poihipi. He said not to worry as she would soon see the brooch as the man who then had it was in the North Island but would soon cross to South Island to some Jubilee Celebrations (Pakeha) coming off. The man duly turned up and the brooch was recovered from him as the matakite had foretold. (The brooch had been given to man by a female relative of the loser as he was leaving for North Island and transaction was kept secret.)

Dreams (moemoea) did not go by contraries (as with the Pakeha), and were regarded as warnings or omens (tohu). The tohungas could explain them.

My informant had never heard of water gazing divination (whakaata) in Nelson.

WAIRUA-ATUA

'The wairua was the human spirit,' said the narrator. 'An atua was a demon. The former could not haunt you but the atua can. I have never heard of moths being called wairua-tangata, so I do not know how the name was given.'

SUPERNATURAL THINGS

On this subject the collector's Nelsonian informant seemed to have very little to say but after some gentle pressing he said he had never heard of maeroero, or wild men of the woods, in Nelson, but that some of the hills were said to be the haunt of the fairies known as patupaiarehe but he had no particulars about them, or goblins, or ogres.

As for taniwha, one was said to inhabit Lake Kaiaua (Croixelles). Its name was (or is) Rapahoe but he had not heard of its having eaten anyone in the days of its activity. It was turned into a rock and as such stands there yet. Its reputation still survives and it is an uncanny spot to meddle with, for it is (or was) said that if any Maori goes poking about this rock, some near relative of this audacious person will die.

In regard to supernatural things as affecting human beings he considered that the forms of witchcraft called makutu and whaiwhaia were, as far as he knew, much the same thing, although the former was said to be the more deadly of the two. [This, he added, was a subject he had puzzled over a good deal, for when he was a boy he had been brought to believe that the former invocation of evil, that is, makutu, would kill anyone, but he later found out it had no power against, or over, Europeans; yet he could not divest himself of the idea that if any tohunga could still produce strong enough makutu he could still kill people who believed in it, although he would have no power over those who defied him. Personally he had defied any of the old Maoris to makutu him. H.B.]

Add to Supernatural

My informant had never heard of 'warning voices' in Nelson, but had heard it said that in the North Island near Masterton when the people went 'bobbing' for tuna (eels) and had caught a goodly number a voice would say, 'Don't catch any more.' It was a wairua or taniwha who issued this warning to them.

Narrator had never heard of an evil spirit called pukaatua but Pukeatua (Devil's Knob to Pakeha) bears an ill reputation on Banks' Peninsula as it is said you can hear fairy voices from the site of the old-time pa near there.

My informant had never heard of rakau-haere (trees which travel about) in Nelson, but he knew a rock there which was said to appear or disappear at will. A man named Rapahoe was drowned in Lake Kaiaua (Croixelles) and was turned into a rock shaped somewhat like a shark (or taniwha). Narrator had seen the rock but he never saw it disappear as old people said it could do.

He had heard of the kahuitipua who once inhabited Nelson as well as rest of South Island. They are spoken of as atua (spirits) or kehua (ghosts).

He had never heard of maeroero being in northern part of South Island, the Nelsonians claiming that these eerie gentry lived down at Milford Sound.

Some North Island people speak of a winged racwe having once inhabited Taranaki, but my informant had never heard of such men in Nelson.

WESTLAND

CONTENTS

Section
V	Paints, dyes and Scents	521
VIII	Medical lore	521
X	Customs	522
XII	Greenstone	522
XIII	Canoes, etc.	524
XV	Vegetable Foods	524
XVI	Ichthyology	526
XVII	Ornithology	528
XVIII	Entomology	530
XX	Botany	530
XXI	Meteorology	531
XXIII	Mythology	532
	Visit to Bruce Bay in 1908 or 1909, Maori Account	532

Note: Other Sections missing as no information available

SECTIONS REPRESENTED

V Paints, Dyes, and Scents — VIII Medical lore —X Customs —XII Greenstone — XIII Canoes, etc. — XV Vegetable Foods — XVI Ichthyology — XVII Ornithology — XVIII Entomology — XX Botany — XXI Meteorology — XXIII Mythology

Note: Other Sections missing as no information available.

Note: As I did not get to Marlborough, Nelson or Westland in the limited time at my disposal, for Westland information I sought out three Maoris in North Canterbury who had once lived in Westland and these pages are the result. H.B.

Pa or Blue Colour — Nihotuka or Toothache — Komuka or Damper — Tangiwai or Glassy Greenstone — Marakamu or a Kind of Greenstone — Hoaka or Sandstone (grinder) — Kiekie and its Edible Fruits — Haparu or Young Grayling — Kotuku or White Heron — Koka or Native Crow — Waipapaku or River Rapid — Patete or a Kind of Ferntree — Houhou or 'Five Fingers' — Tikapu or Mountain Lily — Tikumu or Mountain Daisy — Toropakihi or Green Lizard — etc.

[[SECTION V: PAINTS, DYES AND SCENTS]]

COLOURS

The collector asked one of his informants what the old people over in Westland called various colors but he said the only one he remembered as noteworthy was he had heard blue called pa.

[[SECTION VIII: MEDICAL LORE]]

MEDICINAL LORE

The cure for toothache (nihotuka) on the West Coast, said one of my informants, was to get a lizard, lay it across the decayed molar and bite it in two and let its blood run into the hole in the tooth. 'This was superstition again,' he added. The toropakihi (little green lizard found in grass) was the lizard used. The collector asked re the blood of a lizard and was told it was a brownish fluid, scanty in quantity, and it left a stain – showing it was a form of blood. Another cure for toothache was to use the juice of the flax root (not the pia or gum of the plant, as sometimes stated). Old Horipere (a Kanaka who usually resided about Bluff) got a sufferer to lie down and poured this juice in her ear and four hours later my informant heard her say she was cured. This old 'medicine-man' used to give a pannikin of flax-root water as a purgative – it was very drastic. Hori (paralytic fits) from eating karaka berries raw, tutu seeds, or too much kiekie or tiori, could be treated by burying patient in sand (up to neck presumably) to stop convulsions twisting them too much. [Man who said this has been in North Island. H.B.]

[[SECTION X: CUSTOMS]]

CUSTOMS

A Maori lady who visited Westland twenty years ago said that while at Arahura for some months she saw no customs different from those she was familiar with in Canterbury.

One of my informants on Westland matters said that he was sure that putting clay round birds to cook them in embers was a trick the Maoris had picked up from the Pakeha.

[[SECTION XII: GREENSTONE]]

GREENSTONE

Considering that two of his informants – both very intelligent men – had spent a year or two each in Westland – 'the home of the greenstone', the real Te Wai Pounemu – the collector got disappointingly little information about the greenstone. One seemed to have neglected the study of the subject. The other was a little better and after some cogitation gave a few items about it. He had seen various greenstone articles there, but of course was too late in the day to see Maoris working it and never thought to inquire. It was a subject seldom mentioned in 1884 and 1885 but he heard one or two facts at odd times. Tangiwai was a glassy stone found on the West Coast but he had never heard the name koko-tangiwai. Inanga, inaka or ina' (as it was sometimes called shortly in hurried pronunciation) was a whitish-colored greenstone and was regarded as the best of the lot. Marakamu [This is a new name to the collector. H.B.] was also of a whitey color but was thicker in the grain than inaka. You could see through clear pieces of tangiwai but you could not see through either inaka or marakamu. He had heard the name aotea as denoting a variety of greenstone but it was a kind he had never seen. These were all the names he could recollect that he had heard during his sojourn in Westland. In searching for the valued pounemu it was a good sign to dream of a person. If you found a lump or block you thereupon named it gratefully after the person, or main person if there were several, who had appeared to you in your dream. The hoaka was a coarse kind of stone, probably sandstone, used to grind the greenstone, but although he had heard the name he knew nothing about where it was procured or how it was used. He had heard the dark or cloudy spots in the greenstone called tutae-koka and was told that this name was given to them because they came there through the violation of tapu done by the servant of one of the early Maori navigators and explorers of the West Coast. This navigator was called Tamatea-pokai-whenua and he was searching for his missing wives who had been turned into greenstone round there. The name of the slave was Hapuku and it was while cooking some koka (New Zealand Crow) that he violated the tapu and hence the flaw in some pieces of greenstone and hence they are called the tutae (excrement) of the koka that Hapuku was cooking. The collector stated that he had read the name of the slave was Timuaki and that he was turned into the mountain – still known as Timuaki – near Arahura; but his informant was positive that the old people in Westland always called that slave Hapuku. Timuaki, he added, was one of the early canoes which came to the South Island but he was sorry he could not say who was captain of this canoe, nor relate its history.

Add to Greenstone

Up the Arahura River, said my third informant, at a place called Tuhua, it was said that the Tairea canoe could still be seen but transformed into a reef of greenstone. According to rumour, as he heard it, you can see two men in the canoe, one at each end. The country has sunk, so it is said, since the famous Greenstone Canoe made her first and last trip up the river where it now reposes and it is now in a deep and precipitous gorge and those anxious to inspect the locality have to descend by ropes (so 'tis said). The water rises and falls over the Waka-Pounemu according to the state of the rainfall, etc. and sometimes you can see its outline and then again it is buried under rushing torrents of water. [My informant added that R. Taiaroa, of Taumutu, went to see the place and he advised me to see him, but unfortunately the collector has not met Mr Taiaroa since this information was given. H.B.]

[[SECTION XIII: CANOES, ETC.]]

CANOES

The collector has no information re canoes used on Westland coast but one of his informants said that to cross the turbulent West Coast streams the Maoris made mokihi of koradi sticks but the collector has no further notes about this but may get some on next trip.

TORCHES

The torches used when spearing flounders (by torchlight) round in Westland, said my third informant, were called rama. They were made of kapara (the heart of the red pine tree) which is resinous and burns well. This kapara was split up into long sticks which were tied together and this was set alight, constituting the torch.

[[SECTION XV: VEGETABLE FOODS]]

VEGETABLE FOODS

Round on the West Coast, said one informant, was a sort of food which did not grow on the East Coast. This was the kiekie and you could get two kinds of 'fruit' from the same tree. When it comes into bloom it has thick-set leaves, like the magnolia shrub of Pakeha gardens, and of a white colour and these can be eaten. The name of this food was tawhara. The leaves turned brown and rotted if not eaten. In each cluster of leaves is the fruit, the tiori, and if the leaves are not eaten it ripens nicer than if left to grow exposed to a cold world. This fruit is a soft, waxy, yellow stuff 'like a banana' and shaped something like a ure to which it is sometimes compared. It is straight and usually about four inches or so long by one and a half inches thick perhaps. This is a rough drawing as supplied by a hurried sketch made by my informant of the leaves with the fruit in the midst of them. He finished his remarks on the kiekie by saying if you ate too much of either tawhara or tiori you would in all probability get a very bad headache.

    A fern (he forgot its name but thought it was piupiu) over in Westland was eaten. Its leaves could be boiled and eaten as a sort of cabbage. The old people used to roll this fern round wekas and other birds consigned to the umu (earth-ovens) and when the cooked (or steamed) birds were taken out the fern was devoured as a kinaki (relish) to the flesh. It tasted very palatable.

They also ate the tender young fronds (rito-o-mamaku) of the mamaku variety of the treefern. It was put in the umu by itself sometimes and it took longer, he thought, to cook properly than any other native food. He could not compare its taste with that of anything else he had tasted because it had a peculiar gummy flavour – a taste of its own. It was a soft, watery taste – an acquired taste – and was inclined to make the eater feel 'gassy', or such was his opinion. You could also take the young mamaku and take the heart out and tao it in the umu. Such a tree would not grow again, but when the ponga was cut down for fencing posts it re-grew from the stump. He had never heard of any treefern called wheki, but he had heard the name katote. On the West Coast the katote looked like a young nikau to him but he did not know if it was eaten. In regard to edible berries the rehua is a plant with bluish berries. It is a creeper and the wekas (woodhens) are very fond of the berries. These are something like the tapuku in appearance only this is a white berry. The patotara is a plant two or three inches high – it has prickly leaves and it grows on poor ground. It grows one stem and there are five or she berries of a yellowish color on this. He had eaten them and found them more tasty than the rehua berry.

Another informant (in Canterbury) speaking of other matters mentioned that the kiekie was on the West Coast and that you could eat the 'tawhera' and 'tiore' of it.

Another stated you could get hori (fits same as caused by tutu poisoning) from eating too much kiekie or tiori, but the collector has no details of this.

Add to Vegetable Foods

The kiakia [he called it kiakia not kiekie and I noted the same fact with one or two other speakers – evidently a dialectical variation, as pounemu for pounamu and kumera for kumara, etc. H.B.], said one of my informants, grew on the West Coast, but not in Canterbury. The tawhara (taf-a-ra) is flower and fruit combined. What the Pakeha calls 'Five Fingers' grows inside and gets ripe in April and May, each being something like a banana in shape and very sweet to the taste. The Maori called this tirori. The tawhara has a sweet taste too, but is somewhat watery. The patete is a ferntree which he had eaten when on the West Coast, and he considered it identical with the katote of Canterbury and Otago. The hinau tree grows in Westland but he never saw the berries of it eaten, although the tataraheka (lawyer) berries were devoured with relish. He never saw the kumera grown in Westland during the three years (1884-5-6?) he was there, and he never heard of aruhe (edible fernroot) there. A little koareare (edible portion of raupo) was got in the lagoons and was eaten; and some kauru (from the cabbagetree) was also eaten but was not very plentiful. He had never heard of the Maoris there (or anywhere else, for that matter) eating the roots or any part of the speargrass plant. Bush berries were plentiful.

A Maori lady, who visited the West Coast twenty years ago, told the collector the only food she saw at Arahura which she was not accustomed to in Canterbury was the tiroti or kiekie.

POTATOES

When in Westland my Tuahiwi friend noticed that over there the Maoris grew several varieties of potatoes much more largely than others. These were the repe, the karaponia (Californian) while the big kidney potato they called waitaha and the popular derwent they knew as katote. Bush clearings on the West Coast grew (and grow) prolific crops of potatoes.

Add to Potatoes

The West Coast, said one informant, is wetter than Canterbury and when there he noticed that the Waitaha, or 'White Rock', potato, grew very well indeed. The bush soil seemed to suit potatoes judging by the abundant crops.

[[SECTION XVI: ICHTHYOLOGY]]

WESTLAND INFORMATION
FISHING

A Tuahiwi Maori, who once spent two or three years in the Province of Westland, told the collector that when there he had seen the pikipiki, a black kind of kokopu or cockabully, and moreover had assisted to eat it. It was very bony.

Over there he had noticed a peculiar way of catching the grayling or upokororo. This fish has a habit the moment it catches a glimpse of a person of disappearing. It darts out of sight in the twinkling of an eye and invariably its meteor flight is downstream. The hapara is the young of the grayling and is little bigger than a smelt yet inherited instincts are strong and it does the same disappearing trick that marks its parents. It is a very delicate morsel as if it is caught one day it must be eaten the same day. The Maori says it is not eatable next day as it goes into a jelly or mash whose Maori name my informant had forgotten.

The habit of the grayling in darting away when it sees a biped on the bank struck the Maori as very unsportsmanlike so he sought a means to circumvent such an unreasonable characteristic. Sometimes a shoal of upokororo will heke upstream but my informant had never heard any reason for this fact. If a man saw a shoal anywhere in a river he would back away from the bank with quietness and celerity and hasten away to inform his companions. These would put nets [of the kind known as kaka and described in both Murihiku and Canterbury notes.

H.B.] under the first or second shallow (waipapaku) below where the fish had been noticed and would quietly hold them there against the force of the current. (Westland rivers are prodigal of rapids). Then a man would walk up to where the grayling were opposite and the scared fish would dart off downstream and right into the nets of the men waiting for them. Another way my informant had heard of catching upokororo when they were in shoals was to make a drain (awa awa) with a hole (parua) and they would follow the current into the hole. The mouth of the drain was then blocked (puru) and as no more water came in the rest drained or dried away leaving the poor grayling stranded on dry land. This way is reminiscent of one method of catching eels in Canterbury but my informant had never heard it given a name in Westland.

Add to Fish

The people of the West Coast, said one of my informants, caught the mataa or whitebait in the same ways as the Canterbury people did. They would get them by the kohao method – placing a koko or very closely-woven net or basket on a long stick and kohao the tiny fish out of the rivers and creeks up which they were swarming in apparently endless lines. As an alternative or an addition to this method they would place a basket facing downstream and in the morning lift it out well-laden. The basket was open-mouthed and had no contrivance to hold the mataa prisoner but they would swim into it and fiddle away inside it for hours. The stronger the current the more they remained in the basket and he had known them to stick there all night.

He had not seen sharks nor octopi caught and did not know about them.

Add to Fish

The upokororo (grayling) was a shy fish, said the third of the collector's three informants regarding Westland, and its young were called haparu. These fish are caught in the shallows with 'scrim' since the Pakeha came, and before that with flax nets (as detailed previously). He knew very little about the inaka (minnow) and its migrations. There was no kelp on most of the West Coast so the inaka could not spawn among it there. The people would sometimes drag nets from boats for flounders (patiki) or would spear them by torchlight in the Arahura River. He had seen old Kere (Kelly the Pakeha called him) at Maitahi (Bruce Bay in South Westland) use a handy spear he had made himself. It had a bone hook at one end to gaff eels while the other end had a hard, black point (of some material unknown to the narrator) lashed on with whitau. This end effectively speared flounders. The whole spear was well and truly made and its neat workmanship reflected credit on its maker and owner. The old man used both ends with skill and adroitness. Another informant said he had never seen the inaka spawning anywhere. The West Coast was mostly a long sandy beach without kelp but observation of the migrations of the minnow was prevented (in his day, at least) by the fact that sluicing had rendered the streams too muddy to see the fish in them.

Add to Eels

My third informant said he had caught eels over in Westland (where he was born and reared). The 'bob' there, he thought, was called putiti, and not punoke as in Canterbury, and the stick which held it was called matire. The bob was tied to the end of the stick. When you felt a tug, the art of 'bobbing' was to ease off a little and then as the stick began to twist in your hands you would know its teeth were firm in the toothsome 'bob' and then you gently work it upward toward you. Do not wildly heave it over your shoulder but pull eel straight to you and quietly deposit it in the parua (hole) by your side and patu (kill or stun) it with a heavy stick or waddy. Sometimes you would get two, and sometimes three, eels on your bob at one time but he knew no Maori name for such luck. If the bank was not suitable to make a parua into which to drop your catch (and often in densely wooded Westland it was not suitable) a simple but ingenious plan to hold 'Brer Eel' was adopted. A rohe consisting of a waha or mouth of piritia (supplejack) and a body of net (made of whitau) would be placed in the stream and the eels caught would be dropped into it. The mouth of the rohe is on water-level but the eels keep down below the surface and will not escape from it. A stone or two will keep the net taut at first. The 'bobber' shakes the eels off into the rohe, and lifts it and bears it away at the conclusion of his sport. Narrator said he knew nothing about the spawning of eels. The rivers in Westland had not closed mouths like so many Canterbury Rivers so the eels (and other fish) had free passage in and out at all times. [Under the heading 'Fish' see description of an 'eel gaff' which my informant saw in remote South Westland. H.B.]

[[SECTION XVII: ORNITHOLOGY]]

BIRDS (WESTLAND)

In his Canterbury Notes last trip the collector got a lot of good information re wekas or woodhens. The man who gave that welcome korero (talk), on this trip informed the collector that almost all that he had said about wekas was derived from the old people in Westland where he lived during the mid-eighties. At that time the Maoris used guns to shoot pigeons and other birds. Kiwis and kakapos were not then about Arahura and Hokitika but were in the bush further South. Another man who spent some of his youthful days in Westland said he had been down near Okarito and on a sandbank which was almost an island he had seen the kotuku (white heron) breeding. There must have been about sixty of them or so in that locality. He understood that they usually nested in trees like some of the shags did, but here they had their nests, which seemed to be sticks, in the sand. The female birds sat on the eggs and he was greatly struck with the sight of the males stalking majestically round the nests in a big circle one after another like a file of soldiers. They were presumably on guard. He wished to go there and inspect the place better and closer but old Keri Tutoko would not allow him, saying the place was tapu. Down in the Fiords there was said to be a certain tree which was the only tree the kotuku settled on. *[Note: My informant and I met the young Maori who had told him this. The young fellow had been in Preservation Inlet and had seen the particular tree the birds settled on, and had seen them on it, but he did not know the name of that tree nor what kind it was. He had seen kotuku round Inlet but there were no nests there that he knew of, nor did he know where they bred. H.B.]**

Round on the West Coast, continued my informant, he had seen the koka (crow) come round travellers' heads hovering about like fantails, so perhaps if the people of old ate them they knocked them over with sticks. [Strange to say my informant said he had never heard the beautiful, mellifluous notes of the koka. He seemed surprised to hear it had such a reputation. H.B.] He did not know how the kakapo had been caught in the old days but when he was there it was hunted with dogs on moonlight nights. You could hear them 'booing' at certain seasons. Tutoko's dogs were smart but were not quick enough to prevent him bagging one in a net on the end of a long stick and he brought it to Canterbury and kept it as a pet for months. It lived on raw potatoes and scraps, etc. Round on the Coast when you saw the flax chewed into strips you knew the kakapos were about. The kiwi round there laid a tremendous egg for its size and the old Maoris told him it took the bird six months or more to hatch the 'whoppers' it had laid. Calling birds by blowing with leaf in mouth was called whakapipi in Westland. Wekas would be caught by using two sticks. The short one (paruru) would have a branch tied to it (or after the pakeha came, a red rag) and would be shaken to bring the inquisitive bird near. The long stick (paihere) had a noose and when bird's head was in this the snarer thrust the stick forward instead of pulling it upward. If he did the latter the bird's foot would come up like lightning and it would probably kick the noose off, but the skilful manipulator brought the tautening of the cord from the rear of the bird and so prevented such a manoeuvre.

He had seen the pigeon nest in ti (cabbage-trees) at Okarito, Westland (and also the pakura nest on mikimiki shrub at Martinborough, North Island). He wondered if the parera (grey duck) carried its young away as he had seen the young hatching and gone back in fifteen minutes to find all had gone. This would happen even if the nest was under a tussock and no cover near.

Add to Birds

My third informant on Westland matters once paid a visit to Mahitahi (Bruce Bay) and to Jackson Bay (whose Maori name he had never heard). There is a kaik at Bruce Bay (the most isolated Maori settlement in New Zealand) and it took him three days on horseback to reach it from Hokitika. He had seen the white heron (kotuku) on his travels, but did not know how it was caught. When he was at Mahitahi (or Maitahi) pigeons were shot with guns but he saw the inquisitive weka (woodhen) being caught with a noose on a stick but he forgot the Maori names of these. The longer stick had a slip-noose at its end and a shorter stick with something dangling on it was used to attract the bird as is customary in this time-honoured method of snaring this bird.

[[SECTION XVIII: ENTOMOLOGY]]

EDIBLE GRUBS

Over on the West Coast the big, white, fat, timber grubs were found plentifully, usually in the matai (black pine). They were called tuka, or sometimes uhu [a form of North Island huhu. H.B.] and were either eaten raw or cooked as the fancy of finder dictated.

THE TUATARA

One of the collector's two principal informants re Westland in mentioning that the old Maoris there told him that it took the kiwi bird at least six months to hatch its eggs, continued, 'And they also told me it took the tuatara seven years to hatch its eggs but I could not swallow this latter fact.' The tuatara, he added, lived on a rock island in the ocean near to Okarito. He had not seen them but he was told they were 'fine big fellows'.

[[SECTION XX: BOTANY]]

PLANTS

Houhou a shrub about nine feet high was very common in Westland. Its leaves were, if I understood aright, like the five fingers of a hand. My informant said the railway station called 'Hoho' was named after it (Another corruption of

Maori names round there, he added, was the siding Te Kinga which should be Te Kainga). Going over to the West Coast via Arthur Pass and Otira Gorge he had seen the mountain lily and the mountain daisy and the Westland folk said these were called Tikapu and Tikumu respectively. He had heard old Mrs Mutu speak of these and other names. He had never heard of anise nor of the plant 'vegetable sheep', and he thought musk was an 'importation'. Mokimoki was a fine fern which scented the ground – it might be the New Zealand musk. He had only seen it on a visit to the North Island – perhaps the South Island was too cold for it.

The hinau tree used to grow on Banks Peninsula at Little River (Wairewa) once but it still grows in Westland. He never knew the berries of it to be eaten at either place, but on the West Coast the wild pigs certainly fattened on hinau berries.

The pakehas on the West Coast called the poka or ponga treefern, the 'bungi' or 'bungey'. They made fencing posts that would last for ever practically and when cut down, re-grew from stump. As far as he knew the Maoris ate no part of the ponga.

He never heard of haumata grass nor of a berry or plant called rerewa.

The horseshoe fern or parareka did not grow in the South Island – only the North.

Add to Plants

My third informant on Westland said that over on the West Coast he had noticed silver and yellow pines which he had not seen on Eastern side of South Island but he forgot their Maori names. Over there he had eaten miro berries as a boy and other berries whose names he forgot.

Another informant said that flax grew along the rivers in Westland so that the people of old had this inestimable boon as well as had the more open centres where one expected better flax, than in bush country. He had never heard any criticism on the quality of the flax there.

[[SECTION XXI: METEOROLOGY]]

WEATHER LORE

One of my informants said that he recollected hearing the older people in Westland say that the kahukura (rainbows) were a sign to the Maoris. If you were going a journey and one faced you it was a bad sign = stay at home; but if it was parallel to your projected route it was a good sign = haere (proceed). A number of Natives were coming across to Canterbury (via Otira and Arthur's Pass) and an old lady would not come as a rainbow lay athwart the road to the Mountains. She implored the others to desist but the young men (narrator included) set out and had a good trip across in splendid weather. Later when the old lady judged the signs more propitious she set out but had an extremely unpleasant time through heavy rains and storms. The old people used to judge the prospects of seasons by observing the flowering of plants, abundance of koradi sticks, etc., but my informants were unable to supply this lore.

[[SECTION XXIII: MYTHOLOGY]]

MYTHOLOGICAL

*A very ancient tradition (or 'yarn' as my informant gravely termed it) says that a Maori ancestor called Tama-taku-ariki [not Tamatea-pokai-whenua, the captain of Takitimu, as sometimes stated, although there is no doubt Tamatea explored the Southern Fiords. H.B.] searched the West Coast for his missing wife. He started at Nelson and went as far as Milford Sound at least (if not further) and being unsuccessful returned and according to my informant found her in the North Island [See Murihiku Notes. H.B.]. He was wearing a pokeka or raincoat of rough texture and in the haste and eagerness of his search, shreds and fragments of this coat were torn off by the clinging vegetation and held. These shreds eventually fell to the ground where they germinated and grew as the kiekie tree – a mythological name for which is Te Pokeka-a-Tama. This frantic navigator did not come to the East Coast of the South Island at all, hence there is no kiekie to be found on that side but only on the wild and rugged West Coast whose shores he examined for his lost wahine.**

VISIT TO BRUCE BAY IN 1908 OR 1909. MAORI ACCOUNT

Mrs Jacobs, of Morven, in March 1936 told me that twenty seven or twenty eight years earlier she had visited Westland. There was then no Maoris at Jackson's Bay, but some at Maitahi; spoke English as a rule. Now only two or three families still there. Her husband came from there and married her and lived here until Rawiri te Maire, her grandfather, died and then they went on a visit to Westland to her husband's father, Hakopa Kaapo (she spelt it). This man was born on the East Coast, but married a Katitoa woman of Westland and he settled there after his marriage, although she thought the Katitoa had no interest south of Mafera (Greymouth).

At Makawhio they grew kumera and she saw them. The taro grew too. It is like the kumera but longer; it is like the artichoke but with a darker skin.

There were plenty of birds, such as ka-ka-po, kivi, and koko (or tui).

Their ways, she thought, were different to here – far more Maorified. The Maoris here cook in ranges or in camp ovens and bread is baked in either, but over there she found them baking it in the ashes like damper and calling it kornuka. They laughed at her when she mentioned umu and said it was not done there, although one or two of the older people had seen it operating elsewhere – but not in South Westland.

Some of the huts were of poka ferntree and thatched with wiwi rushes, of which there were acres growing higher than her height. Some huts were copied from Pakeha and were of wood, roofed with tin. They had mats for sleeping in and pokeka mats as rainproof coats. She thought most were away from Makawhio but that a few still lived at Maitahi. When she was there some spoke good English, but there was also a lot of Maori talk and she considered they had a more Maorified outlook than in South Canterbury.

She heard no talk of taniwha there but one in Marlborough. At Oaro creek there is a hole haunted by a taniwha, whose name she forgot. At top end is clear water and at the bottom end, the same, but the centre of the pool is a bright vivid green – an emerald green. At times there is scarcely any water and it is safe. At other times it is full and unsafe as the water shoots up and down again like a spring in action and shows the presence of the taniwha.

APPENDICES

APPENDIX 1

Edited remains from first draft of Murihiku volume

Section
- I   Habitations and Buildings 537
- II   Clothing 539
- III   Flaxwork 540
- IV   Personal Adornment 540
- V   Paints, Dyes, and Scents 541
- VI   Face-carving and Wood-carving 543
- VII   Games and Music 543
- VIII   Medical Lore 544
- IX   Disposal of the Dead 544
- X   Customs 545
- XI   Weapons 546
- XII   Greenstone 547
- XIII   Canoes, etc. 550
- XIV   Domestic Science 551
- XV   'Ichthyology', etc., Fishes and Fishing 551
- XVII   'Ornithology', Birds and Birding 552
- XVIII   'Entomology', etc., Insects, Worms and Lizards 553
- XX   'Botany', etc., Trees and Plants, Vegetation, Herbage 553
- XXII   The Religious Element 554
- XXIII   Mythology 555
- XXIV   Superstition, Wizardry 565
- XXV   Folk-Tales and Sayings 567
- XXVI   History Jottings 568
- XXVIII   Names of Things, Contact with Pakehas 570

APPENDIX 2

Glossary of Names for Flora and Fauna 579

APPENDIX 1

EDITED REMAINS FROM FIRST DRAFT OF MURIHIKU VOLUME

SECTION I

HABITATIONS AND BUILDINGS

Add to Whares

One old man in telling a story about Maui, who was projecting darts along the beach with his brothers, said the legend went on to say the dart went so far and so strongly that it broke the gable-end of his father's house. He thought it was rubbish to say a boy's dart could split a big board but of course Maui's atua could do so easily enough.

*At Temuka {the collector was told that in a chief's house there used to be four mainposts as a rule.}.**

The name of the meeting-house at Temuka (European workmanship) is Te Hapa-o-Niu-Tireni and it implies that in the payment for New Zealand some of the Maoris were passed by and their claims neglected. The road through the kaika at Temuka is called Huirapa after the Kaitahu-Katimamoe ancestor of that name.

The old Maori kaika of Moeraki was not at the present township nor on the site of the whaling station at One-kakara but was on the opposite side of the little peninsula and facing South. The only buildings now on the Reserve are the little Native Church and a well-built Hall. This Hall (European made) is called Uenuku (after the son of Paikea) and the attached kitchen is called _____ after the wife of Uenuku. The Maoris did not have streets as we do, so every dip, eminence or point had a name for convenience sake, and the spot on which the hall is built was called Tahuri-korari. The old kaika of Moeraki was not fortified but there was a pa (Te-Raka-a-Hine-Atea) on a hill near Katiki (Nga-Tiki) three miles away.

A European who came to Southland in January 1857 says the Maoris at Riverton built his parents a house of ferntrees and clay. They made it in two days but it stood thirty years. (It is said the whalers showed the Maoris the use of clay or 'cob'.) Another European tells me that in the Waiau Valley in 1868 a Maori (from Colac Bay) made the diggers three excellent huts of totara bark.

He cut two niches round a tree six or eight feet apart as required, then made a slit between them, and patiently and skilfully worked off the bark with a sharp stick, getting an unbroken roll which he put on a framework. (It was a woeful waste of good trees, as the trees died.)

According to the muttonbirders the climate down on the islands is noticeably milder than the mainland [they were all shivering when the collector saw them about the Bluff].

[Relevant to the Maoris having carved figures of ancestors against the poutokomanawa of the big whares, the two old Maoris who visited the Otago Museum with the collector took a great fancy to the two figures there and Rehu named the one near the cases Tukoroua after a forebear of his – a titi island south of Stewart Island is named after him – while Kurupohatu named the one near the door Te Ruawai after his ancestor who fought at Lake Kaitangata.]

Add to Buildings

At Moeraki the hall was called Uenuku but he did not remember the name of the kitchen attached to it. At Waikouaiti the hall is called after Huirapa and the kitchen after his wife, Maririhau; and other places also had their places of assembly.

FORTS

The collector has not yet gathered definite information about pas and pa-construction but in his notes finds several items which may be given here although they are not very connected.

One old man said: 'At the mouth of Buchanan's Creek, Willowbridge, (South Canterbury) there was a proper pa but no fighting occurred there that I know. My father planted some greenstone on its site but on going back years later could not find a trace of it. It was all ploughed and he could scarcely recognise the place. The name of the pa was Te-Kai-a-Te-Atua and it was called after another pa of the same name at Kaiapoi.'

An old woman said: 'Mary Hill, at Waihola, was called Poutakahiamaru. There was a pa there once. Some miles distant is Ram Island, now called Jeffries' Farm and where the farmer has a pump once stood the pa, Whakaraupuka.'

An old man in speaking of the North end of Stewart Island said the Pa of Tukete was at Raggedy. A beach inside Gull Rock was known as Te Pa-whakataka which meant 'to prepare a pa' but he had never heard the origin of the name. One Maori in describing a fight said that one warrior bounded on to the patatara (of a pa).

Another man mentioned the Te-Raka-a-Hine-Atea pa at Kartigi and the collector tried to find out the origin and meaning of the name and also the names of the gateways but could get no particulars whatever. [Named after Maui's father and latter's mother.]

Add to Fortifications

One kaumatua said: 'Pas were at Pahi's (near Orepuki), Preservation Inlet and Stewart Island down this way. When I was up at Temuka I saw part of the Waiateruati pa near there.'

Three of my informants remembered the old pa at Tau-o-te-maku on Ruapuke Island: 'I remember when a small boy seeing the great rimu posts with men with pawa eyes carved on top. How did those great posts get there as the virgin bush is two miles away? *They were set in about ten feet apart and a man was carved on top of each.** An old man and woman, Ohua and Te Hiki, were then living in it.'

'In Rauparaha's time rumors of the fight coming to Ruapuke caused the pa to be built. Poupou were placed in the ground and kaho (battens) lashed on. Two gates, whose names I do not know, had men's faces carved on the posts. It was never completed as Hinehaka, a prophetess, told them to stop work.'

I have seen the remains of the pa at Ruapuke. There were big posts (poupourahi) at intervals and some were carved but I do not recollect the details. The posts were thicker than a large telegraph pole and there was a good area of ground inside the pa of Tau-o-te-maku.'

SECTION II

INFORMATION RELATING TO CLOTHING

Add to Clothing

One woman told the collector that her father, who died some years ago, used to wear an old pokeka as a raincoat. It was a long, bushy one and as he was over six feet high, he looked quite imposing in it. What became of it she does not know but she has not seen it for years.

A rip near Dog Island is called Takai-pokeka (roll up your raincoat) and he thought it was named because the breakers rolled over the hu (spit) like a pokeka being rolled up.

Heretatua (tie belt) at Rakiura is named because after a canoe wreck a man swam to a rocky face, tied his belt to a projecting tree and clambered ashore.

The collector asked what, exactly, the kauheke was, and the 'mine of information' replied it was a kind of houi (ribbonwood). It was a small sort, and its dark skin (kiri) could be stripped (tihore) and its inside skin chewed as a food, but he thought that to say its leaves could be worn in the hair was a yarn. The people would wear a circlet (kopare) of kakaha leaves for those who died in war. The kiri, or bark, of those two trees – kauheke and houi – were the only ones so used as far as he could recollect.

SECTION III

INFORMATION RELATING TO FLAXWORK

Add to Flax-work

While the collector was chatting at Puketiraki, two of the tauas (grandmothers) were scraping flax and thereafter one continued steadily, swiftly and deftly plaiting (rereka) flax baskets to hold potatoes and such things. Some small, dainty whitau baskets she was executing for a lady in England, who had been kind to some district Maori soldiers at Home, were splendid examples of such work.

SECTION IV

INFORMATION RELATING TO PERSONAL ADORNMENT

Add to Ornaments

An old man said: 'My grandfather, whom I remember well, used to tie up his hair in a koukou and stick a heru in it.'

*At Temuka is also preserved a long straight hei made in the old days.** Its name is Kahotea – probably because it is made of the kind of greenstone of that name.

HEI-TIKI

The plough turned up an ancient heitiki years ago at Pakihi-kawai (Georgetown, near Temuka) and it was now in the possession of the people at Otakou (Otago Heads). An old saying ran: 'Matua hine i whaka-rakatira i tane, ma te tane i whaka-rakatira te wahine' (means – a girl of low rank becomes high-class by marrying a chief and a common man is elevated by marrying a chieftainess). If such a girl was betrothed to a chief and was given a heitiki to wear she became tapu.

SECTION V

INFORMATION RELATING TO PAINTS, DYES AND SCENTS

KAKARA OR PERFUMES

PAINTS

{*The 'mine of information' narrated: 'Our red paint is made from what you call haematite and we call maukoroa.} A man dreamt it was to be found in the hills at Kaitangata and he woke and went to the place he saw in his dream.** If you dream and go to sleep again you will forget the places seen in the dream but this man got up and went straight to the spot and marked it. The maukoroa is not a clay but is dug out of the hill like the form of a man and the place where the heart would be is the purest maukoroa and is for the best people. Once, very long ago, a maeroero took a woman away. The husband of the latter followed and rescued the woman. To keep her safe at night he tied her to a tree but the maero again got her. The man made a house and painted it red and painted all the trees around red too. Then he recovered his wife and the two went to the house and painted themselves red. The maero came looking for the woman and he looked in the hole in the top of the whare and he saw the two people sitting there all red. So he sat on top of the whare and sang a song and went away. The man took his wife home and was not bothered with the maero again. [Note: The old man sung the song said to have been sung by the maero and the collector has a copy of it.]

Add to Paints

*A Maori said to the collector: 'Haemetite or maukoroa is found in various places, one of these being a cliff on Huriawa Peninsula, near Waikouaiti. It was taken out of the cliff and was first burnt and then was ground down. Oil from the ate (liver) of the shark was mixed with the powder and formed a lasting paint.** Some Europeans saw the maukoroa cliff and knew it should make good paint and took the haemetite and mixed it with linseed oil but it was not a success. It soon washed off the houses on which it was put. *Shark oil is the only successful thing to mix with it but the white man won't catch the sharks to make a real, good paint so the maukoroa is not used to-day. I have seen whata legs at Purakaunui painted red with it – probably to preserve them.** The maukoroa at Huriawa has quite a wide reputation – so good is it that some years ago when the church officials decided to paint the Maori Church at Otaki in the North Island they sent a man down to Otago especially to procure the red haematite from the cliff near Waikouaiti.'

Near Port Molyneux {a flat stone is said to have been used as a 'table' on which to pound the maukoroa.}

Add to Dyes

None of the collector's informants had heard of a tree called makatoatoa from which dye is stated to have been made. At Puketiraki the collector was told that 'The toatoa is a small tree which grows on Mount Cargill.'

At Temuka the collector was told: 'We never heard of the makatoatoa but from the toatoa we got reddish-brown (whero) dye.'

[In regard to word aroaro the collector said he thought it meant the front of anything and he was told it had that meaning also. If a person had his back turned you would hear the saying 'Huri mai tou aroaro' (turn your front) but the front of a cliff was akanui – 'te pari akanui mai' (the cliff faces toward us). What the North Island Maori calls 'red-hot' the collector cannot say.1

SCENTS

The people from the Te-kai-a-te-Atua pa at Willowbridge had gone to Waimatemate (now called Waimate) and the women went out one evening and singed the taramea but in the morning could find no juice. The men in a jocular mood had forestalled them by getting up early and surreptitiously removing the juice. Hence the hill to the south side of the Kapua-hurihia gorge at Waimate is now called Urutane (men's gathering or collecting).

Add to Perfumes and Scents

The old taua (grandmother – she is a great-grandmother) from Henley said that Kopuru moss grew at Otago Heads {kopuru is a fine moss which grows on rocks.}. It grows at Roaring Bay, near The Nuggets, and has a pleasant scent.

SECTION VII

FACE-CARVING AND WOOD-CARVING

Add to Tattoo

Happening to ask an old man if the Maori name of Green Island was Popotea or Papatea (both forms are used) he replied: {'The name is Papatea'}.

Add to Tattooing

The collector was told that all who were tattooed in the tuhi method were jocularly called 'ka hipi o John Topi' John Topi's sheep). John Topi was the head chief of Ruapuke and Stewart Island and this style of tattooing was jokingly said to be his brand. This would seem to imply it was confined to the extreme south of New Zealand when the white people came.

SECTION VII

INFORMATION RELATING TO GAMES AND MUSIC

Add to Games

*The well-informed kaumatua had not much to say re games: 'We call a race pure but sports are kahau. Wi is a kind of game of the prisoners' base style with plenty of running and when I was a boy I have even seen the men playing at it.'**

Add to Musical

Pu means a call or blowing a noise and Pakeha guns were so-called. Once upon a time, just after the people round Foveaux Strait had got a musket or two they went up to fight the Canterbury people near Banks Peninsula. The latter Maoris heard the Southerners were coming with pu and thought these were trumpets. At Little River one taunted the invaders: 'Go back and rear children for us to kill.' A Southerner up with the pu (gun) and shot the taunter dead. His body rolled down the cliff and his startled mates fled from the new pu which could not only make a noise but kill men as well.

SECTION VIII

INFORMATION RELATING TO MEDICAL LORE

MEDICINAL LORE

'Old Bill', a Kanaka who died on Ruapuke thirty years ago, prided himself on being a great 'native doctor' and he used goai extensively.

Add to Medical Lore

He did not know who the ancient Tukete was, but a modern man of this *name lived on Rakiura (Stewart Island) some eight or nine generations ago and was prodigiously fat. He suffered from papapuni, a stoppage of the action of the bowels for which narrator** had heard no cure and did not think there was one. He could not 'ka riro ki te tiko' (go *and evacuate his bowels) but got some relief from 'spewing' (ruaki). When he was killed his slayers got four or five baskets of fat from his body. Narrator had never heard of another case of real papapuni save the historical one of Tukete.**

POISONS

The mine of information said that when he was a young man he worked for a pakeha who made tutu wine and very good it was as well as being non-intoxicating. The berries were not found on the tree species of tutu, only on the plant. Pukoro was the name of the flax bag through which the berries were wrung.

SECTION IX

INFORMATION RELATING TO DISPOSAL OF THE DEAD

DISPOSAL OF THE DEAD

In the old kaika at Moeraki there are four burial grounds. The first is Tawhiroko on a hill, the next is Uhimataitai on the Tutakahikura beach, the next is Kikipuku near the Uenuku Hall while the fourth is at the church and is called Kawa. In addition there is on Tikoraki Point a 'Halfcaste Cemetery' of whaling days. The Maoris here were in the habit of burying the personal effects and bedding with the corpses until quite recently but a happening some years ago has made them chary of doing so. A Maori who had bought a new outfit just shortly before his death was buried with his clothes and bedding as was customary. That night a European dug up the grave and was thereafter seen wearing the hat, suit and boots of deceased and presumably was also using the dead man's blankets. Now after the burial a funeral pyre is made of the deceased's clothes, pillow, bedding, etc. This is also done at some other centres.

The same kaumatua before entering the urupa not only deposited his smoking requisites on the ground outside but sprinkled his shoulders and hands with a greenish fluid which had been made by the bark of the goai (kohai) being steeped in water. This sprinkling, he gravely remarked, was a very old custom but no more information was forthcoming.

Add to Disposal of the Dead

A man told the collector that there was a burial cave called by the name Whakare-ka-iwi (throw away the bones) and situated near Otago Heads.

SECTION X

INFORMATION RELATING TO CUSTOMS

CUSTOMS

*A European to air his knowledge of North** Island Maori said to a Southern woman 'Hei konei ra' (farewell). Now in the South 'konikoni' means to go on all fours and crawl, and the woman looked at the pakeha puzzled-like and then replied indignantly 'No! I won't go crawling about for you or anybody else.'

And one lady of the collector's acquaintance is proud of the fact that her father was a 'whaka-tutane' from the Kai-Tahu chief, Tuahuriri.

Pregnancy: What customs were adopted during this period by women the collector cannot say except that he was told for a time before the expected arrival the expectant mother must not wear clothing belonging to another woman. What would happen if she did was not stated but it would clearly be something very unlucky.

Tapu: This great institution of the old days still carries weight although now tinged with pakeha innovations. A European who went to Riverton in 1857 says his mother gathered dry mikimiki wood off a Maori burial ground and burnt some. There was great consternation among the Maoris and under their chief Paroro they considered this descecration of the 'taputapu'. In the end the Maoris made his mother take the unburnt wood and replace it on the ground. When his family left the house lent them in the Kaik no Maori would go into it and it fell to pieces of decay.

After that Matiaha, the chief, installed a big, iron printing press in it and it was thereafter called whare-parehe (parehe = press) but it still kept its tapu character. No food was allowed in it – Matiaha and his assistants ate outside. They said karakia when they came out of the whare-tapu. It was Matiaha's intention to print a Maori history, etc., but he died before the idea was carried out, and the whare was left tapu – deserted. It stood near the present Hall {and some years ago some Maori larrikins burnt it down} as 'a lark', ruining the press.

Add to Customs

The 'mine of information' {had not heard that whistling was abhorrent to the people of old.}. A Waihao Maori [[H. te Maire]] {said he had heard that spittle could be makutu'd}.

The 'mine of information' said that in olden times, and now with the modern potato, planting was always done as near new moon as possible so that the crop would grow well. He had never heard of planting being done at the dark o' the moon. At te-toru-o-kara (the third night of the moon) in months of September and October is favorite time of planting even to this day. Another aged man [[H. te Maire]] said that things planted at new moon followed the example of the moons as they come up and grew well.

SECTION XI

INFORMATION RELATING TO WEAPONS

*Taiaha. Name of the head (usually carved) is arero. The head was te arero (the tongue).** {Stones} found on the gravel beaches at Waitahuna, at Pomahaka and elsewhere. One stone would be dashed on another and when broken this left sharp edges called mata and it was these mata edges which were used to scrape the embryo spear.

You could strike fire with kohairaki and after the Europeans came they were used as flints. *{The huata} made of manuka. Manawa threw a spear and killed the father of** Tukiauau, and Tuparitaniwha from a cliff speared Tuhokairaki just as the latter *reached the water. I can not say how far a spear was thrown in combat.' {The spear point} could be** driven through a two-inch board. Kaunia killed the chief Rakitauhopo with a timata which he threw at him when fighting was going on up the Waitaki Valley.' *Kaunia's spear point whistled when he made it and this was a good omen.**

Regarding the modern use of taiaha one woman said that in the fifties a fight was only just averted at Taiari and one old warrior was provocatively using a taiaha. An old chief in Canterbury who habitually used one as a staff nearly killed a policeman who threatened him with a revolver. The Maoris at Temuka presented Captain Halsey of H.M.S. New Zealand with a valued *old taiaha.**

One of the old men mentioned that before the big flood of 1868 he was in the Ohinetukutuku bush at Kaitangata and saw the stump of a big totara tree which had been felled by toki. The cuts showed it had been cut by an expert who was both deft and strong.

Add to Weapons

*A well-informed kaumatua said 'I never heard of the toki-titaha.** Titaha means sidewise, (aronui is in front), so toki-titaha must be an axe for *chopping.** ... Although I have never heard the term toki-titaha I have no doubt some trees *would be easier cut with such a thing than with an adze. The toki was also used as a weapon for the history tells us that Tu-te-makohu had a famous toki. I forget its name but** the Wesleys at Glenavy and the Waaka family at Temuka are his descendants and might know. When Tutemakohu died at Otaupiri the toki was buried and has never been found. Though the toki was *his weapon he killed Kaweriri with a pukahu (a stick sharp at both ends and used to spear** eels, bore holes or as a staff) which he picked up. I think his toki must have been straight like an axe. The history also says that Tirokotakanewha killed Kahutupuni (on Otago *Peninsula) with a toki.'**

SECTION XII

INFORMATION RELATING TO GREENSTONE

Pounemu or Greenstone — Oro or Polishing — Hoaka or Grindstone

GREENSTONE

*The collector was shown a piece of greenish stone which his ancient friend said was called matua-o-pounamu because according to legend it is the mother of greenstone.** It was sent him from Arahura. A man called Whakarewa a Katimamoe chief living at Te Awa-mokihi near Moeraki heard of Raureka's exploit in crossing the Southern Alps and he set out to find greenstone. Arrived at Arahura he dreamt he saw a woman (whose name the narrator forgot) in the water at a certain place. Next day he saw the place of his dream and looking he saw a piece of Matua and then the real pounemu. He and his men brought much greenstone back overland to their home, one valuable piece being two feet square but thin. The chief took ill and is said to have deposited the greenstone square in an adjacent lagoon. The narrator has seen the place but no one has found the store yet. After Whakarewa's trip people began to go over to Arahura on regular expeditions for the precious pounemu. My informant also had a small piece of koko-takiwai from Milford Sound which had been brought round to Murihiku to make into tautarika (earrings) but this had not been done.

Describing the stone hammer in the Otago Museum to two old men both declared they had never seen such a thing nor heard any name for it but both surmised it was meant for breaking pounemu. The patu-aruhe for beating fern-root was usually a stone or of wood but was not a hammer. *The kurupaka was the kind of stone used for breaking greenstone and the old people of a bygone generation said it was the only stone which would break pounemu.**

Another informant said that greenstone could be found in Mount Te Koloka (opposite Bucklerburn at Lake Wakatipu) at a cliff called Te Horo. It was just ordinary greenstone which was found there. *There were only two kinds of greenstone – kokotakiwai and pounemu** – and he did not know the names of the divisions of these. In old days there was a real pa at the mouth of Buchanan's Creek at Willowbridge and although there was no fighting at it greenstone was buried there. The pakeha ploughed over the site and destroyed the landmarks and the 'cache' has not been found.

Add to Greenstone

At Temuka the collector sought information relative to the pounemu or greenstone. As at other places they knew nothing regarding the 'headless figure' in the Otago Museum but suggested the head had been so poorly carved that it had been ground off in disgust and the place polished. *There were two main kinds of hoaka (grindstone) used, the coarse one being called hoaka-taratara and the finer one hoaka-manihi. The coarse one was used to take the edges off or for the rougher work while the fine whetstone could impart a polish. The old people used to put greenstone in the sea for the salt water to polish and they say it made a good job of it. Working greenstone on a hoaka is called oro but to place it in the sea to take the edges off and to polish is called mate-moana-e-oro. The pieces in the sea were tied to rocks and it was the swishing back and forward by the unceasing wash of the waves which accomplished the work. To split the pounemu (or to break it) my informants only knew of a long, tough stone called kauri.**

They went on to say that some of the old people had said the pounemu was originally a takata (man) and that others said it had been an ika (fish). In the latter contention the fish panako and pipiki *are mentioned as being famous fish of that time, being the only ones to swim over the hiku (tail) of the pounemu as it was lying in the bed of the stream. For this reason (because they were the only fish plucky enough to essay the feat) they have enjoyed a great reputation (and as far as the collector can gather were once regarded as sacred, the only fish apparently to enjoy such an honor). The panako is a kind of kokopu and the pipiki a kind of minnow. A song was made about this episode of which only the last line seems to be remembered, viz. 'Nana ika ke hiku o te taniwha'. The pounemu is here alluded to as a taniwha.** It is also said the pounemu was once a man who was subsequently turned into stone but nothing further seemed to be known on this topic.

An old man at the Bluff mentioned that he was descended from Raureka the woman who left Westland and arrived at the mouth of the Rakaia River in Canterbury where she told the people of the greenstone. Her sole companion on the trip was her tame kuri or dog. When the narrator was a young man he went round to the West Coast with others and they found some pounemu in the Gorge River, near Cascade. It was in the bed of the river and they broke up a lump of the pure stuff and brought it back to Murihiku. The greenstone found at Poison Bay, near Milford Sound, was better than that got in Milford. *Kokotakiwai, he scornfully added, was not considered a proper greenstone at all.**

The well-informed kaumatua said that he had heard the old people say that greenstone was once a people. The wives of Tama of the Tairea canoe cleared out and when their canoe was upset at the mouth of Arahura River they were turned into pounemu. According to what he had heard Raureka was the first one who brought greenstone to the East Coast.

In some old Maori manuscripts the collector copied the name is always written pounemu (not pounamu) as Te Wai Pounemu (the South Island). An old woman at Bluff had a long straight piece of (narrow) greenstone suspended on her breast. She said it was an au and that the kind of pounamu in it was kawakawa.

The 'mine of information' considered the collection of Mr Fels of Dunedin (of greenstone) far and away the best he had seen. *He said the old Maoris used the term waimarima to describe the beautiful color in the best pounemu. The well-informed kaumatua said that kurupakara was used to drill holes in greenstone. He never heard of a hei-matau.** The headless figure (in Museum) might have been made purposely to depict some chief killed that way.

Add to Greenstone

An Otago Heads Maori told the collector that when he was a young fellow he went shearing and ran across greenstone at two or three places. This was fifty years ago when he and several other Maoris mounted their nags and went shearing in the backblocks. Near Glade House, Te Anau, he noticed a block of takiwai and broke off a bit and took it away with him. It was a nice clear piece he had and you could see the sun through it. He also saw some in the water at Lake Manapouri. Then the party went to the head of Lake Wakatipu and while here he visited a quarry whose whereabouts had been preserved by tradition. It was through the bush from Kinloch and up a hillside where two landslips were but he did not know the name of the place. *The name of the kind of greenstone got from there, he understood, was aotea and it could be distinguished by certain cloudy defects in it. This was explained by a tradition which said the greenstone there was burnt once and bore marks or signs of the fire since.** The kokotakiwai was also procured in that locality. [Note: This old man as a visitor to the place where the collector saw the headless tiki [See Canterbury Notes] was shown that curiosity and at first said it was uri but soon amended his statement by saying it was of aotea from the 'burnt pounemu' mountain at Wakatipu. H.B.] After inspecting the old quarry at Kinloch the party continued their shearing tour to Wanaka and Hawea and then returned home by leisurely stages down the Waitaki River and the coast. In Dunedin he gave pieces of greenstone to two Englishmen (tourists) who were delighted to meet a pure-blood Maori and they gave him two return gifts – a beautiful stone from Mexico and a crystal from South Africa.

The collector was told of a beautiful toki of perfect greenstone found at Henley and sold to the then manager of the Bank of New South Wales at Dunedin for forty pounds.

Considering that the South Island is Te Wai-Pounemu the amount of information available from South Island sources about the greenstone is very meagre.**

SECTION XIII

INFORMATION RELATING TO CANOES, ETC.

HE RAKAU-WHAKAPAPA

Mr Richard Taiaroa, of Taumutu, when conversing with collector, *said his late father had owned a rakau-whakapapa (notched genealogical stick) which was said to be the only one in the South Island. Narrator had once seen it when taken by** his father to the Bank of New Zealand, Dunedin, where his father had it deposited with his greenstone curios and with valuable family papers. *It is three-sided and has a row of notches down each ridge twenty one on** one ridge, almost the same on another and five on remaining ridge if he recollected aright. It is still in the Bank at Dunedin (and if an illustration of it was desired for publication he would give an order to Banker to let such be taken).

SECTION XIV

INFORMATION RELATING TO DOMESTIC SCIENCE

Add to Cooking

The 'mine of information' said an umu was a proper earth-oven, a big thing, a finished production, but kohua, he understood was a North Island name for a small hole in the ground.

SECTION XVI

INFORMATION RELATING TO 'ICHTHYOLOGY', ETC. FISHES AND FISHING

The Southern Maoris called the cowfish – upokohue and the {porpoise terehu.}
   Add to Crabs and Crayfish and Shellfish
   The kakahi, he continued, was the only shellfish he knew in inland waters and was formerly very plentiful in streams on the Waimea Plain. The Waikakahi River (now called Waikaka) near Gore, was so-called by the ancient Maori because its bed was liberally besprinkled with kakahi.

SEALS AND SEALING

My informant narrated a laughable occurrence. A nice sand beach near Kakanui was the resort of whakahau and one day one was up on the beach. Two Maoris broke an eight foot rail off a fence but they could not hit the sealion so they lassoed it and tied the rope to another rope lying handy. This latter was round a horse's neck and before they could intervene (if they could have done so for laughing) the horse was pulled into the sea. A tug-of-war ensued but the rope broke near the horse and the sealion continued out to sea 'with one and a half ropes on him' as my informant said.

SECTION XVII

INFORMATION RELATING TO 'ORNITHOLOGY', BIRDS AND BIRDING

Another man said the morepork was regarded with superstition. He thought nothing of this until the following incident occurred. Two other young fellows and he were sleeping on a cutter in a lonely part of Stewart Island near a precipitous bush-clad shore. They had just got into bed when they heard a morepork calling and coming nearer and nearer until it alighted on a moonlit piece of the deck. *Here it called 'peo-peo, ko-u, ko-u' until they became scared.** They agreed to rise together and did so, my informant hurling a tomahawk at it but missing it. It soared up and away. At daybreak next morning an old Maori who lived three miles away rowed up and demanded 'Why did you try to kill the ruru last night?' They were astonished and asked how he came to think they tried to do such a thing but all he would say was 'I know'. As he rowed away they remembered it was currently reported that an owl was his atua and that is the only explanation they ever got of the mystery. *An old woman said: {'The white titi is a sign of death.'}**

Add Birds

*An old woman said the ruru (morepork) was an uncanny bird, at least those which were atuas were to be avoided.** ... of impending events and went on to relate an incident where she said one such** atua bird had tried to warn her. She and another woman were sleeping in a round whare with a hole in the centre of the roof and this bird settled there and began to talk to them. They could not understand what it wanted to tell and presently *it scolded them and then left. They were in a tension of nervous excitement for some time after but gradually quietened down. Next day two of their relatives were drowned.**

Add to Birds

The old people sang at tangis in the kaiks a song, one line of which was 'Huna kutuku te huna te moa te huria te tipua.'

At one time in the Kaik he had a dish of sparrows to eat and they tasted all right. Imported vermin had done more to kill out the Native Birds than all other causes. The ferrets had killed the birds and then the rabbits had killed the ferrets (indirectly). Ferrets like a varied diet and when the Native birds were done they had to live on rabbits only and got the mange. The last he saw some years ago were all mangy. The weka, which was the finest ratter ever he saw, could beat a ferret in a fair fight but the wretches sneaked behind and jumped on the bird's back and so got at its neck. [Note: This informant's description of bird-snaring methods is given in a paper by H.B. [[1920b]] in *Transactions of the New Zealand Institute*. H.B.]

The old lady from Henley told the collector the people from there made {*a habit from time immemorial up to about fifty years ago of going inland in the due** season after wekas.}

SECTION XVIII

INFORMATION RELATING TO 'ENTOMOLOGY', ETC., INSECTS – WORMS AND LIZARDS

One old man said he did not know about tree lizards but at Kaikaiawaru near Puwai landing on *South Cape Island (a muttonbird isle) {he saw a black lizard}. Another old man said {the hairy lizards were known of old as moko-tua-huruhuru}.**

An early settler told the collector he had never seen the two-feet long lizards, but he had seen tree lizards. *He was once bushfelling with a Queenslander at Henley and in removing the bark of a tree a** lizard appeared. His mate shouted 'goanna' and killed it at once thinking it was harmful. A neighbor of his says he has *seen the tuatara lizard at Owaka within the last few years.**

SECTION XX

INFORMATION RELATING TO 'BOTANY', ETC., TREES AND PLANTS, VEGETATION, HERBAGE

*The collector's introduction to the subject of potatoes as edibles from a Maori standpoint was in this wise.** One old man asked him what he would call a mountain pass and he replied he thought 'kopi' was the word. 'No,' was the answer, 'tarahaka is a pass; noti is a narrowing in a range, but kopi. You not know what kopi is. Kopi is potatoes left in water till they are soft and rotten. My Golly! They have an awful – what you call it – pong!' *The Maoris at Temuka said: 'Kopi is the taewa or mahetau left in a spring or running water for four to six weeks according to the quality of the water.'**

In a roomful of Maoris one young man said he had seen the vegetable sheep plant when mustering on Pakati (Mount White). He doubted if the old Maoris had ever seen it as there were no ovens (umu) there at that height, but an old Maori said the people of old traversed all the ranges and although he had never seen the 'vegetable sheep' he had seen ovens on the summit of Wairuaapo (Lammerlaws, in Otago). The old lady from Henley said she remembered camping on Strath-Taieri when a girl.

SECTION XXII

INFORMATION RELATING TO THE RELIGIOUS ELEMENT

Add to The Tuahu, etc.

Although not definitely connected with tuahu procedure another note may be added here. Going through his notes of bygone years the collector notices that he has twice been told that the pile of rocks to one side of the Waimumu Gorge was a sacred place resorted to for worship in olden days. If not exactly resorted to by those at a distance travellers passing within hail went there to karakia. The name of this spot is apparently forgotten. One informant continued: 'On the other side of Hokanui there is a mass of rocks near where the Otamatea runs into the Mataura. [Near Stony Creek. H.B.] These rocks had names. One had an uncommon name – a curious name I always thought, but I cannot recall it just now. It was a resting-stone for travellers.' From this it appears there was nothing sacred about the second group of stones but that the former ones had some element of worship connected with them. Many other places may have had the same idea associated with them but the record of them has disappeared as the old people died.

SECTION XXIII

INFORMATION RELATING TO MYTHOLOGY

Takaroa or Ocean God — Raki or Sky Father — Papatuanuku or Earth Mother — Maui or A Demi-god — Tinirau or A Sea-Deity

From this section I used parts about rainbows, formation of Wakatipu, shape of earth, the sun's course and earthquakes.

MYTHOLOGICAL

It is rather late in the day to collect Maori mythology as the old priests who knew it have long since passed away, but ever and anon, as the collector talks with the old folk still left, fragments of ancient beliefs, etc., crop up and these are herewith given.

Two of the old men sung a song dealing with the creation, stars, etc., and in answer to a question, one said he reckoned that Mirimiri (star) was our Jupiter and he went on to say that he considered the heavens were stars. [Whether this is an ancient belief or a suggested idea from 'modern spiritualism', the collector cannot say.] The old man, in a mystical manner, continued: 'From earth you travel through fourteen heavens before you enter the one the Maori race came from. I do not know the names of those heavens, only that there were fourteen of them. The heavens are stars and you must pass them till you come to the right one. In the old story he once told me (see *Journal of the Polynesian Society* 8. H.B.), Rona went to the moon to live. In that story the word 'aroaro' means 'the face of a rock'. Lately astronomers have found out there is life on the moon but the old Maoris knew this. The true history will come out by-and-by. At tangis you hear some of the ancient names in the songs. People now think tangis are no good but they do not know the true nature of these occasions, telling as they do of the soul going the long journey through the heavens to its final destination.' In reply to a question he said he had heard the name Irihia but nothing concerning it and went on: 'In creation, according to the old Maoris, the first thing was love; then thought; then a thing was formed in the ground like a Maori hillock and this brought seed; then something like a potato; then the sun, moon and stars; and then man, the first being Maku.' In reply to a question if Io was not one of the first human beings created he said Io was the start of the history of the barracouta fish. Io was a person but was associated with various fish in a story which is told elsewhere in these notes, (see Fish). [Note: The collector has a rough copy of the 'star song' but it is not yet accurate enough to hand in.]

In an account given in McNab's [[1907]] *Murihiku a* European writing in 1823 says the Maoris worshipped Kowkoula. This is evidently meant for Kahukura (or Kaukura if the 'h' is deleted, as it sometimes is) so the collector inquired of one old man who replied: 'Kahukura was an atua. It was the "ghost" of Te Whakaemai, who lived in my grandfather's time, and he could pray to it and so bring on thunder and rain. Kahukura was a god of wind and rain. He used to have some fish or taniwha at sea to do his work and he could bring them ashore when he wished. He was the god belonging to the Kai-Taoka and other branches of the Kai-Tahu people and lived at Catlins or Tautuku, and also at Waikouaiti.' (In reply to a further question he said he had never heard of 'Rockiola' or 'pararoy' also mentioned in *Murihiku*). [The expression that such a god was 'ghost to someone' has been used to the collector several times and evidently means that the tohuka spoken of invoked that god solely or to the exclusion of others. There is a high hill, and also a stream between Catlins and Tautuku, known as Kahukura; while the celebrated god which Te Wera kept in a cave on the peninsula at Waikouaiti was called Kahukura. On his next visit to Puketiraki the collector has been invited to visit this cave in company with a local Maori.]

The doings of Maui furnish an apparently inexhaustible crop of stories and anecdotes to the Southern Maoris as every time the collector goes among these folk he hears of exploits of Maui which are new to his ears. In describing the boyish game of projecting pukakaho reeds along the beach one old man said that Maui played this game and it was known long before Maui's time. His four older brothers could only send their darts a small way but Maui sent his so strongly and so far that 'it went right to his mother's house where it broke the gable-end or matapihi. It is all tommyrot to say a boy's dart could split a big board but it must have been his atua at work. His brothers were angry but his mother said "Don't hurt your little taina." His father did not say anything. Then Maui and his brothers went into the bush to get pigeons. The older brothers had a pukaikai or spear but Maui had not so he used his ten fingers as tara and in two pokes he got twenty birds. When he got home with his twenty pigeons he found his brothers had only got one bird with their pukaikai.' At Temuka it was pointed out to the collector that Mahuika who had the custody of fire in the story of Maui is a man in southern lore, not a woman as is said in North Island traditions. A thoughtful Maori said to the collector: 'Te Maui sought to save mankind in Maori legend, something like Christ did by conquering death. Maui's idea of conquering death was to crawl through Hine-nui-o-te-Po but as you know he failed. Matiaha Tiramorehu, at Moeraki, years ago composed a waiata (song) about Tane and Hinetitama arguing over death. The result of this argument was that Tane was to stay on earth and look after the children of mankind and endeavour to preserve them while she went to the underworld to try to drag them down to her.' The collector drew this informant's attention to the fact that some Maoris said Maui endeavored to enter the Great Lady of Night by the exit from the womb (from which man is born) but that others say it was her mouth he wriggled into. He thought over this for some time and then said 'It was her mouth and nowhere else.' The collector may add he thinks this is a modernised version of that item.

An old man said: 'Whaitiri was a cannibal woman who lived in the heavens. She heard of a man named Kaitakata on the earth and came down to marry him. She thought from his name he was a man-eater so she took a slave with her and when she was near Kaitakata's home she killed the slave but Kaitakata would not eat the flesh. This was before our ancestors ate men and Kai-takata may have been named for some drowning fatality or after some fish which had eaten men perhaps. A Maori [who died in the Gore Hospital in January 1920] was called Kaitai (food of the sea) in memory of someone who was drowned in the sea so Kaitakata may have been named in the same manner. Whaitiri did not know this about Kaitakata's name and she came to him to have a husband who ate the same food as she did, but she found he was not a man eater. She married him, however, and they had a son Karihi who was named after the lower line of a fishing net, while another son was called Puka after the weights which keep the lower line down. Another son was the most famous of the lot. This was Tawhaki who climbed up to heaven.' This was all on this subject as the old man went on to describe fishing nets. (The collector noted that he pronounced Karihi as Ka-rihi.)

The southern Maoris narrate the story of Rata in great detail. Matiaha Tiramorehu had a boat at Moeraki which he called Niwaru after the name of Rata's famous canoe.

A name applied to some tree(?) in Hawaiki was Poroporo-huariki and this name was brought to New Zealand. The southern Maoris use this name as a figurative term for Turanganuiarua (Poverty Bay).

*'When they see rainbows the (Southern) Maoris know Te Ao-Matara, a tapu man of old (mentioned in the Tuhaitara whakapapa) is travelling about. It is his sign. His wife ran away but saw a rainbow and knew he was coming. After some trouble he got her back.'**

Add to Mythology

In the first place Maui was a menstruous cloth thrown out on a bramblebush by his mother, said an old man. His poua (grandfather) happened to pass, and carried it on and it developed into a child which he nursed until the boy could run about. Then one day the other brothers were playing the game of kokirikiri or kotiritiri where you project a koauau dart with a stick and Maui came along and joined in. Although only a little boy he sent his dart so far it broke the maihi (gable) of his grandfather's house. His mother appeared and said to the other boys 'Where did you pick up that boy?' and they said they thought he was a poriro (bastard). Maui said to his mother, 'I'm yours' and when she doubted this, he repeated, 'I'm one of your own.' After some talk her mahara (memory) recollected the rag and she took Maui in as a son. Te Raka was his hakoro (father) Hine his hakui (mother) and Murirakawhenua his poua. Maui destroyed some gardens but the narrator did not know this part of the tale. Maui took food to his grandfather but he ate it himself. The old man died and Maui took his kawae (jawbone) but buried the body. When the people went to visit the grandfather they found he was dead and buried, but the narrator never heard Maui was punished for this. Next the brothers went birdspearing with a pukaikai [See Bird section] without Maui, so the latter went into the bush and, using his ten finger nails as pukaikai, in two thrusts he had twenty birds while his brothers only got one or two. His mother was very pleased with the twenty pigeons. Then Maui made a whiri rope and koro-mahaka-erua (two nooses) and put them over the hole where the sun comes up. His three brothers were there and when the sun's head came up they pulled the nooses tight, two being on each side tugging. The sun was very angry and shouted, 'Let me go', and the brothers got scared and were going to let go, but Maui would not consent. 'Let the atua-tahae go,' they implored Maui but the latter harangued the sun and then beat it lustily after which they let it go, and the sun continued its course slower and more subdued. It went off with the nooses on its shoulders but these eventually burnt off. Then Maui's brothers went fishing thinking he was at home but all the time he was under the tataa (bailer) of the canoe. They were disgusted but said, 'Let him stop on board but we won't give him a line, a rod, or a hook.' He had these secreted on board but he had no bait and they would give him none so he hit his nose and waited till the blood came out toto-karukaru (clotted) and this he used as bait. Maui's matere (rod) can still be seen in the lower jaw of the maka (barracouta) and his line in the coil in the kakihi (limpet). He threw over his baited line and soon had a gigantic 'bite'. The boat rushed about like mad. The brothers shouted 'Let go.' 'Not so,' said Maui, 'I'm not going to let it go – this is the fish I came out for and I'm going to stick to it.' The boat went along at a great angle – the gunwale on Maui's side flush with the water and Maui straining every nerve while the other three brothers hung on to the other side to try to keep the boat straight and calling to him to let go. Then up came Te Ika-a-Maui, the fish of Maui, with the houses standing, the fires burning, dogs barking, children crying, women singing and everything going on as usual. The North Islanders don't like to think they were pulled out of the ocean like this, but so it was. This island was Maui's canoe. Then Maui followed his father and using his maro to be the white on his breast when he went into the shape of a pigeon he settled on his father's ko but you know that story. Then Maui went to his other poua (grandfather) Mahuika to get fire. The old man gave Maui a finger each time but Maui put eight of them out in a pool so the old man set the forest alight. Maui only escaped burning by changing himself into a kahu (hawk) and even then he was well singed. Before this the kahu was of a darker color but since then it has always had a burnt color (as at present) to commemorate Maui's escapade. He said karakia and rain came on, then heavy rain and then snow and the fire was quickly quenched. Mahuika rushed round to save some of it. He tried the kapuka (broadleaf) and other trees but they were no good. Finally he managed to hide some fire in these five trees: hinahina, kaikomako, totara, kahika and haumaukoroa; and there it may be found to this day.

After the above recital one of the two old men present sang a song about Maui having a conflict with Tuna who was apparently cut in two, the head portion originating the koiro (conger eel) and the tail portion turning into ordinary eels; also a song re Maui's exploits generally, and also one about the stars.

A description of the Maoris in Southland in 1823 (published [[1907]] by R. McNab) says they supplicated Kowkoula, the atua or spirit who ruled the world during the day, and Rockiola the spirit of the night. It is also said the leading chief was a pararoy. The well-informed kaumatua said 'Kowkoula is evidently meant for Kahukura or Kaukura, the God of the Rainbow. Rockiola, I take to be intended for Rakaiora who is a god of some sort. Rakai means to comb your hair and dress up and ora means life but I cannot say what Rakaiora was the god of. Pararoy is probably meant to be Pararo as there was a head chief of that name at Riverton in the early whaling days.' The 'mine of information' said that 'Kahukura was a great devil in the fish portion of living things. He was sometimes a whale, and again a kokopara, or an eel or a shark. I think Rockiola should be Rakaiora who is the god of the Karetai family. [The leading family on the Otago Peninsula.] I do not know the facts about that god but any member of that family should be able to tell you.'

Add to Mythological

An old man told the collector that Maui sat on a whale's back for three days and nights; and he wanted to know why the Pakeha should not believe the story of Maui as well as that of Jonah. [Note: He had evidently got the story of riding on a whale from the traditions regarding Ruatapu, Tinirau, Kae and others, and mistakenly attributed it to Maui. H.B.]

Some years ago an old Maori and the collector were sitting in the bush and we saw a pigeon wagging its head continually as its custom is. The old man said the bird was a kereru (or also often called a kukupa) and that it kept nodding its head because Maui when a pigeon (in shape) could not speak but simply nodded his head to everything his father, Te Raka, addressed to him as he sat perched on the ko (spade) in his father's garden in the underworld. Maui was first a menstruous cloth (maro) thrown into the sea; but the collector 'knew the story well enough', he concluded, without giving any more details.

The collector once asked an intelligent poua (grandfather) at the Bluff how the name Murihiku came to be given to the southern end of the South Island. He considered it was applied because it was the tail of Maui's fish. He thought Maui pulled up both the North and South Islands at the same time.

'Raki (Rangi) and Takaroa (Tangaroa) were brothers away in the dim ages. Both were gods,' said an old man in speaking about a whakapapa (genealogy).

Another veteran briefly told the collector the myth about creation as he had heard it from a learned old man of the South many years before. His breezy narrative proceeded: 'Papatuanuku was married to Takaroa, but Raki saw she was a nice-looking woman and claimed her as his wife when Takaroa was away. I was not told there was a family with the former marriage but with the latter there was a big lot of children, Tane being one of the sons. There was no daylight between Raki and Papa then and the family were living in a thick fog. Tane wandered out of it and then went back and told the rest that they were living in a mirk and that it was better outside. So the children made up their minds to part their parents. They got posts to prop Raki up but I forgot the names of those props. The parents were cuddling one another so the children had to chop Raki's arms off before they could lift him. After they got him raised up they put stars on him to decorate him and make him look pretty. I have no recollection of the sun and moon being mentioned in the story. Then Tane's wife cleared out and he went to the heavens to look for her.'

Speaking some years ago to the collector an old man said: 'Wahieroa was a famous man. It is said he had an earlier name but that he was re-named Wahieroa like this. His canoe was capsized at sea and he got into a long log of wood floating about and drifted to a pa on the seashore. The people took it for firewood and when they went to carry it out of the wash of the tide he made himself light (by karakia) until they got it up the beach and then he made himself heavy. As they moved along this happened several times until they left the log in disgust. A girl came along and tried the weight of the log and as he made himself very light she picked it up and carried it home for firewood. When she arrived at the whare the log turned into a man, Wahieroa, and she became his wife and consequently Rata's mother. As you know, Wahieroa travelled to Matuku's land and was killed there. His son asked the mother where the father was and she replied he was at the setting sun, so when Rata was big enough he set out to find the land where his father, Wahieroa, was killed.'

Speaking to the collector four years ago, the 'well-informed kaumatua' said: 'Tura and Whiro were brothers. The eldest son of Tura was Iraturoto. Another son, Tauira-o-hua was born on a strange island. Tura and Whiro went out in a canoe and got to this island where Tura either stepped ashore to explore it or dropped overboard to swim ashore to see it better. While he was doing this Whiro cleared out with the canoe, and also with Tura's wife, who was aboard, leaving Tura stranded on that island. There was no fire there as the people were maeroero ['fairies' – he explained this term. H.B.] and so Tura made firesticks and lit a fire. He married a fairy woman by whom he had a son, Tauira-o-hua. When Tura became old his hair turned gray and his wife deserted him. In his loneliness he called out to Iraturoto who was hundreds of miles away and such was the power of that message that Iraturoto came with a canoe and took the old man back to his old home. I can whakapapa from Tura to me, but I reckon he was never in New Zealand. By descent Tura came from Te Kahui-anu who were a bad people thrown out from the heavens to the po by Tane.'

Kopuwai (the collector was told some years ago) was a giant in Rapuwai or Waitaha times (South Island). He was a big lizard up the Mataau (Clutha) and ate birdsnarers. One day he caught a party and ate them except Kaiamio whom he kept for a wife. She cut raupo for a mokihi in a lagoon. The giant had a cord tied to her wrist so one day she undid it and tied it to some reeds and slipped down the river on the mokihi. The North West wind was blowing and the giant slept till night when he awoke and found her gone. He smelt about like a kuri (dog) and scenting she had gone down the river he drank it at a draught. It filled up again at once. The girl was safe at her kaika and told the people Kopuwai slept when the North West wind blew. At a suitable time three hundred people from Kaitangata went up and got him and his two-headed dogs sleeping in his cave. They set fire to brushwood and burnt them. There was a hole in the top of the cave and a scale flew out and turned into a pair of lizards – the start of lizards in New Zealand. The dogs were petrified and are now at Duntroon. The cave was at the foot of the Old Man Range. The people found it had several parts, one of which was filled with human bones.

An old Maori told the collector he considered Murihiku should be in the North Island as Maui fished it out – not the South Island. The tail should be Cape Maria van Dieman. A recent version – not one given by the old people – said Tane fished out the South Island but there was no history to this effect.

Add to Mythological

[I note someone, perhaps E. Best, has put a question mark re 'whera'. Tregear gives this as whewhera and meaning as 'spread out or flattened'. H.B.]

The old man from Otago Heads being in a garrulous mood narrated: Hineteiwaiwa went in search of Tinirau and said to each fish she met, 'E te ika nei!, E te ika nei! E hara, E hara koe te ika kokirikiri a Tinirau.' (This fish! This fish! No! You are not the darting or moving fish of Tinirau.) Then, continued narrator, ka tauhuri te ika te ki atu ki a Hineteiwaiwa (the fish turned and answered her). The hori was the first she questioned and he very rudely replied 'Kiko hauka, kumu hauka, tara hauka' (euphemistically this may be interpreted as 'You smell horrid'). Then ka riri a Hine, ka takahia e Hine te ika ka wheratia hoki e Hine era ika. (Hineteiwaiwa was angry and trod upon and spread out those fish) – hence is the kutuhori (sole) its present shape. Receiving derisive replies from each fish she met and questioned she dealt with each in retaliation. She trampled the moeanu (sand fish) into the sand, where it still resides; she scratched the paikea (humpbacked whale) and you can still see the marks of her fingernails in the corrugations down its front; she threw her maro (waist-cloth) at the mako-repe (elephant fish) and it stuck to that fish's nose forming the 'trunk' which hangs from it. The canoe of Tinirau when he cleared from Hineteiwaiwa was called Te-reperepe-tautini-a-Tinirau and this is the jellyfish. The narrator did not wish to tell lies about those old tales so would frankly admit he did not remember the start of the story, its ending, nor whether Hine caught Tinirau. Others might recollect it better than he.

Another good story, if his memory worked properly was that relating to Kae. Kae is now used as a word to mean a person who has one or two teeth out in the front of the mouth. Tinirau owned two whales or atuas – one was Tutunui and the other, a wahine whale, was Keakea. Kae went a holiday to Tinirau's place and when departing he asked for the loan of a whale to bear him back home. He said Keakea was too small so Tutunui was lent, but he was warned by its master not to take it too close inshore and Kae promised compliance with this request. When nearing the shore at Kae's place the whale shook itself as a signal to him to dismount but Kae callously ran Tutunui ashore and moreover put him in the umu to cook. In the night Keakea who missed her mate followed the trail and when near the shore 'sung out like a cow' and when no answer was returned she knew Tutunui was dead. Now Tinirau had three 'taipo' sisters, one of whom was named Ruawahine, narrator thought, but the names of the others he forgot. Tinirau called these women up and gave them instructions how to encompass Kae's doom. They asked how they would know Kae and were told he had a tooth (niho) missing in front of his mouth and if they made him laugh they would notice this defect. These women by sorcery pulled the land of Kae and the land of Tinirau close together and stepped over and then gave a kick backward and the two lands fell back again and receded to their former positions. (This was what the old people said but for himself he thought this part of this old Maori yarn was a 'damn lie', said narrator.) When the three women stepped ashore at Kae's place they were taken to the guest-house as manuhiri or 'new chums' (strangers or visitors) but they would not eat. Then they played and sang at each house in the pa except Kae's as it happened, and Kae invited them to come to his house at night and they went. They sang hakas and played pois and danced posture dances throwing their waewae (legs) up in a grotesque manner that made everyone laugh but Kae, whose bed was at the poutokomanawa. Then in one dance one of the women advanced almost on to the top of Kae and lifted up her kakahu (garment) in such a suggestive manner that he could see the kumu and Kae laughed and they saw the missing tooth's gap and knew it was their man. Kae wished them to continue their performance but they begged off as they were 'tired', they said. Kae went to sleep and the women by the exercise of the rotua incantation made him sleep sound. They put him in a tata fishing net and he was snoring. They pulled the lands close together again, stepped over and then kicked the other land away to its original position. They carried Kae up to Tinirau's house and a woman who was up on the tahu (ridgepole) awoke Tinirau when she saw them coming. Kae had been made sleep by rotua and now he was awakened by karakia to find himself in a different country and confronting the man whom he had lied to and whose pet he had treacherously cooked and eaten. One of the three women bit his face and he sang out in pain, another bit his side and the other bit the other side of him. Each time he screamed, and was told that Tutunui did not sing out when he was cast into the fire and the flames burnt his skin. They ate him alive did those avenging women. That was the end of the story, said the narrator, but he was sorry he did not take more notice of details when he was a boy. Now he was greyheaded he regretted this neglect.

Rotua ki moe (enchanting a person to sleep) was not like the Pakeha waving his hands in front of a man's face for the tohuka could go outside and the man inside would go to sleep all the same; or again the tohuka could karakia a man at a distance to sleep. The narrator did not know how this mysterious thing was done.

The narrator then began to sing the song about Paikea, Ruatapu and others. Whatitata, he explained, was the mother of Ruatapu (not of Paikea) and when walking along the beach she found the bone of a man named Paraoa. She took this bone home and made from it a heru (comb) for Ruatapu's brother, Te Kautia-te-Raki. One day Ruatapu surreptitiously used this comb and unwittingly put it back in the wrong place. Te Kautia knew it had been used and told his father, who angrily told Ruatapu he was a poriro (bastard) and in revenge Ruatapu drew the puru (plug) of the Tutepawharaki canoe and saw the rest drowned. Ruatapu hit his nose and put his finger in the blood and tried to pani (paint or smear) a streak of this on the one who could swim ashore but it would stick on no one but Paikea and this young man got ashore with the message that the Tai-a-Ruatapu wave was coming. Come it did and the only ones who escaped, te-morehu-o-te-whenua (the survivors – or remnant – of the land), did so because they heeded the warning and climbed Puke-Hikuraki (or Pukekihikuraki).

Another story was about Tama-taku-ariki whose wife Rukutia was run off with by Tutekoropaka. He searched the West Coast to Milford Sound and hence the kiekie grows down that side of the South Island to that place. It is te-pokeka-a-Tama because it grew from the strands of his pokeka (raincoat) torn off in his bush travels and left in the rough vegetation of that part. He never came down the East Coast of the South Island, consequently no kiekie is to be found on this side. He went back (to the North Island presumably) and found Tutekoropaka living in a whare in a secluded part of the coast, the path to the whare being hid by tatarahika (lawyer vines) which the searcher passed through by a karakia [which collector had not time to take down]. This opened the way up for him without leaving a trace of his passage. Night came on and Tama said a brief karakia 'ki hia mimi, ki hia tiko' (this is to create a desire to obey the call of nature) and Rukutia came out and talked to Tama a little and then in again. Soon after Tama repeated his words as above and again Rukutia arose and went out for a brief conversation. After she had gone in some time Tama repeated for the third time his words and Rukutia obeyed the karakia and out again and after sexual intercourse went in again. Tutekoropaka was by this time very suspicious but Tama pronounced a rotua-ki-moe which put him to sleep and Tama went away. Four days later he came back in a canoe. Rukutia was up on the roof and she saw Tama coming in his waka and she sang a song to him, a song which made Tu very angry. Then she ran down to the shore and swam out to meet Tama who, however, greeted her (to put it mildly) in a very cutting manner. Tama cut her in half and with a few insulting remarks to Tu left latter the kumu or lower half of the body, 'the part he liked best', while he himself took the top half away in the canoe. Tama planted the head of Rukutia in the ground by his whare where it seemingly grew for next year Rukutia re-appeared and was his wife again. Such was the yarn, added narrator; he did not vouch for its truth but so the old people told it to him.

This narrator also had something to say regarding the great Maui: Maui had three brothers but he was himself a taipo or demon. He was first a maro-toto (menstruous cloth). Maui may have had four brothers – narrator had heard both numbers (three and four) stated in this connection. Maui was in six great 'killings': 1. Irawaru – his brother-in-law turned to a dog. 2. Te Ra – the noosing of the Sun to make it go slower. 3. Mahuika – a man down in the Reinga. Getting fire. 4. Murirakawhenua – a woman, an old witch. He was sent with food to her but he ate it en route and kept this up till she died from starvation and he then took her jawbone. 5. Hauling up the Fish – this fish is the North Island of New Zealand. His brothers said 'Let it go – it is an Atua-tahae' (evil demon) but Maui persisted and pulled up the land, on which women were singing, fires burning and dogs barking. When Maui pulled up the fish he called it Orokoroko, the name Te Ika-a-Maui being given by subsequent generations. 6. Hinenuiotepo – This lady, the goddess of death, was the great-grandmother of Murirakawhenua. Maui crawled up the tiko and loosened up inside generally and came out her mouth without anyone laughing. This first trip was quite successful and Maui said one more trip would kill her as he would bring out her vital organs which he had loosened but this time the brothers laughed and all was up with Maui and also with the human race's hope of immortality, or of never dying in this body. These were the six 'killings' of Maui and to say there were more was to add words to those of the old people. He had heard it suggested that Maui killed Tuna but this was not so. The old people used to mention about the slaying of Tuna and although narrator could not name the man who did the deed he was positive it was not Maui.

Add to Mythology

'Maui', remarked the 'mine of information' in reply to a question, 'killed Tuna, because that great fish tried to get Maui's wife. Maui cut a big awa (ditch) and pulled the eel into it. The water went away and Maui cut Tuna in half.' The narrator further stated he had never heard of legendary winged people or men able to fly in the air. Rakiora was a god of the rainbow and Rakaiora was a ghost or god of the Karetai family. *If the whaitiri (thunder) rolls in the daytime and you see two rainbows the smaller one is Rakiora. The Maoris of old did not know the earth is round-shaped like what the Pakeha says but thought it was flat and they said the ra (sun) went down one side in evening and up the other the following morning. Earthquakes were called ru but he had never heard the old people tell of the origin or history of them. 'Te whenua kai te oioi' (the earth is shaking) is an expression used when ru is on. It must be caused by big fires underneath the earth's surface he thought. He knew no name for comets nor had he ever heard the old people assign any reason for the tides of the sea.

Another Maori said that Kahukura was the god of the rainbow. He had never heard of Rakiora and did not know what that name (or Rangiora) meant.** He knew little about mythology except that Raki was the heavens above and Te Reika the world below the earth. He had heard of no kahui-rere or winged people in South Island.

The Henley lady referred to the famous 'shining stone' called 'Te Konohi-o-Tawhaki', which lay on the beach near Otago Heads. Some sixty years, or so, ago it disappeared and it was not now known where it went. Perhaps some of the old people buried it. *She used to ask her seniors where the sun went when it disappeared into 'te rua o te ra' every evening but they could not tell her.** Maui's fishing line is said to be represented in the thread of the kakihi shell; and his matau (hook) in the formation of the 'roro-o-te-upoko' (brain) of the hapuku (groper).

SECTION XXIV

INFORMATION RELATING TO SUPERSTITION, WIZARDRY

Wairua or Human Spirit — Atua or Evil Spirits — Tohu or Omens — Moemoea or Dreams — Rotua or Hypnotism — Whaiwhaia or Sorcery — Makutu or Witchcraft

WAIRUA-ATUA

Then later still on the titi islands I was cutting wood and saw a man pass along a little-used track. He had a military coat on and I remember noticing the square shoulders and broad back of the owner. One of our party had a soldier's coat with him and at dinnertime I asked what he was doing to be so much out of his way as to be on the track I saw him on. He denied having been there and his mate backed him up in this so we went to see into the matter. The track was there black and muddy but no footmarks were on it so we came to the conclusion it must have been a wairua or spirit. I never used to believe such tales but I do now for when I got back from the islands I received a wire to say my son had been killed at the war. An atua was a ghost, a demon or a supernatural being.

Sandy Low, an old whaler, shooting pigeons at Table Hill, Tautuku, shot a maeroero but it only laughed at him and took the pigeon he had shot. 'Sanny' said its hair went down to its feet. [*A Waihao Maori [[H. te Maire]]{ said that for rotua-ki-moe}.**] Narrator's father saw the gate at Glenavy magically opened and the engine stop [See *Journal of the Polynesian Society* by Henries Beattie [[1920c]]]. The Maoris came to North side of river (and train to South side) and their drays and carts were on bridge before the train appeared. The wheels of the engine went revolving without its gaining ground until all the traps were across the bridge and then the wheels went forward again. There was a lot of talk about it at the time but no word of an official prosecution as the drivers were extremely puzzled over the occurrence. Narrator was asked to go up to Omarama the time the trouble with the military was on (1879) but he declined as he considered it foolish to threaten to fight much superior forces. The soldiers took his father prisoner and he stopped troopers from firing and Maiharoa held his hand up too. Maiharoa was of the same rank as his father but was the tohuka and the authorities only wanted the chief. He had heard that Maiharoa filled the air with *voices, but narrator did not know how it was done, or what it was called.**

WITCHCRAFT

The collector was puzzled as to the difference between three forms of witchcraft mentioned by Southern Maoris, viz makutu, rotua and whaiwhaia.

SECTION XXV

INFORMATION RELATING TO FOLK-TALES AND SAYINGS

Korero-tawhiti or Folk-lore — Parau or Fables — Whakatauki or Proverbs

The above [[Section XXIII, Murihiku]] story was told by an old woman in a roomful of Maoris at Temuka and everyone laughed at the idea of the seal that if he stopped with his winged friend, the quail, he would be killed for food. The translation is only a rough one that the collector picked up at the time.

The rourou is the flax plate of the Maori. It was said Te Pariwhakatau was the name of a place (and there is such a place-name up near Kaikoura) but it seems to the collector that in the brief waiata it might be a man's name. Although some of these tales can still be heard it is very hard to get explanatory details at this date – now the older generation has gone.

Later note: The question marks were, I think put there by Elsdon Best, but the words are as given to me, and are plain to a Southerner. Taki = tangi. Taukiri = an exclamation of surprise. Kai = kei. Puru is a strange word and is Maorified form, I believe of English word 'bull' and hence came to mean 'beef' or 'meat'. What the original word was in the pre-Pakeha rendition of the seal's lament I know not, but possibly some word like kame, kome or kamu. H.B.

SAYINGS, PROVERBS, ETC.

A number of proverbial sayings are scattered throughout these notes but the collector has one or two left which he has not been able to classify under the various headings preceding.

'Koukou mai e te ruru kihai i mawhitiwhiti kihai i marakaraka te upoko nui o te ruru tereko he po he po he ao ka awatea.'

This is a saying that was repeated by the old people when they heard the morepork call in the early morning as it was a sign that dawn was near. The collector would not have got this saying but part of it was given as portion of a poi-waiata (see under Poi) and my informants at Temuka wrote out the above saying to show that its inclusion in a poi song was erroneous. No translation of the exact meaning was given but may be procurable later.

'Takata te mohio, takata te pai, he whakatauki i mua.' This was a saying of one of the collector's old friends (now dead) and means 'The man of knowledge is a good man is a proverb of old' or simply 'Knowledge is a good thing'. He employed this saying relative to the preservation of ancient lore.

The next saying is not a proverb but occurred when one old man was explaining the use of weapons. He said one man might thrust his mere or patu at one of the opposing side saying 'Ko koe taku hoa o whai hoariri' (You are my companion, my fighting enemy). This was not an established saying but was said sometimes.

SECTION XXVI

INFORMATION RELATING TO HISTORY JOTTINGS

Arai-te-uru or 'Emigrant Canoe' — Maioriori or 'Morioris' — Maeroero or 'Wild Men' — Kati-Mamoe or 'A Tribe'

TRADITIONAL

When the celebrated Arai-te-uru canoe was wrecked at Matakaea Point a man named Puketapu went south looking for wood. He found it at Owaka and attempted to carry a big load back but his kawe (of flax) broke and he had to mend it with pukakaho (toitoi reeds). He dropped some wahia (wood) at Otepoti (and this now forms the Dunedin Town Belt), and another piece at Waitati, another log at Waikouaiti and these started the bush that now grows at those places. Just as daylight came he dropped the rest of his faggots in one heap at Otuwhata (Goodwood) and was turned into stone (Mount Puketapu). Down his broad back you can see the marks of his kawe – one watercourse is lined with flax and the other with toetoe to witness to the truth of the narrative while the timber he dropped last of all stretches away below him. *Two others of the Araiteuru's crew went for water. Aonui went south and found it at Mataau (Molyneux). He dawdled on journey for daylight came on and he was turned into the tall basaltic pillar called Cook's Head (on Tokomairiro Beach). Pakihiwitahi went northwest to the source of the Waitaki and came back with an ipu (bowl) of water and also with a hoaka (stone for grinding) he picked up. He was turned into a mountain too (the one on which the McKenzie Memorial was built) and near its top is a strong flowing spring shaped like an ipu, the overflow from which forms the Whataparaerae Creek, while the hoaka is found lower down. The sail of the Araiteuru was petrified into a broad flat rock under Matakaea. There it lies with the morua (seams) plainly visible and also the hole at the top to attach it to the mast.

A man named Taki had a fishing taumanu on a point at Lake Wanaka. It was floated off by a taniwha called Takaroa and this was the origin of the 'floating island' story. This taniwha is said to also go to sea as well as proceed up the river to the lakes. Another taniwha is said to live round at the rocks in Open Bay, Westland, yet the well-informed** kaumatua said he had never heard of the famous shark, 'Kaitiaki-o-Tukete', in Foveaux Strait. (It is wonderful how stories are known to some old men and not to others who live in the same district. H.B.)

MAORIORI (OR MORIORI)

When the collector visited Kawhakaputaputa in March 1920 old Hori Paraire was dying. (He died a day or two later.) Hori was said to be a Moriori from the Chatham Islands. He was a short, thickset man, with white hair and broad features and somewhat darker skin than the usual (Southern) Maori. His age was supposed to be about seventy six. He was called George Hori by Europeans and had been a good shearer, etc. The well-informed kaumatua told the collector that 'Geo.' was a Maioriori (he pronounced it) and that his (George's) uncle Wharekauri had been here in Southland before him. George came over from the Chatham Islands with a Maori minister who had been there a considerable time and in the South Island of New Zealand he lived first at Kaiapoi and then at Rapaki and then over forty years ago [nearer fifty I think. H.B.] he came to Murihiku to see his uncle. He liked the South and married and lived at Colac till his death. He was an intelligent man and could read and write. He knew the Maori language when he came, but in any case (said my informant) the Maioriori tongue is much the same as Maori. He had never heard Hori speak of Maioriori history but had heard the old people in the South when he was a boy speak about it. They said the Maioriori left the South Island in Waitaha times. A fight occurred over a woman (a putau perhaps, see Customs) at the Rakaia River and the defeated people went to live at Manuka beyond Akaroa on Banks Peninsula. A big fishing canoe was blown away and it was thought to be lost but afterwards a canoe came from the Chatham Islands and said how the original canoe had reached there and the people had founded homes there. My informant said he had never memorised the name of the woman, the name of the fight or the name of the canoe but the people of old knew all those details.

The name Moriori happening to be mentioned in a roomful of Maoris at Temuka one woman said that the Morioris had 'a choking or gasping way of speaking', and she endeavoured to give an imitation of their method of utterance.

TRADITIONAL

*Maeroero: Tradition says that these fearsome 'wild men of the woods' had fingernails of such a length that they could kill wekas (woodhen) by thrusting them at the birds. The nails were then useful in scraping the birds, and after that was over these beings would stick the birds on the ends of their nails and toast them at fires by the kohiku method.

The Maeroero were able to make fires. An account given the collector states that before the Europeans came to New Zealand the Maoris would be canoeing along the sea-coast at Tautuku and would see smoke ashore. They would land but would find no one at those places. The ashes and smouldering embers would be there but the Maeroero who had lit the fires had fled.**

One good lady (a full-blooded Maori) after mentioning about the Arai-te-uru canoe going ashore at Matakaea (Shag Point) said to the collector in a puzzled tone: 'I do not know [[how]] this history was preserved at all, as the canoe was wrecked on the rocks, and by morning the crew were turned into hills, so how their children or descendants came into being, or heard about the story, I do not know.'

TRADITIONAL

Katimamoe – Horomanu Patu (also called Pukuheti) was the last pure-blooded Kati-Mamoe chief, said one of my informants who remembered him. The old man, he continued, used to declare that he had seen the moa *(Dinornis)* when he was a boy; and also that when he was a youth out fishing with John Topi Patuki (who died in 1900 aged about ninety years) they had seen the maeroero on the shores of Foveaux Strait.

When the collector interviewed R. Taiaroa, the latter mentioned he had stored away in his possession a mat which was said to be solely of Kati-Mamoe workmanship. He thought it was the only Kati-Mamoe mat now in existence, but, unfortunately, the collector did not see it.

SECTION XXVIII

INFORMATION RELATING TO NAMES OF THINGS, CONTACT WITH PAKEHAS

NAMES OF THINGS

Tahu = roof, umu = whirlpool, whakatauki = proverb, pakaru = broken, arawhata = stairs, hauata = don't worry, nohoaka = seat or chair, unu = drinking, hoaka = grindstone, hoariri = enemy, tautarika = ear-rings, kaimatiro = loafing, tota = sweating, huika = confluence of rivers, ka kahuru = ten in number, aroaro = front of a thing, aumaha = heavy, kino = bad, rehu = disappearing, Waiata-o-manu = song of birds, kaitiaki = guardian, papare = to ward off, whakakopa =

bird wheeling in flight, matai = watching, inatao = cold, matari = very cold, pona = ankle, rekereke = heel, taotao = toes (or taotao-waewae), matikuku = toe nails (or matikuku-waewae), kuha = leg or thigh, kumu = behind or posterior, atiati = calf of leg, turi = knee, tuki = elbow, waewae = foot, papa = 'bottom' or lower part of back, hope = spine, tuara = back, niho = teeth, raho = testicles, kaokao = ribs, keke = armpits, kiri = the skin, hauku = dew, naka = shift over, horokeke = to drop down when legs exhausted, kao = lying flat, awetanga = cuddling, tara = splinters, rupinga = sleep, ao = handfuls, wahia = firewood, pepeke = doubled up, koekohe = waving arms about, wiri = shivering, whakarere = to leave a thing, tuku = to let go, whakareraki = a dull day, piki = a plume, whaiwhaia = witchcraft, puke te wai = a flood, tahae = a vagabond, atua = a demon, wairua = a spirit, ruku = to dive, ika = (any) fish, manu = (any) bird, tipuna = ancestor, mahaka = twins, te toka = the south-west, tarai = to adze, orau = cooking-house, teitei = lofty, whatakai = food storehouse, he = a mistake, tika = correct, huruhuru = the hair, rae = the forehead, tukemata = the eyebrows, konohi = the eyes, tarika = the ears, ihu = the nose, waha = the mouth, pahau = a beard, kaki = the neck, pito = the navel, puku = the stomach, manawa = the heart, upoko = the head, rikarika = the hand, Matikuku-rikarika = fingernails, taotao-rikarika = fingers, kutu = lips (human) or beaks or bills of birds, taotao = (animals' and birds' toes are also called this name).

Add to Names of Things

Crown of the head = papaka o te upoko (synonymous tumuaki), Sides of the head = akaka (or akaaka), Back of the head = hemihemi (same as in North Island), Eyelash = kamo, Eyelid = whare o te kohohi, Eyeball = taka. The eye is konohi but collector could get no name for its pupil. Bridge of nose = tau, Nostrils = pokaihu, Upper Lip = Te kutu-oruka, Lower lip = Te kutu-oraro, Mouth = waha, Roof of mouth = tapawaha, Tonsils = tohetohe, Ear = tarika, Ear lobe = rore o te tarika, Cheeks = paparika, Spine = kakao o tuara, Chest = poho, Breasts (of woman) = u, Lungs = pukapuka, Kidneys = taki, Heart = manawa, Arm = peke, Wrist = puna, Knuckles = punapuna, Thumb = konui, Little finger = koiti, Other fingers = taotao, Big Toe = konui, Little Toe = koiti, Other toes = taotao, Palm of the hand = papanui o te rika, All toe and finger nails = Matikuku. The proper name of foot was raparapa and the leg waewae (so the collector was told) but now waewae = foot and kuha = leg. (Kuha was originally the name of the thigh.) According to one informant io = thigh. The back of the leg = remu. To carry a thing on the back = whakawaha, To carry a child in mat on back = taukawe, To carry anything at all = pikau, Small bits of anything = kawetoweto, Snoring = kokoro, Blind = pohe, Rubbing over = tuparu, Wai tera = Who is that?, Kaupo = swim at night, Taupo = land at night (from boat), Tini = smoking a pipe, E aha te kata = What are you laughing at?, hangai or hakai = opposite, whiriwhiri = choose or select, tetahi = one (or another), timuaki = leader (synonymous with tumuaki), weheka

= separated or divided, puta = to come in sight, whakaae = to consent, riteka = likeness or custom, tikaka = policy or rule, kohi = to collect or gather, rori = to bind, collect, or gather, pana = expulsion, mate = grievance, koa = glad, hiahia = desire, kape = leaving out, manako = to like, mene = to assemble, moemoea = a dream, tono = a demand, to bid, taea = reached, accomplished, whaka whiwhi = to present, tuku = to give up, to allow, to send, to begin an action, putake = root, reason, cause, an ancestor, patipati = flattering, cajoling, not to be trusted, whaka wa = to accuse, to demand an investigation, hanga (or haka) = a work, a fabric or a property, Wai-mori = freshwater (according to one couple). Waimaori is the common name for it and I suggested they meant wai-moriori but they clung to the assertion that wai-mori was correct.

At the Bluff the collector was told Manauri = dark; Kotea = fair. None of his informants knew the meaning of Te-raka-a-Hineatea.

*The Maoris now say for sunrise 'Puta-mai te ra' (coming here the sun), but formerly they used the poetic or figurative term 'Haea te pu ata' (tear open the dawn, or split the dawn open). Ata is really the reflection caused by the sun before it appears, but is now often employed to express the idea of dawn.**

Add to Names of Things

The Maori name of Dunedin is Otepoti. The old lady from Henley and the 'mine of information' both agreed the name meant 'boat landing' as te poti = 'the boat'. 'It was a tauraka-waka (landing place) and the whalers gave the Maoris whale-boats and a landing there,' said the aged man. This does not agree with the usual translation.

In speaking to the 'mine of information' the following items cropped out in conversation: To have an eye knocked out or its sight lost was 'oti karotia te taka'; to swallow food is 'horomaka kai'; in a family of boys a man's first son is matamua, his next tama-tuarua and so on, the last being called a potiki; kakau is a handle, but kakau [northern = ngakau. H.B.] is inside you – it is your heart; kupu means word, roko is news and karere is a message; whakawaha is to carry a child, or indeed anything, on the back; boys used to be called tamariki-tane, girls kotiro and old men koroheke. A gift is called aroha, the same name as love or affection, as it springs from these.

An intelligent woman informed the collector that kai was simply a modern form of ancient kei. E aha tau (note: tau is abbreviation of tahau) means 'What do you want?' If you were furious with a person and went to 'slate them and they asked your errand (as above) and you had altered your mind, you would answer E pai (not kai te pai) = good.' Kauhou is 'breathing', and 'Teretere ana te kauhou' means 'the breathing is too fast' (i.e. unnaturally rapid). Hehe is panting after exertion.

[As an example of the difficulty the collector has in procuring names and information take this passage from his notes when interviewing Henare te Maire, seventy seven years old, who with Tikao shares the honor of being the two best-informed kaumatua left in South Island: 'He could not give the name of the pupil of the eye; he had never heard of toheroa, nor kopata, nor putara, nor whakapepepa, nor pakuru, nor rerewa, nor ririwaka, nor wainamu, nor tapairu regarding wheke, nor centipedes, and could not give Maori measures, nor names of eclipses, comets – etc., etc.' He gave some good information along special lines, but above illustrates difficulty of investigation. H.B.]

MAORI AND PAKEHA IN THE SOUTH

During the collector's talks with the Southern Maoris their modern life and ideas frequently cropped up and a compendium of the more interesting items is herewith given. Anything which they are not sure of (this applies to the introduction of plants and amimals) they attribute to Captain Cook. The collector has been told that Cook brought the kuri or dog, and the kiore or rat as well as other things. One old man said: 'Captain Cook brought the pig or poaka and potatoes of the horeta variety. He showed the people at Rakiura (Stewart Island) how to cultivate these potatoes.' The introduction of the pig and potato may be as stated but that Cook showed any Southerner how to plant and tend the succulent tuber is a modern addition.

The Natives' first acquaintance with pakeha necessaries of life is interesting. One narrated: 'After the pakeha came the Maori saw him eat cheese and when the Maori saw soap he thought it had to be cooked and eaten so he put it in an umu. He thought it was the fat of some animal or fish and he called soap motu-ruaraki (motu means fat), but when he opened the umu all he saw was some froth on the stones. He reckoned sugar was seed and although it tasted sweet he would not eat it in case it was harmful, so he sowed it broadcast. All this happened at Saltwater Creek whaling station at Otipua before Timaru was a town.' Another said: 'When the whites came the Maoris planted tacks in the ground and a month later on investigating why they did not grow they found them all rusty. They also put soap in the umus and it all melted away. Queen Victoria gave the people from Akaroa southward the sum of £2000 and the Maoris asked for it in pennies. These pennies were very many and of great weight and the Maoris thought they were getting a tremendous sum.'

The dog tax was never very popular with the Maoris and one old man counts it to his credit that he once saved the life of a constable collecting it – a sort of 'Do good to your enemies' stunt. The policeman was deplorably drunk and fell from the saddle, his foot catching in the stirrup and my friend rescued him. This policeman was always called Te Whiti by the Maoris of Southland because he once had dinner at a Maori house at Colac Bay and would talk of nothing but Te Whiti and Parihanga. (Parihaka, in Taranaki.)

When one of my informants was a girl a stirring episode occurred at the Taieri. She was born in 1843 and this episode occurred in 1849 or 1850 when the settlers were starting to take up the country. A Maori had, either accidentally or purposely, pushed a youth's head on to a wheat mill and it was split open (although he subsequently recovered). This youth had relatives at Moeraki and Waikouaiti and a taua (warparty) came down to avenge his injury. The women and children, including my informant, were sent up the hill to hide until the storm was past. The men sharpened weapons and one old fellow (Heremaia Toitu) went out and danced provocatively, flourishing a taiaha, before the advancing party, but better counsels prevailed and peace was preserved. Two or three Europeans assisted as peacemakers.

Tumaruraki was a Maori who was wrecked on the Snares and made a canoe of such materials as he could and reached the mainland or Stewart Island. Much later a pakeha who was marooned on Solander Island, made a boat of sealskins and reached the mainland. The Maoris thereafter called him Tumaruraki.

The Maoris early saw the advantages of education and sometimes made schools of their own with indifferent success. One such was run at Waitaki by an old Maori in the early days. A woman who attended says: 'I often laugh when I think of my schooling. We all walked round in a circle (porini) and then squatted and sang, Twicey one are two, twicey two are four' and so on. That is all the schooling I got.' One of the best-informed Maoris the collector knows is self-educated. A full-blooded Maori who read 'The Lady of the Lake' thirty years ago, recited Scott's famous poem to the collector, and made explanatory remarks and commented on beautiful passages, in a manner worthy of deep admiration.

At Moeraki the collector was told the name of a point was Te Heti o Matiaha and asking what this name meant he was told 'heti' was the Maori attempt to say 'head' of the whalers. (It should be upoko in Maori.) This point was formerly called Te Heti o Paitu but after Paitu left it was renamed. Pahi was chief here before the white men came but when they did he removed to Te Waewae Bay where is a place named after him. Paitu was chief at Moeraki then, but sold the country round to Teschmakers for a gold watch but the Commissioner stopped the transaction and Paitu shifted to Riverton and Matiaha became chief. This Matiaha Tiramorehu, whom Stack [[1898]] in 1877 called the greatest Maori authority in the South Island, is spoken of as a noble man. Of gentle demeanor he ruled wisely and would allow no drink in the kaika. He had a remarkably pretty daughter but unfortunately she died two weeks after she was married. He died in 1881 aged eighty six and a stained glass window in the little Church is in memory of him. On the tombstones in the graveyard the collector read Rawiri te Mamaru seventy nine, Hamiora Weka one hundred and twelve, Horomona Mauhara ninety four and Hira Mauhara one hundred and ten.

About 1875, according to one of my informants, a Clutha policeman tried to collect from such of the Maoris in the district as possessed firearms a gun-tax. They disputed this imposition and on inquiry it was found the said tax was for North Island Maoris only. For other causes this policeman was soon afterwards dismissed from the force.

At the end of Dr Hocken's [[1898]] *History of Otago* the Journal of Dr Monro is given and in this it is stated that when Tuckett's party visited Southern New Zealand in 1844 they were told that an animal like the beaver frequented Lake Wanaka. The collector asked a Maori regarding this but the existence of such an animal was denied. This old man suggested that a bird, the Kamana (Crested Grebe), built its kohaka (nest) on the water and that as this sometimes floats about it may have originated the story of a 'house in the water'. This bird, the kamana (kam-a-na) was common in Otago before the pakeha killed it out.

Speaking of different races having different ideas one intelligent woman remarked: 'God gave every people ideas but he gave the pakeha the best of all – how to make and keep money. He never gave the poor Maori this idea at all!'

In regard to names given to European things the collector was told that bread was piraua [Piraua = flour while papa (flat) was applied to the whalers' damper bread by Southern Maoris] in the North and papa in the South while sugar was huka in North and tuka in South. Milk is sometimes called the old name waiu (breast water) and sometimes miraka while tea is called ti.

A Temuka boy, Tupairehana, is said to hold the honor of being the only Maori to serve with the Australian forces during the late war and he has two 'wound bars' to show he was twice wounded. He ran away from home with a circus and was in Australia when the war was on and enlisted in the Australian Light Horse. He was called 'Jack' by his comrades and is said to have been a mascot of the whole corps. When the war was over he returned to Temuka and went up to Rotorua to the Prince's reception.

Some time after the Europeans came to Otago a party of Maoris and half-castes went from Waikouaiti up the river to get tutu berries to make old-time tutu wine. A flood (ko puke te wai) marooned them and they were without food until an old man swam to them with a basketful carried on his head.

Add to Pakeha Ways

The use of the word taepo or taipo cropped up. According to the well-informed kaumatua this is a 'pakeha' term and is used by the Maoris so that the pakehas will understand what they mean when they wish to infer the idea of a demon, etc. The correct Maori term should be atua.

The sight of two Maori girls with their olive brown complexions thickly and palpably dusted with whitish powder incurred the disgust of one old man; as also did the sight of a young man with his arm round the waist of a maid: 'When I was a young fellow there was none of that. I lived at a place distant from my girl and infrequent letters contented us. In my courting days there was none of this arms-round-waists business nor "smoodging" ways and the elders told off the girls to their sleeping quarters every night. But if a man had happened to salute a woman on the cheek he would not have got his mouth full of powder in those days. There was no powder on the faces then but nowadays some of the girls look as if they had just walked out of a flour bag.'

The incongruity of English 'smart' phrases on Maori lips is noticeable. At the Bluff one of the older people lamented the fact that so many of the older generation had gone and a young Maori who was listening concurred in this view, solemnly remarking, 'Yes! the old people are now pushing up the daisies.'

A Maori named Tarawa was drowned in the Mataura River (in the sixties) and the collector was told by a European that it was strange a man whose name meant 'salt water' should be drowned in fresh water. While all the Maoris agreed that waitai meant saltwater no one could say what Tarawa meant until the 'mine of information' said it was the name of one of the sons of King David in the Old Testament.

PAKEHA

An old Maori complained to the collector that the younger Maoris were now using the word hapa (shop) from the North Island instead of the word toa (store) to which he had been used. This word 'toa' is now sometimes used for 'door' and you may even hear an old person say 'paia te toa' instead of the correct 'paia te tatau' (shut the door).

An old Maori travelling in the express pointed out one township through which the train was passing as Te Kuri. This was Hampden the creek by which is Te Kuri. Similarly Palmerston South is known as Waihemo, Warrington is Okaihau, Christchurch is Otautahi, Dunedin is Otepoti and so on. These names were used by the passing generation, the present generation only uses the English names.

None of the collector's informants had heard of the reputed 'beavers' in Lake Wanaka (see Hocken's [[1898]] *Otago*). Tregear's dictionary gives name as kaurehe. The collector kept asking for months regarding animals like beavers, until he dropped across the word 'kaurehe' in searching for another word. Thereupon he asked two old men about the kaurehe and they knew at once what was meant. From their descriptions it appears that the kaurehe is a traditional water-monster of fearsome characteristics. Their information appears in the Canterbury section of these notes.

Add to Pakeha Ways

An old Maori from Puketiraki went into the iron foundries at Dunedin and was much edified at seeing holes drilled in iron but when a knife sliced an inch thick sheet of iron like butter he looked amazed, felt the iron, gazed at the knife and ejaculated in startled tones, 'It must be sharp.'

The newer generation of Maori calls the inland kakahi, 'the freshwater pipi', and boils them. Some of these kakahi are as big as oysters and are said to eat very well.

There was an old mill for grinding wheat at the kaik at Tuturau. It was said to be 'part of the price given the Maoris for New Zealand in 1840'. It belonged to Tuhawaiki and he gave it to Reko as the Maoris grew a little wheat at Tuturau. The sole remnant or relic of the old mill was hunted up and the collector was instrumental in getting it placed in the Southland Museum some time ago.

The fine old Maori lady who died at Tuturau in December 1919 was a district institution. Whenever there was a fete on in Mataura and the Pakeha girls wished to appear as Maori maidens they besought the good offices of the amiable dame who not only gave the desired advice and help, but would often make flax paraerae (sandals) to complete the effectiveness of the costumes.

Before they were properly acquainted with flour, the Maoris put it in the umu as it was (without mixing) for four or five hours but needless to add they were greatly disappointed with the result.

Add to Pakeha Contact

An elderly man said he had never seen the kiore or native rat except once in the Museum. His father said it was a cleanly animal and good eating. To this information a matron added that when she went to school at Henley the white children taunted her and other Maoris as being cannibals and rat-eaters. She did not know anything about the rat, but felt the slur keenly.

An old woman said that she could eat any Native food but could not bear the look or taste of rabbits.

One of my informants is better known by everybody as 'Tommy Billy' than by his proper Maori name.

As at European settlements the Maori children varied in cheekiness or impudence. Numbers lent courage to be insolent but the fewer numerically the better the conduct.

Taiaroa has a map of South Island which he says cost his father £100 to fill in. It has only Maori names and Canterbury is very fully marked, Central Otago fairly well, but Murihiku is very poorly represented.

A Maori woman who has lived in Canterbury some years said: 'I wish I was back in Otago where the Pakehas were more friendly and the pleasant Scotch tongue was heard.'

Add to Pakeha Contact

The collector saw a couple of photographs of old Matene Wera Korako (who died at Henley twenty years ago at the reputed age of one hundred and twenty one years). These were taken by a photographer named Moore (?Muir) who went with McKegg, 'and an English lord', to the kaik for the purpose. The old man looks solemn and the collector was informed he was very adverse to being taken but was finally persuaded into it. Pakeha settlers have told the collector Matene had a fine, aristocratic face, with a Roman nose.

A Maori matron told the collector that when a girl at Otago Heads she found some large silver coins on the site of an old whare. She was going for the cows and the site was exposed by a subsidence of soil. She noticed there was a great heap of pipi shells nearby. Her mates and she were excited at finding these strange, big coins and rushed home with a handful of them. They cleaned the coins and her taua (grandmother) said they were doubloons. She pronounced the word dob-loons and they called a new cow Dobloon in memory of this. Narrator's father went to the old whare (which had been uncovered by a minor landslip) and religiously gathered up every fragment of it, dug up the stumps of posts, and buried the lot in the urupa (cemetery).

A European, a professional man (a surveyor) at Invercargill, who has always taken a great interest in the Maoris, has blossomed out into a sort of honorary faith-healer to the Maoris. They consult him for all manner of things. One asked where a ring was lost and was told to look in a certain cow-bail at Ruapuke Island and there the missing article was duly found. He told a woman at Temuka what medicine to take, and if she has faith she will be cured. A Kaiapoi man went down to Invercargill about his gout and was told not to let his mind worry. He came away saying he felt better than he had for years. The gentleman believes in mental therapeutics and the Maoris have great faith in him.

The Maoris would have better health if they exercised the precautions of even the average European but no doubt the requisite knowledge will come after some generations of education or after they are absorbed into the white race in the South Island.

APPENDIX 2

GLOSSARY OF NAMES FOR FLORA AND FAUNA

In the first column are names from the manuscript and in the second column are either Beattie's description of the item or a brief designation of its general class (fish, bird, plant etc.), according to the context in which the name occurred. In the third column are suggested scientific names based on the references at the end of the glossary. In many cases these are educated guesses and none should be accepted as certain.

ABBREVIATIONS

HB	Herries Beattie [indicates where he expressed uncertainty about name or spelling]
Can	Canterbury
Mur	Murihiku
Nel	Nelson
NI	North Island
SI	South Island
Tar	Taranaki
Tem	Temuka
Tgr	Tregear [compiler of dictionary HB used as reference]
( )	encloses information on source of the word or locality of use
[ ]	indicates information added to clarify class to which item belongs
aa etc.	indicates macron in MS

A

aka	a vine	
akakohia, kohia	plant	*Passiflora tetrandra*
akapipi, see kuku		
aka-puatawhiwhi	kind of vine	
akatea	plant	
aka-tororaro	kind of creeper	
akatotara	creeper, vine	
ake	tree	
akeake	tree	prob. *Dodonaea viscosa*
akerautaki	tree	poss. *Dodonaea viscosa*
akerautangi	tree	poss. *Dodonaea viscosa*
apora (Can), hapura (Mur)	apple	*Malus* spp.

arokehe	kind of eel	*Anguilla* spp.
aruhe, rarauhe, rauaruhe	fernroot	*Pteridium esculentum*
aruhe-rakau	fernroot	prob. *Pteridium* spp.
aua	mullet, herring	prob. *Aldrichetta forsteri*
awheto	insect	

B

bidibidi, see piripiri
bubu, see pupu

F

falariki, see wharariki		
fereti	ferret	*Mustela furo*

G

giegie, see kiekie
goai, see kohai

H

haata (Mur)	horse	*Equus caballus*
haka	a white clematis	prob. *Clematis* spp.
haka hiwihiwi	shellfish	*Guildingia obtecta*
hakekakeka	kind of mushroom	*Auricularia polytricha*
hakeke	tree	*Olearia ilicifolia*
haki	native holly	*Olearia* or *Senecio* spp.
hakihaki	tree	
hakopa	ladybird	
haku	king fish	*Seriola* spp.
hakuai	legendary bird	
hao	kind of eel	*Anguilla* spp.
hapara, see haparu		
haparu, hapara	young grayling	
haparu, see also upokororo		
hapu	kind of kumera	*Ipomoea batatas*
hapuka, see hapuku		
hapuku, hapuka	groper	*Polyprion oxygeneios*
hapura (Mur), see apora (Can)		
harakeke, harareke	flax	*Phormium tenax*
harareke, see harakeke		
harore, harori	kind of fungi	*Pholiota aurivella*
harori, see harore		
hature, haturi	mackerel	*Trachurus* spp.
haturi, see hature		
haumata	kind of swamp grass	
haumata (Can), see matata		

haumatangi	kind of toetoe	poss. *Cortaderia* spp.
hea	hare	*Lepus europaeus*
heihei, see tikaakaa		
heno (Tgr), see hino? [HB]		
hinahina, mahoe (NI)	whitewood	*Melicytus ramiflorus*
hinau	tree	*Elaeocarpus dentatus*
hinereta, see hinerata		
hinerata (Mur), kiore (Can), hinereta	English mouse	poss. *Mus musculans*
hino? [HB] or heno (Tgr)	bush wren	*Xenicus longipes*
hipi	sheep	*Ovis aries*
hiwaiwaka	fantail	*Rhipidura fuliginosa*
hiwihiwi	fish	prob. *Galaxias brevipinnis*
hoe-moana, kukupati, pati, patikuku	'oar of the ocean' – shellfish	*Atrina zelandica*
hoho	brown duck	*Anas chlorotis*
hoho	shoveler duck	*Anas rhynchotis*
hoiho (Can)	horse	*Equus caballus*
hoka	red cod	*Pseudophycis backus*
hopa	kind of potato	prob. *Solanum tuberosum*
horepara	big black eel	*Anguilla* spp.
horihori	kind of flat-fish	prob. *Rhombosolea* spp.
horihori, kutuhori	sole	prob. *Peltorhamphus* spp.
horihori-wai, 'tuna Pakeha'	a white bellied eel	*Anguilla* spp.
horoeka	grasstree	prob. *Pseudopanax crassifolium* poss. *Dracophyllum* spp.
horokaka	plant	*Disphyma australe*
horopito	pepper tree	prob. *Pseudowintera colorata*
houhou	five finger tree	*Neopanax arboreum*
houi	ribbonwood	prob. *Plagianthus betulinus*
huanga	kind of shark	
huarau	kind of shark	
hue	gourd, calabash	prob. *Lagenaria vulgaris*
hue-Maori	gourd	prob. *Lagenaria vulgaris*
huhu (NI), see tuka		
huia	bird	*Heteralocha acutirostris*
hutuwai, see piripiri		

I

ihupuku	sea-elephant	*Mirounga leonina*
ikamaru	fish	
inaka	tree	prob. *Dracophyllum longifolium*
inaka, inanga	minnow	*Galaxias* spp.
inaka	kind of pawa	*Haliotis* spp.

inanga, see inaka		
iro	maggot of blowfly	*Calliphora quadrimaculata*
iro, see also rako		

K

kak [kaak], see kaka		
kaeaea, see karearea		
kaha	shag	*Phalacrocorax* spp.
kahawai	fish	*Arripis trutta*
kahia	white-bellied shag	*Phalacrocorax* spp.
kahika (Mur), kahikatea (NI)	white pine	*Podocarpus dacrydioides*
kahikatea (NI), see kahika		
kahikatoa, see kaikatoa		
kahikomako, see kaikomako		
kahio	worms in fish	
kahu	harrier hawk	*Circus approximans*
kaihe (NI)	ass	*Equus* spp.
kaikaatoa, see kaikatoa		
kaikai-haroro, see kaikai karoro		
kaikai-karoro, kaikai haroro	shellfish	prob. *Paphies* spp.
kaikatoa, kahikatoa, kaikaatoa	tree	poss. *Kunzea ericoides*
kaikomako, kahikomako	tree	*Pennantia corymbosa*
kaio, ngaio	bullkits, sea nuts	*Boltenia pachydermatina*
kaio, see ngaio		
kaio	kind of worm	
kairaka, pakeha piopio	skylark	
kaiwhiria (NI), see rautawhiri (SI)		
kai witi, see manukino		
kaka	parrot	*Nestor meridionalis*
kaka (SI), kanga, kaak [kak]	maize, Indian corn	*Zea mays*
kakaha, takakaha (Moeraki)	plant	prob. *Astelia nervosa*
kakaha	kind of grass	
kakahi, kakahi-wai-maori	freshwater shellfish	*Hyridella menziesi*
kakahi-wai-maori, see kakahi		
kakahi-wai-tai	shellfish	
kakaho	reed	prob. *Cortaderia* spp.
kakapo	ground parrot	*Strigops habroptilus*
kakariki, kawariki (NI), pare waka, porere, porete, powhaitere	parrokeets	*Cyanoramphus* spp.
kakariwai	robin	*Petroica australis*
kakaruai	robin	*Petroica australis*
kakihi	limpet	
kakihi-tere	shellfish	
kakiihi	shellfish	

kaleko, see kareko		
kamahi, kamai	tree	*Weinmannia racemosa*
kamai, see kamahi		
kamana	crested grebe	*Podiceps australis*
kamukamu	marrow, pumpkin	prob. *Cucurbita* spp.
kanae (NI)	mullet	prob. *Mugil cephalus*
		poss. *Aldrichetta forsteri*
kanakana	lamprey	*Geotria australis*
kanakana-wairaki, wairaki, wairaki-kanakana	young kanakana	*Geotria australis*
kanga, see kaka		
kanohi-o-Tawhaki	shellfish	poss. *Turbo smaragdus*
kapitana	calabash, = Captain	prob. *Lagenaria vulgaris*
kapiti, see kareko		
kapuka	broadleaf tree	prob. *Griselinia littoralis*
karae	rainbird, petrel	*Pterodroma* spp.
karaerae, see mako karaerae		
karaka	tree	*Corynocarpus laevigatus*
karamee	plant	
karamu	shrub/tree	*Coprosma* spp.
karaponia	Californian potato	prob. *Solanum tuberosum*
karara (Nel), ngarara	general name for insects	
karara-moko-huruhuru	green lizard	*Naultinus* spp.
karara-mokomoko	kind of lizard	
karara-papani	kind of lizard	
karara-toro-pakihi	spotted lizard	prob. *Leiolopisma* spp.
karara-tuatara	lizard?	prob. *Sphenodon* spp.
kareao, see pirita		
karearea, kaeaea	sparrowhawk	*Falco novaeseelandiae*
kareko, kaleko, kapiti, karengo	kelp, carrageen	*Porphyra columbina*
karengo, see kareko		
karetu (SI)	a grass	
karetu (NI)	a grass	poss. *Hierochloe redolens*
karewao, see pirita		
karewarewa	bush hawk	*Falco novaeseelandiae*
kariparaoa	kind of potato	prob. *Solanum tuberosum*
karo	plant	poss. *Pittosporum* spp.
karoro	black-backed gull	*Larus dominicanus*
karuru, koruru	shellfish	
kata	small leech	
kata	snail	
katipo	type of spider	*Latrodectus katipo*
katote	type of ferntree	prob. *Cyathea smithii*
katote, katotee	kind of potato	prob. *Solanum tuberosum*
kauheke	tree	poss. *Hoheria* spp.
kaupare	kind of shark	

kaurehe	kind of lizard	
kauri (SI), kauritawhiti (Tgr), mimiha (NI)	gum, resin or pitch	
kauritawhiti, see kauri		
kauru, see ti		
kawakawa	wild swede or turnip	poss. *Brassica* spp.
kawakawa	peppertree	*Macropiper excelsum*
kawakawa	kind of fern	
kawariki (ND), see kakariki		
kea	bird	*Nestor notabilis*
keikei	plant	*Freycinetia baueriana banksii*
kekeno	fur seal	*Arctocephalus forsteri*
kekerengu	insect	poss. *Platyzosteria novaeseelandiae*
kekerewai, manu-a-Rehua	insect	poss. *Pyronota* spp.
kereru	pigeon	*Hemiphaga novaeseelandiae*
keroa (Nel)	daddy-long-legs	
keroa (Mur), waeroa (NI), naeroa (Nel)	mosquito	*Culex pervigilans*
keru (NI), see puhi		
kewa	right whale	*Balaena glacialis*
kiakia, see kiekie		
kiekie, kiakia, giegie, Te Pokeka-a-Tama	plant	*Freycinetia baueriana banksii*
kihikihi, see kihikihiwaru		
kihikihiwaru, kihikihi, kikiawaru, terakihi	kind of cricket	
kikiawaru, see kihikihiwaru		
kikihi, see kihikihiwaru		
kikihiwaru	dragon fly	
kikopu	kinds of potatoes except parareka kind	prob. *Solanum tuberosum*
kilimoko, see kirimoko		
kina	sea-egg, sea urchin	prob. *Evechinus chloroticus*
kina, kiore	hedgehog	*Erinaceus europaeus*
kiokio	kind of fern	prob. *Blechnum* spp.
kiore, see kiore-maori		
kiore (Can), see hinerata		
kiore, see kina		
kiore-maori, kiore tawai	native rat	*Rattus exulans*
kiore-moana (Tgr), see kiore-tawhiti		
kiore-tawai, see kiore-maori		
kiore-tawhiti (Mur)	seahorse	*Hippocampus abdominalis*
kirimoko, kilimoko, kiripapa (Nel)	a small manuka	poss. *Leptospermum scoparium*

kiripapa (Nel), see kirimoko		
kirirua	big black eel	*Anguilla* spp.
kivi, see kiwi		
kiwi	kiwi	*Apteryx* spp.
kiwi-ma	kind of kiwi	*Apteryx* spp.
koareare	raupo reed	*Typha orientalis*
koati (NI), see naninani		
koau	shags	*Phalacrocorax, Stictocarbo* spp.
koauau	kind of kelp	
koau-mapua	freshwater shag	*Phalacrocorax* spp.
koau-pango	black shag	*Phalacrocorax* spp.
koau-pateketeke	king shag	prob. *Phalacrocorax carunculatus*
koau tai	shag, grey sea shags	*Phalacrocorax* spp.
koauteko	kind of shag	*Phalacrocorax* spp.
koekoea	long-tailed cuckoo	*Eudynamis taitensis*
koekohe, kohekohe, koikohi	trumpeter fish	*Latris lineata*
koeo	small variety of pawa [paua]	*Haliotis* spp.
kofitifiti, see kowhitiwhiti		
kohai, kowhai, goai	tree	*Sophora* spp.
kohekohe, see koekohe		
kohepiro	plant	
kohia, see akakohia		
kohitihiti	sand wasp	
kohitihiti	daddy-long-legs	
kohuai, see kokuta		
kohuai, kohuwai	kind of moss	
kohukohu	mildew on posts	
kohuwai, see kokuta		
koihi	fish	*Mendosoma lineatum*
koikohi, see koekohe		
koiro	conger eel	prob. *Conger verreauxi*
koka	native crow	*Callaeas cinerea*
kokekehe	kind of eel	*Anguilla* spp.
kokihi	plant	*Tetragonia tetragonioides*
kokirikiri	leather jacket fish	*Parika scaber*
koko (Mur), see tui		
kokoeka	grass tree, lancewood? [HB]	poss. *Pseudopanax crassifolium*
kokomuka (SI), koromiko (NI)	shrub, veronica	*Hebe salicifolia* or *H. stricta*
kokopala	fish	*Galaxias* spp.
kokopara	cockabully	*Galaxias* spp.
kokopu	bullhead	*Gobiomorphus gobioides*
kokopu	native trout	*Galaxias fasciatus*

kokopura, see kokopara		
kokoto	shellfish	
kokuta, kohuwai, kohuai	green scum on stagnant water	
komutumutu, see kopapa		
konini, see kotukutuku		
kopa	shellfish	
kopakopa	shellfish	
kopakopa	plant	*Plantago* spp.
kopapa, komutumutu	trevally fish	
kopara	kind of potato	prob. *Solanum tuberosum*
koparapara (Mur) or makomako (Can)	bellbird	*Anthornis melanura*
kopata	plant	*Geum urbanum*
kopekapeka, pekapeka	bats	*Chalinolobus tuberculatus* or *Mystacina tuberculata*
kopuru	seaside growing moss	
kopuru, purua	mould	
koradi, korari	plant	*Phormium* spp.
korakiraki	kind of eel	*Anguilla* spp.
korari, see koradi		
koreke	quail	*Coturnix novaezealandiae*
koroama	sardine	prob. *Sardinops neopilchardus*
koroama, see also marakuha	fish	prob. *Sardinops neopilchardus*
koroamo		poss. *Sprattus antipodum*
korohea (Tgr), see korowhio korokio	shrub	*Corokia buddleioides*
koromiko (NI), see kokomuka (SI)		
koropio (Tgr), see korowhio (Mur)		
korora	small penguin	poss. *Eudyptula minor*
korowhio (Mur), koropio (Tgr), korohea (Tgr)	native thrush	*Turnagra capensis*
koruru, see karuru		
kotare	kingfisher	*Halcyon sancta*
kotimana, punitanita	Scots thistle	*Cirsium vulgare*
kotokoto	kind of eel	*Anguilla* spp.
kotore-moana		
kotuku	white heron	*Egretta alba*
kotukutuku, konini	fuchsia	*Fuchsia excorticata*
kotuku-wai-tai	little blue heron	*Egretta sacra*
kouka	biggest kind of eel	*Anguilla* spp.
koukou, rurukoukou	morepork	*Ninox novaeseelandiae*
koura	crayfish, crawfish	*Jasus* spp. *Paranephrops* spp.
koura	kind of potato	prob. *Solanum tuberosum*
kouraraki	whalefeed	

koura-wai-maori	freshwater crayfish	*Paranephrops* spp.
koura-waitai	saltwater crayfish	*Jasus* spp.
kowhai, see kohai		
kowhitiwhiti, kofitifiti, mahitihiti	kind of grasshopper	poss. *Paprides nitidus*
kowhitiwhiti, see also pakau, toetoe		
kowhiuwhiu	kind of tree	
kuaka (Mur)	kind of muttonbird	*Pelecanoides urinatrix*
kuaka (NI), see pouaka (Mur)		
kuao	young eels?	*Anguilla* spp.
kuku (NI)	mussel	prob. *Mytilus aoteanus* or *Perna canaliculus*
kuku, see pipi		
kuku	pigeon	*Hemiphaga novaeseelandiae*
kukupa	ring fish	
kukupako	black teal	*Aythya novaeseelandiae*
kukupati, see hoe moana		
kukuruwhitu	bird	
kumara (NI), see kumera		
kumera, kumara (NI), kumera-maori, hapu, Te roa mahoi, kumera moutere	sweet potato	*Ipomoea batatas*
kumukumu	gurnard	*Chelidonichthys kumu*
kupenga	plant	
kura	king of the birds [extinct? bird]	
kuri	dogs	*Canis familiaris*
kuri-kowao, see kuri maori		
kuri-maori, kuri kowao, mohorangi, ruarangi (NI)	native dog, Maori dog	*Canis familaris*
kurupatu	bird	
kuruti	bird	
kuta	cress, watercress	prob. *Nasturtium* spp.
kutu	louse	poss. *Pediculus* spp.
kutuhori, see horihori		
kuuhi	goose	*Anser domesticus*

M

maataa [mata]	insect	
maataa, see mata		
mahetau (SI), taewa (NI)	potato	*Solanum tuberosum*
mahetau, see also hopa, kariparaoa, katote, katot ee, kikopu kopara, koura, taewa, noinoiraki, papaka, parareka,		

patiti, raramu, repe, rope, waitaha		
mahinahina	shrub	poss. *Melicytus ramiflorus*
mahitihiti	grasshopper	prob. *Paprides nitidus*
mahoe (NI), see hinahina		
maire	tree/shrub	*Nestegis* spp.
mairehe	kind of eel	*Anguilla* spp.
makaa [maka], mangaa	barracouta	*Thyrsites atun*
makamaka	shrub	
makamaka	fern	
maka-tahalaki, see maka-taharaki		
maka-taharaki, maka-tahalaki, maka-tikati (Can)	kingfish, Jewfish	prob. *Rexea solandri*
maka-tikati, see maka-taharaki		
makihikihi	plant	
mako	tree	poss. *Aristotelia serrata*
mako	shark, blue shark (Moeraki)	poss. *Isurus oxyrinchus*
makohuarau	spiny dogfish	prob. *Squalus* spp.
mako karaerae, karaerae	kind of shark	
makomako (Can), see koparapara (Mur)		
makomako	shrub	*Aristotelia serrata*
makorepe, see repe		
makoururoa	kind of shark	
mamaku	treefern	*Cyathea medullaris*
manawa	kind of eel	*Anguilla* spp.
mangaa, see makaa		
mangatara, see mangotara		
mango	general name for sharks	
mango, see also huanga, huarau, karaerae, kaupare, mako, makokaraerae, mako ururoa, mako repe, manga tara, mango tara, matawha, papaki, takapani, taniwha, tatare, tupa, tutaahuna, tutahuna, tutauna, ururoa		
mangotara, mangatara	kind of shark	
mania	tussock, patiti tussock	
manu-a-Rehua, see kekerewai		
manuka	tree/shrub	*Leptospermum scoparium*
manu-kai-hua-rakau	thrush	*Turdus philomelos*
manuka-pouri	black manuka	poss. *Leptospermum scoparium*
manukino, kai witi	sparrow	*Passer domesticus* or *Prunella modularis*

manutane (Can), see tikaakaa		
mapara	white pine	prob. *Dacrycarpus dacrydioides*
mapou	shrub	*Myrsine australis*
mapua	shag	*Phalacrocorax* spp.
maraki	a kind of dried fish	prob. *Sardinops neopilchardus*
marakuha	sardines	
marakuha, see also koroama		
marare, marari, ngehe	butterfish, kelpfish	*Odax pullus*
marari, see marare		
mariri	a small paua	*Haliotis* spp.
mata	big, black beetle	poss. *Platyzosteria novaeseelandiae*
mata	whitebait	*Galaxias* spp.
mata	kind of fern	poss. *Histiopteris incisa*
mata	kind of toetoe	poss. *Cortaderia* spp.
mata, mataa [mata], maataa [mata], toitoi	fernbird	*Bowdleria punctata*
mataa [mata], see mata		
matai	black pine	*Prumnopitys taxifolia*
matamoi, matamoii [matamoi]	grayish eel	*Anguilla* spp.
matamoii, see matamoi		
mataruna	mushrooms	
matata, haumata	bird	*Bowdleria punctata*
matata, see also mata		
matawha	kind of shark	
matika	musk [plant]	
matipo	shrub	poss. *Myrsine australis*
matirewa, see matoreha		
matohe	butterfish	*Odax pullus*
matoi	shrub	
matoreha, matirewa	cutty grass	poss. *Gahnia* spp.
matua-a-iwi	returning inaka	*Galaxias* spp.
matuhi	kind of bird	*Xenicus* spp.
matuku	bittern	*Botaurus poiciloptilus*
mauku, see patiti		
ma uku uku, mauukuuku [maukuku]	kind of grass	
mauukuuku, see ma uku uku		
merene	water melon	*Citrullus vulgaris*
miki	shrub	poss. *Cyathodes* spp.
mikihoe, mikioe	plant?	
mikimiki	stinkwood	poss. *Coprosma* spp. or *Cyathodes* spp.
mikioe, see mikihoe		
mimiha (NI), see kauri		

mimiha	kind of seal	Order Pinnipedia
mingi	plant	
miro	tree	*Prumnopitys ferruginea*
miromiro	tomtit	*Petroica macrocephala*
miuweka	merganser ?	?*Mergus australis*
moa	extinct moa	Dinornithiformes
moamoa	fish	*Genyagnus novaezelandiae*
moeanu	skipper, 'sandfish'	poss. *Scomberesox* spp.
moenu	fish	
moeraro, see tororaro		
moeriki	bird	
mogi, see moki		
mohoao	kind of flounder	*Rhombosolea retiaria*
mohoperuru (NI)	bird	
mohorangi, see kuri maori		
mokakariki (Nel), see mokokakariki (Can)		
mokarakara	red/black butterfly	poss. *Vanessa gonerilla*
moki, mogi	fish	*Latridopsis* spp.
mokimoki	fern	*Phymatosorus scandens*
moko-huruhuru, mokotuahuruhuru (Can), pirirewa (Tar)	kind of lizard	
moko-kakariki (Can), mokakariki (Nel)	kind of lizard	prob. *Naultinus elegans*
mokomoko	kind of lizard	
mokopapa	tree lizard	poss. *Hoplodactylus* spp.
moko-tua-huruhuru, see mokohuruhuru		
mouku (NI), piupiu (SI)	kind of fern	poss. *Asplenium bulbiferum*
muheke	squid	

N

naeroa, see keroa (Mur)		
naki (SI), see puhi (SI)		
namu	sandfly	*Austrosimulium* spp.
naninani	goat	*Capra hircus*
naonao	midge	
naupiro	anise	*Angelica montana*
nei (Mantell)	grasstree	poss. *Dracophyllum* spp.
neinei	fish	
neinei	tree	poss. *Dracophyllum* spp.
ngaio, see kaio		
ngaio, kaio	tree	*Myoporum laetum*
ngarara, see karara		
ngaro	kind of fly	

ngehe, see marare		
ngeru (NI), see puhi (SI)		
nikau	palm	*Rhopalostylis sapida*
noinoiraki	kind of potato	*Solanum tuberosum*
noke, noki	earthworms, worms in children	
noke-ma	white [earth] worms	
noke-pako	black [earth] worms	
nokepango	'black' worms	
noke-tuatara, noki-tuatara	ordinary red [earth] worm	
noke-waiu, noki waiu	big white [earth]worm	
nokewhero	red worms	
noki, see noke		
noki-tuatara, see noke tuatara		
noki-waiu, see noke waiu		

O

oe (HB)	plant?	
okaoka, ongaonga	nettle	*Urtica* spp.
ongaonga, see okaoka		
oue	kind of flax	poss. *Phormium* spp.

P

paala (SI) [pala], see puru		
paara [para]	frost fish	*Lepidopus caudatus*
paawaa [pawa], see pawa		
paikea	humpback whale	*Megaptera novaeangliae*
pakake	hair seal	*Phocarctos hookeri*
pakau	kind of grasshopper	
pakeha pioioi, see kairaka		
pakirikiri	rock cod	prob. *Lotella* spp.
paku	kind of moss	
pakura, pukaki, pukeko	swamphen, swampturkey	*Porphyrio porphyrio*
panako	fish	poss. *Galaxias* spp.
pao	kind of flax	*Phormium* spp.
papaaka [papaka]	kind of eel	*Anguilla* spp.
papaii	kind of speargrass	*Aciphylla* spp.
papaka	general name for crabs	
papaka	kind of crab	
papaka	kind of fernroot	prob. *Pteridium esculentum*
papaka	kind of potato	*Solanum tuberosum*
papaka kokoriki	kind of crab	
papaka rerere	kind of crab	
papaka-roharoha	kind of crab	
papaka-taniko	kind of crab	

papaka-tuatini	kind of crab	
papaki	kind of shark	
papakoura	plant	
paparaki	cabbage	Brassica spp.
paraki, see patete		
parara, parikoko	bird	Pachyptila vittata
parareka (Tgr)	horseshoe fern	prob. Marattia salicina
parareka	kind of potato	Solanum tuberosum
paratawhiti	horseshoe fern	Marattia salicina
parera	grey duck, wild duck	Anas superciliosa
parera-kowhio	blue mountain duck	poss. Hymenolaimus malacorhynchos
paretao	kind of fern	
parewaka, see kakariki		
parikoko, see parara		
paritea	kind of wild swede	Brassica spp.
parooaroo [paroaro]	plant?	
parumoana, see paru-o-te-moana		
paru-o-te-moana, parumoana	kind of seaweed	
patakaroa	kind of starfish	
patake	little teal	Anas spp.
patangaroa	kind of starfish	
patangatanga	red jacket fish	
pateke	teal	prob. Anas chlorotis
patete, paraki	fish	Retropinna retropinna
patete	kind of ferntree	poss. Cyathea smithii
patete	plant	
pati	kind of seaweed	
pati, see hoe moana		
patiki	flounder, flatfish	Rhombosolea spp.
patiki, pipi-poro	shellfish	
patiki-horihori, horihori	sole	Peltorhamphus novaezeelandiae
patiki-kutu-horihori	sole	Peltorhamphus novaezeelandiae
patiki-wai-maori	freshwater flounder	Rhombosolea spp.
patiki-wai-tai	a sea flounder	Rhombosolea spp.
patiki-wai-whai, waiwhai	saltwater flounder	Rhombosolea spp.
patikuku, see hoe moana		
patiti, mauku	common tussock	Poa spp.
patiti	kind of potato	Solanum tuberosum
patohe	fish	Paratrachichthys trailli
patotara	plant	Cyathodes fraseri
patotara	yellow bellied flounder	Rhambosolea leporina
patutuki	Maori chief, rock cod	Notothenia angustata
paua, see pawa		

paukene	pumpkin	*Cucurbita* spp.
pawa, paawaa [pawa], paua	shellfish	*Haliotis* spp.
peho (Tgr), see peopeo		
pekapeka, see kopekapeka		
penemauroa	maidenhair fern	poss. *Adiantum* spp.
penu	small penguin	
peopeo, piopio, peho (Tgr)	morepork	*Ninox novaeseelandiae*
perei (Tgr)	plant	
pi	bee	poss. *Apis mellifera*
piharau (NI)	lamprey	*Geotria australis*
piharenga	kind of cricket	poss. *Teleogryllus commodus*
pihipihi (Akaroa), tauhou (NI), titiri pounamu (Temuka)	ringeye	*Zosterops lateralis*
pikao	kind of grass	*Desmoschoenus spiralis*
pikiarero	plant	*Clematis* spp.
pikipiki	kind of cockabully	prob. *Galaxias* spp.
pikiraki, pikirangi (Can)	mistletoe	*Elytranthe tetrapetala*
pikirangi (Can), see pikiraki		
pikopiko	kind of fern	*Polystichum richardii*
pimiromiro	tomtit	*Petroica macrocephala*
piopio, see peopeo		
pioioi	lark, ground lark	*Anthus novaeseelandiae*
pipi (Nel)	general name for shellfish	
pipi (SI)	general name for mussels	
pipi (SI) akapipi, kuku	mussel	prob. *Mytilus edulis aoteanus*, poss. *Perna canaliculus*
pipi (NI)	shellfish	*Paphies australis*
pipiki	fish	
pipi-poro, see patiki		
pipiwharauroa	shining cuckoo	*Chalcites lucidus*
piripiri, hutuwai, bidibidi, bidibid	plant	*Acaena* spp.
piripiripohatu	fish	*Cheimarrichthys fosteri*
pirirewa	tree	
pirirewa (Tar), see mokotuahuruhuru		
pirita, kareao, karewao	supplejack [vine]	*Ripogonum scandens*
pitakataka	fantail	*Rhipidura fuliginosa*
pitau	part of raupo or koareare	*Typha orientalis*
piupiu, see mouku		
piupiu	maidenhair [fern]	poss. *Adiantum* spp.
poaka	wild pig	*Sus scrofa*
poaka, see pouaka		
poaka	black torea, kuaka	*Himantopus leucocephalus*
poanaka	plant	
pohata	kind of wild swede	*Brassica* spp.
pohata	plant	
pohio	skua	*Catharacta* or *Stercorarius* spp.

pohio	kind of gull	*Larus* spp.
pohowaiki, see pouhawaiki		
pohue	plant	*Calystegia* spp.
poka, ponga (NI)	treefern, bungee	*Cyathea dealbata*
pokaka	tree/shrub	*Elaeocarpus hookerianus*
poketara	puffball	*Calvatia* or *Lycoperdon* spp.
pola, see pora		
ponga (NI), see poka		
pongarongaro	gnats or midges	
popohua, see popohue		
popohue	shrub	
popohue, popohua	white clematis	*Clematis* spp.
popoiakore	kind of seal	
popoikore	hair seal	*Phocarctos hookeri*
popokarua, see terehu		
popokorua	ants	*Monomorium antarcticum*
popokotea	native canary	*Mohoua* spp.
poporokaiwhiria	kind of tree	
popoti, see terehu		
pora, pola	'Maori cabbage'	*Brassica* spp.
poraka (NI)	frog	*Litoria* spp.
porapora-patiki	'small flounder' (Moeraki)	*Rhombosolea* spp.
porere, see kakariki		
porete, see kakariki		
poroporo	Maori gooseberries	*Solanum* spp.
poroporo	kind of flounder	*Rhombosolea* spp.
poroporo-tawhiri (SI), see rautawhiri (SI)		
porotata	kind of mushroom, fungi	
pouaka (Mur), powaka, kuaka (NI), poaka	godwit	*Limosa lapponica*
pouaka	kind of grass	*Poa triodioides*
pouakai	bird	
pouakai	bush or quail hawk	*Falco novaeseelandiae*
pouhawaiki, pohowaiki	English rat	*Rattus* spp.
powaka, see pouaka		
powhaitere (NI), see kakariki		
pua-ata-ata	silvery [fish]	*Retropinna retropinna*
puaihakarua	soldier fish, red jacket	*Helicolensus* spp.
puaiwhakarua	fish	
puataata	young minnow or silverbait	poss. *Galaxias maculatus*
puatata	fish	*Retropinna retropinna*
puha, puwha (Tgr)	sowthistle, ordinary kind, bush thistle	*Sonchus* spp.

puha-taratara	kind of sowthistle, bushthistle	*Sonchus* spp.
puhi (SI), naki (SI), tori (NI), ngeru (NI), puti (SI), puhihi (SI)	cat	*Felis catus*
puhihi (SI), see puhi		
pukahu	moss in swamps	
pukakaho	toetoe reeds, reeds	prob. *Cortaderia* spp.
pukaki, see pakura		
pukanikani	shellfish	*Aulacomya ater maoriana*
pukatea	kind of tree	
pukawerewere	spiders, general term for most insects	
pukeko, see pakura		
pukio, pukiu, upoko-takata	niggerheads [plant/grass]	poss. *Carex secta*
pukiu. see pukio		
pukutuara	reptile?	
pukutuora	an aquatic monster	
punawe, see punui		
punitanita, see kotimana		
punuatuna	young eels ?	poss. *Anguilla* spp.
punui, punawe	plant	*Stilbocarpa* spp.
pupatiti	kind of tussock	
pupu	common variety [shellfish]	*Turbo (Moedlia) granosus*
pupu or bubu	periwinkle	poss. *Littorina* spp.
pupu kaiwhiri	shellfish	poss. *Cookia sulcata*
pupu-kari-kawa	shellfish	
pupu koihi	shellfish	*Penion sulcatus*
pupu-korama	shellfish	
pupu-ma-takata	shellfish	
puramorehu	fish	
puramorua	pigfish	*Congiopodus leucopaecilus*
purau	plant	poss. *Bulbinella* spp.
purehurehu	insect	
puriri	tree	*Vitex lucens*
puru (Can), paala [pala]	bull [cattle]	*Bos taurus*
puru	mould	
purua, see kopuru		
puruheka	fungoid growth, or mildew	
putakitaki, putangitangi	paradise duck	*Tadorna variegata*
putangitangi, see putakitaki puti (SI), see puhi puwha (Tgr), see puha		

R

rako, iro, rango	blowfly, bluebottle	*Calliphora quadrimaculata*
ramarama	pepper tree	prob. *Pseudowintera colorata*
ramarama	kind of tree	poss. *Lophomyrtus bullata*
rangiora	shrub	*Brachyglottis repanda*

rango, see rako		
rapiti	rabbit	*Oryctolagus cuniculus*
rapoka	sea leopard, sea-devil	*Hydrurga leptonyx*
raramu	Derwent potato	*Solanum tuberosum*
raratahurihuri	finback, ?blackfish	poss. *Balaenoptera physalus*
raratawhiriwhiri	blackfish	poss. *Globicephala melaena*
raratawhiriwhiri	seal	poss. *Arctocephalus forsteri*
rarauhe, see aruhe		
rari	New Zealand ling	*Genypterus blacodes*
rari	fish	*Macruronus novaezelandiae*
rata	ironwood	*Metrosideros robusta*
rata	kind of vine	*Metrosideros fulgens*
rauaruhe, see aruhe		
raukiokio	kind of fern	
raupo	bulrush	*Typha orientalis*
rauriki	kind of sowthistle, or bush thistle	*Sonchus* spp.
rau tawhiri (SI), poroporo-tawhiri (SI), kaiwhiria (NI)	black maple (settlers), matipo (townspeople)	*Pittosporum tenuifolium*
raututu	kind of flounder	*Rhombosolea* spp.
raututu	sole?	*Peltorhamphus* spp.
rawaru	blue cod	*Parapercis colias*
rehua	plant	
rekareka	kind of water plant	
reko, riko	kind of eel	*Anguilla* spp.
rengarenga (Tgr)	plant	
repe, Te Maro-o-Hine teiwaiwa, makorepe	elephant fish	*Callorhynchus milii*
repe	kind of potato	*Solanum tuberosum*
reperepe-o-Tautini, reperepe-tautini (Akaroa)	jellyfish	
reperepe-tautini (Akaroa), see reperepe-o-Tautini		
rerewa	plant	
rerewaka	kind of grass, plant	
rerewaka	pied stilt	*Himantopus* spp.
riko, see reko		
rimu	freshwater weed	
rimu	kelp – ordinary kind	*Durvillaea antarctica*
rimu	red pine	*Dacrydium cupressinum*
rimupuka, rimupuku, rimurapa	kind of kelp	*Durvillea antarctica*
rimupuku, see rimupuka		
rimurapa, see reimpuka		
rimurimu	carrageen (pakeha), kind of seaweed	
rimurimu	pink coloured seaweed	

rimurimu	red swamp growth	poss. *Azolla filiculoides*
ririwaka (Tgr)	sedge	poss. *Scirpus fluviatilis*
riroriro	grey warbler	*Gerygone igata*
riroriro (HB)	native canary, whitehead	*Mohoua* spp.
ro	stick insect	*Argosarchus horridus* or *Clitarchus laeviusculus*
rohutu	tree ?	poss. *Neomyrtus pedunculata*
rongaronga	midges	
ropi	kind of potato	*Solanum tuberosum*
rori	shag, small sea shag	*Phalacrocorax* spp.
rori	shellfish	*Scutus* spp.
roriki	a water plant	
roroa	shellfish	*Resania lanceolata*
roroa (SI) see toheroa		
ruarangi	Maori dog	*Canis familiaris*
rua-whenua	big white worm	
runa	plant	
ruru	morepork owl	*Ninox novaeseelandiae*
ruru koukou, see koukou		
ruru-whenua (Mur), whekau	big morepork, open country owl, laughing owl	*Sceloglaux albifacies*

T

taaki	donkey	
taewa (NI), see mahetau (SI)		
taha	plant	poss. *Lagenaria vulgaris*
tahoehoe	shellfish	
taiwhatiwhati	shellfish	prob. *Paphies* spp.
takahe (Can), see takahea		
takahea (Mur), takahe (Can)	bird	*Notornis mantelli*
takakaha (Moeraki), see kakaha		
takapani	kind of shark	
takapo	shrub	prob. *Gaultheria antipoda*
take-harakeke	kind of eel	*Anguilla* spp.
takirikau (HB)	kind of flax	prob. *Phormium* spp.
takitaki	turkey	*Meleagris gallopavo*
tamuri	snapper	*Chrysophrys auratus*
taniwha	kind of shark	
tapairu	kind of octopus	prob. *Octopus maorum*
tapuka, see tapuku		
tapuku, tapuka	snowberry	*Gaultheria* spp.
tarahikoau	kind of tussock	
tarakihi, warehou	bream (Moeraki)	*Seriolella brama*
taramea	ordinary speargrass	*Aciphylla* spp.

tara pirohe	whitefront tern, barracouta bird	*Sterna* spp.
tara puka	black bill gull	*Larus bulleri*
tarapuke	bird	*Larus* spp.
tarapunga	sea martin [bird]	*Larus* spp.
tarata	white maple (settlers)	*Pittosporum eugenioides*
tara-whaka-rara	Caspian tern	*Hydroprogne Caspian*
taro	plant	*Colocasia esculenta*
tarutaru	grass	
taru whenua	ordinary grass of the plains	
tata	brown duck	*Anas* spp.
tataa	spoonbill duck	prob. *Anas rhynchotis*
tataki	a grass	poss. *Gahnia lacera*
tataki	kind of thrush	poss. *Bowdleria punctata*
tataraheka, see tatarahika		
tatarahika, tataraheka	lawyer [vine]	*Rubus* spp.
tataramoa	kind of bramble	*Rubus* spp.
tatare	kind of shark	
tatariki	yellowhead, canary	*Mohoua ochrocephala*
tauhou (NT), see pihipihi		
tautini	kind of crab	
tawa	kind of tree	*Beilschmiedia tawa*
tawai	beech or birch	*Nothofagus* spp.
tawai-whero	red birch, black birch (settlers)	*Nothofagus* spp.
tawake	kind of penguin	
tawaki	big penguins, ordinary-size penguin	
tawhiwhi	vine	poss. *Parsonsia heterophylla*
Te-Aitaka-a-Puka	whale, cowfish	poss. *Tursiops truncatus*
Te Haumaataa	kind of grass	
Te Maro-o-Hine teiwaiwa, see repe		
Te Pokeka-a-Tama, see kiekie		
terakihi, see kikiawaru		
terehu, popokarua, popoti	porpoise	poss. *Australophocaena dioptrica*
te rerewa	plant	
Te-roa-mahoi	kind of kumera	*Ipomoea batatas*
Te-tatau-o-te-whare-o-Maui	daddy long legs	
tetehe	shellfish	
tetere moana	shellfish	*Anchomasa similis*
ti, kauru, tii, ti-whanake	cabbage tree	*Cordyline* spp.
tieke	saddleback [bird]	*Philesturnus carunculatus*
tii, see ti		
tikaakaa (Can) [tikaka], heihei (NI), manutane (Can)	rooster	*Gallus gallus*

tikaka	fowls	*Gallus gallus*
tikapu	mountain lily	
tikumu	mountain daisy	*Celmisia* spp.
tio	mud and rock oyster	*Crassostrea* or *Ostrea* spp.
tio kohatu, see tio pohatu		
tio paruparu, tio pati	mud oyster	*Ostrea* spp.
tio pati, see tio paruparu		
tio-pohatu, tio-kohatu	rock oyster	poss. *Crassostrea glomerata*
tiori	plant/shrub?	
titaiwaka, see titakataka		
titakataka, titaiwaka	fantail	*Rhipidura fuliginosa*
titi	muttonbird	*Puffinus griseus*
titiaweka	tree	
titiripounamu	rifleman	*Acanthisitta chloris*
titiri pounamu (Temuka), see pihipihi		
titi-wahine	kind of titi	*Puffinus* spp.
titi wainui	kind of titi	*Puffinus* spp.
ti-tohea	dwarf cabbage tree	prob. *Cordyline pumilio*
ti toi, toi	plant/tree?	prob. *Cordyline indivisa*
titoki	tree	*Alectryon excelsus*
ti-whanake	cabbage tree	*Cordyline* spp.
toatoa	tree	*Phyllocladus* spp.
toetoe	grasshopper	
toetoe	toetoe reeds	prob. *Cortaderia* spp.
toetoe herekau, toetoe mata, toetoe-matai, toetoe-paka, toetoe pakau, toetoe pukio		
toetoe, see also haumatangi, mata, pukakaho		
tohemango (NI), see toheroa		
tohemaunga (NI), see toheroa		
toheroa (NI), roroa (SI), tohemango (NI), tohemaunga (NI), tupehokura (Otago), whakai-a-tama (Can)	shellfish	*Paphies ventricosa*
toi, see ti toi		
toitoi, see mata		
toitoi (HB)	marsh rail	
toitoi	New Zealand creeper	*Finschia novaeseelandiae*
toitoi	shellfish	poss. *Cookia sulcata*
toitoi-pakau	plant	poss. *Cortaderia* spp.
tokoeka, tokoweka, totoweka	kind of kiwi	*Apteryx* spp.
tokoraki	king penguin	poss. *Aptenodytes patagonicus*
tokoweka, see tokoeka		

torea	redbill, oyster catcher	*Haematopus finschi*
toretore	shellfish	
tori (NI), see puhi		
toritori	shellfish	poss. *Mytilus edulis aoteanus*
toro	fish	*Leptoscopus macropygus*
toroa	albatross	*Diomedea* spp.
toroku, torongu	black hairy caterpillar	poss. *Metacrias* spp.
toromiro	True lovers's knot [fern]	
torongu, see toroku		
toropakihi, tupakihi (Nel)	lizards, grass lizard	poss. *Leiolopisma* spp.
tororaro, moeraro	vine	prob. *Muehlenbeckia* spp.
totara	tree	prob. *Podocarpus totara*
totoara	robin	*Petroica australis*
totokipio	diver, dabchick	*Podiceps rufopectus*
totoria	mollyhawk	*Diomedea* spp.
totoripa	dusky plover	poss. *Charadrius* spp.
totoweka, see tokoeka		
towai	tree	prob. *Weinmannia* spp.
tuaki, tuangi	kind of cockle	*Chione stutchburyi*
tuangi, see tuaki		
tuaraki	black [earth]worm	
tuatara	tuatara	prob. *Sphenodon punctatus*
tuatini	kind of shark	*Notorhynchus cepedianus*
tuere	blind eel, slime fish	*Eptatretus cirrhatus*
tuere	lamprey, blind eel	*Geotria australis*
tui or koko	bird	*Prosthemadera novaeseelandiae*
tuiau	flea	
tuka (Can), tukarakau, uhu, huhu (NI)	white pine grub	*Prionoplus reticularis*
tukarakau, see tuka		
tuke	kind of cockle	
tumatakura, see tumatakuru		
tumatakuru, see whino		
tumatakuru, tumatakura	wild Irishman shrub	*Discaria toumatou*
tuna	eel	*Anguilla* spp.
tuna, see also arokehe, hao, horepara, horihori-wai, kirirua, kokekehe, korakiraki, kotokoto, kouka, mairehe, manawa, matamoi, papaaka, reko, riko, take harakeke, tuna hau, tuna heke, tuna kai noke, 'tuna Pakeha', tuna raka, tuna tai, weko, winiwini hao		
tunahau	kind of eel	*Anguilla* spp.

tunaheke	kind of eel	*Anguilla* spp.
tuna-kai-noke	kind of eel	*Anguilla* spp.
'tuna-Pakeha', see horihori-wai		
tuna-rakau	kind of eel, wooden eel	*Anguilla* spp.
tunatai	a yellow eel	*Anguilla australis*
tupa	yellow shark	
tupakihi	kidney fern	*Trichomanes reniforme*
tupakihi (Nel), see toropakihi		
tupari	tree	
tupehokura (Otago), see toheroa		
tuupehukura	shellfish	
turakiao	kind of fern	
turokio	shrub	
turokio	long kind of cutty grass	
turokio	kind of fern	
turukio	fern with a long leaf	poss. *Blechnum discolor*
tutaahuna	kind of shark, dogfish of pakeha	
tutaekereru	plant	*Parsonsia heterophylla*
tutae-kereru	vegetable caterpillar	
tutahuna	kind of shark	
tutaki	thrush	*Bowdleria punctata*
tutaki	kind of grass	
tutauna	kind of shark	
tuterakihaunoa	sperm whale, 'sparm' whale (whalers)	*Physeter macrocephalus*
tutu	plant	*Coriaria* spp.
tutukiwi	bird	*Coenocorypha aucklandica*
tutuna	kind of grass	
tutu-rakau	tree	poss. *Coriaria arborea*

U

uhi	yam	*Dioscorea sativa*
uhu, see tuka		
upokohue	cowfish	
upokohue, see also Te Aitaka-a-Puka		
upokororo	grayling	*Prototroctes oxyrhynchus*
upokororo, see also haparu		
upokorua	ant	
upoko-takata, see pukio		
ururoa	kind of shark	

W

waerau	centipede	

waeroa (NI), see keroa		
waharoa	smelt	*Retropinna retropinna*
waina	introduced American sweet potato	
wairaki, see kanakana-wairaki		
wairaki-kanakana, see kanakana-wairaki		
wairoa	daddy-long-legs	
wairua-takata	moths	
wairua tangata	kind of moth	
waitaha	'white rock' potato	*Solanum tuberosum*
waiwhai, see patiki-wai-whai		
warehou, see tarakihi		
waruwaru mahitau	plant?	
waruwaru taiawa	plant?	
weho	kind of mushroom	
weka	woodhen	*Gallirallus australis*
weko	'stockwhip' eel	*Anguilla* spp.
wera	general name for whales	
were	centipedes	
weta	insect	*Hemideina thoracica*
whai	skate	
whai	stingray	*Dasyatis* spp.
whaiporapora	kind of stingray	prob. *Dasyatis thetidis*
whaiuku	kind of stingray	prob. *Dasyatis thetidis*
whaiwhai	kind of flounder	*Rhombosolea* spp.
whakahao, whakahau	sea lion	*Phocarctos hookeri*
whakahau, see whakahao		
whakai-a-tama	shellfish	*Mactra* spp.
whakai-o-tama, see whakai-a-tama		
whakaira-tama	white mussel	poss. *Paphies ventricosa*
whaoriki	plant	
wharangi	kind of tree	*Melicope ternata*
wharangi	kind of paua	*Haliotis* spp.
wharariki, falariki	mountain flax	*Phormium cookianum*
whareatua	puffball mushroom	*Langermannia gigantea*
whauhi	ribbonwood	prob. *Plagianthus betulinus* poss. *Hoheria* spp.
whawhai	kind of flounder	*Rhombosolea* spp.
whe	kind of caterpillar	
whe	small stick insect	poss. *Clitarchus laeviusculus*
whekau, see ruru-whenua		
wheke	octopus	*Octopus maorum*
wheke, see also tapairu		
wheki	ferntree	*Dicksonia fibrosa*

whetiko	pupu [shellfish]	*Diloma subrostrata*
whino, tumatakuru	gorse	*Ulex* spp.
whio	blue mountain duck	*Hymenolaimus malacorhynchos*
whioioi	sandlark	*Anthus novaeseelandiae*
wi	snowgrass	poss. *Juncus* spp.
wi, see wiwi		
winiwini-hao (Temuka)	small kind of eel	*Anguilla* spp.
witara	weasels	*Mustela nivalis*
wiwi, wi	rushes	poss. *Juncus* spp.

REFERENCES

1. REFERENCES USED FOR INTRODUCTION

Andersen, Johannes, *Maori Life in Ao-tea* (Christchurch: Whitcombe and Tombs, 1907).
Anderson, Atholl, *Te Puoho's Last Raid: The march from Golden Bay to Southland in 1836 and defeat at Tuturau* (Dunedin: Otago Heritage Books, 1986).
___ *Race Against Time: The early Maori-Pakeha families and the development of the mixed-race population in southern New Zealand* (Dunedin: Hocken Library, 1991).
___ 'Anne Wharetutu Newton fl. 1827–1870', in *Dictionary of New Zealand Biography, Volume 1: 1769–1869*, ed. W. Oliver (Wellington: Allen and Unwin and Department of Internal Affairs), pp. 308–09.
Beattie, Herries, *Pioneer Recollections: Chiefly of the Mataura Valley*, volume 1 (Mataura Ensign, 1909).
___ *Pioneer Recollections: Chiefly of the Mataura Valley*, volume 2 (Mataura Ensign, 1911).
___ 'Traditions and legends collected from the Natives of Murihiku' Part 1, *Journal of the Polynesian Society* 24, 1915, pp. 1–15.
___ 'Traditions and legends collected from the Natives of Murihiku' Part 2, *Journal of the Polynesian Society* 24, 1915, pp. 17–26.
___ 'Traditions and legends collected from the Natives of Murihiku' Part 6, *Journal of the Polynesian Society* 26, 1917, pp. 61–72.
___ 'Traditions and legends collected from the Natives of Murihiku' Part 7, *Journal of the Polynesian Society* 26, 1917, pp. 73–77.
___ 'Traditions and legends collected from the Natives of Murihiku' Part 8, *Journal of the Polynesian Society* 27, 1918, pp. 79–103.
___ 'Traditions and legends collected from the Natives of Murihiku' Part 9, *Journal of the Polynesian Society* 28, 1919, pp. 42–51.
___ 'Traditions and legends collected from the Natives of Murihiku' Part 11, *Journal of the Polynesian Society* 28, 1919, pp. 212–25.
___ 'Traditions and legends collected from the Natives of Murihiku' Part 12, *Journal of the Polynesian Society* 29, 1920, pp. 128–38.
___ 'Traditions and legends collected from the Natives of Murihiku' Part 13, *Journal of the Polynesian Society* 29, 1920, pp. 189–98.
___ 'Traditions and legends collected from the Natives of Murihiku' Part 14, *Journal of the Polynesian Society* 31, 1922, pp. 193–97.
___ 'The Southern Maori, and Greenstone', *Transactions of the New Zealand Institute* 32, 1920, pp. 45–52.
___ 'Nature lore of the southern Maori', *Transactions of the New Zealand Institute* 52, 1920, pp. 52–77.
___ 'LIII – Acknowledgements', *Otago Daily Times*, Dunedin, 6 June 1931.
___ *Tikao Talks: Traditions and tales* (Dunedin: Reed, 1939).
___ *Moriori* (Dunedin: Otago Daily Times and Witness, 1941).

___ *Maori Place-Names of Otago* (Dunedin: Otago Daily Times and Witness, 1944).
___ *Maori Place-Names of Canterbury* (Dunedin: Otago Daily Times and Witness, 1946).
___ *Maori Lore of Lake, Alp and Fiord* (Dunedin: Otago Daily Times and Witness, 1945).
___ *The Maoris and Fiordland* (Dunedin: Otago Daily Times and Witness, 1949).
___ *Our Southernmost Maoris* (Dunedin: Otago Daily Times and Witness, 1954).
___ ed, *Folklore and Fairy Tales of the Canterbury Maoris* (Dunedin: Otago Daily Times, 1957).
Best, Elsdon, *The Maori*, 2 volumes (Wellington: Polynesian Society Memoir 5, 1924).
___ *The Maori Canoe* (Wellington: Dominion Museum Bulletin 7, 1925).
___ *Games and Pastimes of the Maori* (Wellington: Government Printer, 1925).
___ *Fishing Methods and Devices of the Maori* (Wellington: Dominion Museum Bulletin 12, 1929).
___ *Forest Lore of the Maori* (Wellington: Dominion Museum Bulletin 14, 1942).
Buck, Peter (Te Rangi Hiroa), *The Coming of the Maori* (Wellington: Maori Purposes Fund Board, 1949).
Dawson, Les, *Taproots Revisited: The whakapapa of Wharetutu and George Newton*, (Invercargill: Taproots Publishing, 1986).
Garven, Peter, *The Genealogy of the Ngai Tahu*, 3 volumes (Christchurch: The Author, 1974).
von Haast, Julius, 'Address', *Transactions of the New Zealand Institute* 10, 1878, pp. 37–56.
Harlow, Ray, *A Word-list of South Island Maori* (Auckland: Linguistic Society of New Zealand, 1987).
Hocken, T.M., *Contributions to the Early History of New Zealand (Settlement of Otago)* (London: Sampson, Low and Marston, 1898).
Jacobson, H.C. and J.W. Stack, *Tales of Banks Peninsula* (Akaroa: The Akaroa Mail, 1914).
MacDonald, David, 'New Zealand Collections III: The Beattie papers', *Archifacts* 3, 1974, pp. 4–7.
McNab, Robert, *Murihiku and the Southern Islands* (Invercargill: William Smith, 1907).
Ngai Tahu Maori Trust Board, *Original Beneficiaries as listed in Maori Land Court Order, dated 12 March 1925* (Christchurch, 1963).
Ngai Tahu Maori Trust Board, *Ngai Tahu Kaumatua alive in 1848, as established by the Maori Land Court in 1925 and the Ngai Tahu Census Committee in 1929* (Christchurch, 1967).
Oppenheim, R.S., *Maori Death Customs* (Wellington: Reed, 1973).
Phillipps, W.J., *Maori Houses and Storehouses* (Wellington: Dominion Museum, 1952).
Shortland, Edward, *The Southern Districts of New Zealand* (London: Longman, Brown, Green and Longmans, 1851).
Skinner, H.D., 'Culture areas in New Zealand', *Journal of the Polynesian Society* 30, 1921, pp. 70–78.
___ *The Morioris of the Chatham Islands* (Honolulu: Bishop Museum Memoir 9, 1923).
___ *Comparatively Speaking*, edited by Peter Gathercole, Foss Leach and Helen Leach (Dunedin: University of Otago Press, 1974).
Smith, S. Percy, *Lore of the Whare-wananga: Part I, Things Celestial* (Polynesian Society Memoir 3, 1913).
___ *Lore of the Whare-wananga: Part II, Things Terrestrial* (Polynesian Society Memoir 4, 1915).

Stack, James, 'Sketch of the traditional history of the South Island Maoris', *Transactions of the New Zealand Institute* 10, 1877, pp. 57–92.
_____ *Kaiapohia* (Christchurch: Whitcombe and Tombs, 1893).
_____ *South Island Maoris* (Christchurch: Whitcombe and Tombs, 1898).
Starke, June (ed.), *Journal of a Rambler* (Auckland: Oxford University Press, 1986).
Taylor, Nancy, *Early Travellers in New Zealand* (Wellington: Oxford University Press, 1959).
Tregear, Edward, *The Maori-Polynesian Comparative Dictionary* (Wellington: Lyon and Blair, 1891).
_____ *The Maori Race* (Wanganui: A.D. Willis, 1904).
Williams, H.W., *Maori Dictionary*, 5th edition (Wellington: Government Printer, 1917).
Wohlers, J.F.H., 'The mythology and traditions of the Maori in New Zealand', *Transactions of the New Zealand Institute* 7, 1874, pp. 3–53.

2. REFERENCES USED IN COMPILING GLOSSARY

Allan, Harry Howard, *Flora of New Zealand*, volume 1 (Wellington: Government Printer, 1961).
Ayling, Tony, *Collins Guide to the Sea Fishes of New Zealand* (Auckland: Collins, 1982).
Brownsey, Patrick J. and John C. Smith-Dodsworth, *New Zealand Ferns and Allied plants* (Auckland: David Bateman, 1989).
Burton, Maurice, *Systematic Dictionary of Mammals of the World* (London: Museum Press, 1962).
Child, John, *New Zealand Shells* (Auckland, Periwinkle Books, 1974).
Coffey, B.T. and J.S. Clayton, *New Zealand Water Plants: A guide to plants found in New Zealand freshwaters* (Hamilton: Ruakura Agricultural Centre, 1988).
Crowe, Andrew, *A Field Guide to the Native Edible Plants of New Zealand: Including those plants eaten by the Maori* (Auckland: Collins, 1981).
___ *Native Edible Plants of New Zealand* (Auckland: Hodder and Stoughton, 1990).
Daniel, M. and A. Baker, *Collins Guide to the Mammals of New Zealand* (Auckland: Collins, 1986).
Dawson, Stephen, *The New Zealand Whale and Dolphin Digest: The official Project Jonah guidebook* (Auckland: Brickrow Publishing, 1985).
Falla, R.A., R.B. Gibson and E.G. Turbott, *The New Guide to the Birds of New Zealand and Outlying Islands* (Auckland: Collins, 1979).
Firth, Susan, Martyn Firth and Elizabeth Firth, *Ferns of New Zealand* (Auckland: Hodder and Stoughton, 1986).
Foord, Malcolm, *New Zealand Descriptive Animal Dictionary: The common names of the animals, native and introduced, large and small, on the land and in the waters of New Zealand and her outlying islands* (Dunedin: M.R.R. Foord, 1990).
Forster, R.R and L.M. Forster, *Small Land Animals of New Zealand* (Dunedin: John McIndoe, 1970).
Gill, Brian, *Collins Handguide to the Frogs and Reptiles of New Zealand* (Auckland: Collins, 1986).

Graham, David H., *A Treasury of New Zealand Fishes*, 2d ed. (Wellington: Reed, 1956).
Healy, A.T., Standard common names for Weeds in New Zealand: Including casuals, economic plant escapes, and agricultural seed impurities, *2d rev ed. (Hastings: New Zealand Weed and Pest Control Society Inc, 1984).*
Laidlaw, W.B.R., *Butterflies of New Zealand* (Auckland: Collins, 1970).
Miller, David, *Common Insects in New Zealand* (Wellington: Reed, 1971).
Moore, Lucy B. and Elizabeth Edgar, *Flora of New Zealand, volume II: Indigenous tracheophyta, monocotyledons except gramineae* (Wellington: Government Printer, 1969).
Morton, John and Michael Miller, *The New Zealand Sea Shor* (London: Collins, 1968).
Paul, Larry J., *New Zealand Fishes: An identification guide* (Auckland: Reed Methuen, 1986).
Powell, AW.B., *Native Animals of New Zealand*, rev. ed. by B.J. Gill et al. (Auckland: Auckland Institute and Museum, 1979).
_____ New Zealand Mollusca: Marine, land and freshwater shells *(Auckland: Collins, 1979).*
_____ *Shells of New Zealand: An illustrated handbook*, 5th rev. ed. (Christchurch: Whitcoulls, 1976).
Pownall, Glen, *New Zealand Shells and Shell Fish* (Wellington: Seven Seas Publishing, 1971).
Reader's Digest Complete Book of New Zealand Birds (Sydney: Readers Digest, 1985).
Robb, Joan, New Zealand Amphibians and Reptiles in Colour *(Auckland: Collins, 1980).*
Salmon, J.T., New Zealand Flowers and Plants in Colour *(Wellington: Reed, 1976).*
Strickland, R.R., Nga Tini a Tangaroa: A Maori-English, English-Maori dictionary of fish names *(Wellington: MAF Fisheries, 1990).*
Svrcek, Mirko, The Hamlyn Book of Mushrooms and Fungi *(London: Hamlyn, 1983).*
Williams, Dale, *Home Fruit Growing in New Zealand* (Wellington: Government Printer, 1985).

INDEX

INDEX OF PERSONAL NAMES AND PERSONIFICATIONS

Adam, William, 11, *13*
Albert, Prince, 264
Amo, 264
Andersen, J.C., 364
Ao-marere, 487
Aohikuraki *see* Te Ahuhikuraki, 372, 373
Aonui, 569
Aotea, 286
Apanui, 344
Apes, Elisha William, 26
Aroaroakaehe, 435
Arokaihe, 426
Auhunga, 285
Awhioraki *see* Kahukura, 401, 440
Awhiorangi *see* Awhioraki, 401
Beattie, Christina, 10
Beattie, Herries/James Hemes, 9–32, 35, *37*, 40, 51, 55, 65, 97, 127, 179, 295, 321, 328, 329; *see also* General index: *Journal of the Polynesian Society, Pioneer Recollections* Volume 2, *Tikao Talks, Transactions of the New Zealand Institute*
Beattie, Herries (son of JHB), 10
Beattie, James, 9
Beattie, Margaret, 10
Beattie, Mary, 10
Benham, Professor, 274, 467
Best, Elsdon, 12, 15, 30, 59, 298, 562, 567
Bill (a Kanaka), 544
Bishop, H.W., 173
Bloody Jack *see* Tuhawaiki, 430
Boultbee, John, 30
Britt, Charlie, 158
Buck, Peter, 12, 30, 73
Bullen, F.T., 38

Caddell, James, 185
Cameron, Mrs, 193
Cameron, Eruete Poko, 23
Carroll, James, 324
Chapman, Frederick, 18, 26
Christ, 243, 412, 557

Colac, 'old' *see* Matene, Korako, 25
Colenso, W., 62, 36
Connor, Jack/Kona/Kana, Tieke, 26
Cook, Captain, 120, 187, 401, 462, 463, 488, 573
Couch, Mrs, 28
Couch, Wira, 28
Coupar, Louisa, 24
Coupar, Stewart, 24
Cowan, James, 18, 444
Crane, Elizabeth (Mrs), 25

David (in Bible), 281, 576
Davis, Harry *see* te Maire, H., 26

Ell, Mr, 463

Faitt, Denham, *115*
Fels, Mr, 550
Forbes, J.A. 12
Frere, Reverend, 270
Fulton, Dr, 187

Gilroy, Mrs, 442
Gilroy, Paddy, 38
God (Christian), 380, 412
Goliath (in Bible), 281
Great Lady of Death *see* Hinenuiotepo, 398
Great Lady of the Night *see* Hinenuiotepo, 405, 557
Green, T.E./Thomas/Tom, 23, 28, 277, 282, 367, 374, 433, 445, 460, 464, 468

Haere, 404
Haereroa, Tiemi Kupa *see* Kupa, Tiemi Haereroa, 39
Hakeke, 250
Hakopa, 211
Halsey, Captain, 547
Hamo, 433
Hamua, 375, 438
Hansard, Mr, 60
Hapu-matua, 301
Hapuku, 523

Hari, Leah, 265
Harlow, Ray, 30
Harper, Colin, *115*
Harper/Harpur, Mere/Mary (Mrs), 26, 65
Harrison, Reverend, 466
Hateatea, 366, 378, 452
Haupere, Hoani *see* Tommy Billy, 27
Hekehekeinuku *see* Rangi, 395
Hekehekeipapa *see* Papatuanuku, 396
Hekuru, 442
Hemo *see* Hamo, 433
Hempleman, G., 430
Henry (son of Rita), 446
Herd, William A., 324
Heslop Brothers, 251
Heuheu, Mrs, 209
Hikaiti, 440
Hikatutae, 273, 429, 438
Hikutauataua *see* Maui, 393
Hine, 391, 558
Hine *see* Hineteiwaiwa, 562
Hine-ahu-one *see* Hinehauone, 58
Hineao, 414
Hinearoaropari, 384, 392
Hinearoraki, 384, 385, 388, 392
Hinehaka, 212, 539
Hinehauone, 58, 384, 385, 389, 391, 392, 399
Hineiteiwaiwa, 423
Hinekaitaki *see* Hinekaitangi, 428
Hinekaitangi, 443
Hinekakara, 437
Hinekato, 439
Hinemateroa, 414
Hinemoa, 259
Hinenuiotepo, 58, 391, 397, 398, 403, 406, 557, 565
Hinenuiotetoka *see* Hinepunuiotetoka, 400
Hinepaaka, 417
Hinepoupou, 478
Hinepunuiotetoka, 391
Hinepunuiotoka *see* Hinepunuiotetoka, 384

Hinepunuiotonga *see* Hinepunuiotetoka, 398
Hine-putauhinu, 488
Hinerautu, 441
Hinerauwharangi, 488
Hineroa *see* Hinemateroa, 414
Hineroriki, 384, 392
Hinerotia, 384, 392
Hinerotu, 415
Hinetakahere, 386
Hinetaumai, 464
Hineteiwaiwa, 424, 562
Hine-te-ngahere, 404
Hinetitama, 58, 384, 391, 397, 398, 403, 406, 557
Hineturepo, 386, 404
Hinewahia, 24
Hinewera, 415
Hocken, T.M., 12, 354, 575, 577
Hohapata, Pita Te Kahupuku, 29
Hori, George *see* Paraire, Hori, 569
Horipere, 522
Hotu-Mamoe, 442
Howell, Captain, 24, 193
Huareare, 364, 404
Huiarei, 434
Huirapa, 429, 537, 538

Inaka *see* Inanga, 286
Inanga, 284, 285
Io, 58, 131, 132, 370, 394, 395, 396, 402, 556
Io Whatamai, 395
Io Whatata, 395
Io-tatamai, 402
Io-whatata, 402
Ira-turoto, 442
Irakehu, 444
Iratahu, 434
Iraturoto, 561
Irawaru, 386, 387, 391, 404, 565
Iriraki *see* Irirangi, 372, 443
Irirangi, 414, 438

Jack *see* Tupairehana, 575
Jacobs, Mrs, 532
Jimmy the Boy *see* Caddell, James, 185
John the Baptist (in Bible), 383
Jonah (in Bible), 560
Joughin, Reverend, 408, 467

Kaapo, Hakopa, 532
Kae, 560, 562, 563
Kahore, 439
Kahu, Hoani Korehe, 23, 27
Kahu, Tiriata (Mrs), 27, 39
Kahu *see* Kahungunu, 437

Kahu (family), 23
Kahukuni, 416
Kahukura, 200, 285, 363, 373, 383, 400, 401, 428, 440, 446, 513, 556, 559, 560, 565
Kahukura-te-paku, 372
Kahungunu, 437
Kahurangi, 285
Kahutia-te-Rangi, 433
Kahutupuni, 547
Kaiamio, 561
Kaiapu, 279
Kaiheraki, 416
Kaikaiawaru, 401
Kaikoura, 150
Kaiporohu, Hoani, 24, 39
Kaitai, 557
Kaitakata, 557
Kaitiaki-o-Tukete, 569
Kana, Tieke *see* Connor, Jack, 26
Kapa, 440
Kapu, 439
Karaka, Arama, 135
Karaki, 378
Kararahuarau, 434, 435
Karetai (family), 560, 565
Karetai, 463
Karetai, Ripeka, 28
Karihana (Mrs), 27
Karihi, 136, 160, 401, 557, 558
Kaukura *see* Kahukura, 200, 556, 559
Kaunia, 547
Kawakawa, 284, 285, 286
Kaweriri, 547
Keakea, 562
Keama, 419, 420
Kelly *see* Kere, 527
Kemp, Major, 257
Kere, 527
King/Kurupohatu, Eruete Kingi/Kurupohatu, Kingi Ruru/Ruru/Ruru, King, 23, 24, *50*
King, Joseph, 36
Kipling, R., 35
Kirikiri, 426
Kirikirikaehe, 435
Kirikirikatata, 435
Kirk, Professor, 263
Kiwa, 396
Kohikohi, 24
Kokiro, 440
Kona, Tieke *see* Connor, Jack, 26, 39
Kopuwai, 351, 435, 561
Korako, Hoani, 98, 205
Korako, Matene Wera, 578

Korekore, 217
Koroko, 143, 370, 371, 378
Koroko (tohuka), 27
Kowkoula *see* Kahukura, 556, 559
Kuini *see* Tiiti, 25
Kupa, Tiemi Haereroa, 23, *25*, 39
Kupe, 286, 316, 405, 408
Kurupohatu, Eruete Kinihi/Kingi *see* King, 24, 39, 254, 538
Kurupohatu, Kingi Ruru *see* King, 24

Lot, wife of (Bible), 375
Low, Sandy, 566

Maaka, Epipha, 29
McDougall, June, 23
McKenzie, Mary, 10
Mahine-a-Rangi, 241
Mahora-nui-a-tea, 364, 395, 404, 407
Mahuika, 336, 384, 385, 386, 387, 388, 389, 390, 395, 557, 559, 565
Mahuraki, 427
Manure, Tiori/Newton, George Mahure, 24, *25*
Maiharanui *see* Te Maiharanui, 275
Maiharoa *see* Te Maiharoa, 250, 270, 371, 381, 382, 418, 421, 422, 436, 440, 567
Maka, 29
Makea, 428
Mako, 279, 439
Maku, 364, 404, 407
Manawa, 547
Mantell, W.B.D., 24, 245, 356
Marakamu, 286
Marama *see* Maramahuakea, 359, 364, 399, 404
Maramahuakea, 364, 404
Maririhau, 538
Mark, John, 445
Martin, Mrs/Matene, Hinehou, 25, 28
Martin, 'old' *see* Matene, Korako, 25
Maru, 95, 312, 401, 417, 439
Maru-kaitangata, 489
Marukore, 429
Matakarepo, 160
Matamata, 214, 405, 406, 420
Matauira, 439
Matene, Hinehou/Inehou *see* Martin, Mrs, 28, 39

INDEX OF PERSONAL NAMES AND PERSONIFICATIONS   609

Matene, Henare, 28
Matene, Koroko/Matene, Koroko Tumeke/Old Colac/Old Martin, 25
Matene, Puru see Pitama, Teripa Te Hauraraka (Mrs), 28
Matiaha see Tiramorehu, Matiaha, 546, 575
Matiherangi, 433, 434
Matiora, 446
Matiu, Hoani/Matiu, Hoani, Tamahika, 24, 39, 97, 436
Matua, Henare, 395, 418
Matuku (woman), 561
Matuku see Matukutangotango, 432, 433
Matukutangotango, 432
Mauhara, Hira, 575
Mauhara, Horomona, 575
Maui, 72, 86, 141, 186, 203, 207, 252, 308, 320, 331, 336, 341, 347, 364, 383, 384, 385, 386, 387, 388, 389, 390, 391, 392, 393, 395, 398, 400, 402, 404, 405, 406, 407, 424, 435, 458, 537, 539, 555, 557, 558, 559, 560, 562, 564, 565, 566
Maui-Tikitiki-a-Te-Raka see Maui, 398
Maui-tikitiki-o-Te-Ranga see Maui, 385
Mauimua, 385
Mauipae, 385
Mauipae see Maui, 398
Mauiroto, 385
Mauitaha, 385
Mauiwaho, 385
Mautakitaki, 398
Mawete, 444, 447
Mawiti see Mawete, 444
McGregor, Mr, 230
McKegg, Mr, 578
McNab, R., 60, 135, 556, 559
Moki, 273, 279, 414, 428, 429, 437, 438, 443
Moki the Second see Moki, 231
Moki-a-Ruahikihiki see Moki, 231
Moki-tawhiri-ruru, 231
Moko, 361, 426, 443
Mokopapa, 349
Momo, 430
Monro, D., 354, 575
Moore/Muir? (photographer), 578
Morehu, 403
Morrell, Captain, 60
Mu, 401

Mumuhako, 398
Munchausen, Baron, 144
Murirakawhenua see Mahuika, 384, 389, 392, 395, 399, 558, 565
Mutu, Miss, 414
Mutu, Mrs, 531

Nani, 27
Newton, George (father of G.M. Newton), 24
Newton, George/George Mahure see Mahure, Tiori, 24, 39
Nga-toko-ono-a-Hemo, 433
Ngatoro see Ngatoro-i-rangi, 427, 452
Ngatoro-i-rangi, 427, 435
Niho, 410
Noah (in Bible), 433
Nukuroa, 427

Ohua, 71, 149, 539
Old Colac see Matene, Korako, 25
Old Martin see Matene, Korako, 25
Omurirakawhenua (jawbone), 388
Oppenheim, Roger Stanley, 30

Pahau, Tikini (Mrs), 250
Pahi, 185, 574
Paikea, 433, 434, 435, 537, 563, 564
Paipeta (family), 23
Paipeta, Pita, 27
Paipeta, Wikitoria, 27
Paitu, 574, 575
Paka, 378
Pakihiwitahi, 435, 569
Palmer, William, 25
Papa see Papatuanuku, 58, 396, 397, 402, 403, 404, 560
Papatuanuku, 383, 395, 396, 403, 555, 560
Paraire, Hori, 569
Paraoa, 563
Pararo, 560
Pararoy see Pararo, 556, 560
Parata (taniwha), 396
Parata, Tame (MHR), 18, 26
Parata, Wi, 442
Pari, 81
Paroro see Pararo, 546
Patu, Horomanu, 570
Patu-whenua see Te Maiharoa, 418
Patuki, John Topi, 570

Paul, 11
Paul (apostle), 207
Paurini, Bob, 421
Philips, Mr, 298
Phillipps, William J., 30
Piper, P. (Mrs), 39
Pitama (family), 23
Pitama, Teripa Te Hauraraka (Mrs)/(nee) Matene, Puru, 28
Poho, 444
Poihipi, 516
Pokeka, 378
Pokene, 464
Pokuku, Wi, 136
Porora see Wohlers, J.F.H., 383
Porourangi, 433, 434
Potaura, 378
Power, William see Te Paro, Wiremu, 24
Pratt, Rugby, 203
Puaho see Puoho, 410, 444
Puaka, 202, 439
Puhi-kaiariki, 436, 442
Puhi-manawanawa, 436, 442
Puhi-o-Rakaiora, 436
Puhi-rere, 442
Puka, 136, 557
Pukekohatu (tipuna), 481
Pukekohatu, Rora, 481
Puketapu, 568
Pukuheti see Patu, Horomanu, 570
Pukurakau, 106
Punahere, Caroline, 26
Punahikoia, 443
Punga, 403
Pungawerewere, 432
Puoho, 163, 212
Pupene, Hamuera Te Aomutu, 29
Puraho, 489
Purakau, 367

Ra see Rehua, 395
Ra see Tama-nui-te-ra, 404
Rakaihaitu see Rakaihautu, 445
Rakaihautu, 408, 440, 441, 445
Rakaihikuroa, 241, 452
Rakaiora, 436, 513, 559, 560, 565
Rakaitauheke, 95
Rakaitekura, 372
Rakaraka, 253
Rakatehurumanu, 434
Rakaunui, 452
Rakawahakura, 444
Rakeihikuroa see Rakaihikuroa, 452
Rakeinui see Rakaunui, 452
Rakena, Reverend, 465

Raki *see* Rangi, 58, 370, 402, 404, 555, 560
Rakihikaia, 428
Rakiora, 200, 565
Rakiraki, Jack/John Puahu, 39, 112, *113, 115*, 149, 214
Rakitamau, 437, 438, 443
Rakitapu, 163
Rakitauhopo, 547
Rakitauneke, 405, 420
Rakiwhakaputa, 444
Rangi, 383, 394, 395, 396, 397, 402, 403, 412
Rangi-nui *see* Rangi, 402, 403
Rangi-roa *see* Rangi, 403
Rangitakapumaro, 414
Rangitawhanga, 439
Rapahoe, 517
Rarotimu, 343, 394, 395, 396, 400, 402, 407
Rata, 402, 432, 433, 437, 441, 558, 561
Rauparaha *see* Te Rauparaha, 212, 223, 539
Raureka, 548, 549
Rauru, 441
Rautu *see* Tama-Rautu, 403
Rawaho, Jane *see* Tinirauwaho, 24
Rehu, 23
Rehu, Henare Te Kooti, 26, 39, *51*
Rehu *see* Rehu, Henare te Kooti, 538
Rehu, Mr, 460
Rehu, W., 321
Rehua, 58, 363, 395, 397, 399, 404, 406
Reiri, Flora (Mrs), 6
Reko, 577
Reuben, 29
Riahiko (grandchild of T.B. Taiaroa), *233*
Rickus, James, 270, 446
Riki-o-waio, 445
Rita, 446
Robelia, Nicholas, 26
Roberts, Peter *see* Te Kahupuku, 29, 471, 492
Roberts, W.H.S., 18
Robertson, Abner, 417
Robertson, George, 272
Robertson, Mr, 516
Rockiola *see* Rakaiora, 556, 559, 560
Rohe, 405
Rokoitua, 441
Rokokohuai *see* Rongokohuwai, 414

Rokomai, 200
Rokotaitawhi, 444
Romatiki, 26
Rona (servant), 399
Rona, 399, 434, 556
Rongokohuwai, 414
Rongomai *see* Rokomai, 200
Roro, old, 261
Rotopikoro, 150
Ruahikihiki, 439, 440, 445
Ruaimoko, 349, 399, 400, 403, 423
Ruaitawhaki, 439, 440
Ruapapa, 430
Ruatapu, 213, 397, 433, 560, 563, 564
Ruawahine, 563
Rukutia, 564
Ruru *see* King, 24
Ruru (father of King), 24
Ruru, King *see* King, 24
Ruru, Kingi, 50
Ruru, Pirini (Mrs), 405
Ryan, 27
Ryan, Piripi, 27

Sandfly *see* te Awha, Rawiri, 149
Sanny *see* Low, Sandy, 566
Scotch John, 190
Scott, W., 574
Selwyn, Bishop, 297, 298
Shortland, E., 18, 136, 298, 303, 308
Skinner, H./Henry D., 9, 11, 12, 14, 15, 16, 23, 35, 36
Skinner, W./William H., 11, 14
Smith, S. Percy, 12, 15, 23, 60, 80
Smith, W.W., 11,
Spencer, James, 24
Spencer, William *see* Te Paro, Wiremu, 24
Stack, J./James W., 27, 98, 108, 280, 417, 426, 437, 441, 443, 464, 487, 493, 575 *see also* General Index: *Kaiapohia, South Island Maoris, Transactions of the New Zealand Institute*
Starke, June, 30

Tahukumea, 397, 403, 406
Tahumutu, 414
Tahununu, 212, 382
Tahupotiki, 433
Tahuwhakairo, 397, 403, 406
Tai te Kiteraki, 464
Taiari, 452
Taiaroa (family), 98

Taiaroa, Hori Kerei, 19, 233
Taiaroa, R./Richard/Riki Te Mairaki, 27, 205, 231, *309*, 414, 523, 551, 570, 578
Taiaroa, Tini Kerei Burns (Mrs), 27, *233*
Taiarorua, 378
Taiehu, 425, 426, 440
Taikawa, 24
Tainui (family), 284
Tainui, Ihaia, 493
Taiororua *see* Taiarorua, 367, 370
Tairea, 435
Taituha, 277
Taituha, Momo, 205
Takaroa (taniwha), 569
Takaroa, 396, 401, 402, 404, 555, 560
Takatahuruhuru, 121, 149
Takawa, 438
Taki, 569
Taki, Paora/Paori, 27, *28*, 413, 444
Tama, 284, 286, 405, 426, 513, 564
Tama *see* Rona, 434
Tama *see* Tama-taku-ariki, 549
Tama *see* Tamatakutai, 437
Tama-nui-te-ra *see* Rehua, 404
Tama-Rautu, 403
Tama-taku-ariki, 532, 564
Tamahoru, 439, 440
Tamakino, 279
Tamarereti, 397
Tamatakutai, 437
Tamatea *see* Tamatea-pokai-whenua, 416, 427, 435, 437, 442, 443, 532
Tamatea-kaimatamua, 427
Tamatea-nui, 427
Tamatea-pokai-whenua, 427, 443, 523, 532
Tamatea-roa, 427
Tane, 58, 59, 193, 363, 383, 384, 391, 395, 396, 397, 398, 402, 403, 404, 426, 513, 557, 560, 561, 562
Tane-aniwa, 200
Tane-nui-a-Rangi *see* Tane, 403
Tanemahuta *see* Tane, 403
Tanetiki, 429, 438
Tangaroa *see* Takaroa, 396, 401, 402, 560
Tangatahuruhuru *see* Takatahuruhuru, 188
Tangiwai, 284
Tanner, Mere/Kui (Mrs), 25, 39
Tapui, 275, 381

Tarawa, 576
Tarewai, 282
Tarewati, 26
Tau, Reihana, 28
Tauira-o-hua, 561
Tautini, 372, 414, 423, 438, 443
Tauwhare, 282
Tawha, 381
Tawhaki, 136, 160, 401, 513, 514, 557
Tawhirimatea, 399, 400, 403
Tawhiriwhiri *see* Tawhirimatea, 400
Tawhiti, 403
Taylor, R., 210
Taylor, W.A., 50, 127, 309
Te Ahuhikuraki, 372
Te Ahuhu, 397, 403
Te Ake, 279, 414, 415, 439
Te Amaruraki *see* Te Amarurangi, 397
Te Amarurangi, 403
Te Ao-Matara, 200, 558
Te Ao-tauwhetuku, 414
Te Aotarewa, 440
te Awha, Rawiri, 149, 163
Te Haere, 150
Te Heni, 442
Te Hiki, 539
Te Hiku *see* Te Hikutawatawa, 372
Te Hikutawatawa *see* Tuahuriri, 372, 373
Te Hori, Pita, 250, *251*
Te Ihutakaru, 463
Te Ikamaru, 140
te Kahu, Tare Wetere, 205
Te Kahukura, 438
Te Kahupuku, 29, 471, 492
Te Kakau, 380, 419
Te Kapo, 143
Te Karaka, 445, 446
Te Kaue, 95
Te Kautia *see* Te Kautia-te-Raki, 564
Te Kautia-te-Raki, 564
Te Kene, Turia Morokiekie, *25*
Te Mahana, Atiru, 24
Te Maiaki, 378
Te Maiharanui, 430
Te Maiharoa, 27, 110, 135, 381, 418, 441, 567
Te Maiharoa, Taare Reweti, 23
te Maire, H. (Mrs), 26, 39
te Maire, Henare/Davis, Harry, 26, 27, 135, 199, 205, 206, 208, 39, 546, 566, 573
te Maire, Rawiri, *26*, 199, 532
Te Maiwaho, 397

Te Maiwerohia, 375
Te Maku, 395
te Mamaru, Rawiri, 575
Te Marama, Tuhituhi, 23
Te Maui *see* Maui, 557
Te Mautai, 444
Te Muru, 320
Te Paho, 378
Te Papatua-a-Mauheke, 414
te Paro, Wiremu/Wiriama/Power, William/Spencer, William, 24, *25*, 39
Te Po ko uatipu, 394
Te Puaho *see* Puoho, 410
Te Puoho *see* Puoho, 27
Te Raka, 384, 385, 387, 558, 560
Te Rakaitauheke, 439
Te Rakiihia, 28, 418, 419
Te Rakitamau, 443
Te Rakitauneke, 214
Te Rakitaurewa, 439, 440
Te Rakiwhakaputa, 272, 431, 445
te Ramarama, Whatiua, 433
Te Ranga, 384
Te Rangi, 383
Te Rangi-whaka-puta *see* Te Rakiwhakaputa, 431
Te Rangi-whaka-upoko-i-runga, 384, 397
Te Rangiangaanganui, 282
Te Rangihiroa *see* Buck, Peter, 73
Te Rangihorahina, 415
Te Rangiorahina (male taniwha), 415
Te Rangiorahina *see* Te Rangihorahina, 415
Te Rauparaha, 27, 39, 223, 249, 275, 280, 282, 285, 374, 425, 430, 431, 439, 444
Te Ruahikihiki, 279, 414
Te Ruawai, 538
Te Taoho, 79
Te Uira, 24 te Ururaki, 27, 39
Te Ururaki, Mihiata, 27
Te Wahia, Hanna/Fanny, 26, *127*
Te Wahine maru kore *see* Hineao, 415
Te Wao-Nui-a-Tane, 398
Te Wera, 156, 379, 556
Te Whakaemai, 556
Te Whiti (policeman), 574
Te Whiti, 260, 574
Te Kautia-te-Raki, 564
Tekotu, 427
Teone, 27
Terehaka, 250

Tererewa, 399
Teviotdale, David, 14
Thomson, Mary Roden, 10
Ti-a-Tauwhetuku *see* Te Ao-tauwhetuku, 414
Tiiti/Kuini, 25
Tikao, Rahera, 27
Tikao, Tamati, 27
Tikao, Teone/Hoani J./John Taare/C., 18, 24, 27, *227*, 298, 394, 403, 406, 408, 418, 467, 471, 573
Tiki, 57, 58, 59, 207, 242, 370, 394, 396
Tiki-au-waha, 58
Tiki-auha *see* Tiki-au-waha, 58
Tikiauaha, 396
Tikikapakapa, 396
Tikitohua, 396
Timuaki, 523
Tini (grandchild of T.B. Taiaroa), *233*
Tinirau, 401, 423, 433, 555, 560, 562, 563
Tinirauwaho/Rawaho, Jane, 24
Tiori/Turia, 12, *13*
Tipua-tawhirowhiro, 371
Tipukerekere, 400
Tiramorehu, Matiaha, 371, 378, 397, 546, 557, 558, 575
Tiriwa, 398
Tirokotakanewha, 547
Titikura, 398
Tohu, 260
Toi *see* Toi-te-Uatahi, 441
Toi-te-Huatahi *see* Toi-te-Uatahi, 441
Toi-te-Matahi *see* Toi-te-Uatahi, 441
Toi-te-Uatahi, 464
Toi-ua-tahi *see* Toi-te-Uatahi, 441
Toitu, Heremaia, 574
Tokitoki, 185
Tommy Billy/Tom Billy/Haupere, Hoani, 27, 577
Tomoana, Henare, 257
Topi, John, 250, 543
Topi, Maurice, 205
Torikiriki, 403
Transvaal, 464
Tregear, E., 49, 53, 62, 80, 87, 113, 123, 167, 168, 172, 212, 229, 234, 235, 238, 241, 243, 244, 250, 256, 272, 276, 278, 283, 298, 303, 312, 322, 342, 353, 367, 393, 395, 397, 399, 435, 474, 477, 480, 488, 508, 510, 511, 562; *See also*

General Index: *The Maori-Polynesian Comparative Dictionary, The Maori Race*
Tu *see* Tutekoropaka, 564
Tu *see* Tutepopoarangi, 439
Tu *see* Tuteuretira, 439
Tu te Makohu, 375
Tu te Rakipaoa, 464
Tuahuriri, 256, 373, 375, 378, 414, 438, 443, 444, 545
Tuarawhati, 428, 443
Tuauau, 27, 370, 371, 378
Tuckett, 575
Tuhaitara, 200, 429, 558
Tuhawaiki, 24, 430, 577
Tuhokairaki, 547
Tukarekare, 440
Tukete (the earlier), 441, 444
Tukete, 84, 444, 445, 538, 544
Tukete-te-rua *see* Tukete, 444
Tukiauau, 547
Tukorero, 67, 225, 428
Tukorotepaka *see* Tutekoropaka, 286
Tukoroua, 538
Tumaro, 372
Tumaruaki, 574
Tumaruraki (a pakeha), 574
Tumatataa, 374
Tumeke, Matene Korako *see* Matene, Korako, 25, 28
Tuna, 141, 404, 406, 559, 565
Tunarere, 211
Tupai, 399
Tupairehana, 575
Tupakihi, 378
Tuparitaniwha, 547
Tupurupuru, 437
Tura, 266, 267, 363, 416, 428, 437, 440, 441, 442, 561
Tura-katahi, Patea, 252

Turakautahi, 231, 252, 373, 378, 417, 438, 439, 444
Turakipo, 414, 415
Turoa, Tupe (Major), 343
Turongo, 241
Tutaemaro, 429, 438
Tutaka *see* Tutakahinahina, 443
Tutakahinahina, 442
Tutakakino, 341
Tutanekai, 258
Tutekawa, 67, 225, 272, 279, 424, 428, 429, 437, 443
Tutekoropaka, 286, 405, 564
Tutemakohu, 547
Tutepiriraki *see* Tutepirirangi, 429
Tutepirirangi, 438
Tutepopoarangi, 439, 440
Tuterakihuanoa, 58
Tuteuretira, 439
Tutewaimate, 361, 426, 443
Tutoko, Keri, 529
Tutunui, 562, 563

Uenuku, 408, 433, 435, 437, 482, 537
Urihia, 143
Uru, Mr, 460

Vangioni, Mr, 274, 467
Victoria, Queen, 264, 574

Waaka (family), 547
Wahakai, 439
Wahieroa, 402, 432, 437, 561
Waitai, 408, 443, 444
Wales, Prince of, 395, 575
Waruwarutu, Natanahira, 367, 378
Watkin, J., 198, 199, 201, 203, 204
Watson, Teone, 28

Wehikore, Mere, 24
Weka, 401
Weka, Hamiora, 575
Wesley (family), 547
Wesley, Elizabeth *see* Whaitiri, Takai (Mrs), 24
Wesley, Tom (Morven), 205
Wetere, Hoani Korako *see* Korako, Hoani, 205
Wetere, John Takai, 24
Wetere, Tare (Otago Heads), 209
Whaitiri, 446
Whaitiri (god), 399
Whaitiri (Mrs) T., 39
Whaitiri (woman), 557
Whaitiri, Arihia, 24
Whaitiri, Takai (Mrs)/Wesley, Elizabeth, 24
Whaitiri-paku, 441
Whakarewa, 548
Whakatau, 211
Whakatohe, 280
Whakuku, 428, 443
Whalagi *see* Wharaki, 430
Wharaki, 430
Wharekauri, 569
Wharetutu, 24
Whatitata, 563
Whatiua *see* te Ramarama, Whatiua, 433
Whatu-Mamoe *see* Hotu-Mamoe, 442
Wheke, 279, 415, 439, 445, 468
Whiro, 561
White, John, 23, 404
Whiua, 275
Wild, L.J., 357
Williams, H.W., 152
Wohlers, J.F.H., 42, 45, 95, 207, 229, 256, 383, 453, 38
Woods, Mrs, 26

INDEX OF PLACE NAMES

Acland's Run, 417
Africa, 441
Ahuahu, 427
Ahuriri *see* Napier, 460
Akaroa, 27, 38, 223, 257, 259, 261, 265, 274, 275, 279, 287, 300, 304, 307, 316, 326, 330, 331, 333, 339, 345, 370, 380, 383, 399, 407, 408, 409, 414, 415, 416, 421, 430, 440, 441, 444, 460, 463, 467, 488, 569, 574
America, 241, 441

Aoraki, mountain, 452
Aorangi, 407
Aotearoa *see* New Zealand, 216, 445
Aotearoa *see* North Island, 460
Arahura, 429, 493, 522, 523, 526, 528, 548
Arahura River, 286, 523, 527, 549
Arahuru [i.e. Arahura], 197
Arowhenua, 24, 27, 174
Arthur's Pass, 531
Ashburton, 437

Ashley River, 324, 360
Asia, 441
Atlantic Ocean, mid, 324
Auahituroa Channel, 149
Auckland Islands, 130, 446
Auckland Peninsula, 390, 436
Australia, 42, 426, 575
Awa-kaeaea, 168

Banks Peninsula, 192, 214, 224, 240, 245, 247, 275, 285, 295, 302, 306, 307, 314, 316, 326, 330, 333, 338, 341, 348, 350,

355, 356, 357, 358, 361, 362, 381, 407, 413, 414, 416, 422, 427, 430, 453, 461, 466, 488, 512, 517, 538, 543, 569
Bay of Islands, 269
Bay of Plenty, 442
Belfast, 349, 354
Birdling's Flat District *see* Waikakahi District, 407
Birdling's Flat *see* Waikakahi, 317, 325, 416, 443
Blenheim, 282, 374
Blenheim District, 510
Blue Mountain *see* Maunga-a-whiu, mountain, 506
Bluff, 11, 23, 24, 25, 39, 68, 74, 76, 94, 108, 118, 128, 155, 157, 176, 179, 205, 276, 279, 442, 444, 522, 538, 549, 550, 560, 572, 576
Bluff Hill, 158
Bobby's Head, 184
Brightwater, 488
Bruce Bay, 527, 530, 532
Bruce Bay kaik, 530
Buchanan's Creek, 538, 548
Buchanan's *see* Otawiri, 300
Bucklerburn, 548

Cam River *see* Whakahume, river, 224, 318
Campbell Island, 341
Canterbury, 27, 39, 131, 185, 221, 224, 240, 248, 259, 264, 265, 266, 268, 269, 283, 291, 299, 301, 302, 304, 307, 317, 320, 330, 332, 348, 350, 358, 359, 360, 361, 376, 406, 412, 413, 414, 416, 423, 425, 428, 451, 461, 463, 471, 491, 522, 525, 526, 527, 529, 531, 547, 549, 578
Canterbury, North *see* North Canterbury, 521
Canterbury, South *see* South Canterbury, 313
Canterbury Plains, 361, 437
Cape Maria van Dieman, 562
Cape of Good Hope, 425, 436
Cargill, Mount, 542
Cascade, 549
Catlins, 187, 556
Cave, 444
Central Otago, 64, 124, 175, 187, 578
Chatham Islands, 14, 88, 356, 445, 446, 447, 460, 569, 570
Cheviot, 465, 488
Christchurch, 28, 270, 576

Clinton, 167, 168
Clutha, river *see* Mata-au, river, 111, 561
Codfish Island, 24, 109
Colac, 569
Colac Bay, 24, 59, 67, 145, 149, 155, 158, 200, 212, 218, 220, 236, 446, 537, 574
Colac Bay kaika *see* Oraka kaika, 218
Cook, Mount *see* Aoraki, mountain, 452
Cook Islands, 196
Cook Strait *see* Raukawa, 375, 414, 429, 438, 460
Cook's Head (pillar), 569
Corsair Bay, 468
Croixelles, Lake *see* Kaiaua, lake, 502, 517

Devil's Knob (Nelson) *see* Pukeatua, 517
Devil's Knob *see* Marokura Hill, 257
Dog Island, 539
Dunedin, 92, 98, 158, 167, 193, 323, 452, 550, 551, 572, 576, 577
Dunedin Harbour, 314
Dunedin Town Belt, 568
Duntroon, 562
Dusky Sound, 122

East Coast (NI), 232, 308
East Coast (SI), 125, 285, 524, 532, 549
East Polynesia, 12, 14
Egypt, 374
Ellesmere, Lake *see* Waihora, lake, 38, 149, 279, 285, 303, 308, 310, 313, 314, 316, 317, 320, 322, 336, 337, 344, 348, 357, 360, 370, 425, 428
England, 184, 250, 464, 466, 540
Europe, 467
Evening Island *see* Poutama, island, 183
Eyre *see* Ohapuku, 319

Falafala, island *see* Wharawhara, island, 36
Fiordland, 24
Forsyth, Lake *see* Wairewa, lake, 135, 314, 317, 325, 424
Foveaux Strait, 9, 16, 23, 47, 90, 129, 157, 161, 376, 443, 39, 543, 569, 570
France, 356, 467
French Farm, 383

Gallipoli, 260
George, Lake *see* Ourawera, lake, 149, 163
Georgetown *see* Pakihi-kawai, 540
Geraldine River, 439
Gisborne *see* Turanga, 136, 252, 295, 407, 429, 454, 461
Gisborne District, 88, 302
Glenavy, 27, 547, 566
Goodwood, 147, 184, 568
Gore, 9, 11, 12, 115, 431, 552
Gorge River, 549
Governor's Bay, 444
Green Island (near Dunedin) *see* Okaihae, island, 165
Green Island *see* Papatea, island, 183, 543
Greymouth *see* Mafera, 532
Gull Rock, 165, 538

Haere (tuahu), 208
Halswell, 444, 446, 447
Hampden, 576
Hanmer, 427, 438
Hart River, 320
Hart's River *see* Kuaowhitu, river, 314
Hataitai, 438
Hauloko, lake *see* Hauroko, lake, 198
Hauroko, lake, 198
Haurongo, lake *see* Hauroko, lake, 198
Hauroto, lake *see* Hauroko, lake, 198
Hawaii, 391, 463
Hawaiki, 60, 241, 245, 250, 252, 261, 266, 270, 271, 274, 276, 285, 301, 347, 351, 361, 366, 376, 395, 396, 401, 402, 405, 407, 420, 423, 426, 427, 428, 431, 433, 435, 436, 437, 440, 441, 442, 445, 452, 482, 488, 558
Hawaiki pamamao, 202
Hawaiki-nui, 270, 391, 441
Hawaiki-pamamao, 270, 433, 441
Hawaiki-roa, 270, 391, 441
Hawea, 550
Hawke's Bay, 256, 375, 390, 395, 418
Henley, 24, 25, 26, 28, 45, 69, 70, 72, 79, 83, 89, 175, 192, 254, 542, 550, 554, 572, 577, 578
Herbert, Mount *see* Te Ahupatiki, mountain, 357

Heretatua, 539
Hidden Island *see* Putauhinu, island, 342
Hikuika, mountain, 361
Hillgrove *see* Waipouri, 124
Hinemateroa (clump of trees), 414
Hinepaaka, tapu tree, 417
Hitawerewere Pa, 431
Hokanui, 555
Hokanui, hills *see* Hokonui, hills, 431
Hokianga, 254, 408, 443, 467
Hokitika, 528, 530
Hokitika, river, 429
Hokonui, hills, 184
Hoputoroa, island, 172
Houipapa, 192
Hui-o-Rangiora, 402
Hukanui, 431
Huriawa Peninsula, 541, 542
Hurunui, 432

Inch Clutha, 164
Invercargill, 158, 163, 263, 578
Irwell River *see* Waiwhio, river, 314
Island Bay *see* Whakamoa, 350
Israel, 207

Jackson Bay, 530, 532
Jeffries' Farm, island *see* Ram Island, 538
John Bull's Head, rock *see* Whaka-renga-mahe, 130

Ka Mokaikai, saddle, 408
Ka Mokaikoi, saddle *see* Ka Mokaikai, saddle, 279
Kahukura, cave, 556
Kahukura, hill, 556
Kahukura, stream, 556
Kai-a-te-Atua, pa, 208
Kai-a-te-Atua, tuahu, 208
Kaiapohia Pa *see* Kaiapoi Pa, 280, 430, 439
Kaiapoi, 16, 29, 67, 223, 224, 225, 226, 230, 237, 247, 251, 258, 265, 268, 273, 274, 278, 280, 297, 298, 301, 317, 320, 360, 373, 374, 376, 405, 410, 418, 429, 430, 437, 439, 458, 460, 462, 466, 471, 503, 538, 569
Kaiapoi District, 223, 224, 246, 250, 252, 302, 317, 320, 516
Kaiapoi Pa, 224, 229, 230, 231, 249, 255, 324, 345, 378, 401, 439

Kaiapoi Pa *see also* Te Kohanga-a-Kaikaiawaru, pa, 439
Kaiaua, lake, 502, 517
Kaikaiawaru, 554
Kaikarae (correct form) *see* Kaikourai, 167
Kaikoura, 86, 202, 211, 247, 279, 301, 302, 414, 426, 444, 460, 480, 488, 499, 501, 567
Kaikoura Mountains, 429
Kaikourai, 167
Kairaki Beach, 503
Kaitakata *see* Kaitangata, 418
Kaitangata (lake), 538
Kaitangata, 59, 149, 150, 163, 213, 418, 541, 547, 561
Kaitorete District, 425
Kaituna, 240
Kaituna, hill, 427
Kaka Point, 23, 24, 25, 113, 115
Kakanui, 552
Kakanui *see* Kakaunui, 452
Kakaunui, 452
Kakautawa *see* Foveaux Strait, 460
Kanawera, island, 224
Kapua-hurihia, gorge, 542
Kapuka, 24, 39
Karitane, 65, 97
Karitane mission station, 24
Karoro Creek, 74, 216
Karororangi, mountain, 514
Kartigi, 45, 538
Katiki, 430
Katiki *see* Kartigi, 537
Kawa, urupa, 545
Kawa, creek, 205
Kawatiri, 460
Kawhakaputaputa, 569
Kelvingrove, 184
Kikipuku, urupa, 545
Kilmog, Mount, 193
King Country, 511
Kinloch, 550
Koau, kaik, 224
Kohurau *see* Kurow, 106
Koromiko, siding, 38
Korotuaheka, 270
Korotuaheka *see* Waitaki Mouth, 41, 123, 135
Koukourarata, 245, 337, 405, 443, 467
Kuaowhitu, river, 314
Kuauwhiti, 320
Kurow, 106

Lakiula, island *see* Rakiura, island, 36
Lammerlaws, mountains *see*

Wairuaapo, mountains, 554
Leeston, 27, 320
Little River (river), 381
Little River *see* Wairewa, 27, 147, 149, 299, 320, 323, 343, 413, 431, 447, 516, 531, 543
Little River District, 273
Little River *see* Wairewa, 447
Long Bay, 274
Long Island *see* Kanawera, island, 224
Long Island *see* Te Kanawera, island, 182, 183
Longbeach, 437
Lyttelton, 112, 331, 341, 348, 349, 373, 413
Lyttelton Harbour, 88, 256, 279, 332, 333, 339, 411, 427, 431, 444

Mackenzie Country, 439
Macquarie Island, 157, 165
Mafera, 532
Mahinaapua, river, 438
Mahinapua, lake, 429
Mahipuku, mountain, 514
Mahitahi *see* Bruce Bay, 530
Mahunui *see* South Island, 390
Mahuraki, hill, 413, 427
Mairaki, 417
Mairaki Point, 415
Maitahi *see* Bruce Bay, 527, 530, 532, 533
Maitahi (near Nelson), 488
Makawhio, 211, 532, 533
Makihikihi, 186
Manahune, 439
Manapouri, lake, 550
Manawapopore *see* Manawapore, 149
Manawapore, 149
Maniatoto Plains, 175
Manu-whaka-rau, 165
Manuka, 569
Manuka Pa, 446
Manukau, 460
Maori Reserve, Moeraki, 537
Maori Reserve, Taieri, 73
Maori Reserve, Tuahiwi, 224
Maori Reserve, Tuturau, 172
Maori Reserve, Koukourarata, 245
Maranuku, 25, 39
Marlborough, 430, 533, 539
Marokura, hill, 257
Martinborough, 529
Marua-i-nuku, 407
Mary Hill *see* Poutakahiamaru, hill, 538

Mason Bay (Stewart Island), 24
Masterton, 517
Mata-au, river, 135, 561, 569
Matainaka Lagoon, 139, 140
Matakaea, 376, 426, 435, 569, 570
Matakaea Point *see* Matakaea, 568
Matangiawhia, 372
Matangiawhia Pa, 372, 373, 443
Matau, mountain, 514
Matau-a-Maui *see* Hawke's Bay, 375, 390
Matau-a-Maui *see* Napier, 427
Mataura, 151, 577
Mataura Falls, 150
Mataura River, 150, 151, 555, 576
Mataurua, hill, 408
Mataau, mountain *see* Matau, mountain, 514
Maukiakia, beach, 192
Maukiakia, island, 178, 192
Maunga-a-whiu, mountain, 506
Melanesia, 390, 442
Mercury Bay *see* Ahuahu, 427
Mexico, 92, 550
Milford Sound *see* Piopiotahi, 167, 168, 285, 493, 517, 532, 548, 549, 564
Moana-nui-a-Kiwa, 396, 400
Moeraki (West Coast), 163
Moeraki, 26, 28, 48, 59, 60, 66, 70, 72, 79, 112, 118, 119, 131, 144, 147, 152, 153, 156, 159, 178, 179, 192, 197, 205, 208, 213, 218, 220, 257, 311, 313, 354, 371, 378, 403, 426, 430, 439, 504, 539, 538, 544, 548, 557, 558, 574, 575
Moeraki kaika, 218, 537
Mokamoka, 279, 444
Mokoia, island, 259
Molyneux, 169
Molyneux *see* Maranuku, 25
Molyneux River *see* Mata-au, river, 135, 139, 189, 200, 569
Monck's Cave, 468
Monument Hill, 324, 411
Moreanuku, 384
Morianuku *see* Moreanuku, 274, 384
Morven *see* Waihao, 124, 199, 205, 208, 532
Motu-kauiti, bay, 468
Motukarara, island, 348, 453
Motunau, 349
Mount Sommers Run, 417

Murihiku, 34, 46, 56, 63, 64, 66, 82, 84, 86, 87, 90, 96, 120, 122, 130, 301, 330, 360, 416, 435, 444, 446, 451, 452, 462, 491, 511, 535, 538, 548, 549, 560, 562, 569, 578
Muriwaihoata, river, 405
Murray's River (on Stewart Island) *see* Otaku, 24, 213
Mussel Beach, 427
Muttonbird Islands *see* Titi Islands, 165, 216

Napier, 160, 257, 346, 424, 437
Native Reserve (at Koukourarata), 245
Neck, The (Stewart Island), 24
Nelson, 16, 29, 192, 372, 414, 427, 438, 443, 449, 451, 469, 477, 484, 485, 487, 494, 497, 506, 515, 517, 532
Nelson District, 173
Nelson Province, 448, 474
New Brighton, 333
New Brighton Beach *see* Oruapaeroa, 308, 326
New Plymouth, 11
New South Wales, 464
New Zealand, 12, 15, 43, 72, 73, 75, 81, 95, 112, 128, 129, 162, 185, 187, 202, 203, 216, 241, 243, 247, 258, 266, 275, 284, 285, 292, 300, 301, 303, 306, 308, 316, 334, 336, 341, 343, 346, 347, 354, 363, 376, 379, 384, 390, 391, 396, 405, 406, 407, 408, 426, 428, 433, 435, 436, 437, 440, 441, 442, 443, 445, 446, 452, 460, 467, 474, 480, 488, 490, 496, 499, 503, 507, 511, 530, 540, 537, 558, 561, 562, 565, 569, 570, 577
New Zealand, southern *see* southern New Zealand, 79, 543, 575
Nga-Tiki *see* Kartigi, 537
Ninety-Mile Beach, 418
North Canterbury, 9, 223, 224, 301, 357, 408, 521
North Island, 41, 45, 57, 64, 86, 98, 110, 126, 129, 160, 192, 195, 210, 230, 243, 248, 254, 257, 259, 264, 275, 278, 283, 286, 292, 293, 298, 301, 302, 304, 320, 335, 336, 345, 347, 348, 353, 359, 360, 361, 364, 371, 373, 376, 390, 393, 406, 414, 415, 418, 424, 427, 429, 430, 431, 436, 437, 438, 441,

443, 445, 446, 460, 464, 484, 489, 509, 511, 516, 531, 532, 560, 562, 564, 565
North Island *see also* West Coast (NI) North Otago, 51, 73, 124, 199
Nuggets, The, 172, 542
Nuku-tawhangawhanga, plain, 402, 404

Oahu, 391
Oamaru, 193, 232, 426, 427, 435
Oaro Creek, 533
Oceania, 95, 405
Ohapi, 317
Ohapi River, 148, 325
Ohapuku, 318, 319
Ohikaparuparu *see* Sumner, 446
Ohikuparuparu *see* Sumner, 414
Ohinetukutuku, Bush, 547
Ohonu, 286
Okaihae, island, 165
Okalhau *see* Warrington, 576
Okarito, 529, 530
Okiri *see* Little River, 323
Old Man Range, 562
Omarama, 567
Omata, 142
Omawete, 444
Omawiti *see* Omawete, 444
Omimi, 174
Onawe, pa, 230, 255, 280, 430
Onawe Pa (Akaroa), 444
One-kakara, whaling station, 537
Onuku, 223, 274
Opawa, 415
Open Bay, 569
Opihi River, 135, 148
Opuaha, 439
Opukutahi Reserve, 415
Opunake, 81
Opurere, 188
Opurere Falls, 150
Oraka, 39
Oraka, creek, 137
Oraka, kaika, 218
Orariki, 279
Orautahi, 79
Orepuki, 45, 38, 539
Oreti River, 163
Orokoroko, 390
Orokoroko *see* North Island, 565
Oruapaeroa, 308, 326
Otago, 36, 83, 92, 98, 103, 120, 128, 131, 140, 167, 205, 214, 269, 330, 354, 503, 525, 536, 542, 554, 575, 578

Otago, Central *see* Central Otago, 64
Otago, North *see* North Otago, 73
Otago, South *see* South Otago, 69
Otago Harbour, 60
Otago Heads, 27, 49, 60, 68, 70, 73, 79, 83, 91, 96, 98, 99, 116, 123, 124, 131, 138, 141, 151, 156, 192, 209, 245, 313, 463, 540, 542, 545, 562, 566, 578
Otago Peninsula, 60, 103, 118, 124, 175, 192, 547, 560
Otago *see* Otakou, 431
Otaki, 307, 412, 431, 542
Otakou *see also* Otakou kaik, Otago Heads, 16, 60, 98, 205, 245, 430, 431, 460, 463, 540
Otakou, kaik, 83
Otaku (on Stewart Island), 213
Otamata, river, 555
Otarama, 417
Otaupiri, 547
Otautahi *see* Christchurch, 576
Otawiri, 279, 300
Otehore, hill, 419
Otehore Pa, 274
Oteoka Hill, 361
Otepoti *see* Dunedin, 452, 568, 572, 576
Otipua, 148, 573
Otira, 531
Otira Gorge, 531
Otokia, 11
Otu Lagoon, 505
Otutohea, Bush, 443, 467
Otuwhata *see* Goodwood, 568
Otuwhata, Bush, 192
Ourawera, lake, 149, 163
Owaka, 554, 568
Owhaka, harbour *see* Lyttelton Harbour, 431
Oxford, 189, 190, 339, 352, 353, 358, 512
Oxford, Mount *see* Tawera, mountain, 353, 360, 417

Pacific Ocean, 95
Pahi's (pa), 539
Pakati, mountain, 554
Pakihi-kawai, 540
Palmerston, 576
Papakaio, 192
Papakura-a-Takaroa, 404
Papataipuhi, cave, 488
Papatea, island *see* Green Island, 183, 543
Papatotara, 177

Papatowai, 191
Papawai (Wairarapa, NI), 28
Paradise, 274
Parakakariki *see* Sleepy Cove, 274
Pareora, river, 148
Parihaka, 81, 260, 574
Parihanga *see* Parihaka, 260, 574
Parika, 110
Paringa *see* Parika, 110
Pariwhakatau, 439
Parnassus, 427
Patea, 341, 414
Paturiki, pa, 437
Pekapeka, 273, 430
Picton, 487
Pigroot, 124
Pihanga, mountain, 225
Pikopiko-i-rangi, 405, 406
Pikopiko-i-whiti, 391, 392, 399, 402, 405, 406
Piopiotahi, 168, 285
Poho-areare, pa, 415
Poison Bay, 549
Polynesia, 286, 390
Pomahaka, 121, 195, 546
Pomahaka River, 150, 188
Popotea, island *see* Papatea, island, 543
Poroporo-Huariki, 407
Port Adventure, 158
Port Cooper *see also* Wakaraupo, 431
Port Cooper *see* Lyttelton Harbour, 431
Port Levy *see* Koukourarata, 245, 337, 405, 443, 463, 467
Port Molyneux, 60, 71, 112, 216, 542
Port Molyneux district, 74
Pou-a-moko *see* Woodend, 301
Pourikino River, 142
Poutakahiamaru, hill, 538
Poutama, island, 183
Poverty Bay, 136, 429
Poverty Bay *see* Turanganuiarua, 558
Preservation Inlet, 529, 36, 539
Pu-o-te-ra, 174
Puai, 224
Puerua Stream, 139
Puharakekenui, 420
Puke-atua, hill, 453
Puke-Hikuraki, hill, 564
Pukeatua, 517
Pukekihikuraki *see* Puke-Hikuraki, hill, 564
Pukeokaoka Island, 176

Pukeone, mountain, 514
Puketapu, mountain, 568
Puketeraki *see* Puketiraki, 26, 452
Puketiraki, 48, 65, 66, 67, 88, 118, 126, 127, 147, 160, 174, 250, 355, 452, 540, 542, 556, 577
Pukeuri, 199
Pukeuri, hill, 258
Punakoura, 155
Punatarakao Creek, 208
Purakanui *see* Purakaunui, 45, 88, 173
Purakaunui, 60, 137, 542
Purau Bay (near Lyttelton), 300
Purupurukene River, 142
Putauhinu, island, 342
Puwai, landing, 554
Puwaitaha, saddle *see* Ka Mokaikai, saddle, 408

Quail Island, 339
Queenstown, 323

Rabbit Island, 36
Raggedy, 538
Rakahuri, river *see* Ashley River, 360
Rakaia, 306, 417
Rakaia Gorge, 331, 426, 438
Rakaia River, 417, 549, 569
Raki (heavens), 565
Rakitamau, garden, 198
Rakitata, 214, 298
Rakitata River, 135, 268, 308, 417
Rakiula, island *see* Rakiura, island, 36
Rakiura, island, 36, 39, 157, 178, 215, 444, 452, 460, 539, 544, 573
Ram Island, 538
Rangiora, 16, 23, 466
Rangitata River *see* Rakitata River, 268
Rapaki, 23, 27, 28, 223, 224, 225, 232, 238, 239, 241, 254, 271, 278, 332, 337, 358, 360, 407, 408, 411, 413, 427, 445, 448, 461, 462, 466, 467, 569
Rapanui, rock, 431
Raroheka, 386, 388, 406
Rarohenga *see* Raroheka, 388
Rarotonga, 391, 407, 445
Raukawa, strait, 429, 460
Reika *see* Reinga, 384, 403
Reinga, 226, 274, 376, 384, 395, 397, 398

Rerenga-wairua, 384
Ringaringa Beach, 84
Ripapa Pa, 444
Riverton, 11, 24, 72, 78, 98, 127, 135, 172, 179, 193, 206, 537, 546, 560, 575
Riverton Beach, 135
Roaring Bay, 542
Roto-nui-a-Whatu *see* Kaitangata, 149
Rotorua, 258, 427, 575
Rough Ridge, 187
Ruapehu, mountain, 427
Ruapuke, island, 16, 39, 42, 66, 67, 69, 70, 74, 76, 119, 124, 155, 166, 185, 200, 207, 212, 539, 543, 544, 578
Ruataniwha, kaik, 224
Rurukoukou, 168

St Andrews *see* Otipua, 148
Saltwater Creek, 315
Saltwater whaling station, 573
Samoa, 253, 36
Sandy Bay, 172
Selwyn River, 314, 323
Shag Mouth, 14
Shag Point *see* Matakaea, 376, 442, 570
Sinclair, Mount *see* Hikuika, mountain, 361
Sleepy Cove, 274
Snares, islands, 574
Solander Island, 574
South Africa, 426, 436, 440, 550
South Canterbury, 87, 124, 129, 139, 192, 195, 197, 313, 315
South Cape, island *see* Kanawera, island, 224, 554
South Coast (SI), 125
South Island, 14, 45, 57, 76, 106, 129, 209, 247, 259, 273, 275, 283, 284, 285, 292, 293, 308, 330, 345, 353, 365, 376, 378, 379, 390, 404, 405, 406, 414, 425, 426, 427, 428, 429, 431, 435, 437, 439, 441, 442, 443, 444, 445, 446, 447, 452, 460, 463, 464, 468, 488, 489, 493, 509, 510, 511, 513, 515, 516, 517, 523, 531, 551, 560, 561, 562, 564, 569, 573, 575, 578
South Otago, 69, 73, 210
South Otago district, 199
South Taranaki, 406
South Westland, 528
Southern Alps, 284, 331, 356, 426, 439, 506, 548

southern New Zealand, 79, 87, 185, 39, 543, 575
Southland, 42, 78, 148, 173, 197, 205, 256, 263, 410, 431, 436, 452, 536, 537, 559
Sparrowhawk Stream *see* Awakaeaea, stream, 168
Stephens Island *see* Takaporewa, island, 506, 507, 509
Stewart Island *see* Rakiura, island, 16, 24, 26, 42, 48, 79, 84, 94, 133, 157, 165, 176, 178, 200, 211, 213, 215, 216, 444, 460, 535, 536, 538, 539, 543, 544, 552, 573, 574
Stony Creek, 555
Strath Taieri, 28, 175, 554
Studholme, Lake *see* Wainono, lake, 160
Styx *see* Puharakekenui, 420
Sumner, 333, 414, 415, 431, 446
Sydney, 464

Ta Anu-Matao, 384
Table Hill, 566
Tahi-marae Pa, 81
Tahu-a-Te-Kaumira Range, 199
Tahuri-korari, 537
Taiari *see* Taieri, 452, 39, 547
Taieri, 11, 99, 574
Taieri, kaika, 42
Taieri Maori Reserve, 73
Taieri River, 110, 130, 137, 152, 158, 187
Taikunui *see* Tokanui, 190
Taireasee South Island, 460
Taitapu, 446
Takahaka *see* Cheviot, 426
Takaka, 485
Takapo, lake, 228, 357, 426
Takaporewa, island, 506, 509
Takitimu, mountains/range, 64, 167, 358, 416
Takitu *see* Belfast, 349
Tamahua, island *see* Quail Island, 339
Tamaipi, 106
Tapoa, bay *see* Corsair Bay, 468
Tapuaenuku, 407
Tapuaenuku, mountain, 429, 514
Taranaki, 81, 247, 263, 350, 435, 441, 460, 517, 574
Taranaki *see* South Taranaki, 406
Tasmania, 177
Tatakahikura, beach, 545
Tau-o-te-maku, pa, 539
Taukahara Bush, 413

Taukiepa, island *see* Kanawera, island, 224
Taumutu, 27, 136, 205, 226, 231, 241, 242, 244, 269, 273, 298, 303, 309, 314, 322, 367, 370, 381, 443, 448, 449, 523, 551
Taupo, 209
Taupo, lake, 320
Tautuku, 214, 556, 566, 570
Tautuku whaling station, 25
Tawera, 354
Tawera *see* Oxford, 352, 439
Tawera, mountain, 353, 360, 417
Tawhiroko, urupa, 544
Tawhiti-a-Rua, 407
Tawhiti-nui, 270
Tawhiti-roa, 270
Te Ahupatiki (in Lyttelton Harbour), 431
Te Ahupatiki, mountain, 357
Te Aitanga-a-Hinemateroa (clump of trees), 414
Te Aka Matua, 370
Te Anau, 550
Te Anau, lake, 163
Te Ao Marama, 370
Te Aruhe-a-Pora *see* Pigroot, 124
Te Awa-mokihi, 548
Te Awatuiau, 185
Te heti o Matiaha, point, 574
Te Heti o Paitu *see* Te heti o Matiaha, point, 574
Te Hono-ki-Wairua, 270
Te Horo, cliff, 548
Te Ika-a-Maui *see* North Island, 390, 559, 565
Te Kai-a-Te-Atua, pa (Kaiapoi), 538
Te Kai-a-Te-Atua, pa (Willowbridge), 538, 542
Te Kai-a-te-Atua, kaik, 223, 224
Te Kainga (correct form of Te Kinga), 531
Te Kanawera, island *see* Kanawera, island, 182
Te Kare Tua Tahi, 370
Te Kinga, railway siding, 530
Te Kohaka-a-Kaikaiawaru, pa *see* Te Kohanga-a-Kaikaiawaru, pa, 401
Te Kohanga Pa *see* Te Kohanga-a-Kaikaiawaru, pa, 439
Te Kohanga *see* Kaiapoi, 437
Te Kohanga-a-Kaikaiawaru, pa *see also* Kaiapoi, pa, 439
Te Koloka, Mount, 548
Te Kore, 370

Te Kuri, creek, 576
Te Kuri *see* Hampden, 576
Te Manuka Pa *see* Manuka Pa, 444, 446, 447
Te Marokura (a flat), 407, 408
Te One-ki-pikopiko-i-whiti, 389, 391
Te Pa-a-Moki, 231
Te Pa-a-Te-Ikamutu, 231
Te Pa-o-Te-Korua, 231
Te Pa-o-Te-Rangiwhakaputa, 273
Te Pa-whakataka, beach, 538
Te Papatua-mau-heke (clump of trees), 414
Te Pariwhakatau, 217, 567
Te Po, 384
Te Po ko Matipu, 370
Te Po TuaKahuru, 370
Te Poho-o-Tamatea, hill *see* Mahuraki, hill, 427
Te Poho-o-Te-Mahaki, hill, 413
Te Puia, pa, 407
Te Pukehapopo, 433
Te Pukekihikurangi, hill, 433
Te Raka-a-Hinaatea Pa, 430
Te Raka-a-Hinaatea Pa *see* Te Raka-a-Hineatea Pa, 430
Te Raka-a-Hine-Atea, pa, 537, 538
Te Raka-a-Hineatea Pa, 430
Te Reika *see* Reinga, 565
Te Reinga *see* Reinga, 406
Te Rerenga-Wairua, 460
Te Taumutu *see* Taumutu, 460
Te Umukaha *see* Temuka, 417
Te Upoko-o-Mahuraki, hill *see* Mahuraki, hill, 427
Te Waewae Bay, 575
Te Waha-a-Parata, 396
Te Wai Point, 180, 181
Te Wai Pounemu *see* South Island, 284, 522, 550
Te Waipuna Pa, 444
Te Whakatakanga-o-te-ngarehu-o-te-ahi-a-Tamatea, 427
Te Whata-a-rama, 417
Te Whiwhi, hill, 199
Te Whiwhia, 370
Temuka (cemetery), 270
Temuka, 14, 23, 27, 41, 68, 71, 72, 73, 74, 75, 76, 78, 81, 109, 110, 112, 116, 119, 126, 128, 136, 143, 144, 145, 146, 147, 148, 149, 155, 160, 166, 211, 218, 220, 224, 228, 236, 252, 254, 270, 291, 295, 305, 317, 320, 344, 354, 374, 382, 417, 418, 421, 439, 446, 458, 465, 35, 39, 537, 539, 540, 542, 547, 549, 554, 557, 567, 568, 570, 575, 578
Temuka, kaika, 218
Temuka, kaik, urupa, 270
Ti-a-Tauwhetuku (clump of trees), 414
Tiimaru *see* Timaru, 460
Tikao Bay (Wainui), 27
Tikoraki Point, 545
Timaru, 232, 573
Timaru Lagoon, 147
Timingi, mountain, 514
Timuaki, mountain, 523
Titi Islands, 42, 45, 84, 121, 159, 171, 174, 176, 179, 183, 185, 186, 187, 190, 192, 195, 215, 224, 343, 349, 353, 358, 511, 566
Tokanui, 172, 190
Tokomairiro Beach, 569
Tokomaru, 271
Tolaga Bay, 271
Tonga, 356
Transvaal, 464
Tuahiwi, 16, 23, 25, 26, 28, 29, 224, 242, 244, 248, 254, 270, 284, 301, 306, 321, 349, 355, 358, 367, 409, 429, 448, 453, 461
Tuahiwi, urupa, 274
Tuahiwi District, 224
Tuahiwi Reserve, 224
Tuhiraki, hill, 441
Tuhua, 523
Tukoroua, island, 538
Turanga *see* Gisborne, 372, 407, 429, 433, 460
Turanganuiarua, 558
Tutaipatu, lagoon, 318, 339
Tuturau, 24, 150, 206, 212, 410, 444, 539, 577
Tuturau Maori Reserve, 172

Uenuku, 452
Uhimataitai, urupa, 545
Upper Mavora Lake *see* Manawapore, 149
Urutane, hill, 542

Volcanic Region (NI), 435

Wahu, 391
Wai-aniwa, 200
Waianakarua, 192
Waiateruati, pa, 539
Waiau, river, 177
Waiau, valley, 537
Waicola *see* Waikoula, 168
Waihao, 26, 124, 199, 315
Waihao River, 313, 322
Waihemo River, 144
Waihemo *see* Palmerston, 576
Waihola (in south?), 163
Waihola, 538
Waihola, lake, 123, 142, 165
Waihora, 279, 303
Waihora, lake, 279, 285, 314, 320, 360, 425
Waikaka, river *see* Waikakahi, river, 552
Waikakahi, 280, 326, 407, 416, 437, 443
Waikakahi District, 407
Waikakahi, pa, 230, 254, 276, 428
Waikakahi, river, 552
Waikanae (NI), 324
Waikato, 464
Waikawa, 16
Waikirikiri, river *see* Selwyn River, 314, 317
Waikokopura, 137
Waikouaiti, 26, 45, 59, 64, 65, 77, 139, 140, 198, 199, 201, 203, 218, 246, 300, 453, 538, 541, 542, 556, 568, 574, 575
Waikouaiti (peninsula), 556
Waikouaiti, kaika, 218
Waikoula, 168
Waimakariri, river, 287, 310, 317, 318, 319, 354, 361
Waimarino, river (NI), 353
Waimataitai, lagoon, 147
Waimate, 11, 26, 27, 192, 199, 354, 39, 542
Waimate Gorge, 137
Waimatemate *see* Waimate, 199, 542
Waimea Plains, 44, 552
Waimumu Gorge, 555
Wainono, 160
Wainui, 27
Waiora-a-Tane, lake, 398
Waipapa, 439, 440
Waipawa Creek, 158
Waipouri, 124
Waipuna, 268
Waipuna Hill, 272, 381, 444
Waipupu, fishing camp, 231
Waipupu, pa, 231
Wairarapa (NI), 28, 225, 254, 438
Wairarapa, lake, 390
Wairau, 27, 481
Wairewa, 27, 261, 268, 279, 300, 303, 323, 326, 361, 444, 446, 464

INDEX OF PLACE NAMES 619

Wairewa see Little River, 531
Wairewa, lake, 135, 279, 314, 317, 325, 381, 382, 424
Wairuaapo, mountains, 554
Waitahuna, 546
Waitaki, 574
Waitaki Hills, 435
Waitaki Mouth, 41, 110, 123, 135, 136, 199, 258, 270
Waitaki Plains, Lower, 199
Waitaki River, 135, 192, 199, 200, 287, 313, 351, 435, 550, 569
Waitaki Valley, 197, 547
Waitarakao, 147
Waitarakao Lagoon, 147
Waitarakao see Washdyke, 139
Waitati, 568
Waiteruati Pa, 439
Waitui, 438
Waiwhakaheketupapaku, spring, 269
Waiwhio, river, 314, 317
Wakapatu, 213
Wakaraupo see Whakaraupo, 431
Wakatipu, lake, 131, 144, 167, 170, 548, 550, 555
Wallacetown, 163
Wanaka (settlement?), 163
Wanaka, 550
Wanaka, lake, 144, 167, 354, 569, 575, 577
Wanganui, 341

Warepa see Wharepa, 418
Waro-nuku, cave, 433
Warrington, 576
Washdyke, 139, 147
Wawau, 407
Wellington, 263, 270, 390
Wellington Harbour see Whanganui-a-Tara, 390
Wellington Province, 373, 428
West Coast (NI), 407, 414
West Coast, 121, 247, 285, 298, 342, 355, 373, 405, 437, 493, 494, 499, 522, 523, 524, 525, 526, 527, 529, 531, 532, 549, 564
West Coast Fiords, 122, 145, 167, 168, 529, 532
West Coast Sounds see West Coast Fiords, 90, 192
West Dome, 375
Westland, 16, 110, 187, 192, 211, 213, 265, 340, 373, 429, 437, 438, 500, 519, 521, 522, 523, 526, 528, 530, 531, 532, 549, 569
Westland Province, 526
Weston, 10
Whakapuaka (Nelson), 29
Whaka-renga-mahe, rock, 130
Whaka-renga-pohatu, rock see Whaka-renga-mahe, rock, 130
Whakaamoa, pa, 407
Whakaari, island, 460
Whakahume, river, 224, 317

Whakamoa, 350, 440
Whakapuaka, 471, 492, 515
Whakaraupo (correct form of Wakaraupo), 279, 431
Whakaraupuka, pa, 538
Whakare-ka-iwi, cave, 545
Whakatane, 343
Whakatipu, lake see Wakatipu, lake, 452
Whakatipu-waimaori (part of lake), 452
Whakatipu-waitai (part of lake), 452
Whanganui, 299, 343, 460
Whanganui River, 427
Whanganui-a-Tara, 390
Whangaparoa, 427
Wharawhara, island see Rabbit Island, 36
Wharekauri see Chatham Islands, 460
Wharepa, 418
Whataparaerae Creek, 569
White, Mount see Pakati, mountain, 554
White Island see Whakaari, island, 460
Willowbridge, 538, 542, 548
Wilsher Bay, 25
Woodend, 230, 318, 339, 345, 430
Wyndham, 142

Zulu land, 440

GENERAL INDEX

Page numbers in *italic* type refer to sections on the subject.

adornment, personal, *54*, *56–59*, 60, 163, 165, *241–45*, 246, 248, 273, 332, 343, 420, 451, 459, *478–79*, 480, *540–41*
aeroplanes, 347
albinos, human, 265, 401, 463; titi, 179, 182, 183, 184, 212, 553; weka, 171, 409
alcohol, use of, 465
animals see bats/pekapeka, crocodiles, fish, frogs, introduced animals, kaurehe, lizards, otters, pukutuara, rats, sea lions, sea elephants, sea leopards, seals, shellfish, tuatara, whales; see also insects etc; sea creatures

animals, beavers, see kaurehe
archaeology, 14
astronomy see stars atahu, 210, 422
atua, 57, 58, 183, 213, 376, 377, 378, 396, 409, 415, 418, 420, 432, 447, 453, 463, 513, 516, 517, 537, 553, 556, 557, 559, 562, 565, 566, 576; birds, 212
Aurora Australis, 200, 363, 400, 513
Australian Light Horse, 575

B.P. Bishop Museum (Honolulu), 15
Bank of New South Wales, 550
Bank of New South Wales (Gore), 16

Bank of New Zealand, 98, 551
bats/pekapeka, *190*, 336, 346, 347, *508*
beavers see kaurehe bedding, 43, 44, 46, *228–29*, 338, *473–74*, 533
beds, 43, 44, *228–29*, 264, 279, 280, 466, 471, *473–74*, 485
Bible, the, 213, 380, 383, 431, 576
bird hunting, 42, 69, *163–84*, 207, 212, *334–35*, 374, 473, 477, 489, *504–08*, 510, *552–53*, 558, 566
calling, 529
dogs, 163, 164, 165, 170, 188, 336, 338, 339, 340, 342, 351, 529

guns, 170, 172, 528, 530
hooks, 338
nets, 338, 529
of kereru/pigeons, 557
of titi, 24, 77, 94, 169, 176, *177–80, 182–84,* 215
of tui, 175, 335
of weka, 553, 570
seasonal, 28
snares, 163, 165, 166, 169, 170, 172, 173, 174, 175, 334, 335, 337, 338, 339, 343, 345, 468, 504, 505, 506, 529, 530
spears, 172, *173,* 175, 337, 338
stones, 170
bird skins, 47, 243, 343
birding preserves, 175, 178, 182, 184, 345, 353
birds, 38, *163–84,* 189, 215, *334–45, 504–08,* 523, 524, 525, *528–30, 552–53*
abnormal, 183
atua *see* atua, birds extinction of, 553, 575
introduced, 460; chickens/fowls, 318, 418, 421, 467
kinds of
cuckoo, 241
dotterel, 507
ducks, 325, *505*
parera-kowhio/blue mountain duck, 505
parera/grey duck, 505, 529
grey teal, 505
hakuai *see* birds, mythical
hawks, *167–68 see also* kaeaea, kahu, karewarewa
huia, 241, 468
kaeaea/sparrowhawks 507
kahu/harrier hawk, 387, 388, 506, 559
kaka, 71, 100, 122, 174, 175, 216, 241, 245, 259, 290, 417, 445, 481, *504,* 505, 507, 508
kakapo/ground parrot, 100, 215, 351, 506, 529, 532
kakariki/parewaka/porere/parrokeets, 100, 183, 216, 290, 505, 507
kamana/crested grebe, 575
karae, 211, 409
karewarewa/bush hawk, 506
karoro/seagulls, 160, 216, 331, 409, 503, 506, 507
kea, 118, 344, 506
kereru/kukupa/native pigeon, 64, 71, 173, 175, 186, 193, 214, 241, 248, 290, 386, 387,
417, *504,* 529, 530, 557, 558, 559, 560, 566
kiwi/kivi 47, 232, 236, 351, *506,* 529, 530, 532; kiwi-ma, 506; totoweka, 506
koau/shags, 276, 318, 416, 505, 529; koau-pango/black shag, 505; koau-pateketeke/king shag, 500, 505
koekoea/longtailed cuckoo, 56, 100, 506
koka/native crow, 215, 216, 506, 521, 529
koreke/native quail, *169–70,* 217, 506, 567
kotare/kingfisher, 507
kotuku/white heron/white cranes, 56, 71, 90, 241, 243, 273, 505, 507, 521, 529, 530; nesting and roosting sites, 163, 529
koukou/morepork, 409
kura, 507
kuruti, *506,* 507
makomako/bellbird, 290, 505
mata/fernbird, 507
matuhi, 500, 507
matuku/grey or blue bittern, 505
maunu, 351
moa, 57, 167, 345, 361, 426, 507, 570
pakura/pukeko/pukaki/swampturkey, 325, 387, 388, 398, 505, 529
pimiromiro/tomtit, 507
piopio/morepork owl, 38
piopio/thrush, 38
pipiwharauroa/shining cuckoo, 203, 506
porere, 507
popokotea/yellowheads/native canary, 507
pouaka/powaka/poaka/kuaka/godwit, 38, 506
pukaki, 325
putakitaki/putangitangi/paradise ducks, 64, 505, 507
rail, 507
rerewaka, 507
riroriro/grey warbler, 507
rock-wren, 507
ruru/morepork, 81, 100, 211, 212, 371, 409, 419, 506, 552, 553, 568
sparrows, 553
swans, black 325
takahea/takahe, 210
tarapunga/sea-martin, 506
thrush, 507
tieke/saddleback, 215, 506
titakataka/titaiwaka/pitakataka/fantail, 388, 398, 405, 507
titi/muttonbirds, 44, 62, 114, 127, 138, 165, 177, 178, 179, 180, 183, 184, 189, 190, 195, 212, 291, 353, 506, 507, 509, 553; titi wahine, 178; titi-wainui, 178
titiripounamu/rifleman, 507
torea/redbills, 409, 506
toroa/albatross, 47, 54, 66, 77, 215, 479, 506
totoara/robin, 507
totoria/mollyhawk, 215
tui/koko, 71, 175, 248, 290, 352, 505, 507, 532
waxeyes/'glass-eye'/white-eyes/ringeyes/blight-birds, 507
weka/woodhens, 47, 63, 64, 83, 84, 87, 113, 118, 171, 174, 175, 186, 189, 195, 217, 248, 290, 291, 292, 319, 351, 352, 356, 409, 417, 465, 477, 506, 507, 529, 530, 553, 570
whioioi/sandlarks, 507
mythical, 432; hakuai, 177, 183, 184, 343; Manu-nui-a-Tane, 441; Te Manu-a-Tane, 441
origin of, 396
sex of, 216
Boer War, 464
bone, human, 88, 90, 271, 272, 273, 274, 388, 392, 432, 558, 562, 563, 565
bone, use of, 57, 129, 158, 236, 296, 343, 433
birding, 173, 338, 504
carving, 252
ear decorations, 54, 56, 241
fasteners, 47, 56, 232, 235
fishing, 131, 133, 143, 148, 337, 386, 500
hair combs, 56, 242
hei, 56, 57
musical instruments, 78, 79
sealing, 333
sewing, 53, 144, 235, 241, 242
shellfish picks, 160, 330
tattooing, 64, 66, 249
bone, whale, 78, 100, 101, 149, 235, 241, 249, 282, 308, 334
Botanical Gardens, Christchurch, 240
botany *see* plants and trees

canoe accidents, 539, 561, 569, 570
canoe anchors, 433
canoe making, 434
canoe paddles/hoe, 100, 105, 107, *108*, 109, 110, 111, 147, 281, 282, 287, 314, 492, 495; steering, 111
canoe sails, 54, 109, 111, 511
canoes/waka, 38, 59, 60, 67, 103, *108–11*, 124, 130, 133, 154, 165, 208, 209, 212, 246, 247, 252, 260, 284, 285, *286–88*, 290, 308, 317, 336, 337, 344, 363, 369, 376, 377, 380, 381, 389, 392, 396, 401, 407, 411, 415, 420, *425–28*, 434, 435, 436, 440, 444, 445, 446, 459, 463, 478, 479, 481, 488, 492, *494–96*, 524, 561, 562, 564, 574
kinds of
double, 286, 495
dug-out, 287, 337
log, 110
outrigger, 109, 286, 468
single, 110, 287, 288
unua, 109, 110, 286, 287, 288
named
Aotea, 427, 435, 436
Arai-te-tonga, 197
Araiteuru, 196, 247, 285, 351, 375, 376, 426, 427, 435, 442, 568, 569, 570
Arawa, 427, 436, 452
Greenstone canoe/Waka Pounemu *see* Tairea, 523
Horouta, 301, 441, 442
Huruhurumanu, 441
Kapakitua, 425, 440
Mahunui, 389, 390, 405
Makawhiu, 372, 438, 488
Manuka, 301, 441, 442
Niwaru (boat), 558
Pukekohe, 488
South Island (Maui's canoe), 559
spirit, 202
Tainui, 427, 436
Tairea, 284, 285, 286, 426, 523, 549
Takitimu, 202, 351, 375, 376, 416, 426, 427, 428, 435, 436, 437, 442, 445, 452, 532
Te Hauwai, 375, 438
TeWaka-a-Rangi, 426, 441
Te Waka-a-Tamarereti
Te-reperepe-tautini-Tinirau, 562

Timuaki, 523
Toitoi (boat), 412
Tutepawharangi/ Tutepawharaki (of Ruatapu), 397, 433, 564
Tutepawharangi (of Tane), 397
Uruao, 202, 441
Wakahuruhurumanu/ Wakahurumanu, 202, 425
Waka-Pounemu *see* Tairea
Canterbury Museum, 468
Carnegie Institute (New Plymouth), 11
carrying, loads, 54, 98, 274, 275, *280–81*, 295, 297, 323, 341, 568
carrying, people, 280
carving and carvings, 45, 59, 60, 66, *67*, 99, 104, 161, 208, 244, 249, *250–52*, 255, 343, 366, 371, 378, 435, 438, 471, 472, 478, 479, *481–82*, 495, 507, 538, 539, 543, 546
boxes, sticks, 98, 236, 373, 468
buildings, posts, 41, 67, 223, 225, 226, 229, 230, 372
canoes, 67, 108, 109, 110, 286
household utensils, 240, 295, 296
Kaiapoi monument, 231
of skin *see* tattooing, 480
of stone, 549
on trees, 468
carving designs, origins of, 252
cattle *see* introduced animals, cattle caves, 88, 156, 269, 273, 312, 387, 388, 426, 432, 434, 487, 488, 545, 556, 561
burial, 274, 488
cemeteries, Pakeha (Temuka), 270
ceremonies, 99, 205, 206, 242, 267, 272, 274, 277, 278, 287, 301, 365, 371, 376, 377, 382, 383, 459, 472, 487
chewing gum *see* gum, chewing
chiefs, 25, 199, 200, 205, 207, 214, 277, 381, 382, 410, 414, 424, 427, 428, 429, 431, 438, 439, 443, 444, 445, 446, 447, 464, 541, 543, 545, 546, 547, 548, 559, 560, 567, 570, 574, 575
white, 463
childbirth, 28, 93, 116, 261, 264, *266–67*, 372, 409, 489
caesarian, 267, 428

children, unborn, 86
Christchurch Exhibition, 223, 230, 282, 299, 333, 428, 435, 437, 464
Christchurch Hospital, 262, 263
Christchurch Museum, 76, 79, 98, 123, 193, 252, 296, 348, 349, 476
Christchurch Star, newspaper, 444
Christianity, 207, 275, 410, 422, 423, 466
churches, 206, 537
Moeraki, 545, 575
Native/Maori Church (Otaki), 431, 542
St Stephen's (Tuahiwi), 301
Wesleyan (Taumutu), 231
clothing, *46–52*, 91, 92, 122, 165, 228, *232–38*, 279, 282, 338, 350, 374, 387, 423, 432, 438, 441, *475–77*, 510, 532, 533, *539–40*, 559, 564
footwear, *52*, 72, 156, 217, *236–38*, 237, 475, *476–77*, 577
leggings, 52, *236–38*, 459, 468, 476, 477
maro, 86, 106
of mourning, 90
rainwear, 47, 195
clouds, 247, 363
coins, silver, 578
colours, *62–63*, 245, *246–47*, 479, *521*
comets, 201, 513
Commissioner (of Lands?), 427, 575
cooking, 82, 87, *111–17*, 120, 121, 124, 125, 126, 128, 129, 132, 153, 155, 158, 159, 165, 166, 169, 208, 248, 261, 262, 263, 264, 268, 273, 280, 288, *290–94*, 295, 297, 298, 300, 301, 302, 304, 306, 308, 311, 326, 327, 330, 333, 335, 336, 337, 339, 343, 347, 348, 352, 353, 419, 420, 426, 439, 458, 462, 466, 472, 490, 494, *497*, 498, 502, 506, 509, 522, 523, 524, 525, 530, 533, *551*, 570
cooking shed/wharekauti, 292
counting, 99, 179
creation, 205, 380, 394, 395, 397, 401, 403, 556, 560
crocodiles, 188, 354
Cruise of the Cachalot (Bullen, FT), 38
cultivation, 107, 108, 120, 179,

182, 198, 199, 203, 282, 286, 289, 301, 302, 303, 334, 346, 374, 375, 380, 386, 393, 408, 441, 454, 462, *496–97*, 498, 513, 526, 546, 548, 560, 573
by the stars, 303
kumera, 301, 387
customs, 27, 28, 44, 69, 77, 91, 92, *93–96*, *98–99*, 124, 205, 207, 209, 212, 236, 254, 255, 269, 270, *275–81*, 305, 316, 344, 376, 408, 419, 434, 443, 454, 485, 487, *488–90*, *522*, 540, *545–46*
hoki/hongi, 94, 275, 276, 485, 488; origins of, 488
kai-tangata, 271, 277, 280, 283, 288, 472, 488, 493
tapatapa/name giving, 275, 277, 279
taramea collecting, 63, 248

dances and dancing, *81–82*, *260*, 467, *484*
war, 98, 253, 478, 484
death, by drowning, 26, 212
death, disposal of the dead, 71–78, *88–92*, 209, *269–74*, 369, 380, 381, 384, *487–88*, *544–45*
bone-scraping, 88, 269, 273, 487
canoe burial, 88, 488
cave burial, 88, 90, 269, 272, 273, 274, 487, 488, 545
cremation, 88, 209, 214, 252, 269, 272, 273, 274, 415, 429, 430, 434, 438, 487
earth burial, 88, 90, 271, 272, 280, 485, 558
preservation, 88, 89, 241, 244, 269, 271, 273, 430, 487
sandhill burial, 90, 271, 487
tree/platform burial, 88
water burial, 88, 252, 269, 272, 273, 274, 487
death, origins of, 397, 403
decoration, 46, 48, 71, 102, 104, 105, 225, 471, 500
taniko, 46, 232, 234, 236, 475, 498
A dictionary of the Maori language, (Williams, H.W.), 152
directions, 196, 198, 199, 359, 400
divination, *209–10*, 420
dog catching, 69, 187, *188–89*, *350–52*, 510
dog hair, 475, 510

dog skins, 46, 47, 232, 234, 243, 350, 351, 432, 438, 475, 476, 510
dogs, 165, 166, 170, 175, *187–89*, 210, 264, 338, 339, 340, 342, *350–52*, 374, 386, 414, 432, 435, 467, 489, 529, 565
bulldogs, 106
kuri, 163, 164, 172, 187, 188, 278, 338, 339, 340, 342, 350, 351, 352, 371, 386, 506, *510*, 549, 573
two-headed, 561
domestic science *see* cooking; household utensils
Dominion Museum, 298
dreams, 212, 213, 262, 373, *410–12*, 415, 493, 516, 541, 548, 566
dredging, 151, 158, 161 dyes, 47, *60–62*, 63, 66, 236, *245–47*, 468, 475, 478, *479*, 511, 512, 541, *542*

early settlers (European), 9, 11, 193
Early Settlers Museum (Dunedin), 12
earth, the, 202, 363, 383, 384, 395, 402, 407
earth ovens, 43, 61, 111, 114, 116, 117, 119, 120, 121, 122, 123, 126, 132, 154, 155, 158, 165, 166, 202, 206, 217, 300, 327, 336, 351, 372, 471, 497, 501, 506, 524, 525, 533, 551, 554, 562, 573, 577
hangi, 290, 292, 293, 295, 297
kapa-maori/'koppa-maori'/kopa-maori, 291, 292, 293, 330, 335, 337, 382, 432
puna/puna-ti, 290, 291, 293
umu, 290, 292, 293, 294, 297, 301, 302, 304, 310, 316, 326, 333, 335, 337, 338, 341, 343, 352, 353, 374, 379, 382, 415, 445, 462, 468
earthquakes/ru, *204*, 399, 400, *514*, 565
East Polynesian culture, 14
echoes, 434
eclipses, 201, 400
education, 574, 578
entomology *see* insects, etc; tuatara
epidemics, diarrhoea, 262
influenza, 86, 263, 270, 410, 464

measles, 86, 261, 264, 463
rewharewha/maremare, 264
whiu, 86
Ethnological Research Board, 15
exploration, 523

fairies *see* tribes/hapu, patupaiarehe
fastenings, 47, 52, 56, 57, 233, 234, 235, 238, 241, 282, 476, 477
feasts Aruhe-taratara, 445
Pohatu-parimurimu, 445
feathers, 44, 46, 47, 49, 54, 56, 71, 90, 98, 100, 104, 105, 106, 163, 171, 174, 178, 184, 233, 281, 291, 479, 491, 495
bedding, 228, 338
clothing, 228, 232, 234, 236, 336, 338, 339, 341, headband/hair ornaments, 241, 243, 244, 273, 343, 468
needles, 235, 241
nose/ear ornaments, 242, 420
removal, 112, 165, 290, 293
ferrets *see* introduced animals, ferrets
fertility, women, 266
fieldwork, of H. Beattie, 16–29
fire, 471
origin of, 391, 435
use of, 89, 102, 103, 205, 208, 248, 249, 256, 273, 283, 337, 382, 487; in land clearing, 289
fire making, 114, 196, 290, 292, 294, 388, 546, 559, 561, 602, 292
trees, 388
fires, grass, 82, 175
fires, tapu, 208, 209
fires, Te-ahi-a-Ue, 435, 452
fires, underground, 204, 427, 435, 452
fires, volcanic, 427
fish, 38, *129–53, 307–33*, *500–03*, 524, *526–28*, 552
fossil 331
kinds of
aua/herring, 501
blue bone, 501
bully, 343
dogfish, 322
green-bone, 501
haku/king fish, 500, 501
haparu/young grayling, 521
hapuku/groper, 116, *133*, 134, 212, 295, 333, 392, 566

hature/mackerel, 500, 501
inaka/inanga/minnow, 138, 147, 279, 290, 339, 343
kahawai, 500
kana, 150
kanae/mullet, 501
kanakana/piharau/lamprey eels, 107, *141–43*, 146, 147, 148, 150, 151, 187, 316, 320, 321, 323, 418, 502
kauri, 127
kelp fish/ngehe, 501
kohekohe/trumpeter, 392, 501
koiro/conger eel, 141, 324, 405, 559
kokirikiri/leather jacket, 501
kokopala, 150
kokopara, *137*, 560
kokopu, *137*, 147, 549
kokopu/bullhead, 501
kukupa/ring fish, 501
kopapa/trevally, 501
koroama/sardines, 177
kumukumu/gurnet, 501
ling, 392
maka-taharaki/maka-tikati, 501
maka/barracouta, 116, *131–33*, 177, 293, 295, 341, 500, 501, 556, 559
mako-repe/elephant fish, 423, 562
marakuha/sprats, 177
marare/butterfish 304, 501
mata/whitebait, 137, 139, 290, 298, 299, 339, 501
minnow, 142, 549
moeanu/sandfish, 423, 562
moki, 304, 392, 501
ngehe/kelp fish, 500
pakirikiri/rock cod, 501
panako, 146, 549
patangatanga/red jacket, 501
patete/paraki, 135, 279, 501
patiki/flounders, 116, 143, 144, 150, *152–53*, 279, 289, 339
patiki-kutu-horihori/kutuhori/horihori/hori/sole, *152–53*, 423, 424, 562
perch, 142
piharau, 316
pipiki, 146, 549
pua-ata-ata/silvery, 500, 501
rawaru/blue cod, 501
repe/Te Maro-o-Hineteiwaiwa/elephant fish, 423, 424

stinger eel, 338
tarakihi/warehou 501
trout, 142, 502
tuna/eels see entry under 't'
upokororo/grayling, 146, 501
waharoa/smelt, 501
warehou see tarakihi
mythological, 403; waro (re Maui), 395
origins of, 396
sex of, 310, 314, 325
fish foods, 116
 mako-karaerae, 332
 mango-maroke, 332
 maraki, 116, 133, 246, 278, 308
 moi, 132
 paku, 116, 132, 316
 patiki-maroke, 116
 pawhera, 116
fishing, 24, 42, 124, *129–56*, 201, 207, 212, 305, *307–33*, 374, 385, 392, 413, 416, 426, 458, *500–04*, *526–28*, 552, 559
 bobs/putiti, 528
 by the stars, 315
 canals, 139, 147, 149, 502, 527, 565
 gorges, 307
 of crabs, 503
 of eels, 27, 112, 115, 117, 124, 143, 144, 145, 146, 168, 192, 194, 288, *316–26*, 348, 354, 374, 404, 413, 420, 425, 426, 440, 443, 473, 502, 509, 517, 547
 of kanakana, 107
 of koura/crayfish, 155, 326, 504
 of salmon, 465
fishing camps, 231, 408
fishing canals, 289, 314, 316, 320
fishing hooks, 129, 131, 133, 212, 273, 307, 308, 314, 332, 334, 385, 389, 458, 478, 487, 500
fishing lines, 61, 195
fishing nets, 129, *133–37*, 135, 136, 137, 307, 308, 310, 312, 314, 316, 322, 331, 500, 501, 526, 527, 558, 563
 origin of, 405
fishing pa, 191, 308, 314
 pa-kanakana, 145, 148, 149
 pa-tuna, 145, 148, 152, 307, 502
fishing preserves, 175, 311, 345
 kanakana, 151

fishing sinkers, 120, 129, 130, 143, 390, 463
fishing spears, 289, 502, 527
fishing traps, stone, 149
fishing up land, 389, 391
flax, use of, 49, 51, *52–54*, 61, 67, 68, 70, 71, 75, 76, 77, 78, 79, 80, 83, 86, 100, 102, 103, 109, 110, 111, 115, 132, 135, 136, 137, 139, 143, 145, 146, 161, 169, 174, 180, 182, 228, 233, 235, 236, *238–41*, 245, 246, 247, 248, 249, 254, 256, 258, 259, 281, 290, 291, 294, 295, 297, 307, 308, 310, 312, 314, 317, 318, 319, 320, 322, 323, 326, 331, 337, 338, 339, 340, 341, 344, 360, 419, 452, 453, 468, *475–77*, 522, *540*, 544, 568
floods, 361, 426, 432, 433, 575
 of 1868, 547
 Parawhenuamea, 361, 433
fog, 514
folk tales, *215–17*, *423–24*, 567
food, gifts, 140
food exchange, 278, 291, 490
food preservation, *44–45*, 114, 116, 124, 132, 133, 140, 144, 147, 155, 158, 160, 177, 189, 190, 203, *229*, 246, 291, 292, 296, 297, 302, 308, 312, 314, 316, 325, 326, 332, 335, 337, 344, 352, 462, 472, 489, 494, 499, 501, 503, 506
food storage, *44–45*, 60, 93, 114, 120, 124, 132, 133, 155, 158, 223, 226, *229*, 296, 297, 302, 332, 353, 354, 462, 498
footwear see clothing, footwear
fortifications, 45, 103, 223, *229*, 471, 492, *538–39*, *474*
frogs, 325

games, pastimes, sports, 25, 28, *67–77*, *80–81*, 93, 99, 212, 228, *253–60*, 303, 308, 327, 358, 372, 452, 468, 478, *482–84*, 493, 543
 darts, 75, 76, 106, 253, 281, 482, 537, 557, 558
 poi, 47, 49, 70, *80–81*, *260*, 476, *484*, 563
 teka, 372
 whai/cat's cradle, 69, 257, 434, 482
giants, 388, 390, 426, 432, 434, 435, 444, 561
Gibraltar of the South Island, 231

Glade House, 550
God (Christian), 207, 213, 409, 575
gods, 58, 106, 131, 193, 200, 202, 207, 208, 211, 244, 278, 285, 349, 359, 363, 367, 370, 373, 374, 375, 382, 383, 388, 389, 393, 395, 396, 397, 398, 399, 400, 401, 406, 420, 423, 428, 446, 463, 556, 559, 560, 565
gold miners, 12
Gore Hospital, 557
Gore Standard, newspaper, 12
Great War *see* World War I, 374
greenstone/pounemu, 29, 54, 56, 57, 62, 67, 71, 90, 100, 101, 103, *108*, 116, 137, 236, 242, 244, 274, 281, 282, 283, *284–86*, 377, 420, 435, 437, 467, 478, 481, 491, *493–94*, 521, *522–23*, 538, 540, *548–50*
Kahotea block, 493
Te Taka block, 493, 494
gum, chewing, *127–28*, 296, *305–06*, 494, *499*
kauri (fish), 127
kauri (shellfish), 127
kauri, 128, 305
mimiha/pakake, 128, 305, 499
pikiraki, 305
puha, 127, 128, 305, 499
gums,
flax, 83, 100, 262
rimu, 64
taramea, 63, 248, 249, 542
tarata, 100, 248, 249, 480

H.M.S. New Zealand, (ship), 547
habitations, *41–45*, 59, 60, 103, 184, 190, 195, 205, 208, *223–31*, 272, 283, 314, 358, 372, 382, 393, 405, 412, 419, *471–74*, 481, 484, 489, 494, 510, 511, 533, *537–39*, 541, 564, 578
round houses, 41, 42, 43, 183, 223, 224, 226, 471, 553
hair styles, 56, 106, 164, 242, 243, 244
haka, 47, 48, 49, 81, 98, 106, 243, 260, 467, 478, 484, 563; koekohe, 82
halfcastes, 35, 38, 94, 104, 144, 176, 193, 242, 263, 270, 272, 317, 347, 367, 373, 410, 424, 431, 468, 507, 509, 545, 575
Hauhau, religion, 422

headless figure, 242, 243, 244, 478, 549, 550
healers and healing, 262, 378, 413, 544, 578
health, 86
hearths, 42, 472
heavens, 59, 201, 247, 363, 364, 376, *383–84*, *396–99*, 402, 406, *513–14*, 557, 561
heitiki *see* ornaments, heitiki
history, traditional, 12, 14, 18, 49, 80, 84, 94, 102, 103, 105, 124, 143, 156, 204, 256, 274, 281, 365, 367, 371, 374, 379, 384, 398, *425–47*, 468, 516, 546, 547, 548, *568–71*
History of Otago (Hocken, T.M.), 354, 575, 577
Hocken library, 15, 16, 18, 29, 40, 51, 367, 378
Hoho Railway Station, 530
horses *see* introduced animals, horses
household utensils, 47, 53, 54, 61, 63, 100, *116–17*, 161, 290, 293, 294, *295–96*, 297, 426, 435, 461, 466, 494, *497–98*
basins/bowls, 48, 61, 249, 292, 399, 441, 480
ipu, 61, 64, 66, 109, 111, 114, 119, 179, 182, 183, 189, 249, 290, 292, 426
humans, origin of, 396

ichthyology *see* fish
informants, of H. Beattie re 1920 project, 16–29
insects, etc, 85, *185–87*, 199, 240, 307, 334, 340, *346–48*, 349, *508–09*, 530, 554
bees, 212, 486
beetles, 170
butterflies, *185*
fleas, *185*
flies, 138, *185*
kutu/lice, 216
leeches, 176
moths, 185, 336, 347, 516
ro/stick insect, 186, 347, 410, 508
spiders, 176, 185
spiders, katipo, 87, 185, 268, 486
tuka/tukarakau/uhu/huhu/white pine grub, 186, 342, 346, 347, 348, 380, 509, 530
weta, 186, 347, 508
whe, 347, 410, 508
worms, 115, 132, 143, 187,

319, 320, 325, 336, 340, 346, 348
insects, introduced, 123, 185, 460, 508
introduced animals, 451, 460, 461, 553
birds *see* birds, introduced
cattle, 82, 262, 333, 351, 358, 414, 467, 486
dogs *see* dogs,
ferrets, 553
horses, 137, 138, 140, 211, 262, 264, 358, 414
mice, 336
pigs *see* pigs 351, 401, 414, 465, 466, 467
rabbits, 339, 553, 577
rats *see* rats
sheep, 146, 195, 212, 265, 325, 344
weasels, 184
introduced plants, *see* plants, introduced
iron foundaries, 577
islands, 164, 561
floating, 569
Israelite, religion, 422

Journal of the Polynesian Society, 12, 35, 59, 205, 274, 380, 421, 423, 429, 452
Journal of the Polynesian Society (H. Beattie articles), 212, 253, 416, 418, 420, 430, 434, 440, 441, 443, 556, 566
Ka-tara-o-kai *see* Aurora Australis, 200
Kahotea (hei), 540
Kaiapohia (Stack, J.W.), 30, 96, 228, 285, 298, 302, 367, 370, 373
Kaiapoi Debating Club (Maori), 324
Kaiapoi Factory, 224
Kaiapoi Mill, 228
Kaiapoi Pa, monument, 231
kaika, 41, 44, 56, 59, 70, 81, 86, 140, 151, 188, 207, 208, 217, 223, 224, 226, 258, 270, 271, 336, 337, 353, 360, 377, 467, 474, 537, 544, 546, 553, 561, 575, 577, 578
karakia, 57, 58, 64, 66, 82, 85, 86, 90, 167, 188, 204, *206–07*, 208, 209, 210, 234, 242, 249, 261, 266, 267, 272, 274, 278, 282, 285, 365, 367, 369, 370, 371, 372, 373, *374–75*, 376, 377, 378, 379, 380, 381, 382,

388, 392, 393, 399, 404, 408, 413, 414, 415, 417, 418, 422, 423, 428, 435, 442, 452, 487, 515, 516, 546, 555, 559, 561, 563, 564
kaurehe (animal), 350, 354
kehua/ghosts, 206, 213, 517

lagoons, 68, 74, 77, 88, 109, 137, 141, 142, 163, 226, 247, 269, 318, 339, 413, 505, 548, 561
lakes, 141, 142, 163, 164, 166, 231, 287, 330, 338, 339, 351, 414, 425, 429, 569
land alienation, 29
land claims, 418, 464, 537, 567
land sales, 537, 574, 575, 577
language/dialect, 43, 46, 114, 159, 160, 161, 177, 185, 198, 210, 223, 280, 284, 331, 334, 335, 336, 339, 341, 342, 343, 345, 348, 349, 350, 447, 451, 453, 458, 473, 475, 476, 481, 501, 502, 503, 525, 545, 567, 576
   English, 465
   Maori, 36, 56, 106, 114, 117, 161, 183, 401, 459, *460–63*, 474, 503
   Polynesian, 442, 464
language/dialect *see also The Maori-Polynesian comparative dictionary*, Tregear, E. (in Names and Personifications index); wordlists
legends *see* history, traditional
lightning, 206, 399, 400, 513
Liverpool University, 324
lizards/karara, 25, 27, *187*, 190, 214, 279, 340, 346, *348–50*, 354, 381, 382, 418, 420, 434, 453, *509–10*, 521, 522, *554*, 561
   mokopapa/tree lizards, 508, 512, 554
   mokokakariki/bush lizards, 409, 410
   karara-tuatara, 354
   moko-tua-huruhuru, 554
   origins of, 434, 561
   toropakihi/green lizard, 521

mahika kai, 23, 151, 207
makutu, 93, 205, 209, 210, 211, 261, 262, 277, 279, 320, 366, 367, 370, 371, 374, 378, 379, 380, 412, 414, 417, 418, 419, 420, 438, 490, 513, 516, 517,
546, 566, 567
mana, 58, 197, 206, 208, 267, 364, 373, 374, 375, 376, 377, 382, 388, 397, 399, 400, 417, 418, 421, 422, 428
Manchester's bookshop and stationery business (Waimate), 11
Manukatahi (residence), 419
manuscripts, 9, 15, 16, 23, *29–31*, 151, 207, 282, 460, 550, 551
Maori Council, 262
Maori Land Court, assessors, 27
Maori life in Aotea (Andersen, J.C.), 364
Maori Parliament, 28, 416
The Maori Race (Tregear, E.), 151, 225, 234, 259, 273, 276, 277, 324, 351, 414, 417, 454, 488
The Maori-Polynesian comparative dictionary (Tregear, E.), 30, 42, 47, 51, 62, 86, 195, 226, 253, 260, 264, 282, 289, 291, 305, 336, 337, 352, 354, 356, 365, 384, 387, 388, 432, 453, 458, 459, 474, 577
maps, 30, 578
marae, 89, 271, 278
marriage, 94, 95, 275, 277
matakite, 365, 378, 410, 421, 422, 437, 513, 516
Mataura Ensign, newspaper, 10, 12
Mataura Paper Mill, 151
mauri, 267, 376, 379, 380
McKenzie Memorial, 569
Medal of the British Empire (MBE), 1967 award, 11
medical lore *see* sickness/disease/remedies
meeting houses/Maori halls, Huirapa, 538
   Maririhau (kitchen), 538
   Matiti, 41
   Moki, 231
   Te Hapa-o-Niu-Tireni, 229, 537
   Te Whare-o-Pohutukawa, 403
   Tuahiwi Hall, 252
   Tuahuriri, 224
   Tutekawa, 224
   Uenuku, 205, 538, 545
   Wheke, 225, 445, 467, 468
Memoirs, Polynesian Society, 442
menstruation, 86, 265, 267, 358, 423
meteorology *see* weather
   meteors, 201, 202, 359, 360, 400, 513
mice/hinerata *see* introduced animals, mice missionaries, 36, 38
moa-hunters, 14
mokai, decoy birds, 334, 335, 339, 343, 504, 507
   pet birds, 335, 336, 343, 344, 387, 388, 481, 507, 529
   pet dogs, 188, 351
   prisoners, 210, 430
   retaliatory abuse, 96
   slaves, 90, 94, 96, 231, 271, 281, 287, 288, 432, 433, 443, 472, 489, 523, 557
mokihi, 109, 135, 137, 286, 339, 438, 468, 494, 496, 524, 561
months, 404
moon, 201, *202–03*, 359, 360, 361, 364, 375, 383, *399*, 404, 407, 434, 496, 497, 514, 556
   calendar, 362, 399
   effects, 266
   fishing by the, 310, 314
   origin of, 404
   planting by the, 27, 303, 546
moonlight, 148, 164
Mother Nature, 480
mourning, signs, 269, 270, 271
Murihiku (McNab, R.), 41, 60, 135, 556
museum exhibits *see* Canterbury Museum; Otago Museum
music, 478, 484
musical instruments, *77–80*, 214, *258–60*, 339, 416, *483–84*, 499, *543*
mythology, 25, 131, 136, 141, 160, 197, 204, 205, 366, 371, *383–08*, *532*, *555–66*
Maui, *384–93*

naming children, 464
Native Land Court, 446, *see also* Maori Land Court
navigation, 202, 363, 365, 380, 401
needles, 53, 232, 235, 236, 238
   bone, 64, 66, 158, 241, 476, 480
   feather, 241
   shellfish pick, 330
   tattooing, 249, 274
   wood, 158

New Zealand, Tourist
Department, 285
New Zealand Government,
47, 178
New Zealand Institute, 12, 14
New Zealand Land Wars, 467
noa, 206, 266, 271, 272, 377

ogres, 197
oils (or fats), 59, 114, 120, 126,
133, 141, 154, 178, 182, 184,
189, 245, 246, 247, 248, 261,
264, 291, 292, 296, 304, 305,
324, 326, 468, 534
oils, birds, 59, 83, 114, 290,
291
kereru, 64
putakitaki, 64
titi, 62, 179, 248, 299
tui, 335
weka, 63, 64, 83, 84, 295,
340, 480, 485
oils, fish, 62, 312, 314
tuna/eel, 64, 83, 298, 299
oils, human, 85, 273, 381, 439,
445, 544
oils, plant
castor, 267
linseed, 541
miro, 249, 299, 512
olive, 263
taramea, 89
titoki, 192, 248, 357, 512, 38
oils, pig, 262
oils, porpoise, 333
oils, rat, 295, 299
oils, seal, 261, 267, 333
oils, shark, 59, 83, 332, 333,
479, 480, 502, 541
oils, whale, 296, 334
omens *see* signs/omens
origins of, *see* specific topic
ornaments, 56, 100, 238,
241–45, 248, 420, *478*, 479,
481, 540, 550
ear, 54
hei, 91, 241, 493, 494
hei-tiki, *56–59*, *241–45*,
478, 493, *540–41;* origins of,
242, 244, 478
nose, 56
tiki, 274
Otago Museum, 9, 12, 14, 15,
16, 23, 49, 51, 52, 54, 68,
102, 103, 104, 105, 107, 110,
111, 114, 130, 131, 133, 146,
154, 155, 157, 160, 161, 162,
170, 171, 178, 180, 183, 186,
187, 223, 230, 234, 238, 243,

282, 345, 468, 478, 498, 538,
548, 549, 550
Otago Museum, 1920 project, 9,
10, 14, 23
Otago University Museum *see*
Otago Museum, 9, 10, 15
Otago Witness (newspaper),
65, 36
otters, 354

pa, 45, 78, 207, 210, 212, 223,
229, 230, 231, 244, 258, 273,
274, 283, 289, 351, 353, 428,
430, 431, 437, 438, 439, 444,
446, 447, 517, 537, 538, 539,
542, 548, 561, 563
model, 468
sites, 23, 27
paints, *59–60*, 67, 73, 89, 109,
213, 243, *245–47*, 332, 369,
419, 468, 478, 479, 495,
541–42
pakeha contact, 35, 78, 84, 86,
87, 93, 99, 111, 112, 114, 123,
138, 141, 157, 175, 178, 182,
184, 202, 205, 206, 262, 267,
272, 311, 322, 339, 363, 373,
380, 384, 395, 409, 413, 416,
417, 423, 446, 462, *463–68*,
485, 488, 515, 543, 548, 560,
563, 565, *573–78*
peoples, 260, 282, 289, 307,
431, 465
Fijians, 282, 299
Hawaiians, 36
Kanakas, 78, 242, 244, 340,
407, 544
Maori, 396, 407, 428, 436
Polynesians, 437
Rarotongans, 428, 435, 464
Samoans, 36
Tahitians, 36
photographs, 467
pig hunting, 466
pigs, 106, 119, 198, 235, 300,
351, 371, 401, 414, 465, 466,
467, 498, 531, 573
Pioneer recollections, v2
(Beattie, H.), 356
placenames, origins of, *431–32*
recording of, 12, 18, 23, 24,
26
tapatapa, 279
placenames *see also* the
Placenames index
plaiting, 49 53, 54, 135, 228,
232, 234, 235, 236, 240, 241,
254, 288, 432, 476, 540
bark, 51

by kanakana, 323
hair, 242, 244, 478
of boned fish, 116
rat tails, 353
plant foods, 25, 27, *117–29*, 263,
296–07, 498, 499, *511–12*
aruhe/fernroot, 105, 117,
123–24, 125, 179, 240, 279,
283, 295, *296–01*, 342, 437,
468, *524–26*, 548
chewing gums, *127–28*,
305–06, 499
honey, of plants, *119*, *122–23*,
124
hue, *302–04*
karaka, *302*
kauru, 119, 121, 123, *124–25*,
229, 240, 280, 283, 293, 295,
296–99, 417, 525
kiekie, 522, 524, 525
kumera, *301–04*
mushrooms and fungi, *128*,
306–07, 499
pukapuka/raupo bread, *123*
rehia, 125, 126, 304
seaweeds, *125–27*, *304–05*,
499
tutu wine, 125, 126, 575
plants and trees
plants, 44, 52, *191–96*, 247, 292,
296–07, *355–59*, *511–12*,
524–26, *530–31*, 554
trees, 38, 52, *191–96*, 292,
355–99, *511–12* introduced,
99, *120*, 255, 257, 290, 292,
451, 453, 461
kinds of plants and trees
aka vine, 44, 83, 137, 145,
146, 149, 225, 274, 286,
289, 291, 317, 473, 502;
aka-puatawhiwhi, 485; aka-
toropapa, 426; aka-tororaro,
43; akatea, 228, 317, 323, 426,
472; akatotara, 45
akakohia, 479
ake, 282, 491, 497
akeake, 316, 337, 481
akerautaki, 316
akerautangi, 493, 495, 502
apple, 348
aruhe/rauaruhe/rarauhe 148,
152, 278, 279, 336, 377, 441,
498, 503
bramble, 558
cane, 42
clematis, 318
ferns, 43, 169, *196*, 321, 323,
445, 466; parareka/horseshoe
fern, 531; penemauroa/

maidenhair fern, 480, 508; piupiu, 215, 236, 524; tupakihi/kidney fern, 508 ferntrees, 498, 537; katote, 122, 525; mamaku, 441, 482, 499, 525; poka/ponga/'bungi'/'bungey', 43, 224, 335, 336, 345, 471, 474, 498, 504, 525, 531, 533
fungi and mushrooms, 27, 128, 291, 306–07, 499; hakekakeka, 499; hakeke, 248; harori/tree fungi/tree mushroom, 129, 494, 499; toadstools, 264
gorse, 255
grasses, 42, 106, 158, 163, 165, 195, 325, 344; haumata, 345; kakaha, 91, 132, 174, 243, 340; karetu, 63, 72, 253, 265, 476; matoreha/ordinary cutty grass, 48; ikao/cutty grass, 48; pouaka, 82, 85, 114, 267; rerewaka, 111; tarutaru/taru, 175, 180; tataki, 42, 174, 176; tutuna, 111; upoko-takata, 174
harakeke/harareke/korari/koradi/flax, 42, 43, 44, 46, 47, 48, 49, 51, 52, 68, 78, 82, 85, 109, 116, 122, 130, 136, 137, 144, 145, 149, 151, 162, 164, 169, 174, 177, 214, 225, 228, 236, 237, 238, 240, 243, 255, 262, 286, 287, 288, 289, 290, 292, 325, 344, 346, 361, 416, 471, 473, 475, 476, 477, 482, 483, 484, 494, 496, 497, 498, 501, 502, 503, 505, 506, 524, 531, 532, 568; oue flax, 240; pao/variegated flax, 240, 477; takirikau flax, 240; wharariki/mountain flax, 53, 238, 240, 475, 477, 498
haumaukoroa, 559
heather, 290
hinahina/mahoe/whitewood, 245, 246, 262, 345, 350, 480, 505, 559
hinau/pokaka, 468, 479, 490, 499, 497, 502, 511, 531, 525
horopito/pepper tree, 508
houhou/'five fingers', 521, 530
houi/ribbonwood, 47, 49, 51, 90, 189, 234, 286, 288, 321, 349, 398, 453, 476, 478, 539, 540
hue/hue-Maori/taha/gourds, 63, 112, 257, 295, 296, 302, 483, 497, 498

inaka, 42, 224
kahika/kahikatea/white pine, 38, 189, 288, 335, 347, 559
kaii, 131
kaikatoa/kahikatoa, 77, 104, 108
kaikomako/kahikomako, 388, 559
kaio/ngaio, 84, 90
kakaho reeds, 335, 361, 431, 471, 472, 496
kamahi/kamai, 61
kapuka/broadleaf, 67, 190, 482, 511, 559
karaka, 38, 268, 302, 486, 522
karamu, 82, 206, 247, 262, 263, 417, 479
karo, 64
kauheke, 49, 51, 91, 122, 453, 539, 540
kauru, 278
kawakawa, 417
kawakawa/pepper tree, 485
keikei, 498
kiekie/kiakia/giegie/Te pokeka-a-Tama, 122, 247, 494, 499, 503, 505, 521, 524, 525, 526, 532, 564
kohai/goai/kowhai, 82, 83, 84, 85, 133, 174, 179, 223, 243, 247, 262, 263, 282, 283, 289, 295, 296, 316, 333, 337, 361, 398, 544, 545
kirimoko, 83
koareare/raupo/bulrushes, 44, 70, 71, 80, 81, 82, 109, 111, 121–22, 123, 163, 177, 229, 254, 287, 292, 316, 339, 344, 345, 431, 468, 471, 472, 482, 495, 496, 498, 525, 561
kohepiro, 486
kokihi, 61, 66
kokomuka/koromiko/veronica, 38, 83, 85, 262, 263, 485, 487
kopakopa, 485
korokio, 114
kotukutuku/konini/fuchsia, 114, 203, 214, 293, 350, 511
kowhiuwhiu, 511
kumera/sweet potatoes, 38, 226, 229, 278, 289, 301–04, 334, 375, 387, 406, 426, 441, 442, 472, 494, 497, 498, 499, 532
kupenga, 486, 508, 511
kuta/cress/watercress, 292, 294, 319
macrocarpa, 270

maire, 100, 243, 283, 289, 295, 296
maize/Indian corn 99, 257, 292
makamaka, 127
mako, 64, 79, 135, 173, 295, 337
makomako, 128
manuka, 43, 63, 71, 76, 83, 102, 104, 105, 108, 112, 117, 143, 147, 150, 156, 173, 177, 189, 226, 229, 235, 243, 256, 263, 273, 282, 283, 288, 289, 295, 296, 311, 317, 325, 332, 333, 337, 338, 348, 350, 405, 432, 443, 453, 467, 481, 495, 497, 498, 502, 503, 504, 506, 508, 509, 546
manuka-pouri/black manuka, 493
matai/black pine, 189, 206, 347, 398, 482, 511, 530
matoi, 67
miki, 340
mikimiki/stinkwood, 87, 114, 143, 189, 340, 529, 546
mildew/puruheka, 291, 497
miro, 149, 248, 249, 502, 511
mokimoki, 248, 480, 531
mosses, 63, 86, 196, 353; kohuwai, 148; kopuru, 63, 265, 480, 542; purau, 498
moulds/puru, 291, 497
mushrooms see fungi and mushrooms
musk/mountain musk/New Zealand musk, 63, 248, 531
naupiro/anise, 63
New Zealand cedar, 314
nikau palm, 38, 471, 478, 482, 499, 511, 525
okaoka/nettle, 405
papaii/speargrass, 248, 498
patete/treefern, 335, 342, 521, 525
patotara, 170, 340, 510, 511, 525
pikao/pingao, 234, 237, 282
pikiraki/red mistletoe, 207, 305
pines (native), 186, 247, 509, 531
piripiri/hutuwai/bidibidi, 83, 175, 335, 480, 505
pirirewa, 350
pirita/kareao/karewao/kaio/supplejack, 71, 79, 136, 137, 139, 145, 146, 155, 228, 256, 259, 263, 288, 289, 310, 316,

317, 318, 323, 326, 331, 474, 490, 493
pohata, 229, 334
pohue, 292
pohutukawa, 241
pokaka, 48, 61, 236, 246, 247, 511
popohue, 317, 318
poporokaiwhiria, 511
pora, 226, 229, 294, 454
poroporo, 258, 505
poroporo-huariki, 558
potatoes/mahetau/taewa, 53, 70, 99, 116, 179, 202, 203, 206, 226, 229, 238, 279, 289, 291, 292, 332, 334, 346, 419, 463, 472, 497, 498, *526*, 540, 546, 554
horeta potatoes, 573
puha/bush thistle/sowthistle 87, *119*, 127, 128, 253, 263, 264, 268, 292, 294, 335, 486, 499
pukakaho reeds/toetoe reeds/toitoi reeds, 41, 75, 223, 224, 256, 338, 345, 482, 494, 557, 568
pukatea/bukatea, 511
pukio/niggerheads, 224, 336, 472
pumpkins, 289
punitanita/Scots thistle, 485
punui, *121*
puriri, 384, 511
ramarama (of Nelson), 482, 511
ramarama/pepper tree, 68, 263, 511
rata, 100, 104, 133, 157, 398, 417, 485, 505
raukiokio, 473
rautawhiri, 205
reeds, 228, 316, 413 *see also* kakaho; koareare rehua, 525
rekareka, 262
rimu/red pine, 64, 263, 335, 524, 539
rohutu, 68, 511
roriki, 261, 268
runa, 84, 262
rushes, 42, 43, 165, 316, 338, 471 *see also* wiwi seaweeds, 125, *499*; karengo, 499; kelp, 72, 78, 79, 132, 138, 153, 158, 178, 182, 258, 291, 305, 316, 483, 527; bull kelp, 179; koauau kelp, 75, 77; rimu kelp, 138, 142, 177, 179, 344, 385, 499; rimurapa, 499; pati

304, 332; rimurimu seaweed, 316
speargrass *see* papaii; taramea, 248, 498
sweetpea, 453
takapo, 170, 340
tapuku/snowberries, 170, 340, 525
taramea/speargrass, 63, 89, 248, 249, 480, 498, 542
tarata/lemonwood/white maple, 100, 205, 248, 249, 480
taro, 445, 497, 498, 532
tatarahika/lawyer vine, 405, 525, 564
tataramoa bramble, 186
tawa, 511
tawai/beech/birch, 61, 189, 314, 352, 353, 417, 479, 500, 511
tawai-whero/red birch/black birch, 236
ti/tii/cabbage trees, 48, 69, 90, 111, 172, 232, 234, 236, 237, 238, 255, 262, 267, 280, 286, 287, 288, 290, 294, 340, 477, 498, 525, 529; ti-tohea/ dwarf cabbage tree, 47, 476; ti toi/toi, 90, 177, 232, 236, 238, 240, 243, 475, 476, 498; titoi, 47; ti-whanake/cabbage tree, 476
tikapu/mountain lily, 521, 531
tikumu/mountain daisy, 47, 90, 233, 236, 238, 261, 521, 531
tiori, 525
titiaweka, 42, 84, 224
titoki, 248, 249, 512, 38
toatoa, 51, 60, 61, 62, 63, 77, 247, 479, 542
tobacco, 206, 270, 381
toetoe, 53, 75, 130, 225, 228, 257, 262, 289, 290, 361, 377, 471, 472, 473, 493, 568; haumatangi, 477; mata/ toitoi, 494, 506; toetoe-pakau, 495; toitoi-pakau, 494 tororaro/moeraro, 137, 145, 146, 151
totara, 42, 45, 72, 108, 109, 111, 131, 149, 177, 182, 184, 189, 223, 229, 291, 292, 295, 314, 317, 335, 373, 398, 435, 482, 497, 502, 506, 511, 537, 547, 559
towai, 131

treeferns *see* ferntrees
tumatakuru/Wild Irishman, 114, 325, 381, 405, 418
tupari, 42, 224
tussocks, 43, 44, 111, 132, 180, *195*, 228, 234, 475, 477, 529; mania, 43; patiti/ mauku/tussock, 41, 42, 43, 47, 132, 144, 148, 152, 175, 224, 236, 237, 294, 316, 317, 325, 342, 473, 477, 498; snowgrass, 49
tutaekereru vine, 155
tutu, 78, 79, 87, 259, 268, 483, 486, 522, 525, 544, 575
tutu-rakau, 78, 79, 259, 480, 483
uhi/yams, 497, 498
vegetable sheep, 344, 554
vines, 146, 180, 228 *see also* aka whaoriki, 486
wharangi, 479
wheat, 426, 435, 577
wiwi/rushes, 42, 43, 224, 319, 320, 325, 340, 419, 503, 509, 533
plants, origins of, 405
seeds, 426
sex of, 357
Po, the, 384, 395, 404, 407
poems, 'The lady of the lake', 574
poha, 77, 98, 112, 114, 116, 125, 126, 133, 147, 153, 155, 159, 177, 178, 179, 181, 182, 183, 184, 189, 195, 291, 499, 506, 511
kiore, 353
mata, 159
titi, 6, 177, 280
poisoned sticks, 188
Polynesian Society, The, 11, 15, 442
pools, 106, 156, 174, 206, 210, 278, 380, 382, 487, 533
population, Maori, 87
porpoise hunting, 333
porpoises (terehu/popokarua/ popoti), 154, 333
Poututerangi/Potutarangi/ Poututorangi (pole), 383, 396, 397
pregnancy, 489, 545
preserves, 298, 345, 462
preserves, birding *see* birding preserves preserves, fernroot, 298

GENERAL INDEX   629

preserves, fishing *see* fishing preserves preserves, planting, 454
preserves, rats, 353
printing press, 546
prisoners, military (European), 567 *see also* mokai, prisoners
publications of H. Beattie, 12
Pyramids, the, 374

qualifications, 464
quarry, traditional, 550

rabbits *see* introduced animals, rabbits
rain, 197, 370, 375
rainbows, *200–01*, 202, 359, 363, 400, 401, 426, 428, 446, 513, 514, 531, 558, 565;
Kahukura, 363; Rokomai, 363
rainfall, 375
rakau-whakapapa, 252, 551
rat catching, 188, *189–90*, 254, *352–54*, 488, 490, 508, *510–11*
rats, 44, 112, 176, *189–90*, 291, 300, 345, *352–54*, 490; English/pakeha/pouhawaiki 189, 190, 266, 352, 353; kiore/kiore-tawai/kiore-maori/native, 44, 45, 140, 188, 189, 190, 211, 218, 226, 248, 278, 292, 293, 336, 350, 352, 353, 354, 490, *510–11*, 573, 577; kiori, 573; river crossings, 352, 353
relationships, 448
relationships *see* wordlists, relationships
religion, *204–09*, 365, 555
reptiles, 214 *see* crocodiles; snakes; tuatara
river crossings, 352, *see also* rats, river crossings
Rongopai, 275, 431
rotua, 210, 417, 421, 422, 516, 563, 564, 566, 567
round houses, *see* habitations, round houses, 553
rua, in sea, 396, 415
rua, of birds, 165, 177, 179, 180, 182, 183

salt, 115
  use of, 182
sandhills, games on, 70
sanitation, 223, 226, 264, 473

scents, 25, 27, 28, *63–64*, 194, 195, 245, *248–49*, 356, 478, *480*, 541, *542*; mokimoki, 63; taramea, 249; tarata, 249
Schools of Learning, 242, 204, *365–71*, *376–77*
Schools of Learning, wharekura, *204–05*, 249, *365–66*, 367, 370, 371, *376–77*, 378, 380, 381, 417, 515, *516*
wharemaire, 249, 365, *366*
wharemauri, 376, 377, 379, 394
wharepurakau, 365, *366–70*, 516
scientific names, 30, 162
  birds, 163, *170–71*, 210, 570
  fish, *130–31*
  insects etc, 186
  lizards, 187
  shellfish, *161–62*, 328, 329
  sea creatures,
    crabs/papaka, *155–56*, 160, *326–27*, *503–04*; papaka-rerere, 500, 503; papaka-roharoha, 504; papaka-taniko, 504; tautini crab, 423
    jellyfish/Te-reperepe-tautini a-Tinirau, 316, 423, 562
    kaio/ngai/bullkits/sea nuts, 159, 307, 326, 330, 331
    kina/sea egg/sea-urchin, 63, 140, 153, 158, 292, 307, 330, 331, 503
    kiore-moana/kiore-tawhiti/sea-horse, 56, 140, 244, 330, 479
    koura/crayfish/crawfish/lobster, 99, *154–55*, 155, 292, 327, 330, 331, 502, 503, 504; koura-wai-maori/freshwater crayfish, 155, 326; koura-wai-tai/saltwater crayfish, 155, 326
    muheke/squid, 153
    sea-cat, 479
    starfish, 140, 331
    whai/stingrays/skate 87, 112, *156*, 172, 313, 338, 493, 504
    wheke/tapairu/octopus, *153*, 312, 313, 385, 489, 501
    sea creatures, *see also* porpoises, sea lions, seals, sharks, whales
    sea elephant/ihupuku, 157, 479
    sea leopard/rapoka/sea-devil, 156

sea lions/whakahau/whakahao, 156, 157, 552
seal skins, 49, 156, 234, 235, 476, 574
sealers, 24, 36, 39, 66, 156, 205, 235,
sealing, 83, *156–57*, *333–34*, 500, *552*
seals, 49, 54, 56, *156–57*, 217, 235, 261, 267, 307, *333–34*, 500, *552*, 567, 333; kekeno/fur seal, 49, 83, 156, 157; pakake/hair seal, 156, 157, 217, 333; popoikore/popoiakore/hair seal, 156, 333; raratawhiriwhiri, 154
seasons, 203, 361, *362–63*
sewing, 53, 156, 236, 241, 288
sharks, 59, 116, 129, 141, *153–54*, 209, 241, 278, 279, 292, 295, 307, 322, 324, *332–33*, 410, *501–02*, 541, 560, 569; karara, 434; mako, 153, 279, 392; mako-huarau/spiny dogfish, 141, 153; matawha, 500, 501; tuatini, 493, 501
sheep *see* introduced animals, sheep
shellfish, 53, 57, 114, 125, 129, *157–62*, 158, 216, *326–32*, *503–04*, *552*
  cats eye, 159
  hoemoana, 160
  inaka, 500, 504
  kaikai-karoro, 503
  kakahi/freshwater pipi, 159, 216, 552, 577
  kakihi/sealimpet, 112, 159, 178, 216, 559, 566
  karuru/koruru, 78, 159, 503
  kauri, 127
  koeo, 100, 158, 159
  koruru, 78
  patiki, 503
  pawa/paua, 64, 100, 129, 133, 158, 159, 160, 235, 242, 248, 307, 308, 331, 385, 437, 480, 500, 504, 539
  pipi/akapipi/kuku/mussel/blue mussel, 38, 46, 48, 53, 54, 90, 100, 116, 158, 159, 160, 240, 267, 269, 270, 276, 278, 279, 283, 307, 480, 503, 578
  pukanikani, 158
  pupu/bubu/periwinkles, 158, 159

630 TRADITIONAL LIFEWAYS OF THE SOUTHERN MĀORI

rori, 158, 159
tahoehoe, 158
taiwhatiwhati, 159, 160, 503
tio/oysters, 74, 100, *157–58*, 307; tio-paruparu/mud oysters, 157; tio-pohatu/rock oysters, 157, 159
toheroa/tohemango/tohemaunga/tupehokura/whakai-a-tama/roroa/clams, 159, 160, 503, 504
toitoi, 78, 259
toretore, 158
toritori, 159
tuaki/tuangi/cockle, 158, 159, 277, 311, 503
tuke, 159
wharangi, 500, 504
shells, fossil, 331
shells, use of, 266, 269, 276
shelters, 144, 174, 175, 192, 195, 199, 232, 335, 358, 466
maimai, 42, 43, 226, 335, 337, 339, 357
pahuri, 42, 43, 147, 228, 317, 345, 471, 473
papakaurewa, 504
ponga whare, 342
uhi, 325, 503
wharau, 226
sickness/disease/remedies, *82–88*, *211*, *261–69*, *293*, 305, 356, 369, 374, 379, 380, 382, 398, 415, 463, *485–86*, *521–22*, 524, 525 see also epidemics
blindness, 72, 84, 159
colds, 82, 333, 409
constipation, 83, 124
diarrhoea, 83, 373, 437
disability, clubfoot/bumblefoot, 85, 438 gout, 84, 214, 411, 578
hori, 300
inbreeding, 264
influenza, 410
leprosy, 84, 370, 417
madness, 419
measles, 463
papapuni, 544
pneumonia, 412
poisoning, *87–88*, *268–69*, 485, *486*, 522, 525, 544; fungi, 306; honey, 486; karaka, 302, 344, 486; katipo bites, 486; kiekie, 269; kohepiro, 486; tiori, 269; tutu poisoning, 486

running mouth, 159
six fingers or toes, 85, 99
 toes/fingers rotted off, 211
skin, diseases, 293, 485, 512
 whawhaia, 417
 wounds, 214, 439
sickness, in animals, 262, 306, 486
signs/omens/tohu, 99, 102, 169, 171, 179, 182, 184, 186, 200, 204, *222–23*, 282, 347, 349, 350, 408, *409–10*, 412, *415–16*, 513, 516, 531, 553, 558, 566, 568
 bad, 183, 211, 212, 341, 371, 379, 409, 410, 416, 436
 good, 212, 416, 547
 of death, 211, 212, 409, 415, 416, 422, 553
signs, weather see weather signs sky, 247, 402, 426 black streak, 513
skylore see Aurora Australis; lightning; rainbows; stars
smoking, 463
snakes, 354
snares, bird see bird hunting, snares
snares, rats see rat catching
snoring, 420
snow, 47, 197, 245, 388, 438
South Island Maoris (Stack, J W), 250, 367, 393, 487
Southern Districts of New Zealand (Shortland, E), 298, 303
Southern Lights see Aurora Australis, 200, 360, 363, 436, 513
Southland Freezing Works, 150, 151
Southland Museum, 577
spiritism, *419–20*
spirits, 84, 93, 98, 212, 213, 274, 277, 378, 401, 402, 406, 408, 409, 414, 417, 419, 420, 421, 429
 evil, 86, 169, 206, 213
 guardian, 420
springs, 88, 120, 142, 269, 317, 320, 324, 371, 380, 399, 420, 462, 487, 554, 569
 hot, 427
sea, 305
stars, *201–02*, 297, *363–65*, 375, 377, 380, 383, 397, 398, 404, 513, 556, 559

Aotahi-ma-Rehua/Autahi, 201, 202, 363, 364, 404
Haere-ahiahi/Evening star, 201
 falling/shooting, 200, 365, 400, 513, 514
Hiratai, 404
Hirauta, 404
Kopuparapara/Venus, 202
Maki-motumotu, 404
Manako-tea, 404
Manako-uri, 404
Matariki, 202, 363, 364, 497, 513
Meremere, 202, 363, 364, 404
Mirimiri/Evening Star/Jupiter, 201, 202, 363, 556
morning, 212, 363
Ngakapa, 363, 364
Ngaputahi, 497, 513
Puaka/Puanga/Rigel/Evening star, 201, 202, 323, 363, 364, 401, 404, 497, 513
Pungarehu, 404
Southern Cross, 202
Takurua, 201, 363, 364, 404
Tawera/Morning Star, 201, 364, 497, 513
Te Ahum, 404
Te Ika o Te Raki/Milky Way, 201, 202, 359, 363, 365, 404, 513
Te Kahui-whetu, 404
Te Kore, 404
Te Mahana, 404
Te Parinuku, 404
Te Pariraki, 404
Te Waka-a-Tamarereti, 411
Te Wewera, 404
Teka/Southern Cross, 202, 497, 513
Tokopa, 201
Were-te-Au-maria, 404
Wero, 201, 363
Wero-te-kokota, 404
Wero-te-ninihi, 404
Whitikaupeka, 404
Stephenson Percy Smith medal, 11
stone, carving, 250
stone, kinds of, 100, 101, 102, 103, 106, 117, 168, 281, 283, 285, 290, 427, 435, 481, 491, 494, 521, 523, 548, 549, 569; Moeraki boulders, 426; Oamaru stone, origins of, 435; see also greenstone/pounemu

stone, turned to, 284, 285, 286,
    351, 375, 376, 426, 434, 435,
    478, 517, 549, 562, 568, 569,
    570
stone/s, use of, 103, 117, 158,
    159, 166, 188, 208, 288, 374,
    436, 515, 546
  carving, 67, 252
  cooking, 61, 111, 114, 121,
    182, 290, 293, 295, 297, 382,
    445
  cultivation, 303
  fishing, 136, 147, 148, 149,
    152, 308, 316, 320
  flaxworking, 46, 47, 48, 116
  food preparation, 105, 124,
    132, 154, 296, 548
  games, 68, 70, 72, 253
  greenstone working, 54
  mourning, 90, 92, 269
  tattooing, 65
  tuahu, 208, 209, 374
  water burial, 88, 269
suicide, 269, 271, 440, 464
  by pining, 478
  origin of, 271
sun, 201, 360, 364, 375, 383,
    389, 391, 395, 398, *399*, 402,
    404, 407, 434, 558, 565
snaring, 389
superstition, *214*, 254, *408–23*,
    516–17, *566–67*
swamps, 163, 166, 168, 195,
    196, 230, 231, 246, 318, 336,
    339, 344, 345, 356, 362, 479,
    507
  nei, 196
  re, 196

Tai-a-Ruatapu, tidal wave, 564
taipo, 393, 408, 409, 418, 419,
    421, 563, 564, 576
Takai-pokeka, rip, 539
Tales of Banks Peninsula,
    (Jacobson, HC), 381
tangi, 23, 89, 90, 91, 98, 151,
    254, 259, 269, 271, 276, 291,
    296, 305, 465, 553, 556
taniko *see* decoration, taniko
taniwha, 137, 154, 208, 213,
    214, 376, 396, 404, *414–15*,
    423, 425, 433, 453, 517, 533,
    549, 556, 569, 577
tapu, 89, 204, *205–06*, 207, 208,
    271, 272, 273, 274, 276, 277,
    279, 295, 365, 366, 371, 373,
    374, 376, 377, *381–83*, 412,
    438, 515, 541, 546, 558
  bird hunting, 377

canoes, 442
fire, 371, 374
fish, 137
fishing, 377
men, 280
people, 377, 380, 440
place, 252, 267, 269, 274, 276,
    373, 408, 529, 555
removal, 277, 371
trees, 206, *417*
violation of, 523
tattooing, 62, *64–66*, 96,
    131, 245, *249–50*, 251, 276,
    277, 351, 366, 371, 413, 478,
    480–81, 489, *543*
  of women, 250
  origins of, 250
  styles, 64, 66, 249, 250, 543;
  origins of, 250
taunting, 96
tax, on dogs, 574
tax, on guns, 575
Te Aute College, 36
Te Konohi-o-Tawhaki (shining
    stone), 566
Te Rama-o-Tawhaki *see* Aurora
    Australis, 513
Te Tai-a-Ruatapu, flood, 433
Te-Ika-a-Maui (Taylor, R), 211
teeth, shark, 56, 241, 242, 282,
    283, 332
teeth, use of, 56
Temuka, town clock, 418
Temuka Leader, newspaper, 271
Teschmakers, 575
The Maori Race, 79, 85
The Wonders of Western Otago,
    285
thunder, 197
tipuna, 41, 43, 58, 84, 91, 96, 99,
    103, 118, 119, 123, 128, 129,
    138, 141, 145, 154, 156, 161,
    183, 197, 199, 217, 230, 232,
    234, 240, 248, 249, 252, 264,
    267, 270, 274, 275, 276, 277,
    282, 283, 286, 296, 301, 304,
    314, 326, 333, 339, 351, 353,
    356, 363, 381, 382, 386, 401,
    408, 409, 410, 414, 417, 428,
    429, 430, 436, 437, 439, 443,
    452, 453, 459, 472, 474, 481,
    482, 488, 489, 504, 509, 514,
    552; names, 414
tides, 396, 407, 515
Tikao Talks (Beattie, H), 383
tohu *see* signs/omens/tohu
tohuka, 27, 53, 82, 86, 89, 106,
    154, 188, 204, 205, 206, 207,
    208–09, 210, 211, 212, 213,

234, 249, 250, 252, 262, 266,
267, 271, 272, 274, 277, 278,
282, 342, 365, 366, 367,
370, 371, 372, 374, 375, 376,
377–81, 382, 383, 395, 408,
410, 412, 414, 415, 417, 418,
419, 421, 422, 423, 427, 438,
442, 443, 475, 476, 480, 484,
487, 489, 514, 515, *516*, 517,
556, 563, 567; women, 209
tohungaism, 264
torches/rama 108, 143, 144,
    147, 183, 184, 286, *288–89*,
    311, 365, 392, 413, 494, *496*,
    506, 513, 524
Transactions of the NZ Institute,
    35, 45, 62, 197, 215
Transactions of the NZ Institute
    (HB), 553
Transactions of the NZ Institute
    (JWS), 62, 348
Treaty of Waitangi, 464
tree felling, 289, 297, 547, 554
trees *see* plants and trees
trees, enchanted, 214, 408, *414*
trees, kotuku roost, 529
trees, moving, 214, 414
trees, sex of, *193–94*, 512
tribes/hapu, 96, 106, 209, 276,
    298, 345, 353, 379, 396, 408,
    437, 440, 452, 484
  Hawea, 425, 436, 440, 441,
    445, 446
  Hoaka/Hoanga, 285
  Huirapa, 429
  Irakehu, 27
  Kahea, 429, 436, 440
  Kahui-matangi, 406
  Kahui-matua, 442
  Kahui-rere, 406
  Kahui-roko, 441
  Kahui-tipua, 416, 441, 517
  KaiTara, 487
  Kai-Tahu/Ngai-Tahu/
    Gaitahu 88, 107, 231, 232,
    250, 275, 295, 302, 308, 372,
    373, 376, 378, 401, 413, 424,
    428, 429, 430, 431, 436, 437,
    438, 439, 441, 443, 444, 445,
    447, 537, 556
  Kai-Taoka, 556
  Kai-Tuhaitara, 443
  Kati-Ira, 440, 442, 443, 444
  Kati-Kuia, 415, 447
  Kati-Kuri, 408, 430, 444, 446
  Kati-Mamoe/Ngati-Mamoe,
    87, 100, 107, 108, 149, 214,
    231, 279, 309, 406, 407, 414,
    418, 419, 420, 425, 429, 430,

436, 437, 439, 441, 442, 444, 445, 446, 447, 537, 548, 568, 570
Kati-Matamata, 405
Kati-Rakaihautu/Kati-Rakai, 440, 447
Kati-Toa, 430, 532
Kui, 435, 436
Maeroero, 60, 102, 214, 267, 276, 314, 402, 413, *416*, *425*, 541, 561, 566, 568, 570
Moriori/Maioriori/Maoriori, 88, 256, 425, 444, *445–47*, 468, 568, *569–70*, origins of 12, 14, 15
Mata, 285 mythical, 406
Nga-Puhi, /Kapuhi 266, 273, 436, 442
Nga-Rauru, 441
Ngai-Tahu *see* Kai-Tahu, 23, 27, 295, 308, 373, 376, 431, 436, 437, 447
Ngai-Tara/Kai-Tara, 408, 415, 423, 437, 446, 447
Ngati Kahungunu, 241, 437
Ngati Porou, 437, 448, 1
Ngati Tukoro-a-te-awa, 343
Ngati Wairangi, 437
Ngati Wairua, 437
Ngati-Tuahuriri, 373
Ngatiawa, 275
Patea, 438
Patupaiarehe/fairy people, 401, 402, 413, 425, 428, 517, 561
Pounemu, 285
Rakitane, 415
Rapuwai/Rapuai, 267, 416, 425, 437, 440, 445, 561
South Island Maori, 11, 12, 14
Tamarereti, 397
Te Kahui-anu, 561
Tini-o-te-para-rakau, 402
Turehu, 401
Tutumaiao, 435, 436
Waikato, 436
Waitaha, 64, 107, 140, 228, 231, 279, 425, 436, 440, 441, 443, 445, 561, 569
tuahu, 204, *207–08*, 209, 230, 249, 252, 365, 366, 369, 370, *371–74*, 377, 382, 473, *515–16*, 555
tuatara, 187, *348–50*, 507, *509–10*, 530, 554
tuna/eels, 44, 64, 83, 105, 112, 114, 115, 119, 121, 129, 139, *141–52*, 155, 214, 273, 278,
279, 283, 289, 290, 291, 292, 300, *316–26*, 320, 339, 393, 404, 405, 412, 420, 425, 430, 440, 462, 490, 493, 497, *502–03*, 509, 517, 527, *528*, 547, 559, 560, 565
kinds of
tuna-rakau/wooden eel, 144, 147, 150
tunatai eel, 144, 147
hao eel, 144, 147, 148, 502
horepara eel, 144, 147, 150, 502
horihori-wai eel, 144, 147, 502
kirirua eel, 144, 147
korakiraki eel, 500, 502
kotokoto eel, 112
mairehe eel, 502
matamoi eel, 144, 147, 502
papaka eel, 144, 147
take-harakeke eel, 502
origins of, 141
tutae, 523
tutumaiao *see* Aurora Australis, 400

universe, origins of, 402
University of Otago, 9, 14, 35
urupa, 92, 99, 208, 269, 270, 443, 444, 473, 515, 544, 545, 546, 575, 578
'Halfcaste Cemetery', 545

vegetable foods *see* plant foods
ventriloquism, *209*, *421*
visions, 262

wahi-tapu, 473
waiata (text), 81
waiata, 9, 80, 81, 91, 137, 201, 217, 253, 259, 286, 343, 363, 364, 379, 391, 397, 399, 400, 402, 403, 404, 407, 415, 436, 447, 452, 478, *483–84*, 541, 549, 553, 556, 557, 559, 563, 564, 567; Te Tere o Takitimu, 442
Wairau Mission School (of James Stack), 27
wairua, 213, 226, 274, 376, 379, 380, 382, 384, 398, 409, 441, *516*, 517, *566–67*
wakawaka *see* preserves
warfare/battles, 14, 24, 39, 49, 78, 85, 91, 94, 95, 96, 99, 100, 101, 102, 104, 105, 106, 107, 110, 163, 205, 234, 236, 243, 245, 253, 254, 255, 256, 258,
261, 264, 267, 269, 271, 277, 278, 281, 282, 285, 306, 366, 369, 371, 372, 373, 381, 408, 419, 425, 429, 430, 432, 433, 437, 438, 439, 440, 442, 443, 444, 445, 446, 467, 476, 487, 538, 544, 547, 561, 569, 574
Aruhe-taratara, 445
dance, 260
Kaihuaka, 279, 381
Kaihuanga, 272
Kakakaiamio, 440, 445
Pohatu-parimurimu, 440, 445
Tarahaukapiti, 105
Te Aruhe-taratara, 440
Tuawera, 415
Ua, 442
Ui, 442
Whakamarama, 443
warning voices, 416, 425
water, 205, 206, 210, 380
use of, 274, 382
water pollution, 528
weapons, 87, 90, 99, *100–07*, 114, 132, 133, 156, 157, 165, 194, 213, 236, 252, 274, *281–284*, 333, 334, 335, 358, 363, 366, 374, 377, 425, 428, 429, 433, 443, 467, 468, 484, *491–94*, *546–547*, 568, 574
axes and adzes/toki, *102–03*
Aumapu (axe), 452
Awhiorangi (axe), 363, 425, 435, 440
guns, 424, 430, 543, 547
Kahotea (mere), 282
Kahotea (patu), 284
mere or patu, *101–02*, 491
paiaka, *104*, *491*
pouwhenua, *104*, *492*
sealing, 333
spears, *102*, *491*
taiaha, *100–01*
weasels *see* introduced animals, weasels
weather, *196–201*, 197, 198, 199, *359–62*, 514, 531; signs, 199, 201, 211, 360, 361, 363, 364, 400, 409
weather lore *see* weather; winds
weaving (raranga/whatu), 46–54, *232–40*, 292, 387, *475–77*, 489, 494, 540
whaiwhaia, 211, 378, 379, 563, 566, 567
whaka-oriori/lullabies, 80
whakapapa, 9, 14, 18, 26, 28, 94, 95, 96, 98, 200, 275, 276,

GENERAL INDEX   633

277, 311, 343, 344, 365, 370, 373, 379, 382, 387, 394, 395, 396, 399, 400, 402, 408, 423, 424, 428, 429, 433, 434, 436, 437, 440, 441, 442, 452, 464, 489, 516, 551, 560, 561; Po, 395; Rarotimu, 400, 402, 407; Tuhaitara, 558
whakatauki, 81, 95, 156, 157, 193, 197, 198, 217, 282, 334, 362, 364, 372, 420, 423, 424, 425, 437, 458, 540, 567
whaleboats, 572; Manawatu, 413; whaler, 430
whalers, 11, 24, 26, 49, 60, 74, 78, 80, 86, 87, 96, 112, 114, 115, 157, 190, 195, 205, 213, 256, 259, 261, 291, 293, 333, 336, 409, 424, 430, 464, 507, 537, 566, 572, 574, 575
whales, 129, 153, 154, 208, 209, 305, 307, 333, 376, 423, 560, 562

black fish, 154
bowhead, 154
kewa/Right/black whale, 110, 154
paikea/humpbacked whale, 154, 241, 562
aratahurihuri/finback whale, 154
aratawhiriwhiri, 154
Te Aitaka-a-Puka, 154
uterakihaunoa/'sparm'/sperm, 56, 154
upokohue/cowfish, 154
whaling, 78, 157, 185, 198, 333, 346
wharekura, wharemaire, wharemauri, whare purakau *see* Schools of Learning
wheat mills, 574, 577
whenua/afterbirth, 93, 266, 267
whenua/ground, 93

whistling, 102
winds, *196–200*, 207, 272, *359–62*, 398, 400, 424, 442, 513, *514–15*
causes, 305, 316
origin of, 398
use of, 336
witchcraft (atahu/makutu/rotua/whaiwhaia), 204, *210–11*, *417–19*, 567
women, origins of, 403
wordlists, 9, 23
body parts, *454–58*, 486
introduced plants and animals, *460–63*
relationships, *218–19*, *448–51*
things, *451–54*, *571–72*
World War 1, 260, 332, 356, 374, 465, 467

zoology *see* animals